Shamanic
Secrets
for
Physical
Mastery

SPEAKS OF MANY TRUTHS
AND ZOOSH THROUGH
ROBERT SHAPIRO

EXPLORER RACE
MATERIAL
MASTERY SERIES

Other Books by Robert Shapiro

THE EXPLORER RACE SERIES

EXPLORER RACE: THE ULTIMATE UFO SERIES

THE MATERIAL MASTERY SERIES

SHINING THE LIGHT SERIES

The Sedona Vortex Guidebook (with other channels)

EXPLORER RACE

Material Mastery Series

Shamanic Secrets for Physical Mastery

Speaks of Many Truths
and Zoosh through
Robert Shapiro

Light Technology
Publishing

ISBN 1-891824-29-5

Published by
Light Technology Publishing
PO Box 3540
Flagstaff, AZ 86003
1-800-450-0985
www.lighttechnology.com

FLAGSTAFF COLOR GRAPHICS
COMMERCIAL PRINTING SPECIALISTS

FLAGSTAFF COLOR GRAPHICS
4030 E. Huntington Drive
Flagstaff, AZ 86004
1-928-526-1345

Foreword

Whether you be a native person or an insightful person, a yogi or a good Buddhist, it is in the nature of the understanding of all life, of sensitive knowing, compassion and heartfelt feeling, that all life is sacred—to be loved and to feel love when that love is freely given. This book is about ways to give love and receive love from beings who wish to give and who wish to receive. It is about how to live in a gentle way, how to walk gently on the land, how to give the land what it needs and how to respectfully receive from the land what it gives. It is about benevolent magic. It is about life, which is magic in its own right. It is about the respect that we all desire and deserve. It is about giving, receiving and walking together in harmony.

—Speaks of Many Truths
through Robert Shapiro

Preface

Sometimes I will say something that is meant to prompt the reader to stop and think, "What does he mean by that?" Sometimes incomplete information is given by a teacher because it is meant to prompt the reader to stop, put the book down and consider what that might mean in more detail. This is why sometimes things are not meant to be clear. It's why sometimes things are apparently vague, because the student, the reader, is meant to fill in the best he or she can with his or her own inspiration.

Teachers teach not only by instruction, but by allowing students to participate even in thought as they are learning. This can be useful because it trains students to act to the best of their ability on their own. After all, what will the student do when the teacher is no longer available, eh?

Over the years we have sometimes given things that are not totally complete, and as good spiritual students you have done your best to fill in the gaps for yourselves. Those gaps stand in place as long as they stand until something else comes up in the future that relates to them and we or someone else through Robert gives you more details. That's when you have a moment where you see something more uniquely, more specifically, or it even prompts your own inspirations. That's how the teaching works.

We cannot give you a complete and thorough explanation of every single thing because it is important for you to have life experience, which often prompts you to think in new and different ways. That alone is helpful for your inspiration and to draw conclusions that are workable and become portions of your wisdom.

—Speaks of Many Truths
through Robert Shapiro
May 2004

Contents

07943   017483

List of Gestures

August 11, 1999: Beginning a Different Way

Speaks of Many Truths
July 26, 1999

ell me about the effects of the August 11, 1999, lineup of planets. What is the aftermath? How will this affect humans?

To me, aftermath always means application of what you have learned in new and often more useful ways. It means this time you have been living through. It has been meant to strip from you your old adaptation. You must, as a soul, adapt to Earth ways when you come here. You cannot do things the way you have done them on other planets with the same wisdom and enthusiasm. You must do things here the way they are done. Sometimes this is not much fun, but you get better and better at it. Then after a while you don't remember that you ever did it another way or that there *is* another way.

Discomforts Bring Up New Skills and Strip Away the Unnatural

You have come to moments in the past that have been intended to bring up your soul and spirit skills, usually in a dramatic situation—as you know, in an emergency, this disaster, that disaster. Then suddenly everyone works together for the betterment of all beings. But that type of thing can only happen so much, until disasters cause more harm than good—and you have seen much of this. So now it is better for you to have an opportunity to become aware of things you have been doing that can be done in a different, better way that is in greater alignment with what is natural for you.

This time you have been living through has been designed to strip away the unnatural, just as an actor would leave the character he or she plays in the theater, then go home and be himself as best he can. It is the same way for all people. Many of you will have had some discomfort through this time recently, but sometimes that is to get you to ask for help if you don't know how or are ashamed. Some of you have been taught to be ashamed to ask for help, as if there was something wrong with you for asking this. This is unfortunate in your cultures now, but it is a fact. Sometimes you are put into a position where you must ask for help, then you discover that it's not so bad. People are often happy to give it, and they give you new, better ways to be and to act. Then you don't have to do things the way you used to, which was ofttimes painful or uncomfortable. You got used to the pain because you thought this was the only way to do it.

For those of you in situations like this, you have had to unload some behaviors that you could do in a different, better way or that other people could do for you. You have had to say, "Well, that's just how it is." Others of you have had a different opportunity. Maybe you have lots of skills you want to offer or didn't even know you had, and you were put into a position where those around you—or people you maybe didn't even know—suddenly needed you to do something. Much to your surprise, you discovered that you could not only do it, but that you were good at it! That's the time you have been living through most recently.

Don't feel bad about some discomforts that come up. These are all intended to lead you to the same place—to do what you naturally do best and to let go of what you don't do so well. You have all had to learn how to do many things that you don't do so well. Sometimes it was necessary; other times it gave you some compassion for those who will be continuing to do these things when you don't have to do them anymore.

You all are beginning to learn now that a finger can be a finger and a toe can be a toe, and sometimes toes can do things like fingers and fingers can do things like toes, but it is always easier for fingers to be fingers and toes to be toes. (That's something we say to our youngsters, but it is very profound.) Some people can do some things very well and other things not so well, but they try.

You are all being reminded that you do not have to do the same things. Some of you can do some things and others other things. You are being reminded that some of you do some things easily because you were born to them, and others, if you don't do a thing so easily, there's probably something else you were born to. If you haven't been asked to do it yet, you *will* be, so you'll discover it if it's remembered. Generally speaking, if it's hard to do, if it seems completely unfamiliar, if you feel completely lost doing this thing, most likely you were not born to it. Things that come easy, natural to you, these you were born to.

A Time of Rediscovering the Whole and What Skills You Were Born With

I always thought that the things you were born to were the things you had done before and that in this life you were to learn new things. Is that not the way it works?

My understanding is that in this life, yes, you are born to *discover* new things, but now you are in a different time—a time now of rediscovering the whole. Every person is part of the whole spherical One. In the whole spherical One of each planet—or sometimes even each family (but usually each planet)—there are always certain people who do certain things well. Other people don't do those things so well because they were born to do something else.

Now is a time of rediscovering the One (the planetary One), then becoming more than that. But start out as the *planetary* One. In my time it is more like the tribal One. In your time it has expanded to be the planetary One, and it is now a time to rediscover that. So in the next few years, not much more than that, everybody will discover at some moment or another what is natural for you, what you were born to, skills you were born with—talents, you call them. You might not do them full-time, but you will discover them.

If you are in doubt, ask your friends. You might say, "Have you ever noticed anything that I am really good at?" At first you will laugh, but after you get over the joke, then say, "Will you notice me a little bit the next few times we are together and tell me if there is something I'm just good at that you notice or can think of now?" Most people will not need to do that, but some of you might, and it's okay to say such a thing to your friends.

Too Much Individuality

What was the catalyst? What happens so that suddenly the old way we lived was changed?

You went too far into individuality. You began thinking of the individual as a sphere in his or her own right—such as each individual being a planet—the individuality of each being more important than the whole of all beings. You got to the break point with that. If you went any further, you would not be able to keep soul capacity; all souls on the planet at any given moment would not be able to feel, on a spiritual level, union with all other souls. If you do not feel that way, then mass death takes place.

So something happens in August?

> **What Really Happened: The Third Wave**
>
> **1:** The first wave, who wanted to awaken, were previously pulled gently.
> **2:** The second wave, who wanted to awaken, were previously *pushed* gently.
> **3:** The third wave, peaking on August 11, 1999, do *not* want to awaken but are being massively pulled *and* pushed, using astrological pressure.

No, it has been building to this for hundreds of years.

And this year . . .

This year is the time to notice that individuality is not meant to be the goal, but the *means* to the goal: exploring individuality to discover the whole of all beings. Normally one explores the whole of all beings to appreciate that, but in recent years cultures have been exploring individuality. You have gone as far as you can go with this.

We start perceiving ourselves as part of a greater whole instead of each being an individual whole?

Yes, but it cannot be a philosophical or mental conception. It is not about *thinking* about it that way. It is not symbolic; you have been presented with all of that already. It must be something for which there is *physical* evidence. In the past, in disasters people are put into situations. Some people are good at climbing, other people are good at thinking, some people are good at following, other people are good at directing and so on. In disasters you discover these things very quickly out of necessity, but disaster often causes much harm. And now with more people *everywhere* on the Earth, it is not possible to have too many disasters without causing great harm to people. There are so many people, you know. So other kinds of pressures must be created that affect the planet, such as motions of celestial bodies. These things affect the planet, and you, being made up of Mother Earth's body, are also affected. That is why motions of celestial bodies affect *you*. Astrology is real.

August 11: A Trigger to Discovering New Abilities

So the lineup of planets that will happen in August will trigger this?

Correct. Because this is a way to create things without floods, fires, earthquakes or volcanos.

So we each feel a pressure to become part of the whole.

A pressure, exactly. Or circumstances will happen more often where your "born to" talents must come to the surface. If it is not pressure on you, it is pressure on somebody who knows you or pressure on someone you happen to be nearby, say, at the scene of an accident. If you have something you are good at (maybe you don't know it) and someone says to you (here you are, walking by—innocent bystander, eh?) or just says to the crowd, "Run down to that drugstore! We're all out of something. Run down as fast as you can get there, and run back." Obviously, the heart patient does not volunteer, but somebody suddenly gets a feeling, drops everything, runs down, runs back, and discovers, "I didn't know I could run like that!" That is a simplistic example, but it could happen. This is a dramatic example I've picked because it is appealing, but ofttimes things are much more subtle.

For instance, you are visiting the home of your neighbor who has recently given birth. The child is having a problem, crying, coughing, something—not enough to call the doctor, but you get the feeling of what is wrong with the child. "Try this," you say. You are not even married, never had any children; your only experience with children is being one yourself. But suddenly you say, "Try this." Your neighbor tries that and immediately the baby is happy, fine. Your neighbor looks at you and says, "How did you know that?" And you say, "I don't know." [Laughs.]

You've discovered a hidden talent. Maybe you have the capacity to . . . it's not thought, it's just something you say immediately. You discover you have a connection to youngsters, babies. Somehow you are able to know what they need as a simple, sudden thing. "Oh, do this," and maybe just change the position of the baby. "Oh-oh, that's okay, that's fine." Then the young mother says, "Oh well, my other kids didn't need that, but I guess this one does. Thank you very much. If I have another problem, I'm gonna call on you." Everybody jokes and laughs, and maybe you think about it later: "Where did *that* come from?"

I've got goosebumps.

See?

Humans, then, need to really start focusing on what is called in business their core competency, right?

Yes, these skills you must know about, because you need to discover that you have undiscovered talents, talents you were born with. But most of you do not know of your talents in such a way that you are using them all the time. Oh, you might say, "Gee, I've always been able to swim really well." Like that. You have discovered the kind of talent that would be discovered in your school system, because the school you went to had a pool. Or maybe you discover you're a good athlete or something because your school has a good athletic program, or you're good at math. But most talents are not discovered in schools; most talents are discovered in circumstances of *life*. [Laughs.]

Now circumstances are changed a little bit so people have the chance to discover talents they didn't know they had. Then they can say, "Oh-h-h, I can do *that*!" That is very important, because once you discover a talent, you will be aware of it. There might be a circumstance again in the future where such talent is needed, and you might have some competence. This doesn't mean that everyone who gets an inspiration *all* the time has that talent, but you will recognize it if it just comes natural, easy, or someone gives you a tiny amount of instruction and suddenly you are really good at it—a quick learner, they sometimes say.

Are you saying that we may have been doing things because of circumstances in our life, and they're not what we were born to do?

They're not what talent you were born with. You just adapted to this because your culture says everybody must do everything. Some people were raised to believe that it is not okay to ask for help. Somebody down the street is good at math; you aren't, but you struggle along with math. You study, study, study, and you get to be adequate. The person down the street hardly studies at all, and he is a whiz at math.

So you should be doing something else—is that what you're saying?

Probably you were not born to math, you were born to something else. You are a whiz at something else; you just don't know about it yet. Everybody is born for different things. They don't know what they are because the system you live in, the culture, is not set up like ancient cultures, where people's talents were often discovered. They did not have the same education for everyone. In your culture, there is the same education for everyone—opportunities are very limited to discover people's talents. Usually, the culture is *also* very limited. You get out of school, get a job, get married, have children, like that. This is a very fixed way of living. There is not much variety, not much opportunity to discover what you might be good at because it's such a fixed culture.

But this is the time when we have to start to do what we love to do. Is that what you're saying?

Exactly, and what you love to do is very often what you are good at, and *naturally* good at. In circumstances of things being different, it has been very important for you this year to be very flexible. People who are rigid this year are having trouble, but if you are flexible, adaptable, you will be able to learn this easily and perhaps in ways that are fun. If you are rigid and unable to adapt, and are controlling or living in circumstances of *feeling* very controlled, you might require drama. So be more flexible.

There's the inertia of habit, also. If someone's done something for twenty years, it's hard to start over.

When they've done it that way, that's right. You don't have to start over. Remember, starting over is too much, if done in the way you have been doing things. You can't do that. "It took me twenty years to learn how to do this so I can do it well now." Do you understand? But when you discover the thing you are good at, it takes you a week or two to get *really* good at it, not twenty years.

So you're really talking about every human beginning to do what he or she wants to do and suddenly enjoying life.

I am talking about *discovering* what you are good at. Maybe not everybody feels they can do that right away, but it's an opportunity to discover. Only a few people on the planet—in terms of percentage, 10, 15 percent—are doing what they are naturally good at. Most everybody else is doing something that they are just doing. They learned how to be good at it but were not born to it.

So when someone finds what he is good at, then he needs to have a career change or do it as . . .

You need to take note that you are good at this thing. You don't necessarily need to throw your career away. But you need to consider, "Now I know of at least one thing I am good at that I didn't know about before. I wonder how this could be used in a career. I've racked my brain; I don't know. I think I'll ask my friends; I think I'll ask others." You are now in a position to ask people you will never meet through the telephone, computer, other things: "I discovered I was very good at this. Is there a job where this is involved?"

You don't know about it, your friends don't know about it, but somebody on the other side of the Earth says, "Oh yeah, how 'bout *this?*" And you say, "I don't know." This would be the thing you discover you can do. You say, "Oh, how wonderful!" Then because of advice from friends, others, people who live miles away, people you don't even know, you discover, "Here's something *else* I can do that I didn't know about," similar to the thing you've discovered. Then somebody else says, "Well, what about *this?*" and you discover, "Oh, there's that, too, and it's kinda like what I been doing, yes." Then you discover there is even more.

Do you understand? You discover things that are related, that have their foundation in the thing you've discovered you can do. Pretty soon you discover all kinds of things that are natural abilities that open up new avenues for you to do in a career that would be easy.

New Jobs Created, New Designs and Technology

During this time and for the next three to five, maybe seven years, fully half the world's jobs will be created. When people start doing what they are *good* at doing, an explosion of creation and creative energy goes into this, because when you are happy doing what you are doing, it is like a celebration. You no longer are just trying to do the best you can at something that's hard for you. You find that it is easy and fun to do the best you can at something that is fun to do. You can put creative energy into this, and it's not hard; it's simple.

Lots and lots of jobs will be invented in all fields, not just technology: medicine, healing, food preparation, lots of new kinds of cooking, making garments, making decorative objects, making furniture. In the next few years, society will begin to form the nucleus of things that have appeared as benevolent pictures in science fiction, like futuristic furniture (not just funny-looking stuff that would be uncomfortable to sit in, but things that would actually be comfortable).

For instance, Robert is currently sitting in a flat chair, but what if the chair was shaped like a doughnut but well-padded, so that the rounded portion of the person's bottom kind of hangs a little bit in the chair and looks beautiful sitting there. Before you sit in it, you say, "This has got to be uncomfortable." Then you stretch back and you discover, "I've never found a chair so comfortable in my life." So futuristic-looking things will suddenly be designed to be more comfortable and more beautiful.

The world will be re-created like a celebration. Everybody wants things, everybody is doing things they enjoy doing. People make lots and lots of money, and can buy lots and lots of stuff.

A renaissance.

A renaissance, a good word. So this is coming now. This is coming for your people and can only happen when people are loving what they do because it comes easy, or at least the core thing comes easy. Things that are allied to it are also easier than what you've been doing. But if you go too far, you get to the point here [makes expansive gesture with arms spread wide]—thing is not quite so easy anymore.

We went too far.

That's right, you went too far. You don't do that anymore because there is somebody else who does that thing, and you don't have to take the bad with the good. You just know, "Oh, somebody else does this. If I have been discovering this, soon I will meet these people. If I do not know them, I'll ask friends. If friends do not know these people, then I'll ask others I don't know on the computer. Somebody will tell me, 'Oh, this person is doing something like that, too. You two ought to get together.'"

So this is a very positive thing that is happening. What's been building up for all these years, culminating with the astrological configuration in August, is going to change the way we perceive ourselves and the way we live.

Exactly. It is the beginning of better times. Of course, it will not always be so wonderful. Things will still happen that make you unhappy, but this is the beginning. And remember, sometimes opportunity is disguised as difficulty. Difficulty often means you must do things differently, better; it does not mean you can't do things anymore. You may not find that different way right away, but you *will* find it. Then you'll do it differently, in a better way. Then it is very easy and you won't look at doing that thing with dread like before. Now you say, "Oh, fine."

For example, nowadays very often people dread going to the dentist's office: "Oh, pain. Somebody fooling around in my mouth—I don't like that." Very soon, without any discomfort—no needles, nothing—you'll go to a dentist's office that will have not only current technology, but more that's coming—no pain. You'll just relax, listen to music, watch a video, and the dentist will work. It will not be uncomfortable at all. There will be no needles. Something will be put into your body with no break in the skin. An adaptation of a previous invention is coming.

So you'll see new things coming. Surgery will be the same way pretty soon. No needles, no pain. Having surgery will be like having someone work on your car—it's fine. "I go to the doctor, she does this thing, and I heal up real quick afterward."

Social Skills

There will be a revolution in such things for other technology also, including interaction with social skills. Right now you might want to do something to help people: "These people don't get along with each other. How can I help?" It's hard. You go to school, learn many, many ways; it takes years and years. You get out and it is still a struggle, but some people discover in this time or soon after that they are good mediators, good between people: "Oh, why don't you this? Why don't you do that?" People say, "Oh yeah, I didn't think of that. Good idea! We can do that. Fine."

See, people help each other. Lot of times people *want* to help each other; they just don't know how to do it because they are trying to do a job they don't find easy. They try to apply what they were taught, which worked in some other situation at some time. But that application does not work in this situation, so they need to have a different application, not only for the individuals involved but for the circumstances, both inner and outer—to say nothing of the inspirational moment. If you are good at that, then you go there. You are with those people for just a moment, and an inspirational moment happens. You say this and this, you try this and this, and everybody says, "Oh, yeah! That's terrific!" because you are good at that.

That's wonderful!

Then life gets easier, it is more fun to live—there's no stress. Stress goes away and people live longer, happier, healthier, more comfortably.

A Period of Birth Control

There will be some things that people won't like. For example, for a time there will be birth control—not unpleasant, not cruel—that will be required by a world government. Some people will be very sad because they cannot have lots of children, but their rational minds will say, "I understand. For one thing, children who don't have parents need to have parents. Maybe one of these children can live with us. Oh, boy! Wonderful!"

Then after that, you have to take a hard look at civilization. Too many people are enough. "Let's not kill people off in battles. Let's just decide not to have so many children for a while." This comes initially by government enforcement, and people will feel very unhappy about it, will try to fight it sometimes.

All people will be able to agree in thought, in theory, that this is a good idea but won't want to give up the opportunity to have children. Children will not be taken away from people and redistributed, not that, but when a couple comes together, the government might say, "You can have no more than one child. Sorry." So the couple is allowed to have one child who survives. If maybe there is an accident and the child does not survive . . . sad, very sad. You grieve for a while, then you can have another child. This gradually reduces the population—not in a cruel way, but it is necessary.

This will happen all over the planet, all governments?

Yes, this has to do with a world government. It is not coming immediately, but it's coming. It's necessary to shrink the population gradually, gently.

Earth Changes from Digging and Tunneling

What about the earth changes? Are they going to continue—the high winds and floods, the volcanoes and the earthquakes?

There will be some, but the more you can adapt to these benevolent ways . . . especially shrinking the population gently, making a commitment to doing it and saying, "We'll make the best of it. If my wife and I cannot have a child or we only have one child, it is okay, because almost everybody in the neighborhood has one child. Sometimes many children get together and we're with them. We all kind of share each other's children, and this is fun. Then we can sometimes be around many children. It is fun. We're just not responsible for them all, all the time. So it is all right, not a terrible sacrifice."

When you do this, then the planet can find a way to have these planetary motions without causing catastrophes. But it must sometimes do extreme motion in an attempt to live with the effects of human beings' activities on Earth—primarily mining, drilling and tunneling. These have a profoundly damaging effect on Mother Earth. Much of what you need can simply be taken out of places where you have dumped things that you don't need and re-created into things you do need.

Recycled.

Yes, recycled. A good place to begin is to start digging in old dump sites now to retrieve things that have been buried, trash. Take it all out and recycle. We can recycle almost everything except some chemicals, but in time we'll be able to recycle all that, too. Mother Earth is now reacting to all that digging in her body and melting the polar icecaps, as you have noticed. Some of this might cause a little problem for a while—water problems, rain problems—but ultimately this will give you virgin land. So it's not so bad. Just don't dig in the Earth. If you dig in virgin land, it is like poking a needle in a baby. It's cruel. If there is too much cruelty to a baby, the baby goes away. Mother Earth does not feel good about what you are doing in her land and her virgin land. Her function of going away simply means flooding, as has happened before, or else she will take all of her water inside her. There will be no water. Everything will dry up. This is not usually done with volcanos; it's usually done on a planet like this by water. The earth change that is to be looked at with the most important eye is water.

Do you see that people will start listening?

They must.

Oh, that's excellent. That's good news. It's so delightful to get good news.

It's good news.

Cellular Clearing of Traumas and Unresolved Events

Speaks of Many Truths
July 27, 1999

his is Speaks of Many Truths. Greetings.

Greetings. Before we talk about clearing cellular memory of stored trauma, would you explain what cellular memory is and how the body stores memories?

Cellular Memory

When anything happens to an individual, there is very little storage as long as there is complete resolution. Resolution does not mean resolving only a problem; it might equally refer to some observation or interaction, for example. Resolution means, in this sense, completion.

On the other hand, if there is any portion of it remaining unresolved—not only thought, which is actually a minor aspect, but any portion of the physical self of any individual that does not feel totally at peace with this, "at peace" meaning complete—there is an attraction in that portion of the physical self. You might actually feel a sense of a tingle or a touch sensation there, or something that would bring your attention to that physical place.

Often you might connect the two events, though they are not related in your experience. But the assumption that a situation—unresolved in any way—goes to specific parts of the self is past-oriented. Past-oriented refers to the way things have been. You and your world are building on the future timeline, so you are running roots to your Now time. As a result, many things have changed or are in the process of evolutionary change. In this case, evolution is future-rooted.

For instance, here is an innocuous experience: You meet someone on the street who looks familiar. He says hello to you, and you say, "Hi, how are you? I hope you're all right." You chat briefly and go on, not remembering that person's name. It is not critical. You go on with your life, yet your physical body feels a discomfort because it has not remembered that person's name, even though that person has remembered yours. But it is not a big thing.

Wherever that discomfort originated . . . for example, in the solar plexus: If the solar plexus does not have much going on (if it is not taking in too much or creating or activating too much), then it will park itself there for a time. But because so much of material creation is generated or experienced—both going out and coming in—in the solar plexus, at some point the solar plexus will dump this off, and it will usually filter down from there (not up, unless it was a frightening experience or something like that).

If it was innocuous, such as the incident described, it will filter down, settle somewhere, usually in the hips, thighs, buttocks or legs, and remain there. Should you have other experiences like this, it will not create a problem at all. But should you have many, many such experiences, especially if you are someone in business or in a demanding service occupation (someone in the medical community or a pilot), then you would very quickly build up a reservoir of sensitive places in your body that would need to have physical resolution.

Physical Resolution and the Power of Physical Exercise

Physical resolution is different from and, to my way of feeling, far superior to mental resolution. Very often, as in the case of our innocuous example, you might not see that person again and you may never remember that person's name, so mental resolution might not be possible. Yet vigorous exercise, a vigorous walk, a swim, a hike, something where you are using the lower parts of your body and swinging your arms vigorously, maybe a run—after fifteen to twenty minutes, this will tend to transform that physical discomfort.

In your time, with running it is different. You almost always run on man-made material, streets and so on. If you ran on the beach in the sand, for instance, that would work. But if you had nowhere else to run, you would have to run on concrete or what-have-you with rubber shoes. That will do some good, but generally speaking, hiking on the land or running on the soft material or swimming does better. It can be other things, but short, vigorous body motion from the base of the rib cage down—and maybe more with the rest of your body—is what works.

How it works, as much as I understand it, is that the discomfort is like a speck, a physical, subsurface speck on your leg. If you were to see it under a magnifying glass, it wouldn't look like a clot, but it might look slightly denser either in the tissue or the gland, since it is in a capillary. It is a speck that will catch your eye. There may be a slight ripple where one might not normally be in a physical body. That's the best way I can describe it. After vigorous exercise, sweat glands open up and so on, forcing things to the surface, and through some chemical reaction in the body, the discomfort is transformed.

The Transformative Power of Ceremonial Dance

In my time [Speaks of Many Truths lived in the 1600s in what is now the western United States], sometimes people would run barefoot, or most often there would be dances in which you would dance the dance of yourself. This would not be something vague. It was the dance you did when you were a child, when you could stand up. First you would get up and fall down and get up and fall down, but eventually you would establish some dance. Adults would be dancing, then you would do *your* version of the dance.

That would be encouraged in a child. Then, as an adult, you would do your version of the dance, perhaps vigorously, if you did not feel right, if you felt a little uncomfortable and you couldn't say why—you just felt uncomfortable, but the rest of your life was okay. Then you would do the dance as a ritual. I have heard that some tribes in my time do a sweat, but my people did not do that. We did this dance. You have sometimes seen this illustrated pictorially and even in your moving pictures.

This works. To me, it works best to a drumbeat, but you might try it some other way. Don't do it to music, because your body will try to adjust its rhythmic motions to the music. Drumming is okay as long as the drum starts slowly and the person who is beating the drum has some idea that you are attempting to transform or get rid of something. The drummer might pick up the pace a little bit or tap the drum in a particular series of drumbeats, like this: bum, bum-bum, bum-bum-bum, bum-bum-bum. This gives you some idea.

A drumbeat might start out like this—bum, bum, bum and so on. It will start out rhythmically, slowly. As the person begins to move, the drummer does not set the rhythm for the dancer; the dancer's motion sets the rhythm for the drummer. Remember this, drummer, because the drummer is very important. If you see people beginning to move faster and faster, you can pick up the pace a bit—bum, bum, bum, bum and even quicker. But you might get a series of staccato movements, sudden jerks and sudden motions, turning around. The dancer turns this way, turns that way. That's where you might come up with bum-bum-bum or bum-bum.

That's how it began in my time. Your drums exist in your time, so you could do it. The mechanics of it is a ceremonial dance, which I recommend is the best way, because it can even be done indoors in your modern time if necessary—provided the neighbors are not overwhelmed by a loud drum. That is the best way to transform, I believe.

You are saying that the memory is stored in the blood, capillaries and tissues?

The "speck" does not refer to a speck of dust or dirt. Let's call it a density. It could happen like that. This is not to scare you. If you could look at the living capillary, you would notice that for no reason you could understand, the flow of blood moves back and forth around this thing, but you don't know why. You would look at it and say that there is nothing there, and ask why the blood is apparently going around something—like water going around a tree in a stream. But there it is.

At other times you might get a sensation of something on the wall of the capillary. Blood flows around it, but you don't see anything. I'm going to call this the basic capillary design [Fig. 1-1].

Future Support Systems Are Changing Present Patterns

This is now after . . . what do we call it, the shift? Is what happens in August 1999, a shift to the future timeline? Is there pressure on us to connect to the future timeline?

A moment. What begins in August (it is a beginning in many ways) is like . . . picture holding a ball. Normally, a baseball, for instance, has predictable stitches. That is the way a baseball looks, the way it's stitched. Everybody who likes baseball knows how a baseball looks. But say you hold the baseball at its top and bottom. Suddenly you turn your hands like this: you turn your top hand one way and your bottom hand the other way. The baseball in the center stays fixed, but the top and bottom of the baseball twist. The stitch pattern no longer looks the same, yet the overall baseball is the same.

It's like that. Things are happening now to force a change in the pattern without changing the overall flow of life. You get to do a life, but you must do it differently. In this way, this is a support system from the future. In the past there have been encouragements to do this. Generally,

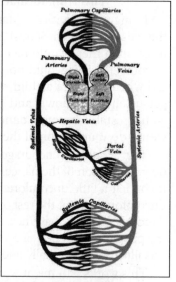

Fig. 1-1. Basic capillary design. (See Henry Gray, F.R.S., *Gray's Anatomy,* 15th ed. [1901; reprint New York: Bounty Books, 1977] 456.)

encouragements happen at different times in the lives of individuals, but here you have something happening at the same time for everyone. This is useful, because people will be able to say, "Why? What's all that? Holy cow, that's really something!" In short, you will be able to consult with each other. Mostly it will be little jokes you will make.

What is occurring is that you are gradually being *forced* to do things differently. In the past the force has been gentle. Now the force is more demanding, because methods of living life have been false for many people—adapting to things you don't do well, doing the best you can at them.

Like an assembly line.

Yes, but now it is needed on an individual cell basis, to say nothing of what your world and the planet need from you. You are actually needed to begin creating solutions for problems you have been unable to resolve before this, such as what to do with atomic waste. "Hide it, bury it in the ground"—that's the worst possible thing! If you put it in the ground, it won't take long before it contaminates the water that you, the animals, the planet and everything drink. It won't take long before everybody is poisoned. So burying it is the worst possible thing, yet that's happening all over. There will need to be solutions, but you have not been able to come up with them knowing what you know, doing what you do. You must have solutions, but the solutions are not present now in your time, nor have they been present in your past. The solutions are available only in the future.

Anyone's Discomfort Is Everyone's

So you must force yourself to get on track with your natural abilities, to stimulate overall creativity, working yourself toward the future where all the solutions for all your unsolvable problems reside—diseases and, perhaps more importantly, communication techniques between peoples. Think about how many angry words and battles in families, to say nothing of between countries, could be avoided if people could simply speak and communicate, not just with words, but with gestures, touch, feeling, everything. The other person completely understands you and has compassion for your position, then he speaks back to you and you completely understand him and have compassion for his position. It's not just that he sympathizes with you, it's not just that he says, "I feel your discomfort." It's that your discomfort becomes his own. He must resolve it, not only for your sake but for his sake, because your discomfort literally becomes something he physically feels.

Many tribal peoples know that if one person in their tribe is suffering, they all suffer. This is not a mental concept; it is the physical, outer world for us and other sacred peoples living in a sacred fashion. You have forgotten this. You have been able to harden your heart, you think, and think your thoughts. You make decisions that will hurt others because they are good for some, and you think with your mind that this does not harm you, your business, your family, your country, whatever your group.

But in fact, as a result of these decisions (or even in the absence of your decisions), if people are suffering on the other side of the world, people you have not met, *you* are suffering physically on a day-to-day, moment-to-moment level because those people are suffering. You might ask, "Where is the evidence of that?" I will say, look to the diseases that are unsolvable and sometimes strange—you use the word "bizarre." Earth organisms—viruses, bacteria—have been here forever. They were here when you were all born, they were here hundreds of years ago. They are here now in my time, but they are not harming us. Why? Are we so much stronger? No. It is because we honor the discomfort of any member of our group. Even if we are mad at that person, we still honor that discomfort and seek to resolve it in every way we can.

The Amoral Mind and the Heart-Centered Future

You try to put a shield around your heart and not feel things, but not because you are cruel. You don't feel safe to open your heart, and for good reason—I give you that. You try to make small decisions, as you call them, with your mind. But the mind is completely without morals. You model the computer after the way you think, and as you've all noticed, computers do not have morals. They make decisions modeled after the logic in your mind, which does not take heart or feeling or love into consideration. Even if you try to build that into a computer, it cannot have the depth of any human being's heart, though it might try to imitate it in some slight way based on what you've put into it.

Here is something to understand: In your future timeline, all decisions are made by the heart. No decisions are made with the mind, even the most simple—"What hat should I wear today?" "Do I want to put maple syrup on my cereal or do I want to use sugar?"—simple things, you understand. *All* decisions are made with the heart. "Do I want to go visit my relatives?" Heart. The mind is not involved at all. So you see, it's not about a different way of *thinking*. This is why Zoosh and others talk to you like this. It's about a different way of *feeling*. It's a way of noticing how you feel, learning how to know what feelings mean when they communicate to you, such as in the love-heat exercise (this exercise is also referred to as heart-warmth/physical-warmth in this book). Do you have heat for this? Then it's good. Have you no

The Love-Heat/Heart-Warmth/ Physical-Warmth Exercise

—Robert Shapiro

I am giving what we're calling the love-heat/heart-warmth/ physical-warmth exercise in a way that Speaks of Many Truths taught me how to do it. Take your thumb and rub it very gently across your fingertips for about half a minute or a minute. And while you do that, don't do anything else. Just put your attention on your fingertips. Close your eyes and feel your thumb rubbing slowly across your fingertips. Notice that when you do that, it brings your physical attention into that part of your body. Now you can relax and bring that same physical attention anywhere inside your chest—not just where your heart is, but anywhere across your chest, your solar plexus area or abdomen—and either generate or look for a physical warmth that you can actually feel.

Take a minute or two or as long as you need to find that warmth. When you find it, go into that feeling of warmth and feel it more; just stay with it. Stay with that feeling of warmth. Feel it for a few minutes so you can memorize the method and, most importantly, so your body can create a recollection, a physical recollection of how it feels and how it needs to feel for you. The heat might come up in different parts of your body—maybe one time in the left of your chest, maybe another time in the right of your abdomen or other places around there. Wherever you feel it, just let it be there. Don't try and move it around—that's where it's showing up in that moment. Always when it comes up and you feel the warmth, go into it and feel it more.

Make sure you do this when you are alone and quiet, not when you are driving a car or doing anything that requires your full attention. After you do the warmth for five minutes or so if you can, or as long as you can do it, then relax. And afterward, think about this: The warmth is the physical evidence of loving yourself. Many of you have read for years about how we need to love ourselves, but in fact, the method is not just saying, "I love myself," or doing other mental exercises that are helpful to give you permission to love yourself. Rather, the actual physical experience of loving yourself is in this manner, and there are things you can do that are supportive of it. But in my experience and the way I was taught, this is the method you can most easily do.

The heat will tend to push everything out of you that is not of you or that is not supporting you, because the heat, as the physical experience of loving yourself, also unites you with Creator. It unites you with the harmony of all beings, and it will tend to create a greater sense of harmony with all things. You might notice as you get better at this and can do it longer that should you be around your friends or other people, they might feel more relaxed around you or situations might become more harmonious. Things that used to bother or upset you don't bother you very much, because the heat creates an energy, not only of self-love, but of harmony. Remember that the harmony part is so important. You might also notice that animals will react differently to you—maybe they'll be more friendly, perhaps they'll be more relaxed, maybe they'll look at you in a different way. Sometimes you'll be surprised at what animals, even the smallest—such as a grasshopper, a beetle, a butterfly, a bird—might do because you're feeling this heat.

Because it is love energy, it naturally radiates just as light comes out of a light bulb. Remember, you don't throw the heat out, even with the best of intentions. You don't send it to people. If other people are interested in what you are doing or why they feel better around you, you can teach them how to do this love-heat/heart-warmth/physical-warmth exercise in the way you learned or the way that works best for you. And the most important thing to remember is that this method of loving yourself and generating harmony for yourself creates harmony for others, because you are in harmony. Remember that this works well and will provide you with a greater sense of ease and comfort in your life, no matter who you are, where you are, what you are doing or how you're living your life. It can only improve your experience. The love-heat/heart-warmth/physical-warmth exercise is something that is intended to benefit all life, and in my experience, it does benefit my life.

heat for this? Then it's not for you right now. Do you have discomfort? Then it is bad for you right now. It's very simple. Practice is required to get it right, but the technique itself is simple.

This is how all decisions are made in the future, and it is that future timeline that you must attempt to create, because it is there that every single solution to every single problem you now have exists—not just toxic waste, but whether you should buy red shoes or green shoes. Think about all the little things that you'd like to have help with. The heart decision is quick, easy [snaps fingers]. Quick, simple. But a head decision? "I don't know. These green shoes are pretty. These red shoes are pretty. I can afford only one pair of shoes. What to do?" This is something everyone can identify with. It's a simple thing, but you have all come across this. Sometimes you are embarrassed; other times you are just upset.

So you must do things the simple way now. You must recognize that greater incidences of cancer . . . is cancer caused by a virus, by bacteria, by a mutated strain? No. All these things have been on Earth for thousands and millions of years and didn't bother humans in the past. They bother you now because there are people all over who are suffering, and everyone is affected by everyone else's suffering.

Let Your Heart Become the Decision-Maker

You cannot make a mental decision to resolve their suffering, though it is good that you want to. "Let's send this government some money. Hopefully, they will give their people the food, the medicine, the shelter they need, and people will feel better." It's very nice that you have been doing that, but it is not enough. You must also clear your body with dance or vigorous exercise as we discussed. Then when you notice discomfort around you and you do not have anything unresolved—let's say that you are just sitting there and suddenly you feel discomfort—it's safe to say it is probably discomfort belonging to somebody else. Then what do you do? I will tell you. You do heart-warmth, which is why heart-warmth is critical. Know that you are halfway there with everything.

Go into your heart and feel the warmth. It may not be in the heart; it might be in the solar plexus or somewhere across the chest, on the side of the chest, wherever you find it. When you notice the warmth, go into it. Feel it more. Stay with it for five, maybe ten minutes. Maybe you can't stay with it for that long; maybe all you can do is stay with it for a minute. Do that. Don't be distracted. When you are done, the warmth will probably go away and you won't feel that discomfort anymore. You may have resolved somebody else's pain or helped to resolve it where someone is feeling it. You will probably never meet that person.

How have people had pain resolved in the past without humans knowing how to do this? In my time we know how to do it because we are closer to plants, animals, Mother Earth and so on, but in your time you are distracted by your pursuit of mental perfection.

How have people had many things resolved in the past? All trees, all plants, all animals, including many who are exposed to humans—cows, horses, sometimes dogs, cats (not always dogs and cats, but sometimes)—if they are exposed suddenly, they feel this pain (not their own) and immediately go into focus in that moment of heat. If you are around such a being, plant, blade of grass, animal or stone, if you are used to the love-heat exercise, you might suddenly notice, "Oops, suddenly there's love-heat." You didn't do anything to bring it on, but it is there. It is probably someone around you whom you might or might not be able to see—a rock, a rabbit, a spider, an ant—doing love-heat for someone else.

Because you are used to it, you notice it. If you can stop and help, do so. Go into love-heat yourself. You will probably instantly or very quickly feel much greater heat than you normally feel because somebody else near you is doing love-heat. You help them do what they are doing, and between the two of you the heat is much stronger. So it is of benefit to both you and the other being. You might see the other being or you might not—most likely not.

But it will help somebody else whose suffering will affect you, because you are in fact all one. In the future timeline everyone is crystal clear that you are all one because then you are all doing love-heat regularly, all the time. You are, at that point, able to do it and do other things. By then you will no longer have to drive; you'll have vehicles that take you around that follow built-in electronic pathways. This is not so far in the future; such things are being experimented with now. So you might be in a vehicle and still do love-heat.

Using Love-Heat to Release Trauma

That's excellent for a little innocuous discomfort. What about children who are severely abused and traumatized, who literally create a wall around those memories so they won't remember them, just to be able to function? When it is a storage of trauma that massive, how do you deal with it?

The same way—love-heat. A traumatized person cannot bring up love-heat easily. Let's say you know of such a person, now an adult. How do you know that this person may have been traumatized compared to the person who is just very mental and has difficulty focusing on bringing up heat, feeling heat?

Many times you try to help this person bring up heat. You give him instructions, you take him through step by step. You create for him, perhaps, a peaceful, safe environment, a comfortable environment. He can't do it. Could a psychologist, therapist or counselor probe his past in a professional manner to see if trauma might be possible? That's acceptable when done by a professional or well-trained counseling person, one who has been instructed, who has experience. They don't *have* to have a paper degree to say they can do it, but they might.

A more likely situation is where you help people to do this. Maybe you have helped many; maybe many people you know in the area already can do it. Maybe you (two people) get together once a week to do love-heat in general so that all the extra radiated heat feels stronger, or perhaps three, four, five people are doing it, many people are doing it. Heat is powerful, and everybody feels better almost immediately, especially if out in nature, where trees, grass, animals, mountains, maybe everybody pitches in. Everybody feels better.

After that you might say to this person, "We are going to be doing this ceremony with this heat, this transformation, to make everybody feel better." Have that person come after you have been there for maybe a half-hour, and when the person comes, assign someone to welcome him, to walk him from his vehicle. Make him welcome; don't just have him park outside and find his way to you.

Send somebody out, maybe two people, to meet the person and bring him in gently: "Come, you are welcome. Come into our place of meeting. We want to do what we can for you. You are welcome." If the person does not want to come, that's it. Do not force him. But if he wants help, then bring him into the center of the circle and make sure the people who can do heat are at least ten to fifteen feet away from him.

Provide a comfortable chair with no metal for the person; it might be a completely wooden chair. Just have something comfortable for him to sit or lie on, but no metal. Have him sit down or lie down, what-have-you. Then with all eyes closed in the group, have everybody face the person in the center and focus into their heat.

You're not to direct the heat at the individual; you do not send heat at a person. Just do the heat, and it will naturally radiate from you. That's why you keep your eyes closed. Try not to think of sending heat to the person. Sending it to him doesn't work so well because it takes it out of you entirely. If you send it to him so that the person will receive it, it will be willful on your part. It's as if you come up to someone and say, "I have a better way for you. I'm sending this to you to make you feel better." Perhaps that person doesn't want it even if it *would* make him feel better.

The heat must be freely offered but never forced. So don't look at the person. Close your eyes and just radiate in the usual way in the group. Then the person can take in as much or as little as he wants. Do so the first time with this person for anywhere from five to ten minutes. The person might or might not feel heat. He is not to be asked; people are not to say to him afterward, "Do you feel any better?" because he might feel that politeness requires him to say he is better.

Just say, "You are welcome to come back next time we meet." That's all, like that. If the person wishes to leave, two people are assigned to escort him down to his car. If he would rather walk down to his car on his own, fine, but let him know that he is welcome. Maybe he will come back the next time you meet.

You can do other things. Forty minutes or so into the program you are doing—I call this a program now—have the person sit in the center again while you are feeling the heat. Not everybody will feel the heat at all times—they don't have to—but most people will feel the heat most of the time. Then that person can stay in the center of the circle for fifteen minutes. He can even do this the next time for twenty minutes, but never more than that.

Try this three, four, maybe five times. If the person still does not feel heat, then wait and try again in a year or two. Don't force it. The person has to be ready. You can instruct the person in the center of the circle as to what you are doing; someone can run him through the instructions before he goes into the center of the circle. But perhaps you have tried it with him already, and he knows the technique but can't get to it. So the person thinks it does not work, and the others understand.

You can wait and try it again. Maybe the person can try some other time with somebody else. Or perhaps something will happen in his life and he will do it on his own. Maybe he'll sit on a rock at the beach, suddenly feel heat and discover, "So *that's* what it's supposed to be." Sometimes people don't understand, go into the heat, feel it more, and then they can do it on their own. Some get it right away; others take time. Most people don't take this long, but I give you this explanation because it is the simplest thing to do. But by all means, if that person knows where that trauma is, go see a therapist regularly. Talk about it. But do this, too.

Where Trauma Is Stored in the Body

For persons who have experienced a long period of trauma, is this a large problem?

A big question. You want to know if it is in the capillaries and so on?

Yes.

When there is severe trauma such as that, the kind of trauma where a person goes numb in certain circumstances—maybe later in life this person is having sex with a loved one but feels numb and can't participate very well and doesn't know why: "Something is wrong with me." This person might think back, "This may have to do with earlier trauma." First, she could maybe go to a therapist, and second, she could try heat, or vice versa, or at the same time. The main thing is, where does all that excess trauma go?

Obviously, many traumas make for too much restriction in the capillaries, but if there is severe trauma like this—especially where one is apparently having something purposefully forced upon her by another, as opposed to a natural disaster where one does not feel that Mother Earth is personally attacking her but that it is happening to everyone—such trauma, as in childhood abuse, tends to be stored in the bone marrow.

Can that lead to bone marrow cancer and things like that?

Maybe, maybe not. This is not fixed.

What about leukemia? Is trauma a cause of leukemia?

No.

Releasing Trauma through Vigorous Exercise

Since it's stored inside dense bone, would you have to check with a clairvoyant to see if you were actually releasing it?

The best way to release discomfort is through vigorous physical exercise, as I said. But what about the person who might be paralyzed or something like that? Then you do as much vigorous physical exercise as you can. What if your arms and legs can't move? This is a rare situation, but if you cannot move your body at all, the next best thing is to have somebody else move your body for you.

A physical therapist.

Have a physical therapist move your body vigorously, move your legs vigorously. Please describe what I am doing.

You are putting your hands straight out in front of you and to the sides very quickly.

This is for your legs. Move the legs vigorously, but in a natural pattern of the leg joints. Someone can do this for you, but she must move vigorously so she doesn't take it on for you. If she moves your legs slowly, it might just ease into her because she is not being vigorous enough. So therapists will have to also be vigorous.

Another possibility is that you can open and close your eyelids. Put all of your attention physically into fluttering, opening and closing the eyelids. You don't have to do so firmly, just open and close them quickly; then at some point you will have to stop and then start again. Do what you can.

So trauma is stored in cellular memory?

You can call it cellular memory, but it is better to use the terms I have mentioned. Other people have referred to cellular memory and will describe cellular memory in other ways. I recommend that the term cellular memory be used, but also other terminology such as capillaries. If you are looking for a singular descriptive term, cellular memory may not be the best. As I said, there are many descriptions of what that is.

Working with a Healer to Release Discomforting Energy

What about a sensitive or a clairvoyant working on you energetically? Can he or she release these patterns from you?

Yes. Clairvoyants cannot release the trauma, but they can release accumulated energy. For instance, say you have trauma that is in the bone marrow or capillaries. That trauma might make your auric field around those areas thinner. As a result, you might more easily attract discomforting energy floating around in the air. Some people call this possession, but I do not see it that way; it's just discomforting energy. Maybe sometimes it would be an entity.

Most likely clairvoyants—but let's say psychic healers, it's a better term—would be able to remove the entity and/or discomforting energy. They might be able to remove some of that energy, but since it is intended that you as an individual transform this—because you are not just a victim of this but created it by putting yourself in the situation where such a thing might occur (maybe you wish to learn material-mastery techniques in this life and needed to give yourself profound motivation to do so)—some may be leftover for you to do. It is almost always impossible for someone outside yourself to do all of this.

If the psychic healer attempts to remove it all, it can hold, but only for a short time. If you do this and then have techniques you can do, you will be able to get cleared out and then maintain yourself. But if you do not maintain yourself, the person who is clearing you out will have to clear you every five minutes or every hour, something like that. Eventually that healer won't be able to do it anymore, even if he or she has the capacity to do it with others, because your spirit has signaled a message to the healer's spirit, saying, "Don't. This individual needs to discover material mastery, transformational methods he can use for himself. That's why there is such profound need."

Then such a person might benefit by asking the psychic healer what to do: "What is your technique?" Or by asking the physical therapist, "What do you do?" Or by asking a physical or martial arts instructor or a racing, running or swimming instructor, "What is the way to swim to feel the most vigorous, to feel good? What do you like? How do you like to swim best?" Maybe you swim in the pool, a vigorous stroke. Or maybe a gentle backstroke works best for you. It's different for everyone.

In other words, you must ask different people and try different things. Never give up. Eventually you will find your way and in the process perhaps learn how to do a lot of things that are good or fun to do. Some things won't feel right, and then you'll say, "That's not it," and go on to the next thing.

Is this a promise for the people who read this book, that no matter how severe their trauma has been, how deeply they've been hurt or how much it impacts their life at this moment, they can clear it?

I cannot make such promises—that requires Creator. I can only say that I believe it is possible, I cannot give guarantees. There are no guarantees in life. If I say, "It's guaranteed you can do it," and then a tree falls on you the next day, I have lied.

How can you say it, then? It's probable that they can do it? It's possible that they can do it?

"Possible" is good word because it gives permission. If we say "probably," they feel like they *should* do it. Probable is where they *should*; possible is an encouraging word. It seems like a small thing, but encouragement is a nurturing way to learn something, whereas demand is always associated with pain. That's why I said before, no demands, only suggestions. Change it, you see, so it doesn't sound like a demand to the person.

Some people respond more frequently to demands because they have been in demanding situations, especially a younger person, but continuing demands add to their reservoir of discomfort. Eventually discomforts show themselves in some fashion. Maybe you connect to the pain of childhood, maybe you don't. This is why military service, with the best of intentions, is now inflicting a great deal of pain on soldiers—men and women. But in the future, military service will be very different; it will have to do with adventure, exploration, discovery. This is why scientists might be in the military. It's adventurous sometimes, discovery—it's fun. It's about teamwork, doing things together.

Star Trek is coming, right?

Star Trek, yes, but also deep-sea exploration. Also learning how to communicate with animals in the way those animals want to communicate, not in the way you want to make them communicate. Don't make chimpanzees speak your language. Learn to speak *their* language—not the sounds they make, but how to talk. It is not so difficult. One helps the other. The future military is about adventure, good things.

The Future Timeline and the Year 2012

The August 11 [1999] eclipse won't automatically put us on the future timeline, but will it put pressure on us to move to it?

Here's a good example: Say you are walking in a stream. The stream feels good—it's a hot day, cool water, very nice. The course of the streambed begins to slant down a little bit, making it easier to walk, because the water also flows that way. The stream is still not deep enough to sit down and float in, but it's easier.

What about the dimensional degree? We were at what, 3.4798 or something like that? Does this change that dimensional point?

You've moved up a little bit—you're now at 3.48.

We were there once. So we've come back to that?

Yes, you came back to that a little while ago. You achieved 3.48 again before August.

Some people are saying that we humans were programmed to terminate by the year 2012.

Terminate, meaning?

Die, leave.

All human beings? No, no. The time 2012 is a rough estimate made from the past. Two thousand twelve encompasses the time you are in now. What this means is the end of time as you have known it—not the end of life, the end of *time.* Now you are shifting to a different timeline. That's what it means. This has been grossly misunderstood in your time to mean the end of life, but it does not mean that at all.

You might ask me how Speaks of Many Truths, living in the past, can talk about future things. You must understand, I connect to Robert through a window. If I spoke through Robert from the past, from me directly through Robert, it would be past-oriented, but I speak through Robert through a window in time—it's different. A window in time can go to anchor a future timeline just fine and come back that way.

So many channels now are having to alter their methods for the sake of improving the signal. That's why channeling a shaman being may be easier, because a shaman is used to shifting into energy patterns to function in the best way possible, whereas other beings might be rooted in other times, in a past timeline. It may be difficult for them. They can do it, but it takes time.

Clearing Cellular Memory: An Overview Technique

How do we clear cellular memory? You were saying . . .

Heat and vigorous action is the simplest, quickest method. The old method of psychological analysis is not so good in the long term but useful in the shorter term. Long-term psychoanalysis treats only the mind. Psychology must become well-involved with the spirit, the physical self and the feeling self—holistic psychology. Then we'll have "whole" as in a circle psychologist, a whole psychoanalyst, using all those things as some psychologists are doing now.

Then the patient gets better quicker and frees up the psychologist's time to work with many more patients. Many, many people could benefit from this wholistic technique. Many people now do not go to a psychologist because the process is too wordy for them, but if psychologists did things on physical, feeling, spiritual and verbal levels, then there would be something for everyone. Psychologists would have ten times as many people, maybe a hundred times as many people, and all would get to feel better faster.

My concern is that there are six billion people out there, and many of them have traumatic cellular memory or habits or patterns or mistaken conclusions. There is much trauma stored in people, and it needs to be cleared now.

Using a material-mastery technique as we have been discussing . . .

All right, but . . .

You want to say [clap-clap], all cleared up now, but it cannot be quick-quick. It's done by the individual.

So we don't go into individual things like diseases or addictions or past-life memories or, like you said, toxic waste? Are these unrelated to this topic?

No, we are doing an overview now. Let's look at it: Sensitivity—yes, people might have one hand that is more sensitive than the other, or an individual might feel gently down the body, feel some place that's sore, not bruised. Most people notice a sore place when someone is giving them a massage. Take your thumb, go down a little bit from the solar plexus, press in. If it is sore at half an inch or an inch, that means some kind of discomfort needs to be resolved.

> **Tapping the Body's Wisdom**
> Find a sore spot on your body that you didn't know about. Touch it and ask your body, "Is there something you want to tell me? What does this mean?" If you don't get words, ask for motions or for an inspiration through a dream. If you still don't get a response, go to a bodyworker and ask the same question.

Now, move your hand around the body—take one hand and squeeze an arm, moving your hand down as you squeeze the arm gently. Do that gently, then more firmly as you come back up. Notice some spot that is sore. Maybe you rub a muscle and notice it is sore there.

The main thing is that if you find some place sore like that (maybe the muscle needs to be rubbed out, maybe not; perhaps it is just a sore point in your body), the first thing you do is talk to your body as if it were someone and say, "Do you have something you are trying to tell me?" This is the overview technique. If you can get words, get words. If not, reach around if you can and touch the sore point. If the soreness is in a spot you cannot touch in your back, lean against something so it presses slightly on it—just enough that you feel it, but not enough that you make it worse or traumatize it.

When you ask, "Are you trying to tell me something?", if you cannot get words, then ask to be given motions before you go to sleep—maybe the body moves its arms and legs in some way. Then ask for inspiration or a dream to write down that you can remember in the morning or in the middle of the night if you wake up: "What does this mean?"

If this does not work, then go to someone who does bodywork. Sometimes bodyworkers will pick up messages from a body, a sore point. Tell the person, "I've got this sore point in my body, and I'm not sure what it is. I think my body is trying to tell me something. Can you pick it up?" Go to somebody else to help you. This is a material-mastery technique. Eventually you will learn how to do it yourself.

So I am saying, "Would there be certain types of messages stored in this leg or this knee or this elbow? Can we do with our bodies the same things we do with Earth?"

Can we?

Yes, in a manner of speaking, but it's a little different. We're going to try to relate the parts of the body to circumstances. Let me give that some consideration with my advisers. [Pause.]

Release Point for Resolving the Old Pain of Accidents

Reach around to the base of your skull. Come up to the top of the indentation and touch the bone outside of your skull.

Right where the skull starts.

That part of the human body. This is not for everybody; this is a general trace. I must say general, because people are individual. Each one is his or her own world. But, generally speaking, in that part of the body we tend to retain and support all accidents. Let's say you fell down when you were a child and bumped your knee. If it didn't get completely resolved—maybe an adult cleaned it up, put on a Band-Aid, but was busy taking care of another child and you didn't get completely comforted—then the capillaries right around that part of the bone, skin or tissue will retain the unresolved accident.

It might also be a subtle accident. Maybe you said something to someone that you realize hurt his or her feelings. You didn't mean it that way, but you can't do anything about it. You can't take it back; the damage is done. Equally, someone might say something to you that hurts your feelings. You feel it. Maybe you tell that person, maybe you don't, but it hurts your feelings. It is an accident, not done with intention, but it gets stored right there in the back of the neck.

What do you do about it? How do you resolve it, aside from the general methods you've given before?

Reach around with the middle finger of the right hand. Touch there to the bone, that spot. Then put the index finger down right below it. Hold it for a moment and say, "I would like to have resolution, completion and comfort with the old pain of accidents from here. I would like to have this happen for me in the most comfortable, benevolent way."

Tomorrow we will come back to this exercise.

Feeling Is Our Body's First and Primary Language

Speaks of Many Truths
July 28, 1999

Welcome. *You seem very friendly and jovial and humorous. In my perception you used to be kind of crotchety and cantankerous. Is the energy different here in Hawaii [where this channeling took place]?*

Let us say that there are many factors at work. One, the energy is gentle and more benevolent here. Two, you are feeling a little better. You must understand that it is a connection. If you are exhausted and unhappy or if you are refreshed and having a pretty good time, it makes a difference.

You make a connection to me?

It is necessary, as has been stated before. Those in the room, especially those asking the questions, interact; they are part of the unit of exchange.

Gestures for the Physical Body

Now we will continue from yesterday. We were starting to discuss the hand gesture to release discomforting memories incrementally. In the previous book [*Shamanic Secrets for Material Mastery*], hand gestures were given to do things that might be massive, because Mother Earth can do massive, multileveled things all the time. Those were the type of gestures.

But with a human being, we must go slow and gentle, so I will not give hand gestures to release and clear everything at once. You tend to think of releasing something as it going out from the body, don't you?

Yes.

That is not the way releasing ever takes place unless done very carefully by a practitioner. Generally speaking, release takes place . . . it goes into the body and the body processes it in the usual manner. These will be gestures, unless otherwise stated, that will allow release to take place incrementally and slowly. If you are going to release this place [points to the base of the skull]—*especially* in this place—then it must be done very slowly.

More Instructions for Releasing the Old Pain from Accidents

Here are more instructions for the person releasing in the base of the skull: For this place, make the gesture once a day. Try to make it at the end of the day—before you go to sleep, for example. That way the

Gesture for the Slow Release of Old Pain from Accidents

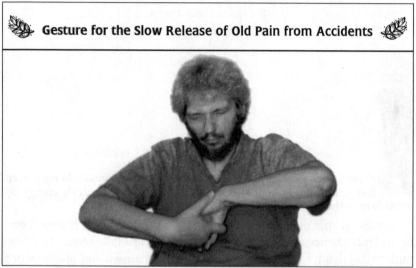

Fig. 2-1a. Here is the gesture to release old pain from accidents, held in the body at a point at the base of the skull. Hold for at least thirty seconds. Do this once a day for thirty days, preferably before sleep.

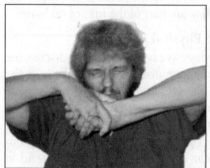

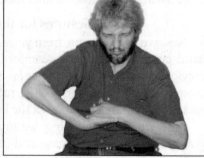

Fig. 2-1b. Another view to clarify the position of the hands.

Fig. 2-1c. A third view.

activity will begin in dreams, which is the most gentle place for most people. Continue daily to make the gesture this way before sleep for thirty days.

Then wait at least thirty, maybe sixty, or—if you are feeling odd or unusual or if you have some discomforts from something else—up to ninety days before you begin the next procedure with the next part of your body. When releasing from the human-being body, you must go slowly and gently.

Now, here is the gesture to release incrementally from that part of the body [Fig. 2-1]. Realize that it is very complicated. As always, we'll show these things once.

Yesterday we discussed minor discomforts that may be experienced. What would be an example of something severe?

You would know if there is something severe because over the years you would have had some kind of trauma there. It doesn't mean that you would have had a terrible injury, but perhaps you might have bumped your head there more than once, enough to remember. This goes for any part of the body. If you continually bump some place in your body . . . maybe you bump into the wall or the door when you get out of a vehicle. If you bump your head or arm or leg, bumping the same place regularly, then you will know that the area has something that needs to be released.

Release Point for Difficulty in Embracing Your Home Location

Let's move on to the next release point. I know you have interest, so we'll go right to interesting places.

Toes?

The right foot, yes, between the big toe and the second toe. Touch there, right between them.

Put your finger down between the two toes where you hit the connecting tissue?

That's right, right there. Not this toe or that toe, but right between. This place has to do with the difficulty in embracing a physical home. Your physical home has to do, not with the building in which you live, but with the ground upon which that building stands.

The exceptions to this need for release might be that you are not intended to be there. There might be better land for you somewhere else. Explore that first. Yet if you feel attracted to an area or you know it's right for you by all the methods of consultation you use, but you still feel uncomfortable—maybe you keep bumping your toes in that area—then you must do something to release that part of your body. In this case, it does not mean there is memory there—it might mean that, but more likely, because it is a part of the foot, the forefoot, it has to do with embracing the land.

As you know from the previous book [*Material Mastery*], if you want to be on the land, embrace the land and receive information (as you would say) or get feeling from the land, when you walk, put your forefoot down first, then your heel. When you do not want any support from the Earth, you put your heel down first. That is what many native peoples noticed immediately with newcomers—they put the heel down first. The peoples took that to mean that those newcomers in old times either did not want support from the land or did not know how to receive. In short, they took it that the newcomers were ignorant.

Resolving Resistance to Your Home Location

This place I mentioned, the spot between the toes, is not a place to store the discomfort, but rather is a signal. Therefore, you do this gesture [Fig. 2-2]. You will know after three days: If the area does not

Gesture to Release Resistance to Your Home Location

Fig. 2-2a. This simple gesture you do for only three consecutive days. Hold for at least thirty seconds. Make the gesture before you go to sleep at night.

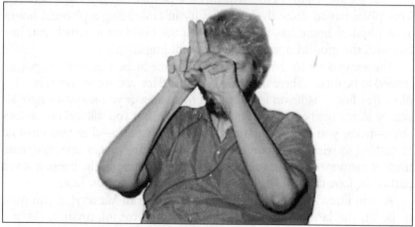

Fig. 2-2b. A second view, for the sake of clarity.

release—if you still bump your foot or if you still feel uncomfortable on the land you are occupying—then the message is a real warning. It might not be something wrong, you see; it might be something right. Maybe the land is giving you a message that for some reason—it could be many reasons—this is not a safe place for you to be. This is not always the case, but sometimes the land will warn an individual, "It is not safe here."

In that case, if you're still feeling uncomfortable after three days and have checked everything else (such as the use of a wand [Fig. 2-3] as we discussed in *Material Mastery* [Chapter 11]), that it isn't this person or that person or this event and so on—if you have trekked through all of that and it is not that, then you have to ask yourself, "Is the land trying to warn me?"

🌿 Using the Left Hand as a Wand 🌿

Fig. 2-3a. Here is the wand, using the left hand.

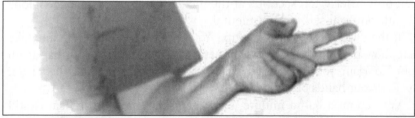

Fig. 2-3b. Detail showing position of fingers for the wand.

If you get a feeling (warmth) that land is trying to warn you of something, then you must pursue with your consultants, with your body techniques of knowing, what the land is trying to warn you of. Let's give an exercise for that.

Card Technique for Clarifying Body Messages

We have given the exercise about heat [see pp. 7–8] and we talked about warmth in *Material Mastery*. This is what to do:

A. Making the Cards: Make four cards, using simple 3 x 5 index cards from an office supply store. On the side that has lines, take a simple pencil, nothing fancy. You don't have to press too hard. Write DANGER, not small. It doesn't have to be between the lines, but it doesn't have to come out to the edges of the card, either. Turn that card over so the blank side is facing you. Then write on the next card: CAUTION. Turn that card over and lay it face-down.

Then write on the next card: SAFETY. Turn that card over and lay it face-down. On the last card write OPPORTUNITY, and turn that card over and also lay it face-down. Move the cards around in front of you. Sit in front of a table, for instance, in a place where you feel comfortable.

B. Using the Left Hand as a Wand: Move the cards around and around for at least a minute so you have no idea what card is what. Then separate them on the table using the wand, which is your fingers, like this [Fig. 2-3].

Now take the wand and aim it. Don't touch the cards, but aim your left hand, your left arm, clearly toward a card and say (not to the wand—the wand is a receiving unit), "Is this the message for me?" Aim without touching anything; don't lean your arm on the table while you're aiming at the cards. Make sure there's plenty of space between each card.

C. Noticing Heat in Your Body: What you are doing is checking in your physical body to see if there is heat in the place you focus on in the heat exercise. Anywhere—across the chest, the solar plexus area, the upper abdomen—notice if there is heat. If there is no reaction, wait only briefly, ten seconds at the most. You'll have to be conscious of your physical self; it's not mental.

If there is heat, it will come up. You will feel it. Take note mentally here, how much heat did you feel there? Then relax. Put your hands on your lap again; you can cross them or not, though it's probably better not to. Rest your hands on your legs.

Wait about a half a minute, something like that. If the heat is still present, go into the heat and feel it for a time, as long as you want to enjoy it but probably no more than a minute or two. It might be very strong heat, so you don't want to shove it away. For the circumstance of this teaching, heat means yes, but there are degrees of heat. It might be very strong heat, which would mean a very significant yes. Or it might just be mild heat, which might mean a possible yes or "there is more to this" or yes with variables.

Then relax. Repeat the process with the other cards so that you go through this process four times. Take note. When you point at a card, if there is distinct discomfort in the same physical area, don't go into the discomfort and feel it more. Just take note: "Discomfort. Doesn't feel good."

D. Separating the Cards That Trigger Heat: Then take your other hand (not the wand), in this case your right hand [Fig. 2-4.]. Take that

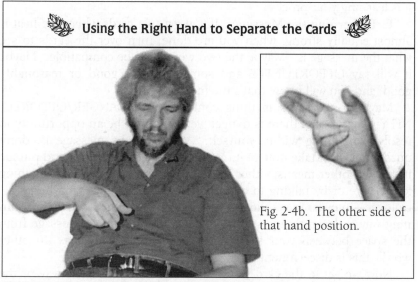

Using the Right Hand to Separate the Cards

Fig. 2-4b. The other side of that hand position.

Fig. 2-4a. Use your right hand to move the cards. This is similar but not quite the same as the left-hand position—notice that the fingers are touching.

card with distinct discomfort and move it off to the side.

Do that with all the cards. Suppose you get no reaction at all—no heat, no discomfort, nothing. Just leave those cards where they are. More likely you may get a little bit of heat for one, maybe a lot of heat for another. When you get any heat at all with a card, put those cards close to each other. Then check again the other cards where there was no reaction. No reaction? Slide it aside. Don't put it next to a card where there is discomfort; just slide it aside.

Put those cards where you felt heat next to each other but not touching, moving them with your right hand, not exactly in the wand position but similar. Keep a good distance between the cards, four to six inches. Then point and say, "Is this the message?" using the wand hand, and note any heat. (I'm explaining much more than needs to be explained to try to make it clear.) Take note of which card you feel the most heat for. If you feel almost the same heat for more than one card, then there is more than one answer.

Then rest. Always rest for a minute or two between steps, between pointing at the cards. If you get a lot of heat, then you can enjoy it, but rest eventually allows heat to dissipate.

As you begin this exercise, your body is learning your process and how to communicate to you in physical signals you can understand, at the same time wanting to provide heat, which is love. Your body is learning this exercise with you, not because it cannot do it, but because it is learning your process.

E. Discerning the Message: If you get two cards where the heat is almost equally strong, when you are done, turn over the cards to see what the message is. Maybe the two words will be compatible. Maybe it will say OPPORTUNITY and something else good or reasonably good, and you will know that's the message.

Maybe it will say something confusing, like DANGER/OPPORTU-NITY. That means there is danger, yet there may be an opportunity to resolve something within yourself. Whatever the message is, don't question it. Just take note of it. Write it down, remember it and pursue it through other means, either by your own spiritual ways of obtaining knowledge or by talking to counselors or other people—maybe an astrologer—in order to get their point of view or method. That is a beginning way to learn things so that you do not just have a message from the space between your toes with no idea what it means. In other words, this is discernment work.

Now we get to the card where there is no response one way or the other. Turn the card over and look at it. Let's say that it says DANGER. There is no reaction to it. If it says DANGER, then come up with other words that describe that. You might write EXTREME HAZARD on a card, meaning worse than danger, or another word, something less than that, meaning slightly dangerous. We try to get finesse on this one, you understand?

Clear the tabletop and start over again. With the card where there was discomfort, just take a finger and flip it off the table, but don't look at it if it lands right-side up on the floor and you might be able to see the word. Turn it over with your foot or something, but don't touch it, because you are still working. Take the other card on which you have written EXTREME HAZARD. Spin that around and try again. If there is still no reaction, then set it aside. That is not the message. Sometimes when it is not the message, it comes through as discomfort, and sometimes it comes through with no reaction in your body. You have the knowledge.

You can, if you like, turn over the card where you got the discomfort. Know that that word is not the message. Or you don't have to turn it over at that point. It's probably better if you *don't* turn it over, because you've got discomfort and you might get more discomfort by turning it over. You can turn that card over last, but by the process of elimination you will know.

Release Point and Gesture for Releasing the
Pain of Unresolved Relationships

Now we go to another area where the body might store discomfort, a place between the fingers [Fig. 2-5]. This place will often hold disappointments in love relationships, sadness having to do with an unresolved relationship, someone you wish you had been with. Or

Release Point for the Pain of Unresolved Relationships

Fig. 2-5. Here is the place between the fingers. This is the spot, between the middle and the fourth finger of the left hand—not the fingers themselves, but this point between them that I'm touching.

maybe someone wishes he or she were with you, if it was strong enough or if he was nearby—for instance, maybe he sat near you in class in school when you were younger and wanted to be with you, but you weren't interested. If the person was sitting near you, the person's disappointment and pain might still go into your hand because of his proximity to you.

But most often it has to do with *your* unresolved pain. Maybe a person you loved died and you still love that person, or perhaps a person you loved got interested in somebody else. In any event, this point has to do with unhappiness in love.

Make the gesture [Fig. 2-6]—again, always before sleep; then dreams can act on it first. You will still be acting on it, but it will start with

Gesture to Release the Pain of Unresolved Relationships

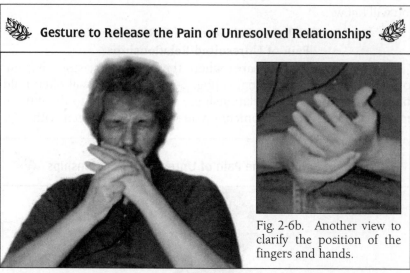

Fig. 2-6b. Another view to clarify the position of the fingers and hands.

Fig. 2-6a. This is the gesture. Hold for at least thirty seconds. Do this before sleep once a week for no more than six weeks—a total of six times.

dreamtime, see? It will be gentler. Make the gesture once a week because you must proceed with great caution. It's a very tender area for most people, even for people who think of themselves as tough. It's just as tender for the warrior as for the gentlest person you can imagine. It makes no difference, so proceed with caution.

Fig. 2-6c. A third view.

This process takes three times as long as the other processes I described before. The difference there is that you make the gesture once a week for no more than six weeks. So you will make the gesture six times and that's it. That may be sufficient.

Be very careful with these gestures, please. Try to do them as accurately as possible. Except for those who are physicians, acupuncturists or people in medical professions who have consciousness, it might surprise you to know that every place on the surface of the body has to do with activating or stimulating either that place or often other places on the body.

Working with Energy Fingers inside the Body

Interestingly enough, it is the same for the inside of the body. In advanced work in, say, acupressure—healers who work inside the body without breaking the skin know this—sometimes you reach with extended fingers (energy fingers) inside the body of a person. You press up on the skin or bone, not always on the same place. You press here to do one thing, but press from the inside up to do another thing. The beings [who are showing gestures to Speaks of Many Truths] are reporting that you press a little above the wrist on the left hand to do one thing, but when using the extended energy fingers and pressing up in that area from the inside, it does something else. So the body has active stimulation points on its outside and inside.

Sometimes, for instance, when working to heal the heart of an individual, either from physical trauma or (in some cases, but not all) feeling trauma, the discomfort might go into his or her rib cage. So here's what you do. Below the rib cage, go in up to the pancreas. Move your energy fingers very gently inside the pancreas in specific ways, making gestures. Move this way and move that way. Back, forth, in and out. Back and forth, sometimes on the surface of the pancreas, sometimes on the inside. Sometimes you make your fingers very small, touching only a tiny part of the pancreas, moving around. This stimulates the heart to heal.

Release Point for Money Difficulties

I want to talk about something that many people are very concerned about. Many are concerned about having enough money, and others are concerned because they need to be rich. In their own mind, they know they need to be rich. Maybe they have a big family, many people depending on them, cousins, aunts, children, and they are only one person. They need to get rich so that they can support everyone until those family members can support themselves. These things happen very often.

They might have been working for a long time but are still unable to get rich past a certain point. They can support themselves, but with sacrifice. They live in poverty and can send some money to their family, but they are barely surviving. They need to get actually rich; then many people can get rich. Not so limited.

This area in the body is a little difficult to describe. Behind the solar plexus is a muscle at the base of the sternum [Fig. 2-7]. It is not on the outside of the body, but on the inside of the body where the solar plexus is.

Releasing the Constriction of Wealth

This gesture [Fig. 2-8] will gently free up any memories that have to do with the constriction of wealth, such as "wealth is not safe." Many,

Release Point for Money Difficulties

Fig. 2-7. The release point is not on the outside of the body, but inside the body where the solar plexus is, where the bone ends and the soft part of the body begins. It is right behind this point, at the base of the sternum.

many people say things to youngsters. Some people say this, some say that. When you are a child, you often feel that it is not safe to have any money because people will be jealous of you or you won't be able to be "one of the boys or girls." You hear many, many things like this. You think it does not affect you, but it affects everyone all the time.

Even people in your time, people who have so much money that other people cannot even imagine it, are affected by this. If they would release this area, they would have even more money. You might ask, "How is it possible for everyone to have so much?" For one thing, not everyone wants or needs to be rich, but it is possible because the creation of new technology, *heart* technology, is just beginning at the ground floor. We've hardly begun, but it will eventually be the only kind of technology. This is going to create tremendous wealth. Some of it will be a new form of wealth that you have not yet considered. As a result, much of this will be available.

Gesture to Release the Constriction of Wealth

Fig. 2-8a. This is the first step of the gesture, the first hand position. Bring your right hand up slowly. The gesture must be made sitting. It's best to do so with your back to the north. If you can't do that, do the best you can.

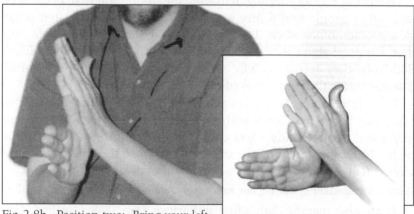

Fig. 2-8b. Position two: Bring your left hand up slowly, resting atop your right thumb. Hold for at least thirty seconds without moving your body (to the best

Fig. 2-8c. Another view of the second hand position.

of your ability), with your eyes closed. Do this once every third day before you go to sleep at night, for two or three weeks.

This freeing up has to do with the original process as described at the back of the skull. Use the standard method, in terms of how often and how much time to wait between applications. You can hold longer, up to a minute (it won't help to hold any longer than that), but you must hold for at least thirty seconds. This will begin to free up things that might be holding you back.

> **The Standard Method**
> The standard method is to make a gesture at least thirty seconds before you go to sleep at night, once every third day for two or three weeks. This is the gentlest way to do it.

You might ask, "What is being freed up?" Very often what is being released slowly to be processed through the body will be old remarks. Maybe as a child you had a nickel. The other children didn't have a nickel; they had a penny. Because you were not very close friends, you didn't pool the money. Maybe someone said, "You've got more than we've got." Perhaps you felt good about that, but maybe you felt embarrassed, shy. That goes in your memory. That means that having more wealth is a reason to be embarrassed, shy, which restricts wealth. You might feel like that.

So it's about specifically removing certain stored pieces from the body's computer memory?

Removing memory. Memory in the body is always stored in feeling. We use a computer analogy because people can understand that today. It's removing memory-feeling, removing the feeling you have because of what other people said if they were close to you (children often stand close to each other when they are very young). Maybe the other children felt good about their pennies, then you came along with a nickel. Suddenly they felt like, "Oh, we are disappointed in the penny," whereas before the penny looked pretty good.

I'm talking about fifty years ago when children could go to a little store, maybe go into town with their parents, and have a penny to buy some penny candy. You could have something to show for a penny, but with a nickel you can buy a lot. I use this analogy for the reader. The questioner can remember such times.

What is the dynamic of moving our hands in a certain way? Why does it work?

Remember that the body's first and primary language is feeling. Unhappiness is stored in feeling. Gesture is feeling. Even if you reach up and scratch your head, that's feeling. You are scratching something that itches, but it is all communication with feeling. Asking the body to communicate in words is not natural to it.

Some of you could say, "This does not seem right, Speaks of Many Truths, because the mouth, lips, tongue—all of these instruments can speak words." Yet what if I told you, as Uncle Zoosh used to say, that your mouth, lips and tongue were not intended to speak words but to make noises you would call grunts? Sometimes these noises are understandable to you, such as *mm*. This could mean "good food" or "I understand." This sound is very often universal or cross-cultural; many cultures might understand that *mm* means, "Yes, I understand." But that is what is natural for the body—a sound that is understood to have meaning but is not a word.

How Humans Received Language

How do you get the overlay of the sound that has meaning? How about the word that has meaning?

Words come from the Earth dweller being exposed to the sky dweller. People came from the sky, and the sky dweller often had a specific sound that was different all the time, not just *mm*, but a very elaborate sound. Eventually people understood that this was not just *mm*, but specifically something else. Then the well-intentioned sky dweller often taught language to interested Earth people.

Almost all root languages stem from sky dwellers. This good-hearted gesture from the sky dwellers was so that Earth people could describe their world. Seems like a good gesture, yes? But it turned out to actually work against the body's method of true expression.

The sky dwellers in ancient times did not understand what was happening on Earth. They thought that Earth dwellers were nice, primitive individuals; "We could give them little bit if they show interest, if they have talent." How was the first word from the sky dwellers taught?

Imitation?

No, the first word from the sky dwellers was demonstrated to Earth dwellers. The sky dweller first said his name, which was not a sound like *mm* but an elaborate word, consisting of many sounds. For instance, the name "George Albert Smith" would not be a typical sound for an Earth dweller who is accustomed to saying only *mm*. The Earth dweller recognized that this was something different. He understood conceptually, through hand signs and gestures from the sky dweller, that these sounds as given had to do with this person specifically.

Then the sky dweller might have gestured to all his companions and used a term to describe his people. He might have drawn a picture in the dirt where the Earth dwellers lived, astronomically, and then where the sky dwellers lived. Or he might have pointed to the sky, if it was nighttime, and made pictures on the ground, making it clear that the sky dweller was from there, saying these words.

In short, the sky dwellers, like any explorers, wanted to communicate with the beings they had just met. Sounds from Earth dwellers were so basic, they could not speak of the things the sky dwellers wished to speak of, though the sky dwellers knew these sounds, too. But the sky dwellers could not ask Earth dwellers the things they wanted to know about. So the sky dwellers felt it was a goodhearted gesture to teach the Earth dwellers a basic language, maybe not even the sky dwellers' language, but a language that has been taught to many people all over where the sky dwellers have gone. It was a language that was easy to understand, maybe with a small vocabulary. That's how language started, but with words, not the body's method of communication, which is sound. It is a simple but profound truth, yes?

Sound: Our Fundamental Communication

So we have to get back to that beginning, communication-wise?

You don't necessarily have to get back to it, but you need to recognize that everything the body does has to do with material mastery and everything the spirit or soul does has to do with spiritual mastery. Put these two together and you have a vehicle in which your personality, which goes on life after life, can learn more about spiritual mastery and material mastery.

The body is made up of Mother Earth, as Grandpa Zoosh says, and can learn other things because Earth herself is spiritual, material, teaching, dimensional and is now completely a quantum master. She is no longer working on quantum mastery [as discussed in previous *Explorer Race* books] but *is* a quantum master, so you have the opportunity available to you to learn lessons in all of these areas, because your body is made up of Mother Earth.

You do not have to get rid of words, but you can remember that foundational communication has to do with sounds. You would say normal sounds or grunts or meaningful sounds such as *aah*, meaning "feel good"—that sound is also cross-cultural. Now, because everybody has the same meaning and everyone understands these sounds, at least in your culture, this must be considered a root language for you. Your root language is not English, not Spanish, not French, not Russian. Your root language is the sound you make with the body through your mouth.

Something taught in some spiritual modalities is called toning, where you might get in the shower and let your mouth emit sounds that you don't think about, going up and down the scale.

If you make a conscious effort to go with musical sound, you may just be making sound and may not be necessarily stimulating any profound healing, or you might be doing so only to a minor degree. But if you allow your body to make the sounds it chooses to make through your mouth . . . maybe sometimes the sound could be musical, maybe toning, but no words, not even a beautiful word like Om (that is a word). It may be that in the shower, you'd say, "Aah," because you feel warm and comfortable. Very often people get into the shower and make that sound.

Take note the next time you make that sound for any reason. The sound is being made because feeling is being expressed—*aah*. Everyone knows that means "feel good." It is easy to just not think about it. These sounds are at the profound root of body-speak.

Then movement must be another basic form of communication?

Certain movements you take for granted; you could put your hand over your heart, meaning something about your heart. If you are sad, if you are happy, maybe you see a child walk for the first time and you put your hand over your heart. *Aah* isn't stated, but that means, in this case, "Isn't that wonderful?" It's a natural gesture that doesn't need to be spoken—very profound.

How Gestures Release Feelings in Your Body

I am still not clear how moving a hand in a certain way in relationship to another hand triggers the dissipation of a bad feeling.

You do understand, for example, how acupuncture works. The meridians of the body have been studied for years and years by people who have found that this is accurate, but to be perfectly honest, sometimes points are different on different people. So an acupuncturist with many years experience knows that not all points are the same for everyone. Using that as an example, you can understand how stimulating a certain point might prompt healing in another part of the body.

These gestures work similarly. The body has certain material mastery rhythms. We know that one of the body's material-mastery rhythms has to do with the heart pumping. When the heart stops pumping, it means you're not in the body anymore. This is mechanical, obviously. A plumber or a doctor would understand that the heart must pump liquid around the body in order to keep you alive. Liquid does many things, but if the heart is no longer pumping (or if the plumber says that the pump is no longer working), things will stop.

It is like this: The body is now a material master. The mind, the mental part, is not a material master for most people, but your personality, your mind, resides in a body that is a material master—the physical body. Everyone's physical body is a material master and constantly gives you lessons in material mastery.

I start with the heart pumping blood, because the heart is also the source of great love. Love-heat takes place where the heart is: across the chest, the upper abdomen—in short, close to the physical heart. So blood not only goes through the heart for medical reasons, as you understand—physical, scientific reasons—but goes through your heart to give the blood love.

So sometimes things that seem perfectly obvious after you hear them are easy to forget because they are so basic, you don't think about it. This is the material-mastery lesson about why gestures are given.

Any gesture.

Yes, any gesture. Why? Because the body communicates not only in material mastery to itself, but to the world around it. The heart knows this. A baby sitting or lying in a crib, moving around, kicking his legs, wiggling and so on—one thinks he is experimenting with his body. But sometimes gestures have to do with what the body is doing. Do you know that very often, when a baby tries to pull his legs up and then kick . . . you've all seen babies do this at least once. The baby pulls his legs up and then kicks out with both legs at the same time; he seems to be experimenting, moving his body, enjoying it.

Doctors think this means one thing, but not always. What does it mean in body language? It means the baby wants to have his feet on the soil of the Earth, wants his feet to touch the soil of the Earth. In short, the body is trying to reach Earth.

This is a message, not just from an individual baby. Babies in their cribs do these things quickly, as soon as they can move. This tells people around them that the baby is communicating as well. He does not just want his feet on the Earth. The baby communicates to all human beings who look at him that the soul comes into the physical body here to be on Earth. That's what that gesture means.

Did you know about that in your time and pick the baby up and put him on the floor?

We knew. Remember that in my time, there were no books, not so many words—very few for my people. So we had lots of time. We had to live, have food and do the things other people do. But we had lots of time to observe nature, observe animals, observe Earth, observe our own bodies and the bodies of our children, and learn what things mean.

Plus you're taught.

Yes, we're taught, but we learn and give a lot of teaching to each other. Oh yes, we know.

Is there anything to the idea that just as there are meridians and lines of energy in the body, they are also within the aura? Are you touching magnetic lines or any lines of energy in the aura itself with these movements?

There's a slight difference. All parts of the body are in motion at the microscopic or atomic level. Moving beyond the microscopic level, we see that certain parts of the body are in motion all the time, blood and so on. Generally speaking, much of the body is not in motion all the time. But the auric field is *always* in motion. Every split of a second, energy radiates out, some is being absorbed, brought in . . . it's constant. So you cannot just reach to a point in the aura and say that this point means this and this point means that. You can sometimes do this, but only on an individual to individual basis. Still, it is a good question.

Clearing Severe Trauma Incrementally

The original question here was, how do people clear severe trauma? But first you spoke about minor things instead of severe trauma.

What you are not clear on is that this works for clearing minor things, but for severe trauma the idea is to treat it incrementally. There might be many, many thousands of minor things, and any one gesture might clear all of them. But let's say there is a huge trauma. A gesture will not clear it all at once, or the body could get sick, traumatized, possibly even die, because the trauma must be processed through the body. So the gesture might, in fact, release only some of it. The next time you could try a new gesture, maybe do more and so on. That's what I mean by incrementally.

These gestures work on the major traumas, then?

Yes. I have just not been talking about major traumas. I use the word "incrementally" to mean bit by bit.

Are you going to go into diseases, which are really weaknesses of the body?

Right now I am going one step at a time. I understand that you want me to pinpoint and say what gesture will get rid of cancer in the body, for instance, but is not like that. Cancer does not fall into the body from the sky. The body is predisposed for illness; as these traumas, these upsets, these sadnesses in the body accumulate, if they are not addressed and released by the methods being given, then disease comes.

Disease does not fall out of the sky for most people, with the exception of a child born with disease. If there is a birth disease, it almost always has to do with the soul wishing to begin such a challenge for its own education. The child is not cursed from a previous life, but this is the soul choosing to see what it can do with this body, this life, in this way.

For now we'll work on releasing certain things, what this part of body means and so on. We'll continue, then, in the second part of this book to talk more about my life.

About the shamanic teachings that have been given you?

I'll talk about my life the way I live it.

Release Point for the Unexpected, Both Positive and Negative

The whole left knee joint—the top of some bones, the bottom of other bones and the big bone in the center—has to do with moving through the unexpected in the most benevolent way for yourself. The unexpected can be anything from trauma and discomfort to unexpected bountiful gifts, but *where* you move through them is important.

Sometimes somebody jumps out from behind the door and says, "Surprise!"—gives you big gifts, a party and so on. But if you do not feel safe to be unexpectedly surprised like that, you might fall down and hurt yourself and put a damper on the party. That usually does not happen, although it happens more often than people realize, but this is about moving through the unexpected benevolently.

You might also be driving down the street and all of a sudden—bang, crash—there is an unexpected sound from outside of your car. Not a car crash, but just an unexpected sound. You are startled; you react and maybe then continue to drive on. "What was that?"—curiosity is natural. But you go on. That is moving through benevolently. Your body is going to react, but you go on.

But maybe someone lights a firecracker—bang!—and the entire body does not feel too good. There is too much stuff stored in the knee, perhaps. The immediate reaction to a firecracker on the sidewalk is to turn away from the loud sound right into a light post and then have a *real* bang. We want to clear the left knee so your reaction can be equal in proportion to the stimulation.

Some people think that they are just nervous and are going to react like that, but I'll tell you a little secret: People who seem to be nervous when they are born are not nervous but have a great deal of creative energy that is meant to be applied. If you have child who seems to be nervous, get him or her to do as many creative projects as possible. Don't just buy a kit and build a plane, because that's not too creative. That's just doing one thing after another. It's better to buy paper and paint and create something yourself. "What should I paint?" "Anything you like." When it's finished, if it doesn't look like the real thing . . . well, practice. Maybe your child can go to a summer art class and learn a little bit of technique, but mainly encourage creativity in him or her. Nervousness is not natural.

When children are hyperactive, do you equate that to nervousness or is that something different?

For one thing, hyperactivity is not a real thing, though I do not wish to discount people who live with a so-called hyperactive child. Most children are hyperactive at one time or another. That's normal. It is normal for a child to want to run and play all of the time. If a child is like that twenty-four hours a day week after week and year after year, then okay, maybe the child is hyperactive. But this means that the child needs creative things to do or might need to be an athlete, if the child is physically able. Maybe he or she wants to play baseball, perhaps swim—then let the child do that all the time if you can. But generally speaking, such things were not treated as a disease in my time. Some children are more quiet and other children are more active. It was the same thing in my time.

Resolving the Trauma of the Unexpected

Following is the gesture to clear traumas having to do with the unexpected out of the knee. What traumas might there be? Things happened that were unexpected—good, bad, it doesn't make any difference—and you might not necessarily have reacted too well to those unexpected things. Mothers, fathers and people around babies know this a lot. Let's say that a teacher comes into nursery school and the children are playing around on floor, maybe one or two parents are there. The teacher claps his or her hands, as teachers often do with older children. Some children will stop and look up. Most children are not too impacted by the traumas of life yet, but at least one or two children will immediately cry because a sudden sound like that has to do with the unexpected. Children who immediately cry when hearing that sound—not done harshly, but done suddenly—are having trouble with the unexpected and their left knee needs to be cleared.

So as an adult, if you jump at any loud noise, you definitely need to clear your left knee [Fig. 2-9], again using the standard method. This is especially important because this book is going to be read largely by adults. If you are a nervous person, you could benefit from doing this gesture.

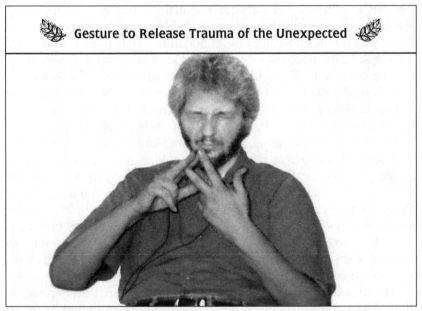

Gesture to Release Trauma of the Unexpected

Fig. 2-9a. Here is the gesture to begin to clear the left knee. Hold for at least thirty seconds before you go to sleep at night. Do this once every third day for two to three weeks.

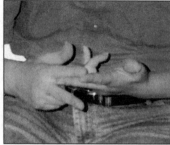
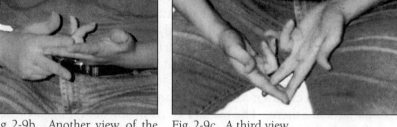

Fig. 2-9b. Another view of the finger position.   Fig. 2-9c. A third view.

The standard method is to make this gesture for at least thirty seconds before you go to sleep at night, once every third day for two or three weeks. This is the gentlest way to do it. Many nervous people do not know that it is important to be gentle with themselves. They might know this mentally, but they have patterns and habits. Gradually, as you begin to clear, it will be easier to relax. Then you will know that you are no longer nervous and have cleared your left knee completely. For the average nervous person to totally clear using the standard method, it might take a year.

How do you know when your left knee is cleared? You still might be nervous sometimes, but sometimes something that appears to be nervousness can actually be a natural body reaction. So how do you know? You will know because minor things that used to cause nervousness do not disturb you anymore. Don't judge on the basis of major things, though. If somebody comes into the room or office you're in and slams the door, that is not a minor thing; it is a sudden sound out of the context of the sounds you normally hear. Don't use that as a basis. Rather, if someone near you in that room makes an unexpected sound, but it's not unusual, and it doesn't cause you to tighten up in your solar plexus area or around your shoulders, then the knee is clear.

What if you start to have those feelings again? Then begin the procedure again, but it won't take as long to clear. Once you have cleared, the procedure can be easily repeated. If you've been chronically nervous your whole life, then you can, if you choose, do this gesture once a week for three weeks as a maintenance program or once every six months, even if you are not feeling nervous. But if there is not clarity, just try to pay attention to your life. How is it going? All right?

Do not expect yourself, after a lifetime of reactions and nervous actions, to get completely better immediately. But there should be significant improvement.

Releasing the Neck Stress of Expectations

Do people tend to store their stresses in the back of the neck?

People's first reaction usually happens in the solar plexus area. Then tension goes up the spine into the shoulders, across muscles under the side of the neck and then to the back of the neck—usually that route. Where you hold the tension that prompts a nervous reaction is less important, but not unimportant.

What about people who store tension or stress in the back of the neck?

Discomfort in the back of the neck almost always has to do with what you are expected to do—other people's expectations of you or your expectations of yourself. The gesture for that is a little different: Touch the bridge of your nose with your right thumb and place your forefinger on your head [Fig. 2-10]. On a big hand, a person's finger goes up farther; a small hand doesn't go as far.

🌾 Gesture to Clear the Neck Stress of Expectations 🌾

Fig. 2-10b. Then place the first finger on your forehead. Hold for thirty seconds. Do this once every third day for two to three weeks, preferably before you go to sleep at night.

Fig. 2-10a. Touch the bridge of the nose with your thumb. Try to line up your thumb as shown, using your right hand.

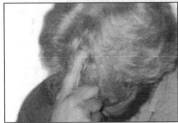

Fig. 2-10c. A different view of the finger placement.

Fig. 2-10d. This will clarify the position of your fingers. Do this with your hand, then place it on your head as shown earlier.

The bridge of the nose is the key.

The bridge of the nose is the key, exactly. Perform this using the standard method. This will tend to relieve expectations, both inner and outer. It's very helpful.

We'll go through the body and show different things—not everything, but we'll try to give mostly examples. This book is about more than that, though.

Relieving Tension Headaches or Earaches from Visual Traumas

Some people feel some discomfort here in their temples. Now, sometimes there is tension that might lead to a headache or take on the form of an earache or even a headache that radiates around the area where the ear is, but not to the jaw.

Gesture to Clear Effects of Visual Traumas

Fig. 2-11a. This is the gesture. The thumbs do not touch the top of the head, but hold them about an inch or two right above the middle of the top of the head, above the crown chakra, for at least thirty seconds. Do this before you go to bed once every third day for two or three weeks.

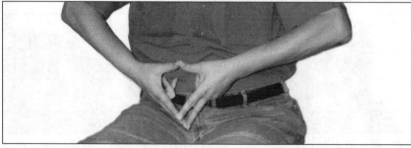

Fig. 2-11b. A different view to clarify the position of the fingers.

This area has to do with pain based on what you've seen visually that might impact you. Maybe you are being driven in a car and can't stop— you're driving along and see where a dog has been struck by another car and you are sad. A dog has lost its life in a traumatic way. It's something you see with your eyes.

Maybe you see a child, but you can't go to the child for some reason. Your culture does not encourage it with you being in a vehicle. The child is very thin, not trim and athletic, but emaciated. What you see is traumatic to that part of your body. Or maybe you are watching television, seeing sad things happen to different people.

There are many, many different possibilities if you're getting lots of tension or headaches or earaches in that area. This is different from a child getting earaches; this is adults—let's say nine years old and up. Then it might be good to clear that area using this gesture [Fig. 2-11].

Above the crown chakra?

Yes, above the crown chakra is sufficient.

Using the standard method?

The standard method, yes.

Releasing the Sadness of Nonacceptance

Now, let's discuss this area.

The joint of the right arm, the inside of the elbow.

This has to do with not being accepted by those around you. When you want to be accepted and liked and so on, but you're not—that sadness goes there. This often needs to be cleared.

You can see that a lot of this book has to do with youngsters, because most often traumas and sadness in childhood are felt for the rest of the life.

Gesture to Release the Sadness of Nonacceptance

Fig. 2-12b. A different view to clarify the position of your fingers.

Fig. 2-12a. Here is the gesture. Hold for at least thirty seconds before you go to bed at night. Do this once every third day for two to three weeks.

Yes, that's the point of this book.

The gesture of release is very simple [Fig. 2-12].

The Care of Newborn Babies

It is hard to imagine, but imagine a physical body being born. It's a highly sensitive body. Think of sensors in science fiction books. Sensors tell us this and sensors tell us that—but this is a fictionalized format.

Take that but greatly amplified—that is how you are in the physical body. Babies are born profoundly sensitive; they are sensitive inside their mother's bodies. They come through the mother's body as they are born into this world. That is why it's vitally important to both mother and child to be as gentle as possible and, once the baby is born, to not separate him from the mother—to just be born and handed to the mother, not taken by doctors or nurses, not weighed by them, not slapped. (Babies believe the slapping is on purpose, even though it's not.) A gentle birth. The baby comes out and goes to the mother. The mother holds the baby. If they need to wash the baby off, wash the baby off while the mother holds him. It's okay if the mother gets some blood on her; wash the mother off too if you want, but let the mother hold the baby. Nobody else should hold the baby for quite a while, because the baby has been inside the mother's body. When he comes out he must, at the very least, be held by her.

How long before somebody else should hold the baby?

The mother might have to sleep—if so, prop up pillows around the mother and the baby so that they sleep together. The mother and the baby should not be separated for the first four hours. But if the baby must be held, this must be done very gently and tenderly. If you require or wish to do something medical during the first four hours, let the mother hold the baby.

If medical trauma, even well-intentioned, takes place, the first thing the baby feels, not thinks, is, "Not safe." The baby knows he's safe inside his mother. Then the first message, on the feeling level, when he comes out of his mother is that he's not safe. Babies do not think in concepts, just outside of mother versus inside of mother. If the outside is not safe, frightening, he might stay frightened the rest of his life just about that, to say nothing of other things.

Imagine the science fiction version of sensors expanded to the seventeenth power. Not just in greater amplitude of sensitivity, not just in babies . . . as sensitive as babies are, we never change; adults are no different. They're still just as sensitive, though they have built up the debris of unresolved trauma.

Which dulls the sensitivity?

Which dulls your awareness of increased trauma but does not decrease the trauma and its aftereffect, mentioned earlier in this book.

The Early Times before the Explorer Race and the Birth Process

Why is this thing perpetuated? I don't understand why it's been allowed. Why has birth trauma been ongoing for thousands of years?

Not so long. Think about the history of Earth in this position in this solar system. People lived here before the Explorer Race showed up, some people such as myself. I am not part of the Explorer Race, you understand.

Many, many native peoples—African people, native people in northern Great Britain, Scotland, native people all over Canada, South America and so on—many of these peoples are not part of the Explorer Race. They had to prepare the Earth back thousands of years. Some tribes might have started having Explorer Race souls four, five, six hundred years ago.

That's all?

That's right, not much before then; it was very occasional. This person, that person. This is my perception. This tells you that the bulk of Explorer Race people have been here recently. The Explorer Race is on a different path, learning lessons of creator training, so explorers must have a tremendous amount of consequences—consequences of actions, thoughts and so on. But ancient peoples in more ancient times . . . some tribes were not too wise. They hadn't been there that long and didn't understand how the birth process went.

Some others, having been here for a while, knew how the birth process went—gently or surrounded by gentleness. Maybe the mother-to-be and her first child go into a woman's hut. There's an older woman there to show her what to do. Very gentle. She is just there to help and so on. Maybe if it's a breech birth, the grandmother or midwife would have to reach up inside the mother and turn the baby around, but she knew how. The midwife was a very old woman and skilled.

But going back further than that when people originally . . . many peoples, native peoples, older peoples, lived by water out of necessity. You need water to drink. Maybe in later years they took ships out to go here and there, but that's many years later. Many other people lived by streams and so on—it must be fresh water. Sometimes there was even a warm pool of water, considered to be sacred by native peoples. Ofttimes, but not always

If there was a pool, they would have a wet birth?

Yes, they gave birth in the water. All children live inside their mothers in water. The first lesson is very basic: This is a water planet. You might ask yourself, if a human child is inside its mother in water, what about a duck, for instance, in an egg. What does that say? Is the baby chick surrounded by water? What does that suggest?

Ducks originally come from a dry planet.

That's right. A basic observation, which is very important at all times. A water-birthed baby comes out swimming, so he or she is familiar with water—born in water, cushioned by water, hearing water sounds and the sounds of her mother's body, but always she swims through the water. The child comes out of her mother in birth swimming, knowing how to swim. It's very unusual for a child to come out of her mother and sink to the bottom of the pool—that's very unusual, very rare. I have heard of one of these circumstances, but the midwife can reach in and pull the baby up to the surface. Recognize that that soul has never been on a water world ever before.

Most of you born here have been on a water world at one time or another, so babies come out swimming. You know this as an individual. Very often a child is fed later on by parents, spoon-fed. Eventually the child wants to feed herself. She says, "I want to do it." What if a water birth takes place? The child comes out swimming and immediately is able to help herself. A child who swims out of her mother will have more confidence in the physical world she finds herself in because she is able to act on her own behalf immediately.

A water birth is the best. It's best in saline-type warm water, but it can be done in mineral water associated with ground water. It's not recommended at your time to use ocean water; most ocean water is now too polluted. But you can create a saltwater bath to have a water birth. The child born this way might be more friendly with sea creatures, and the sea creatures also might be more friendly with the child. I know of experiments done in your time with children born in saline pools with dolphins—very interesting experiment. [There is a wealth of information available on water births on the Internet, in your favorite bookstore and at your local library.]

Release Point for Trauma of Birth Separation from Mother

What about a child who is slapped, beat on, pressed against cold metal and injected with a needle? Where is he storing all that trauma?

It goes to different parts of the body, but usually the initial trauma, especially separation from the mother, which is a terrible trauma . . . after four hours, the mother's sister, for instance, who is in a loving state of being, can gently pick up the baby. She can gently hold that baby, coo to the baby or sing, gently making sounds, not words. When you make words, you unconsciously use sounds.

You might make a sound in a word without knowing it—for example, *uh-oh.* You all know that sound means "I don't feel good" or "Oh, no," but that sound could be incorporated even in a one- or two-word sequence in one person. *Uh-oh.* Remember, because he is a highly sensing being, a baby will hear natural sounds first, but he does not understand words—to the baby's benefit, naturally.

So sounds are very important. The making of sounds, happy sounds and not words, is important. Not even just happy sounds, but when holding the baby, you must be happy and loving the baby. You must feel it. You can't just say, "I love the baby. Give me the baby." This statement is not borne out of feeling.

So where does the trauma of separation from the mother get stored?

If the separation takes place traumatically, it resides back here, where the left buttock begins to blend into the back of the left leg. It goes right in there and stays there for a lifetime, even if the baby is breastfed.

By the way, breastfeeding is always the best way—from the breast, not any other way. Breastfeeding is vital for the baby's health, as many people know, and also for the baby to continue to recognize his mother as a source of support. The mother is representative not only of a loving being, but she also is the first person the baby contacts in his Earth experience. So if someone else picks up the baby and, though well-intentioned, shoves a bottle into his mouth, the baby says, "What is this? I don't like this too much." If he's hungry, he will figure it out and eat, but this is not too pleasant.

The mother's milk is most important. Do the best you can. Sometimes you will not be able as a mother to provide mother's milk for the baby. The next best thing, if you must provide a bottled product, is to hold the baby while genuinely feeling love for him. The best thing for you to feel is heat in the chest or upper abdomen so the baby feels safe. Then pick up the bottle and put it in his mouth, all the while feeling heat. You do not have to make sounds to the baby, but you can if you like. Make happy, good-feeling sounds.

Resolving Birth Trauma

What is the gesture to clear the trauma in the left rear of the hip?

Refer to Fig. 2-13. Again, use the standard method. I have not said this before, but it's important to say: Clear only one area at a time. You can clear multiple areas at the same time only if your body does not give you too much discomfort signaling that this is not good. You can also do this if you are in good shape physically—athletic, healthy, not sick, without any chronic illness, that kind of thing. But if you have some trauma, discomfort, chronic illness or something like that, do one thing at a time; complete that process and then go on to the next thing. I suggest you don't try doing too many things.

Remember, proportion is not a factor of transformation—a lifetime

Gesture to Release Separation Trauma

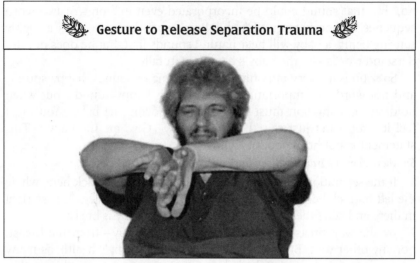

Fig. 2-13a. Here is the gesture to clear trauma in the left rear of the hip. Hold for at least thirty seconds. Do this before you go to sleep at night once every third day for two to three weeks.

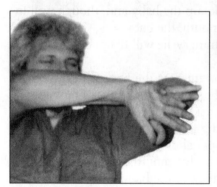

Fig. 2-13b. A different view.

Fig. 2-13c. A third view. The actual position is when the fingers point forward as shown in Fig. 2-14a.

pattern of unhappiness as compared to just bits. The same gesture done in the same way still clears it; proportionality is *not* a factor.

Release Point and Gesture for a Lack of Self-Confidence

If people have pain above the ankle and below the knee in the front, is it something about stepping out into the world?

It primarily has to do with confidence. The left side has to do with self-confidence, which you create by doing things on your own and feeling good about them. The right side has to do with confidence given to you by others—parents and grandparents saying, "You did that

well," and so on. This is confidence that comes from others.
That makes sense.

So we'll continue with that, clearing that area [Fig. 2-14].

Gesture to Release a Lack of Self-Confidence

Fig. 2-14b. A different view, to clarify the position of the hands.

Fig. 2-14a. This is the gesture, just like this. Hold for thirty seconds, preferably at night before you go to bed. Do this every third day for two to three weeks.

How do you know these things?

I know.

You knew them consciously before this book?

Yes.

And this works for lack of self-confidence from both what one has experienced and what one has been given by others?

Yes, exactly.

So it clears both of them at the same time?

Yes. Much of this has to do with having one's personal self-confidence crushed when one was a child, being told "wrong" too often, being disapproved of. But if you can, accept this and transform yourself. Unfortunately, in your time and your culture, this has been going on for a long time. Many people are like this, but not everyone.

Your friends, people you're exposed to, are going to give you confidence, but most important is that your mother, father, sisters, brothers, aunts, uncles and grandparents give you this. It's not just them saying, "Oh, isn't that wonderful," every time you do something, but saying it when you do something that you're good at or something that is a nice thing. Then your parents, uncles, aunts, grandfather, grandmother say, "Good for you, well done," like that. That is external confidence. It's not that you *deserved* to be praised; something about deserving to be praised has gotten well out of hand in your time. Different people have different qualifications for "deserving."

This seems like approval, but when it is felt on that leg, it helps to give a person confidence in doing the right kind of thing. It is a good thing, and that child did it just right because she received approval from a beloved family member.

Children often cannot get approval for what they do.

The parents do not know how; maybe they did not receive it when they were children and approval is completely unknown to them. It's a sad thing in your time. Part of the reason that so many people now are sick with diseases that did not exist in my time and why there is crime and stealing—this kind of thing is unknown to my people—is because children have to gain confidence by interacting with other children who are disapproved of.

If you learn as a child that the only kind of attention you get from adults is disapproval, you might unconsciously attempt to get disapproval from other adults all the time when you grow up, because disapproval takes the place of love. Then you seek disapproval because that's all you know.

There are whole cultures across the United States where it got passed from generation to generation. They didn't receive this kind of love and understanding because the parents couldn't give it.

That's right. They are not bad people; they did not know, were ignorant. That's what these books hope to moderate. Think about circumstances, not just feelings in the body, but conditions, patterns of behavior that are full of sadness.

The Subconscious as Physical Feeling: Help from Various Sources That Cooperate

What about what we call storing things in the subconscious? How does that relate to the storage in various parts of the body that you're discussing?

The subconscious is an idea to people who believe the mind is everything and thought is everything. The actual subconscious has nothing to do with the mind at all. The subconscious *is* physical feeling.

And what if you're cut off from your physical feelings?

They are not cut off, but . . . when people say conscious mind, subconscious mind, unconscious mind, they use this instead of physical body, feeling body. The whole construct is completely not true. "Subconscious" has come to be the word for that which cannot be thought about but comes close. That's because it is in feelings. If you try to find the subconscious in the mental construct of conscious/subconscious/unconscious, it is a long, hard journey. If you go to a psychoanalyst for ten, fifteen years, he or she will do the best he or she can to help, but if you go directly to the physical body, you might be able to clear much, much quicker.

The best way for many traumas to heal would be for a spiritual psychologist to work with a bodyworker, a healer and maybe a channeler, too. Bring them all together—even a shaman, a medicine woman maybe, all different people. Each practitioner would contribute his or her own expertise and sensitivity, and all insights would be shared.

The psychologist says to a medicine woman, "I think it might be this." The medicine woman would say, "I feel it might be this thing." These things might feel different but could be related. The psychologist thinks this could be the cause, but the medicine woman could say, "Look at this person's body." She might feel that something is missing, an herb. A mystical man could look at the person's body and say a feeling is missing, this feeling needs to be generated, but that's all. This would all be very brief, not this talk, talk, talk. This way the practitioners have some idea that everything each and every one of them sees (assuming they know what they are doing) is all connected—different parts of the same cause.

Well, maybe soon we'll have multidisciplined healing groups.

It is very important, because different people respond to different treatments. But mostly people have access only to a certain kind of treatment. Maybe a psychologist will say, "I know this treatment is right for this person, but it's not working." So that psychologist could go to a medicine woman or mystical man and describe the patient and ask the medicine woman or mystical man what he or she thinks or feels.

If the person can go, good, but maybe he can't go. Maybe the person does not feel good about the medicine woman or mystical man because there is religion involved, for instance—he does not believe in that. Then the psychologist would go ask. Or maybe it could work the other way. Maybe the medicine woman or medicine man is working with a person very much involved in thought. He or she might go talk to a psychologist friend and ask, "What do you think this person might need?" See, they'd share information.

I hope that is our model for the future, where there is one of each.

Yes, skills and occupations need not disappear; they simply need to be applied differently, more gently, benevolently. Surgeons don't have to go away immediately, but ultimately it will be best for them to . . . not quite yet, but eventually, no more surgery. This is probably a society and culture where we may be attached to surgery for a time, but eventually there will be no more of that. You could say, "But people fall down . . ."

. . . and break their leg.

But there won't be that kind of trauma then. There won't be surgery because surgery won't be needed.

Good night.

The Resolution of Fear, Trauma and Hate

Speaks of Many Truths
July 29, 1999

reetings.

Is fear a thing in itself, or is each incident stored somewhere—for instance, fear of heights, fear of water, fear of open spaces, fear of success, fear of failure, fear of love, fear of being alone, fear of dying and on and on like that. Is fear a thing in itself, or is each type of fear separate?

Fear of any particular thing is based on a learned experience, whether it is something that was learned by your own personal experience or someone frightened you about that thing. It is the *experience* of learning the fear. The trauma of learning the fear, whether it was something that didn't go right for you and had a consequence you didn't like, or whether others prompted that fear through their actions or statements to you—that is the trauma that would go into the capillaries.

For instance, you as a youngster go for a walk on a trail with your friends. You pass through an area where the trail is a little rough and maybe not too complete. Your friends jump over some part, but you are not sure about jumping. The worst that can happen is that you might fall ten, twelve, fifteen feet. So you try it, but you miss the other side of the trail and fall down.

Now, if this is a simple act of falling and landing on something soft and not hurting yourself, it may not be traumatic, but if you fall and there is a wound or an injury, that trauma would perhaps go into some part of your body.

Release Point for Trauma-Induced Fears

Let's talk about trauma-induced fear. Most trauma-induced fear resides in a very specific area. Remember when we talked about the area behind the solar plexus? Trauma-induced fear exists here. Let's start at the sternum. Go about two inches in either direction on the surface, then go up the bone a distance of about two or two and a half inches.

Then all the way across? A rectangle?

No, it is just a shape.

Oh, it's a line on the bottom and a line that comes up in the center.

Very good, thank you. In that place reside fears prompted by traumas. It is important to know that, because there is an opportunity here. Most often any fear-prompted trauma, any experience like that, even if you don't remember why, if you approach or come close to having an experience based on or having a history of such fear-caused trauma, the first place in your body that will signal you is this area. Most likely you will either feel a rather slight tension there or you might feel a dull ache.

This is on the edge of the bone above the solar plexus?

It is the exact place I mentioned. We are moving along the base of the rib cage on either side and then up a couple of inches in the center.

Is it in the bone or in the capillaries?

No, it's in the tissue, on the surface. So if you can be alert to that discomfort, you will immediately know—this is where it's complicated—that your body is warning you, "Danger, be careful," an instinctual message, or that you are confronting a situation having to do with an old fear.

The problem is that you don't know which it is?

No. I'll tell you how to know.

Identifying Your Body's Fear Message

This is how you can use your auric field a little bit. Take your hand (I recommend the right hand) and hold it in front of that area briefly. If the discomfort goes away (the pain and the tension), it probably means that it is a message of an actual potential danger, an instinctual message.

Because it's coming into your aura?

Yes, and you are blocking it that way. If, on the other hand, the tension or discomfort does not go away, it has to do with the memory of the pain. This gives you clear-cut physical evidence that you can use, and when practiced properly, it can allow you to discern. If you know that the felt message has to do with an old fear, it does not mean to ignore it. It means that you know you'll be doing something that recalls some previous trauma.

You may be able to ignore it or modify it based on your actions. It might be possible to turn this way or that way, but if not . . . say, for instance, that you have a fear of heights and you are in a train moving along. You have been moving through the city, but eventually the train moves through the country. You have been on that track before and you know there's a long railroad bridge coming up that goes over a precipitous drop to a river below, as bridges often do.

You are sitting there, you are safe; perhaps you are in your own compartment. But because you've traveled that route before, you know that you will get upset. You can look out the window, and when the train goes around the curve, you can see that bridge coming up and you get that discomforting feeling in your body. Probably you know it has to do with that fear, but test it.

Hold your hand in front of your body, perhaps four to eight inches in front. If the tension is still there, you know this most likely has to do with your fear of heights. If, however, the tension of discomfort goes away, then it might not be danger because you are going over a bridge. Maybe there is somebody in the car you are riding in who might pass by and do something annoying, maybe not to you.

Or perhaps there is danger to someone in your immediate proximity, someone sitting next to you or right in front of you or behind you, without a metal barrier between you. That person is the one for whom there is some danger, and his or her instinctual body is feeling that danger at that moment, although he or she might not know what it means. A metal barrier will usually prevent you from feeling this, but if the person is sitting close to you (perhaps you are sitting in a middle seat and people are on both sides of you), it might mean danger to that person.

Danger can be a lot of things. It could be something annoying or upsetting. Maybe a child will go by and make a loud noise. If you have children of your own, that sort of thing doesn't bother you, but perhaps your seatmate would be startled and upset. It could be something like that, or something more extreme.

So don't automatically assume that the bridge and the train will fall. Most likely that is not going to happen. They build those bridges to last. It is something to take note of, however. If you can, hold your hand there in front of your body for a few moments, until the train goes over the bridge (don't worry about people around you wondering why you are holding your hand there). After the train crosses the bridge, if you notice that the discomfort goes away, it doesn't mean it was your discomfort. It could mean that the person sitting near you or on either side of you was also terrified, maybe more afraid of heights than you are, and that he or she relaxed.

But remember, this could also mean that there is danger in that area to yourself or others from a negative energy. When you feel that discomfort initially, even before you put your hand there, ask your benevolent spirits and angels to protect you. See this protection within you. Don't automatically radiate it out to others; don't assume the danger isn't for you.

Yet your body functions in a very subtle way. A danger signal might also have to do with something far away. You are going over a bridge, but the discomfort doesn't seem to be associated with your old fear of heights. Perhaps there is some danger in the immediate area but not close by. For instance, a deer might get a feeling of danger three-quarters of a mile ahead. This instinct in the animal is the same instinct that I am teaching you all how to feel.

So it is possible that within three-quarters of a mile in any direction there is danger for you or perhaps something you will be affected by. It could even be something bizarre, such as a plane suddenly losing altitude. You are in a train now, and the private plane is within a half mile of the train and people can see it. They are startled, but the plane regains altitude and everybody is safe. Nevertheless, the danger message was accurate.

You see, your body works just like the deer's body. You might very well get a danger message three-quarters of a mile away. When you practice this, you get good at it. You can get messages that are beneficial, not only warnings of danger, but perhaps warnings for benevolence, something good, love, something wonderful three miles away. Then you can find it. It might be twenty miles away, it might be a thousand miles away, but this is a beneficial thing, see? Follow that warmth, go there. Something good will be waiting for you.

Resolving the Fear

I am putting the base of my right hand in the center of my chest [Fig. 3-1]. This has nothing to do with where fear is located. Take your time getting up [to take photos]. Remember, you're not a teenager.

Well, I'd like to go back to my teenage period and do it right this time.

No, I don't think so. Think of how your life was when you were a teenager. That's what lives to come are for. Do you ever wonder about reincarnation? You have attitudes about how you would do it if you could do it over again. Do you know that most people who want to return to Earth in times of growth and change might have a reincarnational life at the same time of their last life—the same time, same experiences, same events—generally the same circumstances, but a different life? They die, come back and attempt to do it over again. People do that all the time. I am not necessarily recommending it, but I'm not saying not to do it. People are trying to live their lives over again, seeing if it would be different, hoping it will be better.

🌿 Gesture to Clear Fear 🌿

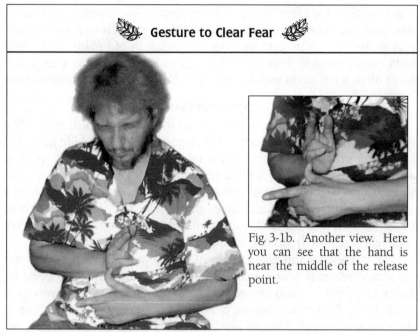

Fig. 3-1b. Another view. Here you can see that the hand is near the middle of the release point.

Fig. 3-1a. Here is the gesture to clear fear. Put the base of your right hand at the solar plexus. Hold for thirty seconds at night before bed. Do this once every three days for two to three weeks.

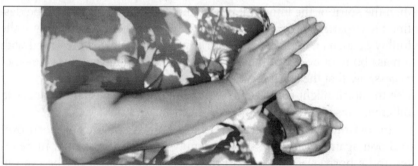

Fig. 3-1c. A third view of the hand/finger position.

Of course, they forget who they are. What often happens is, you come up with different variables, all the possible solutions. It may be an improvement, maybe not, but you'd be surprised how often people do this.

Is there any difference between the trauma we experience in this life and what we bring into this life to clear? Is it stored in the same place?

For the sake of clarity, you do not bring trauma in, you bring desires. You cannot bring memories of trauma into life on Earth as it is now.

The reason you are screened to have ignorance—screening past memories, future memories, knowledge/wisdom—is not just to re-create your reality, but also to prevent you from bringing in old pains or discomforts. Since you will have gone through a clearing process after death, more often it has to do with keeping you from bringing in spiritual bias.

Spiritual Bias

Spiritual bias is who you are between lives in your spirit state. You may have certain fixed attitudes. When you live a physical life here, you learn, you grow, you change, but it takes awhile for the total spirit to adapt to what is learned. Sometimes a spirit, if it is very fixed in its attitudes, might accept the evidence of that one life, then come back to a similar time, maybe the same time, and do life over again two or three times. It then might take the accumulated body of experience and say, "All right, I definitely need to change my attitude about that!"

The veil you go through to prevent you from remembering who you are and to re-create your experience of all you know when you come in, also screens out spiritual bias so that it does not restrict your exploration of life here. Sometimes you are protected from many things, but one of the things you don't think of being protected from is spiritual bias, because bias is usually based on previous experience or an attitude that spiritual beings may have as a result of some ignorance on their part that they have occasionally been reluctant to give up. When this happens, then the spirit or the immortal personality (as Zoosh calls it) will be destined to experience life after life that will allow that spirit being to see the futility of such an attitude. The spirit world ultimately is presented with a mass body of evidence that shows that other things are possible—not necessarily that the spirit is wrong, but that other things are possible—or else the spirit might continue to explore many subtleties and nuances in different lives in order to really show itself that it's right.

In just my simple experience I have known souls to be born over and over again to the same tribe or family, which is unusual, or more often to be born over and over in the same general area, maybe even in the same neighborhood, so that circumstances are similar and the soul can prove that it's right. It tries to put itself in the circumstance so that it can say to its teachers at the end of that life, "See, I was right."

If a soul is like that, of course, it is not too evolved. But many souls are not, and the teacher might reply, "It seems so." However, in a situation like this, the soul would either try to rationalize this, as souls might do when they are very young in experience, or it might accept that from the teacher and say, "How about trying a life like this?" Then it would go down and do that.

That's how sometimes people will live many, many lives or many similar lives. This can happen on other planets as well, but usually there's no resistance. There things evolve and you remember your previous lives, so you have no reason to have as much spiritual attitude.

But some of the ETs have attitudes about humans, and they end up coming here. They look down and judge us, then they come and experience it and leave, saying, "Well, it's harder down there than I thought. I understand them now," or something like that.

Yes, exactly. It is very easy to stand off at a distance and say, "How can they do that? What's wrong with them?" I am not trying to justify behaviors, but in your time it is very easy to stand off at a distance and point the finger at a criminal or someone who has done something that is in the news, and you say, "How can he do that? What's wrong with him? Is he a monster?"

Yet if you have the capacity to examine his life, how he came to be like that, you will discover that he is not a monster, that he had a moment of opportunity when he could have done this or that. Maybe he did that and you hear about it as a crime. But he might have done the other thing, in the case of the example, and then you wouldn't hear about it.

That's really clarifying, in terms of the reincarnational cycle.

Spiritual Desire for Resolution

There seems to be evidence that people can have fears from past lives—for example, a fear of heights or a fear of relationships. How is that stored—not the actual trauma, but the predisposition?

Yes, there is then what is called the spiritual desire. If you have had some terrible experiences—say you fell off a cliff and died at the point when your life was just getting better—it's probably pretty traumatic. Then you might have a tremendous sense of being unresolved, while at the same time feeling very shy about going too close to the edge of a cliff. Sometimes it can be too close to the edge of something high; sometimes it can even relate to a broader context, like being too close to the edge of an issue, but that's rare. I mention this so that you can understand how these things can be blended into other avenues.

The soul cannot bring in traumas, but it can bring in desires—a desire to know more about this, a desire to resolve this, like that. With a desire to resolve something, for example, the soul, when manifested in the physical self, would be exposed to circumstances that would help it resolve its fear of heights.

Or not?

Or not. Maybe its fear of heights continues. If it builds up to an extreme (gets worse), there will be a long pause between physical lives during which the soul might be nurtured, might go to other planets where things are more gentle and benevolent and work out a great deal of that discomfort on other planets, in other lives. In terms of Earth years, it might spend thousands and thousands of years on other planets working out the bulk of that fear.

Then it might come to a similar time (this, of course, is not linear time) when one had a life on Earth before and have a life after working out the bulk of the trauma. The soul has the capacity to pull through the resolution on benevolent planets for how to deal with this on Earth. It doesn't necessarily have any memory of that, but it may have a sense that this is resolvable and might then attempt to find a method to resolve it. One of the things the soul might be taught on other planets is to learn how to trust that it is safe to ask for help. The soul will then come in and still have that fear but in a manageable state, and it will ask probably everyone it knows, "Help me; can you help me with this?" Eventually, as it gets older, the soul would talk to counselors and to adults with experience, trying different things.

Overcoming the Fear of Heights

In my time we'd be taught how to fly with the birds. The person who comes in with that fear of heights, perhaps a youngster, eventually that soul would be taught to experience the beauty of flight. But you don't immediately go and fly with the birds. You would take this person to the place where he feels the safest, not up on top of a hill. Probably this would be somewhere surrounded by mountains or hills, but where he is down on flat ground in the valley. You would have him sit on the ground or where he feels comfortable, where the worst thing that can happen is falling off the rock--the rock is not too high (not making fun of this fear), but very safe. You've done some work with this student; maybe he has learned how to share energies with a tree or you may have taught him how to share energies with the deer in a deer body and so on, so he knows how to be in the body of a being.

Then say to him that you're going to ask a bird to come along. He might like birds; maybe he has a favorite bird that is in the area. You are going to ask that he extend himself, staying flat on the ground. Maybe even put your hand on his knee or some such thing.

If he has a desperate fear, you might put your hand on the part of the body you know that fear is associated with, most likely the solar plexus. The shaman, the mystical man or woman, would put his or her hand on the student and say, "It's all right. You are going to ask a bird you like. Maybe you like the hawk, for example; you find the hawk beautiful. You are going to ask brother hawk to fly from the top of this mesa to the top of another mesa and soar very gently, slowly." Have the student glance up at the hawk. He knows what it looks like; he doesn't have to stare at it. While he's here solid on the ground, he is going to extend himself to be in the hawk. Even though the hawk has its eyes open, he is in the hawk, eyes closed.

The student's job, with his eyes closed inside the hawk, is to feel the warmth of the Sun on the bird's body, perhaps to feel the motion of feathers as the bird moves. (Feathers, you understand, are not just stuck there, are not just wings, but are individual. Birds can move an individual feather on their bodies; feathers can be moved to some degree like fingers and toes. People do not always know this.) So you ask the student to feel the motion of the feathers or of the breeze. The bird is soaring slowly in an updraft, so there is not much breeze. In short, the student's eyes are closed inside the bird. He doesn't open his eyes on the ground and doesn't open them in the air, either. The bird's eyes are open, but the student's eyes in the bird are closed.

The student flies in the bird for a time. That's pretty safe. He does this maybe five or six times. After that, because of his previous training of being in a tree, being in the air and so on, the person feels the tremendous sense of the subtleties of flight. The bird moves a little bit, very tiny movements—one feather, then two feathers—and the bird actually changes direction or goes up or down. The bird is most likely a master flyer. To survive, the hawk must be a pretty good flyer. The student does this five or six times so that he really has confidence in that bird's ability to fly. This is not done one time after another. The student might have one flight in the bird one day with eyes closed, then examine it. Maybe you don't take the student out for another three days while he examines his memory of the experience.

After five or six times, the student has a lot of confidence in the bird's capacity to fly. Then the next time the bird flies, the student gets in the bird, and this time he opens his eyes but does not look down, only up at the clouds. Because the student is physically sitting on the ground, he can do this and feel safe, but he is still going to keep his eyes closed in his body on the ground while opening his spiritual eyes in the bird. If he asks the bird to look up, the bird will do so. The bird is cooperative with such things when done properly, when done with reverence.

So the person has a gentle experience confronting this fear. First, he learns confidence in the bird, flight, body and subtleties, and then he can look up and feel safe. He only does that for a little while, practices that two or three times with the bird looking up . . . maybe two more times with the bird looking up and then side to side. Of course, every time he goes first with his eyes closed in the bird. He does it in progression, eyes closed, feeling the bird's body, everything, so that he is building on strength, what he's known and felt it's safe to be confident in.

The student still has his eyes closed on the ground. Then the student in the bird opens his eyes and tells the bird that it is okay for it to look wherever it wants. The bird looks up, but of course, being a hawk, it looks for food, so the bird naturally looks down most of the time. It only looks up and from side to side to check for predators that might be dangerous to it.

By that time the student is very confident in the bird's capacity. He feels safe, plus he knows he is sitting on the ground. He can feel the rock under him, he can reach down with his hand and touch the soil, move his hand around in the dirt. He is on the ground. He knows it, and yet he also flies with the bird.

The student builds up confidence slowly like this. It might take many months. After doing this with the bird, then the student takes a hawk feather. The hawk will have given him the feather, or he will have gathered the feather from some other place. The student with the hawk feather then goes through a similar experience. The student now as the hawk knows how the hawk flies. He starts out standing on the rock and goes through an imaginary flight across the canyon. His eyes are open—he looks up, looks down.

Now, obviously, the student is maybe five inches above the ground, but it's important to gentle the fear. We are not actually treating the fear; we are building confidence in the capacity to be up high, teaching something new rather than confronting the fear. We can confront fear and work on that for years, going in many different directions and discovering many different fears, but never teach anything new.

The quick way to build great strength and also give the person hawk knowledge, energy and spiritual capacities is this way, by teaching new things. So start out with a rock. Have the person put his arms out, moving, but with his eyes open. Have a hawk feather on his body, at least one, but maybe one, two or three hawk feathers in whatever mystical place on the body you feel like or whatever the student feels confident with.

After the student has done that for about a week, five or six days, have him process the feeling of confidence. The student wants to immediately run up to the top of the mountain—he wants to go for it. It felt good, the hawk confidence. He is safe now with hawk energy. "Let's go up to the top." But you say, "No, go slowly." Next time you are out with the student, go up the trail on the side of the mesa. Go up maybe twenty feet and do the same thing. The student will be the hawk as experienced before. Gradually, gradually, gradually. When you get to the top of the mesa, first go to the center of the mesa. Then the student gets closer and closer to the edge. By the time you get him to stand on the edge, his eyes are open and he feels terribly confident.

Arms out?

Arms out, flying as a hawk. This might take a year, another year. It's a process.

Building Strength from Fear

You might ask, "Why not go faster?" I say that this is the most important thing so the student can understand that the fear he came in with is not just something leftover as trauma from a previous life. No, that is what encourages the student to seek, to have something that is strong so he feels strong in this. It encourages him, drives him, motivates him. We believe in our time that when you arrive with such fear, you need that, that the person who came in with that will someday need to do a great deal of flying.

Maybe you are going to learn hawk medicine. Maybe you are going to have to fly physically (not necessarily fly like a bird, but stand on the top of a mountain)—for instance, be taught long vision, which is a form of flight. Then you would have the capacity to fly. Your body is on top of the mountain in a sacred place, but you can fly like a hawk over the next mountain to see what's on the other side.

Maybe you will fly over to the other side of the world to name something for your people or for someone who needs to know something— or *you* might need to know something. Maybe you are going to have to fly not only around the Earth in this way, but to other planets to discover what things are happening on those other planets for yourself or for others in your tribe or even for people around the Earth whom you will never meet. Maybe you are going to become a shaman or a mystical person in your own right.

In short, you might come in with what seems to be a fear to be resolved, but which is actually prompting you to learn techniques that you will use to help yourself and others on the planet, in your tribe, on other planets, everywhere.

Why do I talk this way with such passion? Guess.

So the person will understand that this fear is a strength.

A strength to come. What else? *I came in with such fear.*

Really? What fear?

The fear of heights. My teacher went through that exact process with me, which is why I know it so well. My teacher never considered that there was something wrong with me because I had a fear of heights. He always told me from the very beginning, "Don't worry about this thing. We can do something about it. It has to do with something that is going to be a gift for you, and you will help others on this planet, all over the world. This thing that seems like a terrible fear to you right now is a sign by which I know you are going to be a mystical man."

As a mystical man, your long vision is teaching not only your own people in your time, but everyone who reads this book four hundred years after your life in that time.

You see, my teacher does not see fear as a weakness but as a strength to come that will help people everywhere on Earth in all different times. My teacher can see not only what I'm going to be doing in my life living in the tribe, but also what I'm going to be doing with you, working with other people, working with all the beings I will work with in the future. My teacher knows all this and presents this thing—that to me feels like fear and makes me feel less than the other boys—as not fear at all, but a great gift.

Because I believe in my teacher, I know I can have confidence. I know that even though I still feel the fear, I can be sure that I will be able to resolve this because I believe in my teacher. I love my teacher and know that my teacher can help me. He has taught me many things already. By that time I am about seven or eight years old in Earth years.

Who was your teacher?

I will see if I can tell you my teacher's name . . . not now. I will tell you my teacher's name someday. He is a physical person, of course. Wonderful, yes? [Publisher's note: Later we learned that his teacher's name was Reveals the Mysteries.]

Yes. Thank you so much for sharing that.

This is important, because it is very easy in your time for well-intentioned people to explore the fears of an individual and use the rational mind to explain them. But exploration goes on and on, because fear leads to many avenues. That can be perhaps intellectually useful, but the fast way is to work on strength, how we resolve it by learning strength. Eventually, strength becomes stronger than fear. Then the new strength does not overpower the fear, but the fear develops confidence in the strength you have in your own physical body to resolve this.

The fear is like a helpless child. I am not saying fear really is this, but I am using this as an example. The fear, like a helpless child, trusts the physical body in which it resides and has confidence from the physical evidence of step-by-step teaching that this new strength will completely protect it. Fear simply dissolves, goes into the body, passes through the body in a natural process and is released and resolved for all time—meaning, of course, for that individual's soul.

Other Fears: Resolving the Fear of Water

Can we say that this example, using the fear of heights, will also work for water, closed spaces, success and failure, being alone, love and many other fears?

Yes.

Does the strength of each one build on that body of trust?

Yes. Think about it. You might have had a life on a desert planet, for instance, maybe all your lives on desert planets—you never saw water before. Then the teacher says, "Maybe it's time for you to try a planet where there is desert but also water." He shows you water (between lives, of course), people playing in it, drinking it, washing, using it for ceremonies, cooking food in it. You see that this water looks like a very useful thing and maybe it's fun, too. But you go to that life, and as things evolve, you have an unpleasant experience in the water.

The first time, a frightening thing happens, maybe not even to you. For instance, maybe someone you know or love drowns in water. This is your first experience with water. You say that you don't blame God, you blame the water; you say that the water is at fault. How can it take your beloved away from you? And you never go near water again in that life.

So in the next life there is a similar teaching. For instance, in my time my people live near water. Not close, but within walking distance, there is an underground pool of water and also a stream that runs almost all the time, making sounds. Plus it rains sometimes, of course. Either I notice or other mystical people or elders or brothers or sisters of the person notice that this person is afraid of the rain and doesn't like to wash. The person drinks water but is not comfortable drinking water as it is—he won't drink it out of his cupped hands and will only take liquid in the form of something having been cooked in it maybe. Then he drinks that liquid.

There are many different evidences of this fear, and often the family is in the best position to notice these things. They begin to test it, taking the person down to the water. If you shake water like this on a person, you can feel the fear. You can easily find out if the person is afraid of water without traumatizing him. (You don't have to throw him in the water and make things worse.) Then you can say, "Okay, there is a fear of water," and begin to do similar things to what I described before, meaning incremental steps.

The teacher knows the fear of water means that this person will probably be doing something with water in the future that will be wonderful for our people. The person comes in with fear, and people show him that he is drawn to water for resolution of that fear. Then, as a result of the teachings about water and building up confidence about water, he will someday have things to offer to us or other peoples about water. So this is not considered fear, but is considered a gift, an attraction.

So start slowly. Take a small vessel, something we make, and go down to the stream or even the underground pool of water and get water at its clearest. The underground pool comes through the rocks—very clear, cool, very refreshing, full of minerals. We drink that water and become very healthy. Bring some of that out.

Of course, by this time you will have built up a relationship with this person, you understand. Don't immediately start him on this. You will have worked with this person for five or six months already, perhaps, so there would be basic knowledge. By that time, the student has confidence in who he might love or at least like, because teacher and student must be matched up. Perhaps a small tribe has one mystical man, one mystical woman, but a larger tribe has more than one and often many people are learning.

The Student Who Was Afraid of Water

So here was somebody I worked with: My own teacher is still alive in the tribe, and several others, but the student is matched up with me, and I work with him. I take the student to a place near where the underground pool is, but he is not required to go there. I say, "Sit, be comfortable." I sit down on a rock in the sun and wait. I go get something and bring it back. "You wait, rest, be calm." So we do. He has regular homework that I give him to interact with animals, plants, rocks, so he does his homework.

I come back when he is involved with his homework, focused in spiritual work. Then I show him. I stand off at a distance, five or six feet, and I tip a vessel over a little bit—not so great that it pours out, but so he can see it is water in there. He stops his homework by then and looks at it, nods his head and acknowledges. He goes, "Um, water, okay"—something like that.

Then I take my finger from my left or right hand, whatever feels right for the student—in the case of this student, the left hand feels better. I take my first finger (fingertip only, the soft part of the finger) and just barely touch the water so that the fingertip is just moist. Then I reach over to the student. I don't touch him but move my moist finger around and around in front of the student. The student is not wearing a shirt, me neither (warm months); we are not dressed. I move my finger around the outside of the student, first just in front of the student so that he can see it from a distance of about a foot and a half or two feet—maybe three feet because the auric field pushes out in places where it doesn't feel the water is safe. When my fingertip dries, I dip it back in the water and cover the whole auric field so that the auric field is sampling or touching the water, but from a distance. I go over it with just my fingertip. Then I do the same thing with two fingers in the vessel.

Do you see the auric field?

I do not necessarily see the auric field. Maybe I see it, maybe I feel it, maybe I know it. The main thing is that I am aware of the energy of the auric field pushing. This all happens in one day.

The student is probably standing, but maybe sitting. If he gets tired, he sits. Maybe I sit too sometimes. I do it with two fingers, the same thing, then three fingers, four fingers, five fingers (we call it a finger but you say thumb). Eventually I put my left hand in the water and touch the auric field.

By that time the auric field is used to being touched with water and no longer has much resistance. At various times, the closest place where water feels safe is four inches from the physical body, but in other places it is still a foot to a foot and a half away. I'm still only doing the front of the body. That's it for that day.

I ask the student to go home, rest, eat and examine what he felt during this experience. Then he is asked to do homework to examine his feelings about this for the next few days, working with other people in between, of course. I tell the student that he can talk to me about his feelings or not, or just examine those feelings.

The next time out, we do the same process with one finger, but I do it behind the body. The student trusts me, but even so, I might be at times six or eight feet behind him because the student cannot see. Sometimes I stand upwind, sometimes downwind. If I stand upwind, the student can use his sense of smell and have some idea of where I am. If I stand downwind, the student can't use that and can only use his auric field to feel me. So he is involved in the auric field very much.

We do this as a second step because I want the student to use his auric field. I want the auric field to be involved intentionally with water. So one finger, two fingers, three fingers, the same thing. Eventually I use the whole hand. It seems like I am washing the auric field, but not really. I am just touching it top to bottom in the back. I might have to do this process behind the student two, three, four, five times until I get close to him, meaning within a foot or a foot and a half, very slowly. This is the process.

So the next step: I have noticed where in the front and in the back of the body I came closest with my hand. This means that this area of the body feels the safest with water. Now we start having fun. This student at that time feels the safest with water at the bridge of his nose, so I take one finger, dip it in the water and touch the wet finger to the bridge of the nose, but move the finger in very slowly. The student is perfectly calm; he knows I'm not going to do anything damaging, knows what's going on. The student takes note of his feelings all the time, so he knows where discomfort comes up in his body. That's why I go very slowly, because discomfort might come up right about this time.

So I move very slowly and can feel a slight resistance, slowly, slowly, slowly. If I cannot touch the bridge of his nose that day, then I get as close as I can. I tell the student to examine his feelings, not to analyze. What "examine feelings" means is to remember the circumstances and to feel those feelings again. Examining feelings is not a thoughtful process, but a feeling process. My belief is that if feelings are coming up, they need to express themselves, so the more you can feel those feelings, the better. So the student is encouraged to feel feelings. We do that and eventually I am able to touch the bridge of his nose with a wet finger. This is a slow process. The process with the fear of water is sometimes longer.

But this is an extreme case where he doesn't drink or touch water.

He has to drink water, but not out of a stream.

Many people are afraid of getting near the water, but . . .

They are afraid of that too, but I use an extreme example so that I can give you more subtleties.

This is a very extreme example. Go on.

Eventually, cutting through many steps but to touch various bases (this is a long, long example), I am able to touch my wet hand to his body, front and back. The student still has feelings of discomfort but trusts me because we work together. Because he allows feelings between experiences, going home and examining his feelings, he becomes a friend with the fearful feelings associated with water.

Those feelings become so familiar because the student feels those feelings so many times due to our work. Now when those feelings come up, when he is being touched by wet, he no longer feels those feelings as uncomfortable. Those feelings are now familiar, not just frightening feelings that he doesn't normally feel, but regular feelings, feelings he has all the time. We germinate these feelings, let these feelings express themselves.

After my wet fingers touch the whole body, we find an area of the body where the feelings of the fear of water are most concentrated. In this person it is the part where the abdomen touches the leg on the left side, almost at the hip bone but in and down about an inch—right in that spot. That's where the body is the most reluctant to have water touch it, so we know that the feelings are concentrated in that area. There are feelings in other places, but that's where they're concentrated.

So I work with that part of the body, talk to it. I get words sometimes or feelings. That part of the body tells me what to do. With this person, I then say that we are now going to the water. We take as many days or as many different times as necessary to walk close to the stream. We walk to a sandy spot, with not too many stones. The water at that point of the stream is about two or three inches deep. At other points the stream is maybe a foot deep, but there it is not very deep, only two or three inches. It is like a sandbar in a river, only smaller because it is a stream, and it is also comfortable to lie on. The sand, being white sand, is especially comfortable. I take him there and say, "This is well water. Well water comes from somewhere, goes somewhere."

Then I reach my hand into the water and touch the person in that spot many, many times. Eventually I can feel that the spot no longer has a problem with me touching it with water. Then I have the student get close to the water, but not in it. We don't build up to him lying down in water yet, but we're close. He reaches down with his hand and touches water to that spot. In time the feeling that the student identifies as discomfort with the water begins to fade. It's not there anymore because the student is so familiar with how that feels physically. He can tell instantly when the feeling becomes less. Every time the feeling becomes less, the student reaches down and picks up a little more water. Eventually, instead of just touching a finger to the water and dampening the spot, he scoops up handfuls of water and splashes it on the spot because that spot now feels safe with water.

Next, we keep going in slow, incremental steps so the student can lie in water. I'm jumping way ahead, but it starts out very slowly: put one toe in, put the next toe in. This type of thing might take three years, as I say, working with the student. Eventually the student no longer has discomfort associated with water, and because it has gone very slowly, gradually, gently, the student has profound confidence with water. The body not only feels safe with water, but looks forward to being touched by water. Eventually the student learns how to swim, but that requires a considerable walk to a small pond. Again, slowly, slowly teach that.

There is something else also going on here. I'm not just helping a person become confident around water, but around many different exposures to water. Water touches the auric field many different times. It touches different places on the body. The student learns to drink, likes water from here and so on—in short, he is also studying water.

Because the student could not actually drink water in the usual way (out of our hands as we usually do), he has had to study different versions of water in his earlier fearful state of water. So he has all this different knowledge about water, and by this time water is no longer his fear but his strength. Now I leave that person alone for a time. I say, "Now you are fine with water, after you learned to swim. You are fine with water, everything is okay." By that time he is enthralled with water, and we know—mystical people, tribal people, brothers and sisters, everyone knows—that this person now likes water. We are very confident that this person is going to learn more about water, because from all the teaching steps, the person is totally aware of his physical body and his feelings.

Now, the physical body was memorizing during this process. The student can bring up feelings at a moment's notice when recollecting experiences with water. In short, he can understand how anybody's physical body could react to water, having worked with the self. For starters, he will know the water cure for anybody else who comes in with a fear of water. If I am not available or no other mystical people are available, the student might be able to help another person with the fear of water because he knows all the steps and has the patience. That is the beginning step on the path toward his being a mystical man.

But what was his gift in the end? What's the end of the story?

There is a river a long distance from us. This student was the first one to build a boat, to go down the river to see what's there. He put us in touch with other people we didn't know who were there, and we came to be great friends with that tribe of people. They are great friends with us. We traded things back and forth, and eventually we liked each other so much, we all lived together. We had separate tribes, different cultures, but we lived in the same place. It turns out we lived in a nice place.

In short, this person delivered new family and friends to us. We were downriver about thirty-five or forty miles, but we had never done that before. We were not water people. We did not build boats or travel distances. We walked, as land people.

He went alone the first time?

He went alone. He built his own boat; he had an inspiration and built an outrigger, not unlike they do here on the island of Hawaii. First he used his hands and discovered that they were not very good. Then he made a rudimentary paddle. Eventually he taught everybody else boat-building, navigation, all these things, and both tribes were eventually able to preserve themselves much longer.

My tribe was once invaded many years later. I was no longer alive at that time, but the tribe was. By this time, the tribe had become known for being boat-builders and fishermen. They had many big boats.

A warring force came to invade the tribe. By that time my people and the other tribe were known as water people and were no longer known as land people. So they got into boats and went away, safe for another hundred years. Very nice. He was a very important person to the tribe. He came in with a fear of water, but actually his fear was used to attract him to strength, which leads to inspiration, which leads to a great gift to all of our peoples.

You understand that when we work with young people, they have been reared in sacred surroundings, spiritual surroundings, so these are fears that are noticed. These fears are not caused by life experiences. The best time to notice these fears is when a child is very young and has not had traumas—but, of course, in your time often there is birth trauma. The child is taken away from his or her mother, slapped on the bottom. It's harder to tell then. But if there is not birth trauma or if there is a gentle, loving birth . . . it is possible to have a loving birth without it being a water birth.

I'd say, just pay attention to the child. Notice if the child is frightened of something for no reason you can think of. Then that's the gift; his or her fear will lead to the gift.

How to Work with Your Fears

For people who are reading this book, how do they deal with their fears? They use the gesture, but how can they extrapolate from this to find their gift?

They would try to use a similar method, as I say, in very slow increments, for any fear that they feel. Try to think of the things you might be afraid of. Try to think back. What fear goes back as far as you can remember (not just something you know you can put your finger on)? If you were okay with heights and were suddenly afraid of heights when you were fourteen years old, it isn't that. If you can remember your early years, go back and try to remember things you were afraid of, if there was more than one thing.

Explore old fears in this life first, and seek the help of a spiritual person such as myself, people of your day who will very gradually teach you not about fear but about strength, giving you the gift of that thing. That's what you can do now as an adult. You must use your memory, trying to remember the oldest fear you have, where you can never remember being without that fear.

Can one do this by oneself?

I recommend that you work with somebody else. Say you are fifty years old, for example. You have had a lifelong fear and maybe many other fears as a result. You may not trust yourself that much. You need to work with somebody slowly, not every day, but often having at least three days in between to examine your feelings. Work with somebody else because you can build up confidence in the way that person works. I recommend that you have a relationship already, so work with him or her on other spiritual matters for perhaps four, five, six months. Don't just immediately go for a cure of this fear, which is, in fact, actually a discovery of the strength that the fear was meant to guide you to.

So there are two issues here.

You do need to work with somebody else, because by the time you are, say, fifty years old or even thirty years old, you may not have enough confidence in yourself. I don't mean mental confidence—I mean *body* confidence. It is always better to have somebody else to work with. It will be a slow process, but you will not just resolve fear, you will discover a gift that most often you had no idea you possessed. *There's the level of fear as a gift, and then there is the level of fears we have accumulated in this life that we can use the gestures to dissipate. Is that true?*

Yes. We launched into things about the tribe because, as you can tell, I am attempting to influence parents in ways of bringing up their children so that parents, doctors and counselors do not take it for granted that trauma is to be expected. I want to encourage people to look for signs, and with patience, such as described with these two individuals (fear of heights and fear of water), you can discover that if your child seems to have been born with such fears and you can't put your finger on how the fear began, then you have discovered that your child has a great gift to offer. A child's fear leads you to discover this gift.

So I am attempting to encourage a change in the way children are reared, because we cannot wait for a magical cure from God to make everybody better. Some of this will come, but you must demonstrate to God or Creator that you are prepared to take actions as well as receive gifts.

A gift is given to you of a physical body on Earth at a time of great learning potential, and Mother Earth is a spirit in that body—all of these things start out with a gift. That's the way Creator sees it. It doesn't see you as stuck on Earth; Creator sees Itself as giving you the gift of this life on Earth as you experience it.

So Creator already sees you as having a gift. This is a most important attitudinal adjustment. Then you can explore what to do with that gift. You demonstrate to Creator that you appreciate the gift by taking action, by utilizing the gift. In other words, Creator is giving a toy to a child that can be used only for profound learning. If you give a child an educational toy, you don't want the child to just settle down, to go do something else. If the child wants to do that, that's fine. But in this case of giving spirit or soul a physical body on Earth in these times, you must use the body or else not go on living in some way. You are going to use the body or step out, go on elsewhere. Creator already gave you a gift and wants you to use that gift to discover, to demonstrate that you are prepared to do so. Creator will give you other things, will help you, but you must demonstrate to Creator that you appreciate that gift and use it to learn.

The New Generation of Children

How does this relate to the new children coming in with different DNA and a totally different type of potential?

Who says their DNA is different?

There's the Indigo children and Rainbow children and the psychic children of China and the children who are immune to AIDS. There seems to be a large influx of them in the last ten or twenty years. They're different, aren't they?

Children come in with an energy of difference, but the DNA must be the same, with minor variables that have been here for a long time. Do you know why it must be the same?

No.

In DNA—you call it the building blocks of life—there are not only apparent molecules that make up life as you understand it, but remember, every molecule, every atom, every particle of DNA is alive and has potential to offer. This is a learning time. There is more learning going on here on Earth now in your time than at any other time of the Explorer Race.

Would Creator take that away so that you can't learn? No. All children have the gift of DNA. It's just that a thousand years ago DNA was not interacting with energy brought in, in the same way. Energy of spirit comes in, soul energy—each soul energy specific to that soul personality. The soul energy stimulates the DNA to do certain things, but in DNA from person to person, aside from specific unusual things, the basic chemical analysis of DNA as a substance is the same. It *must* be the same, because it must be able to respond to the stimulation of the soul's energy to deliver what that soul needs to learn in that life and ultimately what it will teach in that life, as we have discussed. But DNA is broad. This soul stimulates DNA in the body to do this; a different soul stimulates the same DNA in another body to do a different thing.

So how can we say there's more potential?

I mention this not to judge other people who say differently, but I must speak what I know and what is shown to me. What is different is that souls coming in now have energy that stimulates things in the DNA that have always been there, but that have not been stimulated in these times to deliver what DNA has always been able to deliver. These souls with these energies have not been here before in these times (they might have been here at some time in the past).

So we're saying that there is a new wave of souls, which is what they are calling the Star children. You're saying that they don't have the fears and limitations we did?

If they don't have the fears, what does that mean?

They don't have the gift.

Exactly. If they don't have the fears, they don't have the gift. Are they to be denied the gift? As they grow up, their generation might have gifts needed by their generation. If they are denied these fears or these desires to learn, then gifts needed by their generation will not be available.

Seeing Life as a Gift

It is important to look at the process of life as a gift. It is very easy to look at traumas and discomforts and unhappiness, because everybody experiences things here, and whether you have the most wealth or the least wealth, everybody is going to have some unhappiness, some pain, some discomfort. It is very easy to look at life here as hard, yet that's why it's short. Life here is short compared to life in other places because it is hard in many ways.

Because we have all lived lives in other places that are more benevolent, it is very easy to quickly feel like life here is a burden. But life here is about learning, teaching and sharing. As a result, there are things you have to do to stay alive—everybody has to do them—but loving, teaching and sharing are a part of life. You go to school to do these things, yet school takes place during your whole life here. That's why life here is short.

But isn't it going to lengthen now as things become more benign?

Remember, life everywhere else is lengthened. It might become slightly more benign, but it's still school. We're not going to lengthen it too much. Maybe the average life span in twenty-five years will be another ten or twelve years more, but that's all, because it's still school. You don't want to be here for a thousand years. If you were here for a thousand years, you'd learn the same thing you came in to learn over and over and over again. You wouldn't learn new things; you'd learn the same thing.

Say life here was a thousand years or even more, as is typical for many other planets, but you came in to learn something that you could learn easily here in a short amount of time, a life span. Why hang around? Why hang around for eight or nine hundred years to learn that same thing and be put in a position to learn those same lessons in varying degrees over and over and over again, when you already learned them in the first sixty years of your life.

Why can't we renegotiate after sixty years and learn something else?

Keep making new bargains with your soul? Creator gave you the gift of life here about learning. Creator does not *make* you a creator. If Creator made you a creator, you would make lots of bargains with your soul, but your soul comes here to learn. It knows what it knows. You can try to bargain with your soul, but remember, your soul does not communicate in words. So how are you going to bargain with your soul?

The soul will communicate in benevolent, gentle feelings. Maybe you can prompt feelings with sign language a little bit, act out a little bit, but don't try to rationalize the soul. The soul will not pay any attention to that. It is interested in spirit and a little in feeling—spirit and spirit feelings, but only the most gentle feelings.

Negotiation with the soul is probably not going to work unless you use profound symbolic secrets, but when you use shamanic secrets to change the purpose of the soul, everything you are exposed to in life changes. You cannot change one thing without changing everything.

Maybe life is going pretty well except in one area. You would like to improve this area, so you change your contract with the soul and your whole life changes. Maybe you lose 90 percent of the things in life that you wanted. You managed to change that 10 percent, but at what cost? Think about that.

Pain and the Body at Soul Review

If the soul feels only benevolent feelings, then where is all this suffering and agony we're experiencing going to go?

It does not *ever* go to the soul; the soul cannot feel that, cannot handle it. It would damage the soul severely.

So what is the use of it? What is the goal?

It goes in the body. The body is the material-mastery teacher, not the soul. The soul does not know anything about material mastery.

But we have to leave the body here?

Yes.

So how can we take the wisdom?

Between lives you access the experience learned. How? You access accomplishment. For instance, perhaps you are a long-distance runner, maybe you came here to learn how to run. Maybe you never ran before, you were always a water being, for example.

You become a long-distance runner and experience lots and lots of pain, but you also experience lots of exulted feelings of accomplishment. The soul can feel such feelings of accomplishment in the afterlife (between lives), so it can experience that benevolent thing. The soul can also look at pictures of life, not to experience the pain, but to be taught by a teacher that this is not a good thing. It has physical evidence of that because it experiences good feelings. Maybe a person is running, running, running, and then she can't run anymore. She is exhausted, falls down, has cramps in her leg. Maybe before that the soul has a feeling of great accomplishment in examination with its teacher over a few years, but then the soul looks down and it no longer feels great accomplishment or happiness. Suddenly there is no feeling at all. The soul looks to its teacher and says, "I don't feel anything." The teacher says, "What do you make of that?" If the soul has had an experience before of not feeling anything, it says, "This must be unhappiness, discomfort, not pleasant—correct?" The teacher says yes.

You cannot take pain to the soul, the soul being the pure essence of love and innocence. Love and innocence cannot experience pain on the same level. If the soul does, it can be crippled or injured indefinitely. Then it will require healing that only very profound beings can give. So the soul is protected from feeling pain. Pain has to do with life, a given life experience. Life is meant to teach, to learn, so when out of the body, the soul does not need to know that then; it just needs to learn in a gentle way.

Remember, most lives take place in a benevolent place. If the soul is injured with pain, it will never go to a benevolent place and have life again until it is cured. Once upon a time, previous creators came along with a wand and cured, then said, "Wait, this isn't working. I can't take the pain out of these souls one at a time. It's not working. Let's veil the soul and have the soul teachers examine the life but not have the souls feel the pain. That works. Then I can do other things. Otherwise I spend my time healing souls and doing nothing else."

Relationship of Soul to Personality

You are a spirit, an immortal personality. You know who you are; you know what you've done. What is the soul in relation to who you are?

What is my soul in relationship to who I am? Picture sitting in a very comfortable chair; it holds you very comfortably. Put your legs up, rest your arms, lean your head back. Be very comfortable. That is soul. It supports me gently.

It supports you?

It supports me gently but does not interfere. The chair does not jump into the body when you sit in it. The chair does not grab you and hold you. The chair does not push you out. A comfortable chair gently supports you.

So we are independent of our soul?

No, no, no. You *are* your soul, but the soul must be protected. Let's say the soul is a circle [draws Fig. 3-2]. Your life is a point on the circle (X). Maybe these points are other lives (different lives going on at different times and so on).

Where are you on the circle in relationship to that soul or, by extrapolation, to anybody's soul?

I told you that I am not so different from the stage where you are. I just know who I am, I know what I am doing and I know why.

That's a little different.

Not too much. It is not like I am on this level and you are on another. Not so different.

The Soul's Purpose for a Life

I have an issue with the soul. Souls don't seem to know what they are doing.

Oh, the soul knows what it is doing; it comes here for a purpose. Maybe it'll

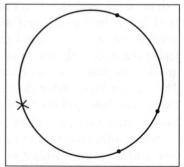

Fig. 3-2. The soul as a circle and your current life a point (X) on that circle. The other points on that circle represent other lives.

come with a fear of heights; maybe it'll come with other things. Maybe it wants to run or wants to resolve a fear of heights—a given gift, as we discussed. The soul does not come wanting to do many, many things; it wants to do only a couple of things. When it is between lives, the soul can talk about many things with its teacher. But when the soul is actively involved with life, it has only one or two things it needs to do. Have you ever had a talk with someone, like you and I talk? When you talk, you start out with one thing you want to talk about, then that discussion leads to many, many things. You can relate to that. You started out talking once upon a time, and it led to the *Explorer Race* series of books.

Many, many things branch out. The soul comes with a way to look at it, with a foundation—like building blocks, as many as it takes. The soul comes with building blocks, maybe one, maybe two things. Everything that you become branches out from those things. Understand clearly, the soul has not done this capriciously, come with two things. The soul has discussed this many, many times with its teacher. The teacher tries to encourage the soul, "Better come with just one thing." But the soul is maybe ambitious: "Oh please, I want to come with *two* things." The teacher is not in a position of approving or disapproving but is just an adviser, so the soul comes with two things, like two taproots for a tree.

Normally the tree has one main taproot. Two taproots usually mean two trees or two legs. So you have to do two lives' worth of stuff. You say, "I can do it. What do you think?" And the teacher says, "I really don't recommend it." Why? Because he or she doesn't have confidence in you? No, he or she has seen other souls try to do this and has seen the results. But you say, "I can do it," so the teacher says okay.

The teacher tries to suggest to you without saying, without programming, as you say, that things could go badly—just to give a suggestion by way of talking. But the soul is excited and enthusiastic, ambitious perhaps, so you take two root things you want to start with, and just like one conversation leads to many things, these root things lead to many things in your life.

That's why souls do not choose to change that. Think right now: taproot, tree, then tree trunk, branches, leaves and so on—the whole cycle of a tree's life. All this has to do with the taproot or one of the original things the soul wants to do. If you decide to change the purpose for your soul coming in, the soul sees that as illuminating *all* that.

If you step away from the tree, the soul is no longer in the tree and the tree dies. The soul sees that as either a form of death or your rejecting all or at least part of what that soul came in here to learn. The soul is reluctant to do that because it has spoken with teachers, advisers, guides, everybody, and has decided with everybody's support to come here and do that.

Then you—meaning your soul and you, combined with your life—say, "No, let's do this." Maybe you are right, but perhaps you don't have to change your soul's intent. Maybe because of a series of discomforts, one after another, you want to get your soul to change its purpose; perhaps it is not the soul's purpose to have those discomforts repeating. Maybe it needs to do this thing, whatever is happening, in a different way.

Seek help, get advice, talk to people. That's why people go to counselors and so on, to find new and different ways to do things. Perhaps you can resolve the problem without destroying the soul's original intent.

The Individual within the One

If that's a soul, then where is the Creator part of us? The larger part? Is the soul part of the greater being?

You are all one. We examine the soul as a separate being here in the way scientists examine a slide under a microscope. They see material on a slide as a drop of liquid, one thing. They look under the microscope and see smaller particles and smaller things that make up one thing. They look under more and more magnification, and smaller and smaller and smaller particles make up this liquid.

We are looking at the soul as part of the liquid of all being. We are examining it as if it is separate, but if you pull back from your point of view, you can see that the soul is part of something else. Pull back further and look—one soul of *all* beings. Pull back further—one soul of all creators of all beings. Pull back further—one soul of all universes, creators, all beings . . . in short, keep pulling back. Feel the liquid, for the sake of example. Liquid as a substance becomes bigger and bigger and bigger, yet all are part of one thing.

A wave that comes in from the ocean is a single wave made up of uncountable numbers of particles, all individual things doing something together, but they are experienced as one thing. Likewise, the soul is a portion of Creator and beyond, but we examine it on a small scale.

How does our immortal identity relate to the soul? Reality is beyond the understanding of the soul, isn't it?

It is like you want a graph: "Where does the total accumulation of identity or immortal personality reside?" It resides everywhere. It resides in yourself now. The basic personality is recognizable from life to life and resides in the greater portion of you—perhaps nearby sometimes (near you spiritually and sometimes physically), perhaps not nearby at other times—and it keeps going out, relating. So the total you can be found all over, everywhere.

The total can be found all over anywhere, maybe not concentrated in one spot. For the sake of example only—these are not actual numbers—maybe ten thousand particles make up the total you. Those particles can be all over the place but can still function as the total you, even though one portion of you might be far beyond measurements of numerical quantity. It doesn't make any difference; it does not have to come close to you physically to function as part of the total you.

Are you in your spirit body, the total you?

No, there are other parts in other places because I am focused in the personality of my life as I lived it on Earth in my time. I know that I have lived other lives at other times and have had other experiences, but I still experience life as I lived it on Earth—wear clothes, live on the same land, can see people in my time, be in my time. I choose to be in time, talking through. In short, I experience an extension of life as I lived it.

But I have lived other lives in other places and may be able to tap into that sometimes, utilize that knowledge and wisdom if necessary. But most often I do not look there first.

Is what you call the God-given talent each person brings into a life related to the taproot, the thing one is born to do?

It might be at least partially related to that building block in the soul. Most souls come in with one thing they want to do and everything else branches out from that. It might be related to that, yes.

How do we get to what you call the taproot of the soul or the original building block?

Why get to it? After this life you are very much aware of it. Some things you don't need to know; they can complicate life. Have you ever had somebody come to you at work and bring you a new thing you can use, perhaps a product, something useful? Their job in the company is to give people there new things they can use to make life simpler for them.

But instead of just giving it to you, the person sits you down and explains all the technical details of it that you don't need to know. You just need to know how it works. You just want to take it, use it, work with it—you don't need to know how it was formed chemically. In short, sometimes too much information is not good.

I see. I did stray.

Straying is good. We discover other things. We stray, but never too far from the main path.

So all the fears can be worked out with that technique?

The technique meaning incrementally slow steps as described, with plenty of time to build up confidence in one's own physical body.

And in addition, we can use gestures to begin to help. We also have the heat; we can use the heat of the heart.

That's right.

Do we attempt to bring up the love-heat before we do the gestures [see pp. 7–8]?

You can if you like.

Does that make it go faster?

No, fast is not a factor. Forget faster, always faster: "How can I get there quickly?" That is not just for you, but for many people. One thing we know about getting there quickly—we'll miss things on the way. What do we have to do then?

Go back and see what we missed.

And when we go back, we usually are unhappy to go back. If we had gone slower, we would have enjoyed the discovery as we had it, but when we moved ahead, we had to come back and do that discovery. Then we resent the discovery; the thing does not work well for us. We get annoyed with the process of life and then begin to mistrust life. Don't rush. Rush is a big mistake, always.

The only time I know that rushing is worthwhile is when you run from danger chomping at your heels—fire or a bear. Rushing is very important then, but otherwise, take time and notice.

Release Point for Hate

What about hate, rage? That leads to how we turn things to self-destruction, being accident-prone and all that. How do we work with this?

Most people are not born with hate. They learn this. It is a learned experience. The resolution of hate is very important. Hate can be held here, where the ribs come together—this bone, the sternum, but out here, away from the body.

About a foot away?

About a foot away, but in front of that spot (the solar plexus). Usually it is held there, because if hate is held inside the body, even if you say or do nothing to those you hate (it might be an individual for some reason; it might be a group of people), it can shorten your life catastrophically. It will almost always make your life miserable. Sometimes hate is necessary as a temporary lesson, for you to work with it, or it is trying to lead you to what is causing it or what you came here to do. Or maybe one of your experiences involves some trauma, which leads to hate. Or perhaps other people have told you that hate is valuable. There are many different possibilities.

Usually, if you are going to have your full life cycle, you cannot hold hate inside you. Hate is summed up in one very simple phrase: *Hate is completely equal to self-destruction.* Self-destruction sometimes takes the form of hurting other individuals, but it is still self-destructive because you don't always remember that you are all one and you are hurting yourself.

What does Zoosh say? That when you hurt yourself or somebody else, it is self-destructive, self-violent, right? Hate is very dangerous in general. It is better to resolve things before they get to hate. But you asked how to make the gesture to begin to resolve hate.

Sometimes hate is very subtle and you're not conscious of it. You hate someone or something or some circumstance and don't even know about it. Sometimes a way to recognize that hate is present is if you have a disease that you were not born with. This is not an absolute, because diseases come up for you to learn many things. But sometimes diseases come up because you are hating something or someone or some event and don't remember it. It's just there.

Or it might not even be physical disease or discomfort; it might be just a constant source of tension. There are many possibilities, different reasons, different evidences of hate. We will not spend too much time examining hate because we cannot talk about it without feeling it. Did you know that?

No, I didn't. Isn't cancer often the result of hate not dealt with?

It can be, but it can also be self-anger not dealt with. It can also be a lesson one is learning. Cancer can be a disease for some other reason, but I pick that example—self-anger or disappointment with life. But it can be other things. It is not just one thing, it is not "this equals that." With life, everybody has different subtleties, so most of the time you cannot give ironclad rules.

If you suspect that you are hating something for no reason that you can think of—you are tired almost all the time and this is a regular thing, but you can't figure it out, you can't think of yourself as hating—examine. Think, think. Hate is not a thought, it is a feeling. It can be demonstrated and expressed and considered as a thought, but hate is a feeling, and it can become a pain you get used to that finds itself in some part of your body (sometimes described as your weak point) where you tend to not feel so good sometimes. Hate might be in there and you don't even know it.

Releasing Hate

The gesture to begin to release hate is important for about 75 percent of Earth's population. Most people in most cultures (but not all) are led to believe that hate is not nice to express, so disease or discomfort develops inside the body. Then you get used to thinking, after a while, "That's just where I have a pain, and that's that." That's how many people often have small to large portions of hate in them. It can be hate—not necessarily always, but it can be.

There's no specific place where it can be stored, then?

No. In this case, it might be anywhere, but it is always in a place in your physical body where you come to recognize that this place hurts all the time or where pain periodically comes up. It is not a functional problem, but pain.

The gesture to begin to release this pain must be done slowly one night a week before sleep [Fig. 3-3]. Before you do the gesture, feel love-heat energy. That could be useful. If you cannot do that, if you don't know how, then do the gesture. Hold the gesture for no more than thirty seconds. Try to do it before you go to sleep at night. Do this for maybe three months.

🌿 Gesture to Release Hate 🌿

Fig. 3-3a. This is the gesture. Hold for no more than thirty seconds. Do this slowly, one night a week before sleep for three months. If necessary, you can slow it down to one night every three weeks.

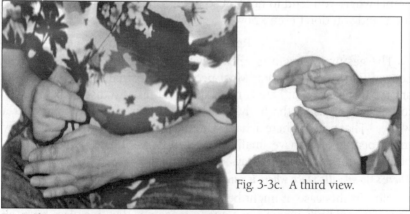

Fig. 3-3c. A third view.

Fig. 3-3b. A second view of the hand position.

The gesture is not designed to immediately disseminate hate; it will release it slowly. You could not take it; it would kill almost everybody, for hate is a powerfully destructive force. So it must be released very slowly in increments. It must also be released slowly because maybe you sleep with somebody, maybe you have a mate. If it is released slowly, then it can go through the natural process of the body and pass through the body as liquid or a substance. You might experience some discomfort, but it will be not be major. They won't be extreme, but discomforts will usually come up someplace where you usually feel pain in your body. So do this no more than thirty seconds, as stated.

You can do this so that you feel uncomfortable in that spot where you sometimes have discomfort, or you can slow it down to one night every three weeks. But do it at least as many times as would equal one night a week over three months. Keep track in a book.

Sometimes there are different gestures for different people. Make the gesture, and if it doesn't feel right, move your hands apart. Move your hands around slowly while holding the gesture in position until it feels right for you. You can see that I am holding it gently in front of my solar plexus.

I can continue for a short time only.

We will get together again tomorrow. Thank you very much.

Dealing with Fear, Pain and Addiction

Speaks of Many Truths
July 30, 1999

This is Speaks of Many Truths. Greetings.
Welcome.

Deal with the Fear of Living by Encouraging Life

I'm wondering if the fear of dying isn't the biggest one of all. Is that something we can address?

The biggest fear is not the fear of dying, it's the fear of living. If you look at the fears you've mentioned, to say nothing of the hundreds you haven't, the biggest fear is that of living. That's why religions that have sprung up through the years, especially in your time, tend to address dying as well as being born as something that goes with God. But the fear of living is unquestionably the biggest fear.

How can we address that?

Much of what I've been saying has to do with encouraging life. In your time perhaps the biggest problem is that when children are born, they are expected to want to live. Therefore, very few individuals ever encourage them to live. The only children who are encouraged to live are those born with disease. Even then they are exposed to medical and other techniques that do not encourage life, though they may treat the symptoms.

Therefore, I would recommend that the first year of life be involved in welcoming and encouraging—not saying, "We are going to have fun playing baseball," because that doesn't mean a thing to a baby and it also puts off love and life for the future. I'm not talking about telling the baby about what you're going to do but about how you feel now, how you love them, how you are happy to have them there every day.

Saying it once isn't enough. Saying it once a month or once a week isn't enough. Say it every day. A foundation of encouragement lets the baby know that you welcome him or her, and that's vital. Be aware also that you cannot be talking on the phone, talking to somebody else, painting your fingernails, scratching your leg *and* talking to the baby to encourage or welcome him or her. You must be doing *only* that, and you must ask yourself, "Am I truly encouraging the baby, or am I just saying the words?" If you know that you are encouraging the baby, welcoming and loving the baby, then you know that is good, but if you have doubt, here is some simple homework.

Homework: Learning How to Welcome Others

Find a good friend or your mate, and sit facing each other in chairs, not in bed. Look at each other and say, "I'm so happy you are here. Welcome." You can repeat that and say other words along those lines. Close your eyes when you do this if you like. This might be better for couples especially. Do you know why? Because couples have a history, and they will see things in the other person's eyes that may or may not be there, so closing the eyes makes it easier.

Say these things to the other person, and when you are done saying them, before the other person says anything back to you, ask, "Do you feel welcome?" Understand that this is not a test or a competition. It is to find out if what you are feeling and radiating is being received by the other person in a way in which he or she can feel welcome—not just feel what you are radiating, but *feel welcome*.

If the person feels something else, he or she might not be able to distinguish between what is welcome and what's happening. Ask the person, "How do you feel?" This question is not to be answered on the basis of what the person thinks, but strictly how he or she feels physically. "Are you relaxed? Do you feel welcome? Do you feel loved?" In words like that, physically. "How does your body feel?"

The reason I'm emphasizing this is because so many people in your time respond with a thought when asked how they feel. Therefore, it's good to practice this way. Then the other person does the same thing.

Communication Is Physical

Remember that you are trying to develop skills to *feel* what you are saying. In reality, all communication is done with feelings. In your time that has been forgotten, and most people try to communicate with words, yet their feelings often do not match their words.

For example, if you are talking on the phone and having a conversation about something that's annoying—maybe it's about work, maybe about people, whatever it is—and your youngster or your wife or your husband comes up to you and says, "I'm not feeling very good and I need a hug" . . . the person does not really *say* that he needs a hug, but that is what it is. Do you say, "Hold on a minute, please," set the phone down and get into a feeling of life or affection with the person or encourage or welcome him, then give him a hug, pat him, stroke his head and say, "It will be all right"? Or do you just continue talking on the phone and reach an arm around the family member's shoulder and say, "It's all right" and give him a squeeze? That doesn't do it.

Communication is first physical, with radiated feelings. That's how animals know. Anybody who's ever petted a cat or an attentive dog knows that, because if you are not paying attention to it when you are petting it, it is going to poke you. It might even give you a little fake bite (not breaking the skin) and say, "Hey, I'm a person. Pay attention to what you're doing here." It's not that the animal is jealous or simple-minded. It's that the animal realizes that it is teaching you how to devote your total attention with feeling and touch. In short, the animal is giving by receiving; it is teaching you a most important thing.

It is very important then, this circumstance you have. Nowadays you have those phones that you can carry around, and maybe you are hugging the baby and talking to the baby and the phone rings. What do you do? Reach for the phone and ignore the baby?

In your time you call it priorities. You have to ask yourself what is more important—your family, wife, husband, children, baby or the telephone. Now, I know that sounds simplistic. You could say, "Well, it might be an important call. It might be from a family member, or it may be something related to work that I need to know right now." But I would say that, most likely, you are doing that work in order to support your family, in order to give you and your family a good lifestyle, not the other way around. You are not having a family so that you can have fun or challenge away from work. It's the other way around. You work to support your family. Family is first.

So this assignment to practice with a good friend or mate is to discover whether the words you say are accompanied by feelings that the other person can feel that connect equally to the words you are saying. Your partner might not say that she feels welcome necessarily or encouraged, but she might say that she feels relaxed and comfortable. That's a good response, too.

Try to be truthful with each other. It's also possible that tensions you have before you do this exercise could affect it, so try to relax each other. If you are just friends, lie down for a moment and try to relax completely and let go. Do whatever you do to relax completely, gently. Then sit and face each other so that you can be receptive and not carry a lot of extra tension.

This is a lot of homework, but I do not expect you to do all of this all the time. These are different things you can do. Do whatever feels best to you to achieve your purpose here, which always has to do with learning and becoming more in a way that is benevolent for you and others.

Releasing the Fear of Living

I never thought of the fear of living before.

There are many fears out there that you can see in your friends and yourself. You can try to adjust them one by one. Think of this: Even though it might seem absurd, many times you will be afraid of doing something because you don't know how, you are afraid you are going to be ridiculed, you might look foolish and on and on. But dying you don't have to learn how to do. It's easy; it just happens. There is no right or wrong way there, just the act of death. The real fear has to do with pain.

And annihilation.

Oh, but you know sleep is very much like that. I will tell you something: You go into a deeper state of unconsciousness (no awareness) when you are in sleep than when you die. When you die you are totally conscious. You don't sleep, you don't go into a quiet time; you just go from one stream of life straight into another, with communication with friends and people you've known and loved and looked forward to meeting again. It is straight into something else; it is not deep. So if you can sleep, you can die. It's true.

But many people don't have this absolute assurance that this is going to happen. That's part of the fear, isn't it?

The reason is because in sleep, many people do not remember their dreams, so they feel that sleep is like an unconscious state, like they got banged on the head and fell down and are unconscious. That's what it seems like to them. But even if you get hit on the head and fall down, things go on that you may not remember.

So people compare death to deep sleep, in which they can't remember anything—as you say, oblivion. But, in fact, it is not like that. If you've ever had a good dream, a fun dream, you wake up and it's like, "More, more," you understand? It's much closer to that, because it would be fun, wonderful, the best. If you want to know what death is like, think of the best dreams you've ever had. It would be better than that, but that would at least give you some idea. I'll give you a gesture that will help people to release their fear of living.

There are three stages or positions [Fig. 4-1]. This gesture is not done suddenly but gradually, in steps. Do this once every three days for two weeks, then wait.

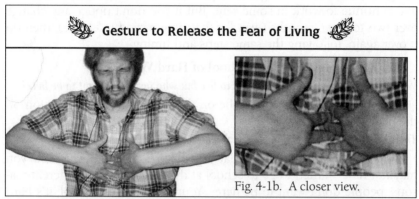

Gesture to Release the Fear of Living

Fig. 4-1b. A closer view.

Fig. 4-1a. Position one: Fingertips are centered in the solar plexus, the point where your ribs come together at the base here, where the soft part starts. Do this for about a minute unless it is uncomfortable, but try to do it for at least thirty seconds. Most likely, it will be comfortable.

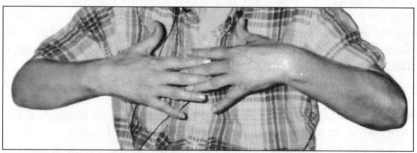

Fig. 4-1c. Position two: The fingers straighten out and lift off the chest. Do this step for a minute. This is comfortable.

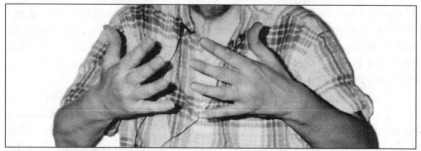

Fig. 4-1d. Position three: This might feel a little uncomfortable, but try to hold it for at least ten seconds, maybe thirty seconds, but no more than that. Do the entire gesture once every three days for two weeks, then wait a couple of months. If things don't get better, repeat the gesture.

In the next few months things might start to get a little better; you might gradually feel more relaxed or confident about life. If not, then repeat the gesture exactly, then wait. If things get better and you notice things getting better in regards to your fear of living, then let it go. It will continue to work in some way. But if you don't notice any change over two to three months (wait for that time period to elapse), then do it over again, following the same steps and timing.

Earth: A School of Hard Work

What about people who aren't afraid to live but who just don't want to be here?

Meaning they don't want to be on this planet or in this location on the planet?

There seem to be people who come here but do not want to.

Now, you must remember that this place is a school. Just like you may not have wanted to go to school at different times for different reasons, people don't want to be here. Your whole life is school; it's hard work. People want to have recess, they want to have a vacation, they want to have fun. This is not the place for that, even though there will be times when you have good times.

But mostly it is hard work, from one end of life to the other. That's why most people don't get to come here very often. It's a lot, and it might take many lifetimes in more benevolent places to assimilate it all. Know that if you have that feeling (and it is not uncommon), be assured that most of your lives on other planets are thousands of years long.

I think I can almost guarantee that the life you have here, unless you are very young, will be less than 110 years. Babies being born now might have a life span of 125 years because of changes in medical science and so on and, hopefully, changes in people's lifestyles.

It is a short time that you are here relative to the length of most of your lives. Tell yourself that. If it does not comfort you very much, then say, "I will find many fun things to do." And don't just say that in a *drudgery* way: "I will find many fun things to do." In other words, don't say it in a depressed fashion. Promise yourself, as you would make an oath with a friend, that you will find many fun things to do so that life here will be tolerable. Of course, eventually it *will* be tolerable, and then you will have fun things to do so you will get through.

I realize that is not really the answer you were looking for. You might want to say, "How can I connect to the other planets?" But I see no advantage in that. You knew what you were coming here to do. This is about work and also about love and fun and fun things to do. But the primary function of this place is about work. You won't be here forever.

I do not recommend trying to go out of your body and connecting to other planets, doing these kinds of things. If you do that—and some people have been doing that in your time—can you guess what can happen? You get so distracted with being elsewhere that you discover at the end of your life that you didn't do what you came here to do, so you get in line to come back. So try to embrace it and make sure you have fun things to do in order to make it bearable during the times when it isn't.

More Than One Soul Extension on Earth at the Same Time

That brings up something else. You said people would have to come back, but earlier you said that some people will keep coming back to the same time frame to get it right.

From their perspective or attitude. Trying to do it right means trying to get it the way their attitude says how to do it.

What I'm asking is, can there be several extensions of the same soul wandering around at the same time? Or are there alternative realities?

You mean on Earth, for instance?

Yes.

This is frowned upon. As long as you are well apart from each other it might be all right, but the effect is not so very different from identical twins, although you do not have all the pleasures of the identical twin, only the discomfort. You all know that if anything should happen to your identical twin, you, as the other twin, will feel it. You might not feel the physical pain, but you may suffer. Your life might never be the same because literally a portion of you has died.

This could also happen to other life on the planet within the context of planetary energy and so on. You wouldn't necessarily experience the pleasant experience as an identical twin does of the other person, but you might feel the grief. It is very complicated, but this is the simplest way I can describe it.

So this is frowned upon because it is considered to be a distraction. Also, in a rare circumstance that happens once in a while because a soul wants to do it, you might meet this other person physically. Most likely within a few minutes, not much longer than that, you would be confused about your own identity. Such confusion could last a very long time, even if you part from that person. You might take on traits, desires, hopes, dreams and so on from the other person—both of you might do that and become completely confused about your personal identities. I have heard of this happening typically for months, but sometimes for the rest of your life. So, of course, this is considered interference.

Well, how do they come back, then, because they need the same kind of awareness level on the planet and the same level of technology, and even fifty or one hundred years would make a tremendous difference?

No. You are thinking in linear time. They come back to the same time.

After the other person is gone?

No. Say you have a life. You are born in 1946, you live life and then you die. You decide that you didn't get it the way you wanted it, so you go back to 1946 and live it over.

How do you keep from running into the other party?

You don't, you're not allowed. You don't run into the other part of you.

But you are both there. Only one Earth and just one time period. It's the same reality even if you go back in time.

Most people do not do this, you understand. We are splitting hairs. We are talking about something that takes place once every . . . in your lifetime on Earth, this will happen to another soul living on Earth maybe about two or three times. It is very rare. Most souls do not have such a stubborn attitude.

I've often heard about counterparts.

Counterparts are different. What I was talking about before had to do with counterparts. It didn't have anything to do with coming back to the same time and living over again—that's not counterparts. Counterparts are two portions choosing to be born around the same time or within the same life cycle (they might not be the same age). That's what I was talking about.

Suicide

To continue the same thought, people who do not want to be here sometimes attempt suicide, which is totally against what they came here to do. Are there teachings or gestures for that?

Yes, but not all suicides relate to unhappiness. Sometimes if you were intended to live longer, you wait on Earth in a state between worlds until the beings come to welcome you. You are in terrible mortal agony in the hospital, and it looks like you are going to be that way for a long time. Maybe the hospital is associated with a battleground, so people are not hovering over you every second. Then maybe you can move your arm a little bit, pull out the tube in your arm that is dripping some liquid, keeping you alive. Maybe you could call it suicide, but you are happy to die because the level of suffering is more than you can bear.

You could say, "How can you say that's bad?" Well, if you are of certain religions or philosophies that I would call attitudes, you *could* say that's bad. It's easy for you to say that because you are not lying there in horrible agony. But if *you* were the one lying there, maybe you would pull that tube out, too.

So it is not a crime, not a terrible thing. You do not go to some horrible place. You wait in a quiet place. You are no longer in your body and usually not in such unhappiness. You might be floating in a quiet place, waiting until the end of your life. Maybe you would have died anyway in five years. You just rest in this place; it feels very relaxing. It's a form of semisleep with only pleasant dreams and everything nice. You wait until people come to get you and take you on back through the veils, then you continue on.

But on the other hand, maybe you are just unhappy—your boyfriend or girlfriend broke up with you or something like that, and you are unhappy in the moment and don't want to live. Maybe this has happened before, and you say, "Oh, not again. I can't go on like this." You do not think in the moment that maybe there is some other way to live life, because you have tried. You have asked questions before and here it has happened again, so you believe that it is destiny to go on like this and you can't take it anymore. So you go up on top of a building and jump off.

Maybe, though, what you didn't know is that you would have found resolution in the future and you would have gone on to have children and do other things in life, do benevolent things for people—for all you know, maybe you would have saved someone in a heroic act—many, many things. But you do not, as I say, go to a punishing place. You just go to a quiet place, and there you stay for a long time, not punished. If you need to talk to someone, there would be a voice there to talk to you. You just wait.

Most people do not walk around the Earth in some altered state. This happens occasionally, but eventually there are beings assigned to rescue them. You don't walk around indefinitely, haunting people. I'm not saying that energies do not exist that make other living people uncomfortable, but it makes you uncomfortable so that you will do something about it or tell someone: "I feel an energy over there that makes me uncomfortable." In my time you could talk to a mystical man or mystical woman and they would say, "Thank you very much." Then they would go over there and try to release that energy from that place. If there were spirits there, they would release them, help them to get where they are going. In your time, of course, one can do the same thing, but people have forgotten this. Some people know, though, so you could ask.

Miscarriage and Abortion

Do they usually come back?

They continue reincarnational lives, but sometimes after such considerable trauma, they might say, "I don't want to go back there again." Then the teachers will say, "It's a deal. You don't have to go back for long." They might even say, "You don't even have to be born. You can go back and be inside your mother." Maybe the mother does not want the baby, but you can live inside the mother for a time and then not be born. This happens in your time more than in my time. So the person says, "Okay, I'll go back and have a life for a few months inside my mother, and then she will have an unfortunate miscarriage." Something like that, or in your time it even could be purposeful.

But that is not a happy experience for a baby—can I speak of this, abortion?

Please.

I do not wish people who have sought abortion to feel guilty, but I must clarify one point. It does not make any difference what well-intentioned lawyers, people of the law, judges and so on say about this. When life is blooming inside a mother, it is alive, a living being. Life does not start when the baby comes out into the world; life starts inside the mother. It is important to know that. I am not saying this to justify what groups of people are doing to others. You cannot be, as they say in your time, pro-life if you are shooting doctors. Don't let anyone tell you that. That's not pro-life.

Try to educate people when life begins inside the mother. A baby is not a living human being only when it comes outside; when it is inside, it is also a living human being. Educate people about this. It is a good thing to know.

Starting at what point?

When the egg is fertilized by the sperm.

At the moment of conception?

Yes. There is no randomness. The egg and sperm communicate before the sperm enters the egg. You might ask yourself why *this* sperm, why not any of the millions of others that are in the mother. Remember, each atom, each particle has its own life [see *Explorer Race: Particle Personalities*]. The egg also functions that way. The egg has discernment; it is instructed by Creator, teachers and benevolent beings what to look for.

The egg doesn't just say, "I like the looks of you, but not you." (That's a little joke.) But the egg is instructed on what type of body is needed and wanted for what that soul who is going to enter the body would choose to have. So the egg waits for the exact qualities in the individual sperm. When the egg feels those qualities, it welcomes that sperm. It is all Creator-inspired. There is nothing random. It is not science; it's about life.

I am not trying to say to those who have had abortions or seek abortions or give abortions that you are bad. I am saying, just know that there is a life that wishes to be born through you. If you do not want to have this baby, then it's important (sorry to make this lecture, but I must say this) to acknowledge that the baby wants life. Please allow the baby to have life and make arrangements to see that the baby has a home. The baby could live with somebody else. Ask your sister; maybe she wants a baby. Ask a friend; maybe she wants a baby. If no one you know wants a baby and you don't want a baby, then talk to people in your time who will be happy to take a baby. There are lots and lots and lots of people who want babies in your time and cannot have one for one reason or another. So please let the baby live.

Everything that is happening is happening for a reason. I know there are times when you could say, "The woman did not want to have a baby, a man forced himself on her. Terrible event." Yet there is no conception, no sperm finds its way into an egg, without there being the intention of a baby being born. This does not mean that it is all right for a man to force himself on a woman, but it might mean that the woman is intended to have a child.

This is also important: Speak to women about this these days because so many women are being abused and treated badly by men in your time. If you are afraid that a man is going to force himself on you, do everything you can to protect yourself. Tell people to protect you. Do everything you can to protect yourself and start thinking, "Maybe I'm supposed to have a baby, maybe not with a person I'm afraid of, whom I don't like and would like to go away, but maybe I ought to be thinking about having baby with someone. I don't necessarily have to get married and live the rest of my life with this person, but maybe a baby wants to be born." How do you know? Here is how to find out. If you have a boyfriend already or gentleman friend, don't use birth control.

The Death of the Heart in Rapists

I have been very slow to talk about this with people, because it is very easy for a man who throws himself on a woman to say, "Then I guess I can force myself on any woman because she is supposed to have a baby anyway." Not true, not true. A man who forces himself on a woman, even his wife, when she does not wish to have the love act, every time he does this he causes death within himself—not physical death (as I say, you don't have to learn how to die that way), but rather death of the heart.

You may have a sad life—maybe somebody forced himself on you some other time. But, in fact, when you cause death of the heart doing harmful things to people . . . every time you experience this harmful thing that you do to others, you kill your own heart a little more. It doesn't mean that you are going to die. You seek that even though you don't know it. Rather, it means that you will have to learn how to live and do good things for people. The only way you can do that is, you will have to live the life you have lived over and over and over again until you can find that. It does not mean that you are destined to re-create yourself and be punished; it means that you must live over and over again, not inflicting yourself on others and maybe not having others inflict themselves on you, but you must learn.

I tell you what you have to learn because some of you will read this book: You have to learn that there is *another* way to relieve your terrible pain inside and it doesn't have to do with hurting anyone, including yourself. Here is a first step for all of you who may be reading this, who might have done this thing before.

Resolving the Rapist's Inner Pain

If you are physically able, start to exercise. Some of you know this—run, swim, do whatever it takes to exercise vigorously. The more you move your arms and legs vigorously, the less you will feel the pain.

The next step is to do the gesture I'll give you now [Fig. 4-2]. Do this sequence just before you sleep at night so you will dream about it. Hold the last position at least five minutes.

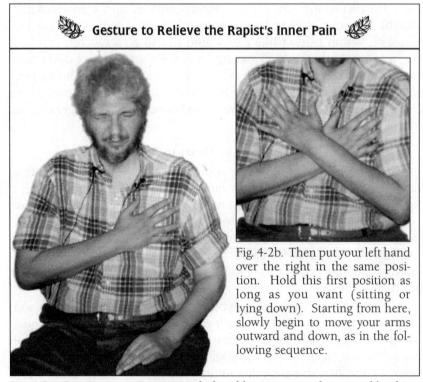

Gesture to Relieve the Rapist's Inner Pain

Fig. 4-2b. Then put your left hand over the right in the same position. Hold this first position as long as you want (sitting or lying down). Starting from here, slowly begin to move your arms outward and down, as in the following sequence.

Fig. 4-2a. Position one: Put your right hand here on your chest, just like this.

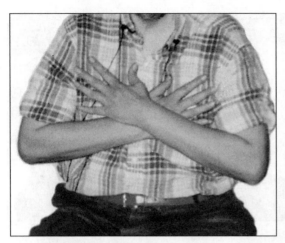

Fig. 4-2c. Position two: Slowly begin to move your hands down your chest, drawing your hands apart until your open fingers point toward your solar plexus (see the following sequence to 4-2j).

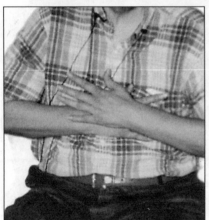

Fig. 4-2d. Position three.

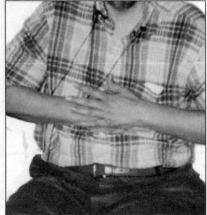

Fig. 4-2e. Position four.

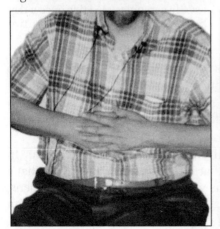

Fig. 4-2f. Position five.

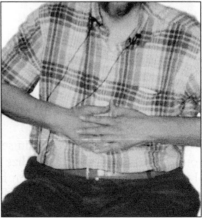

Fig. 4-2g. Position six.

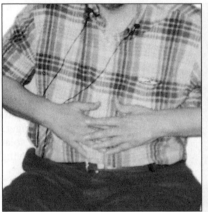

Fig. 4-2h. Position seven.

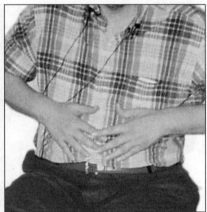

Fig. 4-2i. Position eight.

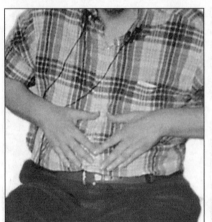

Fig. 4-2j. Position nine.

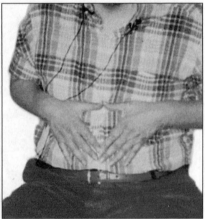

Fig. 4-2k. The final position. Hold at least five minutes. Do this once a day before you go to sleep at night for two to three weeks.

Many steps are given, but I want you and others to know what to do because that gesture will allow you to transform the terrible pain in yourselves that drives you to harm others and, more often than not (you know this is true), to harm yourself.

Is this for anyone who has been . . .

Anyone who has forced himself on his wife or on any woman. In other words, for a rapist. I realize that it sounds harsh, my saying that a husband might force himself on his wife, but sometimes this happens, and I see no difference between that and a rapist who forces himself on a stranger. I recognize that when a rapist forces himself on a woman, there is often other damage done—hitting, hurting, maybe killing. But that is something else.

There is more that can be done, but this is done to give a rapist something to do to resolve the pain within himself that causes him to rape. That is what drives him, regardless of how he rationalizes it in his own mind or fantasizes about it. It is always being driven by his own inner pain that has developed *in this life.* No one is born with the desire and need to rape; it comes about because of circumstances in this life. I feel that in your time this is known but not known widely, just in some circles.

I use your terminology pretty good, okay? I'm getting better at it—I say "okay." I say lots of things now. Practice makes you get better.

You can listen to Robert when he talks, can't you?

I can, but do not usually—do you know why?

Interfering, privacy . . .

Why else? I have a life. I am busy.

I see.

Now I will give some more instructions for that last gesture. Try to do the gesture once a day, and hold the last position. You can hold the first position—your arms crossed over your chest—as long as you want, but try to hold the last position for at least five minutes.

Try to do this before you go to sleep at night, and then you can dream about it. Some of you will have lots of time to do this because you have time on your hands. You know why. But even for those of you with time on your hands, also do it before you go to sleep at night. If you have lots of time on your hands because you are in prison, maybe you don't sleep very well anyway because of the unsettled energy where you are in residence . . . you know what I mean.

So they should do it during the day or at a different time?

Do it whenever you can if you are in prison. If you are not, try to do it before you go to sleep at night or just before that. This will allow things to happen in the dream state that will also help you. It may not cure your pain, but it might. And there's a better chance that it will make your pain less. No guarantees, but I recommend you try it. I have seen this help others.

Addictions

What about those who have addictions to drugs, to alcohol, to food, to gambling? Do they fall under one heading, or are they all different?

Addictions, as you know, always have to do with not receiving love the way you need it. Usually they also relate to not feeling welcome as a child or not being encouraged to live as a child. So much stems back to this, because when a person does not feel welcome, does not seem genuinely loved, he or she will seek satisfaction for those needs in other places.

If you find even temporary satisfaction in food, you might continue to overeat. One might say that we cannot quantify love this way, but if we did, for one part of the love you needed as a child, you would need (given a normal adult life to the end of your natural cycle) over one million parts of food to compensate for that one part of love not received! No wonder people get big or addicted to food. It's the same thing with drugs or any addiction that is destructive. Maybe it's not addictive in small quantities—you have a glass of wine once in a while, no problem. You eat rich food occasionally or even once every few weeks, or you gamble every once in a while with friends, a poker game or five dollar limit maybe once a month. Something like that is all right.

But when it is every day, all the time, it is easy to notice if you are addicted. It's very simple to notice. Are you hungry when you're eating? Do you know what it is like to feel hungry? When you wake up in the morning, you are genuinely hungry, you need to eat—maybe not right away but eventually. You need to eat, you feel hungry. You know what that feeling is. But notice at other times of the day—are you eating because you are hungry or are you eating because it feels good? It might be an addiction. That does not mean you are bad. It does not mean you shouldn't eat. It's just important to know this because it tells you that you need more love.

Resolving Addiction with Love-Heat

You cannot get the love you need as a parent, as an adult, and so you must give it to yourself. Give yourself the love-heat exercise [see pp. 7-8]. Wrap your arms around your shoulders and hug yourself. Do it regularly every day, every chance you get, because you need as much as you can give yourself, not as much as you can give yourself when you have the time.

Because you have not received that love, it is a terrible pain for you. You must have love to live here. All addictions might be self-destructive at some point. You cannot just stop an addiction. You must do something else that gives you love. So do the love-heat or abdomen heat. Know that you must do *something*.

But don't immediately stop your addiction. Let's say you are addicted to alcohol—you don't stop drinking and start doing love-heat. No, you continue your addiction and you do love-heat and love and hold yourself and stroke yourself [Fig. 4-3]. While you are touching your body, it's best to touch the skin, but the next best thing is to stroke down your clothes, stroking downward only, not bringing the stroke back up on the body. By doing this you are encouraging being in your body and being in life on Earth now.

Gesture to Reassure Your Body and Resolve Addictions

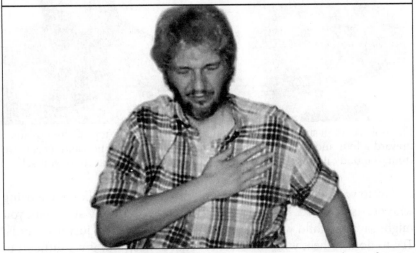

Fig. 4-3a. First rub your chin, then rake your arm with your hand. Stroke your body downward like this, saying to your body, "It will be all right." Do this gesture with love-heat if you can.

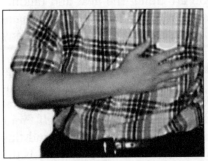

Fig. 4-3b. Position two: Keep moving downward.

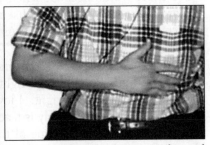

Fig. 4-3c. Position three: At the end of the downstroke, bring your arm outward as much as two feet from your body (see the next four sequences of this movement).

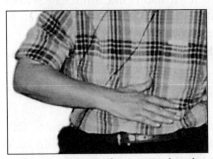

Fig. 4-3d. Position four: Your hand is now away from your body.

Fig. 4-3e. Position five: Keep moving your hand outward.

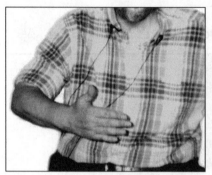
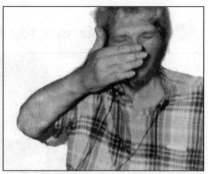

Fig. 4-3f. Position six: Move your hand upward a foot and a half or two away from your body, if your arm is that long.

Fig. 4-3g. At the top of the upstroke, begin the same motion and repeat. Do this as often as you can for yourself.

Say to yourself, "It will be all right," as if you were talking to a being who needs love, like petting a dog or a cat. Include any statement you might say to a child who is hurt or injured, only don't just use words. Try to do love-heat with the stroke. That is best, but if it's difficult to do both, then say, "It will be all right." If you can say, "It will be all right," while you are doing the heat, that's best. Maybe you cannot use those exact words because when you are doing the heat and talking, you are doing heart-speak, as discussed in the previous book [*Shamanic Secrets for Material Mastery*]. As a result, you will not have as many words available.

Say it the best you can, an encouraging statement, not meaning, "You are stupid—it will be all right." Not that, but make it gently encouraging: "It will be all right. I love you, it will be all right." Talk that way to your body. Your body is teaching you how to love yourself. Your mind is discovering the value of this because you feel better, and this shows your mind the physical evidence it craves to know that this is the right thing to do.

So learn how to be kind to yourself. It seems like a nursery school lesson, but this is a basic foundational lesson that has been forgotten in your time. This is simply a reminder.

It sounds like everything starts with lack of love as a child, and we do all these things to—what, make up for it?

Yes.

As a substitute.

Yes, and my feeling is that many addictions are not so terrible. Oh, you could say medically that overeating might shorten your life. It's possible. But you cannot live life without love, so you have to do what you have to do.

Alcohol Addiction

But I agree completely with people who say that overdrinking can not only hurt your life, but the lives of others. You might crash your car into people. Maybe when you drink you become strange and unpleasant. If you have a drinking problem and become unpleasant, you'll know because you won't have many friends. They'll let you know: "You acted pretty strange last night. I don't think I want to see you anymore."

You get hurt, mad and disappointed with life, but you need alcohol because it makes your pain more bearable. You are addicted in that sense; you don't drink because you need it like being hungry, but you drink because you need to soften the pain. This tells you immediately that you are a sensitive person and miss love, need love. Do the love exercises as given, and try if you can, since you are drinking alcohol, to begin by drinking it over ice. This dilutes it but still makes it cold and refreshing, if you like it that way. Or add water. Keep adding more and more water over time so that after a while, when you give yourself more love, you can taste the flavor of the alcohol but it won't have as much of an overpowering impact on you.

Eventually you can just flavor the water with a little bit of alcohol, and then eventually you won't have to drink anymore. That is one way to wean yourself, but don't just stop. You say, "Maybe stopping is good." I say, okay, stop, but immediately start doing the love exercises as given and be sure, if you are weaning yourself, to do the love exercises as often as you can for yourself. I might say more about this in the future.

Releasing the Accumulated Pain from Addictions

We need to give an exercise, perhaps, to release accumulated pain, not from being addicted to something but from the consequences of your addiction, the things you did while addicted. So I will give one gesture for all these addictions [Fig. 4-4].

How profound this is! It needs to get out to all practitioners and psychologists and healers.

I give permission.

Releasing Anger and Rage

What we're dealing with are emotions that are destructive to us. We dealt with hate as one thing, but anger and rage seem to be combined—or are they separate?

If you have anger and rage, you can still benefit from doing the hate exercise [Fig. 3-3]. I would recommend doing the hate exercise for anger and rage, then always doing the love-heat afterward, because it is difficult. You are releasing hate, but remember to do it gently. If you are feeling uncomfortable afterward, try to do the love-heat, because releasing hate, moving it incrementally through the body, can be difficult.

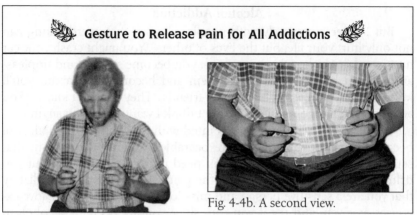

Gesture to Release Pain for All Addictions

Fig. 4-4b. A second view.

Fig. 4-4a. Front view: This will help release the pain that prompts addiction. Hold for at least thirty seconds. Do this once every third day for two to three weeks before you go to sleep at night.

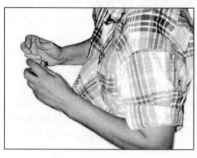

Fig. 4-4c. A third view from the side so the position of the arms is very clear. The position is the same on the other side.

Aren't hate and anger and rage usually intertwined?

Yes, that's why I recommend the hate exercise for all.

Hate is beamed outward or beamed inward—is it the same feeling?

Not the same, but they are related, cousins. Rage and hate are very similar. Anger can be very mild or extreme, but once it gets to the extreme point, then it starts getting into rage. Anger is sometimes good; it can prompt you to do things. Anger is a consequence of something else, so it might prompt you to do something that will resolve the anger and maybe improve life for yourself and others around you. So I cannot just give you an exercise to release all anger at any time. Anger might be necessary sometimes.

Behind anger, won't you usually find fear in some form?

Sometimes, but not always. Sometimes anger is intended to act as a motivating force because for one reason or another you are just not doing anything to resolve whatever is making you angry. Remember, a baby is not *taught* how to be angry; a baby comes in with the capacity to be angry. This tells you that anger is not bad.

When a baby is born, any capacity that the baby demonstrates within the first few days or so or that the baby feels, these are, of course, capacities he or she is born with. All capacities reveal themselves later, but I use this as example. People do not have to learn how to be angry.

You can get angry when someone doesn't get your bottle right away, right?

You can be angry because people don't understand your message and you don't get your bottle, but it is more important to get the breast, not the bottle.

Let's just say food.

Food, love. A bottle does not always include love. From the breast, the baby gets food and love. From the bottle, most often he or she just gets food and not love. It's a very important difference.

That must be one of the advanced lessons because baby bottles came into being only in the last two hundred years or so.

In days gone by, sometimes a mother would die in birth, and if no other woman was available, then a rudimentary form of a bottle was to dribble food down a finger into the baby's mouth. That is an old-fashioned bottle.

Emotion, a Mental Label for Disallowed Feelings

What about diseases? When someone has emotions out of control, will they actually cause disease in the body?

Emotions are never out of control. How does that strike you? Think about it, because this is a regular attitude in your society: emotions getting out of control. But there has never been one person living who has ever had an emotion that was out of control. It is that *they did not know.* Your society is not a sacred society, not living by the way of life on Earth. You do not know what to do with your feelings, so you are really saying that your *feelings* are out of control.

"Feelings" do not identify with the word "emotion." Emotion is a word that the mind uses to identify something it doesn't understand in mental terms. Therefore, if your feelings are unable to be controlled by your mind, then you need to know how to work with your feelings first. When you know how to do that, you won't have to have feelings that scream for attention because the mind refuses to allow them to be.

That's most important. That's why I give you these exercises, including the love-heat. All of this is a foundational exercise for an instinctual method of living in which you use feelings to know where to go, what's safe, how to get there, maybe even how to walk if you are in your body, who to go with and what to do when you get there—in other words, how to live in a sacred, benevolent way for yourself, having as little harmful impact on others as possible. It is important to say this with such specific clarity because in your time children are taught from the moment they are born that if they do not control their feelings, they will be punished.

You might reasonably say, "What do you mean, from the moment they are born?" Children cry only if they are feeling something that needs to be expressed. Sometimes the parent can do something about this and will try different things until he or she finds what works. But sometimes the child is crying for some other reason that has nothing to do with what the parent can do. Nevertheless, the parent can still console the child, welcome it.

Sometimes, especially if the parents are young and there are no grandparents or elders there to help them, someone will at some point tell them that babies cry. So the parent will just let the child cry. The child will learn, after crying and crying and crying and getting no attention—she won't learn this right away but eventually—that the feelings that encourage her to cry will not get her the love she wants. So she learns to distrust her feelings.

Maybe it is urgent attention—maybe she is hungry, something is harming her, she is cold and so on. But she doesn't get that attention, and it is not natural for her as a baby to think. Thought in your society is considered an act of maturity, but what if I told you that *feelings are the true act of maturity and thought is the artificial aspect of your life?* Your devotion to thought has caused you all to be in a place now where the best way to reach you and help you is through thought because that is where you put your attention. That is why you do these books. That is the point. But, in fact, feelings are the true communion with yourself and, as you can see in previous exercises given, with others.

Disease: A Signal to Do Things Differently

How do you work on diseases, then?

Let's save that. Some of you know that you think too much. How often I have heard from people in your time saying, "I know I think too much and I am not doing other things." I am always giving these people homework to bring them into their physical bodies, because their physical bodies will give them the signals that, once they learn how to interpret them (this book will help with that), will help them get what they want and need at its source rather than the substitute thing—where your mind says, "Maybe that will make me feel better. If I have one more chocolate eclair or maybe if I have one more whiskey, I will feel better."

Your mind is not the enemy. This is just what it knows based on previous evidence or experiences you've had. The mind does the best it can, but you are using it separate from the body. Let's say, instead of dealing with disease, that it is always better to learn how to do things that support and nurture the easy way to live (rather than giving you gestures to let go of a disease). A disease is a signal that you need to do things differently. Once you start doing things differently, the disease may moderate.

This doesn't mean that you don't need to go to the doctor and get some support for the symptoms and so on, but in my belief, it is better to treat the cause than the symptom. The symptom can be treated by others. That is why I have been giving all of you this homework.

The Problem with Heroic Medicine

In your time, because of the attitude of medical science and the desire of all people to help each other (you are really there with that), you have the idea of doing heroic medicine—someone has a heart attack and you rush him to the hospital. The doctors and the emergency people all perform urgent heroic deeds done with very specific precision. The person survives the heart attack and goes on and might live a healthy life, maybe with a different lifestyle. The person may have some fun and so on—in short, his life goes on.

But—you know what I am going to say—the heart attack was *intended* to create his death. Death is not the enemy. I realize that this flies in the face of everything people are doing now, but you must understand that not all diseases, as you see them, are the enemy. They might be the pathway so that you can move on.

I mention the heart attack specifically because it is sudden and urgent and often immediate, and if you don't get care, you will often die. That's intended. It may not be that way with all diseases, but sometimes it is. Remember, you are not intended to live long here. That is important to understand.

Let's say you heard that a friend of yours was in a car crash, and you grieve terribly. You love your friend and you miss him or her, and you might say, "Was there something I could have done differently?" Most people killed in car crashes and other violent circumstance like this—that was their exit. Death is not always the enemy. As a matter of fact, death is *never* the enemy. When a person is suffering without death, she just goes on suffering. That would be terrible. Creator would never, never do that.

But if you have a minor injury or disease that is treatable, or a disease where you can receive things from doctors—maybe a tooth problem—where they can fix it and make you feel better, then that's fine, a minor thing. It may not feel minor at the time, but it's minor.

Generally speaking, my belief is, don't try so hard with heroic attempts to keep people alive after a terrible injury. But it's not the same thing if a person having a heart attack can be given a drug to soothe the pain. A heart attack doesn't always kill a person right away; there is just suffering, maybe it's hard for the person to catch his or her breath. In that case it is all right to give things to ease the pain.

What I am saying is that I do not expect medical people, emergency people, to stop doing what they are doing. There is no shame there. I'm attempting to open you up—society in general, not just the physicians. Physicians are not the enemy. Generally, physicians are friends. But I'm attempting to encourage society to remember that often death is also the friend, not the enemy.

But what happens to the life of a man who has a heart attack and then he's miraculously saved and his life changes? There's no problem with that, is there?

No, I am not saying there is a problem necessarily. Maybe he is expected elsewhere to do other things. Those other things, if they are important, will wait, though it is more likely that at the eventual end of his life, those things will not be waiting. There will be other things.

I always used to say that sometimes they have to get out of the show in Pittsburgh or off-Broadway because they are going to star in one on Broadway.

Yes. Nice joke, very good; point well taken.

Pain Relief

But still, humans in the health professions have to continue to do what they do.

Of course they do. The most important thing they do is not only to clear up minor diseases that cause great pain and discomfort, but when they cannot cure a person, it is most important to relieve that person of that pain and discomfort. This is vital. Even in your time this is not fully understood. There is still some belief that it is all right for people to suffer or be uncomfortable. How many times do you hear, "Tough it out. You can take it," or "I've had that pain before. I can live with it." Why? There need to be things you can take so the pain can go away while you treat the circumstance.

Seek out treatment; don't ignore it. Pain is there to be listened to. Pain always means to pay attention, that you need to do something different, better. It doesn't mean to ignore it. If you ignore it and you've had as much pain as that part of your body can give you, your body will respond by finding a way to give you more pain in some other part of your body until the pain gets to the point where you must ask for help or take whatever medication or treatment you have. Why wait?

I cannot tell you how many people in your time ignore pain and go on, then the body produces more and more and more pain until they pay attention. Why wait? I am not criticizing medical people. It's good to ease a patient's suffering. It's almost always good to do that.

Intentional Discomfort

We were saying that within the auric body, within the energy around us, the astral, there are, in my understanding, things impending that haven't actually impacted the physical body yet.

You mean it might or might not happen?

Yes. For the clairvoyants who read this, are there any techniques or gestures to work on these early signs?

How do you mean "work on them"? What is the purpose?

To keep them from reaching the physical body.

To prevent discomforts?

Yes, before they happen.

Remember, some discomforts are intentional. The soul comes in to learn, yes? Maybe you have not learned yet what you need to learn in the way you need to learn it. It is not good to prevent all discomforts. It's better to say, either for yourself or if you are a practitioner working on someone else, "Please allow only the discomforts that this person needs to learn what she came here to learn and for those discomforts to be as gentle as possible to accomplish this." Like that.

This does not rule out discomfort, because discomfort is a variable, as is pain, to lead you to what you need to know or need to do—to other things. That's what practitioners might say while they do their energy work to set the specific standard or set the intent, as people say. You can change that for yourself just by putting yourself in the first person and changing the way it's said.

If you say it for yourself, you can always ask to be helped and supported with inspiration, guides, spirits, angels and so on—whatever things you believe in—to help you to learn in the most gentle, beneficial and benevolent way for you. You can add that, and you can also say, if you choose, "I would like to have the awareness and the ability to resolve this in the most beneficial way for me," because this resolution might allow you to do things better for yourself and others.

A Practitioner's Version of the Gestures

But you are not asking this for others unless you are working on the person as a practitioner. Most of what I talk of in this book is for the individual. But a practitioner can adapt some of these things with his or her own inspiration, perhaps.

The gestures are meant for individuals to do themselves, right?

Yes, always. However, there might be times when the person is unable to do the gestures; maybe he or she cannot move physically. Then practitioners who put themselves in a very spiritual state so they do not take on the discomfort of the individual could do this: Put your right elbow in the exact spot where the hands are supposed to go in any particular gesture. Perhaps your hands or wrists are anchored in a different part of the body than pictured so far, yes? Just as an example. Put your elbow there, but don't press. Just put it there and do the gesture.

That would help the person?

It might. When you use your right elbow, it's less likely that you will take the discomfort on yourself. It would be good to put your hands in the position first and then touch your elbow to the person. If you do this, touch your elbow to the person for no more than ten seconds.

Asking while you are doing it that it be for this person?

No, not necessarily. Asking, as you often do as a practitioner, that energy flow through you to keep you protected, just like many practitioners do before they begin—but keep doing that. Allow the flow to go through you and make it clear by touching your elbow to that person that this is for him or her. If it makes you feel better, you can say that this gesture is for this person you are working on, but as a practitioner it's unlikely that you will need to say it. If your mind needs you to say it, you can. If so, say it out loud.

This would be pretty rare, then, because there are not that many totally paralyzed people.

No, but you might find people who can't move for one reason or another—not only paralyzed, they might be comatose. If you are comatose, you may be moving a little, but it is not common. Or it might be a person in what you call a mental hospital—strapped down, can't move. That's not so common either, but it is another example.

So how would the practitioner know what to do?

Use the book, look at the symbols, signs, all things given. Then put your elbow to the person exactly how I said. I do not understand the question, perhaps. What do you mean, how will the practitioner know what to do?

I was wondering how one would know what the comatose or paralyzed person needed.

The practitioner is reasonably evolved, perhaps, and will be able to get this guidance from his or her own sources. I assume this, or that person would not be a practitioner. It is better to let the practitioner do this rather than yourself, unless you practice, practice, practice. If you are not a practitioner or think that a hospital or institution will not allow a practitioner in there but will allow you to visit because you are a relative, then do love-heat totally while you are doing this—before, during and after.

If anybody asks you what you are doing, say that it's part of a prayer ceremony that you hope will help the person. This is a very acceptable explanation. If that person wants to know more about it, tell her as little as possible unless she is a personal friend of yours. Then tell her a little more, but not much, because she will be speaking to you from a professional position. Say as little as possible because you do not want to talk about the thing you just did. You want the energy to work.

If you happen to see the person later in some social context, you can tell her as much as you feel comfortable telling, but don't tell her in order to educate her because you think she should know. Mostly, she would probably want a simple, short explanation. That's why I say, tell her it is part of a ceremonial prayer meditation, something like that. This is a perfectly acceptable explanation for what is, in fact, true.

An Exercise for People Who Don't Know What They Aren't Feeling
What about people out there who are so mental that they cut themselves off and don't even know what they are not feeling?

That's why we give you the foundational love exercise. Once you discover heat, you have a foundation, and if you want to know what you are feeling, then a quick, simple way to know is to try a thing that actors do in an acting workshop. The teacher tells the student, "Don't just say these words, but get involved in the drama of what you are saying." The teacher says, "*Get* there." Then the teacher sits out in the audience and away from the stage for a moment. "Here's the mood, here's the person." Generally, it will be classic theater of some sort. "Convince me that you are that person in that mood with those feelings right now."

So the actor must put himself into the feeling of the role he is playing and convey that feeling as well as words—in other words, momentary drama to show the acting coach what he can do. Then the acting coach says to try something different instead. She is not convinced.

One of best ways is to go to an amateur acting class like this, because almost all actors know the physical feelings that accompany different emotions, as you call them. Yet almost all people know how you feel in your physical body when you are angry. You've been angry before. Pretend to be angry, like an acting person, or pretend to be happy. Notice how you are feeling in your physical body.

But try not to do too many at once; do one, then relax, study the feeling and don't talk. With the student, I would have the student do something, notice what he is feeling and then go home and memorize that feeling so that he can bring that feeling up at any time—not so that he can process it or think about it or analyze it, as you would say in your time, but so he will recognize that this feeling in his physical body is directly associated with whatever he is working on.

Let's say you are acting happy in your own private acting class— make sure you are happy. You have been happy before, so you might recognize that you are indeed happy rather than just pretending for the sake of the acting workshop. Try to get as involved as possible with being happy so you can recognize happiness. Then examine the feeling in your body that has to do with happiness. Maybe you will take notes on this, maybe not.

More likely it is a matter of *memorizing the physical feeling.* After three days of doing this at least two or three times a day, you will know how you feel in your physical body when you are happy; then try to examine that feeling later. Granted, there will be some variations, especially if during these three days something prompts you to be happy; then you will notice a reaction of *true* happiness.

The acting-workshop style here is the best you can do. It's always best to note that *the action in the body is based on the outside circumstance that prompts it.* In short, try to memorize this physical feeling. Go through this with no more than one feeling every five days using this method. You could even do one feeling a week.

In my time people were not as distracted with so many things going on. But in your time one feeling every five days is probably best. Then you can start another feeling. After a while, you will have five, ten, twelve different feelings that you are able to identify—anger, shame, happiness and so on.

You go through all these different things that we sometimes think of as circumstances but, in fact, are feelings such as shame. After a while, when a feeling comes up in the body, you may know what that feeling is; then you can act on it. "It was a mystery before, but now I know I am feeling shame." Once you identify the feeling, then do a love exercise or another exercise given in this book, perhaps. In short, you will know what you are feeling. When you know, you are empowered. It's when you *don't* know that you are not empowered and life is confusion.

When you say you have a life, is it your spirit life that you're involved in?

I work with other people. Sometimes I work with spirits, sometimes with physical people in my time, sometimes with physical people of your time, sometimes I help people in dreams. There are lots of different things I do.

So you work with people other than through Robert?

I do not speak through anyone else, but I help other people if I am able, just like many others of my type of being help people. I even help a little now with 3.0-dimensional beings . . .

Oh, you started?

A little bit now, yes, with some receptive beings.

As more and more people read these books, will they be calling on you?

Fortunately, I have lots of help. I do not have to do the whole thing by myself. My job to is to give instructions, speak through Robert, get this out in book form. Later, other people, lots of other spirits, will be waiting to help. If someone calls out after reading these books, "Speaks of Many Truths, come help me," if I am busy, someone will take my place.

That's great!

It is that way for all spirit.

But you wait to be asked, right?

I wait to be asked, yes, because asking gives permission. If you are not asked, you don't have permission. Many people are taught through religion that God loves you, God acts for you. That's certainly true, yet if you want God to help, you say, "God, please help me with this." Or you add, regardless of your religion, whatever word you have for God or Creator: "Please help me or send someone who can help me with this in the most benevolent way for me." This way it might be an angel or it might be a guide. For all you know, it might be a human being. God may not be able to come right then, but He will send someone else.

I'm glad you said that. Do you want to say anything else?

We'll continue tomorrow.

Shame, Arrogance, Safety and the Inability to Trust

Speaks of Many Truths
July 31, 1999

We got started a little bit on shame and guilt last night. What about people who can't feel or receive love, or who have sexual dysfunction in their lives?

Releasing Shame

A lot of this has to do with shame, so we will give a release exercise for shame. Sometimes shame has been released in an individual because he or she has actually done something that has hurt others. If it was an accident, genuinely unintentional, shame was probably induced unnecessarily. But if it was intentional, as a child might do, unthinking or unfeeling, then the shame was utilized by an adult to try to encourage better behavior. This is understandable, but it is still not the best method.

If a child does something shameful, walk the child through how the other person felt. You don't have to harm the child the same way, but you must take the child through the experience so that he can feel what he did in terms of its impact on the other person. You might have to induce a little pain, but you cannot simply grab the child and spank him. A child does not understand that. He thinks, "That's the price I paid for my fun." When a person starts to think this, that feeling can lead that person (as has been known on many, many occasions) to a life of crime.

So you must apply training for a child carefully. The explanation to the child, including walking the child through how the other person felt, must fit the situation so that the child understands that that's how the other person felt. Words are not sufficient. It's like a meditative process, not done with vengeance. It must be done very carefully. This was usually left in my time for a grandmother or grandfather to do, because they had received training.

Some people in your time understand how to do this. You cannot just use the meditative process to induce a child to feel pain—then the child will feel only the meditative process—so it must be done carefully, but I mention it just to give a suggestion.

We need to give the exercise or gesture to show how to release shame [Fig. 5-1]. I give this exercise in a way that will allow shame to be released incrementally; since it is cumulative, shame will be released slowly at first, then gradually more and more.

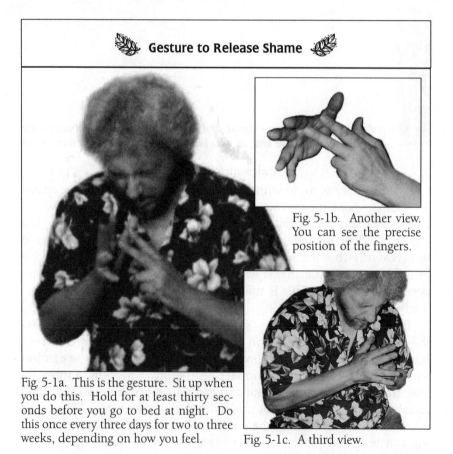

Gesture to Release Shame

Fig. 5-1b. Another view. You can see the precise position of the fingers.

Fig. 5-1a. This is the gesture. Sit up when you do this. Hold for at least thirty seconds before you go to bed at night. Do this once every three days for two to three weeks, depending on how you feel.

Fig. 5-1c. A third view.

Fig. 5-1d. A fourth view.

Fig. 5-1e. Notice that the hands do not touch each other.

Again, always try to do the exercise using the standard method [see page 32]. Sit up when you do this, and try to do it before you go to sleep at night, if possible. If you sleep with another person in the bed, it will not affect them at all, only you. However, for the sake of couples, when doing these gestures, always try to do them after making love; do not do these gestures and then make love. This can cause confusion, because you are starting, a sacred process.

Do this before you sleep, and then allow sleep to take place. How often? Do this gesture once every three days, as is typical to the standard method, but for perhaps two or three weeks. I give you an option: Do it for two or three weeks, depending on how you feel. Remember that this work is all rooted in how you feel, not in how you think, so a lot of this has to do with your body and knowing how your body is feeling.

If after doing this two or three times, you feel uncomfortable, maybe you're going too fast. If you're feeling uncomfortable in your body while you are awake, then you need to skip a process—do it once every five or six days. If that helps but you still feel a little uncomfortable, then cut back to doing it once a week. That should be sufficient.

It is intended to be slow because the effects will be cumulative. If you cut back to doing it once a week, you still want to do it as many times as originally stated (if you did it once every three days over two or three weeks, it would add up to four to seven times). If you went to once every five days or once every week, it would extend the timing, but after that, stop. It is not necessary to do this gesture again unless you feel the need—"I've gone for a long time and forgotten to do this; I could check and see if it is necessary." When checking, then, just do it three times, once every five days. You will know by the way you feel in your physical body if it is helping. If you feel no difference, then it is probably something you completed.

Does that cover guilt, too?

Shame and guilt are first cousins—guilt is the next level, a more extreme version of shame. Shame often prompts guilt, then guilt goes on to manipulate your life and very often the lives of others.

Exercise to Begin to Tell the Truth Instead of Lying

What about someone who either consciously or unconsciously lies a lot? Is that something you can work on this way?

You see, the difficulty with this exercise is that if you are used to lying to everybody . . .

. . . you lie to yourself.

Yes, and you might be living in somewhat of a fantasy world. You must have motivation to release patterns. If you do not have the motivation or are not in touch with yourself sufficiently, you might not be able to do this. But a person who lies to everyone, including himself or herself, might find that he or she can still do the love-heat [see pp. 7–8]. It might be difficult, but it can still be achieved.

If you want to stop lying, that can be very difficult. It might be easier to start telling the truth. Starting to tell the truth, though, will be hard after a lifetime pattern of lie, lie, lie. So I recommend you start to tell the truth about something small and simple; I recommend especially that you do this with a good friend, maybe you have a good friend. One day your friend might ask how you are feeling, and then you can say, if you can, "Well, I'm feeling a little tired today," instead of "Fine."

It is simple. You don't have to tell that person everything you are feeling. Your friend might just say, "Yeah, I feel terrible, too." And then you go on and you think, "That wasn't so hard." In short, begin small. It is much easier to begin to tell the truth than to stop lying. But understand, the reason you started lying in the first place was not only to improve the quality of your life, but also so that people might think better of you.

You will need to begin to tell the truth slowly. Don't rush into it. First you have to discover that it is safe to tell the truth, so begin with simple things like this.

Sometimes not telling the exact truth might have been based on the idea of survival for that person.

Yes, and sometimes it might be about being polite.

Cultural Lies

You are taught in your culture that there are certain simple things you can say that are polite. Sometimes in a culture, such as the one you are living in, instead of saying, "Hello," "Yes," "Greetings" or "Good life," people say, "How are you?" But "How are you?" is not really a question; that's why you say, "Fine." It is a lie both ways.

The person saying, "How are you?" does not want to know. If the person wants to know, she will look at you sincerely and then say, "How are you?" Then she wants to know. But if she just says, "How are you doing?" she doesn't want to know. Then you are supposed to say, "Fine."

This is unfortunate, because it teaches both of you to accept pain as being pain and not as being a message to change what you are doing and how you are doing it. It is built-in training that falsehood or lying is preferred and better than telling the truth. Your whole culture right now uses this so much as its foundation. That is why very often people feel at their wits' end, because they feel a sense of futility.

People feel a sense of futility because they say so many false things to themselves and others, even the polite person, the person not intentionally lying all the time. Many times it is so based on falsehood that you cannot find what is real, so maybe you go out in nature to be around the animals, trees, plants, rainbows, Sun, wind and so on. You know this is real. You feel relieved, relaxed. This is real. Then you go back in your culture and someone will say, "How are you doing?"

Briefly after stepping out of the woods, you want to say, "I feel refreshed, and the woods were wonderful." Maybe you say that, or maybe you just say, "Fine." Then the feeling of futility will build up again later, and you have to go back to the woods. But you cannot always go to the woods.

No, you cannot. We've got sales and advertising, marketing and public relations, whole areas of life that are built on glowing lies.

Lies are lies. It is unfortunate, because once people—especially young people growing up—start to observe their world and pay attention, around the age of nine, ten, eleven, twelve, thirteen, they look at the lies they are surrounded with and feel like, "Well, this is the way of life in this culture." And so they believe this is all right. Then they grow up with confusion and give lots of work to psychiatrists and counselors. But not everyone can see a psychologist or a counselor. Some do not even think it is all right to do so. So, many people just get unhappy and stay that way. They believe that unhappiness is what life is about, when it is not about that at all.

Think of how many people you know who think that life is about unhappiness, suffering and misery. That is because we're raised, sometimes with the best of intentions, exposed to lies. For example, children are often raised to learn how *not* to complain. Something hurts you and you are in pain: "Don't tell anybody. Never speak of your pain." You are hurting, you are suffering, but "Tell no one." So then you learn that life is about suffering within and that you can never get support from anyone. Not only does it never occur to you to ask for help, but if others around you ask for help, you tend to judge them as weak or that something is wrong with them. This tends to limit your world, and if you are the parent of these children, you are ashamed of them.

You can see how this has an effect. Work, life and so on are extremely distorted.

It's also what Isis referred to as self-violence. We're taught to be disciplined, goal-oriented, dutiful and responsible, no matter what the cost. Then Isis comes along and says that is self-violence.

Yes, that's a very good term, because "self" in this case not only means your own self, but also what you inflict on others because of the pain you experience, believing that this is the way life should be. Much pain and disease are prompted by this false culture you find yourself in. People living in a false culture like that very often look for entertainment or release of such internal pain by extreme behavior. Or because they get so exposed to self-violence all the time, they might form a shield around the self, and so they deny pain and expect and demand that others deny pain, too.

They might easily do things that cause guilt and pain to others such as torture. They might make animals suffer so that they can experiment with products to see if those products would be safe to use on humans. It is only a very small step from there to torturing humans to see if those products are safe to use on other humans. This has been done many times under the mantle of science.

Science without Heart

Supposedly science is meant to help people. Science in your lifetime has been used to harm people much more often than to help. This does not mean that science is evil; it just means that science is being misused in a harmful, self-violent way instead of being used in a benevolent way.

That is why scientists are struggling to solve so many things. Until science is a *heart* science—feeling, love is a heart science—you miss many opportunities to know whether you are going the right way or the wrong way. In science now you tend to do a hundred experiments, whereas one would be enough if you were doing heart science. You would feel that this is the experiment to do in order to produce the results you are looking for.

But feelings are shut out of science completely because feelings have to do with life, which has to do with pain, which has to do with unhappiness, which has to do with misery. Feelings are shut out of science, which uses only mental processes. Using only the mental is taking the long, long, long way around and in the process will produce a great deal of violence on the self and others. Science is lost right now, wandering around totally lost. It's trying to find simple solutions to simple problems that science thinks are complex, because science only thinks and does not feel.

Many, many control groups in medical research were denied drugs or were given something harmful. There are many stories now about the violence that science and the government have done to humans.

This also acts as a check (as they say, checks and balances) to keep science from discovering things that might cause you, in your now self-violent state of being in your culture, to bring self-violence to many others—for example, using propulsion to explore space. Propulsion is the slowest possible method. As you know, it is a simple fact that you cannot explore planets very well using propulsion. By the time you get there, astronauts have aged considerably, to say nothing of the difficulties in getting back. You are being kept from discovering and applying a simple method of flight.

Sexual "Dysfunction" and Fertility

What about sexual dysfunction? It's a really big thing that keeps people from expressing themselves.

You mean being unable to have sex?

Well, I think it can work both ways: you are unable to have sex or are feeling driven by a compulsive sexual appetite.

For one thing, being unable to have sex is not unusual in your time because the planet has too many people. One of the planet's messages that goes out to all parts of her body (and you are part of her body) is, "Please do not have so much reproduction." Also, people are getting less fertile, so there is less reproduction. This is not actually a dysfunction. In reality, it is just not to have so many people.

This is not so with animals. Mankind has a great impact on animals, so animals stay fertile unless they, as a species, feel unwelcome by human beings, and then they go away. At the end of their natural cycle, they die and don't come back until there are fewer of that animal and finally no more of that animal on Earth.

This should be made better known so people don't take it so personally.

Well, it is hard not to take it personally because it has been happening for some years. It's like waves. As a place begins to be overpopulated, some people become unable to reproduce. Of course, there also might be other challenges. Individuals born with intention cannot rule that out on an individual basis, but it is usually what happens when a planet begins to be overpopulated. So in more recent years it might be more common for people not to be able to reproduce.

Sexual dysfunction might not be the right term for when a person wants to have sex all the time. This is not dysfunction. The natural state of the human male or female in my time is not to need to have sex all the time, but it is typical for a husband and wife—young people—to want to have sex three, four, five times a day. That's not unusual.

That does not mean they always can do so, but they want to. That's my way of thinking. That is normal. Also, in my time there were not so many people on Earth, so when it became obvious that a woman was with child, in some tribes the man still had sex with his wife maybe once a night—very gently, though.

Many other tribes believed that once a woman became pregnant, no sex was allowed until after she gave birth to the child; then after that she had to heal up for a time. She had to bond with her baby and could not do so while having sex with her husband at the same time. So sometimes there was not so much sex after she gave birth to the baby. The baby had to be welcomed, be close to its mother all the time. Eventually she might be able to have sex with her husband and still have the baby nearby—that is all right, by the way. Babies are not embarrassed by sex.

Are you saying that it is not really relevant right now?

If some people still feel like they need to have sex three, four, five times a day, that's all right. That is normal. There will always be some people who are not affected so much by that, you understand.

Planetary needs.

It's planetary needs, and it might also be that, for some reason, the person needs to have more offspring. You must, of course, have sex with people who want to have sex with you. Maybe a woman knows she needs to have more children. If a woman has a great need to have sex lots and lots of times, sometimes it could mean that a need has gone unfulfilled and she does not feel love and so on. But at least half the time in your time, the woman needs to have a child.

If she is taking something to avoid having children, her desire to have sex might increase more and more and more, so she can't get enough. This is usually because the woman needs to have a child, go through the childbearing process. Then she can relax and that need will go away.

If a man needs to have sex many, many times a day, then he needs to have a child; he needs to foster a child in his wife and go through the life process with the child—not to have sex with his wife when she is pregnant, but to go through the process gently, nurturing his wife, supporting her through the process, then afterward, helping her with the baby, changing diapers, holding the baby sometimes when the baby is upset and the mother needs sleep. The man needs a child. When a man is doing those things, he will find that the tremendous need for sex goes away. Then he just needs regular sex—once a day, something like that.

It is good to know these things because some things are normal and healthy and other things seem to be problem, seem dysfunctional, and you might go to a psychologist. But these are not just physical needs. Very often people might be born with the need to nurture a baby—a man, for instance. Then he goes through the processes described and is able to have that nurturing with a baby, have someone he can love completely and who will love him back completely.

This is a wonderful feeling for a man. It sometimes resolves many problems in him. He completely understands love after that. A man sometimes loves a woman and the woman loves the man, but the man says, "I also want to have sex with the woman," so it is conditional love. But a father loves his baby and the baby loves his father unconditionally. The baby did not give anything to his father that way, and the father did not give anything to the baby that way. The father learns more about unconditional love, both giving and receiving. This is very satisfying and makes the father feel much better.

These things need to be talked about, because the information is not available in our society.

Yes, this is a basic thing that sometimes country people know, but unfortunately in your time many country people are given religions that induce shame and then guilt, and these will almost always lead to resentment, which leads to self-hate, anger, self-destructiveness, self-violence and so on. These religions need to change; they need to be more associated with nature and the way physicality really is, the way spirit really is.

The Creator and Religion

I am not trying to say that what I believe is the only way to believe. Many visions of God are very nice, but if they come entangled with falsehoods about the way life is, then this has nothing to do with the Creator I know. The Creator I know is very loving and nurturing, and wants the best for you. He has put you in a world filled with loving, nurturing beings: animals, plants. They are all complete spiritual beings. Creator exposes you to spiritual humans very often.

That's the loving Creator I know, not the Creator who says, "Go to Earth and suffer. I'll show you." Creator is not like that. The religions that believe this come from self-destruction and self-violence. Those religions will all die out, will all be gone in the future. People will read about such religions for a time. In the future, eventually such history books will not be there anymore, but we will read about it for a time and wonder how people could have done this. This has nothing to do with God. They will scratch their heads and ask, "Why?" and have no idea because God is love.

Weren't many of these religions set up by men who wanted to control everybody?

Yes, these pathways of religion were often set up as political governments to control situations. Sometimes in the beginning, some change in human behavior was necessary, but very often it was just a small group of people who wanted to control things so that they could have what they wanted and too bad whatever everybody else wanted.

But originally they were motivated by the need to get people calm so they would stop fighting and hurting each other. In other words, they wanted to create some sense out of the world and give people common threads they could believe in. Religion can be practical in a benevolent way, but once it is considered the one and *only* way, then you have to convert people, take sides and say, "Believe what I believe or die," or even lesser things, "Believe what I believe or I won't love you"—a terrible thing for a parent to say to a child, but it has happened many, many times.

That is violence. It restricts a child's life. A child feels he must grow up in this very studious religion or "I'll be sorry," but by that time he doesn't remember why (because his parents won't love him). These things are obvious to you now, but most people are not conscious of these motivations, these drives. When they read about it and think about it, they say, "Oh yes, of course." But most of the time they are not conscious of it. So philosophers and speakers like myself have a duty to remind you sometimes so you can say, "Oh, that's right, we know that." You need to be reminded.

Arrogance and Superiority

What about people who have patterns of arrogance and superiority? I don't think they see this as something they need to work on.

People like that are always driven by terrible feelings within themselves. The only exceptions—and there are very few—are those who are brought up by people in very wealthy, powerful situations and taught that they are better than everybody else. But most of those children do not believe it because they come to Earth to learn things.

They might take on some of that attitude, but eventually they go out into the world and discover that things are not like that. Even if they can be safe for a time in private school, some don't believe it. The child might think this as she grows up, but eventually she will make friends, meet someone she wants to marry outside of her group of wealthy people. Then she will learn with somebody she loves; she will *have* to learn.

Generally speaking, though, most arrogant people are driven by the terrible pain of self-shame inside—in other words, "I must keep myself from feeling that pain at all costs," which gradually translates to, "I must keep everyone from knowing I have that pain at all costs. By being arrogant and keeping people away at a distance . . . the further I can keep people away, or as many people as I can keep from me, the less chance they will find out who I am. Who I am is this painful, terrible thing inside of me. It is so shameful, I cannot expose this to them."

Psychologists all know this, but it is really true. The only exception to the rule as mentioned is where people are brought up in a very closed system. In your time, there are not so many situations like this anymore—royalty and such. The bigger the world gets, the more people, the less room there is for royalty.

If someone who felt like that hadn't gone to a psychologist, would he or she start using the shame gesture?

Yes. First look for the shame gesture, and then try to do the releasing of shame and so on. It will be very helpful. Your goal is not to become less arrogant; that will be what happens, but that's not your goal. Your goal is to *feel safe with people*.

Releasing Arrogance by Creating Safety

First do the shame exercise, all right? Then I will also give the exercise for attraction, because almost everybody on the planet needs to feel safe with other people. Sometimes you have a good reason not to feel safe, but you need to know how to feel safe in general—not just with other people, but to experience a feeling of safety inside yourself. Do it often if you can feel this strongly and with love—love-heat and all of this. You don't have to shove it out, throw it out of you; you will just naturally radiate it, and you will tend to be in situations that are safer more of the time.

First go through a program of releasing things you can think of that you might need to release, as mentioned in this book. Try to get more clear. You will know when you are more clear because you will not be driven to do things you don't understand that hurt yourself or others. When you don't feel that so much anymore, then you could perhaps start to use the gesture to create safety.

Creating safety is stimulated within yourself. Zoosh has given the safety exercise many, many times, so I will not repeat that [see Appendix H]. Usually he gives it in a private session, but it's a long, long exercise and takes thirty minutes to describe. We'll just give the gesture [Fig. 5-2].

Consciously you must know that you are attempting to *welcome* safety in you. The Sun supports the Earth. If you can, go outside when the Sun is shining; this is the best way. Then raise your hands toward the Sun, standing up or sitting down if you cannot stand. Do this once a day for ten days.

Then wait a week or two, whatever feels right to you. You have some flexibility. Then do the same thing at night with the Moon. Go outside, but this must be done carefully. It must be very close to the full moon day—for instance, the day before the full moon, the full moon day or the day after the full moon—because the Moon gives lots and lots of energy then. Do the same gesture exactly, but toward the Moon—not when the Moon is just rising, but when the Moon has been up in the sky for a while. You must be able to see the Moon (when it is not

🌿 Gesture to Welcome Safety 🌾

Fig. 5-2a. Here is the first position: Raise your hands toward the Sun, head up.

Fig. 5-2b. Position two: Move your arms down in front of the upper chest.

Fig. 5-2c. Position three: Touch the lower chest. Do this once a day for ten days. Wait a week or two, then repeat the same gesture toward the Moon during the three-day full-moon cycle.

cloudy or raining). This seems obvious, but we say so just in case. Do that once a day for those three days, because you live in the nighttime as well as the daytime. Three days is enough. That will support safety.

You might begin to notice that you don't have to say to yourself, "Safety, safety, safety." Just know that you are out there attempting to create safety.

If you can, do the love-heat exercise while you do that gesture. It may be a challenge, but if you can, good. If you can do the love-heat before the gesture, that is also good. If you can do it after, this is good too, because it reminds your body, spirit, mind and feelings what this is about. You can even say to yourself before you do the gesture as shown, "I welcome safety in me." That's all, very simple. Then do the gesture as described.

After you do the Sun exercise, you might have to wait a week or two just to relax, rest and let things happen. Then do the Moon exercise. You could time the Sun exercise if you want so that the full moon cycle (the day before the full moon, the day after) is a week or two later. But if it does not work out for you somehow, then just wait until the full moon cycle happens and do it that way. To work it must be done one day before the full moon, at the full moon and the day after.

That's beautiful.

It should help if you have feelings of safety. Say, "I welcome safety in me," not with the exercise, but *before* you do it. If you feel better, you can say it once while you do it, but say it only once with that exercise. Then if you are feeling a little safer, be happy. You are welcoming safety inside you.

What about the other side of that, someone who feels very inferior? Is that going to be based on something you've already given?

For inferiority, probably use the shame exercise.

That's a basic one, then.

Yes, the shame exercise works for inferiority.

Doing the Love-Heat Exercise in a Group

What about those who cannot do the love-heat exercise? You said they can join a group, but what if they can't find a group? What if a person is isolated? Does he or she just keep trying?

Keep trying, and tell people about this exercise. Ask them if they can do it. Share it with people you feel good about. Sometimes it's easier for a woman to do this exercise than a man. Women can get to it quicker, but it must be explained slowly. Show it to them printed in the book. If they can do it, then ask if they would mind doing it for a while, practicing for a couple of weeks—once a day or whenever it is convenient. In other words, try to expose some friends to it, people you know, women or men, whoever can do it.

When they get good at it, when there are at least three or more, tell them, "I need to get good at this, but I have been having trouble. Can I try to do the love-heat exercise while you are doing it? Maybe it will help me. Don't send it toward me; just do it and let it naturally radiate. If I sit in the room with you, near you, maybe I can feel it, too."

When a person feels it, then he goes into it immediately to try to feel it more. Then he builds it up slowly. If other people are also experiencing that, it will be easier. In short, people must ask for help. That's very important. Everybody can do different things well, but not everybody does everything well.

This is intended so that you will ask for help. Eventually you'll find people who can do a thing well that you cannot. Keep in mind that maybe there is something you can do well that they cannot, but you don't need to say that. You are in the position of asking them to do something for you, but it will also feel good for them.

They will probably not know how to do the exercise, so they will gain because it will be a good experience for them to do it as indicated. It is not just a hard thing to do, but for them perhaps it will be easier and they will gain from it. Obviously you are to do it because you are attempting to gain a good sense of love feeling for yourself and everything. They can have that, too. You do not need to give up religion. You can be of any religion and do this.

Establishing a Sense of Provable Reality with the Physical Body, Stones and Animals

What about people who can't even trust enough to ask?

Meaning a person who would like to do the exercise but is afraid to ask people because people cannot be trusted?

When a person doesn't trust anyone.

Or anything.

Or himself.

When people do not trust anyone or anything, this is always caused by a life experience. People like this need to see a counselor every day, but they also can help themselves by doing very basic things every day that are provable as truth. This might seem simple or silly, but put your hands together and move them back and forth gently. You can say with absolute certainty, "My right hand feels my left hand moving back and forth, and my left hand feels my right hand." Your sense of touch is truth; you can count on that. It might not always tell you what you need to know, but it is truth.

You can pick up a stone, or if it's a big stone, you can sit down on it or maybe touch it. It is best not to pick up stones in general unless you put the stones back exactly where you found them, especially if they are in the dirt, because they have a life. They are doing something, even though it might not be obvious to you. If you touch a stone, feel its contours, because this is foundational truth for you and helps support trust. In short, do physical things. The more physical things you can do, the more you will be able to believe in something. Begin with the physical.

This is a long, long procedure. Begin with the physical, and if you need more, go to a counselor. But try not to approach it from the position of resolving pain, of trying to make sense out of it. In short, the process with a counselor might work. If it works for you, by all means pursue it. If it does not, then do physical things. You do not have to learn how to ride a bicycle, but try to touch more things that are safe or that are all right to touch. For instance, if you have a dog—maybe get a dog—the dog will trust you absolutely, love you absolutely with unconditional love. You can do the same with the dog, learn that the dog can be trusted.

Maybe the dog has to learn how to behave in the house. Dogs do not build houses; dogs can live on the land. They would never build a house to live in—that is a human thing. So it takes a dog awhile to learn how to live in a house. Maybe you can find a dog at a place where humans keep animals that already know how to live in a house. This could be good thing—or maybe get a cat.

In short, if you live around animals, it's a good way to begin discovering that trust does not mean that the animal will do what you want all the time. But you can learn what the animal is like and discover how much the animal can do for you to adapt to the way you live and also how much you have to allow the animal to be who it is and live its life the way it is—in short, relationship therapy.

In time, if you can love the animal and accept it the way it is, and the animal can love you—there is always hope to love or like humans—if you understand the way you are with the animal, learning how the animal naturally lives its life, that it can do only so much to live life the way a human does and must still be an animal and do things the way an animal does . . . if you are conscious of that, then you learn how to allow the animal to be who it is. You can separate the difference, then, with human beings. Know that any human being can do things the way you do them only just so far. He or she must also do things the way *he or she* does them. If you cannot be around a human who does things the way you do them because he cannot be trusted—if the person hurts you, harms you or hurts or harms others, and you cannot stand that—then pick another friend.

But start with an animal if you are having difficulty and are unable to trust anyone. Start with touching so that you have a basic truth—

physicality. This is real; life begins here. Then go with the animal. Try not to think of the animal as a pet. When human beings think of animals as pets, immediately the animal becomes a lesser class of being. A pet is supposed to do things the way you say, and it becomes all right to discipline or harm the animal, hurt it, for being itself. This is not itself. Understand that an animal can learn and adapt, and it might want to in order to live with you and your ways, but still it must be itself. You must know when an animal must be itself. Animals sometimes show you that you must be yourself.

The Person Who Can't Love Others

Would this process work for further expansion for someone who is so contained and untrusting that he or she can't love others?

I recommend it for such people, if they want to improve their quality of life. They don't *have* to do it, but they can.

I meant, do you agree that not being able to love is pretty much the same process as not able to trust?

It's similar.

What about someone who can't love someone else?

For someone who can't love somebody else, it is usually because of past pain and feeling it is not safe to love somebody else. Do the safety exercise I gave plus the one in the appendix. Much that you do or don't do is because you feel safe or not safe. Of course, as a child you felt innocently safe, but as an adult innocent safety is very rarely there anymore. So you must welcome safety and exercise it like a muscle—relax and do the heat exercise or something like that, or imagine feeling safe. When I talk about "imagining feeling safe," we're getting into Zoosh's safety exercise, which is based on that.

If the person cannot love or won't love, it means the person really does not trust, is not safe. It comes to that. Exercises for that have been given.

It's not safe to be vulnerable?

A person feels it's not safe to open up to somebody else and it's not safe to be loved by somebody else because . . . this is the process, this is what underlies those feelings: It's not safe to be loved because these people might want something from you. In short, if you allow people to do things for you, even people who love you, there is a fear inside you that you might be obligated to them.

When someone does do something for them and they can't avoid it, people who are like that feel that they have to do ten times as much back because they feel obligated. Then love becomes exhausting, and they need to keep love away from them because it is too exhausting. They have to do too much for other people to make it safe.

Could you go a step beyond that?

This exercise is also for people like that, who feel that love comes with strings attached. It might have been like that when they were children, so what they learned about love is that parents love you when you do what they want you to do, but parents do not love you when you do something they don't want you to do. Even after a parent lectures you and corrects you (from the parent's point of view), a parent should still give you a hug to show he or she still loves you. If that does not happen because the parent does not know how to do this, which is often the case, some people might grow up unable to love others, especially if they have similar experiences growing up believing they can be loved, liked or appreciated only if they do many, many things for others.

Sometimes people believe that love is too much work because everything that has to be done for others is exhausting. When you do things on a daily basis for friends or people you meet, not to mention someone you live with, you get too tired and it becomes more trouble than it's worth: "It's too much—forget it!"

Homework to Learn How to Receive Love from Others

There is homework for that (Zoosh gives this homework a lot). It's very hard homework for these people. There are very many people like that, so if you are like that, you are not alone. The homework is as follows: For two weeks, let people do things for you and do nothing in return. In short, you will feel overwhelmingly selfish. When you feel selfish, thank those feelings of selfishness and guilt. Say, "All right, thank you," because they remind you that you are working on how to receive love from others.

You must do so like this. Let's say, for instance, you normally go out to lunch once or twice a week or more with friends. Maybe you pick up the check or at the very least pay for yourself. You never let anyone else pay for you because of feelings of obligation—"Then I must do for them more, more, more"—not because people expect it, need it or even want it. Very often it is embarrassing for them, and they don't want all that. In order to feel safe, you must do all these things for them so you know inside that it feels like enough and for sure you don't owe them anything. So the homework for two weeks is to let people do things for you. If they reach to pick up the check, don't make any effort. They pay for you, fine. Don't say to them, "I'll pay next time." Just say, "Thank you very much," that's all. It's very hard, but it can be done.

After two weeks, you'll begin to have lots and lots of feelings going on inside you. That's the basic homework.

Very good.

This has to do with people who feel there are strings attached. People like that are usually not very successful in relationships unless they marry the childhood sweetheart they actually loved when they were young. Then it sometimes can be successful because they know each other's quirks, so they have no secrets. Then it might work. But very often that is not possible, so it is better to work on this to open up possibilities.

So this goes beyond not being able to receive love; it expands to being unable to receive anything from people.

That's right. It can be a lonely life, because you are here on Earth with human beings and there are more and more humans now in your time, so avoiding people gets harder and harder. Sometimes you just try to harden your heart so that you can't feel them, can't feel anything. Of course, then you can't feel anything for yourself. You get out of touch with your own needs and then life gets distorted, twisted, painful and miserable. It's not good.

Very often you don't know your life is miserable because you are used to feeling that. You most often feel very lonely and do not know what to do about it. It is very difficult. Try this exercise as stated, and also try Zoosh's version of this exercise in the appendix [Appendix H].

The Role of Trauma in Human Life

Speaks of Many Truths
September 18, 1999

This is Speaks of Many Truths.

When we were talking about fears, I said, "The ultimate fear is fear of death," and you said, "No, it's fear of life."

The Fear of Life

Because of the fear of life, you have fear of commitment; fear of commitment actually means fear of life. It's not a progression the other way. If you have that, then there is a fear, but it doesn't mean fear of life as a general concept.

Can you expound on this?

It means the fear of life when it is introduced to anyone in their formative years—the first five years of any given life. That life is often very difficult, not only based upon that soul's previous experiences, but also most challenging because of that soul's expectations. When a soul incarnates into a physical body, there is a general discussion of what the life will accomplish, of certain things that might occur and perhaps even of certain pleasures that might come with that life.

But traumas that might occur in that life are never discussed, not once, because the soul cannot discuss traumas without feeling them. Therefore, the teacher will allude to traumas by saying, "And there might be difficult moments," something like that. That is about as explicit as the teacher, guide or anyone will get in discussing this with the soul.

As a result, the soul comes in and experiences trauma, not only at the moment of birth, as it has usually been experienced in recent years, but also the shock of the way life is around it. On the one hand, there are beautiful, wonderful things. One is born into a family that already exists. One is not usually born as a test-tube child, yes? So as a result, one is born into a dramatic environment. When I say that someone has a fear of life, it means that she has a fear of the life she experienced in her first five years.

Sometimes this will motivate people. It can cause them to turn down a difficult path, say a criminal path, and fight back, become the rebel. It might also cause them to become highly intellectual, to discover other people's ideas and explanations, looking for a meaning for their own early difficulty or trauma. It might cause them to withdraw. And for some people it will not seem to outwardly affect them too much.

But in a moment of tenderness or intimacy they will reveal that trauma in some way, not necessarily by traumatizing others, but often by only partially experiencing intimacy or by being able to do only so much. As a result, one has a society that only functions in a constrained fashion, let's say. That is why I said that the fear of life is the greatest challenge.

In our time, we understood that even a gentle birth was still not easy for the mother or child. So there was a great deal of nurturing and protection. Sometimes the child, whether it was male or female, would not be exposed to male members of the tribe—not even the father or brothers and sisters—only the women, nurturing and loving in order to prepare the child gently for the process of life.

For how long?

I have heard sometimes for several years, but my people were not like that. With my people a child was born and everyone would make an effort to be calm or to not get too excited if the baby was around. Or if they were excited, they would make an effort to be happy and show it by laughing so that the child would grow to see that life could be good. And if people were suffering for any reason, we would to try to have the baby elsewhere for the first five years.

So it is a form of protection. I am not saying you should do this in your time or even that you might or could. I am simply speaking of what I know.

Childhood Trauma

What is the purpose for all the trauma? To this day I don't understand it. Why all the suffering for children?

This society is a school from the moment you are born and sometimes even before that, when you are still inside your mother. You are exposed to these traumas, not because Creator is wrathful or vindictive, but rather because Creator has a deep, abiding faith in the capacity of the souls It allows to be born here to accomplish what they came here to do—to achieve that, to be that . . . to not only rise above such challenges, but to have those challenges actually motivate individuals in order to encourage them on their path.

Regarding encouragement on the path these days: Well, just a few years ago, many people were going into fields of psychology and using the brain and the mind to understand life. But that is, I feel, the long, long path around, to use the brain. Nevertheless, it was popular for a time because society was recognizing the trauma of children and adults and attempting to find ways to make that pain at least understandable, if not to take it away and replace it with something better. In some cases, things were made better, but we are talking about society as a unit.

What percentage of children living today have been physically, sexually, emotionally, intellectually or psychologically assaulted?

Almost everybody.

I don't understand.

When you group it like that—think about it. Here's a circumstance many people can identify with: As a child, you go to reach for an object that is dangerous to touch, and the parent suddenly, out of the corner of her eye, sees the baby reaching for a hot pan or something and screams, "No!" It is scary to the child. This does not mean the mother should not do that, because in that moment, it's much better for the child to be yelled at than to burn himself on a hot pan. But the mother feels guilty afterward. The child cries and she says, "Baby, I still love you," and so on. I'm including that kind of circumstance when you say "intellectually assaulted."

Let's not include that term. Let's omit anything that's for the perceived protection of the child. Let's say instead, assaults on the child's integrity.

Integrity—meaning what? What about being hit? How about that?

Well, let's say physically.

Almost all children get hit by other children or by well-meaning adults.

And it can range from just being slapped for something, all the way to being beaten, so how do you . . .

Yes, or being punched—brothers and sisters punching and so on.

I mean more hard-core assaults, physical and sexual assaults. What percentage of people living now have endured that?

Not that many. I should think less than 30 percent alive now in this time.

How do you know that?

I use long vision.

You can scan the Earth's population in a couple of seconds?

I just look forward in long vision and see a number, then tell it to you.

Okay, less than 30 percent. We're still dealing with an incredible number—30 percent of six billion plus is a couple of billion people.

The Soul's Scenarios for Physical Mastery

Who sets up these lives? If the soul doesn't do it, then who creates the scenarios?

Oh, I didn't say that the soul didn't do it.

You said that the soul couldn't even contemplate it.

The soul can't contemplate it, but souls experience and embrace life with their permission. It cannot be discussed with the soul in its tender state before it enters life. But between lives, when lives are being set up and you consider things and there is distance, then things are discussed, but not in the detail that would cause the soul to flinch and say, "No, I don't want to do that."

But right before life, before you get into the body or the egg or the sperm or what-have-you, it cannot be discussed because it would be like touching the soul.

I still don't understand how the soul can set up something it can't even conceive of or think of. Something else must be operating here besides the soul.

Remember that not every soul is allowed to come here. For the last hundred years, what percent of the souls who occupy this universe have been allowed to come to Earth?

Maybe 1 or 2 percent?

Much less than 1 percent—less than half a percent, much less. It's one of those decimal-point things. Very few, because most souls are not prepared to do what it takes to go to Creator School. Remember that Creator School deals very much with consequences. Creators must be able to live with consequences. They cannot simply say, "Oops, gol darn it! I'll do it better next time." They might be dealing with "oops" and its results indefinitely.

Therefore, before souls are allowed to become creators (I grant there is a distance there), they must experience lives in which every single nuance of their existence is some form of test. It is not a cruel test, yet there is some test going on so that when the life is over and you're back with your teachers talking about what you learned in Creator School (I think it doesn't go quite like that, but I'm putting it that way), you can examine your physical life from moment to moment on a second-by-second basis if you wish, and you can learn something from almost every second of physical experience.

How One Person's Trauma Affects Others

Right now, anybody on Earth who's awake, not sleeping, would be dealing with or experiencing profound traumas, whether there is anything traumatizing them or not.

Any human, right?

Yes, but you are here [draws]. This represents you. Now I'll put in a few other dots to represent other people [Fig. 6-1].

Let's say someone is thinking about a trauma. Here you are. Somebody you don't know—they might be a block or fifty feet away—is thinking about a trauma. The memory of that trauma (something major or what other people would consider minor), first radiates out to here [middle circle], then it might radiate out to here [outer circle].

And all those circles can overlap.

That's right; eventually all these circles are *going* to overlap.

So how on Earth do you go to a mall?

You go to a mall, and you are affected and impacted by all these things. The impact is profound. Let's say you are standing out in the beautiful countryside. A car goes by, people are arguing, but you don't notice that because it is beautiful there. You are looking at the mountain, or maybe you are near the ocean and looking at the sea—maybe you are at the beach and people are having a few spats or perhaps some sort of drama—and you don't really notice these things.

Every time that happens, there is a wave of energy. When people

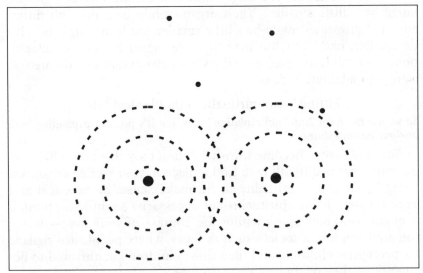

Fig. 6-1. This shows how the trauma energy of one person can affect another, the dots representing human beings surrounded by their energy bodies.

are having good or negative experiences, there are always waves of energy coming off them that have to do with what they are feeling at that moment. If you happen to be nearby, you will be touched by these waves. So to a degree, everybody is feeling traumatized all the time.

Children get used to feeling a sense of anticipation or anxiety if they are raised in a very confined state. Maybe they were raised in an apartment building with lots and lots of people living close together, and yelling could be heard. Then the child might be tense her whole life. But even if you are raised in the country, things will come up.

Physical Adaptation to Earth Life

What I am saying is this: Life here is a very difficult test almost all the time, and most physical bodies wear down. In theory, you could take a normal healthy person of any race or culture born on this planet to another planet where everything is benign (assuming that person could physically live there), and the person might live in that life and that body for maybe three thousand years. This is because the bodies here have been gradually adapted to be physically strong and have internal mechanisms that are very strong compared to another human-type being on another planet.

Another ET-type being might live two thousand years at most, but your physical body could live three thousand years, maybe thirty-five hundred years, because after years of adaptation of the physical body, organs inside the body might get bigger, stronger, vaster. For instance, you might find that on the Pleiades, people might be a little smaller. Their organs might be a little bit different—the intestines might be a little smaller, the heart might be a little smaller, like that. But here they are bigger because of adaptation, not evolution. Evolution does not exist except as a theoretical word, but adaptation does.

Fitting Your Spirituality into Physical Life

So we use the term "spiritual evolution" now, but it's just our expanding back into our natural state?

Yes, it is easy to become spiritual. I don't say this to be challenging, but what is difficult is to find a place in your world, as you are living it, for your spirituality to fit, make sense, be practical and work for you. Being spiritual is not necessarily so difficult, though it might feel challenging within the context of your lives—unless you are born into a society such as I was, where people are vigilant for perceptive children, and then these children are nurtured to become what they might be able to become.

Your life still had many stresses, even though you protected the child. There were survival needs.

Yes, no supermarket.

You still lived less than a hundred years, though?

Much less. Our average life span was thirty-five, maybe forty-five years; some people maybe lived fifty-five years or so.

But I thought you were very old.

I *am* very old—gray hair, very old.

But you don't know in years?

By your count, maybe fifty-four.

Is that all?

Very old. I speak to you now from the time when I was fifty-four, but I went on a little longer than that.

When you said "very old," I imagined you were a hundred years old.

The Gifts That Enable Souls to Handle Extra Challenges

So under 30 percent have this handicap, this extra challenge to overcome?

They have a gift.

Explain that.

A gift means that almost everybody who has this experience has had more than one life of spiritual mastery—not because this is a requirement to go through such a terrible experience, but because to go through it and survive, and in some cases go on to be perhaps a better person than those who injured you, requires the depth of character that precedes the character of this life.

This does not mean that it is acceptable or justifiable to beat children. I understand that if children are playing with fire, something must be done, but not overdone. Nevertheless, people who survive such experiences often have gifts of many previous lifetimes of spiritual mastery. Sometimes they might also have exotic levels of spiritual mastery—a symptomatic condition of people who have been traumatized in some way—such as the capacity to be out of the body.

The body has suffered, but the child's personality suffers up to a point and then suddenly feels numb. This numbness is considered something psychological and needs to be pursued. I grant that therapy is one way to pursue it, but people who go into a numb state, for example, have almost always had at least one life of spiritual mastery where one disengages from the body to be able to maintain a status outside the body. I'm not going to say too much about it, because these types of cultural traces to do things like that have more to do with spirituality in times gone by, not too long before your time.

Also, other levels of mastery might have been reached, such as the capacity to bilocate. Sometimes people at the deepest levels of psychological discussion with therapists or even hypnotherapists, when remembering a beating that has been experienced or a sexual assault, talk about being somewhere else entirely. They could remember the pain and the trauma up to a point—and then they were somewhere else, bilocated to some more benevolent place.

Psychologists sometimes say this is like a memory that is not real, a screen memory, something like that, but in my experience this is real. The person's soul *actually does* have the capacity to literally bilocate. The body is still there, still demonstrating some outward life signs to whoever is abusing that body. The body might be struggling and so on, but the personality is not present.

It would be like a life form, but with no sense of soul personality there. The soul personality is elsewhere. This is why I say that the experience of trauma is not the gift, but I used that word as a "surprise word" response because the gift has *preceded* that experience. Generally speaking, Zoosh says that everybody comes here with at least one life of spiritual mastery, but people who have this type of trauma almost always have had multiple lives of spiritual mastery so that they can survive the experience through bilocation, for example.

How Mother Earth Handles the Overload of Human Trauma

You're talking about the immortal personality as the soul, as the identity, but every human also has an aspect of Mother Earth ensouled with him or her, right?

Yes.

Then Mother Earth is experiencing all this trauma, because Mother Earth's soul can't leave or the body would die, right?

Mother Earth used to experience this trauma, but in recent years (according to your time, for years and years) she has been experiencing less and less of the trauma because she cannot take it. She is past her point of taking it; there are too many human beings in your time. So now she feeds it back in a loop. [Draws Fig. 6-2.]

Here is Mother Earth [big circle]. I'll draw a few dots to represent individuals. Mother Earth used to take this energy, but now she cannot take it, so she loops the energy up and around [see the line looping upward to the left and back around to the top].

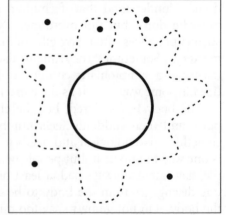

Fig. 6-2. Mother Earth (center circle), having taken on too much trauma, is recirculating it now into her auric field. It then comes down as rain and is processed on her surface.

Then this energy goes into her auric field, not into the physical body, and stays in such a way in her auric field so that it is processed with lightning, clouds. When it comes down in the form of rain, it eventually goes into the people. It must be processed, but she processes it mostly on her surface, not by taking it in. She used to take it in, put it in hot places in her body and transform it, but not now.

How many years ago did that change?

It really started changing about forty years ago from your time. Now more and more she does things that give you responsibility, but she does not immediately thrust . . . she puts it a little farther away from her in some ways, and then she exposes you to it more and more. Eventually she will not take any of it. All the trauma will then be felt not only by the person experiencing it, but equally by the person *causing* that trauma.

How Humans Can Release Childhood Trauma

Say you were raised in an abusive family. Your father and mother struck you, saying, "Don't talk that way to me!" *Bang!* They struck you. When you grew up, you swore you would never treat your children like that. But you find, much to your horror, that in a moment when a child does something, you say, "Don't talk that way to me!" *Bang!* And afterward you almost get sick to your stomach. You realize, "Oh, how could I do this?" Sometimes you learn things you don't want to learn.

Then you know, and maybe in the future you can work on that. But what will happen, for the sake of the example, is that in the next situation, before you go to strike a child, you will get a kind of nauseous feeling, meaning you have learned something unpleasant

The second time?

Yes, you will get that before you strike the child because the experience will be more immediate, all of it happening in the same moment. So you will have a warning, and you might be able to catch yourself in midair. Even if you don't strike the child, but your hand is in the air, the child will feel the pain and might react with pain, fright, crying and tears, even though you didn't hit, because the child feels the complete experience.

This is actually a good sign in Creator School. You do not go to this level of learning and experiencing such traumatic consequences unless Creator allows you to have this. Creator is very careful about what you are allowed to experience: this much, no more, and so on—incrementally, you say.

What happened is that you have some learning of consequences before the fact. When you start to feel your anger rise toward a child, it is accompanied by a nauseous feeling. Anger's energy affects you. Then if you are a conscious spiritual person or perhaps a religious person, you seek consolation in religion, prayer, some spiritual practice or a ceremony to cleanse yourself of this.

It is not something you do once and then never again. You have to stay with it over and over. Then you break the pattern and eventually, someday your child grows up, has children of his own and doesn't strike his own children. So you need to make the effort.

Creator-Assisted Progress: No More Faceless Enemies

But most important, you are progressing in Creator School, everyone. I speak to everyone here. You are progressing because you can see by looking around you that things are different. You have to confront things. No longer can an enemy in war be faceless as in times gone by. When the United States fought Japan, they made the Japanese people into monsters. It became a racial war. If you look back at history, there was a great deal of racial prejudice involved, propaganda that made the Japanese people monsters. I'm not saying that some Japanese warriors and soldiers did not deserve monster rating, but soldiers on many sides might deserve this in different wars. This is no excuse, but it was not a singular experience.

But nowadays, when the U.S. is in some struggle with another country, the people are not faceless. Not only are television cameras and photographers everywhere, but people talk to one another with telephones and computers and say, "Please tell your government, don't drop these bombs. They are not hitting the soldiers. They are hitting my family and friends." So you get upset. The enemy is no longer faceless.

Creator gives you this as a gift to understand that if you do not feel pain in your left hand, you can harm your left hand. Your left hand is still part of your body, but you don't care because your left hand feels no pain. But if you become conscious of your left hand, you cannot harm it without feeling it. It's the same thing in war. When you harm other individuals, you feel it.

Let's talk about war in ancient British times. Soldiers, clan people or what-have-you line up on one side, the other soldiers line up on the other side, and they rush down and fight each other with swords and so on. This is very brutal, but the battle takes place between soldiers or warriors. Although there is a lasting effect on many people, the soldiers and warriors do not distribute bombs all over the landscape to kill all the animals, children and other people.

Mines are like this—little bitty bombs all over everywhere, made to look like things that would cause a curious child to come over and say, "What's that?" *Boom!* Nowadays technology has become almost a satanic influence that way. You can use technology and drop thousands and millions of mines with the rationale that no soldier could cross such a barrier. "We will protect our troops." Yes, all that seems very sensible at the time to soldiers who make decisions and maybe to the politicians who also make some decisions. But when the war is over, a battle takes place elsewhere. People don't go back and say, "Okay, let's pick up the bombs"—they still explode.

War is becoming more fiendish now in many ways, and this is somewhat intentional by Creator. Creator does not want you to suffer, does not support the winning side, any of that stuff. But Creator says, "It is time for you to realize that the aching left hand is *your* left hand." If somebody suffers, you suffer.

The United States and Its Lessons for Creators

The United States finds itself in an awkward position. The United States is a desirable place to be; people all want to come here—they used to, anyway. Now the United States finds itself in the awkward position of growing pains, where it has become the policeman to the world. It is not a good idea, because the United States is a young country. It has certain ideals, methods, beliefs, but is not a universal culture.

The universal culture of the United States is more geared toward popular culture—as they say, whatever is popular in the moment. Right now what is popular is the mind, the creations of the mind and science. The United States' general religion for many people, aside from a form of Christianity, is science. So the United States goes into other countries and says, "You must run your country the way we see it. We don't like what you are doing."

Many times the United States does this with a good heart, but the ultimate effect is a bad heart. For example, if the U.S. gets mad at a leader, say the dictator of Iraq (who used to be your ally), the U.S. then uses many bombs because it's mad at the leader. That affects people. The U.S. is not the enemy—it's experiencing growing pains and must learn that what you do affects everybody. It is a lesson for a creator. It's an old joke: If Creator scratches His head, maybe a toe wiggles somewhere else. Everything affects everything. Creator encourages you all to see this now.

Removing Trauma by Using Gestures and Other Means

We're looking at the techniques you're giving us to remove these traumas from the physical body so the traumas don't influence our behavior.

Removal means you remove a reservoir of something; you might still have some memory. You're not going to suddenly forget it ever happened; you might still dredge up the memory and retraumatize the area unintentionally. But then maybe you could do the gesture more than once. Understand that the gesture is designed to release and in some ways transform, but is not intended to . . .

Do you mean release the pain and suffering—the thing that controls us?

It will clear the residue that tends to prompt certain actions and reactions in you, but it will not cause an instant cure. For many people, it will probably feel better for a time, but then issues might still come up. Then you do these gestures more. And you read more, you think more, you do other things, you talk to friends, you talk to a therapist. In short, it is not intended to be a panacea, but it is intended to create some clearing of old residue. For example, you have a cut, which forms a scab. Then you might have scar tissue for a time, a different color than your regular tissue. Over time, the scar tissue becomes less and less obvious. The gesture is intended to create scar tissue quicker—to heal, in other words, but with noticeable impact.

Heal the scar tissue so that it's more like regular skin.

Heal the wound so that scar tissue can bring things together. The scars are an analogy for healing, as compared to an open, running wound or a scab that looks kind of rough.

Okay, so using this analogy, once we have scar tissue, then these subconscious hates, fears, miseries and old ways of being won't influence us so much?

Or they will be more apparent to you consciously, meaning that you will not be driven blindly by unknown rages stemming from incidents you do not even remember. Rather, memory might be present, and when you feel anger coming up toward somebody, you might be able to relate it to a cause. Then you can think about it, and you might have a greater opportunity for healing. Scar tissue is about the *opportunity* for healing. It's not instantaneous, but it supports your capacities rather than eliminating them from the process.

It doesn't eliminate conscious choices from the process?

No, you have greater opportunity to consciously pursue the healing of traumas. Traumas are not vague anymore. This just means that it's not necessary to struggle through the memory of trauma all the time; your reaction becomes more obviously connected to some previous action. You become, in short, more conscious.

And more able to make choices that change your behavior?

Yes. That person you get mad at all the time—no longer does it become only that "the person is annoying and it's his or her fault." Then it becomes more an opportunity to say, "Wait a minute, this person reminds me very much of that person in grade school when I was young, someone who used to annoy me all the time. It was a shame, you know, because when I first met that person I liked him so much. I felt attracted to him as a friend, and he was nice at first. But then he got to be mean to me, did things to hurt me."

You see, this is why sometimes people will seem to be attracted to something or someone who will harm them. Attraction is still their pattern. This is not the only reason that people become attracted to that which harms them, but this is one example—the original attraction, you know.

You're saying they're attracted to the person who reminds them of the person who hurt them as a child?

The person they *were* is attracted to the child who hurt them when they were a child. They were originally attracted to that child as a friend and there was friendship, but later on came conflict, argument and struggle. Then the original attraction—friendship—turned into something ugly.

Still there is that lingering sense of attraction, and it can even develop into something like this: The child might grow up suspecting attraction in general. If someone is attracted to you and says so, you might become suspicious. If you are attracted to somebody else, you might be suspicious of your own attractions.

That's why the early formative years are so vital. Many societies can be gauged (not judged) on how they treat their children. If children are not nurtured, protected, loved and supported, especially in the first five years, as they grow up, that society would be perceived as having a long way to go for civilization.

Also pay attention to how old people are treated, or people who are different and so on. This is an easy way to look at a society: "How do they treat their children?" You don't have to speak the language. "How do they treat their children? How do they treat their old people?" This is how a civilization is truly gauged.

When people do these exercises, they become more conscious. They clean up their lives, let's say.

Perhaps, yes.

And there will be a radiating effect from them of less rage, less hate, less violence, which will contribute to the planetary mass consciousness. So there will be an effect beyond their own lives, true?

Yes, it will contribute to planetary or global well-being. We remove that much force, pressing down. There might not immediately be force pressing up, but we will remove that much energy from pressing down (using up and down as example here, not as actual directions).

We're talking about two billion people. Even if a hundred thousand people . . .

There are more than two billion people on Earth in your time, yes?

I'm talking about the under 30 percent who had severe trauma.

Oh yes, there are much less than two billion people who have severe trauma.

Let's say one billion.

All right, let's say that, but your definition of severe trauma is a little vague.

I mean people who have been really hurt, and that hurt runs their life on some unconscious level.

The Corrosion of Verbal Abuse

They can also be hurt without ever being touched. You can be yelled at constantly, told you are fool or an idiot. I include that in the number because such trauma disrupts and corrodes life. It is like corrosion. You are young, and it sort of eats into your personality; the older you get, the more your personality is corroded so that you have very little of what you came in with readily accessible to you. By doing some of these exercises, you might be able to redeem or rediscover those capacities, those talents that you might have been punished for as a child. The adults or others you grew up with didn't realize you were demonstrating a talent. All they knew is that you were different, and it frightened them.

People will be affected by this book, or maybe there will be classes and these techniques will spread.

They will go out pretty far eventually.

Motivation, Not Trauma, Can Go to 4D

Can you take these traumas into the fourth dimension?

No.

Does that mean that everyone who doesn't work on this is not going to make it to the fourth dimension?

No, it does not mean that. Remember, the Explorer Race is forming up as a separate unit, and while traumas—in the concept of physical pain, suffering and misery—cannot be taken to a higher dimension, motivation can. You might feel a powerful motivation to do something based on a lesson learned with trauma and so on. You can take motivation, but not the memory of trauma. Nevertheless, motivation is very profound—not just mental, hardly that at all, but *physical* motivation.

People go out for the swimming team in college, and some people get tired and say, "That's it. I can't do any more trips up and down the pool." Other people push themselves harder and harder: "I can do more. I can do more. I can do more." In short, they have motivation from somewhere, from sometime, that drives them on, not to destructiveness but to breakthrough. They achieve something that the school has not seen before or that they have not done before on their own.

This is a motivation that was brought into life perhaps from some trauma in a previous life or, in the case of a person of college age, some trauma from youth. But more likely, such depth of motivation for a young person might partly come from previous experience. I use this as an analogy rather than as an example, because this is the kind of motivation you might see at the fourth dimension, where people will say they strongly feel to do this and this and that.

In the fourth dimension, psychological analysis will not be a factor. People will not say, "Why do you feel this way?" or "Let's explore this." In short, the personality of the person will not be disentangled into tiny little bits and pieces so that you can compartmentalize it, but rather people's motivations will be honored: "Yes, you have the motivation to do this, and you have the desire to achieve this in a certain way. We believe you." They wouldn't say that, but it would be a given that it is believed and not questioned. In the fourth dimension, things are more benevolent. You might have motivation, but not trauma.

Are the people who are living now going to the fourth dimension, or will they end their natural cycle and the motivation they gained from the trauma surface in the fourth dimension in a new body?

It is entirely up to them. People will or won't go to the fourth dimension. They might go to all kinds of other places, but should they ever go to the fourth dimension, it is not linear. Maybe they'll go somewhere and have five, ten lives someplace else, then decide to go to the fourth dimension in time. Then they would pick up right where they left off.

Remember, time is more like this: Strings come down. I extend my hand, go to different lives in different times, not unlike the marionette string, but it's not meant to be manipulated. This is only to illuminate or illustrate the idea of nonlinear time; it's not very easy to do without a visual picture. But you do not have to say that at the end of this life you go to the next life in the fourth dimension and that this is the only way you would have motivation like that.

The present humans on Earth are not going to go into the fourth dimension in the bodies we're in now?

Maybe, maybe not. It's not cut in stone, that one. Probably not, but maybe. It's not impossible.

We cannot take these traumas into the fourth dimension?

You simply would not remember them, but you would have motivation. There would be a blank spot; you would know you had strong motivation to do something, but you could not justify it to people.

If tomorrow (this is not going to happen), we suddenly moved to the fourth dimension . . .

All trauma will no longer exist there.

Oh, it's not that we can't make it because of the trauma but that the trauma will just be gone?

It will be filtered out. You will go through a filter. Trauma will stay on the other side of the filter, but motivation prompted by trauma will remain.

Clearing the Earth of Pain Where Calamities Occurred

So the more we clear with these techniques, the easier it makes it for us and everyone else and the better off the planet will be.

Yes. Someday people will go around to various places on the Earth where there have been terrible calamities, say during World War II at the concentration camps. It was a terrible calamity, not only for the people suffering but for the people inflicting the suffering—calamitous for their souls as well. They had a long, long life review and were very unhappy when they died.

People will go around to those parts of the Earth and do gestures to release pain. This will also release pain from the Earth, make the Earth suddenly do a little better there. Human beings will be born and raised around that area. At the end of the war, you can't just say, "I will never use that land again because it's cursed." That might happen in my time, but in your time so many people have to live somewhere. Once that is released from the land, then people will get along better and feel better in that area.

The people reading this book could go around and do that?

At some point. First do the work for yourself, then do the work in a group of others. Most likely it will be people from that part of the world who do this. It's better for locals to do it, because they are made up of the soil from those places. They release that trauma from themselves, then they go to some place on the Earth where even now it might feel uncomfortable and do that for themselves. Maybe they will do something like this in small groups of six or seven, maybe less, maybe more. Maybe they will have their bare feet on the ground, or they might put their bare backs on the ground and do the gesture.

In that way they can release trauma from the Earth, but I do not recommend doing it this way in the beginning. I recommend that they go near that place, that they don't go right into it; go near it and begin working from the outer circle of that place. Gradually move in like this [moves hand in a spiral motion]. It's hard to describe [draws Fig. 6-3].

Here's the area. I'll write T for trauma. You start out here [1] and do something. Then you go here [2]. Then you go here [3]. Gradually you work your way inward as a group until you get to that area where the trauma took place.

Gradually do that over a long time period, maybe one position a month, not one a day. Go in very slowly to allow your body time; don't lie on the ground—people will want to do that. I recommend

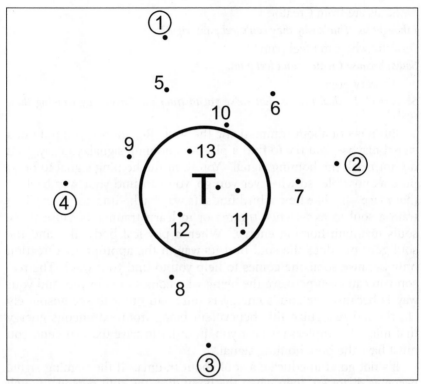

Fig. 6-3. How to clear trauma (T) from the land: Approach from the outside, doing clearing gestures at sequentially numbered spots, slowly spiraling toward the center.

you don't even take your shoes off at first. *Only* when the land feels almost completely cleared can you take your shoes off. People will be attracted to doing this, because it's known by many people that the bottoms of the feet and parts of the back are very open to spiritual energy. But you must protect those body areas when going to places of such great trauma.

If people do that in the future and I am still speaking through Robert, I will be happy to give them very detailed information, including perhaps special gestures on how to work with Mother Earth in that way.

Source Personalities Are Training Our Souls

The Explorer Race came here as three distinct beings or seeds, right?

Three source personalities, let's say.

Did these source personalities create the souls that are creating humans? Or since this is all a creation of the Creator, are our souls of the essence of the Creator? I have a suspicion that we're training the Creator through these souls and that this is part of our agreement with the Creator.

Souls are from Creator.

I thought so. That's why they can't feel pain, right?

Why who can't feel pain?

Souls, because Creator can't feel pain.

Ah, very good.

So part of the deal here is that we've got to train the Creator by training these souls?

But it is not about traumatizing the soul. Remember, you put out a signal maybe. You try to find a place—a homing signal, you say. You do not mask the homing signal. You want the homing signal to be as pure as possible, so wherever you go, you can find your way back to that place. It's like how a bird finds its way back. It is not your job to train a soul to experience trauma or to learn trauma, because those souls maintain homing energy. When a physical body dies and the soul goes on, does the soul find its way in the appropriate direction only because someone comes to help you to find your way? The reason you can even perceive the being who comes to help you find your way is because the soul's energy is pure. In order to see absolutely clearly and recognize this benevolent being from extraneous energy that might be unpleasant near you, in order to have discernment, you must have the pure homing signal.

It's not good to educate a soul about trauma. If the homing signal becomes distorted, then when the body dies, the soul personality will walk all over Earth trying to find its way home. It can't even recognize an angel or a golden being trying to take it back home; it's just completely lost. Souls must remain pure.

So the soul is part of Creator. I've been thinking about this for six months, asking, "Could that possibly be the way it is?"

In this way also, the soul is motivated and understands Creator's desires, even though—as you bring out so importantly, poignantly perhaps—a soul is limited to a minor degree (meaning the soul cannot handle trauma), but this is intentional.

You must remember that as much as we might like to modify Creator, how we'd like Creator to be, in this moment Creator is doing more than billions of things in the same moment. Creator is very involved, very active, doing lots of things. You cannot change Creator in even the most minor way without impacting everyone and everything else.

But that is how we, the Explorer Race, are helping Creator to become more, because He is experiencing what we are innovating and creating, and it doesn't come from Him. Is that a true statement?

Not exactly. A child often accomplishes what the parents are unable to do. If not that child, it might be a grandchild who accomplishes that.

For instance, a child or grandchild might go to college, get a degree and so on.

Creator does not experience pain, but He has compassion for pain. He has had the occasional experience of pain, knows what it is about, but cannot experience pain and be a creator in the way Creator is. Therefore, He gives birth to the Explorer Race to have the same capacities as Creator—let's say the same DNA, for example, but not scientifically like that. So the Explorer Race has the same capacities as Creator but is given built-in motivation to improve on the model, make it better, be able to do more, have greater capacities. In short, to have the capacity to do things that the parent was unable to do.

Creator takes a huge risk doing this, because is possible that the offspring will become renegades or malevolent, destroying the whole creation. Creator takes a terrific risk in doing this, but plans it every step of the way and tries to do as much as possible without actually interfering in the offspring's growth method.

That's why there are so many friends and helpers and advisers of the Creator?

Yes, this is required because Creator is doing more than billions of things in every moment and needs help. So the intention has always been (as stated in previous books) that the Explorer Race will become more, do more and, Creator hopes, accomplish more. Creator knows this is a calculated risk, as you know from previous books.

Everybody had to promise to discreate themselves if it went bad—I mean, the beings involved took incredible risks, too.

Yes, everybody was told that if it starts to go the wrong way, then everything must be . . .

. . . discreated.

Yes, uncreated so that souls, especially pure souls in places other than Creator School, are not impacted. This does not mean that souls incarnated in bodies in other places would be uncreated, per se, as a matter of course, but that something tremendous would be uncreated. The impact will be that the universe will essentially lose its motivation for a time, until another creator comes from somewhere else and takes over and gives the universe motivation.

But the universe might just wander for a while.

We're going to make it.

Always. I think maybe you'll make it.

Maybe? That's not a strong statement.

"Maybe" is a *very* strong statement. "Maybe" represents support and belief. But if I tell you, "Oh yes, definitely you're going to make it," then why should you do anything? Why should you do anything at all? I am not saying, "Oh yes, you definitely are going to make it." I am saying only that maybe you're going to make it, but you must work. Then you can't say, "Oh, that's nice; somebody else will do it. I'm busy, I haven't got the time."

So each human's ultimate connection is to the immortal personality of those original source personalities?

Ultimate connection, of course, goes beyond that.

Yes, I know, but do the souls stay with Creator when Creator leaves?

No, every time Creator births any soul at all into a universe, if Creator leaves that universe, the soul remains.

When we become Creator, what is the fate of those souls?

You take over. You might also create more souls, but you take over what is in place.

Are these souls still the homing device?

The homing device is for an individual manifested personality, a human being, so that the human being can find its way back to the fold (any being, but I say human being because we're on Earth).

We need them now because we've forgotten who we are and we're in this third dimension—or do we use them in the fourth and the ninth and the thirtieth dimensions?

Souls exist everywhere—without exception, from anything I have seen. Everywhere souls exist. "Soul" is a word, but I use the word to mean unifying energy that contains, as Zoosh says, your immortal personality. But it also contains the means and the methods and the love of all beings for the soul, as well as the ability to receive their love.

In short, as a portion of all that exists, the soul personality grows outward in a spherical growth pattern from that point. If you examine some or all of life, everything goes outward in a spherical pattern—personality and so on. It is hard to put in words.

The progression of the three source personalities who then split into many, many, many . . . did each of those personalities then take a portion of Creator as its soul? Souls are really individual, but you say they're unified.

Those three source personalities come into Creator and, like drops of paint, affect Creator in some way. Creator, while birthing other souls through all of Its being, also screens certain souls, like a sieve, through these source personalities. When Creator leaves, these source personalities will stay and become part of the Explorer Race's new Creator.

I'd like to continue this later. I'm trying to understand it.

A source personality does not cause any more than a coloration, a tint perhaps, to souls screened from Creator through source personalities. Picture three color filters. All these souls come out of the mass of Creator, but some souls come through these color filters.

Those are the ones we're connected to as humans?

Yes, those are the ones you are connected to as the Explorer Race. I am specific there because the Explorer Race has not always been only human.

When are we going to talk about that?

Probably not in this book.

Letting Go of Old Attitudes
and Inviting New Energy

Speaks of Many Truths
September 20, 1999

What would you like to say for the book?

What are you interested in doing tonight?

The August Planetary Lineup Has Created New Possibilities

We did the first part of this book before the August 1999 planetary lineup [see the Introduction], which appeared to cause a change of consciousness. Is this book meant for after August? In other words, you didn't decide at first whether you were going to do the book or not. Was doing the book your awareness that everything was going to change and that these techniques would become more workable or easier to use after the eclipse?

I had to see the impact of this on people of your time. In our original discussion about this book, I said I would do it about a year after the first one came out [*Shamanic Secrets for Material Mastery*]. But the alteration of consciousness in your time, which was related to these astronomical events, caused me to believe, after the event, that people would be sufficiently receptive to show enough interest in the second book and perhaps use it in concordance with the first book, with a degree of interchangeability. For instance, if people do not have enough personal energy to achieve a connection with a place on Earth that they feel with the heart sense through warmth or some other way that's meaningful to them, then they might be able to do some exercise in this book that will bring up their energy level. Then they can do the exercises in the first book. Because of the astronomical event, I felt that people might be able to use these two books at times like twins.

As a result of the August event, would you say that everyone on the planet now has the potential or more energy to change?

Yes, I would say that some people did not change, per se, but they now have more impetus or more energy to change. In short, they have much, much more difficulty in staying the same or holding things to themselves. It will require so much effort to maintain what was that it will be utterly exhausting.

Releasing Self-Destructive Patterns

That's a lot of the tiredness now. It has to do with people holding onto those old ways of being. That's why I will give a gesture for release of old self-destructive ways. It's a little different in your time than it is in mine. Here is the gesture [Fig. 7-1]. This gesture is to be done quickly, so practice doing the stages very slowly, one at a time. When you do this slowly, it will not have an effect, but when you do it quickly, the whole thing takes about a second.

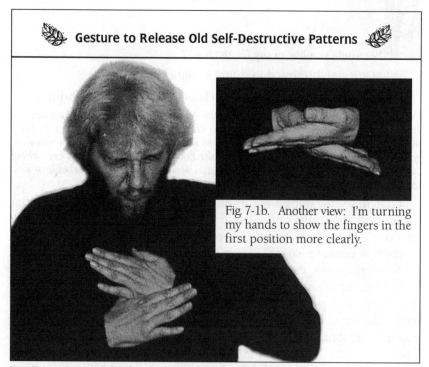

Gesture to Release Old Self-Destructive Patterns

Fig. 7-1b. Another view: I'm turning my hands to show the fingers in the first position more clearly.

Fig. 7-1a. Here is the first position: The left hand is above the right, tucked between the thumb and forefinger.

Fig. 7-1c. Position two.

Fig. 7-1d. Position three: The left hand is sliding down to be more even with the right hand. In the first position, the left hand was above the right hand; in position three, the left hand has almost the same angle as the right.

Fig. 7-1e. Position four: The top of the succeeding downstroke.

Fig. 7-1f. Position five.

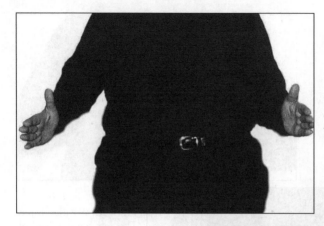

Fig. 7-1g. Position six: Continue down from position four.

Fig. 7-1h. Position seven: End the downstroke with the hands straight down. Do the entire gesture very quickly. It should take about a second. Wait twelve hours, then do either one of the gestures to invite energy.

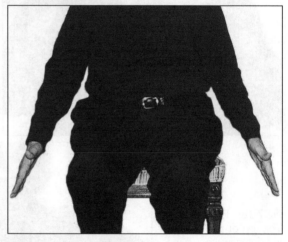

After you do this gesture, wait at least twelve hours to do the next step, which has to do with inviting energy to come into you [Fig. 7-2]. Ideally this would be done in the country with bare feet in some benevolent place to your liking, where you feel welcome. But since not everyone can do that, do it in the best way you know, but try to do it without rubber-soled shoes.

During this gesture, the body is sitting. This can be done initially while kneeling, but we need to get the hands near the ground—not right on it. You need to feel the gesture. It would be best to do this with nobody within twenty feet of you, but do the best you can. Know that if angry people are within twenty feet, you might take on some of their anger. If you can't get away from people for some reason and they are closer than you would like, then wait until the surroundings become as calm as possible to do the gesture, though it won't be at its best.

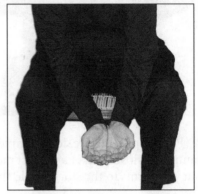

Fig. 7-2b. Position two: Cup your hands and begin to bring them up.

Fig. 7-2a. Here's the first position: Start out kneeling or sitting. Reach down toward the Earth. You don't have to touch the Earth, but you need to come within eight to ten inches of it.

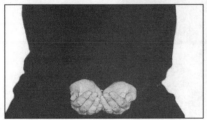

Fig. 7-2c. Position three: The hands are coming up.

Fig. 7-2d. Position four: Continue to bring your hands up. Remember, this is all done quickly and smoothly.

Fig. 7-2e. Position five: Bring your hands toward your chest.

Fig. 7-2f. Position six: Pull your fingers apart across your chest. As you are doing this fluid gesture, say: "I welcome my own energy for me."

Fig. 7-2g. An alternative position six is this last position, bringing your hands to the solar plexus. Use whichever position causes you to feel more energized.

For people who are, for example, prisoners or in a hospital ward and cannot sit close to the Earth, just move your arms. If you must lie down, put your arms to the side and do this alternative gesture [Fig. 7-3].

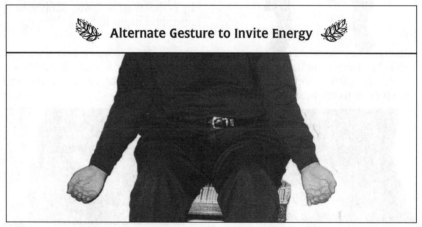

🌿 Alternate Gesture to Invite Energy 🌿

Fig. 7-3a. Here is position one: Do this version of the gesture if you must be lying down. Again, this is a quick, fluid movement.

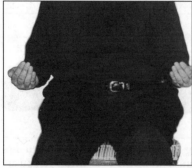

Fig. 7-3b. Position two: Bring your hands up like this.

Fig. 7-3c. Position three: Begin to move your hands toward your solar plexus, as pictured here, or your chest—either one, whichever feels best.

Fig. 7-3d. Position four: Bring your hands to the solar plexus as before. Say, "I welcome my own energy for me."

Fig. 7-3e. An alternate position four: Bring your hands to your chest.

Wait at least twelve hours after completing the gesture to release old patterns in Fig. 7-1 before you invite the Earth energy [either Fig. 7-2 or 7-3]. At this point we want the Earth to give us energy, but it is not her own energy. Interestingly enough, living on the Earth as long as we have, we have put a great deal of our own energy into her. Every time you put a foot on the Earth and walk anywhere, you leave some of your energy there.

So you are not taking Mother Earth's energy; you are really recapturing some of your own energy. When you invite Earth energy (in either way), you can say this so that you will be clear about what you are doing: "I welcome my own energy for me." In that way you will not feel that you are taking in the energies of people around you that you might not wish to take in, and you will not feel like you are taking Mother Earth's energy from her, feeling that she needs it—and she does.

Those two gestures are very useful—letting go of firmly held old attitudes about yourself and sometimes others, and welcoming your own energy, whose levels have been reduced in recent times for you all.

A New Requirement for Your Teachers: A Reverence for the Physical

When there's a large-scale shifting of consciousness such as that caused by the August 11, 1999, event, sometimes the teachers change. Have they changed for humans?

Yes. Teachers now need to be more understanding, accepting and honoring of Earth ways. If teachers are not that way or have little or no identification with Earth ways, an artificial distance is created. This is a time when all people must embrace their own humanity in order to embrace the humanity in others. Teachers will speak of such matters if they have directly experienced some level of Earth experience, either having lived in a body, such as myself, or having been a part of Mother Earth herself—some people will channel the planet, for example.

This does not mean that other teachers cannot be beneficial and helpful, but right now and for the next several years there needs to be a practical address of these circumstances. You are all going through changes intended to bring you into the comfort and pleasure of being physical, rather than the burden of being physical as taught by philosophies that have become popular in recent years (such as the unfortunate idea of original sin popularized by a well-known religion, which makes the body evil to begin with).

When you have an idea like that, you can never be truly comfortable being physical, nor can you ever revere or see God or Creator (however you wish to say it) in your own body or in the bodies of others. Yet you must do that in order to feel the reverence for all life. How can you truly love the animals and plants and be given the gifts from them that they have to offer you unless you have a reverence for life? If you have a reverence for the food you're eating, it will strengthen you more. If you are just putting it in your mouth to fill your empty stomach, it won't give you much energy. No one likes to be taken for granted.

Guides and Teachers

I've asked before about guides but not about teachers. Does each human have a certain number of teachers? Can you talk about that?

There is no fixed pattern. In the past there were often six or seven teachers, sometimes two or three. But teachers (I'm including guides here) can only communicate with you to the extent that you feel safe and sometimes even familiar with them. That's why occasionally, if the teacher is not someone you previously knew, that teacher will at least somehow remind you of someone you previously knew. Perhaps you were once an African tribal person, and whatever your life looks like now (you are a white southerner, for instance), if one of your guides has the persona of an African tribal person, you'd be more likely to feel comfortable and compatible with that guide. You would be more comfortable about heeding and feeling that guide's promptings, which are truly the foundation of inspiration.

If, on the other hand (this is not possible, but only an example), you have never had an ET life and now have nothing but ETs as guides, you might feel uncomfortable with them because there is nothing in your soul's past to relate to them. So now more than ever, guides and teachers must have some familiarity—if not personally, then at least in a tribal sense.

What is the difference between guides and teachers?

Guides are usually learning; they are students. Teachers have already learned what they are teaching about, at least to the extent that they can help you. They might learn a little bit more by having to rise to the occasion and help you with whatever your challenge is, but in short, they are more accomplished. Guides are learning and seeking as much as they are helping, so being a guide is like a training program.

These teachers are the ones who talk to us between lives and help us plan our next life?

Sometimes. They are often the teachers who speak to you at the deepest level of your slumber. But they are not always the ones who speak to you between lives, especially the way Earth is for you now, where there has been such a disconnection between your greater self and who you are now in order for you to experience as much potential for growth as you can.

So it is not always the case. In my time, as I recall, many of my teachers were those I had before and after this life. I am not certain it is quite that way for you in your time, but for some it must be.

Do you usually have the same teachers during your whole lifetime? Are you saying that they may go on for more than one lifetime?

No. If you learn something and start with it and begin on your own, then the teacher may not do much more because it's the teacher's job to inspire you and get you going. Most of this happens when you're very young and can feel comfortable hearing and interacting with the teacher. For most people it happens at the deepest levels of their sleep. Therefore, if the teachers feel that you have started on your own path of this teaching and that any further instruction they might offer you would change the course of that path and perhaps interfere in your own creative process, they will step back until they feel that something they have to offer will be helpful to you.

You said that the teachers have now changed. Did a new wave come in? Are they now different from the old ones?

They are more honoring of Earth traditions. They would not feel uncomfortable with the idea of a soldier sacrificing himself or herself for comrades in battle. This is not to say that other teachers previously didn't admire courage, but all human beings know that this is heroic and is not done because the soldier is suicidal. It is done in a moment's great love and compassion for his or her friends and comrades, not because that soldier wanted to end it all. Some teachers weren't clear about that before, but now they are very clear. I use that dramatic example because such selfless courage is something that many societies on Earth admire.

So all teachers have had a life on Earth?

In the past I don't think that was the case, but now many of them have had lives on Earth, or they have to honor and appreciate Earth. No, I cannot say *all* teachers have had lives on Earth. Certainly beings such as Isis and others might be teachers for people, yet Isis did not have a life of her own on Earth.

No, but she created bodies and experienced that.

That's not the same. It is only the same because of the Earth experience. It's only the same if you are living a life on Earth and are not conscious of lives going on elsewhere. When that is so, you tend to put more commitment into that life.

That is one of the hazards of philosophy (I call the New Age studies philosophy), because as the philosophical student gets more educated, the world gets larger and larger until it encompasses many worlds and then universes. The student will become more and more aware that life is perpetual, and although that might serve you mentally and philosophically and even spiritually in some ways, some people—not all—might use that as an excuse to be less committed to their physical life here on Earth because they know they will go on no matter what.

That is one of the motivations, I believe, behind some of the religions still with you that do not honor the idea of reincarnational life cycles; they felt that people need to pay attention to the life they are living right now. You must understand that rules of religion are usually not created arbitrarily but for some cause that is meaningful to the creators of those rules in that moment, and sometimes it's perfectly understandable and still relevant today.

The Current Heart Expansion

Expansion of the heart is happening for people these days because the heart contains the memory of love in its absolute purest state. It has the capacity to initiate, to harmonize and to bless all beings, including the body in which it functions. In many people the heart is the organ that is now struggling to give you the love and energy it has to offer.

The spiritual connection to the most wonderful beings you all love is always focused through the heart. It is the heart's great joy to offer this first to the person in whom it resides, and from that point, strictly through the radiation of life-force energy, to all others that that life-force energy touches.

If the heart feels restricted or the person is frightened for some reason or shy (which is a form of fear), the heart will get sad. But if the person is having fun—maybe a youngster playing with her friends— then the heart will sing, giving much love and energy to that person and sharing it with her friends in that moment, even if she is near people she doesn't know. It will be shared because the heart knows absolutely that everyone is one.

The heart does not know this as a mental fact. It knows it as a *living* fact. The difference between a living fact and a mental fact is that mental facts are free and open to question (free meaning readily available but not rigid), whereas the heart truth is something that is known on the basis of absolutes. The heart pumps because that's what it *does*. The heart knows love in its purest sense because that's what it *is*.

What percentage of our heart energy is possible for humans at this frequency to hold?

At this moment you have the capacity to experience 17 percent. Most people are struggling around 3 or 4 percent, but the recent astronomical experience had such an impact on all people that it caused much uncertainty. The heart, the pure love of the heart that is the heart's voice, is getting stronger and more insistent that people experience pure love and honor all life within each and every person. Some people are uncomfortable with that.

It does not mean that everybody has to have sex together, but it does mean that people have to at least tolerate the "crazy" opinions of others—or at least take them with a smile, not too seriously—or else others will have the same attitude toward *your* "crazy" opinions.

Is there an exercise for opening or expanding the heart besides the love-heat exercise [see pp. 7-8]?

The heart warmth nurtures the heart.

Is there something we can do that will help us hold more of our heart energy?

I think it is not good to rush that at this time. Right now is not good, because the astronomical impact of that recent event will last over several years, and people do not do so well when they are rushed. They need to take their time.

They need to settle into what happened.

That's right. Well, we should call it a night.

Thank you.

The Waning of Individuality

Speaks of Many Truths
September 21, 1999

This is Speaks of Many Truths. Hold on a moment. The energy distortion is profound.

What is the cause of the distortion?

It seems to be caused by the overlays of choices. The past-anchored timeline is being held onto by many people. The future-anchored timeline is beckoning and some are grasping it, but it creates a jog instead of a straight path to the connection.

The Exploration of Individuality

There is also another factor going on here. Over the years people have become enamored of individuality, but in fact, as you know, not only are you connected to all things and all beings everywhere, but perhaps more importantly on Earth, you are connected to all human beings—everyone is.

There was a veil in place that allowed you to function as an individual, but it is being torn away. As a result, all people are feeling connected with all other people. In my time this is how we knew (we were connected then, you know) when someone in our tribe or even other people nearby were suffering or in need of something. We would be tired or have some affliction we would not normally have.

Then we would go around and ask everybody in our tribe if they were all right. If they were, we would send out emissaries to the nearby tribes and clans and ask them if they were all right. If they were not well, we would do what we could to help them, just as they would do what they could to help us if they were feeling uncomfortable.

In your time this experience has been somewhat lost during your struggle to develop your individual creative capacity. But now the problems the human race is facing are so large and complex that you as individual creators need to function in partnership with others. So you are all beginning to feel each other again.

The Recent Decision to Share Energies with the Suffering

There are people suffering on your world in your time, and many of you are acting as links to relieve the suffering in whatever way you can. As a result, many people are feeling excessively tired. (I might add, it does not matter whether you are the finest-tuned athlete or a sickly person.) Everyone has had an increasingly amplified experience over the past three or four weeks. It's been getting more and more profound, and the comparison between your normal energy as an individual and the amount of energy you have available for you now is, on the average, swinging from maybe a 5 percent loss for some people to a 30 percent loss for others. Taking all people into account, it is overall about a 20 percent average loss.

Now, I'd like to say that this is temporary, but unfortunately I cannot. It's going to require effort. I'm going to recommend that people do breathing exercises, which used to be popular years ago—deep breaths in the morning, especially upon rising, and maybe once or twice again during the day. If you're working in a plant or office, try to step out where the air is a little fresher and take ten to twelve deep breaths, slowly. Don't hold your breath, and don't pant. Just take ten or twelve deep breaths, then relax. If that doesn't quite do it, then take ten more deep breaths. That will help.

I grant that there may be many other things that can be done. I do not know if yoga can be written about; it can be more easily demonstrated. But such breathing exercises are well-known to Eastern studies. This will continue for a time.

Days, weeks, months, years?

I cannot say. It could be as long as three years, but there will be moments when it will get better.

Dealing with the Drop in Atmospheric Oxygen

One of the reasons for this, of course, that we cannot overlook—in your time especially—is the significant decrease in available oxygen. It would be a good idea now for people to stop cutting down trees and to pay attention to the plankton [phytoplankton] in the ocean—in short, all the life forms that exhale oxygen.

With six billion human beings and many other oxygen breathers on the planet, the demand for oxygen is much greater than the planet can provide, and it will be just a short time before the industrial complexes in many different countries realize that there is a need for more oxygen. Ultimately, there will be systems in buildings. You will probably see it first in therapeutic places such as hospitals, but you also will see it in places where people have to be alert, such as military institutions or airport traffic control towers or perhaps even computer-development facilities. They will take bottled oxygen and bleed it into the air conditioning system to raise the oxygen content within the building, the outside air not having significant oxygen. This will gradually be applied in various ways in people's vehicles, but the oxygen will be created by processing water.

That's not good.

Well, it is a short-term solution. Because six billion people and other life forms need water, you will have to come up with something better. Of course, the polar icecaps will melt quite a bit over the next few years, and that will give you a little time to deal with it. Rather than causing a flood or more extreme weather, as you utilize water for oxygen and perhaps use the hydrogen for fuel, there will be an overlap of time in which you will be able to consider other sources.

It might be possible to extract oxygen from stone—that has been looked at for spaceships and so on—but it is perhaps not the best long-range solution. Atmospheric science is probably going to be a very important field in the coming years, so any young people reading this who have not chosen their scientific major in college, look into atmospheric science—the study of gases and creating gases from liquids—and you will be well-prepared for making a contribution in the next ten to fifteen years.

We need the implant the Zeta talked about that allows him to amplify the usable gases in the atmosphere [see ET Visitors Speak, Chapter 19].

That's another reason to prepare yourselves for contact with extraterrestrials. The best way to do that, of course, is to learn how to get along with each other and with Earth life forms you've battled, such as insects, who have a great deal of wisdom to offer you. They know how to make the most out of the least, and when you have a massive population, you must know how to do this.

We really have to take care of our bodies—watch what we eat, exercise and not get too tired. A 20 to 30 percent drain on our energies for years is . . .

It's a possibility, but for some it will be 5 percent. It depends. For people who are living out in the countryside or in the mountains or in places where a more vigorous lifestyle occurs, it would be more like 5 to 15 percent. This is an average, although even there some people would be at 30 percent.

For people in the cities where there is less clean air, these actions are important. Some of the breathing exercises will not help people who are in cities where the air is particularly foul. For instance, certain cities in California are famous for foul air, but certainly they are not alone. Brazil and other countries that have rapid technical development are also going to have to deal with this. That is why bottled oxygen (it will come to be known as oxygen infusion) is a developing industry and will be huge in the future.

Birth Control to Avoid Oxygen Starvation

And even though religion will fight it with the best of intentions, it can't be too far off that some form of required birth control takes place. I am not saying this is a good thing. I am just saying that six billion people is more than Earth can provide for. Why have loss of life through war if it is possible to limit a marriage to one child? It is a sad thing to lose the ability to have seven or eight children, but something must bend. If not, everything will break for everyone.

For example, let's say that the population rises to twelve billion. At twelve billion, oxygen starvation would be a very serious crisis. Most people would require a unit that they would actually wear to infuse extra oxygen into the air they breathe. Twelve billion people would have to live somewhere, and the more places people have to live, the more trees are cut down and the more water pollution there is. I am not saying anything that isn't already known.

Mother Earth will try to hold off from interfering with your population. Of course, she could easily interfere by generating, duplicating and spreading part of her natural organisms, which you call germs. But she won't do that any more than normal, which you expect. She is trying to hold off the best she can to allow you to discover and apply the type of magic necessary for you to adjust your body to live on other gases (which is extremely unlikely, but a lot of people will try to do that), stimulate the Earth to create more oxygen in other ways or use benevolent magic to create needed materials.

Needed oxygen, you mean?

Yes.

How would you go about doing that?

Using Benevolent Magic to Create Oxygen

You wouldn't try to create the materials that would create oxygen. Rather, when you are working with benevolent magic, you must state the need specifically and allow the creative elements of life around you to find their own solution. If you try to lay out a formula based on how you understand oxygen is created, you will limit the capacity of creation to produce what is needed.

Let's give some homework on that. In order to create oxygen in larger quantity, I would like you to try this. This is the gesture [Fig. 8-1]. Hold for ten to fifteen seconds and say, "I ask that there be abundant oxygen for all beings on Earth now." Keep it simple. You must say "all beings" because you are united with all beings.

🌿 Gesture to Create More Oxygen 🌿

Fig. 8-1a. Here is the gesture: The heel of the right hand is touching the chest. Have your back toward the north, and try to do it somewhere outdoors if you can. Hold for about ten to fifteen seconds, then say these words: "I ask that there be abundant oxygen for all beings on Earth now." Do this before you go to sleep at night, once every third day for two to three weeks.

Fig. 8-1b. A second view.   Fig. 8-1c. A third view.

The best way to do this is to have your back to the north. If you can sit out on a rock in the country, that's fine. It's probably better not to sit on the ground, but you can try that if you wish. Take your shoes off if you can, at least your socks, but not if it is not easy or convenient. If you are in the city, try to do it somewhere outdoors, but if you cannot, try to do it on the roof. If that's not convenient or possible, then do it wherever you can. It will help.

Group Gatherings to Perform Benevolent Magic

I recommend these things now because so many factors are operating to challenge individuality. It is difficult for you, especially in some Western societies where individuality has been held as a profound right as well as desirable, but you will discover that now the times are many when you will need to gather.

Don't use only narrow opportunities to gather, such as weddings and funerals, church services and parties. Try to find other reasons to gather in groups of three to five or more. That is a good beginning to prepare you for the spiritual and ceremonial activities you will do in groups of twenty to thirty thousand in the coming years. This won't occur immediately in the Western world, but in other parts of the world it will probably happen within the next few years; in some cases it is already happening. The ceremonies will sometimes be religious, to pray for better circumstances. In other cases they will involve some form of benevolent magic to create the best life "for all beings on Earth" (eventually you will say, "and everywhere else"). You must always say "now," because if you do not, benevolent magic will spread out that capacity to create into time immemorial. One must be specific with benevolent magic or you have to do it over again.

Are you saying that in the brief time period of the last four hundred years, we've changed from a more heart-oriented soul connection with other beings on the planet into this absolute individuality?

It's not absolute individuality, but since this book is going out in English at the moment, it is a concept relevant to English-speaking worlds. Generally, in English-speaking worlds (or countries, you say), this has become a profound characteristic. There are exceptions; some tribes and religious groups have sworn a loving oath to support and sustain each other, and that's good. But individuality was cherished by people in the past because it was so rare and generally only granted to very wealthy or isolated people. Of course, you would at times be lonely, but at other times you would appreciate the space around you.

There was a groundswell, you might say, of interest in exploring individuality in your country, especially in the context of so many people.

Could it be done? Could it be maintained? And could it even be guaranteed by law—which your country sought to manifest.

How Humans Exchange Energy

So one cannot say it is a bad thing, only that it is now an indulgence you may not be able to carry on as much. You are all familiar with people who have more energy than they know what to do with. It's actually intended that people who have abundant energy, even to the point where it makes them nervous and uncomfortable, be around people who don't have much energy—not because the people with low energy are supposed to drain the other individual, but because people tend to charge the atmosphere with their energy.

That's why when nursery school or elementary teachers are in a classroom, they might get tired from the experience, but they can all acknowledge that the air is charged with energy. It is meant that people like this not be burdened with too much energy, because it agitates them and even has some negative impacts on their physical bodies. But it is meant that people like this be exposed to people who don't have as much energy, just to be in the same physical space for a time, until the person who has too much energy feels more relaxed and comfortable because he or she has emanated some of that energy.

You all tend to serve each other's needs all the time, whether you know it or not, so the people who need the energy will simply take it from the atmosphere of the place where the extra-energized person is. The moment when that extra-energized person feels relaxed and comfortable, he will get up and leave, because it is not intended that he be drained.

This was actually a technique used in my time when we needed to keep an elder alive because that elder had wisdom the tribe needed and had not yet passed it on to anybody else in the completeness of what he or she had to offer. The people with too much energy would go into the space where the elder was and leave when they felt relaxed. In this way the elder's life might be perpetuated for a few years, giving him enough time to pass on his wisdom.

Of course, people who are suffering will also be able to draw energy from those who are not. When there are a great many people suffering, there are checks built into the system so that you are not exhausted doing something that requires your absolute attention. So those who are suffering would generally be allowed to pull energy from others while those others are in their deep sleep state. That is why some of you can identify with this experience in recent times: You wake up in the morning after what is usually a restful night's sleep, but you feel exhausted. At times like that, you'll need to try to take a nap during the day. That will help get you through. You might even have to take a nap a couple of hours after you awaken.

If your hours are flexible, try to do that, and it will help. The people who might pull on your energy when you are in deep sleep can only pull on it then; they cannot pull on it when you are taking a light nap of twenty to forty minutes, when most people usually do not sink into deep sleep.

Will there be some sort of balance of energy or less suffering after three years?

It might not be three years; it might go on past that point. I am just saying that you need to know that as an individual who might be in a very safe environment with everything you need, it's not safe because *others are suffering.* It is like an extreme moral lesson. In our time we had our method of knowing when people were suffering. We did that because that's how we were raised, to believe it was of value that all people, at least in our group and in nearby villages, be as energized as possible for the good of all beings. But in your time this has been less, especially with the overemphasis on competition. The idea of competition was originally started to bring out the best in the individual, but it has become way out of balance in your time.

So there needs to be more focus on the fact that you are all united all the time, even when you are in your deepest sleep. It is unavoidable. You need to be reminded of this, and this experience you are having now, however unpleasant, does remind you. I will give other homework in the future to encourage, support and sustain all beings. Some will be magic. Some will be suggestions. Some will even be intentions, because those who are suffering very often cannot take care of themselves.

You know this because you have all suffered in some way and have needed others to help you. Perhaps you cannot go to the other side of the world where people are suffering, but there may be things you can do here—practical, grounded things to help. For those who cannot or are unable to do those things, I will give other exercises in the future that involve magical ceremonies to encourage the betterment of all beings.

Will this motivate people to start thinking about how suffering can be abated all over the world, because it's going to affect each of us?

That's right. It always has in the past, but you haven't noticed it much. Now you cannot help but notice it. It is not a punishment; it is an urgency to become united as one being to prepare you for the union of all beings everywhere. It would not happen at this time if Creator had not felt you were ready to take on such a challenge.

There will be many other different individuals and spirits who will comment on what to do or why these things are happening, and many of those comments will be absolutely relevant, but the main thing to focus on is what you can do to improve the situation for all beings.

Is feeling a connection amongst all beings on Earth a prerequisite for the fourth dimension?

Yes. It's actually a prerequisite for all life, but in this recent time you are experiencing, this sense of disconnection is an anomaly.

So all over the planet, even during ancient times and the Dark Ages, people still had a sense of others on the planet, except for the last four hundred years?

They might not have had that sense, no. But they would have had a strong sense of connection to their own kind, a sense of tribal consciousness and less of a desire for individual freedom. They might have had desires for happiness and wealth and so on within their group, but not for happiness and wealth *apart* from their group. This is something, I think, that can be historically shown.

Clearing the Physical Body

Speaks of Many Truths
September 22, 1999

All right, this is Speaks of Many Truths.

The General Clearing Gesture

Let us do a unified clearing that can be used for all organs. If you wanted to clear the heart, you would start the gesture where the heart is. If you wanted to clear the gut or the intestine, you'd start it where

The General Clearing Gesture
(Here for the Heart)

Fig. 9-1a. Here is position one: Put your right palm atop the back of your left hand, with your thumbs pressed against whatever organ you wish to clear.

the gut is. In short, just move your hands around to that point. Let me just demonstrate the basic gesture (using it here to clear the heart) for the sake of simplicity [Fig. 9-1].

Fig. 9-1b. The second gesture: Pull your hands slowly away from each other and begin a forward motion.

Fig. 9-1c. Position three: Continue the forward movement with the fingers.

Fig. 9-1d. Position four: Continue the separating motion and the motion of the fingers moving forward.

Fig. 9-1e. The final position: The sides of the thumbs are against the chest, forming a triangle with the forefingers. Request that this part of your body be cleared of all old or residual pain that is not performing a benevolent function for you now. This entire gesture takes ten to fifteen seconds to complete. Do this once a day for three to seven days if it is a minor problem. If it is a moderate problem, do it once a day or every other day for two weeks. If it's serious or life-threatening, take about twenty to twenty-five seconds to do the gesture once a day for two to three weeks.

Now let me raise my arms to show you exactly how to position your h___ 's [Fig. 9-2]. This is intended to be done by individuals on them-___ We need to make that clear.

e timing—how long and how frequently?

___uld place your hands in the first position [Fig. 9-1a or Fig. ___you place them over the part of your body you wish to clear.

🌿 The General Clearing Gesture (Another View) 🌿

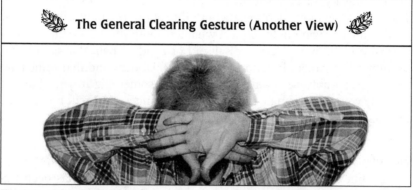

Fig. 9-2a. Here again is the first position: The balls of your thumbs are touching, palms outward, left palm in the outside position.

Fig. 9-2b. Position two: Move your hands slowly upward.

Fig. 9-2c. Position three: Continue the upward movement, the hands now at an angle to each other.

Fig. 9-2d. Position four: Continue upward, creating a greater angle.

Fig. 9-2e. Position five: Slowly increase the angle of the hands to each other.

Fig. 9-2f. The final position: Your thumbs almost form a triangle with your fingers. Again, do this entire movement over a period of ten to fifteen seconds.

Once you get your hands just right, put them on that part of your body. Then make the movement over a period of about ten to fifteen seconds.

If you wish, you might request whatever deity you believe in that this part of your body be cleared of all old or residual pain that is not performing a benevolent function for you now. Understand that some pain might conceivably be prompting you to do something in your life. In this way you will eliminate that which is no longer of benefit but is not a message you might need that could be coming in on the pain level.

Deciphering Pain Messages

Most of us just want to eliminate the pain.

Yes, but the pain is very often part of a message that has been unheard by subtler means. Messages through spirit and form always come in more gently. For instance, you might be sitting, doing very little, or resting or relaxing or perhaps riding somewhere, and you might become suddenly aware of your heart, not because it's beating strongly, but your attention is suddenly drawn there. This would be a type of message that would precede a pain message.

For that matter, you might become aware of some other part of your body. Your attention would be drawn there, not because of a discomfort, but simply drawn there.

How would you decipher that?

First, you would ask yourself (if there are others around you, just think it; if you are alone, say it out loud): "Is a message trying to come through?" If you've done the love-heat [see pp. 7-8], you will probably feel some sense of warmth. Then you can utilize what you know about that part of your body (what it might symbolize, from what I've discussed and what you've read or know about from Eastern methodologies) and inquire on that basis, "Is there a message about this or that?"

If you don't get the warmth, then you would do something like this, in this case linking to your solar plexus (let's say the pain is in your lower right quadrant) [Fig. 9-3]: You have linked to your solar plexus because that may be the place you get the heat. It would certainly be close to it, and it might be a place where you can more easily access an answer. For those who do some form of automatic writing, ask. If you do some kind of channeling, ask. If you don't, then keep asking questions of that part of your body. You don't have to hold that gesture much more than ten to fifteen seconds.

You might even feel something shift inside your intestine, which often gives you an acknowledgment. If something shifts or feels better, a physical balancing might have taken place. Or it might simply mean, "Yes, that's the place." Just ask. Use your methods of information-gathering to find out what it means.

Gesture to Link to Love-Heat When Deciphering Pain Messages

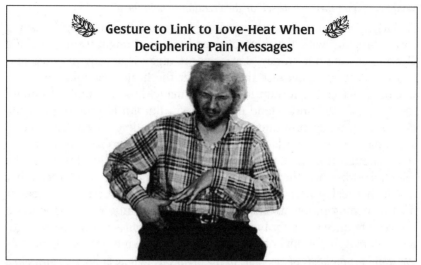

Fig. 9-3a. Here is the gesture. The left thumb is at the solar plexus. The right thumb and middle left finger are touching. Hold for ten to fifteen seconds.

Fig. 9-3b. A side view.

Fig. 9-3c. Another view.

Living Prayer for the Physical Body

You do living prayers for all beings [see Appendix A]. Are there living prayers you can do for your own body and organs?

Yes. You might very well say, "May the discomfort in this part of my body . . ." —wherever the message comes from, whether it is pain or just a feeling. If it is a feeling, you might say, "May the message from this part of my body become clear to me now." "Now" means it is now that you wish to know, though you may not immediately know. But it will probably become clear to you in some symbolic way or in a dream within the next twelve to thirty-six hours. If it doesn't, ask again in a different way.

For people who are not just working to cleanse organs for general maintenance, but who may have a disease or illness, what would be a prayer they could say that would call upon their whole self or the creation to help them?

First, you want to do the clearing gesture. Because you're having some difficulty with that part of your body, you might want to do the clearing gesture once a day. Let's say the organ is already diseased and you know about it because the doctor or the healer has told you. The doctor or healer might want to add how many days you think you ought to do this, if they understand this method. But if it is a minor problem, do the clearing gesture once a day at the same time of day for three to seven days, whatever feels right. If it is a moderate problem, meaning serious enough to require other care (perhaps medication), but it can be maintained by that, then do the gesture once a day or once every other day, if that feels better, for two weeks. If it is a very serious, critical or life-threatening problem, take about twenty to twenty-five seconds to do the gesture once a day for two to three weeks. This is not necessarily going to cure it, but it might help in coordination with other therapies.

We store certain kinds of emotions in the organs as well as in the capillaries and the bones, right?

Sometimes, yes. Sometimes certain organs will hold certain types of feelings; for instance, anger or rage is often held in the gut. What is held in the heart more often than anything else is disappointment. So if you are ever disappointed about anything, clear it by saying, "Well, that didn't work out, but it just means that something else will work out in the future." If you did not go through a process of resolution that causes you to feel better, the residual disappointment will finally lodge itself in your heart. But the clearing gesture should help to release that if it is an old pain of disappointment no longer serving you.

We don't necessarily have to understand the scenario or situation or event that triggered whatever we're holding?

No, we need to keep it fairly simple. If we know too much about the mechanism, we can easily regurgitate the original pain that prompted the disappointment to be in your heart (which you probably would have mentally forgotten long ago) and go through the whole agony all over again on the memory level. It is better in this case to be blissfully ignorant [laughs] of such memory.

Maintenance Clearing to Combat Tiredness and Depression

So just for maintenance, do we need to go through and clear the major organs?

Yes. This can be useful even if you just feel tired or somewhat depressed. The main thing is that because of the statement and the process, you're not going to release anything you need.

Basically, even a healthy person could do this and feel just as good or perhaps a little better, but it shouldn't make you feel worse. If it does, then you're not doing the gesture correctly. Study the photos very carefully and practice the gesture several inches away from your body before you get it just right; go through the whole clearing gesture away from your body before you actually apply it to the point on the body. That way you'll have it right before you do it.

In view of this new situation where we might have less energy available, it would be really important to do the clearing so that we have all the energy available to our natural body, right?

Yes. It will release heaviness brought by the accumulation of residual pain. It ought to be able to give you a boost to compensate for the energy being transferred to other beings.

Excellent. So this is particularly important right now, yes?

Yes.

Clearing Whole-Body Systems

So you gave a gesture that can be used to clear any organ, the unified clearing gesture [Fig. 9-1]. Is there another gesture for the circulation, another for the glands and another for the lymph system?

Let's use this for all parts of the body for now. If we need to be more specific for other specific parts of the body in the future, based on further questions or things people have tried and would like to have more information on, we'll do that in the next book. But now I'd like to engage a certain level of simplicity because the first book [*Shamanic Secrets for Material Mastery*] did not really make any effort to simplify.

Is it what we focus our attention on, then, when we ask for the clearing, whether it's the lymphatic system or . . .

As you suggest, suppose it is something that goes all throughout the body like the lymph, blood or nervous system. Then you would have to begin the gesture at the top of the head. You would essentially do the gesture starting out at the top of the head.

The hand position is over the head as far as the hands can reach.

Yes, above the head, and you'd move the hands back and forth, first to the left, then to the right, over the front of your body. Since you cannot reach the back of your body, you'll have to believe that it wraps around.

Do the gesture maybe two or three times as you go down your body, meant to cover the capillary system. If you want to, you can try to reach the sides and so on, but you obviously cannot do the gesture behind yourself. You're doing perhaps two or three gestures, depending on the speed at which you move down your body. Some of you will do two gestures, some will do three. But move back and forth, in the case of a system that runs through your body, such as your blood.

I'm still not clear. If there are five sequences to the gesture [Fig. 9-1], you do two or three gestures going down?

Yes, you do it *as* you're going down. When you do the gesture, you're going to move like this [Fig. 9-4]: down the body in that style, zigzagging

Gesture for Clearing Whole-Body Systems

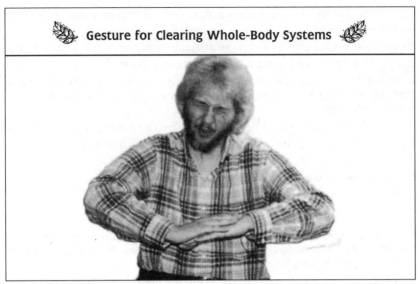

Fig. 9-4a. Here is position one: Again put your right palm on top of the back of your left hand, making sure your hands are positioned correctly. Complete the entire gesture, as shown in Fig. 9-1.

Fig. 9-4b. Position two: This shows the subsequent movement of the hands to clear systems that run through the body. Do the unified clearing gesture [Fig. 9-1] two or three times as you're going down.

Fig. 9-4c. Position three: Continue the zigzag trail.

Fig. 9-4d. Position four: Continue downward.

Fig. 9-4e. Position five: Continue downward in a zigzag pattern.

Fig. 9-4f. Position six: Keep moving downward.

Fig. 9-4g. The final position at the bottom of the trunk—or you can continue down the legs and even do the sides if you wish.

down, first moving to the left from your own perspective.

From the top of the head . . .

Moving from where you are, to your left.

Past-Life Trauma Is Not to Be Cleared

Let's say you want to clear as much trauma from your body as you can. Do you ask for this lifetime and previous ones?

You're talking about your *body*. Your body *is* this lifetime.

But don't we bring trauma from previous lifetimes?

You're going to address *this* life. It is important to not complicate it. If you say, "I want to clear past-life stuff," you might interfere with your past life.

Because it's going on at the same time?

That's right. Suppose you were learning something you came here to learn in this life, and pain was part of the lesson to get you to ask for help. You wanted to find different ways, eventually finding something or many things that worked and eventually exploring philosophical and other explanations of what it is about. You're working on that and you've just about got it. Suddenly a future self of yours clears your body.

End of lesson.

If it was the end of the lesson, that would be wonderful, but the problem is, that would mean the lesson stops and you have to do it all over again.

Oh, the lesson stops in the middle.

Yes, so we have to be very careful not to interfere with other lives. Many, many people will try to clear past lives. Don't do that.

We want to clear the body because we need as much energy as we can get. Do we do one round for so many days of the lymph system, then the circulation and then the organs? This could take forever. Is there no way to do the whole body?

First of all, pay attention to the parts of your body that are either not operating very well, as much as you can tell, or the parts where you feel discomfort at times throughout the day. Do those first, then see how it goes. You don't just begin at A for anatomy and go through Z. Just do the best you can.

If you have extensive knowledge of anatomy, as some medical professionals do, then go ahead—by all means use your knowledge of the anatomy and clear that way. But if you don't—and most people do not—then use the knowledge you have. Many of you will not know, for instance, where the spleen is. You might know only that you have a discomfort there. It hurts, so you do the gesture there to clear that part of your body. You don't *need* to know that it's the spleen. That's very important for those of you who only know where it hurts.

In my time we didn't diagnose diseases on the basis of their names, which of course have descriptions. We just knew that there was pain or crippling or suffering in that part of the body. And different practitioners would perform differently. There's been a long discussion in the past about smell, using various odors to make the smell more natural.

Using the Gestures to Protect, Clear and Charge

Speaks of Many Truths
September 23, 1999

ll right. This is Speaks of Many Truths.

The Origin of the Gestures

Where do these gestures come from? Is this something you brought to Earth from your home planet or something your tribe learned from another tribe?

In the beginning, when our people had difficulties because of the sometimes hostile conditions on Earth, we asked our ancestors to show us and tell us the means by which we could resolve these dilemmas, whether they were between people or were injuries, diseases or hazards—whatever form they might be in. First, they gave us the gestures that worked on our home planets, but only some of those gestures worked here. When all the gestures were not completely compatible with our Earth forms and Earth, we asked them to consult with their teachers, and that took some time. They spoke to us again about a fortnight later and had other gestures. They had been guided by some of their future ancestors, who would still have been in our past, as well as others in our future who traveled to or had access to wisdom beings of Earth. Thus they were able to give us the exact gestures we needed, which more than one mystical person in the tribe memorized over quite some time. To get them just right and memorize them all took several years.

Gestures were even given for circumstances that we would not be likely to experience. We were advised that we needed to memorize these gestures because there would be a time when others would need them. Sometimes they would be people from other tribes. Other times they would be people from the future (or your time) who would ask us to help you resolve your own dilemmas with gestures and other things that might be appropriate to your time.

So you're the only tribe who had these gestures. This is not something that all tribes on the planet have available to them?

I could not say. I have spoken to some other tribes, and some have some of these gestures and also some of their own that we do not have. I've also spoken in long-distance conversations (you know, like long vision) with tribal beings who do not have these gestures but have other things such as dance forms or patterns they make up with more than one person. We do not have these.

You have actually used some of these gestures for your own tribe?

That's why we originally asked.

Was it many generations before you that asked, or was it during your time?

It was before me, yes, but passed on *to* me.

So your teacher taught you and you taught somebody else.

Exactly. If you count the stages in the gestures, it's too much to discuss. But if you just talk about the different gestures for different circumstances, it numbers many hundreds.

The Circumstances in Which We Used These Gestures

You mentioned diseases, dilemmas and hazards. What's the whole range of the use of these gestures?

For example, let's say you had to visit with someone from another tribe within a many-days' walk. It might even be that you had to walk through the general area where a tribe of peoples was passing or living where there was not total peace between you. There would be perhaps, in our time, a safe-transit gesture, you might say, that we would use.

This would allow you to be invisible or for them to see you as benign?

Yes, benign.

What are some more uses?

Perhaps you might have a circumstance where you may need to call a person from another village or even one of your own people who was out hunting perhaps. There would be a gesture to call that person to come back before he or she had planned.

How does that work? You make the gesture and it somehow acts as a communication beacon?

It is true magic. The person would certainly feel an urgency if it was an urgent circumstance. If so, he would urgently pack up everything and leave, even if it was the middle of the night. If it was not urgent but he was needed for some other reason, then that person would simply feel as if he ought to pack up his things and return.

The reason it works, you must remember, is that people in my time would pay attention to such feelings. They would not ignore them. People in your time will often ignore feelings like that and continue doing what they are doing. You hear about circumstances when people do pay attention and rush home to find that perhaps there is a fire, and they save the children or the family, and everything is all right. That's reported as if it were news. But, in fact, these feelings are *often* associated with things, like in my time.

Messages.

Yes, it is sometimes difficult in your time to discern what is a *worry* on your part versus what is a *genuine message*. But you need to identify the benevolent feelings of a message in your physical body compared to the discomforts of a worry. This is something you have to memorize (in terms of the feelings in your own physical body) so that you can discern the difference. Different people will feel it differently, so there is no one way to teach it. You simply have to practice.

You could ask, "Who is making the gestures in our time?" No one—but if there is a need, a message will simply be sent out, as in our time. But if we felt a sense of urgency, we would make the gestures, because that clarifies or sometimes amplifies the message.

Using the Love-Heat Exercise for Protection

We have to start dealing with the negativity on Earth now, and sometimes it might feel like a psychic attack. Is there something people can do when they start feeling someone else's negativity or fears that they know are not their own?

If you're ever amongst several people, try to get together and do the heat together, the love-heat exercise [see pp. 7-8]. If you live alone, try to have a phone chain where you call several people and ask them to do the heat with you. You don't have to keep them on the phone; just call and ask them if they could do it right then, and then hang up. Then you do it, too. That might help. Feel free to also ask your angels and protecting spirits to come help you. But do the heat exercise, because it will tend to deflect and push out of your body anything that is not compatible with you.

With this new sense of unity that just happened, where we will start feeling everyone on the planet and their suffering, where part of our energy is going to help them, there has to be a backwash of stuff from them that we're going to feel, right?

Yes, that's very possible. That's why you need to start these circles or chains where you do the heat. The more people who are doing the heat, the more available energy there will be for others *and* for yourself. Try to do the heat as much as you can during the day and before sleep at night. It is one of the most useful and practical methods to transform and deflect that from you. It also tends to rebuild your physical energy.

Using the Sun Exercise to Build Up Your Energy

Also ask your guides, angels and others you speak with to give you as much physical energy as you can absorb. For those of you who are involved with the planetary bodies, ask the Sun to do this for you. It is most easily accomplished when the Sun is out, but if it is nighttime, ask the Sun anyway. The Moon does other things.

The Moon will work with you during your dreams, whereas the Sun is capable of giving you a great deal of energy, but you must *ask*. Ask for your angels or guides to accompany the Sun's work with your physical body so that everything is done in the most benevolent concordance (meaning alignment) for you.

When we talked to the Void [see Creators and Friends: Mechanics of Creation, *Chapter 10], he said we would eventually learn to ask for energy. At that time, it was to be used as energy instead of electricity. He said there are untold suns that radiate energy that isn't being used, and you can ask that it be directed to the Earth. So couldn't we also ask to increase our own and other humans' energy?*

Yes, do that.

He said there are streams of energy that you can pull toward you, that it was unimaginable energy that wasn't being used by anybody. And they would be delighted to be of service.

Yes, do that. You need to do this. It is urgent. I think you will find that if you do this exercise with the suns, it will be very helpful. Your physical body is set up to naturally draw energy from the Earth, but since the Earth is in such struggle right now, having been mined and polluted so much, the energy you are drawing up from her has sometimes more to do with her pain.

For those of you who are physically able, work hard. This tends to shove energy down to the bottoms of your feet and spherically outward in all directions. If you do not have a job that involves hard work, then dancing helps very much. It would be useful to dance to something rhythmic, to music that is not disrupting or discordant but of comfort to you—physically not just exciting, but comfortable.

If you do not have any of those things readily available but are still physically able, jump up and down. That will tend to dislodge energy in your hips. Jump up and down three or four times—that will shake things up. Then lie down and blow energy out through the bottoms of your feet every time you exhale. Try to line up your feet in such a way that the energy is aimed outdoors rather than indoors if you can.

But the Earth needs energy. This book isn't relating to the Earth, but couldn't we also ask that some of that incredible energy out there from all those suns be directed to the Earth, too?

You can, but she is more likely to do that on her own. In the past, if she needed extra energy, she would ask for that. The energy would come in through her poles and then be disseminated throughout her body along her crystal veins. But because so much mining has taken place, a lot of the energy has not been disseminated to surface areas where mining has disrupted crystal veins.

The inner part of her body still has a good distribution system, but closer to the surface where you are and where people are digging in her, this has been disrupted. That's why energy for her surface is not working as well as it once was.

It's not just mining crystal; they mine crystal to get gold too, don't they?

Or else they mine other things and interrupt crystal veins, or drill or do various things and in the process break through crystal veins. It would be just like cutting through a nerve system. They cut through it, then . . .

Suddenly you can't use your leg anymore. You'd be paralyzed.

Yes.

This book has suddenly become much more important since the revelations of a couple of days ago, correct? [See Chapter 8.]

Its importance is, perhaps, a little more understood.

Clearing Birth Trauma Stored in the Navel

Where do we store birth trauma? I don't think we've discussed that.

Birth trauma is always stored in the belly button. The general clearing exercise given yesterday should be tried there, except that when you get to the last sequence of the gesture [Fig. 9-1e], hold that position over the belly button for a good thirty seconds. Once that part of the body is cleared, it is profoundly easier to embrace life.

It is very difficult to embrace life when that birth trauma is in the belly button because it will continue to cycle around and around. First it will cycle down to the dantien point, to about the second chakra. Then it will cycle back to the spinal column—not into the column, just to it. Then it'll come up near the surface of the sternum and back down through the belly button and around and around and around all the time. It will try to release itself, but it needs assistance.

If you can do that clearing gesture, it will very likely be able to stop that looping. Hold it for quite a while; for thirty seconds. That will clear the birth trauma and allow the physical body to be profoundly more receptive to the energies of life that support nurturing of the physical self. The physical self on Earth is profoundly blocked from being nurtured and energized when this form of trauma remains.

And it's in almost everybody.

It's in almost everybody, yes. There are exceptions—for instance, individuals who have had a very benevolent or benign water birth. This was experimented with for a time in the former Soviet Union, and it is done from time to time in other places and cultures. When the birth is done in water and the child can swim out of the mother and is treated gently afterward, there is usually no birth trauma at all.

These children frequently grow up to be exceptionally strong and bright intellectually or perhaps have unusual spiritual or musical talents. There was a Russian scientist, I believe, who was very well-known for experimenting with water births [Igor Charkovsky].

It would be good to get this kind of information brought back up to the surface, because even though it was popularized for a while many years ago, many people have forgotten about it. Now would be a time when it could be most beneficial.

For the new children.

Yes.

Charging the Navel Area

Once the belly button area is cleared, it is possible to charge this part of your body, but you need to do so in the most gentle way. The best way is to do so in water. Ideally, it would be a mineral spring, but the next best thing might be in the clearest lake, stream or pond you can find. If you are unable to do that, try a man-made saltwater pond.

If there is no other choice, use your own bathtub, but add one-fourth of a handful—equal to about one or two level tablespoons—of sea salt. Put that into the water and stir it well. Don't wash in this water, just get into the tub. Try to sit in such a way that your belly button is covered. If you are a big person, try to use a bigger tub.

Then do this gesture. You might expect a gesture of insertion at the belly button, but don't do that. This is something very simple. Put the right hand like this [Fig. 10-1].

Toward the left hand.

Yes. Hold that position for about fifteen to twenty seconds. If you want to do this also, you can ask that that part of your body be awakened to receive the most benevolent and beneficial energies available for you at all times in this body in this life. (Of course, you say "my body" and "my life.")

Are you still in the water doing this gesture, or are you out?

You are in the water. After that, just rest in the water for another five minutes or so. Try not to think about anything. It will be easier to not think if you have something you can stare at on the wall that is not a picture, something simple.

Or see color in your head?

Gesture to Recharge the Navel Area

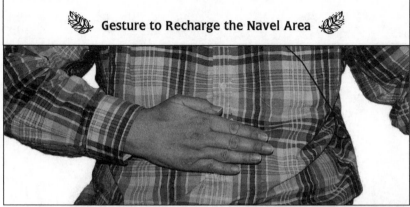

Fig. 10-1a. Three days after the navel area is cleared, you can charge it. While immersed in the water, place your right hand away from the body, about two inches from the belly button.

Yes, but for some people that is difficult. It is infinitely easier to look at the wall if there is a blank spot or a blank tile; just stare at it. If you catch yourself thinking, just say, "All right, it's okay," and go back to just staring for a few minutes. You can set a timer if you like. Then get out of the tub, rest for a moment and drain the water. And then take a shower, if you like, to wash off the salt.

Fig. 10-1b. Place the left hand so it is not quite touching the right hand, but very close. Hold this position for fifteen to twenty seconds, then rest. Do this if you feel unusually tired.

Now, it is not *necessary* to do that with the belly button, but you can do it if you feel unusually tired. The belly button has much to do with recharging or with giving permission for the recharging of the physical body on a regular basis.

Opening the Heart

A lot of people have difficulty in doing the love-heat. We talked about them possibly joining in a group. Is there a gesture you would recommend aimed at the heart when it might be closed or blocked?

One thing that can be done, if you are lying down or sitting in a chair, is to put your left hand on your chest like this, perhaps a little closer to your heart [Fig. 10-2]. Then follow it with your right hand.

Then relax and see if it helps. If it doesn't, take the same position, move your hands a distance of about eight inches from your body and try it there. If that doesn't work, move out another six to eight inches and try it there.

🌿 Gesture to Open the Heart 🌿

Fig. 10-2a. Here is the gesture. The left hand, fingers spread, is placed over the heart area.

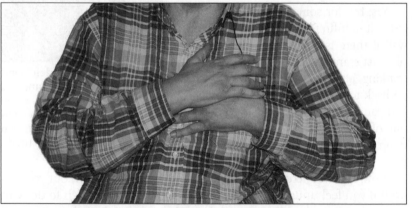

Fig. 10-2b. Follow it with your right hand in this position, then relax.

Because we may be blocked in our auric fields?

That's right. If that still doesn't work, then find someone who can do Reiki. They do not have to be a master. Even first-stage Reiki is sufficient, and there are many, many practitioners of this art available today. And ask them to Reiki that portion of your body, but not to touch your body—to just work in the auric field.

You might begin to feel the heat then. When you feel the heat, go into it and feel it more. Focus *only* on the heat. If, however, you should feel the heat in some other part of your torso (perhaps the other side of your chest or solar plexus), that's fine. Go into the heat and feel it wherever it comes up. I feel that Reiki practitioners would be especially helpful in this way.

Clearing Your Thinking at the Throat

Metaphysically, the throat area activates the will and speaks your own truth or God's truth. Is there anything stored in the thymus, the high heart or the thyroid that we can clear?

Why don't we reach up to . . . what do you call this?

The super-sternal notch is the little hollow in the bone under the throat and above the sternum.

At this spot [Fig. 10-3], do the clearing gesture [Fig. 9-1]. Once this part of the body is cleared, it will be a lot easier for you to think clearly. It is natural to assume that the brain has everything to do with clear thinking, but this part of the body has a great deal to do with that. It is associated with circumstances that occurred when you were very young—from birth to the age of about three months. This is *especially* important if you're the firstborn, because parents are just getting used to taking care of a child then, figuring out how to do things, and as first-borns know . . .

. . . you have to train the parents.

That's right, the parents are making mistakes unintentionally. This is also partly in effect if you are the second-born or third-born and so on, but it is particularly important if you're the firstborn. So when you do the clearing gesture, try to do it slowly. Before I said you are going to do this gesture for ten to fifteen seconds, but here you're going to try to do it over a period of a minute. Hold the last position for about thirty seconds.

Now, I realize that it's hard to know when it's thirty seconds if you have your eyes closed, but you can open them and glance at a clock.

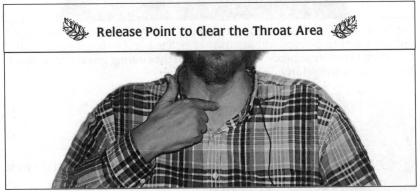

Release Point to Clear the Throat Area

Fig. 10-3. At that point where your bone comes together, up another finger width, about two fingers for the average person, do the general clearing gesture [Fig. 9-1]. Try to do the gesture over a period of a minute, holding the last position for about thirty seconds. Then wait three days before you recharge the area.

Try not to move your body around too much, so have a clock with a large second hand positioned in such a way that you can easily see by opening your eyes and closing them again. Generally speaking, it's good to do these gestures with your eyes closed, because you will have less distraction. But it's fine to glance at the clock briefly.

Recharging the Throat Area

After you've done that, wait about three days. Then you need to recharge the area In order to do that, we're going to use a very simple gesture [Fig. 10-4]. It's not intended to be complex, but we'll show a couple of views for clarity.

This gesture can be held for fifteen to twenty seconds (I think thirty seconds is a little too long). This will tend to recharge the area and al-

Gesture to Recharge the Throat Area

Fig. 10-4a. Here's the position of both hands. The hands are somewhat cupped, but not touching, perhaps within a quarter inch to a half inch, quite close. Hold for fifteen to twenty seconds. This, along with the clearing gesture, may have to be done once every thirty days or so.

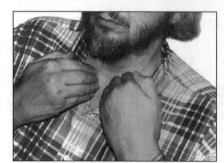

Fig. 10-4b. A second view of the hand position.

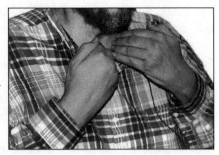

Fig. 10-4c. Another view.

low it to clean out the cobwebs, which might be particularly helpful at this time when you have so very many distractions.

I mention that because you are not using the full capacity of your brain (which is important so that you'll pay attention to your physical body as well). You overload your brain with too many high-speed pictorial images (such as on television or even driving through a community that has many brightly colored cars or buildings). You need to recognize that the clearing gesture for this part of your body might have to be done once every thirty days or so. When you do the clearing gesture, wait three days and do the recharging gesture.

In your time people watch television and movies and play video games. There's so much impact on the mental self that it overflows into the physical self. That's why physical clearing is so important. It is almost like a relief valve, but the relief valve does not flow out of your body. Instead it tends to backflow energy into the auric field around your head. This is what often causes that cloudy feeling, the cobweb feeling in your mind where you can't think fast. Many of you in various professions must think fast. Many professionals, to say nothing of students and everyday people, are often in circumstances where they must think very quickly in order to perform in the best possible way. Please do these gestures, and you will find that they will help.

Fitting the Gesture to the Individual

Can you train a group who would then go out and train other people? This is so important that everyone needs to do it themselves.

It needs to be done on an individual basis first. Know that the gestures might need some minor modification. When you start a gesture—even if it is shown perfectly—if the solar plexus tightens up and doesn't feel good in the body, then you know that the gesture needs to be slightly modified. So you might move the gesture around a little bit or maybe make slight changes in the gesture. You have to play with it a bit, and at some point it'll feel good. Then do it that way.

You see, normally these things are taught one to one. The practitioner shows another individual how to do a gesture to clear him- or herself, and if that core gesture does not work for that individual, slight variations are given on a *one-on-one* basis.

Based on the intuition of the practitioner and the feelings of the student.

Yes, because the physical body of the student is the ultimate guide to whether the gesture is just right for the student. These books will tend to build on each other. That's why the heat is important, but so are discomforts in the physical body. For those of you who cannot feel the heat and use it easily, you will be able to use discomfort in, say, your solar plexus. If you try to use one of these gestures and you get a sudden uncomfortable feeling in your solar plexus area or at the point where your belly button begins or on the right side of the chest, you will know that the gesture needs to be slightly modified. So play with it in order to get that part of your body to relax and feel okay.

Heart Attacks

Did you in your time use these if someone had, for instance, a heart attack or diseases that you wouldn't have doctors for?

If a person had what you call a heart attack, we would let him or her die. We did not try what physicians call in your time heroic methods to preserve life. If the person had something that was a developing ulcer, as you call it, that's when we would do these gestures. We would encourage people; they were never encouraged to keep quiet about their discomforts. They could keep quiet to outsiders, perhaps, but not to the medicine man or woman or the mystical man or woman or their own spouse. They were encouraged to mention it so that care could be given to them as soon as possible. Then it didn't become an ulcer.

In our time, what percentage of heart attacks are meant as an exit? Lighter ones are meant to teach people to change their habits, aren't they?

That's true. A heart attack that is not very serious might occur to encourage you to change your habits, but many heart attacks are pretty serious. The average heart attack is pretty unpleasant. Let's just say that the average heart attack is meant to create an exit, at least 80 to 90, maybe even 92 percent of the time.

This does not mean that people who are saved are staying past their time in a way that is destructive to their souls or to the souls of others. But it does mean that they might be overdue somewhere else where they were expected. When you do end your natural cycle, since it's been extended by modern medicine, you will still need to go to that place where you were expected. You might have to do it in another life, meaning you might have to add a life you hadn't planned on. In other words, it alters your reincarnational cycle.

In modern medicine it's not at all unusual for a person to be brought back and have thirty, maybe forty years with a different health regimen. Then they will have to add something. That thirty or forty years of Earth experience amounts to experiential time elsewhere. So you might add a life, because if you are called to go somewhere else, you still have to go there.

Thank you very much.

The Flow of Energy

Speaks of Many Truths
September 24, 1999

We're asking for more energy now from the infinite suns, from our high self—from everywhere. How do you see this energy actually coming into us? What's the dynamic of its coming into us?

Humans Are Naturally Receptive

Well, the interesting thing about all human beings, regardless of how they consider themselves—whether the human is a baby born totally receptive or a fighting soldier in a unit trained to be absolutely defensive, and those are two extremes—is that they are totally receptive (70 percent of the time in the case of the soldier and 100 percent of the time in the case of the baby). So under no circumstances are human beings anything but receptive almost all the time. Therefore, the focus would be to ask for certain types of energy to be exposed to you to purify you, such as the Sun exercise [see page 192], and to give you energy that you know is good for you compared to all the energy you're constantly exposed to that isn't good for you. You don't really have to try to be receptive. You already are.

The human being is like this on purpose. Creator felt, as much as I can understand, that if soul personalities were going to have a chance to understand the world around them, emulate it and, for at least some people, become engaged with it (and more and more people will do that in the future—I'm talking about mystical people, shamans and so forth, but this is going to become more popular), that people would have to naturally be receptive. So this receptivity is built in, and it is really not possible to stifle it.

If you are trying to stifle it, the best you can do is to try to focus it in certain areas, but most people do not try to do that. Only people who are warriors might try to do that.

What about people who have built walls and defensive positions around themselves because they are hurt, they don't want to be vulnerable?

Even so—if you talk to people like that, ask them to talk to you about their day if they can speak of it. They will tell you about all the things they experienced that reminded them of unpleasant things that bother them. In short, people with walls and so on are still going to be at least 70 or 80 percent receptive because they cannot help it.

Why We Have Certain Blocks

The beingness of the human is something that does not allow you to withdraw from life. Even a person in a room with a simple cot in complete darkness must listen to his or her own breath, to say nothing of the thoughts and visualizations that pop into his or her head at any moment. Therefore, people are not usually aware of their blocks unless they are trying to accomplish something that they do not seem to be able to do.

And yet we know, in certain pursuits, that this lack of ability to accomplish something is acceptable. For instance, if you were to suddenly try out for the Arizona Diamondbacks' baseball team and did not do very well, you might be able to rationally tell yourself, "Well, I'm just not meant to be a professional baseball player." You could say that and feel good about it and laugh it off, and never for one moment would you consider that you are blocked from within from accomplishing the skills of the professional ballplayer.

Or if you were to apply yourself to any skill . . . maybe you suddenly decide you're going to be a physicist and find that you cannot grasp the concepts of physics within the nature of certain of its aspects. You feel like, "Oh well, I guess that's not for me. I guess I'll have to be a publisher." What I'm saying is that if we put this in a different light, maybe it's not that people are blocked so much as it is that people can easily do certain things because of their talents and abilities, whereas other things are more difficult.

This does not mean that something that is difficult cannot be done, but it means that you have to work very hard to do it compared to others who have a talent for it. I need to say this so that those reading this do not feel as if there is something wrong with them. Sometimes blocks are placed by the personality of the individual because you choose to not pursue certain avenues that you have pursued in previous lives.

You might have a talent for those avenues, but you purposely set up the block so that you will not go in that direction, because you have done it so many times and you are definitely intending to pursue something else. You and others have done this and often do this in a given life.

There are people who have been trail masters, as I call them, or guides showing others how to find places and things, who have a certain natural ability to interact with nature yet have decided in this life that they are going to seek out other directions, such as this person I am speaking through now. He has been a trail master many times, but purposely put a block in this life (this was not done before his life but done during his life) so as to not pursue that avenue pursued so many times before. Yet he does have a natural ability to interact with all life, which is why shamanic training was easier for him.

Not to reveal too much, but I am mentioning this as an example because many of you out there, when you read this, will be able to identify with it. So it's very important to recognize that there's a difference between blocks placed in that fashion (as I just discussed) and temporary blocks put up as a result of trauma.

The key is to understand, "Is this a temporary block placed because of trauma, or is it something I do not wish to pursue in this life because I've done it before and I need to do something else?" This is very important to say in this light, because in the pursuit of any attempt at expanding your spiritual identity or even making a broader plateau for the personal philosophy in which you participate, the challenge is simply to understand that you may or may not be intending to do that with your life.

Fear-Based Blocks and Energy Receptivity

This need for more energy by the humans on the planet—we had discussed earlier that maybe one-sixteenth of six billion people have a birth or childhood or teenage trauma that affects them and keeps them from doing what they want now as an adult. Do those blocks keep you from receiving additional energy, for instance?

No, they do not.

Okay, they are just based on fear and keep you from doing certain things, then?

If they are fear-based blocks, meaning temporary blocks . . .

Well, let's just talk about temporary blocks right now.

In that case, they might direct the received energy to certain parts of your body or to certain forms of expressions that are most easy for you. If you don't know how to swim and don't seem to be able to because of some frightful experience when you were a child, the extra energy that you're able to receive from some pure source may not make it easier for you to swim, but it might make it easier to live and walk around and breathe and be able to function.

How does this receptivity work? How do we take energy in?

You take it in through your auric field, which on its own screens that which is best for you and passes it into your physical body—first through the skin, then through the capillaries and then on through the body, not unlike . . . imagine for a moment, imagine sunlight. It is like that.

But also, it is good for those of you who can to ask for your guides or your angels to be there and to make the Sun available to you or whatever source of pure love and energy. Ask for love and light from the Sun to do this for you, or if you are religious—Christian, for instance—you might ask for love and light from Jesus. That is perfectly acceptable; you might ask for this from any religion.

But I say that it is easier to receive the energy from something that naturally and normally gives energy to living beings, like the Sun or the air, because Creator can grant life permission in that sense and give you a portion of Itself but does not in Its own right conduct the process of life for each individual. That is left up to the elements that are available: sun, water, food, shelter and all of this that supports you.

I believe that asking for the Sun itself is most useful, but if you feel strongly about it, you can ask that the light come from any sun or from any star. If you are particularly attracted to a star, then ask that the Sun and a particular star shine as much love and light into you as is most available for you. But I think that it's an advantage using the Sun, because we know how much life the Sun brings. If the Sun were no longer available, how much life would be available on Earth?

Life-Force Energy in the Body

No one has ever mentioned that we take in life force through the capillaries. Is that how it comes in?

It comes into the auric field, then into the skin, then into the capillaries. We know that the capillaries take blood to the tissues, but they do not become excited by the energy. The outer part of the capillary conducts this energy throughout the body. If you can look at the capillary system in the body, you can see that capillaries go all over the place, and working as a network, this system conducts the energy, but on the outside of the capillaries.

That's a new fact. So it doesn't come in through the chakras at all?

It might, but that is not the way I see things.

So what do the chakras do, then? By their purity and activity, do they direct that energy to certain organs and away from certain others?

You do have to understand that chakras are not my way of observing, of seeing. It is not something I even think of. So perhaps I am not the person to ask. It is not something that I consider.

Okay, so the energy comes in. Then is there some system that sends it where it's needed?

The physical body knows where it is most tired, but it also knows where it draws energy from. Very often the physical body will go to certain sources or resources within itself to draw energy. This would, from the physician's point of view, be certain organs, but from my point of view, it differs from person to person. Some people might draw energy from the heart area or from the solar plexus area, but other people might draw energy from other parts of their body entirely: a foot, a hand, an arm.

So the energy will go into the area that needs to be as charged as possible, and when that area is charged, then when the physical body is strained through the stress of some other function of life, the place the body will go to for that extra boost to get through that stress will be the place where the body stores that extra energy.

Ah, so everyone's different?

That's right.

Is it stored in the kidneys and the adrenals?

It is for some people and not for others.

So when you worked with someone, you could see where the energy was needed and could be directed?

That's right, and under certain circumstances, the person might be able to feel that part being charged up. For instance, when you are doing the exercise to recharge yourself, if there is some time between when you've done it and when you do it again, you will feel the recharging quite significantly, and you might notice the energy running almost like water into some part of your body that surprises you.

You expect it to go to your heart and lungs and solar plexus and legs and so on, but you don't necessarily expect it to go to some other part of your body. If you can, notice it, but don't pay too much attention to it because then you could mentally block it. Just notice and think about it later.

Probably, if it's going to somewhere that surprises you, it could be one of two things. Either that part of your body needs that energy right now because it is worn out, something like that, or that is your storage place.

So this is definitely an adventure in self-discovery?

Yes.

Exercises to Cultivate Vertical Wisdom

You did the interesting exercise that clears the cobwebs from the brain by clearing and recharging the throat area, but is there anything to do with the head itself that we can clear to be more straight-thinking? This is what we need right now.

Actually, thinking right now is probably your biggest challenge, because thinking includes everything you've ever been told. Feeling, as I've always said, is infinitely better once you know what feelings to pay attention to and what feelings need to be soothed because they are discomforts.

Is there anything we can do to facilitate using our vertical wisdom [see Appendix I] and move away from linear thinking?

Probably the love-heat exercise is the best start for that [see pp. 7-8]. Vertical wisdom is something that is done most easily without thinking and requires practice.

This is often done by staring at a blank wall, and every time you catch yourself thinking, you stop and continue to stare. It is a boring exercise, but it is intended to be. If you can go for ten or fifteen seconds at some point without thinking anything, then that's progress. Try to get to the point in stages where you can go for thirty seconds to a minute without thinking, and that will prepare you for vertical wisdom. These are little steps, but little steps cannot be ignored.

Those are Zen and yoga meditations, and yet the words "vertical wisdom" were never understood.

Well, it might have been understood by practitioners who went on and on with it. Although those Eastern studies might have brought these forth, they were also known to my people and used when a particular individual showed some capacity for clear vision but had some problem or some sound that would disturb him or her. Then an exercise like this would be given.

That person would be taken to a place where there might be a sheer rock wall that he or she knew very well. Or more likely the individual would be asked to stare at a totally blue sky. Or even if that person would still see things, which is possible with some individuals, we had him or her stare at something right in front of his or her face, perhaps a piece of cloth with no design.

For those of you who don't have a blank wall, you can do that. You can hang a piece of fabric in front of you . . . say, a towel or something that has no design at all, that is ideally white or black or some color you're used to. Something that does not in its own right particularly attract you; it's just there.

From my understanding, these exercises were given long, long ago to many different peoples, but the cultures that have come to be known for them were the ones who wrote them down. My culture and other cultures like mine did not write things down, so we haven't come to be known for them, but that doesn't mean we don't know them.

Trauma Stored in the Back

Don't we have things that we need to clear from the back? How do we deal with the back of our own bodies?

This is awkward, because I cannot reach the back.

I know. That's why I'm asking.

I will not be able to do the gesture on my back—on the back of this person, you understand?

Right, but how did you deal with it in your people. Did you do the gesture for them?

No, we would have them do it in the front. If it still didn't work, we would have a practitioner, myself in my time or others, do it for them, because there are obviously many places you cannot reach—certainly not with both hands.

A lot of people have emotional trauma that they seem to store in their lower back.

And for some, they will store things in their neck.

Clearing the Visioning Process at the Back of the Neck

There's a bulge back here that is associated with the optic nerve. This area is often a place that restricts people's capacity for visioning. But because you can't possibly get both of your hands back there very well and do the exercise there—though you might in some cases, if you have good reach, but as you get older like I am right now, it is awkward—I will give a variation.

Run your fingers down from your left ear—you will be able to find the optic nerve bundle in there [Fig. 11-1]. Now, you might be able to get the clearing exercise [Fig. 9-1] done back there, but for some people it will be awkward. So what I want to give you is a variation of the clearing exercise that can be done with one hand [Fig. 11-2].

This requires for you to hold your arm up like this. Take your thumb and curve it at the end as much as you can (not everybody's thumbs curve back

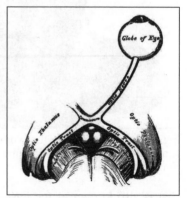

Fig. 11-1. Optic nerve bundle. (See Henry Gray, F.R.S., *Gray's Anatomy*, 15th ed. [1901; reprint New York: Bounty Books, 1977] 721.)

this far), and wrap your thumb around the nerve bundle. Then extend your two fingers. Blow out three times and imagine the air coming out of those fingers.

Now, this gesture requires the use of the breath as well since many people are, in fact, not able to use the other gesture. This is something

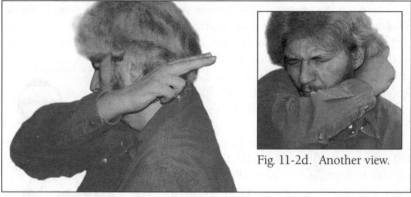

Gesture to Clear the Optic Nerve Area

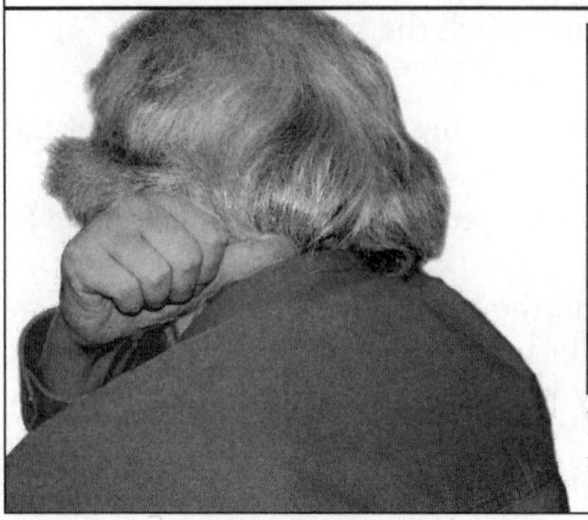

Fig. 11-2b. Another view to show how the thumb wraps around the neck.

Fig. 11-2a. Position your thumb like this at the optic nerve bundle at the back of the neck.

Fig. 11-2d. Another view.

Fig. 11-2c. Now extend your two fingers like this. Breathe out or blow out three times, and imagine the air coming out of those fingers. Do this when you need to clear the visioning process.

that is also known in the East, but I'm giving it to you now in order to clear those nerves that go up into your eyes. It also has to do with very important nerve areas for other parts of your body.

It can be used like this [blows outward]. You know that the air is coming out of your mouth, but imagine it coming out of your fingers. If you do it just so, this allows that area to become a little cooler. You might notice it, you might not. It depends where you are. But if you notice they're cooler, then you know that has done its job. If you don't notice it, don't worry about it, but practice it from time to time if your visioning does not improve.

This is good for the eyes?

It's good for the physical eyes, but it's also good for the visioning process. Sometimes you will talk to people (and many of you can identify with this) who, when attempting to do a creative visualization, are unable to see anything. They have imaginations, but they don't think of themselves as imaginative and have a hard time visualizing things. This is because their mind tells them they have to close their eyes and actually see it. In fact, it is something that they are really remembering and the vision does not happen in front of the eyes as they expect it, but closer to the top of the head.

The visioning process happens up here around the top of the head, and the eyes simply take note of it. This gesture is intended to open up that capacity. As I say, it's particularly helpful for those who already are visioning and also helpful for those who feel that this is something they cannot do.

Now, it's only necessary to call extra energy to come into that area when you want to clear it. And if you have a process you follow for visioning, just continue to follow it—whatever works for you. Different people use different methods.

Trauma Stored in the Bones

You said we store trauma in the bones?

Often you will store trauma in the bones. Sometimes when people develop certain bone diseases, it is a result of stored trauma, but not always. This is one cause of various bone diseases. Very often you will store it in your bones because the tissues can hold it for only so long before they become discomforted.

So if you have not processed the trauma in some way or danced it out, as we might do in our time, then it will drift into the bones. Eventually, the bones will start to ache. By that time, it might be too late to dance it out, but there are still other processes that people can help you with to release it.

Is that a cause of arthritis or stiffening of the joints?

Sometimes it is a cause of that. One of the reasons people get arthritis—I'm talking about arthritis that comes in old age, not the kind that younger people get—is because they were restricted in some way, meaning that some natural talent or ability they had when they were younger was disapproved of. As a result, they were unable to tap into or utilize their natural abilities in their adult life because they were being motivated or restricted by that sense of what's right and what's not right.

In their adulthood, these people are never really able to find the things that they do easily and naturally, or they are unable to find all of them, and sometimes—not always, but sometimes—that is a significant contributing factor to older-age arthritis. Certainly, there are physical reasons for arthritis as well.

So the general clearing would be useful for this, for trying to clear the trauma from all the different bones and joints?

Yes.

Nothing specific for that?

No, not at this time.

Releasing Judgment on Your Hips

A lot of people in your time have ambivalent feelings about their hips. The hips are intended to do several things: one, they are a temporary storage place for discomforts that have not been processed; two, they are intended to be the primary flexibility place in the body; three, they are associated with great strength of the body; four, they are particularly associated with the body's capacity to feel at home on Earth, which is very important; and five, they are also associated with the body's capacity for adaptability.

If we realize that the hips are doing all of this, then we have to understand that this is why the hips sometimes look unusual from person to person. One person's hips might be very narrow, yet they are doing all those things; another person's hips might be very wide, and they are also doing all of those things.

First, you need to adjust something. In your time I recognize that there are certain attitudes that don't exist in my time. So I'm going to address the attitude that is especially prevalent in the Western world (of which you are a part) about people's hips being too big. I want to give an exercise to help you to release judgment on your hips, whether you think they're too big or too small (some people think their hips are too small).

Give me a moment. I have to try different things because it's not something I use in my time. Here is the gesture [Fig. 11-3]. I might add that the best way to do this gesture is sitting, but you can do it standing if you prefer or if it is necessary.

This position is to release judgment. Try to hold the position for at least five minutes. I recommend doing it while you're sitting in an armchair. Do that from three to seven days in a row, as many as you can manage. Seven days is best, but you might not be able to do that. Something will interrupt you or you will forget, but try to do it at least three days in a row. It would be best to do it at the same time of day, so your body will prepare for it.

Before sleep? Is there any better time?

Whenever you wish. But try to do it in an environment where there is nothing going on, no radio, no television, no conversations—in short, as quiet as you can make it. You can use earplugs if necessary. Try not to think too much.

Gesture to Release Judgment on Your Hips

Fig. 11-3b. Another view of the finger position.

Fig. 11-3a. This is not the gesture; I'm just demonstrating the position of the fingers.

Fig. 11-3c. Another view of the fingers.

Fig. 11-3d. A final view for clarity.

Fig. 11-3e. Here is the actual position of the hands for the gesture. Do this while sitting, if possible, and hold for at least five minutes. Repeat the gesture at the same time every day for three to seven days in a row. Wait five days, then do the general clearing gesture [9-1].

These are the conditions that are optimal, but not all of you will be able to create optimal conditions, so do the best you can. If you're not able to create these optimal conditions, then just try to do it at the same time every day for the full seven days. This is the first level to release judgment on your hips. If you do not have judgment on your hips, you do not have to do this. It's only for people who have judgment on their hips, which I recognize is something that occurs in your time.

Clearing and Recharging the Hips

Now, in order to help the hips, you can do the standard clearing exercise as was shown before [Fig. 9-1], and you can do that in the way that was mentioned before. Then wait at least a week or ten days and do this exercise to attract energy that will be of most benefit to your hips [Fig. 11-4].

You want to try to complete this gesture in all of its positions as closely as you can, but as I say, some variance is allowed for what feels right to you. Start at the top and move down to the final position in the time of about ten to fifteen seconds. What you are actually asking, without saying it, is for energy to come from above to your hips. That's what the gesture means.

Gesture to Attract Energy of Benefit to the Hips

Fig. 11-4a. Here is position one.   Fig. 11-4b. Position two.

Fig. 11-4c. Position three.

Fig. 11-4d. Position four.

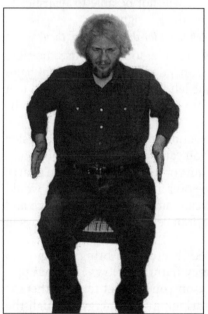

Fig. 11-4e. Position five.

Fig. 11-4f. Position six. Do this seven to ten days after you've cleared this area using the general clearing gesture. The entire gesture should take ten to fifteen seconds. Doing this once is enough, as long as you've cleared. If it's necessary, you can do this three times over three days, but not in a row. Do it at the same time each day.

How long do you do that one? How many days?

Actually, once is enough.

Really?

As long as you've cleared.

How many days between the judgment gesture and the general clearing gesture?

About five.

Then you do the clearing and wait seven to ten days to do the gesture to attract beneficial energy. That's a big one.

Once is enough. If you feel that you need more energy in that part of your body, if you are older and for some reason feeling a little less vigorous, you can do it three times, but not in a row. Do it once and then wait . . . do it over three days. Try to do it at the same time of day.

The best way to do this is outdoors in the Sun, but do it in whatever way you have available to you.

Clearing Shoulder Tension to Allow a Natural Flow of Energy
What about the stress we store in the neck? How do we get at that?

You mean along the shoulders here, in terms of carrying some pains? Again, you will have to use the one-handed clearing exercise with the breath [Fig. 11-2], because you will not be able to realistically put both of your hands over there to do the job right.

You used the right hand. Can you use the left hand for the other side, then?

You can, but I recommend, if you are able, to try and use the right hand for both sides, even if you are left-handed, because the right hand is more of a hand that projects and the left hand is more of a hand that receives. So if you're trying to blow out of the fingers, it is going to be easier with your right hand.

Try to do perhaps four to five exhalations, blowing out for each side depending upon how much tension you carry in that part of your body. You will know, because either it will hurt or it won't. If you don't carry too much, then doing it once or twice over a period of two days would be enough. But if you carry a significant amount of tension there and it's a constant source of irritation, do it once a day for fourteen days in the manner I described.

Now, I'm not going to give you an exercise to bring energy into that part of your body, because energy naturally flows into that part of your body for all of you. The reason you will get tension there is that some of you have difficulty in bringing that energy through the rest of your body, so it backs up and tends to be felt as pain through these shoulder areas.

So clearing that will allow the energy to flow naturally.

It ought to help the energy to flow naturally, but in order for you to feel if that might be a factor for you, it might also be useful to give you this exercise, which is strictly intended for after you do the clearing for as many days as you need to do it. Then the next day, if you want to, you can add this exercise [Fig. 11-5]. You can do it standing or sitting, whichever way you wish.

Now hold that position for about twenty seconds or so (up to a half a minute is acceptable) and blow out three times, imagining the air going down your fingers. Or if you prefer, imagine the air going down your legs, either one.

This is not really intended to clear but to open the avenues by which the energy passes down your body. So we're not really clearing anything out here. We're just opening the avenues to get that energy that's been trapped up in your shoulders down into the rest of your body.

Gesture to Open the Avenues by Which Energy Passes Down Your Body

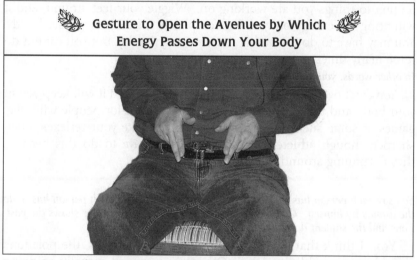

Fig. 11-5a. Reach down to the bottom of your rib cage on either side. This is the hand position; the hands are situated right under the rib cage. Hold for twenty to thirty seconds, and then blow out three times, imagining the air going down your fingers or legs. Do this only after you've done the clearing for as many days as you need to do it.

Fig. 11-5b. Another view. Notice that the fingers aren't touching the body.

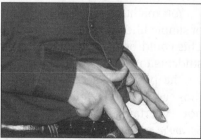

Fig. 11-5c. A third view.

A Simple Grounding Exercise

Some people don't actually occupy their bodies, they float. Are there any exercises for grounding them, for really bringing the whole spirit body down into the physical realm?

Zoosh once gave a grounding exercise that is very simple: Just move your feet around in your shoes, or if your shoes are off, wiggle your feet around. Just wiggle them around. It's best to do it on the ground. This immediately brings your physical attention down to that part of your body, and as a result, your energy rushes down there.

It works best if there are not any other distractions; if the television is on or you're reading a magazine, it won't work as well. But if you are just sitting there, wiggle your feet around. This is particularly useful if you work at an office and feel you need to be sharper or pay closer attention to things you are working on. Wiggle your feet around, and it will bring the energy body down completely inside your physical body. You may have to do this many times during the day, but you cannot do it too many times.

In other words, you're saying you can't overdo it?

You can't overdo it. Do it as often as you like, and it will keep you in your body and make you much more alert. Even for people who play games or some such thing, this will tend to make your reflexes much sharper, though athletes, of course, do not have to do this because they're running around.

Teaching the Gestures

You say each person has to do this by himself. But in yoga, each person has to do the asanas by himself. Could there be a class where the instructor shows the positions and the student does the gestures to learn them?

Yes. I think that would be useful, but if it's a class, the positions should not be held very long. Otherwise, you will actually be doing them. So if you're going to teach the positions, you want to make sure that the positions are done out away from the body as far as the hands can easily reach, so that the body knows this is not the actual ceremony.

You might create illustrations that a person could follow, a booklet of simple line drawings to show the positions with simple explanations. This could be easily condensed, and then in the class you would help students to get the positions just right. But you would allow them to alter the positions according to their body's feedback on the basis of those good feelings in the chest or solar plexus area, what feels right or not. A certain amount of latitude must be allowed.

So you're saying that they can't actually do the ceremony there, that they have to learn the positions and then go home alone and do the ceremony?

Yes, or go out onto the land somewhere and do it.

Clearing and Charging the Spine

The spine has got to be an important focus here, but you can't get to it.

We have a challenge with the spine, but we can get to it. If you can reach your arm around—people with certain conditions might not be able to do this—you can do the one-handed clearing exercise [Fig. 11-6].

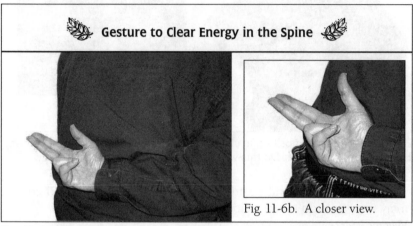

🌿 Gesture to Clear Energy in the Spine 🌿

Fig. 11-6b. A closer view.

Fig. 11-6a. Hold over the area of the spine and exhale three times. Do this at the same time of day for six to seven days. Wait three days, then do the charging gesture.

Hold the position over the spine and exhale three times. If you feel the energy is blocked up there, move your hand down a bit and exhale three times again. Don't just exhale but blow, as mentioned before.

So you can touch the spine anywhere, you don't have to get up to the top of it.

Well, you can't realistically get to the top of it unless you are very flexible indeed. That is a way to clear energy, but to charge energy, one would assume that putting one hand at the top of the head and one at the base of the spine would be the way to do it. But that's not the way I was taught. This is what I was taught [Fig. 11-7].

Do the clearing as indicated, perhaps six to seven days. Always try to do these at the same time of the day if you can, but you might not be able to. Do the best you can. Wait three days, then ask for energy to come into that part of your body in that fashion.

Do this if you feel you need the energy, or if, for instance, you are going to have to exert yourself a great deal, perhaps do some very heavy labors or walk a great distance or anything else you feel your spine might be helping you with. I will do this sometimes when I know I have to walk quite a distance, because the spine gives so much strength to the body.

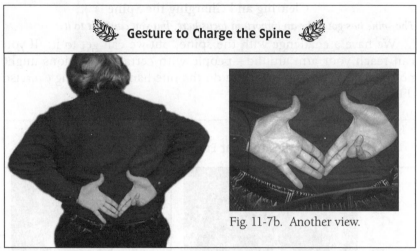

Gesture to Charge the Spine

Fig. 11-7b. Another view.

Fig. 11-7a. This is the position to charge the spine after you've done the clearing. Hold for thirty seconds. Do this whenever you feel you need the energy.

Try to hold that hand position for about thirty seconds. Of course, in my time we didn't have a clock and we used other methods.

What methods?

Oh, sometimes I would simply look at a tree or the animals around me and I would just know how long to hold it. I would look at things in nature or I might ask a specific leaf on a tree to move when I had done enough.

What an interactive process!

They can do that. They are happy to help.

Look what we've lost! A clock cannot give you anything that is of nature. It can't tell you when you've had enough.

That's right, and if you have a connection with the plants and trees in your time, by all means if you are near one, ask, just as I did. But practice with the tree first to see if it will move for you or if it wishes to do so or help you in this way.

This is obviously a tree you were already familiar with?

Yes, or one that is used to seeing you walk by regularly. We had become greeters.

Thank you very much.

Connecting with the Earth

Speaks of Many Truths
September 29, 1999

his is Speaks of Many Truths. Let's talk about this side of the head. I'm pointing to the left temple right around the ear and to some extent the area radiating up a little past the temple into this region of the head.

Above the ear.

The Red Sea Helps Process Sleep Trauma

This part of your body actually relates to a portion of the Earth—it relates to the Red Sea. The Red Sea may be involved in something similar, but for the most part, it is probably doing its own thing. But when it comes to parts of the head, since the head is so highly involved in the nervous system and the running and managing of the body's mechanisms, one sometimes (not always) finds parts of the head relating to a mountain or a body of water.

The Red Sea tends to give energy to this part of the head, usually just before you go to sleep and occasionally just before you wake up. This part of the head relates quite a bit to emotional traumas that occur within sleep. One normally does not consider the traumas that take place within sleep except for nightmares, and yet there are dreams and other events that take place during sleep that the conscious mind does not consider or realize. This usually occurs in those late evening or early morning hours of your personal sleep cycle (I recognize that some people sleep at different hours). Then when you wake up, you are left with a perhaps uncomfortable feeling that is often misidentified because of something or someone in the room, when in fact it has to do with a sleep event.

I've given the clearing exercise before [Fig. 9-1], but let me talk a little bit about the events that might occur. Of course, as I mentioned, there are nightmares, but also sometimes when you are in deep slumber and involved with your teachers, guides and other counselors, they will take you to see something either in your own life or—if it is more useful for the example—in the lives of others (usually on this planet, but not always). Occasionally, this will be a shock—if not an unpleasant shock, then a shock of recognition. Such things do occur at the deep levels of sleep, which is why psychoanalysis is such a valuable tool, because it probes such areas as the unconscious.

Therefore, I feel that this—especially in concert with psychoanalysis or ongoing psychological counseling—is an important area to energize and align with the Red Sea. If it is aligned, there is a better chance that such traumas, shocks or at least discomforts occurring at the deep sleep level might be processed in some way that the conscious mind can recognize and become involved in, which is useful.

Aligning with the Red Sea

So I want to give a series of gestures I feel will help in this process. Here is the first gesture [Fig. 12-1]. Hold this for about fifteen seconds. Let me say that the fingers are not actually touching the head, though

Gesture One to Help Align with the Red Sea

Fig. 12-1a. Gesture one: The fingers are not actually touching the head. Hold about fifteen seconds, then move to gesture two.

Fig. 12-1b. A second view.

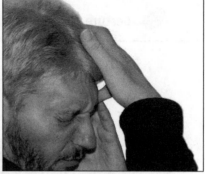

Fig. 12-1c. A third view.

in that first gesture they're very close. But the practitioner (the reader) can play with it until it feels just right, especially if you get heat.

Now here is the second gesture [Fig. 12-2]. Again, hold this for fifteen seconds.

🌿 **Gesture Two to Help Align with the Red Sea** 🌿

Fig. 12-2b. A second view.

Fig. 12-2a. Gesture two: Hold for about fifteen seconds, then do the third gesture.

And now there will be one more gesture [Fig. 12-3]. (Your elbows can rest on the arms of the chair.) Hold this position for fifteen seconds.

Communication in the Deep-Sleep State

This will help to clarify, even purify to some extent, this part of the body's connection with the Red Sea, in hopes that things discussed at deep levels of the sleep state . . . really, your physical body is in a sleep

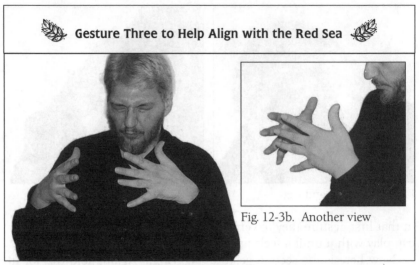

🌿 Gesture Three to Help Align with the Red Sea 🌿

Fig. 12-3b. Another view

Fig. 12-3a. Gesture three: Again, hold this for fifteen seconds. This entire series is done once, so your conditions should be as optimal as possible.

state, but your soul (or as Zoosh says, your immortal personality) is discussing your life as it is going along. So the kind of profound discussions that happen after life (that your soul personality is aware of because it's focused there) also take place all during your life.

Now, we cannot bring this into the total conscious mind because very often it will involve discussions of things that were said before this life or examples of previous lives, concurrent lives or future lives. In short, you might discuss everything that's going on for you in your given physical life as it's occurring now in relation to everything else you've been doing, are doing or might do, if any of those things are important to helping you understand at the soul level what's going on and why.

That's the approach. At the soul level, it's what's going on and why. There is no attempt to make sense of it. The conscious mind needs to hear linear communication, but this communication is happening vertically, meaning that a great deal is going on at every moment of communication, which the soul personality can absorb.

This is part of the reason why when you wake up, your dreams are disjointed. You remember bits and pieces, almost as if you were to take a candy cane and break it up and just pull out a few pieces and say, "Here it is," but obviously there are some things missing. You get the general drift of the shape, but there's a lot missing. It's like that.

So my hope is to accentuate those extra pieces, because very often, especially for people who work regular hours, you will get up with an alarm clock. And as you know, for most of you, your dreams evaporate with alarm clocks.

If possible, we want to create an opportunity to bring up enough of this communication that goes on in your deep level of sleep that your conscious mind might then be able to pull up a piece or two that would be useful to think about or to discuss with counselors, friends, philosophers or what-have-you. That would be helpful in moving through this time of profound transition.

This Time of Transition: Releasing the Old Timeline

As you know, this is a time when timelines are being changed. Everybody is having their limits literally thrown in their faces because they need to let go of the old lines. It's almost like being in the studio, and the film in which you are performing is being rewritten. They literally take your old lines, throw them out and hand you new lines. It not only changes the way the story is told, but it actually changes the way you have to play the character. That's what's really going on now.

The way you have to be in terms of what you demonstrate with your personality must now be in much closer alignment to your true personality. As you know, most of you either feel you must confront or are genuinely confronted with the fact that you have to alter your personality in order to get along with other people in the situations you find yourself in day to day.

But since this circumstance is going on for everyone at this time, everyone is being—you know I want to say gently, but I really can't say that anymore—quite firmly assisted in throwing away their own lines, which have to do with that adaptation to life, and having their new lines, which have to do with their true personality and character, shoved toward them. It's kind of in midstream, though.

Picture yourself holding onto a manuscript with your thumb and forefinger as the script person trys to tug it out of your hands. Meanwhile, the new script is being handed to you, but it's not quite in your hands yet. So it's a very unsettling, sometimes frightening, enervating experience, while at the same time there is a sense of anticipation and even a sense of excitement from time to time—pleasurable excitement knowing that something good is going to happen, something wonderful is going to happen, but you're not sure what. You have no details whatsoever.

That's why I feel that this system or alignment I've been discussing today would be helpful along those lines, and I may give more along those lines in the future since this is so profoundly topical.

This is the first time you've mentioned the physical body connecting to these places on Earth from the point of view of the physical body, and what that means.

From time to time I will mention that because it is a profound reality for certain situations. I won't say it on an ongoing basis because it isn't always so, but in some cases it is. I might not say it in other cases because it would overly complicate the situation, which I really don't want people to do. We must recognize that it is very possible that someone will pick up this book without having read any of the previous books, and we have to allow the book to stand on its own. So I don't want to confuse people.

The North Pole and the Inner Self

There's a spot at the very bottom of the chin—you can all reach and touch your chin, and you can clearly feel the bone here. Many of you have seen what the bone actually looks like. When you move your thumb and push up, you can feel where the bone stops and where the softer tissue begins. Right under the chin where you can feel that . . . if you're talking you can feel your muscles working there. Let's talk about that spot.

Here we have a relationship to a part of the Earth that is unusual—where most people who live on Earth will never go. It is possible that some of you will fly over this spot, especially those of you in the military service, but most of you will never go there. This place on your chin, as I mentioned, is related to the precise (even allowing for wobble) North Pole.

For many people who have gone very close to the North Pole, I realize that the circumstances are difficult, to put it mildly. You might or might not have noticed, but if you had a quiet moment, perhaps in a tent (granted, with the wind howling around you), you might have noticed that this part of your body felt unusually agitated. Of course, if you weren't warm enough, your teeth would be chattering, but most likely you would have planned ahead for such a cold place. So you might feel this.

Now, this might demonstrate itself in an unusual fashion. Those of you who've made this trip there, think back: You might have been either profoundly talkative, much more so than you usually are, or just the opposite—meaning if you are usually talkative or conversational, even on a polite basis, you just didn't feel like talking at all.

This spot at the bottom of the chin is important because it is part of the head. This part of the body has to do with that portion of the inner self (not to sound too psychological, because I will locate it a bit better) that has to do with the levels of personality you actually want to show to people. You are often very shy to do so because of your concerns about what people might think or not think, how they might act or their attitudes—whatever you have been trained in your society to fear. So that's another reason I feel this is an important spot to liberate.

Clearing the Chin to Liberate the Inner Self

Do the usual clearing gesture as given before [Fig. 9-1], and hold those gestures for fifteen seconds. If I don't say anything about holding the gestures, generally hold them for fifteen seconds.

I feel it's important to activate this area a bit. Since the North Pole has more energy than usual at this time and that part of the Earth is becoming more active in many ways, you might actually be able to not only create in your own sense of self, but also in your own body . . . this is right around the solar plexus area, where that desire to reveal the true you resides for most of you (except that once you're already revealed it, it tends to move up in a sort of V-pattern or a spread pattern).

The Melting of the Polar Icecaps

This area of the Earth is moving to a much greater activity level than it has been for a time. Mother Earth has decided that this is an area she can move around and do a lot with because not that many people live or even visit there. So as the scientists who are familiar with the area know, it is becoming much more active.

Now, to some extent the activity might be moving . . . I grant that this is only a possibility, but it might be moving just a little too fast. As many of you know, you are now moving into a time when the polar caps (especially the northern polar regions) are going to begin to melt, slough off, because it's a time to reveal the land that's under there for both spiritual and, to a much lesser extent, residential purposes, though very few people will live there.

For one thing, almost every country on the Earth will want to claim the area for scientific research, to say nothing of spiritual research, which is going to come closer and closer these days. Also, the fresh water that is frozen there needs to be disseminated to a greater degree in the oceans of the world because, as you know, the oceans have become profoundly polluted. There are some life forms in the ocean that not only serve you by exhaling oxygen, but in their own right have been quite decimated by pollution.

And fresh water, especially older fresh water (some of this ice is very old), is much more oxygenated than much of the water you use today. Therefore, it will serve those life forms that will serve other life forms that will, of course, eventually serve you. So this is another reason these regions are melting—not because there's supposed to be a flood to inundate (although I can understand your concerns about these matters because of previous circumstances).

What do you mean by "previous circumstances"?

Well, geologists, to say nothing of the Bible and older books, tell us that floods have made themselves known and can be scientifically tracked as having happened before. Therefore, there are some perhaps well-justified fears that if the polar icecaps melt especially quickly, there could be some significant impact, especially on coastal regions and low-lying states or countries, which might be true. However, if the caps melt just a little more slowly, a little more gradually, not a lot, there will be time to either move populations to higher ground or to alter the ground with massive construction efforts—creating something for such low-lying countries like Japan, for example, or other islands—in which a massive sea wall is constructed, not only around all the cities, but literally around the whole country. In many cases it would be something akin to a platform where you have maybe ten to twenty feet of very solid concrete structure upon which buildings and houses are put.

People will not like that for obvious reasons, but it will make it much safer. I'm not necessarily recommending this, but I am stating it because it will be a good short-term solution. Of course, ultimately the long-term solution is to move to higher ground.

Activating Your Chin to Encourage Physical Confidence and Slow the Ice Melt

I'd like to recommend you activate this area to help you have the physical confidence you need to bring forth these inner personality traits that you'd all really like to show and, most importantly, have others approve of. Of course, society is what it is, and maybe some people won't approve of them. Then you need to have at least the physical confidence to bring up or demonstrate these personality characteristics. Mental confidence, encouragement and psychological counseling alone will not be enough, because many of you have been hurt for various reasons. If you have the physical or body confidence, as I've called it before, you will not be so easily injured by even the most innocuous joke or a stinging comment made by an otherwise friendly person, to say nothing of wisecracks made by people who don't know you.

So let's see if we can activate that area with a series of gestures that will encourage and sustain this type of confidence [Fig. 12-4, 12-5 and 12-6]. Hold each position for about a minute. You can do these gestures three to five times, but I'd like you to space it out over time. Try to do them not more than once every three days. If you wind up doing them once every five days, that's all right, too. Do them the fourth or fifth time only if you feel you might need it.

Remember, this isn't something that we're focusing in thoughts. I want you to use your body feelings as much as possible (as discussed in *Shamanic Secrets for Material Mastery*) because they will tend to give you a clear picture these days of what may be safe for you. So look for that heat. That's why I'm giving you a certain amount of latitude in motion

Gesture One to Activate Physical Confidence and Slow the Ice Melt

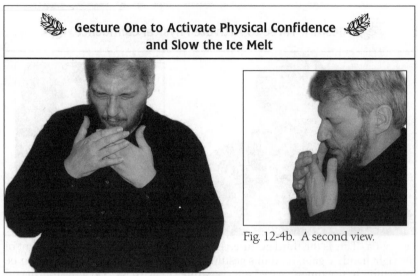

Fig. 12-4b. A second view.

Fig. 12-4a. Here's the first gesture to activate this area three days after it's been cleared. The right hand is slightly touching the left hand, but it is not in full contact. Hold this gesture for about a minute. Wait a few seconds, then move to the second gesture.

Gesture Two to Activate Physical Confidence

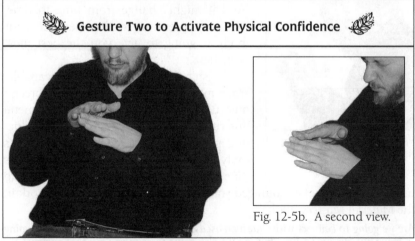

Fig. 12-5b. A second view.

Fig. 12-5a. This is the second gesture. Again, the hands are slightly touching. It can take as long as five minutes to set up this gesture. Hold this for about a minute, then do gesture three.

with the gestures, because the heat in your body will tell you if you have it just right.

If you don't have it exactly the way it is in the picture, but you're getting heat wherever you normally get heat for the love-heat exercise [see

🌿 Gesture Three to Activate Physical Confidence 🌿

Fig. 12-6b. A second view.

Fig. 12-6a. This is the third gesture. Notice that the left hand is now in front of the right hand. Again, hold this gesture for about a minute. This series can be done three to five times, spaced out every three to five days. Do it the fourth and fifth time only if you need to.

Fig. 12-6c. Another view of the third gesture.

pp. 7-8], then wherever you have the most heat, that's how to hold the gesture. And it might change from time to time. Just pay attention to that because your body is going to give you the best message here.

It isn't that your mind isn't capable. Your mind is capable of following precise instructions to the letter or at least general instructions, but it isn't capable of producing physical material mastery at all. It's only capable of understanding it. That's fine, but your physical body is the tool to use. So that's why I encouraged you and gave you a lot of groundwork in the *Material Mastery* book.

Are we going to connect with that increased energy at the North Pole? We're going to bring out our true selves, but are we also going to connect with that energy?

You're not going to consciously connect with it, but doing these gestures will tap that energy very slightly. I really can't give you a number, a percentage, a decimal point as to how much it will tap the energy, but as people begin to do this more and more, it will tap it just enough to slow down the process of the melt and the reemergence of the land by about 1.5 to 1.75 percent, which is just enough. I feel if the process goes forward in its current stage, it won't be catastrophically dangerous, but it might create some hazards that could be avoided as a result of do-ing this thing for yourself (though I cannot guarantee it).

So we're helping ourselves and we're helping the planet?

Yes, although I'd say it's not exactly helping the planet because what you are doing is you are helping other people on the planet.

How fast is this water going to melt? When is it going to start?

Well, it's not exactly clear to me, but it has started already. Those who are working in this field in this part of the world have brought it to the at-tention of others, even if it hasn't been published. But it might have been that they've noticed a little bit more melt or a little bit more motion in terms of the speed of the glacier or glacial movement. So this is probably being noted in the technical manuals at this time, if not for the public.

Is this the Larsen's ice shelf?

I cannot identify with that name.

There's been a lot of talk about that ice shelf melting and causing flooding all over the world.

It might very well be. This simply has to do with feeling a sense of allegiance to life forms other than human beings.

The Polluting of the Oceans and What Must Be Done to Clean Them Up

Plankton [phytoplankton] support human beings simply by exhaling the energy around these beings. The world's population of plankton [phytoplankton] has seriously diminished, and it needs to be much greater, not only for the animals that feed off it, but simply for the oxy-gen it provides you. The more you cut down trees or, for that matter, the more Mother Earth levels areas of trees partly in anticipation for human needs, the more the state of the oceans becomes increasingly critical.

Now, many people—oceanographers, biologists and so on—are probably fully aware of this and have probably been talking about it for a long time, but I need to talk about it as well, because the intention was (as near as I can tell) that eventually Mother Earth would clear land through lightning-caused fires. That might not be her purpose when she's using her lightning—she's usually purifying some part of her body or sometimes stimulating it—but she's also taking into account that more and more human beings exist on Earth in your time, and you need to live somewhere.

Mother Earth does not, as a rule, consider trees too highly as a source of oxygen or even plants on the land as a source of oxygen for human beings, because it was always intended that plankton [phytoplankton] perform that job. But as you know, with the pollution of the oceans . . . this is a serious threat. So as you begin to take a closer look at these things, realize that not only is the pollution of the oceans a problem, but more importantly, that workable, practical and real solutions need to be developed so that no, and I mean *no*—nothing from boats, nothing from land-based sewage companies and so on—*no pollution whatsoever goes into the ocean.*

Now, this can be done, but it would be a very big job. It would take lots of people and would make for lots of employment. And you actually have all the technology now that you need in order to do this work. You just need to make the choice to do so and to use various lands to build the plants to process all the pollution so that none goes into the waters.

Over time you might need to clear a significant amount of pollution dumped in barrels—to say nothing of military hardware that was either unintentionally or, occasionally in an emergency situation, deliberately thrown into the ocean—because in time that will in some cases pollute as well, especially if the dumped material is located near underground earthquake regions or volcanic regions under the sea. The sea itself has a pretty good system for holding in place things that are dropped into it through the incrustation of life forms and sediment, but it is likely that once you get these big factories set up—though they are not actually producing a product, but they will have byproducts that will be useful—and get the system in order, people will start saying, "Okay, let's clear out the oceans."

For those of you in college who are looking around for a career, think about this: This is a growth industry, and within twenty years it will be thoroughly established all over the Earth, because by that time, there will be some form of global organizational system that says, "We don't want to do this, but we must." It will not have an iron fist and govern by bullets and guns, but will simply say, "We must do it. There is no choice. And if this country isn't going to do it or is too poor to do it or doesn't have the will to do it, then we" (meaning the global organizational system) "will go in and do it."

They will have the power to tax, of course, and they will. They'll tax those governments to the extent that the governments can pay, but not to crush them. The poorer countries will have to be supported by the richer ones, but the poorer countries produce the same kind of pollution in many cases, because it's organic pollution that very often causes the problem. Granted, chemicals are a serious problem, but there's much more organic waste.

So the issue is simply that whether the county can afford it or not, the richer countries will have to do this simply because what the poorer country is dumping into the ocean (even if they don't want to) is still going to affect the richer country. So it pays for that country to do it.

Pollution and the Icecap Melt

If you looked at the Earth as a round ball and you were looking down from the top at the North Pole, how many miles out from the center would be free and clear of ice?

Most likely, there would still be some ice that ranges out five, ten or fifteen miles; it would be in kind of a jagged pattern. It might even go out twenty-five miles in places, but that's about it. It's going to melt off quite a bit, and it is possible, depending on which way things go, that all of that will melt off completely.

How much would that raise the oceans and the water on the land now—an inch, a foot?

I do not know. Probably that information is available somewhere and can be accessed, but it will make a big difference. That water has been in reserve, like in a bank. It's been in reserve for all these years in case you need it. You see, if your systems had been in place for the past sixty or eighty years to treat pollution and the oceans hadn't been polluted and all of that business, there would be no talk about melting polar icecaps.

So this is being done deliberately by Mother Earth?

Yes, this is a contingency plan that is to be used by her, and she feels it is needed.

Last week we discussed this new system of humans giving energy to those who are suffering, that we would need that water . . .

The possibility exists that people would want to transform water into its component parts to use in other ways as they have been gradually doing more and more in recent times. So that's another reason you need to have more water. Of course, there is a significant amount of water underground, but most of that water will not be available to you. Mother Earth holds vast amounts of water far underground in places that you have no technological means of getting to without seriously damaging the planet to the point of catastrophic consequences—and I mean quick.

How deep are you talking? Miles?

Many, many miles. Yes.

What about the South Pole? Is that going to stay the way it is?

It is certainly possible that it will melt as well. I feel that the North Pole will start it off, but the South Pole will probably also melt. So people—especially in island nations or, more important, in island nations that are low-lying—will have to make long-range plans about this. Populations will probably have to be moved, if not up, then away.

And there will have to be a very firm authority here. It does not have to be cruel, but there will have to be some understanding that whoever owns the land being inundated by water, that has become a beach, still owns it, but it may in fact not be usable anymore. Now, there will be some struggle over that—wrangling, as you say—but people will have to face this. This is a physical fact, and it's coming.

I want to warn you about this or add my voice to the fact that it's coming so that you can take measures and make plans and understand that as soon as you get a system in place to stop polluting the oceans—and, of course, you'll also have to stop polluting the rivers—if you should do this sooner rather than later, you'll find that within five to ten years of that being in place (as Mother Earth moves slowly forward and slightly backward) that she will probably taper off the weight of the melt.

The Florida Keys?

Yes, many beautiful places. Some countries will certainly be seriously at risk.

Island countries?

Yes, and coastal regions of other countries that are quite low to the surface. Beach property.

Accessing Your True Nature

Okay, that's the connection with the Earth. Let's look at the implications for the self. This allows us to start accessing our true nature, you said.

Well, having physical body confidence to bring up the qualities that are not hidden but that you are shy or genuinely fearful to demonstrate to others. Very often you will see this in a circumstance where someone . . . for instance, perhaps there is a program, a play or a moving picture, and people are there, and they all laugh uproariously at some point, but then they stop laughing. Or perhaps at a party some one laughs uproariously and then catches himself or herself and then stops. This is but one tiny example.

But, more to the point, there are certain happy qualities or thinking qualities or, in short, qualities that people have and know they have (so these are not hidden qualities), yet they are too shy to demonstrate these to the people around them—to family or friends or to people they are exposed to—because they don't wish to be disapproved of. The idea is to increase body confidence so that even if there is some disapproval, you can still demonstrate these qualities regardless.

You see, that's why it's so important. Outside approval will become less important. That's quite valuable, because if the people you see walking around on the street or the people you work with or know or family members were demonstrating their true personalities—and I'm not just talking about whether they're angry, that's not it, but actual character traits in the personality—it would stimulate other people and stimulate solutions and just generally improve the quality of life. So we need to support that.

Clearing the Right Eye and
Activating Your Clear Vision

Since we're focusing on the head, let's stick with that. Now, this eye, the right eye—not the bony structure around it, but just the eye itself (which must be touched very gently, of course)—aside from what it is obviously involved in, is also involved in clear vision.

Now, let me explain what I mean by clear vision. It's quite obvious that clear vision has a physical aspect, but clear vision from my point of view also has to do with several other things. One is mentally understanding something completely out to its various steps, completely and clearly understanding it. And we all know that very often things are so vague that it's hard to get a grasp on what it means in terms of its ultimate ramifications.

Clear vision also has to do (especially with those who are spiritually inclined) with the visioning process—seeing what might be coming, or feeling it or sensing it in whatever way so that you know something is coming. Then you can help your family, yourself, your people (whoever you help) to be aware that this—whatever it is—is coming and to get happy or serious or do whatever you need to do to take this on. That's what I mean by clear vision.

Now, let's try to activate that area in a way that will support clear vision as described. This does not relate directly to any part of the Earth. Always use the general clearing gesture [Fig. 9-1], and then, as usual, wait with any clearing gesture for three days before beginning the other gestures. Some of the gestures from time to time come very close to each other (and I'll let you know when), but that's not surprising since many of them have dual purposes.

All right, here are the gestures [Fig. 12-7, 12-8 and 12-9]. We're going to want to hold these gestures for this particular work about twenty seconds.

Is clear vision like long vision?

For some people, it will help with long vision; for others, it might just help in the visioning processing as mentioned, or possibly even in a vision quest if you're going to prepare for that. If you are unable to get the vision you're looking for, you might also try these gestures when you're out on the mountain or wherever you go.

Long vision is something that is taught as a process, but this could help to prepare an individual for the process and perhaps make the process something easier to learn. It is not really meant to help the physical vision. If it does, that's wonderful, but it's not meant to do that.

Gesture One to Support Clear Vision

Fig. 12-7b. A second view.

Fig. 12-7c. A third view.

Fig. 12-7a. This is the first gesture. Begin this series three days after clearing the right eye. Hold for twenty seconds, then move on to gesture two.

Gesture Two to Support Clear Vision

Fig. 12-8b. A second view.

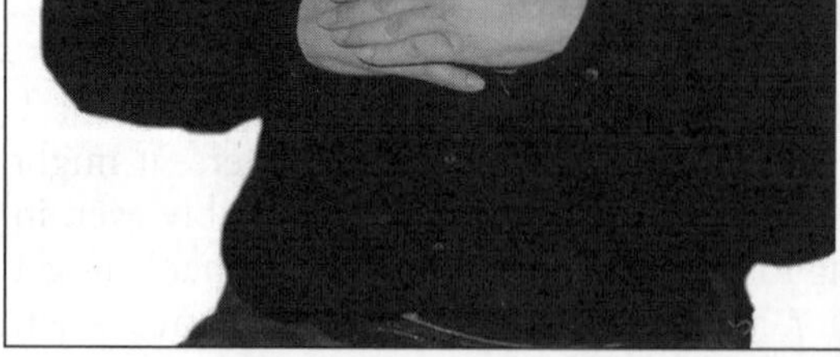

Fig. 12-8a. Here's the second gesture. The hands are not quite touching each other. Hold for twenty seconds, then do the third gesture.

Fig. 12-8c. Another view of gesture two.

🌿 Gesture Three to Support Clear Vision 🌿

Fig. 12-9a. Here is the third gesture. Again, hold for twenty seconds.

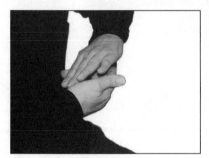

Fig. 12-9b. Another view.

Fig. 12-9c. A third view of gesture three.

Communication of the Heart

Speaks of Many Truths
September 30, 1999

This is Speaks of Many Truths. We talked about the right eye yesterday. Let's talk about the other eye today.

The left eye.

The Left Eye and Feeling the Heart Sensations of Others

When I refer to this eye, again I'm not talking about the bone structure around it, but only the eye itself. This eye has to do with feeling the heart sensations of others. To a minor degree it has to do with being aware of your own heart sensations, but mostly it has to do with sensing the heart sensations of others. The actual sense of that, the actual physical awareness of the heart sensations of others, will probably be felt here on the physical body.

But for those of you having particular difficulty in communicating with others . . . perhaps in some personal or even business relationships, you are constantly having misunderstandings. This might mean that the person who is speaking to you—or that you yourself, for that matter—is not speaking mentally in alignment with the way his or her heart feels. Since the heart signals feelings and since that is the first line of communication your body will pick up, if that person's words are in conflict with his or her feelings, then misunderstandings are sure to ensue—if not immediately, then at some point. It is not always easy for an individual to be in alignment with his or her heart, to speak the heart's feelings, but in a couple of situations, this is particularly important, especially in moments of sincere conversation between the two who are involved.

In order to access a greater clarity with the eye (obviously you also use your eye to see), I'll give a series of gestures that will help you to either have a clearer understanding of whoever's speaking to your heart feelings, or to be more quickly alerted to the fact that what is in a person's heart is not what's coming out of that person's mouth. And if he is a conscious person, you might be able to at some point if he asks you or if there is an opening—and this must be done very delicately—mention that . . . don't criticize him, but what you say is, "You know, there are exercises to attune your heart to your mind." Most people will talk from their mind and not from their heart, suppressing their heart, believing that the mind is better than or somehow superior to the heart's communication. Of course, it's just the opposite.

However, if that person believes that, if you say to him "to attune the heart to the mind," he will be able to hear that. Whereas if you tell him what I've just explained—that the heart is a much clearer communicator, that it is much more likely to speak the total truth of any individual—he will immediately set up blocks and barriers. The mind is always floundering around attempting to find the truth for itself and others. So we don't want to speak to him in that way.

You may know other ways to speak to that individual as well, but never speak to him in a commanding way. This is especially important for business communication. If you try to speak to him in a way that forces him to look at something he's not prepared to look at, he will just entrench his position and, most likely, communication in the future will be worse. So it's a delicate matter.

First, we want to heighten your capacity to know these things, and then you might be able to help others by knowing them. I might add that there are many people on your planet (perhaps 2 percent of the population—in the past it was much less, but there are almost 2 percent on your planet in your Now time) who are born with this natural ability. Often this will make life difficult for them when they are younger, because whatever is coming out of another person's mouth will not be their primary means of understanding that person. The primary means will be whatever's coming out of that person's heart, which will cause many conflicts in communication unless the individual who has that skill is able to express clearly that he or she *hears* feelings louder than words, putting it like that. If that's understood, then people who do this naturally will be able to be the most wonderful therapists in terms of aligning an individual with her own feelings so that she can speak her actual truth.

This is especially important for men, who in your time, in your civilization, are generally divorced from their feelings when they are young, and this gives them an authoritarian way to speak. In short, they are discouraged from speaking their hearts and encouraged to speak their minds in a pattern superimposed by somebody else. This is why so many men in your time are so totally confused, upset and angry. It's because they know something's wrong. They just usually don't know what it is, and for 90 to 98 percent of them, that's what's wrong. Once that's aligned, then everything else will fall into place much more quickly. So this is important.

In the future, people born with such talents will be sought out and have a natural profession. Though they might wish to do other jobs, that will be their natural profession. Nevertheless, this ceremony—I'm referring to the hand gestures as a ceremony because it's done in a way that's intended to be spiritual or sacred—is designed to improve that clarity in the average person who is not born with these abilities.

Clearing the Left Eye and Attuning the Heart to the Mind

First do the clearing gesture [Fig. 9-1], and then wait three days. Then do these gestures. Here is the first gesture [Fig. 13-1]. You're going to hold that first gesture for about forty-five seconds.

Gesture One to Attune the Heart to the Mind

Fig. 13-1a. Begin this first gesture three days after you've cleared the left eye. Notice that the hands are almost but not quite touching. It is so close that there is a sensation of touch. Hold for about forty-five seconds. Then move on to gesture two.

Fig. 13-1b. A second view.   Fig. 13-1c. A third view.

Again, I realize that you don't always have a clock lying around. You'll know how long to hold the gesture if you're utilizing the heat in your chest or solar plexus, wherever it shows up, as you were trained to do in *Shamanic Secrets for Material Mastery* and some of the *Sedona Journal of Emergence!* articles. If it is a little longer than forty-five seconds, that's all right, because as I say, you can't be glancing at a watch when you're holding something like a gesture.

If possible, work with these gestures in a place where a clock is available—it is all right to take a quick glance at the clock, but you want it to be the kind of clock that moves a second hand around so that you don't have to think. If you look at a digital clock, you have to think, but if a second hand is sweeping around from a position starting at the top of the clock, you can get a visual impression. This is much better, because I don't want you to think too much when you're doing this.

You don't want to be doing anything else when you're doing these gestures. Just focus on them. If you have trouble focusing and thoughts are coming up, it will be much easier if you open your eyes and study your hands closely as you do the gestures. Or go into the feeling of warmth in your chest or solar plexus as you are doing them. Then it will be much easier to have more focus.

Do not worry if random thoughts or words come up. That's not a problem. But do not be involved in a thinking process while you are doing this. It can weaken the impact, and that goes for any of the gestures or for any of the circumstances we've ever talked about.

Now let's do the second gesture [Fig. 13-2]. Ideally, we're going to hold the second gesture for about thirty seconds.

Gesture Two to Attune the Heart to the Mind

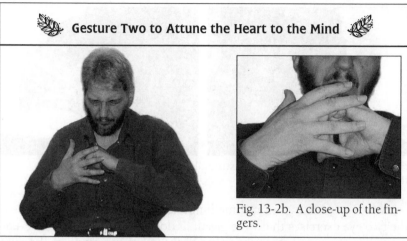

Fig. 13-2b. A close-up of the fingers.

Fig. 13-2a. The second gesture. Hold this position for about thirty seconds. Then begin gesture three.

Fig. 13-2c. A third view.　　Fig. 13-2d. A fourth view.

Now here is the third gesture, which you are also going to hold for thirty seconds [Fig. 13-3].

Gesture Three to Attune the Heart to the Mind

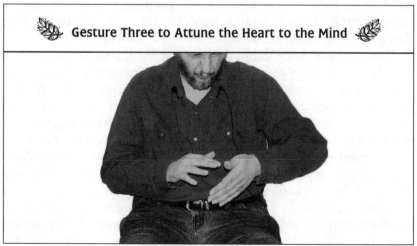

Fig. 13-3a. The third gesture, held for thirty seconds.

 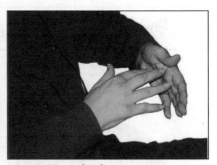

Fig. 13-3b. A second view of gesture three. Fig. 13-3c. A third view.

Now, I want to mention something that's very important in terms of the two eye exercises that were given. It does not matter whether a person is blind or cannot see in terms of the other functions of the eyes. You can still do these exercises and gain in these abilities, so don't be shy about that if you are unable to see. Even if some of you no longer have a physical eye, there will probably still be some residual tissue of the eye in there, even if it is scar tissue. If it doesn't work, all right, but you can try.

Your Natural Means of Communication

The biggest challenge to you all in the coming years—from this day forward, especially—is that you will be learning how to think, speak and act in what is an entirely new way for you here on Earth. Obviously, this is a way that you might think, act and speak in extraterrestrial lives or in higher-dimensional lives. But to go from what you have had here on Earth in your Now time to this process in the course of a life—meaning having to learn it physically compared to just naturally doing it in your higher-dimensional self—is a challenge.

You have been doing things the hard way, but this way—aligned with your heart, speaking your feelings, which will probably involve more hand gestures regardless of your culture or nationality—will come naturally to you because the heart encourages motion. When I say hand gestures, I'm not talking about the motions we've been doing, but general hand motions, how some people talk while moving their hands.

The mind encourages no motion at all. This is because the mind was taught at the very beginning by well-intentioned individuals that it is wrong. When you want to be right as a child (meaning you want to be loved and approved of), if you are told that you are doing wrong by an external authority you look up to or need to pay attention to for any reason, your first reaction is to freeze. This is why when many of you communicate, if you have not been taught the kind of conversation that comes from the heart, your tendency is to not move at all or to freeze. If you've been raised in a culture where the heart is a given part of the culture, then you are often encouraged to move your hands.

I'm not saying one way is right or one way is wrong. I'm explaining that it is natural to have some kind of motion when you are communicating because the heart is in motion all the time. One might say that many parts of the body are in motion all the time, and microscopically, certainly all parts of the body are in motion all the time. But the fact that the heart is the center of your physical being and without it you could not exist is not an accident. (Obviously, the heart is pretty much in the center of your being when you raise your arms over your head.) Creator does these things so that the message on a symbolic or visual or physical front is clear.

The communication of the heart is your natural way to be. You will find that many of the things I talk about now would be to support your natural means of communication. You were all born (with a few exceptions) with certain natural abilities; communication from the heart is one of them. You have your senses—your sense of smell and so on—and all of these things are designed to make it easy to communicate.

But since you want to challenge yourself—and that's important —you have chosen to create a complex web in the society in which you are now living, whatever that might be—any society that does not often approve of heart communication. This is not because heart communication is wrong or head communication is right. It is a challenge and should be totally perceived as a challenge. It does not mean that your culture cannot be honored through heart communication. It means that all cultures must build on the foundational principles of what actually exists.

A quick study of your history books will show that every time a culture has tried to superimpose its own idea of the ideal on what is the actual, it was doomed to fall, even if by brute force it had managed to survive for a time. But if you build even with the tiniest amount of energy (with no force at all) on something that is a solid foundation of absolute reality for your civilization, it takes almost no energy to build a culture that will live indefinitely and yet will benefit all people.

These things may be obvious, but it is important to mention them from time to time because they are very easy to forget in the complex societies you have evolved in your present time.

Aligning the Heart and Mind

You said the exercise was to know if the other person had his or her mind and heart aligned. Does it also align your own mind and heart?

It doesn't align them, but it will let you know. It will be more apparent to you when you are speaking from your head as compared to your heart.

It won't be a painful experience, but you will feel it as something that is separated, almost as if someone other than you is speaking. It won't be otherworldly, in that sense, but it will create for you a heightened sense of distance between what is coming out of your mouth and what is actually being felt in your body.

This is important because it will show you that what you are saying is very often in complete conflict with what you are feeling. Of course, if you are not communicating, you do not have to communicate everything you are feeling every second. But if what you are *saying* is in complete conflict with what you are *feeling*, you will always either be in internal conflict or external conflict—or both of those—in your world with people you meet and situations and objects you interact with. This is especially important, as I say, for people whose lives have become overly complex or who are constantly being nagged by misunderstandings. Either other people don't understand what you're saying, or you yourself feel ill at ease when you say something.

I realize that this may sound impractical. Obviously, there are some times when you may have to compliment someone when you do not believe it, but it is possible to make a compliment to somebody from your heart that is something you can truly believe (meaning you feel the truth of it). Then that person too will feel that you feel the truth of it. In short, many times you compliment somebody and that person doesn't take it in, or he or she says, "Well, all right," or something like that. That probably means one of two things: that person doesn't feel safe accepting your compliment, having something to do with his or her capacity for safety, or the person feels a conflict between your heart and your spoken word and thus cannot take your compliment sincerely.

Now, as I say, this does not always mean that there is something wrong with you giving the compliment in terms of your alignment. By alignment, you understand, we're not talking about what . . . a pen, please [draws Fig. 13-4]. It would seem that we are talking about something like this when you are using the term alignment, you understand, but in fact we are not. That is not alignment.

This is because of the desire in your time for the mind to be equal to the heart, but it never is—and I'll tell you why. In your time you are utilizing a function of the mind that is foreign to its natural condition. The mind is not naturally linear. So your desire to have the linear mind be equal with the heart's

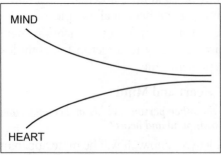

Fig. 13-4. This is not alignment.

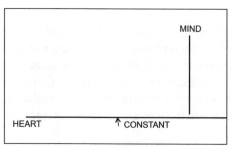

Fig. 13-5. The actual alignment between the heart and the mind.

capacity to communicate is not possible.

The mind truly functions, as has been said before, in an immediate state of what Zoosh calls vertical wisdom [see Appendix I]. So actual alignment between the heart and the mind is more like this [draws Fig. 13-5].

I'm acknowledging linear time by drawing the heart line. This is the actual alignment of the heart and mind. I'm drawing the mind vertically; that vertical way represents the "moment to moment." This would mean that the vertical line is always moving . . . the heart line is a constant. That's why I drew it as straight, because you are in linear time. But whenever you are speaking the heart, the mind contributes the words from your language. So whatever time you are in, whether you are here or here in terms of the chart, the mind moves with the heart. That is the actual alignment.

You are coming into that level of mentality now, which is why many of you are so forgetful. The linear mind requires recollection of the past, whereas the vertical mind does not require that at all. It is only available if necessary, but it is not available if it is not necessary. This is to your advantage, so you don't constantly remember things and hold on to things that may be entirely useless or perhaps even detrimental in that moment.

Now let's go on to the next part of the body that we want to clarify and perhaps heighten. I will not speak of certain parts of the body for this book. I'm not going to talk about the third eye and crown because so many others have. It's just going to complicate matters if I say things. In our time we do things for those parts of the body, but I am reluctant to speak of it in your time because so many volumes have been written about it. Perhaps for the next book.

Well, your perspective is totally unique. What we want from you is everything that is unique, that we can't get from anybody else.

Exactly, I understand now. Let's see what else we will do.

Clearing Your Magical Liver

Let's talk about the liver. It's over here somewhere, yes? Let's do the clarifying exercise to clear it [Fig. 9-1]. Here you want to do that a little bit differently than you've done it before. You want to try to hold each gesture for about a minute. Do the clearing exercise once a day, wait three days, and do it again. Then you're going to wait three days and do it again.

In short, you need to do the clearing exercise in a very *fixed* way. It needs to be done at the same time every day, give or take a few minutes obviously, but by a few minutes, I mean less than five. If for some reason you are unable to do the clearing exercise in that pattern, then wait five days and start over again, because the clearing of this particular organ is very important in your time when there are so many factors impacting it.

Aside from the decreased oxygen level, the pollutants and consumables are making a terrific impact on that organ, which it is really unable to deal with. So after the clearing exercise is done, wait about two days before you begin to do the other exercise that will support it. Let's talk about what the liver does besides its normal function.

The liver of any human being connects with all versions of water on this planet and inside this planet, including certain versions of water that exist at the seventh or eighth dimension. It literally provides you with the capacity to utilize fluids within your body in a way that is most harmonious to the physical body for a given amount of time. This raises the question, how long can you preserve life on this planet?

It would be a fixed amount of time (without radical alterations to the physical body), because those fluids at those higher dimensions allow the fluids in your physical body to function as well as they do, but not as well as they could optimally. This is to keep you from becoming overly enamored with life here and trying to project life here to be six or seven hundred years. Obviously, you have some inclination to do so since some of your holy books refer to individuals living that long, but they lived that long because life here at that time was at a slightly higher dimension.

Those versions of water at the seventh and eighth dimensions have a slightly oily feeling. If you were to rub them between your fingers at the seventh dimension, there would be a definite sensation of some type of viscosity. At the eighth dimension, it would be very pronounced and feel greasy.

These levels of water, as I say, assist the fluid process in your body and also regulate your life span. With a poorly functioning liver (at least a liver that isn't clear in terms of its spiritual ability), you will not only *not* be connected to all versions of water in a good way on Earth, but you will have a very tenuous connection to these seventh- and eighth-dimensional versions of water. It is those things that allow you to be physical, because your natural state is to *not* be physical. To be physical mass, solid, is unnatural for you, and it requires a great many factors functioning in harmony and rhythm to keep you in this unnatural state for as long as you are here in your physical body.

Heightening the Liver's Connection to All Versions of Water

Let's give the gestures now that will heighten and clarify the connection between your liver and all versions of water on and inside Earth, including the versions in the seventh and eight dimensions that, I might add, are the seventh and eighth dimensions of Earth. I was not clear about that before. Here is the first gesture [Fig. 13-6].

Don't we try to get it close to the liver itself? Do we focus . . .

That has nothing to do with . . . it's the hands, not the liver. I can assure you that when we do these gestures again at a later date, if we do, it will not be the same.

Why is that?

 Gesture One to Heighten the Connection between the **Liver and All Versions of Water**

Fig. 13-6b. Detail: This shows the right-hand fingers in the proper position.

Fig. 13-6a. Here is the first gesture. Do this two days after you do the clearing (following the specific clearing instructions for the liver). Hold for thirty seconds, doing this at the same time in the morning and the evening for three days, a total of six times. Then skip a day before beginning gesture two. If possible, do the gestures in this series outdoors.

Fig. 13-6c. Another view.

Fig. 13-6d. A fourth view.

Because the gestures are given in a holy way by teachers—some from the past, some from the future, some from other planets.

We never got around to photographing the other side.

That's all right. The body cannot hold these positions too long, you understand. In any event, should we do these for a special video at some point, they will be gestures that will also work. They will just be different. Some of them might be similar, but many will be entirely different. That is acceptable. The main thing is not whether it's the same; as you know, the main thing is whether it works.

What if you do a gesture one day and a different one the next day for the same purpose?

If I do it differently one day from the next? Then that's the way the teacher is showing me how to do it. Many of the gestures I'm giving you in your time are not used in my time because they are unnecessary. I'm giving you things for your time.

I didn't know you didn't already know them.

It's not a matter of knowing them or not. Occasionally, things would come up in my time. Perhaps somebody somewhere else—not our own people—might need something, and I might need to learn some gestures. But they would be for a condition that would not exist in our tribe.

In your history.

Therefore, I would need to ask a teacher to show me the positions that I would then show the other individual.

And you would see them visually, or would you feel it?

Yes and no, maybe visually, maybe feeling. I pay more attention to how I feel. I might see the teacher at a distance doing the gesture, but the communication that is the most profound and best is the feeling. I go with the nature of the feeling of the physical self. Then I know the gesture will work, even if there might be other gestures that will also work. That is always the case. Gestures always have an impact.

Is that it for the liver?

There is more. Here's the second gesture for the liver [Fig. 13-7]. And here's the third gesture [Fig. 13-8]. Now, there is a final gesture [Fig. 13-9]. I would like you to wait a week before you do it. This is unusual, but that is because the forms of water require time to process this for each individual.

The gesture is done by almost touching the ground. Try to do it in a place where there are no plants growing—a bare patch of ground or sand. In the case of wintertime, try to clear the snow and ice away from the land. However, if you live in an environment where snow and ice is on the surface all the time, as is the case in some places, then you

Gesture Two to Heighten the Connection between the
Liver and All Versions of Water

Fig. 13-7a. Here's the second gesture. Hold about thirty seconds. Do this once in the morning and once in the evening at the same time for three days, a total of six times. Then skip a day before moving on to gesture three.

Fig. 13-7b. A second view.

Fig. 13-7c. A third view.

Fig. 13-7d. A fourth view.

Fig. 13-7e. A fifth view for clarity.

Gesture Three to Heighten the Connection between the Liver and All Versions of Water

Fig. 13-8a. Here is the third gesture. Again, hold this for thirty seconds. Do this at the same time, once in the morning and once in the evening, over three days for a total of six times. Then wait a week before you move on to gesture four.

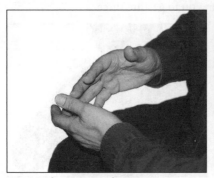

Fig. 13-8b. A second view.

Fig. 13-8c. A third view.

may do it over that surface—again, almost touching but not quite. Hold this last gesture for about fifteen seconds.

And you do these gestures just once?

Do that last gesture just once. Try to do the other gestures in the morning and in the evening. Or if you function under different hours perhaps, I will give you an idea of time: Try to do them anywhere between 6 and 8 A.M. in the morning and 6 and 8 P.M. in the evening. Those are the ideal times. If you cannot do them then, if other times are better for you, try to get it as close to those times as possible.

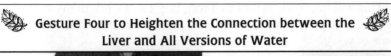

Gesture Four to Heighten the Connection between the Liver and All Versions of Water

Fig. 13-9b. A second view

Fig. 13-9a. Here is the fourth gesture, using the right hand only. Notice that the right hand is almost touching the ground, but not quite. Hold for fifteen seconds. Do this last gesture only once. It must be done outside.

Do these gestures in the morning and in the evening, trying always to do them at the same time so your body can prepare and receive and get the most out of this. You want to do this, as I say, once in the morning and once in the evening, six times. So you go through the first gesture—day one, day two, day three in the morning and day one, day two, day three in the evening. Then wait a day, skip a day. Then again do the next gesture, day one, day two, day three in the morning and day one, day two, day three in the evening, six times.

Then when you're done with the last sequence, wait five to seven days and do the fourth gesture. Always it is best to do these outside. If you cannot do them outside for any reason (which is possible for many of you), that is all right, except for the last gesture, which must be done outside.

Now, for some of you, you will not be able to do that last gesture outside. This is what you could do instead. Try to look out a window to a point on the ground and make that last gesture, aiming that gesture in the precise way of holding the finger toward that part of the ground as long as there are no human beings walking around there. If there are animals walking around, that's fine. (I realize that this is not going to be a factor for many of you, but for some of you it might be.)

This will not work as well that way, but it will work pretty well. Only do that if you are unable to go outside (which might be the case for some of you).

The Mental Desire to Extend Life on Earth

What if we want to clarify that connection to the seventh and eighth dimensions, but at the same time we want to live a little longer? Is there something that can be done to modify that?

You mean you want to live longer here? You want to enjoy life here longer, even though it is infinitely easier everywhere else?

Yes, what if? Maybe we started late and want to catch up.

No. That is the answer.

Well, it was a good try.

Not really, because life here . . . you get used to a level of pain, difficulty and discomfort here because it seems as if that is normal. It may be at your time, especially when life is perhaps unnecessarily complex, but it is totally unknown in other places.

To give you the means to extend your life here would be no different than to purposely injure you, because in your time so many people have no understanding of life away from this planet. There is so much desire to quantify everything through what I would call mental science that the average person desires to extend his or her life as long as possible so that he or she can mentally understand more. But, in fact, it is the heart that develops faith, because of its capacity to know absolutely the truth that life beyond in many ways is a simple fact.

I would not want to extend your stay in such a difficult place for even a day if I could avoid it. I realize this sounds harsh, but it's not because I don't have compassion for you—it's because I *do*.

The Purity of Water inside the Earth

That's fascinating what the liver does. Are there other functions that the liver performs? Is there anything else you can tell us about the liver?

That is the main thing it does. The waters on Earth are very flexible. They appear in many forms, but the waters inside Earth are rarely frozen. They might be in the form of mist or liquid, but the waters at the deep portions inside of Earth tend to be at their purest.

I will give you an example. One drop of that level of purity, one drop of that on or under the tongue, would greatly improve your capacity to resist illness. However, even with the most exotic tools that you have available now (and in the next eighty years), to drill or attempt to obtain that water would necessarily taint it.

Any contact that water has with any human beings living on Earth undergoing lessons in any version of the third dimension or denser (and in some cases the early portions of the fourth dimension) would necessarily affect all of those waters inside the Earth. So they need to be protected because they function with you at a distance. That is why they are so highly purified. Very little of that water is needed for masses of people.

So it's almost like the liver has long touch, then.

The liver has the capacity for this interaction. Long touch is perhaps an appropriate comparison.

More Supportive Gestures

Speaks of Many Truths
October 1, 1999

This is Speaks of Many Truths.   Greetings.
Welcome.

Do you have questions about any other body parts?
How about the adrenals?

Clearing and Assisting the Adrenals

The adrenals in your time will require an elaborate clearing procedure. I'd like you to do the standard clearing procedure given earlier [Fig. 9-1] once a day for two weeks. Always try to do it around the same time every day so your body can get used to it.

This is because, in your time, the adrenals are exposed to so much more activity than they really require or are intended to provide for. This is because of all the artificial stimulants you utilize for medical reasons, for consumables and even sometimes for activities that might not be required to survive but are part of your lifestyle. So we will take the clearing exercise to that extent. After the clearing, wait three days, and then begin the gestures to bring energy into the adrenals and also provide for their sustenance in the future.

Understand that the adrenals of human beings in your time can gain a significant amount of sustenance if they are connected to any sun that you can see or imagine. When I say imagine, I refer not only to the Sun that is in your sky, but also either to that Sun when it is on the other side of the planet and it is nighttime where you are, or—for those of you who are more astronomically inclined—to the suns that are simply representative of much of the light you see from the stars.

But that is up to you. Generally, I recommend the Sun that shines on the Earth, but as I say, it's not a requirement. So the first gestures are involved in assisting the adrenals, and the last gesture will have to do with connecting the adrenals to the Sun.

Here's the first gesture [Fig. 14-1].

Gesture One to Bring Energy to the Adrenal Glands

Fig. 14-1a. Here is the first gesture. Begin these gestures three days after completing the clearing process (following the specific clearing instructions for the adrenals). Hold this gesture for about twenty seconds before doing the next gesture, resting for one or two minutes in between.

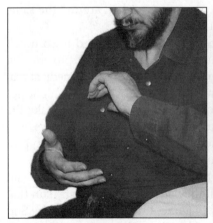

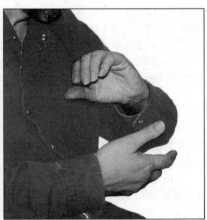

Fig. 14-1b. Another view.   Fig. 14-1c. A third view.

Hold that gesture for about twenty seconds. Then rest for a minute or two (no more than that) before doing the next gesture [Fig. 14-2].

🌿 Gesture Two to Bring Energy to the Adrenal Glands 🌿

Fig. 14-2a. Here's the second gesture. Hold for thirty seconds. Rest for about thirty seconds, then begin the third gesture.

Fig. 14-2b. A second view.   Fig. 14-2c. A third view.

The second gesture is held for about thirty seconds. Rest for perhaps half a minute, then begin the third gesture, which will connect the adrenals to the Sun [Fig. 14-3].

The Adrenal Glands Keep You Focused in the Physical World

Let's talk a little bit about the extended function of the adrenals, aside from their function in your physical self. The adrenals have a great deal to do with ongoing events, not only in your immediate physical world, but also in what I would call supporting universes, what you

---

Gesture Three to Bring Energy to the Adrenal Glands

Fig. 14-3a. This third gesture will connect the adrenals to the Sun. Hold for one and a half to two minutes.

Fig. 14-3b. A second view.

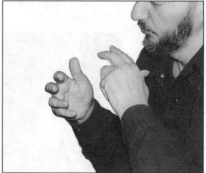

Fig. 14-3c. A third view.

sometimes refer to as parallel worlds. But "parallel worlds" is a confusing, overused term. I don't like to call them that because you are not focused in them. If you were focused in them, they would simply be your world. So let's use the other term.

Therefore, in these other places, these energies are what's really going on. What the adrenals are doing is supporting the barriers—or the veils, if you like—between these worlds to keep firm the world you are focused in. In that sense, they keep you from accidentally drifting from one world into another whether you are awake or asleep. This is especially hazardous for some of you during the sleep time, as you might have very vivid dreams. It is during vivid dreams when this is hazardous, but because you have adrenal glands, the hazard is canceled out. That's what they do.

Say more about these supporting worlds. Is there some aspect of ourselves functioning there?

There might be—I say "might" because for some of you, yes, for some of you, no—and that is another reason. If that is so, it would make it even more hazardous, because if there is any part of you focused over there, the natural tendency in the deep dream state is to be linked with all portions of oneself.

As long as that link happens vertically, you are safe. But if you are near a focus of yourself in some alternate place of existence that is near you, even for a moment, there is a hazard that you might form a bond. But as long as the adrenals are working well, that would not happen.

Overworked Adrenals and the Onset of Schizophrenia

However, let me say something: If the individual's adrenals are working poorly, say at 25 percent or less of their actual optimal capability, and this is in all stages of life . . . I'm not talking about how they work when you are a child versus how they work when you are an adult, just 25 percent of their optimal capability throughout your various ages. If the adrenals are working poorly or below that standard, there is a hazard that you might link at least temporarily with one of these focuses, and if you do, it can create a temporary sense in the dream state of a split personality—meaning that some of you is focused where you are here and some of you is focused in that other place. Now, this does not apply to all cases of schizophrenia, but it does apply to 10 to 15 percent of them. But for most individuals (even individuals who might be biased toward schizophrenia in some way), this does not represent a problem. When you wake up, all is well.

But there is the occasional time when you remain linked. You will know if this happens because you will wake up very disoriented—not just slightly disoriented as you might wake up from a vivid dream, but *very* disoriented—and the disorientation might last for hours and hours. If that happens, you'll know that you need to get some help spiritually from a mystical person or shaman or an individual who can work with these matters. Or if you believe in the mental approach, consult a good therapist.

If you do this immediately, it will probably clear up soon, certainly in no more than a week. But if you just let it go and hope that it will get better, it can create a bias toward schizophrenia even if it goes away (it might very possibly clear up on its own—there's at least a 50 percent chance it will). Even if you didn't come in with it, this can create a bias toward schizophrenia as a possible challenge to you in a given life, adding to the challenges you already came in with. That's another reason the adrenals need to be working well, and it's sometimes the reason that you will be guided or advised to alter your diet in some way, either adding something to it or cutting down on something if the adrenals are being overworked.

Now, this is not generally a hazard with athletes or people who are involved in highly stimulating activities, perhaps running or jogging every day. It would only be the case, for instance, for a professional athlete who focuses the greater part of his or her day on exercise, all day long. This could be a hazard for such individuals, and they especially need to pay attention to it. It might be a hazard for an individual taking some kind of medicine that's a stimulant, or even if someone drinks fifteen to twenty cups of coffee a day, but one does not normally do these things for years and years at a time.

Nevertheless, if you notice or if other people say to you that you seem to have this personality or that personality or "who are you today?"—the kind of little joking remarks people might make to you—then you need to pay attention to this as something that might be going on. If you cannot stop overstimulating your adrenals, then you need to at least approach it mentally so that you can get a grasp of or some idea of what to do or how to recognize the signs of these things in order to find your median or balanced personality.

Alternate Realities

We know so little about alternate realities. The little bit I know is that if you come to a major decision and choose a path, some part of you goes into an alternate reality to experience what you didn't choose. Is it something like that?

That occasionally occurs if it is a major crossroad, but to discuss the mechanics would be very hazardous. I'll tell you why: Many people are so dissatisfied with the lives they are living in your time on Earth that any possibility at all to be involved in an alternate reality—even without knowing whether that reality would be better or worse—would be grasped by them if they knew how to access it. Therefore, I cannot explain the mechanical fundamentals of choosing to move into another reality unless I am speaking to a shamanic student or someone I am training.

Can you look into those worlds as easily as you look into this one?

Yes, generally speaking, looking into worlds that are close to the ones that are associated with each of you, you will find events happening that are like . . . picture for a moment a puzzle. Imagine that you have enough of the main part of the puzzle that you can easily identify it, but there might be a few pieces missing—not enough so that you can't make sense of it and identify it. Those missing pieces might be floating about in that alternate reality. Since it is not a part of your personal self or personal existence or soul, these might be alternates being tried on and off in other realities to see how they feel.

Now, you understand, I am not saying that this has anything to do with the mental process, because it doesn't. It's a way of feeling things at a distance that do not require the feeling to impact your physical self. This is because any feeling that impacts your physical self will be recalled by your physical self and associated with some event, even if it is not directly associated.

Therefore, you are shielded from this, but there is an extended feeling that will go off into those areas. And if that feeling notices something very good or something optimal, then it might request of the soul, the angels, the guides and others who are working with you (the personality) to make such a event or experience or even a portion of an event or an experience occur sometime in the future. Because that feeling is a good one, it is felt that it would be a good thing to be exposed to at some point in the future. So it's an alternate feeling experience, and this is done by the adrenals.

Does a piece ever go off and experience something and come back and join the main personality?

No, that is something more akin to soul pieces moving about. This is different. This would have to do with alternatives of possibility. It might for the most part be very mundane. Suppose you turned right instead of turning left? Suppose you used the hot water to wash instead of the cold water? Suppose you splashed warm water on your face instead of cold? It might be something as mundane as that.

Or it might be something complex. If it is complex, it will not include the entire experience, but something like a taste. If you had a bowl of stew in front of you and you put a wooden spoon in and tasted it to see what it tasted like, it would be like that. It wouldn't be the combined taste of the whole stew, but rather a tiny particle of it that you could miss in your life as it goes on. It could still be processed in this alternate place. If it never comes back, it won't be lost, it won't be missed. But if it does come back, it will simply rejoin some greater thing so that it will not have any noticeable impact.

Most of the time, these pieces do not come back. They are not a part of your personality or your soul. They are simply alternates, other possibilities, explorations. Perhaps in a given lifetime one might have thirty or forty of these that are felt to be something good, where an alternate is discovered or a variable is set up for a future experience.

Maybe as a youngster you were trained to rinse your face off with cold water, but as you got older you discovered that if you rinse your face off with warm water, it is more comfortable. That might have been an alternate that was discovered and set up so that one day, even though you've always rinsed your face off with cold water, you suddenly rinse your face off with warm water. It feels better, and that's what you do from that point on.

So they don't come back to you when you die? Before you go through the veils?

There is no need because they are not part of your soul or your immortal personality.

What are they? How would you classify them? Just free-floating energy?

I would describe them as externals, involved in events you experience.

But does the energy itself go back into the Earth? It goes somewhere, doesn't it?

I do not know.

The Possible Effect of Mundane, Everyday Gestures

As an aside, if we hold these gestures too long, they will have some effect on some part of the body. Sometimes the most mundane things you do have some kind of an effect. For example, here are some typical gestures, having nothing to do with anything sacred, that people do [Fig. 14-4].

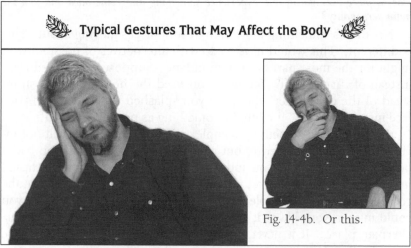

Typical Gestures That May Affect the Body

Fig. 14-4b. Or this.

Fig. 14-4a. Here is a typical gesture, nothing sacred, that may impact the body.

Fig. 14-4c. Another typical gesture.   Fig. 14-4d. And this.

All of these gestures, while being very typical to what anyone might do at a given time, generally do not have an impact on you. But they might actually be a portion of a sequence of gestures that is involved in doing something else, or they might be very close to some gestures involved in some other purpose. That's why sometimes for very sensitive people—people who are very spiritually involved or con-

Fig. 14-4e. Or this.

nected to other worlds because they are a youngster or because they are very old (and are preparing for their transition), or if they are just very focused in the spiritual world—the making of certain typical gestures might very easily feel uncomfortable.

You will find that certain gestures are natural for you and that other gestures feel uncomfortable. If they are physically uncomfortable—meaning if you've had an injury—that's one thing, but if there is no basic physical discomfort and for some reason doing one of these gestures causes you to feel very uncomfortable, it probably has to do with a sequence of spiritual gestures that's not right for you to be doing at that moment. The gesture might be only one portion of a sequence—or even close to one portion of that sequence—that has to do with something that is not right for you to do in that moment.

Conversely, there are certain things that you do because they feel really good. Maybe you do this instead [Fig. 14-4f]. I'm not saying one is better than the other, but maybe you do the gesture and it feels good, and you do that for years and years when you want to just rest or think for a moment. It might be part of a sequence of gestures or close to a sequence of gestures that would be good for you to do in that moment, and that's why it feels good.

Would it be something you learned in another life or in another dimension?

You don't ever have to learn it at all. You probably don't even know it. It's just something that is associated with those series of gestures, and that's why it feels good to you.

That is really good to know.

Fig. 14-4f. And here is a typical gesture that may feel really good.

Clearing the Kidneys

What about our kidneys? They are very important too, aren't they?

Very important. Again we are dealing with something that is hard to reach, though some of you might be able to reach around the side and do the standard clearing gesture [9-1], come to think of it. I think they are close enough to accomplish the clearing gesture, but the kidneys are actually in the back of your body, you understand. If there is ever any difficulty in reaching a portion of your body where some organ resides, then either lie down or sit down and say that you are now doing a clearing for the kidneys, for instance. You don't have to say it out loud; you can think it or you can just know it. But it is useful to focus on it in some way mentally so you don't accidentally clear the spleen or some part of the gut that you've already worked on and perhaps have done something to activate.

So in doing the clearing for the kidneys, again this is something that will need to be done morning and night. I'll be more liberal here: Do it anytime from 6 to 10 A.M. in the morning and from 6 to 10 P.M. in the evening, but usually at the same time every day, if you can. Do this morning and night for, say, five days.

Okay, five days for the kidneys.

Whether you've lived a very benign life or you've lived a life of great agitation, still do it this way for the sake of simplicity. We don't try to group personality types and say this and that and this and that, because you may not know your personality type. So just do it that way. If you wind up doing a little too much, that's all right in the case of clearing.

Kidneys and Your Long Vision

The kidneys have everything to do with long vision. Long vision is the capacity to see things that are not in your immediate environment—meaning you could see something on the other side of the planet if necessary. Occasionally, you might use it to check up on your relatives to see if they are all right or if they need you. I often use it to check up on people in the tribe to see if they might need me when I am off at a distance. This is why it's important for any mystical man or woman to always be training somebody, so that when you are gone, the basic things that you do for the people can be done by the person you are training. Remember that.

Long vision can also be used to explore the planets. It is often used in that way. Perhaps some people from other planets might come to visit you, and they might want to talk to you at a distance. You may have someone in your group who is able to communicate that way, such as Robert does here, but you might also want somebody in your group to describe what that person looks like, what that person's world looks like.

After the conversation or maybe during the conversation, if the person wants to say, "Well, see, it looks like this," then the person with the long vision could describe it in the exact terms the people who are being talked to will understand and appreciate. Sometimes if the person from another planet was speaking through a channel like this, that person may not have the terms, may not immediately know how to say what it is. It may not dawn on that person to say what color it is, for instance.

That's another way, but there are many ways long vision is used. One way it's *never* used is to look at something that does not wish to be seen in that moment. This is why when you're using long vision, you might at some point be concerned about someone (say, a family member), and you look in to see what he or she is doing in that moment, that's your focus, and you see nothing. Or you get some vague sense of that person being present, but you don't see anything else. It's not because the system isn't working; it's because whatever your family member is doing at that moment, he or she does not wish to be seen. He or she might even be asleep, having a particularly intense or meaningful dream.

Most of the time, if that person is asleep and having a dream, you can get a quick glimpse, but not so long a glimpse that your energy impacts him or her. This would change the dream, or if the dream is particularly intense and there is some radiation of the dream around him or her, meaning the energy, you might pick up on that. If you see your relative and he or she is just lying quietly and it's very quick, a split second, that probably means that person is dreaming or visioning.

So you can see into that person's dreams?

Now, you don't *want* to see into his or her dreams.

But if there was some reason to, you actually could do that?

Yes, but that is practically never used. It is only used if somebody is having a nightmare that he or she can't get rid of, and then the technique is a little different. It's not exactly long vision. You have to use something to separate you as the mystical person from the nightmare itself, or what will occur is that you will begin to have the nightmare and so will that person. In that case, you will not have helped that person at all.

There are always other techniques involved for unusual applications such as that. Generally, it's not necessary to use that technique. Generally, if the person describes his or her nightmare, it's sufficient.

In any event, the kidneys are involved in this function—spiritually speaking, of course—aside from their physical function. I know a lot of people say that kidneys have something to do with anger, but they don't in their own right. They are not connected to anger. It's just that if there is too much anger in the body and you are not physical enough—meaning you are not doing any hard physical labor or hard physical entertainment, like dancing (in our time we very often danced our feelings)—then that anger may tend to settle in the kidneys. The kidneys in their own right are not involved in anger, but people who are very angry might have some problem with this. What would normally occur would be that the kidneys wouldn't work right, or they would be overworking, trying to dump that anger the way they process fluid.

So these gestures are going to be helpful with the anger if there's any stored?

No, the clearing will help that. These gestures are designed to somewhat improve kidney function. They might improve kidney function from 5 to 7 percent on the physical level. They *might*—no guarantees. But they ought to improve your potential for long vision. Some of you may be taught this, but for the vast majority of you who are not taught this, it will work for you in other ways.

Say you are worried about the family back home. You're traveling or you are back home worrying about that traveling member of your family. Instead of just being worried, you can reach around to your back and hold your kidneys, if that feels good to you. For some of you that might be comfortable, or you can go like this, placing the flat of both hands on the front of your kidneys [Fig. 14-5].

Gesture to Use Your Long Vision

Fig. 14-5b. You can fold your arms down like this to be comfortable.

Fig. 14-5a. To see if a loved one is safe, reach around and hold your kidneys like this, placing the flat of both hands on the front of your kidneys. As you're doing this, ask, "Is my loved one safe?"

As you're doing that, you can simply ask, "Is my . . ."—whoever it is, a family member—". . . safe?" Or if you are the traveler, "Is my family safe?" or whomever you are interested in. You might quickly get a sensation. Wherever you get the warmth, in the chest or the solar plexus area, you will get it very quickly.

Now, you might not need to touch the general area in front of or in back of your kidneys to do this, meaning that the normal means of the warmth coming in for you as given previously might be sufficient. But it will probably work faster if the kidneys are supported in the way I intend to show you.

Assisting the Kidneys

Here are the support gestures for the kidneys. This is the first one [Fig. 14-6]. You want to hold that for about thirty seconds and then wait for a minute or two. Two minutes might be better.

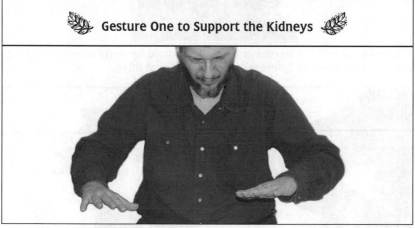

Gesture One to Support the Kidneys

Fig. 14-6a. The first support gesture for the kidneys. Do this three days after clearing. Hold for thirty seconds, and then wait for two minutes before moving on to the second gesture. Do these gestures at a time when there won't be any noise around you.

Fig. 14-6b. Another view.

Fig. 14-6c. A third view.

Here's the next gesture [Fig. 14-7]. I want you to hold that one again for about thirty seconds, and then wait for about three minutes.

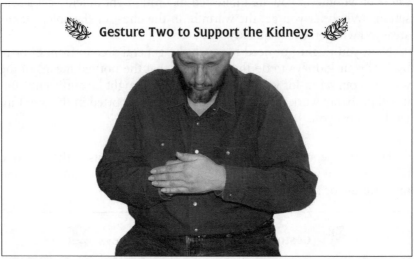

Gesture Two to Support the Kidneys

Fig. 14-7a. Here is the second gesture. Again hold for thirty seconds, and then wait for three minutes before moving on to gesture three.

Fig. 14-7b. A better view of the hand position.   Fig. 14-7c. A third view.

Now, there is another gesture—here it is [Fig. 14-8]. After you do these gestures, if at all possible, sit completely relaxed in the chair, if you are doing this while sitting. Don't worry about the phone ringing. Try to have that turned off, or have somebody else in charge of it without your having to hear any extraneous noise. If you wish to use some kind of earplugs while you are doing this, that might be helpful to some of you.

Do this at a time of night or day or morning when there is no noise around where you are. What I'd like you to do is to rest for at least five minutes, though ten to fifteen minutes might be better. Ideally, I would prefer that you lie down completely flat. Always try, when you lie down,

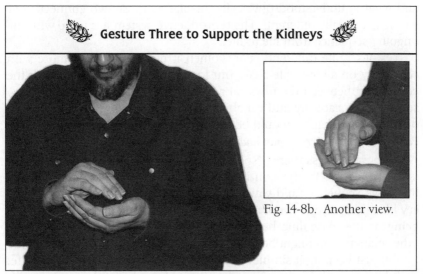

Gesture Three to Support the Kidneys

Fig. 14-8b. Another view.

Fig. 14-8a. The third gesture. Hold for thirty seconds. Then rest for at least five minutes.

to have your head to the north. That's very, very important. If you cannot, then at least lie with your head to the east or west, but try not to lie with your head to the south. There is nothing wrong with the south, you understand. It's just that it's better to have your feet pointing that way. This has to do with the way energy goes around the planet and the way it flows through your body, your body being sort of a miniature Earth in its function insofar as the way Mother Earth relates to you.

That tells you something very obvious, that Mother Earth's energy tends to flow from the North Pole down. So your body's energy tends to flow from the top of your head down, or at least that is how Mother Earth relates to you physically. That's why you put your head to the north.

Three gestures for the kidney. That's it, then?

Yes. We can do one more part of the body involving gestures, but no more than that today. It does have significant impact on this physical body. The reason is that very often I'm holding the gestures longer than they would be held, but even ruling that out, the proper procedure is not being done. I'm not following the clearing and then the waiting. These are all having an impact on this physical body. Sometimes it's a benevolent impact, but sometimes it is not so because of the sequence.

Then you choose the next one.

The Reproductive System and Male/Female Sequences of Life

Let's do the reproductive system. The male reproductive system has to do with the ongoing sequence between what is understood mentally and what is understood physically, insofar as those two connect. For women, it's really different: The reproductive system has to do with the ongoing sequence from life to life.

Yes, it's quite different. For women it has to do much more with continuity on a life-to-life basis, but for men it has more to do with the connecting between the physical awareness and understanding and, to some extent, capacity and capability and the mental. Because of these differences, perhaps it would be better if I gave different gestures.

For the woman, it accesses past and future lives?

It doesn't access them. No, it has to do with the continuity of those lives. It connects the continuity, meaning that for women, in the life-to-life sequence (and you understand, everyone is not a woman every life and everyone is not a man every life), one might be the feminine being or the masculine being in different lives. Of course, on some other planets, you might be something else.

But just keeping it simple here, this is the women's sequence of life, each high point having to do with a given life and there being some differences because a life might be shorter than another life [Fig. 14-9]. Now, I grant that what I'm drawing here is not the optimal for the male. The male's optimal is very similar to the female but not exactly the same. The optimal for the male would be this [Fig. 14-10].

However, this optimal does not have anything to do with the time in which you are living and, for the most part, does not have anything to do with third-dimensional Earth for the male. By optimal then, this

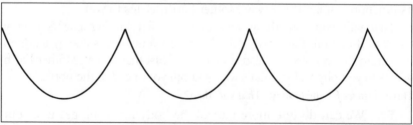

Fig. 14-9. The female sequence of life.

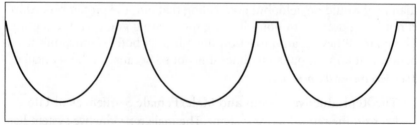

Fig. 14-10. The optimal male sequence of life.

would have to do with benevolent Earth status or occur at a higher dimension or on another planet.

Here is the male sequence in your Now experience also having to do with the third dimension in general. It is quite a bit different [Fig. 14-11].

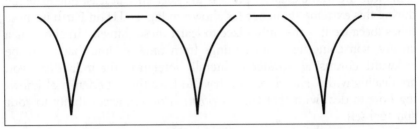

Fig. 14-11. The present male sequence of life.

As you can see, the female has to do with the sequencing of lives. The general feminine structure of life has to do not with the structuring or the accessibility of past and future, but with the continuity that the female feels and is supported or nurtured in, and the continuity that the female provides in nurturing others. That's the female sequence.

The optimal male sequence, since the male is always learning, has to do with a similar continuity, but the gaps are bridged by periods of learning. This means that there is significantly more experience in between lives of studying the given male life. Perhaps if you have another male life to follow in terms of the soul sequence—which may not be linear time but is the soul's sequence (its pursuit of learning)—you would have an even greater time of learning that would stretch out between those lives. If you went straight to a female life, it would be a little less.

I have shown the sequence of what is occurring now because now in the third dimension you still have that significant amount of time in which you are learning, but the life itself in the third-dimensional male tends not to be supported by continuity and it also tends not to provide much nurturing or continuity to others. This is why you need the female to support you with continuity and nurturing.

There are exceptions, of course, and this also has to do with a sense of the male that is not normal (normal meaning what you find everywhere else). The male here—or the soul focused in the male here in third-dimensional Earth—is learning more lessons than the male might learn anywhere else or even in higher dimensions of Earth. Therefore, the male life span is often shorter because so many extreme things are happening.

This is not to suggest that women do not struggle. This doesn't have anything to do with struggle, work, pain. It's not about that. It's what you are learning. Some things can only be learned on Earth in these times in the male form because they would never be considered an aspect of reality for the female form—which is why you tend to find more struggling amongst males.

But it is required to do this; it is not punishment. It's required for all souls who are in the creative process to experience at least one male life during this extreme sequence [as shown in Fig. 14-11] on Earth in these times, because it is the only place to learn these things. In short, as a creator, you come up against things from time to time that might be awkward, confusing, strange or literally foreign in the individuals you are dealing with. Therefore, you have to have the experience of knowing how to deal with that from a position of less accessibility to your spiritual self.

I realize that this makes it sound as if the female is a more spiritual being. I cannot say that this is absolutely true. What I will say is that the female has a capacity—though it's not always that way—to be a more spiritual being in third-dimensional Earth for the Explorer Race.

Also, life out in the rest of the universe is more attuned to the feminine. So as you said, there's no place else to be masculine, the aggressive individual . . . all these things.

That's right.

Thank you for explaining it.

Clearing Male and Female Reproductive Systems

Now we're going to do some gestures for the female and the male. Do the usual clearing exercise [Fig. 9-1]. If you are having some significant sexual dysfunction or you know that you have been traumatized in some way sexually, then I will give you a slightly different sequence for the clearing. If you haven't had those experiences or don't feel you have, the clearing would be the usual clearing exercise done once a day for three days in a row.

If you think or feel you have had some kind of trauma there or you are experiencing something that is clearly an obvious sexual dysfunction—not something that is considered by your culture or society as an abnormality, but an actual sexual dysfunction—then these gestures could help. Perhaps, if you are a woman, it is painful or uncomfortable to have sex, maybe you are small. Or if you are a man, perhaps you have difficulty getting an erection, something like that. I'm not talking about diseases or actual physical injuries that have to be looked after by a physician or healer, depending on what you believe in or what is available.

If there is no trauma, one time a day for three days. If there is trauma, then what?

If there is trauma, then once a day for twelve days. Always try to do it around the same time of day.

Assisting Female Sex Organs

Here are the gestures for the female to give aid and comfort and support to that part of your body. Understand that we're talking about the sexual organs, the tubes, the ovaries and the womb. So in the case of the female, the area of the body spreads up a little bit; it includes the lower abdomen. So although you might not be doing the gesture to give energy to that part of your body by holding your hands in front of there, in terms of doing the clearing, you might want to move your hands up and down in that area of your body.

Here is the first gesture to support that part [Fig. 14-12]. You want to hold this gesture for about twenty seconds. Then rest for a minute if

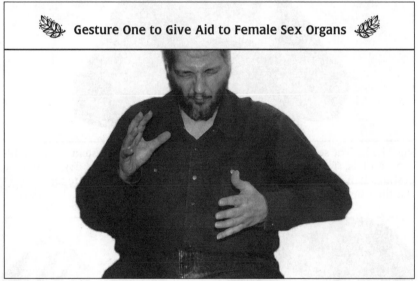

Gesture One to Give Aid to Female Sex Organs

Fig. 14-12a. After clearing, begin the first gesture to give aid, comfort and support to the female reproductive system. Hold for twenty seconds, then rest for a minute if you like before moving on to the second gesture.

Fig. 14-12b. Another view.

Fig. 14-12c. A third view.

you like. You don't have to, but I think it's good to rest for a little while—a half a minute or a minute. Remember that only the clearing needs to be done in front of that part of the body, not the gestures to bring energy and support.

Now do the second gesture [Fig. 14-13]. You are going to hold this gesture for about fifteen seconds.

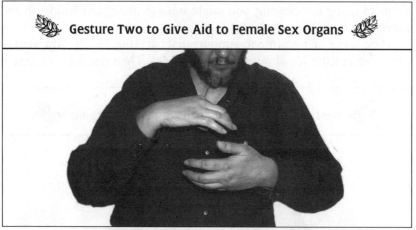

Gesture Two to Give Aid to Female Sex Organs

Fig. 14-13a. The second gesture for the female reproductive system. Hold for fifteen seconds. Then lie down for ten to fifteen minutes and rest. Try to do these gestures at the same time of day. If you believe you've had trauma to this area, do this three times a day for nine days. If not, then do it twice a day for three days.

Fig. 14-13b. A better view of the hands.

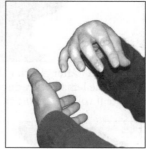

Fig. 14-13c. A third view.

If you think, believe or feel you have had trauma to the area, then do this three times a day for nine days. But if you're not aware of any trauma and everything seems to be all right, then do it twice a day for three days in a row. Unless I say every other day, it's always in a row. Try to do it around the same time every day.

Now, unless there is something else for the female, I will proceed to the male.

So just basically you're saying the clearing just clears and then this gesture recharges and supports? Gives energy to it?

Yes.

Assisting Male Sex Organs

Now, for the male there are the following gestures. Here is the first [Fig. 14-14]. Hold that gesture for about twenty-five or thirty seconds, whatever feels right to you. Then wait for about a minute until you do the next one.

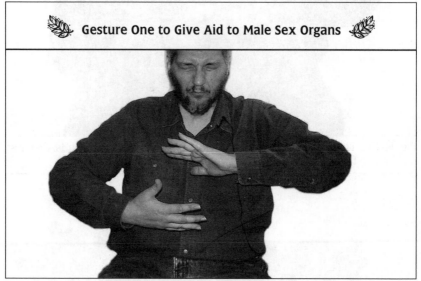

Gesture One to Give Aid to Male Sex Organs

Fig. 14-14a. After clearing, do the first gesture for the male reproductive system. Hold for twenty-five to thirty seconds, then wait about a minute before moving on to gesture two.

Fig. 14-14b. Another view.   Fig. 14-14c. A third view.

This is the second gesture [Fig. 14-15]. Hold that one for about twenty seconds, and then rest for from three to five minutes until you do the last one.

🌿 Gesture Two to Give Aid to Male Sex Organs 🌿

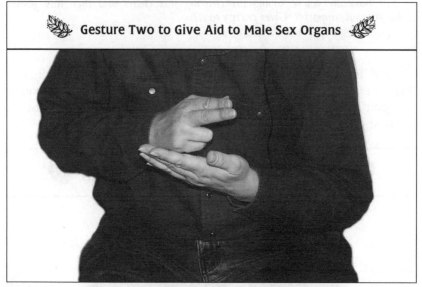

Fig. 14-15a. Here's the second gesture: Hold for about twenty seconds, then rest for three to five minutes before moving on to gesture three.

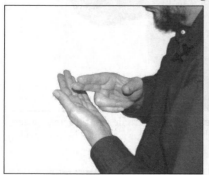

Fig. 14-15b. A second view.

Fig. 14-15c. A third view.

This is the last gesture [Fig. 14-16]. If you can, hold that last gesture for about forty seconds and then rest.

Again, after you do these, I would recommend that you lie down for ten to fifteen minutes. If you fall asleep, do it with your head to the north, of course, and ideally on your back. When I say to lie down, that's what I mean. But if you should fall asleep and sleep longer, that's acceptable. Don't worry about that.

You want to do this sequence once a day for about eighteen days. I recognize that it is a long sequence and it might be a little awkward for some of you to do it every day at the same time of day for eighteen days, but it will probably help.

Gesture Three to Give Aid to Male Sex Organs

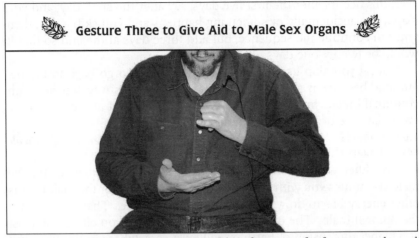

Fig. 14-16a. Here's the final gesture. Hold it, if you can, for forty seconds, and then lie down and rest for ten to fifteen minutes. Do this sequence once a day at the same time for eighteen days, whether you've experienced trauma or not.

Fig. 14-16b. Another view of the hand position.

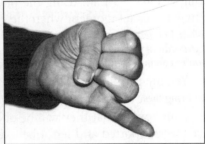

Fig. 14-16c. A third view.

Fig. 14-16d. Detail of left hand.

Fig. 14-16e. Another view.

If there is a day when you forget to do the gestures and this happens during the first five days, start over from the beginning. You'll have to start over from the absolute beginning, including the clearing. If, however, this occurs after the first five days, say after the sixth day, and you skip a day accidentally or something happens and you skip a day, then you can continue the sequence, but add three days at the end so that it would be twenty-one days total.

Now, if you skip *another* day, then you'll have to go back to the beginning, because it sometimes can be modified this way, but not with continual breaks in the sequence. Again, try to do it at the same time every day, give or take three minutes in either direction.

That's really close. Is this assuming no trauma? Is there a different one if the male has had trauma?

No, either way. Now, the combination of these sequences for the male also unites you with another energy (this is just for the male). This other energy has to do with your optimal masculine. That's why I gave the optimal male. The optimal male that exists for you either will exist at a higher dimension of Earth or will exist somewhere in the stars, but you don't have to do anything extra. I've included it so that it will just naturally occur in the sequence given, and this ought to support not only a sense of balance—physically as well as spiritually and on the feeling level—but it might also tend to moderate the way you experience impact, traumas, shocks or surprises that might be unwelcome.

So your tribe gave these. Did all tribes have these gestures?

I do not know. I know that if I am getting gestures that are either adopted to your time or that are for your time exclusively (meaning we don't use them), I am seeing a white-robed individual doing the gestures. That being is doing that and I am following his gestures. Then when we come to the actual gesture, I am using this physical body [the channel's], my physical body and what I feel from the being who is showing me these gestures (he is not with me, but I am seeing with my long vision) . . . I am using the physical senses of all three in order to know the exact moment when the gesture is correct.

What I'm getting at is if yours is the tribe that has these gestures, then this is an extraordinary thing to give to the planet, because your people are gone now. So you're coming from four hundred years ago . . .

Yes, my people are not present.

To bring these to us is an extraordinary gift.

I am hoping that they will be of benefit in your time. Some individuals have reported and felt, I believe, some personal physical wellbeing from the first book [*Shamanic Secrets for Material Mastery*]. Good.

Yes, really good. Thank you so much.

Good night.

Sleeping and Dreamtime

Speaks of Many Truths
October 2, 1999

All right, this is Speaks of Many Truths. Greetings.

Greetings. I've been wondering what you can teach us about dreams.

I can only speak about dreams as I know them. Much of what goes on in the dream world, as far as I can tell, has everything to do with what you do about twenty to twenty-five minutes before you go to sleep. You can do many things during the day, and I grant that some trauma during the day might prompt a dream of some sort that is recalled. But before I go to sleep, I do many fixed things.

Preparations for Sleep and Dreaming

If I am with my people (at home, as you say), then before I sleep there is communication and interaction from myself to them, from them to myself, perhaps in my prayers. If I am between places, out in the countryside, then there is much time talking to the flowers and the soil and the rocks and the animals and so on in the area before I go to sleep.

Either way, the result of both of these circumstances, as far as I've been able to tell, is that the communication is very heart-centered. From what I can tell, that heart-centered communication creates a loving energy before sleep. It also allows me to go to sleep quicker, because it's relaxing. I am being myself, speaking what my heart wishes me to say. And those who speak to me, be they plant or animal or human, are replying in a similar way. That energy affects my dreams. It allows me to remember more of the spiritual instruction as it seems to be in my dreams.

The dreams you often remember in the morning in your time, for instance, will have to do with something that is either going to happen or something that has happened already. So they might be predictions in some way—not to say, "This is going to happen. Remember it," but "Here is some instruction. It will help you for what is going to happen," or "Here is some teaching that will help you to understand what has already happened." These kinds of dreams happen if you do not prepare that way, as much as I've been able to tell.

Twice I dreamt when something was going to happen: once to my people and once when I was out walking from where my tribe was to where a student was. The time I was out on the land, it had to do with a forest fire, what you'd call a brush fire, and I therefore slept in an unusual spot, a place I wouldn't normally sleep: a series of rocks that went out over the river. I usually try to sleep near the water, if I possibly can, and that's where I slept. The fire did come by at night, but because I was sleeping on rocks and nothing flammable, and because it was burning grasses and not trees, it passed quickly. The rocks did not heat up that much.

The other time I had a dream that was instruction, it was about a coming event that had to do with a disease that went through our tribe unexpectedly, perhaps brought by an animal or it might have been brought by a visitor. We weren't ever quite sure about that. I was given pictures of certain plants that I had never really thought about. They were there, they were beautiful and I had a good feeling for them, but I had never given them any real thought.

I took the medicine woman out to show her these plants and told her that they had been very prominent in a dream I had. I asked her what she knew about them, and she said that they had never been used in her time, but that her elder had taught her that they were useful for certain vitamin deficiencies and stomach upsets. I think the disease is called scurvy. We don't have much of that in our time.

And I said that I had dreamt about these plants, I had pictures of them, so maybe it would be good to begin to gather them just in case. She said, "All right." When the disease did strike our village, which was something not dissimilar to what you would call a stomach disorder, she was prepared. She had already made up much of the herbal medication that was needed. She had it ready, on hand for everyone, and we got over it.

Those were the only two times I had dreams about coming events. Warnings. Other than that, the dreams that I have because of my . . . I don't want to call it preparation for dreams because it is more preparation for sleep—or the end of the day, if you like—with my tribal peoples, my family. Wherever I might be, it is simply an acknowledgment and communication with those with whom I will be sharing the land.

Dreamtime Teachers and the Clearing People

But this preparation seems to work to also create benevolent instructions. So when I wake up in the morning, not having to resolve anything from the past or not having any warnings about the future with information I might need, I always remember talking to teachers, one of whom was an elder who instructed me when I was young. Others are clearing people who have not lived on this Earth.

Sometimes they have white robes. Sometimes they are dressed like me, yet I can tell by the way they act that they are just dressed this way to make it comfortable for me, but they do not live here. I remember their words, maybe a word here or there, but usually I just remember their motions, how they look, maybe a picture they've drawn on the ground, and then I think about that. I get up in the morning and I say morning prayers and greet the Sun and animals and plants and so on, but then I think about what I can understand from my dream.

Sometimes the drawing becomes clearer later on. I see something that reminds me of it, and then I think maybe it was a map. Other times, something or someone will come from that place and then I will think again, "Oh, maybe *that's* what the drawing was about."

How to Tell If Dreamtime Predictions Are Genuine

How can people tell if a dream is a projection of their fears or a genuine prediction?

In my case, the prediction for the future did not come with an announcement that people would get sick. None of that. Instead, it was prominent pictures of plants, plants that I recognized but that I hadn't, as I said, given much thought to. So if you wake up and you have a picture of plants or trees or something from which you recognize or consider that there is a helpful herb here, then you ought to try to remember it.

If you have a book, look through it. If you live near the plants, run outside and see if you can find them to remember it. Try not to do too much before you go outside and look for that plant. In short, you want to see physically what it is you saw in the dream vision.

If, on the other hand, the pictures you are left with are frightening, perhaps associated with people, you can write these things down. In your time, I know you write things down. Write it down. If it is a repeated dream, something that repeats itself the same way all the time, it is most likely something you are trying to resolve. But if it gets more and more prominent, if people in the dream get bigger, then you will know that either the event or whatever is involved is something you must immediately resolve in some way within yourself (not suppressing it or controlling it, but resolving it, going into it, feeling it), or that the event it's talking about is going to happen soon. It's coming.

Of course, in my time we also had people who were specialists in dreams and could interpret things on the basis of their feelings. Sometimes interpretations were very similar from one person to the next. Other times they were completely unique, depending not only on the sensitivity of the dream person, but also on his or her experience and on the experience of the teachers.

Dreams and the Physical Body

The physical body can tell you a lot about dreams as well. If you are having frightening dreams, since I think that is what you are really asking about, then you have to explore. Notice how your physical body feels when you wake up from such a dream. That's the first thing to notice. How do you feel and where do you feel it?

If you feel frightened in your throat—aside from the fact that it might have to do with communication, something you said or didn't say, something somebody else said or didn't say—it may have to do with your actual physical life. If you have fear or terror in your solar plexus, it probably has to do with your past in this physical life, and it may not have anything to do with your life at all. It's going to be past-oriented though, and so you have to look at your past. Unless it's a repeating dream that has been regularly ongoing or recurring from time to time, look toward the stimulation you've had recently. Did you watch a frightening movie? Did you read something frightening? I realize that in your time it is a popular activity to be stimulated by the arts in frightening ways. It is a curiosity to us in our time, but I recognize that this is popular in yours.

Either the throat or the solar plexus might refer to something in your past—or in the case of the throat, possibly in the present—meaning you have feelings there. This has something to do, you understand, with your life, but it may also have something to do with something you read or saw along the lines of entertainment. I do recommend that you do not expose yourselves to such things, because your physical body does not tell the difference between what happens to you physically and what happens to others physically in entertainment.

If you read about something or hear about something frightening that happened to others, or if you read or hear about something frightening that is a story that seems to be happening to others, your physical body does not process that as something particularly external. It will not process it on the basis of the actual trauma to others, be it fictional or real, but on the basis of the trauma to your own physical body as you were reading, looking at it or hearing about it.

Just because you don't feel the trauma, since you are used to a level of what you call stress, does not mean that your body doesn't feel it. So your body will process it that way. If, on the other hand, the trauma was something you personally experienced that gave you personal pain, suffering and discomfort, then the feeling will also probably take place in the solar plexus, but it might wrap around to the right-hand side above the belt line.

If you put your hand on your solar plexus and then moved it horizontally to your right side, you might feel it there. If it is there, it might have more to do with your actual life, meaning it has to do with your trauma or it might have to do with your feelings. Generally speaking, if there's something you need to do, you will feel it in your solar plexus and on your right or (possibly for some people) your left side. It usually would be the right side, because just before you're ready to physically move your legs and go somewhere, that's where your energy is stimulated first.

So if it goes to your right side, if you feel something there and in your solar plexus, this probably means there is something you need to do. It might be associated with some level of prediction, but prediction in a dream practically never has to do directly with what you see. It has to do with making preparations on the basis of what you see in case that happens or, more likely, in case something happens for which the preparations you're making for that dream image would also apply. The same preparations would be useful for whatever else would happen.

In that way your dream consciousness speaks to you to stimulate you to get ready for the dream event, even though the getting ready is actually for something else. It pulls that out of your reference mind, meaning your reference images, but in order to take that action you will know that the feeling will take place in your solar plexus area and on your right side for most of you (and occasionally, for some of you, on your left).

Most metaphysicians are taught to interpret symbols in dreams, the images in dreams. You're giving us a more direct application.

That's right. I feel that the physical body is a better teacher because it can always tell the difference between what is strictly a mental experience and what will directly involve the physical self. Your physical body is always functioning in the realm of material mastery, but your mind is neither a spiritual nor material master.

There is no true level of mental mastery that ever applies to the physical world. What is sometimes called mental mastery—the capacity to think and bring things about strictly on the basis of thought—is not truly applicable here. That will usually involve moving things, pushing things around or creating things without their permission. An engineer might look at a river that has flooded once or twice recently and say, "Well, if we build a dam here, we can not only prevent that flood in the future (at least maybe we can), but we can also use it for other things." Although some people might say that the creation of this entire project is a form of mental mastery on Earth, it really isn't because things will be used without their permission, and you can never attach mastery to anything if it is being used without its permission.

Dealing with Your Children's Nightmares

What about nightmares? Can you trace most of that back to the movies people watch, the video games, the input?

In your time, yes, with the exception of people who don't watch such things or don't take in such things (rare exceptions in your time), and also of people who are experiencing an extreme trauma or perhaps some ongoing trauma, such as being mistreated, which often happens to children and women. This happens to some men too, but in your time it is more common for children and women to undergo some form of predatory mistreatment.

So if a child is being mistreated and has dreams in which he is in terror, can you look for a connection there if you can't find any other connection?

What do you mean "look for a connection"?

Between the fact that he may have been abused and nobody knows about it, and the dream . . . and he is living in terror all the time.

First, try to be around when he wakes up in the morning, or if he wakes up screaming, try to be near where he is sleeping. Not in the same bed—in my time it would be in the same room, as you would call it. I do not see much point in having separate rooms unless you do not want to be near your children. But if that is how it is, then you need to get there as quickly as possible.

Of course, he might be crying, but try to ask him, "What do you feel in your body, and where do you feel it?"—not just "Where does it hurt?" but "What do you feel, and where do you feel it?" The child might not understand that, so just say, if you are maybe giving a soothing touch, "Where do you want me to touch to make it feel better?" For a younger child, you might say that. And then the child will tell you where it feels the worst.

Think about that later, maybe consult with people. If you can, talk to a dream person. If the child is very young, bring him with you or ask the dream person to come to you. If you are going to talk to a dream person, it's usually better that you go to where that person is because she will have the place set up in just such a way so she can get the best focus. If the dream person comes to where you are, she will be exposed to all the distractions that are in your place. Although she might draw some conclusions from that, it will still interfere with her capacity, her clarity, unless she has time to be there for a while and set things up the way she needs them to be. But even then, I think it's better to go where the dream person resides.

Where she has her office.

Or her home. On the other hand, maybe the child is a teenager and does not want to go with you to the dream person, doesn't want to have a thoughtful talk. He wants to be comforted. Maybe he is being influenced at school where everything is mental and he needs to process it mentally when he wakes up with a fright.

Then go to the dream person on your own. You don't have to describe the images of the dream unless the therapist talks about them. It is better to describe the places on the child's body where he wanted to be soothed, if he is young, or the places on his body that he said had certain feelings: felt tight in the solar plexus or on the right side, or felt almost choked up in the throat.

Tell that to someone who is a dream master, as you might call it, and she'll say, "Well, then, it probably has to do with this." There will be general areas, but if the child is being stimulated physically—for instance, when you wake up from a nightmare, if you feel like you want to jump under the covers and hide or get up and run or go somewhere or do something—this may have to do with an event, because the physical body is being stimulated to take action.

An event that is coming or that already happened? How do you know which?

I'm talking about an adult trying to understand a child. In the case of the adult trying to understand the child, you have to talk to that child. The more he can tell you about the way his physical body feels, the more you can tell whether it's something that's coming.

The child might not even have pictures or dream images. Children only know how they feel. If, on the other hand, he's not particularly reacting physically, but he has lots of pictures and maybe even words, have him tell you as much as he can. Then, if you do not understand it yourself, talk to the dream specialist.

But the physical body is the best way to know. Of course, with a child you cannot tell very often whether something is a prediction or not. But say you are living someplace where earthquakes are a possibility, and your child is having dreams of earthquakes over and over. Then prepare your home and get all your things together as if an earthquake were coming. It might not be an earthquake; it may just be that you need to have the preparations in effect. Tell the child and involve him in preparing for the earthquake, not only so that he knows you're listening, but so his body will be involved in the preparations and know that the message has been received in some form.

After the youngster helps you prepare as best as possible for, say, an earthquake and everything is ready including food and water to survive for several days—maybe packs you might wear on your back to go up into the hills, all these things different people do—then pay attention to the child's dreams for the next few days and nights. The dream will probably change. It would be very surprising if the child continued to have the same earthquake dream. If that happens and you've done all your preparations, then you could consider moving out of the house for a time. Camp outside if you can. Try being elsewhere. If that doesn't seem to help, then say, "Well, this is about something else." Then you might need to talk to the dream specialist.

But always find out where the child is feeling the discomfort. If he's having the earthquake dream and he is feeling it in his solar plexus and on the right side, it means take action. If he is having the earthquake dream and he just wakes up feeling nervous and shaky with a tightness or constriction in the throat, it may not be something that's actually going to happen. Maybe it is something he is processing from his past, something he has seen or been stimulated about, or perhaps it is a message to make those preparations because they will be needed in some other way.

Your Physical Body's Signs

I don't know that people are trained now to listen to the body and do dream analysis.

I'm giving all of these things because in your time the physical body is completely misunderstood. The feelings felt in the physical body are also misunderstood, and yet they are always the best way to know what has happened, what is happening and, in many cases, what will happen. The mind is not prepared to do these things. If you follow the path of the mind and discount feelings and the physical body, you will be lost.

There was a time a few months ago that many humans were processing for other people on the planet. They would wake up in the middle of the night shaking with fears and tremors and everything. Is that past now? Are we still doing that? Are different beings still doing that?

It's not as much as it was, but generally speaking, if you are processing somebody else's things, you will feel it back here. I am reaching around with the left hand and I'm putting the left thumb and finger a little below the shoulder blade. I'm going to do that on the other side, too. Both sides. Generally, when you wake up, you will feel some tension or discomfort here, but by the time you get down to the hips, it will go away, meaning that it doesn't have to do with anything you have to do.

So if you wake up with tension along the shoulder and the solar plexus, then it has to do with your own life. But if it is strictly over the kidneys, the adrenals, the middle back, then you are probably processing something for somebody else. Maybe it's someone you know, maybe it's someone in the house or someone you care about, but it's probably not you.

And the 5 to 30 percent of energy going toward species consciousness, unity consciousness, that's going from us now—is there any physical feeling from this that you might confuse with these dream symptoms, or do you just wake up feeling tired?

You would probably just wake up tired. Some people might feel something, others will not. If you feel a little tension maybe three and a half or four inches below the knee to about five inches above the ankle along the front of the leg, it probably has to do with that, but most people will just wake up and feel tired.

Dreams Are Not Meant for the Conscious Mind

How can we accelerate the ability to remember the dreams where we're taught something? To bring that into the conscious mind?

You don't accelerate it. Remember, this isn't meant for the conscious mind. When you bring it to the conscious mind, you then think about it. The instruction that is given to you by your teachers at the deep levels of dreams is not meant for your conscious mind.

It's not meant for you to think about, and you know this is true. How do you know? You know because it's given at a time when you are pretty certain *not* to remember it. If it came to you during the daytime when you were able to write it down or pick up a recorder and repeat it, then you'd say, "Well, this is meant for my conscious mind."

But since it comes at nighttime in a dream like this, you can be pretty sure it is meant for your physical self, for your soul self or for your feeling self (part of your instinctual self, you understand). The memories you have of it that you consider in your conscious mind are usually without words or without the full explanation, which tells you that it is not meant for your conscious mind; it's meant for your physical body. And actually, when you remember a dream for which you have incomplete details, especially when large pieces are missing so that you are really not sure or have no idea what it was about, that is simply the way the conscious mind interprets the symbols—meaning the pictures of the dream—and maybe remembers some parts of the conversation.

But, in fact, the actual communication would have more to do with motions in the air. That is why very often if you remember dreams that have to do with spiritual teachers, they are not just sitting and talking. They are moving about. Motion is the best way to communicate with another physical body. If you're a teacher and you're talking to the physical body of an individual and the soul—it will be there whether the person is sleeping or not—you are probably going to be moving your hands around in the air. Some people who see this or remember it in a dream will think that the teacher is demonstrative—meaning she moves her hands—but that's not it at all. The motions have to do with actual communications with the physical self.

Join me right now. I want you to just move your hands around in the air the way I am, and I want you to notice this part of your physical body [points to the chest down into the upper abdomen]. Notice that when you move your hands around in the air, it gives you feelings in that part of your physical body. Isn't it true?

Yes.

That's right. So you see, when the teachers talk to you that way, it is because they are communicating with your physical self. That, of course, also communicates with the spiritual self and in other ways, but the physical way, too. It is not meant for the conscious mind. So do not be concerned if you do not remember the details of such a dream. It was not meant for you to think about.

Dreamtime Communication

So there is teaching that is done in deep sleep with a teacher who talks to the . . . the soul body is what's out there talking to the teacher, isn't it?

Yes and no. The physical body is always prepared for instructions whether you are awake or asleep; it makes no difference. But the physical body is most prepared—and let's say most welcoming—of someone speaking with heart, meaning with genuine kindness and loving communication. Because the physical body is such a receptive instrument for communication, it can be profoundly impacted by frightening things seen on the television or in the movies or imagined in books and so on. It is because the body is always so receptive, waiting for instructions to help it get through life more easily, that it is so easily impacted this way. Of course, you do not get this kind of entertainment impact when you are asleep. Most of you do not sleep with the television or the radio on (though some of you do, and that will impact your sleep and your physical self).

The physical self, then, is fully prepared to receive instructions from a teacher. And everybody, regardless of their station in life or where they live, once they reach into the sleep level that allows dreaming (which usually takes twenty to thirty minutes for many people), they are capable at that time of a much higher or quicker or more amplified response to such physical instructions from a loving guide or teacher.

So your soul body is out there somewhere. It can be anywhere interacting with a loving teacher, and the teacher is talking to the body. What might the teacher say, for instance? What kind of instructions would be given?

The soul, as you say—or your ideal personality—is present, but it does not always have to be completely present (meaning not in its totality) while acknowledging the teacher's communications, instructions, gentle preparations and, even in some cases, attunement of the physical self. The soul self has to be at least partially present so that the physical self will feel safe and involved in the process of life.

But sometimes there will be a long, involved process of gently working with the physical self where there is no communication or instruction whatsoever other than that to the physical self, and the soul self will then often be in more than one place at once. Of course, it's always tethered to the physical body, but while it is with the physical body with that process going on, it also might at the same time be involved in flying about the universes, communicating with other beings or looking at other beings. Because when the soul self is freed, at least to the extent where it is free from its physical obligations, it can do many things and be many places at once.

It's not clear how the soul of the immortal personality out there talking to a teacher, how that gets to the physical. The physical is back lying on the bed. So it goes through the soul, then to the physical?

No. The soul is just in attendance, but it does not pass through the soul. The teacher uses something akin to long touch.

Ah, that's the missing part.

The physical body uses something that is associated with long reach because long reach is also a factor, another thing you can do. This means that you can heighten your receptivity to something, and it draws you toward that something. The physical body has a heightened welcoming level toward that teacher, and the teacher uses the long touch in whatever is being done. As I say, you might consciously remember the teacher talking or maybe not, but moving the hands around is involved in working with the physical self. So long reach and long touch are involved.

That has never been explained before. So what can we do then with our conscious intent to facilitate that? Let's say we want healing, we want attunement, we want guidance, wisdom of the body—can we ask for it?

You can ask for whatever you want, but the teacher will give you what the teacher knows you need. There is no way you can influence the teacher to do something less than the teacher was going to do, but you might be able to entreat the teacher to do something *more*.

It is a possibility, but the teacher will not do it nor make any effort to do it if it would in any way interfere with your life process as it is intended, according to what the teacher knows. If it is not going to interfere in any way with your life process, the teacher *might* do something—but only might.

Ways to Prepare for Sleep

The best way to prepare for sleep is to be involved in a genuine intimate act of love, as between a man and a woman, twenty to thirty minutes before sleep. It might be making love, but it needs to be love, not just self-satisfaction. It needs to be actual love that you feel for that person. That's a good way to prepare for sleep.

If you are having intimate contact with someone and you do not feel love there, try to focus into your physical body as much as possible before you go to sleep. Because you are probably sleeping with somebody else, you might not be able to get up and talk with the plants or what is around you. If there is a plant in the room with you or stones or something like that from the natural world (in a reasonably natural condition . . . for example, a rock that has been moved from its place where it lived or a plant that has been artificially—meaning by man or woman—put in a pot; they obviously do not grow in pots in nature, but that is still reasonably natural), you might have some sense of communication with them. If not, the best thing to do is to focus into your physical body and relax and feel good about your physical body. Try to bring up the heat and so on, and that will tend to prepare you for sleep.

If, on the other hand, you're not having intimacy like that before sleep, try to make peace with all that is in the place you are sleeping. If you are outdoors, it is easier. There are animals, little beings. There might be bigger beings. You can go around, if you are in a tent, and touch or talk.

Put your head out of the tent, maybe. Communicate. Try to touch in the area where you are putting your tent. It's always good to do that before you put up your tent, before you go to sleep. But say you are already in your tent and you are in sleeping garments and so on—perhaps you cannot go out for some reason, maybe it is raining. Then just talk right through the walls of your tent to what is around you. But you must talk out loud. This way the plants and animals especially will know that while you are alone, maybe you are talking to a teacher, but if you are talking lovingly and gently, maybe you are talking to them. Make your peace with them and thank them for welcoming you and so on, or say your prayers. Try to do this for at least twenty to twenty-five minutes before you are actually going to go to sleep or before you make the effort to go to sleep. If you cannot fall asleep right away, then just continue to say your prayers or talk to that life that is around you.

The "Good Life" Blessing

If you are indoors, like most people in your time, in a room with a bed (probably your own room, although maybe you are sleeping somewhere other than your own room), before you go to sleep, walk around the room and touch things, especially with your right hand. When you are touching them, before and during, put yourself into a calm, relaxed, loving state. Try to do the heat in your chest [see pp. 7–8]. If you cannot do that, at least be relaxed and touch everything briefly. You can say, "Thank you for being here in the room with me and keeping me company and watching over me. I will do my best to watch over you, and may you all have good lives," or you can simply say to each object and thing you touch, "Good life."

Because it is a life form, it might have been something before it was that object, or it has its own form of life. You can touch the wall, the floor, the ceiling (if you can). You can touch anything: the pillow, the sheets, the blanket. If you have animals in the room, be sure and touch them before you go to sleep. All these things will help you to have a restful night's sleep.

When I think of how many nights I have worked or read until my eyes wouldn't work, and then fell right asleep—that's not a very good preparation, is it?

Not the best, no. Also, it does not acknowledge what is in your room, especially the parts of your room that give you a comfortable night's sleep. Your bed, your blankets, your sheets, your pillows—these things all make rest more comfortable. But there are often other things in a bedroom, furniture and so on. Go around and touch each briefly, for five seconds or less. Just give a quick touch and say, "Good life." And say it with meaning, "Good life"—mean it when you say it.

Practice saying "Good life" a few times and see how you feel in your physical body. If you feel tense and nervous, then don't touch that which you are saying good life to—just put your hand near it, within about four inches, and say, "Good life." You might be tense and nervous about something. But if you are relaxed and calm and comfortable and can say "Good life" at least calmly, or feel reasonably calm, then touch briefly that which you say "Good life" to.

Contact on the Physical Level during Sleep

So everyone during a normal night's sleep has contact with someone interesting in their life cycle here on Earth, a teacher or a guide, somebody, right?

Yes.

Every single night?

Yes, or whenever your sleep time is, as long as you are going to sleep for more than fifty minutes or, in some cases, forty minutes. Some people sleep in little bits and snatches, such as soldiers in a war. Then you may not always have contact with your guides or teachers every day on the physical level, where they are working with your physical body.

But if you can sleep deeply in that situation, even for that forty or fifty minutes, then you will have that contact. Maybe your buddy watches out for you while you sleep, then you watch out for him or her while she sleeps or he sleeps; then maybe you can train yourself to sleep deeply forty or fifty minutes or more at a time. It makes the physical self seem so much more relaxed to sleep if someone says, "I am awake. I will be here. I will look after you while you sleep." It is very comforting, even if you are in the middle of a war.

What issues do the teachers and the guides address at night? It's not your I-self, right? It's not your immortal personality that you contact? It's always some outside teacher?

I cannot say exclusively what is or what isn't. I can only say what I believe on the basis of my experience. I know that if I wake up in the morning and remember a long conversation that I can make sense of, I will think to myself, "Since I can remember this conversation . . ." —and it is conversation, and I don't remember any physical details with it—". . . this is meant for me to think about." But if I just remember bits and snatches and feelings, then I say, "This has something to do with my physical self and I don't need to think about this at all."

Animal Prayers

Of course, I sometimes have worries like you. I might be worried about a student or someone I am helping or maybe an animal. I might be out on the land and hear an animal at a distance. Maybe it is sick or hurt in some way, and I have been unable to help it or soothe it so that it feels safe around me. And yet it is in this area, but I am getting sleepier and sleepier. Then I might fall asleep a little worried.

But if that happens, I will ask my teachers and elders and ancestors out loud to protect me if they can while they do what they can to help this poor animal who is suffering and who does not trust me. Or I might ask that the spirit who helps that animal or the beings who can help that animal come to help it because it cannot receive help from me. So I will ask perhaps for permission to be safe and for permission to get help for those I cannot help or who do not feel comfortable with my help. When I say that, then I do not fall asleep worried because I trust that it works.

I know it works because it has worked before and it works every time. As you know, when something works, you begin to have faith in it. So in my time you get trained in this as a child because your elders take you out on the land and they will sometimes say, "Oh, you hear the wolf howling or the coyote howling or . . . ." But you are still too young to have been taught how to communicate with the animal in the way it wants to communicate with you, so your teacher might instruct you as a child to ask to be safe with your teacher and that the wolf or coyote get what it needs and be safe. Then when you wake up in the morning and you are safe, you say, "Oh, that worked." By the time you are an adult, you are used to saying that and it works.

It is like a living prayer you say not only for yourself—because it is intended to have an effect in your physical life—but you also are saying it for that animal whom you feel is hurting or sick. For all you know, it might be some cry that the animal makes that you haven't heard before. The animal might be perfectly all right, but if you ask for its spirits and so on to help it and to be kind to it and to give it assistance that it might need—you say it like that, *might* need or *may* need—then you simply give permission for that to happen.

And if the animal needs it, then I believe it might heighten the possibility that help will be present. You know that when you are in pain, even as a human being, it's not always easy to remain focused spiritually. You need to have others ask things for you because you are so involved with the pain. It's the same for animals.

You might have to have others ask so you don't have to, and then eventually you maybe fall asleep exhausted and hope . . . you say your prayers as an animal. Maybe a bear has a cut on his paw, and he climbs a tree just to be safe; then, as much as I understand, he says or feels what he needs. If a human being says it around him, that's good, too.

That bear asks to be protected and safe, because here he is with blood open and running down his poor paw, and he knows he's going to be attacked by those who smell the blood. So he says his prayers and hopes that others will say prayers for him too—maybe others he doesn't always communicate with, maybe human beings, maybe other animals he doesn't normally think about or talk to.

And then someday his paw heals up and he hears another animal in distress—maybe a bird in a tree or another little animal he feels is frightened or upset, maybe even an ant—and he says a prayer for that animal. All animals help each other. You as a human being must acknowledge that you are made of the same thing as animals. So you must help them and trust that they will say a prayer for you when you need help. In your time you can do this same thing as well as other things.

A Living Prayer for Suffering Humanity

In addition, we're now concerned with all of the humans who are suffering on the planet. So before we go to sleep, is there anything we should do in this new time now that the energy is going out?

No, not right before you go to sleep. Right before you go to sleep you go around, talk to things in the room and so on, giving them blessings, because they always give you blessings, making you comfortable.

But maybe sometime well before you go to sleep, say a prayer similar to what I just mentioned for suffering human beings. For instance, you have heard about human beings suffering in earthquakes in some other part of the world, maybe suffering from famine, floods, anything like that. So you say:

"MAY THE SPIRITS AND TEACHERS AND LOVING BEINGS AND HUMAN BEINGS AND ANIMALS AND EVERYBODY AROUND THESE PEOPLE HELP THEM AND NURTURE THEM AND ENCOURAGE THEM, AND MAY THEIR LIVES BE AS GOOD AS THEY CAN BE."

Say something like that, or whatever else you want to say, but if it's about human beings, always include other human beings, because very often these human beings are helping human beings. Don't leave it only up to spirit. People in earthquakes or famines or floods are going to get a lot of help from other human beings. So you want to say a prayer to encourage that.

Say you are there, maybe in a flood. You got your family out, but you have taken a small boat to go back and look at your house and see what is going to be permanently ruined and what you might be able to salvage. So you are there. Maybe you can crawl through a second-story window and look around. "Well, a lot of this is okay." You've tied the boat up outside. Then you hear this cry. You don't know what it is. You go back to your boat and start the motor. Then you turn it off. Maybe you use the oars so you can follow the cry. You go down quite a ways and find a dog on a roof, but the dog is shy.

You say to yourself, "The dog on the roof is hungry, sad and frightened." But it is the kind of dog you are maybe frightened of because you think of it as a guard dog. You approach and talk to the dog, saying, "I will take you to a place where there is food." If you have water or some food there, you try to leave something for the animal if you can. If you can't, then you encourage it (by that time it's weak and tired) to come into the boat.

In short, you try to rescue the animal or do what you can for it. That is obvious to you, but why did you respond in the first place? Maybe you could have said to yourself, "Well, I have family elsewhere and I have been told by all the rescue people that there are no human beings here. All human beings are gone." So you could have said, "Well, maybe it's a bird," and left.

But because someone has said prayer, someone you will never meet, someone on the other side of the world, instead of turning around and going back, which is what you intended to do, you had a feeling, and for no reason you can think of mentally, you try to go help the dog.

Others have prayed and encouraged you, and you are there. Nobody else is there. You go try to help the dog.

It's beautiful.

Prayers work, very often in ways you don't expect. They don't always help when you ask, but very often when they are answered, others have said them for you. It is more likely to work when others say them, because if you are trapped in a collapsed house after an earthquake and are in pain and suffering, it is very hard for you to focus on that prayer. But others are saying prayers. Then maybe help will come.

Maybe you don't get rescued, though. Maybe you die in that collapsed house. That is very sad, but perhaps before you die, sometimes you're asleep or passed out and angels come and talk to you, assuring you that you're going to be all right. There is a place for you, and you're going to see all your relatives. In short, it becomes easier and easier to let go of life, and then, even though you're not feeling so well, you can let go of life easier and pass on. Why? Because other people have asked that spirit and humans and animals and everyone come and help you and nurture you in whatever way they can. It might be spirit or humans, but they find you.

Maybe they get you out, maybe they don't, but at least when you die you go to a loving place with loving beings, see your ancestors and feel all right about your life. When you're passing out of life like that, out of the body, you have a feeling: you'll see threads of color or feel all these prayers that come toward the city you're in where the earthquake was. You can see them streaming in from all parts of the world, even as you are moving out with angels to go to the next place.

You can see all these good feelings and prayers coming toward you, and you have such a good feeling. You know they have helped you, and you know they're going to help others. It is a very good feeling and gives you good feelings about Earth and where you have been. Even if your life has been hard, even if your life ended unhappily, like in an earthquake, you still have good feeling for Earth and its peoples because you see the streams coming from all over the place, streams of good feelings, streams of living prayers sent for you and others.

The Mechanics of Living Prayer

So how would we do more of that? Pray every time we see something on TV or in the newspaper?

That's right. Say a living prayer out loud. Say:

> **"I WILL ASK THAT THESE PEOPLE BE COMFORTED BY ALL THOSE AROUND THEM: SPIRIT, ANIMAL, PLANT, MINERAL, HUMAN. I ASK THAT THEY BE COMFORTED AND NURTURED IN THE BEST WAY THEY CAN RECEIVE AND THE OTHERS CAN OFFER."**

Say something like that, or whatever words you want. Ask for what you want—never ask for what you don't want.

Don't say, "May they be spared suffering." Don't say that. Ask instead for what you want them to have. It is more likely that this will be served, not because God does not want people to be spared suffering, but because material mastery is involved with what you make and how you make it—permission, love and so on. In short, it has to do with creation, but does not have very much to do with *uncreation*. It is much easier to create than to discreate.

Can we offer those same prayers for ourselves if we want to aim ourselves in a certain direction or accomplish certain things or help the whole process? How do you do living prayers?

Yes, but say it only once. I have mentioned living prayer before [see Appendix A]. From my point of view, a living prayer is something you say: "I will request," "I will ask" or "I am asking," "I am requesting," like that. And then you say what you are asking for.

For yourself, you might say:

> **"I AM REQUESTING THAT I BE ENLIGHTENED IN SUCH A WAY IN THIS LIFE SO I CAN BE OF THE GREATEST BENEFIT TO THOSE I MEET AS WELL AS BRING ABOUT COMFORT AND PEACE WITHIN MYSELF."**

Say something like that, if that's what you feel. But say it only once.

It is not about saying it over and over. Things you say over and over again, sometimes called mantras, are a kind of prayer not intended to bring about effect, but actually intended to distract the mind from becoming involved in the thing that the prayer is intended to prevent. If you become mentally involved in the thing the mantra is attempting to prevent, you will probably manifest some of its discomforts within you or around you.

If you are saying a prayer to involve the mind, the mental self, in the prayer itself or saying the statement over and over again, it is an attempt to keep the mind focused on that. Living prayer is completely different from this. It is stated, as I mentioned, and is intended to be said only once.

You say it once, and then Mother Earth and all the energies have it. But if you say it more than once in exactly the same way, then all the energies gradually reduce its happening because they feel that this does not have to do with an actual request you are making, but with some kind of a prayer more associated with religion.

So say the living prayer once, and mean it when you say it, put your heart into it. Then never say it again the same way. You might need to say it some other way. Maybe, for instance, you are fairly enlightened in some ways. Then you meet someone who has a problem, and you almost have what you can say to them, but you know it's not quite right, something is missing. Then you might say:

> **"I WILL ASK FOR THE ENLIGHTENMENT I NEED TO HELP THIS PERSON THROUGH THIS DISCOMFORT SHE IS HAVING, OR THAT SOMEONE SHE MEETS WILL OFFER THIS WISDOM TO HER VERY SOON TO HELP HER."**

This is something that is not quite the same as what you asked before. Maybe you'll get the enlightenment; if you do, then you speak to this person from the heart about the enlightenment you have to help her, if she wishes to hear it. If you do not get it, then you know that someone else got it who will be able to speak to her. You don't have to worry about it at all. Someone else she is going to meet is going to have what she needs to hear, and you can let it go. There's no need to worry.

How's the energy?

About time to stop now, I think.

It's okay with me. This is very beautiful. Beautiful.

And for now I will say farewell and good life.

Good life.

Responsibility and Living Prayer

Zoosh
November 18, 1999

All right. Zoosh speaking.

Oh, welcome! Wonderful.

Preparation for Death on Planet Earth

The channel himself was interested in why people on this planet are profound risk takers and why there are suicidal tendencies, because this is not typical of other planets. On other planets it is not at all unusual, when incarnated, to live eight, ten, twelve hundred years, maybe more. The final cycle of such a life gives the last fifty to eighty years of experiential time, we'll call it, over to the soul's preparation for the transition on other planets—which, to put it simply, on this planet would mean death.

The preparation for transition is vitally important to the soul, not only for the soul to release and also accept what is being offered, but in the soul being able to find its way. You must remember that the universes of all creation are so vast that in order for the soul to find its way, even with the help of guides, it requires a considerable amount of pre-preparation before the moment of actually stepping out of one's physical self.

This has not altered when coming to this planet to incarnate. As a matter of fact, it is even more important here because the conditions on this planet are so extreme compared to other planets where life is often very benevolent. [See the *Explorer Race* series.] One might think that fifty to eighty years of a twelve-hundred-year life is not so much of a percentage, not such a great amount of time. But because of the extremeness of life here, the soul requires that fifty to eighty years of preparation.

When you are born, given the average life and death cycle and ruling out acts of hostility and sudden death—in short, birth straight through to a natural death without my particular diseases or traumas—the average life on your planet might be eighty, eighty-five years on the high side at the moment. So for those born on your Earth, the soul is preparing for death within three to four years of birth, and one can actually see this if one pays attention to children.

You cannot pay attention if you are a parent because you are looking after the child's needs and enjoying the child and your family, but it is possible to pay attention if you are around children in some capacity where they do not require your assistance. Right around the age of three to five, aside from adapting to language and letting go of the usual means of communication one might be born with (which is on the basis of telepathic feelings), one sees a change, an alteration in the eyes of the child. This is partly due to the experience of adapting to one's cultural world as well as to one's family, but it is also due to the sensation that life here is not typical—typical in terms of when one is born on another planet, one never even considers death at all, nor does one consider any risk taking that could lead to death.

If that were the case here, you would have a relatively light, trouble-free childhood. You would not be inclined to take risks as a child. You might still have the sensation of being invulnerable, but you would be less attracted to violence and more attracted to expression, be that in the form of the arts or simple communication, for example.

One sees then, with a child here about the age of five, some changes in the eyes, meaning a sensation within the physical demonstrated self that the lifetime here is short. This tends to create a physical anxiety—not a mental one, not a feeling one—that one must live as much as possible within the short time allowed. Again, it's a *physical* anxiety; no mental or conscious anxiety is involved.

This is why someone might do something. For instance, a parent might say to a youngster, "Why did you do that? Why did you take that terrible risk? Didn't you know that you could get hurt?" And the child says, "I don't know." Sometimes the child says "I don't know" because he doesn't want to tell the parent the real reason, but at least half if not 60 to even 70 percent of the time, he really doesn't know because it's a physical anxiety, not a mental one. So there is no mental explanation for it.

In any event, it is important to know this so that you do not assume that life on other planets has any form of this kind of activity. If you've lived eight or nine hundred years or more, you have established your lifestyle, your personality, within a benevolent expression of itself, and you would not have any particular urgency in your body and in the other forms of your immediate consciousness to rush and do everything. By that time you would have done just about everything so that when the preparation for your transition came along at fifty, eighty years of experiential time, you would not feel denied. You would have experienced so much that the preparation would be a spiritual, loving experience that could be entirely embraced elsewhere. But here it primarily creates a sense of urgency.

A New Level of Creator Responsibility

What's the update on the energies? We had August 11 [1999], and we have the unity consciousness using our energy. What's the planet doing? How is humanity doing?

Humanity is struggling to cope with the responsibility that has been visited upon you. You have to remember that no one on this planet is prepared to have even a small amount—let's say 5 percent—of one's capacity as a responsible creator. From even the most well-educated or wise beings—be it book wisdom, be it life wisdom, be it street wisdom—from even the most grounded individuals, when they are confronted about why they did something a certain way, you will hear rational explanations or excuses.

This needs to go. I want to give people permission to do something you did when you were a youngster. I want to give you permission to say, "I don't know why I did that. It felt right at the time. I'm surprised it didn't work out in a way that felt good." Please give yourself permission to say this. If you do not, you will find in the coming months and years that you will feel overwhelmed by life.

You are now very gradually receiving more and more capacity, responsibility and, to some extent, direction toward responsible creator action. This type of responsibility does not just mean that what you do and how you do it may be questioned by others, because that has always been the case, but rather that the effects upon others caused by what you do may be visited upon you. This does not mean that you will have to suffer for any problem you inadvertently create for others, but it does mean that you may have to work on a spiritual level (I'll give you some instruction in a moment) to resolve problems you might have unintentionally (or even intentionally in some cases) created for others, perhaps in a moment of spontaneous agitation or even in a moment of well-placed but ill-timed action.

A Living Prayer for the Responsible Creator

What to do? If you get feedback or an uncomfortable feeling related to a moment when you did something but you didn't know why, or you did something but didn't expect it to have that impact, there's something you can say. If you meditate, get into that state. If you don't, get into the most spiritual state you can. Don't call on Jesus, Michael and other beings of the angelic realm to solve it for you. You can ask for their *support*, but ask them to support what you are doing and saying; don't give it to them to solve. A responsible creator makes at least an effort to solve it herself or himself.

First invite their support. Try to slow down and stop. Don't suddenly stop for a moment and say it, but slow down and stop. Doing it with your bare feet on the ground is best, but if you can't, then do it the best way you can. Ideally there won't be anybody within five feet of you, so you can say it out loud even if you whisper it. Say, "I will ask" (or alternatively, "I am asking," but the first works better, I feel):

> **"I WILL ASK THAT ANY RAMIFICATIONS OR EFFECTS THAT MAY BE HARMFUL TO OTHERS ON THE BASIS OF MY RECENT ACTIONS BE CALMED, HEALED, NURTURED AND RESOLVED."**

If you prefer, you can simply say "resolved," but I am filling in some optional words for you. Make sure you use the word "resolve," though. That's important.

Try and say it out loud; if you can't, say it in a whisper. It is useful to say that, then just be with the energy for a moment. Don't think. If you find yourself thinking, open your eyes and stare at a wall or something (not a human being). It will be just enough to let it go. Try not to stare at paper with words on it. If you don't have anything else to stare at, look at your hand.

Then let it go and go on. That is actually a form of benevolent magic, which I've talked about before, and also a living prayer, of course. I want to give you these things to say rather than have you say to yourself, "Oh no, I didn't intend that," or "What am I going to do about that? I may never see those people again," which is definitely possible. You simply say something like what I gave you.

The reason you don't give these problems and uncomfortable feelings to Michael or Jesus or God in any form is that it is time to take responsibility yourself. You can ask them to support you and what you are doing in this living prayer, but don't give the responsibility to them.

Know that they are always around anyway and will do what they must, but since the level of responsibility for creation is gradually being eased into your lives now, you need to approach this as if it were a real experience, because it *is* real.

Homework: Watch Your Excuses

So the time of this responsibility is upon you, and except for the very young, most of you are entirely unprepared for it. This is homework: I want you to pay attention in the next two periods in which you are awake—the next two days, let's say. I want you to note how often you make an excuse or rationalize, even with perfect forms of persuasion, that something you did was somehow related to a perfectly explainable cause. This is not to blame yourself, but if you can shift gears and say the living prayer I just gave you in a form that is comfortable to you, if you can say this, just think of all of the excuses you won't have to make. But it does require that when you say it, you really *mean* it. You have to genuinely mean it. You cannot give lip service to it.

I'll tell you a little secret about something you've been dealing with for a long time. Those of you who have gotten used to making excuses or creating unending rationalizations for why you did something, whatever it was, think back: Very often those excuses and rationalizations tended to complicate the situation and make it even worse. It was consistently either a repeating experience in your life or it became blown all out of proportion, if not for you, then for somebody else.

That's because excuses, even though they might be perfectly reasonable, draw your soul's attention to *something that was not learned or understood.* On all other planets it is understood that when one does something like that, one immediately says a living prayer, which has the impact of benevolent magic to resolve the situation.

Stopping Repetitive Stress

Because so many people are affected by what other people do, very often the ramifications spread much further away from you than you can ever know consciously. People come, they go. They are confused, they pass on the confusion—and you may find out about it later in a repeating experience. So let's cancel out all that confusion. Remember, if your soul hears that as something that wasn't learned because no living prayer was said, your soul will insist to its teachers that the experience be repeated as often as it takes until you say the living prayer or do what it takes to resolve the lesson.

If you understand that, you will realize that the experiences you've been having repeatedly, which you often call daily stresses, are not necessary. Remember, I don't care if someone didn't tell you something and that's why you did it, okay? It doesn't make any difference whether the excuse is absolutely legitimate or provable in a court of law. It does not make any difference, because it's not about who is to blame; it's about where the repetitious, unpleasant experience *stops.*

And it stops with you. The moment you or anybody else says a living prayer like this, you transform it. It may not be transformed for everybody, but it will be transformed for you, meaning that those daily stresses become less and less when you say these things. It doesn't mean that if you are with people, you don't tell them, "Excuse me, but this message you gave me was not clear."

Try not to say "wrong," because people hear that as a pointed accusation toward them. If you say it wasn't clear, that gets the point across. "It wasn't clear" means that what was told to them may very well have been mistaken, but it is not an accusatory statement. People, when they hear "wrong" (this is what happens for everyone), immediately become five years old just for a moment on the feeling level. When they were told by their parent or brother or sister or well-intended guardian, "That's wrong; don't do that," they felt bad, unloved, ashamed and ultimately resentful. So don't bring up that battle unnecessarily. Remember to say, "This wasn't clear. This is what it was about, as much as I can understand, and in the future I hope we can have greater clarity, not only in what you tell me, but what others tell you." That is also a kind of sneaky living prayer, because you are saying it to them, but you are including them in your prayer. It is a desire.

It is said perhaps not the same way one says a living prayer, but it is a desire. On another planet you might say, "I will ask that in the future you and I have clear communications always so that we can understand each other and appreciate each other more." That is how it could be said on another planet, but I do not expect you to say that at random to people who might not understand your form of communication. If you can say it to people who *can* understand, then it can work, but don't say it on and on indefinitely because it will become tedious.

Remember, it is not your job to transform the whole world. It is your job right now, with the creation energy being visited upon you, to transform your own self-destructive habits that have been causing repeated daily stresses, because the soul is absolutely aware that you didn't understand something, and that needs to be altered.

One result of recent experiences that affect you and involve you on Earth is that people are feeling overwhelmed with the level of responsibility they have, which is being underscored by others. Although most people don't know about this (because most people don't read this material—we hope to change that at some point), they are overwhelmed by the sudden increase in the level of responsibility for their actions, words and deeds.

So we have reached the point where we have to take responsibility to resolve the negative consequences of our actions.

Yes. Don't assume that by taking this responsibility, everything will become wonderful overnight, but it will begin. If for no other reason, do it for your own personal well-being, because your soul is adamant on this point.

It's not because your soul is structured in a rigid fashion. Your soul recognizes that it is a correspondent, let's say, to guides and teachers, and from its point of view, it is its job to keep you on track. Now, your soul does not always experience the impact of those choices on the physical self and the feeling self—not to the extent you do—but your soul is a tough taskmaster here, slapping the stick into the palm of the hand as a military officer might do.

Your soul is a tough taskmaster because it knows that if you *don't* get this point, you will go round and round in a loop of never-ending, repetitive, stressful experiences because you are caught up in, "He did it," "She did it," "They did it," "I said this because they said that," "I did this because they did that." There is no resolution there. This does not mean that you do not attempt to create clearer communications and clearer actions between individuals, but when those things happen, you can break that chain by saying that living prayer. Even though you yourself may not be entirely responsible, you have been involved in such actions before. Do it for your own sake and for the sake of others.

Are living prayers really for your soul to know that you understand? Is that who you are actually addressing the prayer to?

No, the soul knows; it is not an idiot. The soul knows, based on how you demonstrate your life. You say the living prayer because it is a creation "device." The prayer itself is not an "Oh, please help me" prayer. It's a creation. Living prayer is a creation. "I will ask . . ." is a creation.

For example, you are a creator of a planet—*pouf!* It is no different. It is *pouf!* with your full intention and meaning. That's why I say, stop what you're doing and focus your full intent on it on the feeling, physical level; pay attention only to that living prayer. You say it, then let it go. That is your version on Earth of *pouf!*

It may not happen immediately. You may never know the full impact of what you have said and done, but you might know something, and someday those repetitive stresses will stop because you have taken responsibility for your experience in life. You are not just saying, "He did it," "She did it," "They did it," which guarantees that it continues. You would be pointing the finger for the rest of your life. Think about it.

But at some point do you create the resolution for your actions? Do you take responsibility and create a resolution? So the soul must listen so that it won't push this up in your face again?

Why should the soul believe you? The soul says, "He did it right, so I'll test him." The soul will allow those experiences to keep coming until it is convinced that you are no longer saying it as a measure of self-discipline but because it has become a natural thing to say. It is no longer natural to offer excuses or rationalizations. Once you've moved past that reaction and flow naturally and immediately into this other process, the soul will stop creating those stresses. Then stress might come along as part of the natural process of life. The soul will trust that you have fully integrated that new process into your life and have the full and complete capacity to handle any such experience that comes along in the future. But just because you change it once, the soul is not going to say, "Everything's wonderful." The soul is not a fool.

This is a change of lifetime habits. You were raised by people who often made excuses or rationalizations: "I did that because . . ." You were all raised by people like this, with very few exceptions. You learned that it was okay to do it. In your society the civil legal system is largely based on that, and it is called proof. But we are trying to go past proof here. Proof is not creation. Creation goes beyond proof.

So most people on the planet, then, are creating a recurring series of experiences because the soul is trying to teach them to take responsibility? Is that why they are so overwhelmed?

Yes, but it is not only the soul; Creator is visiting this upon you. The soul is, shall we say, Creator's representative.

So the Creator says, "Wake up, it's time to take responsibility"?

Yes, and it didn't suddenly begin at 5 percent. It's been easing up slowly, but it is almost at 5 percent now.

A 5 percent increase?

No, 5 percent totality, in terms of your creator responsibility. It is now at 4.97 percent, which I rounded off at 5 percent.

So it's going to increase?

Gradually and slowly, incrementally. It is not going to decrease at all.

The Need to Improve Hand-Eye Coordination
and the Shift to Vertical Wisdom

What about the new situation we just learned about in September, where from 5 to 30 percent of people's energy is being used so they will feel the suffering of all other people as a step toward unity consciousness? How are people dealing with that? There's a lot of fatigue and exhaustion.

It continues.

That's all? It simply continues?

There is no change in status, if that's what you're asking.

At least people are bearing up under it. They don't know why, they're just tired.

Yes, correct. A lot of people are getting the dropsies [dropping things] these days. Some of this has to do with the reduced oxygen content in the air, but a lot of it has to do with a necessity to reorient hand-eye coordination. You're going through a period of about three and a half years in which there is going to be this change. It won't immediately lock in after three and a half years, so don't look for evidence, but it's beginning to make the move from horizontal knowledge to vertical wisdom [see Appendix I]. At the end of three and a half years, you won't have vertical wisdom, but you'll be on the path, and the hand-eye coordination is somewhat weakened during this time.

Here's something that's good to do. Children play video games, where hand-eye coordination is improved. If the video game can be nonviolent, that's wonderful. If it can be only slightly competitive, that's useful. But you can also play a pinball machine or move a puzzle around in your hand, trying to get that little ball in the hole and so on. In short, you can do anything that requires precise hand-eye coordination both for fun and as an exercise. You did these things when you were a youngster. You played sports, you went out and ran, you learned how to ride a bicycle. Normally, you wouldn't have to do these things again in your lifetime, but because of this shift now, you have to practice them again. But do it for fun. Find something you can do for pleasure.

The shift is, as you say, the end of what was.

The end of what was, coming to the end now, really stretching past a little bit. But it's the end of linear, shifting to vertical reality. Vertical is so much easier. When you're disciplined under linear, you tend to drag the past along with you. If it's pleasant, that's good. If it isn't, which is most often the case, that's what you drag with you, and it can be very burdensome. But you're going to let that go—all of you at some point—because you're going to have the capacity to tap into vertical wisdom. I'll talk more about that in the future. I'm mentioning it now so that you won't be overly alarmed.

For a short time there will be a tendency to diagnose problems in people who are having these situations. Some people might have to do these fun disciplines in an urgent sense. I do not wish to scare people, but if you're going to have surgery done for any reason, it might be useful to ask your doctor if he or she plays any sports like tennis or golf and so on. Be inclined to have a procedure done on you by someone who does these things rather than someone who does only surgery.

I'm not trying to cast any aspersions on surgeons, but rather I'm saying that hand-eye coordination needs to be something outside your personal discipline to do you any good. If you are, for instance, a long-distance trucker and you always have to use your hand-eye coordination, you would still need to do something beyond your profession to sharpen it and make up for the loss as you bridge through this time.

Once we bridge into vertical wisdom, then . . .

You don't go straight into vertical wisdom but into a stage that prepares you for vertical wisdom. I want to be clear; that's why I'm splitting hairs here. If I told you that you were going into vertical wisdom in three and a half years, you'd be disappointed then if you still didn't know what you needed to know when you needed to know it—and then after that moment, if you didn't need to know it anymore, you wouldn't.

The part-time activity doesn't need to be done for more than ten or fifteen minutes. You can do it longer if you like, but it has to be something that's fun, something that's amusing to you. It can be a sport, but it doesn't have to be.

Can it be games? How many times a week?

Four or five times a week at least.

For days, weeks, months, years? From now on?

From now on for at least three and a half years. If you don't do it, it won't likely be a disaster, but you might find your body wanting to do things that you don't understand. You'll pick up an object and suddenly it's out of your hand. Some doctors will analyze that as part of a pre-Alzheimer's condition that has not been recognized before, having to do with neuromuscular communication. Your mind says to squeeze the object, but the motor reflex opens your hand instead. It might be analyzed as a disease and even treated for a time, but it is a temporary situation for many people.

If you do these fun things, I think you'll find that it will help you quite a bit. It might even improve your work skills unexpectedly. For example, you might speed up your typing capacity on the computer, or if you are in a profession that involves hard labor, you might find that you are much more accurate and tend to make fewer mistakes. You will tend to have fewer accidents on the job and so on. Employers might benefit from something they often do in Japan and other cultures—encouraging employees to do exercises and games and such. In this country companies have often encouraged employees to organize a softball or bowling team. I'm not saying that this needs to be done long or be a big, involved thing that could take a lot of time. But it might be useful to encourage people to do something that is a game, that is fun and not associated with work.

I'm not visiting that upon you, but for employers who are reading this, if you wish to encourage this at some point, that's fine. (Some research has been done on this, by the way, in terms of games that improve work skills. You can look that up under Education on the Internet.)

How to Ask for Strength

People are more tired now, and that's going to continue because of your responsibility level having gone up. You need to begin to utilize what you actually have. You are physically tired. If you are living now in a mountainous area, look out your window if you can see a mountain from there. If you can't, then on your way to work stop when you can see the mountain or mountains. But don't look at a mountain if you know there are lots of antennas there. Look at some point on the mountain where there is the least amount of man-made stuff between you and it. If there are electrical wires visible between you and your view of the mountain, don't do it there, but at some point you will have a clear line of sight.

First ask the mountain to share energy with you—not its own personal energy, because the mountain needs it. Ask the mountain to connect to its sources both beyond Earth and within Earth *if available.* Inside-the-Earth energy may not be available, but the mountain can connect to other planets beyond Earth to feed energy to you that will sustain and strengthen your physical body in the most healthful way for you.

Say it exactly like this:

"I ASK YOU TO CONNECT TO YOUR SOURCES BOTH BEYOND AND WITHIN EARTH, IF AVAILABLE, TO FEED ENERGY TO ME THAT WILL SUSTAIN AND STRENGTHEN MY PHYSICAL BODY IN THE MOST HEALTHFUL WAY FOR ME."

Give the mountain a moment, not much more than ten seconds. Then begin breathing in, taking a deep breath from the mountain. (You can be miles away.) If you happen to notice anything man-made flying by, a plane or a helicopter, just pause. Let your breath out and wait and breathe until that object clears from your line of sight. (If it's a bird, it's all right. It will pass through the bird.) Then breathe in again and exhale. Don't pant. Keep doing that until you feel a genuine increase in your physical energy.

Some of this strength might have to do with deep breathing, but only a little bit. You'll notice an increase, a change in your chest. You should notice it begin to radiate into your solar plexus and into your limbs a bit. It might take twenty or thirty breaths. So breathe in slowly. Take deep breaths. Exhale, then breathe in again slowly and exhale.

You are asking the mountain to do something as an intermediary. It is better for you, being made physically of Earth, to go through the mountain as an intermediary rather than to get the energy directly from another planet. If you did that, you would undoubtedly be staring at man-made objects because of so many satellites hurtling around the Earth. The Earth, however, will bring that energy through without touching any of those satellites (not counting the Moon).

This is a time of creation and the responsibility of creation, and you must have strength. Anyone can do this thing with a mountain, though I grant that many, many readers do not have mountains available to them. Mountains are the best resources.

There is one other resource you can use, and that's part of the reason it has been on the planet. Unfortunately, this resource has been totally misunderstood, and as a result, its numbers have been greatly reduced. If you can connect with a tree whose trunk, as it goes into the Earth, is at least ten or twelve feet in diameter, you can address the tree.

The tree would have been there a long time to be ten to twelve feet or more across, and it can act as an intermediary like the mountain. It's not the best intermediary and can do this for only one, two or maybe three people at a time at most, though one would be best. The mountain is definitely better, but this will work.

Those of you living in areas where it is cold and snowy most of the time usually have mountains available to you. But if you do not—for instance, those who live around the sea or are in the shipping business—look instead at a point on the horizon when the Sun is either rising or setting. Don't stare at the Sun, but at some point near it; you can use that.

Those of you in total flatland with no trees available can also use the horizon. Don't stare at the Sun. Just look toward the sunrise or sunset. Ideally, do this either at dusk or dawn or when it's about to rise above the horizon from your point of view.

I want to give you these alternatives because, of course, not all of you have mountains available.

What about photographs of a mountain such as we have in Shamanic Secrets for Material Mastery?

No, because this is intended to be immediate. This is a response to a personal, immediate need. You're tired and you need something right now. No, a photograph won't work.

For those of you who are in prison, if you can look out a window, ask the clouds to do that. They may or may not be able to. The best thing you can do, if you are in prison or underground, is to remember a mountain, but it must be one you've actually seen. Or remember a sunset you have seen. I'm trying to give you as many alternatives as possible and speak to as wide an audience as possible.

If you are in a place where there are lots of disease organisms, you can either eliminate or greatly reduce the impact of those organisms upon you or you can get stronger. Since the Earth actually uses those organisms—they are part of her body as well as part of the total consciousness of the being here—it is safer for all beings to be stronger. (Don't use that as a spiritual excuse to not take antibiotics if you need them for some reason.)

Meteors

Are meteoroids coming toward the planet?

Meteors that have been traveling through space for some time will not hit the Earth. Some of the materials that burn up in the atmosphere might at some point drift onto the Earth. There is even the chance that a few bits might contact the Earth, mostly in remote locations, but not always. This is usually a good thing. It will be important for scientists to take note of and map where the atmosphere is thinner and the impact of the meteors through this thinner atmosphere. Many scientists have been following this for some time because of the breakdown of the atmosphere close to Earth due to the unintentional side effects of chemicals that have sometimes been put into the sky for industrial/military purposes. It is perhaps beneficial to keep track of this.

In order to welcome these extraterrestrial visits, one might ask the meteors that pass through the atmosphere of the Earth at any time to bring what you need and burn up what you don't need. Say it as a living prayer:

> **"I WILL ASK THAT THE METEORS THAT PASS THROUGH THE EARTH'S ATMOSPHERE AT ANY TIME BRING WHAT WE NEED AND BURN UP WHAT WE DON'T NEED."**

This is the actual position of the hands relative to the physical body [holds arms outward, palms up]. The statement must be said with intent; then let it go afterward. That's the best way to welcome meteors. They've been coming along for years, but if you welcome them, you participate in what they are doing.

Make it clear that you want them to burn up what you don't need in the atmosphere. (You don't want to invite a meteor to come down to the Earth and burn up something you don't need but that you might be alarmed about if it were to burn up!)

Communicating with the Natural World

Speaks of Many Truths
November 19, 1999

his is Speaks of Many Truths.

Astrology Invites a Different Way of Doing Things

People will seek other methods of solution to whatever is annoying them. Sometimes the way you do things is comforting and comfortable, even if it is not the best way ("you" meaning *everybody*). So the astrologic system is set up in such a way as to stir things up now and then. Then it can be more easily seen that the method by which you are doing something could be improved upon.

Generally speaking, if things are stirred up and the method by which you are doing things is only very slightly affected, that means it's probably a very good method. But if it creates disharmonies, problems, delays and discomforts, then the method probably needs to be evolved. That's why astrology is set up that way. It's a useful, if not always comforting, system.

Useful how? So we can look at our process?

Yes, because it is so easy to get into a way of doing things sometimes. To give an extreme example, sometimes people will do things, even by habit, that are delaying, that are not supportive, that might even be considered self-destructive, but they are used to doing it that way and that's the way they understand and have faith in. But when things get shaken around a bit because the astrologic is shaken, then very often you are confronted with delays. And with delays, the methods and systems that are not working well are exposed.

So how does it work specifically? The astrologic?

When this Mercury planet is retrograde, during that time such things as travel sometimes become delayed. Communications can be confusing or upset. Things are not always heard in the way they are meant and so on. Of course, as I say, this has a good side. Whatever isn't working often becomes very obvious, and that can be very useful for the future. It's important not only to recognize what isn't working, but to put it on track in some way, to make plans or write it down, saying, "This thing that I am doing or I have been doing isn't working, and it needs to work better." Make a list, and then work out your method in a different way.

Communicating with the Stars

How did you deal with this in your time? Did you understand astrology?

We did not have the understanding of the astrologic the way you do, but we did have people who understood and communicated with the stars. When things would be upset like that, when the planet Mercury was in retrograde and maybe other planets were retrograde or eclipsed, we would have a person who would keep track of that—not a written record, but memory.

And that way when things came up, instead of doing things the way we always did, we would immediately put in an alternative way to do things. We would immediately shift our methods. Our assertion was that we must always be flexible. That's what we believed or believe.

How could the ones who understood the stars remember over such a long period of time?

They had to remember. Think about your time compared to ours. In your time there is printed word. You read, study, conduct business and work with numbers. None of that existed in my time. There was much more space in the memory to remember things. And, of course, the air was fresher, with more oxygen. Minerals were sharp; visions were clearer. It was not so hard at all. There were not a lot of distractions. There was our life and the life around us, and that was it.

So they could correlate when things didn't go right and look at the position of the stars without having any documentation or anything?

We would talk to the stars.

Tell me more about that.

We would communicate with the stars in the sky at the time things became unsettled. Usually there would be a little warning, meaning that the person who remembered and kept track of these things would know that at about this time, certain things happen.

And if that person did not recall, then something would happen. In short, we never took it for granted that if a child fell down and scratched his or her knee, that it was an accident. We did not believe in accidents. We always assumed that if something like that happened, there may be more to it. So our star speaker would talk to the stars and ask for advice.

Different stars, having different advice and different personalities, would talk. At different times of the year, different stars are available. The personalities of some stars are very cold, you might even say austere, whereas other stars have warm personalities. Some stars have great wisdom and an ability to express it to all peoples. Other stars have great wisdom and knowledge with very little ability to communicate.

So the star speaker would communicate often with the stars who were in the best communication. She would ask a star, "Is there some other meaning behind the child's injury?" And the one star would say this or that, and some stars would say nothing because they had nothing to add. So the star speaker would go on to the next star and so on until she had a composite or a collection of information that would allow her to say, "This is what the stars say to the best of my capacity to communicate with them." Then we would know.

Often stars would say that there might be nineteen or twenty or twenty-two days when it might be difficult to do things the way we usually did them. So that would be a good time to do things in a different way. Then, after that time went by, we would either go back to our usual way or we might discover that doing something a different way was actually better, and we would integrate that into our way of being.

I do not know if all tribal peoples do this, but my feeling is that they must do something like this. Otherwise, they would not survive. They would not have a warning of the unexpected. In your day your scientists tell you when it's going to rain or when there will be a typhoon or something. In our day, if we did not hear about this from the animals, plants, stars or the Earth, well, our people wouldn't survive too long. I'm sure it must be similar for other tribal peoples who are still alive in your time who have survived for a while.

Could you talk to the stars?

I have not done so. I suppose it's something that many people can do. It is not much different than any form of channeling, only with her, our star speaker, it wasn't like this is through Robert. It was a communication. She would be quiet, she would ask quietly, and she would hear the answer through the left side of her head. She would pay attention and check the answer with how she felt in her physical body, the way shamanic people do in your time.

In this way there would be a way to know that this is how it is best expressed. This is what is so for you now.

An Opening for Change

What is happening now? Some people say that they get really angry.

I'm glad you mentioned that, because in this time of heightened consequences and heightened responsibilities, what will happen for everyone is that any anger expressed or a sudden outburst of anger is likely to leave a space in the auric field. When that occurs, it can go one of two ways. If you do not continue to outflow energy, it can be hazardous. You might pick something else up. But if you continue to outflow energy for two or three days, it can create an opening, an invitation to change the way you do everything.

You must remember, almost all adults do everything based upon a very small foundation they established when they were very young that was a safe territory. No more than this—just a teeny little foundation, about a couple of square inches of safe ground that you could establish when you were a youngster. And when they know that, then they build everything on top of that safe territory until they get a teetering pile of chairs stacked up on top of this tiny little space.

If this hole is blown and you are able to continue to outflow energy for a few days, it necessarily expands that space immediately. It allows you to reshuffle everything that you've built on top of it. Generally, following a circumstance like this, all of your methods and approaches built on such a narrow foundation will be almost immediately challenged so that you can see the weakness in them. The weakness might be something you become aware of on your own, or it might be something that is thrown into your face by others because things that you formerly said were not a problem suddenly turn into a mountain. And you thought it was just a molehill.

So thank yourself for this, even though the experience itself is not pleasant. Thank yourself, and say, "Well, I have an opportunity now to change the way I do things to a foundation that is firm and solid and that will work, one that is not based on childhood principles of safety." Childhood principles of safety are vital for the survival of children up through and including their mid-teenage years, but after that, they do not serve the adult very well.

The Need to Breathe

Other people say they are really tired.

That's partly an effect of the times, but I think that you will all find that some of this has to do with the need to breathe. If you pay attention to the way you breathe normally—and that's very difficult to do because when you pay attention, you have a tendency to change your breathing, so you have to sort of just keep an eye on it from time to time—you will notice that you tend to breathe most of the time in a very shallow manner.

When people breathe in a shallow manner, it means that they are basically very frightened. If you know that, you will be able to immediately see how many of the methods you have used are based in the past on that childhood framework of safety. Children tend to breathe deeply, but if frightening things have happened to them, they breathe more and more shallowly. That's because it doesn't feel safe to be seen or to breathe loudly.

This is not unusual. Soldiers, of course, have to breathe shallowly if they are trying to be unseen. It's the same thing if you feel like prey; you tend to breathe shallowly as well. So pay attention to the way you breathe. You could probably acquire an extra 20 to 30 percent of energy if you make it a personal intention to breathe deeply.

You can use yoga breathing exercises if you like; if you find they are helpful, go ahead. But I would say that mostly, every time you think of it, just take a deep breath and exhale. Try to do that more often. It will tend to relieve your physical body of a great deal of the harmful tension you all carry, and it might also, in time, cause you to feel physically safer.

Talking to Faces in Stone

It interests me that you actually lived in a group of people and had this kind of star guidance available.

You must remember that we also had people who spoke to the trees around us and the plants.

And the ancestors?

Sometimes. Usually the animals. We would usually only speak to the ancestors who were obvious in the stone around us. I'll tell you why.

If you look (and you've seen this many times in a place where there are rocky outcroppings), you'll see faces—sometimes they are very obvious and sometimes they are subtle. In our time we believe that if one has lived a very good life, done much service and made a contribution to one's own kind and perhaps others, the stone of Mother Earth will honor that by allowing the face of that individual to appear in stone in a way that the individual could be recognized by people of his or her time.

These are the ancestors we tend to talk to, because they have proven that they are beings who desire to assist or give knowledge and wisdom to our peoples. Sometimes, of course, you fleetingly see someone like this in the clouds, but you do not always see it, whereas the beings in the stone are obvious all the time. So we talk to those ancestors.

For those of you living in areas where faces are obvious in the stone, try this, especially if you have the means or the ability to communicate. Try it and see what the ancestors say. Don't be too attached to them telling you their names. They might be able to make that clear to you, but once their faces are in stone, they've become very unattached to their earthly personalities and more involved in the body of Earth herself. But they will speak to you on the basis of their personal wisdom as well as Earth wisdom. It is something worth doing. I recommend it.

So how would you decide what questions to ask? You would see their faces? Or you would have a question and then you would look for a face? How would that work?

Very often in my time we would know, because we would camp in certain specific places or sometimes live in a place for a long time, and we would have stone seers. They would go and look, often bringing their apprentices with them, and find as many faces as they could see once we got there. But sometimes, when you had a question for which you had been unable to get answers, information or the wisdom you needed, you would just stand and look at the stone and see a face that you'd never seen before who would give you the answer.

Sometimes you would then be able to see that face from that point on. But the most amazing thing, which I found fascinating in my time, is that sometimes that face would be very physically obvious. You could see it physically, and you would connect with that face and get an answer that worked for you. Then the next day you would look, and no matter how much you looked, you couldn't find it. That face wasn't there anymore.

That's something you can do in your time, too. It is a fascinating experience. It does not matter whether you take photographs of it; a photograph might or might not show it. Also, photographs of mountains tend to take energy. Social scientists have misunderstood this. I have spoken of this before, but I will say it again.

Photographs Capture Your Energy

Tribal peoples sometimes did not want their photograph taken, but this was not because they thought it captured their spirit—though they might have said that to the photographer, assuming that the photographer did not have enough depth to understand their spiritual principles. So they would let the photographer believe that. But the real reason was that the photograph would capture some of their energy, and that is sometimes a problem, especially if enough people take enough pictures. We discussed this to some length in *Shamanic Secrets for Material Mastery*.

Yes, we did. We got into the movie stars.

It is good to bring it up again because in your time people are very fond of photographs. But this will pass because people will move from an attachment to the past to a greater focus in the present.

And so photo albums are like an attachment to the past?

It's an attachment to the past. Even though they are very often pleasant memories, sometimes this also brings up unpleasant memories. Such things need to be disposed of, but even if they are, they still exist. The only way to really dispose of them in a way that is truly permanent is to burn them, but I think perhaps photographs are not often burned in your time.

Someday people will say, "Well, this is very interesting, but I'd rather see the place," or as in our time, "I'd rather memorize your face based upon what I can remember, or maybe touch your face if I cannot see as well as most people do." You have glasses; we didn't. Sometimes we needed them, but we didn't have them. So husbands and wives tended to touch each other's face more, to remember it.

A Line of Communication with the Natural World

We have guidance counselors, insurance counselors and financial counselors, and you lived very comfortably with rocks and stars.

We didn't always have as much to eat as we would have liked, but when we had more . . . for instance, when we had more meat, we would dry it for when we didn't have enough. And those days came. We were always happy when we had something put away. That's still popular in your time.

But I'd like to go back to this point. Did you have the understanding that you were born at a certain time and so there was an imprint of you, lines of energies from the stars, or would you just very pragmatically talk to the stars and ask if things were going to be difficult some days?

In our time, when a child was born, it would often be the case for the uncles and the aunts and for the elders . . . children were not born every day. Occasionally, we would have two born in one day—I have heard about that from my ancestors—but it did not happen in my time. So the uncles and the aunts and maybe even the sisters and the brothers (if they were old enough to have responsibility) would perhaps go out to speak to the beings, who would sometimes have something to say about the child.

The star speaker would talk to the stars. The stone person would talk to the stones. And some people would talk to the trees, the plants, the animals. It would be a line of communication.

Now, something that you also need to know—and that was not entirely at all unknown—is that sometimes it would be the other way around, sometimes the animals would talk to us. For instance, I remember once that a rabbit was born with an extra toe on its front foot. That family of rabbits had not seen this before, nor was anybody there in that clan who had. And since I was friendly with that family of rabbits, they asked me if I knew anything about this or if I could find out something for them so they would know whether all the young ones would be born this way in the future or if it meant something—what could I tell them about it, or could I ask all the beings I knew.

So I did that, and finally I spoke to a fairy of a blackberry bush. We could have eaten those berries, but we left them for the bears because it was one of the few things they had to eat there. We'd much rather have them eat the berries then come to our camp.

I asked the fairy, and she said that this particular rabbit was intended to be a clan leader. She would be able to consult with the Earth and have better communication with the Earth through her feet—that's why she was given an extra toe, to have that extra capacity. I passed this on to the rabbit clan leader, who said, "Oh yes, that makes sense." And as far as I know, it worked out well for them.

I want to ask more but just hold it one moment, the Sun is in the channel's face.

The Sun is always welcome, but sometimes in these circumstances it's a little too welcome.

Thank the Sun Every Day

We must always thank the Sun for coming, every day. I have heard from brothers and sisters on other planets that when people forgot to thank their suns for coming, sometimes they did not come.

I have heard from a sister on a distant planet that the sun did not come one day and the people were very frightened. They needed to continue their ancient prayers. They had to ask for an ancient to appear in front of them and instruct them in the ancient ways. That being did appear and instructed them, and they began doing their prayers, and the sun returned. This is one of the homelands, I believe, of some tribal peoples who are no longer on Earth in your time. They are back on their home planet now, and they told me this old story. So this is perhaps one of the reasons that my people and many tribal peoples welcome the Sun every day.

What does it mean, the sun didn't show up? Was it eclipsed or foggy? It didn't actually go anywhere, did it?

She showed me the picture and it looked exactly the way a sun would look if it were eclipsed, except that you couldn't see a brightness around the edge. It was just like a dark disk in the sky. You could just barely see it with a little of the light left over from the nighttime. It was very frightening. So I think it was not an eclipse exactly. It was something the sun could do, and it did.

Effects of Radiation on Humans

From your human point of view, let's go over some of the same questions I asked Zoosh. I asked how humans are doing with the amount of energy we're giving to the process of unity, and he said that everybody is suffering. What can you say about that?

I think that you are actually doing a little better than I expected you to do. There was a moment when it first descended on people that people shuddered. It was a shock, but I think you are doing very well, even though you are all more tired.

There is no question that much of what makes you tired are the electrical and electronic signals through the air. They have become greater in your time—and apparently will continue to become greater.

The electromagnetic and radio waves and all this other radiation are affecting us in addition to everything else?

Yes, they have been for some time. When it was just radio in the thirties and forties, it didn't have much impact. Now it is not only radio, but television and, perhaps more important, the many different waves and bands you are using. All of these things have different impacts on the physical body of human beings. Certainly these impacts are not intended to occur on the human being.

Quite a bit of research has been done to see the impact, but the trouble is that the research has largely been focused on the short-term and long-term impact of this specific frequency or that specific wave, but not on the combination of everything at once. Normally, people compare research papers and essentially speculate, but of course you wouldn't get many volunteers who would want to be bombarded with all those waves and frequencies like that, although there might be one or two. If you did that, you would find, much to your shock, that it is terribly damaging, largely to the nervous system that supplies energy to the muscular system and, even to some extent, to the bone marrow. It has quite a damaging impact. When you add the diminished quantities of oxygen in your time—with your bodies set up to breathe oxygen—and the generally unhealthful style most people live, this is just one more thing.

Now, as I've said in the past—perhaps Zoosh has also said this sometimes in the past—you have been able to avoid this if you live in a high mountain community or in a small town largely surrounded by farmland. But this is not the case so much anymore because of people desiring to be in communication with others and to have that communication available at any time of the day—the communication the average citizen might use with his or her telephone or car phone, for example. Nowadays, there are also all of the different frequencies that the military uses—these have a big impact. And your orbiting bodies, your man-made satellites, all have a cumulative effect, to say nothing of an immediate effect, when combined. So it's a problem.

Here is a suggestion for those of you looking for a good business investment. Some people might be doing this already, but for those of you who are looking for a new business to invest in, you will find that if you can assemble—and it would probably be done initially with a jump suit (a military term, I believe), but eventually it would be done with coats and hats and dresses and pants and so on—it might be possible to put a very thin film, not unlike a metallic film or some slightly metallic residue, between layers of fabric to shield the human body from radiation.

There is a small company even now that has been providing such materials for people working with radiation systems that are more toxic. Not nuclear radiation, but systems in laboratories that might require protective garments and so on. This is a growing business. If these people read this, I would suggest that now is the time to take the business public and go into an investment or a partnership with the fashion industry.

If you wear garments like this (they do not have to be made out of metal, but metal can now be made in very thin coatings and even in different forms and put inside this fabric; then you can add more fabric so that you have two layers of very thin fabric for a hot climate), you would find that it deflects almost all of that radiation. In these circumstances you would find that the energy level for the individual would gradually be restored. You could wear shoes, pants and a long-sleeve shirt, or a dress, or a long skirt and a blouse and perhaps even a hat made out of that fabric (although most likely you would not wear a hat like that . . . perhaps a normal hat, as you wouldn't want to interfere too much with your crown energy area). So if you were wearing something with long sleeves but not gloves, you would find that over a period of weeks for some people and months for others, your energy might be restored by about 20 to 25 percent.

Brilliant idea.

It is not something I can take credit for; it is something that is being done right now, as I say, and it might be possible to find the company that is doing it. I think it was started by a woman who felt discomfort from computer-screen radiation. It would be good to give her credit for this since it is something that she deserves and ought to be receiving some honor for. I believe in the future there might be, much to her surprise, significant honors for her.

We're going to be susceptible to this for years and years and years?

That's right. Your culture is spreading globally and is currently in love with technology. There are many people who are less in love with it, but . . . it is like an infatuation. As you know, among human beings, when there is a time of infatuation, all flaws are unseen. So until the flaws are seen more significantly, the infatuation will continue.

Is there anything else we can do? I'm thinking of a gesture or something.

Yes, let's give a gesture for those of you who are not quickly able to obtain such garments. I do not want to say too much about the way the garments are being made available today, but there are limited quantities available. This person has done the research, and I do not really want to expose that. Let's just say that you cannot easily obtain these garments right away. The best thing to do, then, instead of trying to experiment with it yourself (I do not recommend suits of armor . . . they would work, but they're not very comfortable or practical), would be to make a gesture that would connect you with metallic auras within the Earth that naturally deflect. It isn't necessary to do anything other than deflect this radiation.

Where is it going to be deflected to, though? We're not going to pop it onto someone else who is not wearing these clothes, are we?

It's possible. Does a mirror reflect light?

Yes.

It's possible.

The Coming Need for Social Globalization

That's why I say that in time this will become something that all people will eventually wear until the regulation of the airwaves (which will probably be taken over by an organization affiliated with the United Nations) becomes global. When that becomes global, there will be a very severe penalty for having a transmitter that goes off frequency. Businesses will no longer be fined money; the punishment would be very severe, and the likelihood of being separated from your life and your family could pretty much be guaranteed.

It's going to be that serious?

Well, it's going to be considered that serious by that time. The research will be globally known and understood, globally disseminated. As a result, some countries will have very rigid regulations and others will be less rigid. On top of those will be a more moderate but strictly enforced regulation that is globally enforced. But as I said, in some countries the regulations will be much more strict than that, and to go off frequency even for a good cause will be considered an imprisonable offense. Even if one of your employees does it with the best of intentions, they would come and collect him or her and say, "Ninety days in jail." It won't be the kind of jail you have today; it will be more constructive. But this will be something to consider.

In short, in the future, how the actions of individuals or groups of individuals affect everybody will become the focus of world governments. This will largely be the beginning of globalization on a more social level, instead of only the economic globalization you have now.

Is it the total combination, or are there are some waves and radiations that are more toxic than others?

It is the combination. There are certain microwave energies that are catastrophic, but these are largely known. Little is known by the general public of the impact of the frequencies that are used by different countries' military services. The governments who deploy these military services assume that the necessity to defend the country outweighs any and all side effects, even though research may—or perhaps in some cases, may not—have been done to discover if there are any effects. Some of this research has been done, oftentimes on animals and sometimes accidentally on human beings. When I say accidentally, I mean that the frequency was used in a particular area, and then unexpectedly everybody in that area developed headaches out of nowhere—sometimes severe, long-lasting headaches or even difficulty with vision—that correlated strictly with the deployment of that particular frequency.

Temporary Assistance to Help You Cope with Harmful Radiation

This gesture will connect you to the metallic aura in the Earth [Fig. 17-1]. It is not to be considered a substitute for garments that can protect you from these energy radiations, but it is to be considered temporary assistance.

You cannot hold the gesture long. If you hold it too long, the body will turn to denser material.

Gesture to Connect to Earth's Assistive Metallic Aura

Fig. 17-1a. Here is the gesture to connect you to the metallic aura in the Earth. Do not hold this for too long, maybe thirty seconds. Do this at night before you go to sleep, once every third day for two to three weeks.

Fig. 17-1b. Another view.   Fig. 17-1c. A third view.

You know how you felt in your time. Can you feel these waves through Robert's body when we're talking?

Yes, I can feel them.

It would be so much more obvious to you than to those who live now, who are so used to them.

That's right. You are used to a level of discomfort that you've come to feel is part of life, but if you have the opportunity to have this discomfort removed (which is not common, but possible), then it is quite a shock. For example, pilots who fly in modern airplanes are bombarded with electronic radiation (probably very unhealthful for them, but most of them know this). When they get out of the airplane, they actually can breathe a sigh of relief as the instruments are turned off. It is not good for the pilot and crew to be exposed to this for more than four hours at a time, but many are.

The Future of Aviation Technology

In the future things will be different with airplanes. The instruments will be better shielded. Also, the crews will not be expected to work for more than four hours. This might raise the price of a ticket, but the crew will work for three and a half, maybe a little less than four hours, and then change places with a new crew. They could go back into a separate section of the cabin and perhaps trade off like that for long flights.

But aircraft in general will be different. As you become more focused on how you can help each other, the ideas that have been put forth by many individuals in the past to create a system to move passengers—not unlike the system used to move a satellite from the Earth to the sky—will be put into effect. On a satellite system, you have rockets that fall off and get the satellite up there. With the aircraft, you won't have rockets that fall off, but should a problem occur with the aircraft, the plane will have a separate cabin for the passengers and possibly also for the cargo that will be very strongly strengthened and able to be essentially ejected from the body of the plane.

People might find that they'll be shaken up a little, but . . . also, the seat belts will be different. There will no longer be a lap belt. There will be belts like those used, I think, by people who drive fast cars in your time. They will cross the shoulder and have a lap belt, possibly even a type of harness for the feet. You won't like it. You'll feel trapped, but you will be able to move around somewhat. Should the rest of the plane crash, you will get over your feelings of discomfort and you will essentially be ejected.

At some point, this will be referred to as a safety mechanism. It will be experimented with first in small planes. Such experimentation could take place right now. Obviously, it would be very difficult and dangerous to eject such a passenger cabin at high altitudes, but it would be good to begin the research for companies that make such planes, because it will probably be sold by companies who do business with the private industry first.

After all, if your business officials or your records or perhaps something important to your corporation—some product even—is flying across the sea in an airplane and something goes wrong, you can't easily make up the loss. So you would be able to easily justify the purchase of such an item as a business expense. It might cost several millions of dollars more than the plane might normally cost, but you will simply be able to say, "Well, you cannot purchase insurance like that. This is terrific." And the pod, as it will come to be known, will land in such a way that it will be cushioned, not unlike the cushioning on the bottom of some aircraft . . . what do you call that?

A pontoon.

A pontoon. The pod would be cushioned at the bottom, and this cushion will also be able to float. And while people might sustain some injury, the pod will immediately put out signals. Most likely, navies of the world will respond, and the corporation will have a crew on standby globally to respond to such emergencies.

I am not trying to create fright here. I am suggesting that there is a profound business opportunity in the future that has been considered science fiction in the past, not because it wasn't possible, but because it was considered too expensive. But that will change. So such applications will be very lucrative to the first companies who get involved, because they will sell to companies who can afford to pay for such things. Eventually, these will be applied to the rest of the transportation industry, even cars.

So dying in air crashes should be a thing of the past, then?

That's right. And this is coming in your future, but the research, some of which is happening now, can be seen probably within the next ten to fifteen years (most likely less than that), at least on an experimental basis, but most likely in some application on small private jets, for example.

Taking Responsibility for Your Actions

I can feel the energy, the love that you've communicated. You've given us some advice on one part of this, the energy that we're putting toward planetary unity. Then Zoosh brought up the second part yesterday. We are being overwhelmed now with taking responsibility for our actions. Can you discuss that from your point of view?

It is very difficult. You really need to be more patient with each other, and that is very difficult. If you have an outbreak, confusion, misunderstanding, when the energy passes, you need to say to each other, "I'm sorry. We were not communicating clearly, and it's all right," "My mistake," or "I apologize," or whatever. Then the other person will say, "I'm sorry, too. I didn't mean it." It's important to do these things because you are all feeling this pressure. You will adapt to it though.

You must remember that if life on Earth is about nothing else, you would have to say it is very much about adaptation. You are born, and you are essentially physically helpless and have to adapt to a world. You adapt to the culture. You adapt to the speech. Your whole life is about adaptation. So you will adapt to this, though it will be something you will struggle with in the beginning.

But you have all had experiences like this before. For example, when you go to school for the first time and all these other children are around, it's a little hard. It's fine, but it's a little hard, but you adapt to it and get used to it. Then very often you look forward to going to school to see your friends whom you don't see other times.

So it will be like that. It is something you are starting now, but you will adapt to it. It will be a struggle at first, and then after a while you will look forward to it, because you will have more responsibility to actually alter what you experience in your world in a benevolent way. It just takes you awhile to learn how to do things, and it will be very experimental. So help each other. Say, "Well, I tried saying this the other day, or I tried doing this the other day, and it worked for me." Try to share what works for you—not what you heard worked for somebody else, because only the person it worked for can express it clearly to somebody else.

Zoosh said that Creator had set this up, so we're really trying to accelerate the whole program, right?

They are trying to give you the application and the methods to do what you've been asking for, for so long. It has not been Creator's tendency, much as I know Creator, to interfere in your process. This is not because Creator does not love you; it's that Creator knows that you want to learn how to do it yourself. And so sometimes Creator has to sort of tough it out and not interfere when Creator would love to make things better. But now Creator feels that you have been asking for so long for things to get better that it's time to give you things to learn that you can do to make it better. It is much the same way you learned how to ride a bicycle, which is to get up, fall off, get up, fall off, and then kind of wobble down the road for a ways until you get to know how it works.

Teamwork Will Become Universal

Help each other. This is a time when teamwork will become universal (many of you have been on teams before and are on teams now, even in the workplace). People will be talking a great deal about what works for them. It may not always work for everybody else, but it's good to share these things because it has a very unifying quality to it. It will really make you feel good to tell others what else works for you.

Don't tell them how they should do it. Just say, "You know, I tried this the other day, and it wasn't perfect, but it sure made things better. It worked for me, and you could try it. I don't know if it will work for you." When you share that, you're sharing your wisdom. You give people permission to try it. It might not work for them, but after a while they'll find something that does. Then they'll speak their wisdom about what works for them, and of course, being creative, you'll think of different ways to do things.

He said everybody was overwhelmed. How long will this last? Days? Weeks? Months? Years? I can feel the overwhelm.

That's right, but remember, some of the overwhelm you're feeling is not your own. Remember, you are all becoming more unified now, and so some of the overwhelm you feel from others. You must look clearly at your life when you are feeling overwhelmed. Look around at what you have to do, what you need to do. Prioritize what needs to be done now, and remember that these might not be entirely your own feelings of being overwhelmed. Then relax for a moment. Have a drink of whatever you have, water or lemonade or whatever you drink. Just relax for a moment and go on.

Now, *that* you'll probably process at night. That's why sometimes you'll wake up at night and you don't know why, can't understand why. It's like you're processing that, and it got to be a little too intense. You wake up then, and you say, "Well, okay." Then you go back to sleep.

We've got jewels of wisdom. Good stuff.

Good.

Life Lessons and the Vital Life Force

Speaks of Many Truths
November 23, 1999

The opportunity to drink pure water from a spring gives you so much more vital life force, at least in my time, compared to trapped water that has run through pipes. Trapped water allows you to survive, but the vital life force is no longer present.

So realize that in your time the contributing factors to people having very little energy are based on many things: less breathable air, less vital life force in your diet and water, and very little opportunity to process your true spiritual lessons in your deep dream state because you are processing the stresses of the day.

Exercise to Focus Your Soul and Body
on Your Most Important Life Lesson

As a result, you are now in a curious situation. Now, Zoosh likes to say that beings on other planets might live ten, twelve hundred years, something like that. Interestingly, they really have only one simple lesson (if they can resolve it in that time, because of the benevolent circumstance of their life with no stress). But here, with all of the stresses you are experiencing now and the minimal life force you take into your body to support its life force, you find yourself ironically in the same situation. It's about all you can do in your time to be able to process any one single life lesson, but your souls as well as your bodies are determined to resolve the life lessons you came in with, even if you have more than one.

So here's something to say to your soul and your body. Simply say this:

> **"I'M ASKING MY TOTAL SELF THAT THE MOST IMPORTANT LIFE LESSON BE RESOLVED IN THIS LIFE IN THIS BODY. I AM LIVING NOW, AND THAT IS MY SINGULAR FOCUS. I WILL ALSO ASK THAT ALL EXPERIENCES I HAVE THAT ARE GEARED TOWARD LIFE LESSONS BE GEARED ONLY TOWARD THIS SINGLE, MOST IMPORTANT LIFE LESSON."**

I recommend that you say something like that. Say it at least once when the Moon is out at nighttime. The best place to say it is outdoors. If it is cold where you are living, try to say it with leather shoes on, without rubber insulation on the bottom. Try to say it at least once in exactly the way I described. Then try to say it at least once during the day with the Sun out.

You can say it during the quarter phase of the Moon when it is waxing, then during the full moon, then during the last quarter (it is not necessary to say it during the new moon). If you decide to say it during those times at night with the Moon, you must say it also during the day again with the Sun. You cannot just do so many Moon sayings and only one day of Sun sayings.

One day with the Sun for each day with the Moon.

Correct.

Multiple Life Lessons

That's very wise because there are so many things coming at us now that we can forget about our life lessons.

It is difficult for you because many of you have come in (especially those born in the thirties, forties and even fifties) with multiple life lessons—one, two, maybe even three. Occasionally, one comes in with more, but this is rare. The lives of those of you who have multiple life lessons are much more complicated and difficult and overwhelming to some extent.

Generally speaking, those born in the sixties rarely came in with more than two life lessons—most came in with one or two. This trend stretched into the seventies, but here it was more predominant to have only one, although some had two. By the eighties, almost all of the people born had only one; very few came in with two. Everyone born in the nineties came in with only one life lesson. So far, for those born in the nineties, life is going to be, generally speaking, less complicated.

The exercise I gave is not aimed toward those of you born in the nineties. Of course, you are just a youngster, but if you were born in the nineties, you can ignore this.

What about the thirties, forties and fifties?

These people are more likely to have been born with two or three lessons. Almost no one born in the thirties or even the forties came in with less than two, and it was very common to find three. By the fifties, almost everybody had no more than two, but this gradually waned in the process that I stated. So if you were born in the thirties, you might be particularly overwhelmed right now. Your soul and your physical body are trying to accomplish these three life lessons, and you cannot because you do not have enough vital life force to support that.

Consuming the Purest Water Possible

If you suspect that you are working on more than one life lesson, then try to obtain or go to a place where it is safe to drink fresh spring water (first, find out if the water is safe). Don't just take it home with you in the bottle; drink some right there and drink out of glass. If you are going to put the water in a bottle, put it in a glass bottle. It is not good to drink out of plastic at any time. Even if it is very attractive, it still is not good to drink out of plastic. It's always best to drink out of glass or ceramic—they make glasses and cups out of ceramic—in short, natural material.

Most plastic is not natural material. Therefore, it can only impart stress and discomfort into the water, because in its nature, it is something else. I must say *most* plastic because there is a form of plastic that is almost natural. But I will say that 98 percent of plastic is made from something else, and it was taken from where it was without its permission and brought together. As a result, it is completely uncomfortable, and it can only impart this to the water.

In the case of wood, it is possible to drink out of wood. With wood or even stone, it is possible in some cases to carve the material into something to drink out of. If you drink out of something natural like that, it will impart only its sense of well-being (because it has cooperated . . . it has chosen to be a cup for you to drink out of). You must, of course, ask the material if it will do this before you drink out of it. Making your own cup is always best. You can use it throughout your life.

If you use ceramic, maybe somebody else made it; it needs to be honored and blessed before you take the cup to your mouth, meaning you must speak kindly to it. Do something ceremonial, maybe use the sacred smoke. You can breathe on it. If you are a shamanic or mystical person, hold the cup up to your solar plexus area and (as much as you are able) be the original materials of that cup, so the materials of the cup remember who they are. Then they can come to peace with being the cup.

After you do this, it is helpful to drink the purest water possible. If you cannot, as in most cases, go to the spring and get the water and drink out of it, the next best thing to do is to get spring water that you obtain from some other source—either someone you know got it or has it in a glass bottle, or you go to the store and you purchase spring water in a glass bottle.

Ideally, always get spring water from the place closest to where you are physically living. If you want, you can get spring water from France or somewhere else, but it will not have much support in it for you. Rather, it will have support in it for those physically born in that part of France and, to a lesser degree, those who are physically occupying that land in France. (I'm using France as an example.) It is better to use the water from your own environment.

There is no advantage to buying spring water in plastic rather than turning on the tap and getting water out of it. If spring water is in plastic for more than an hour, the water will lose all of its vital life force. The vital life force in the water will soothe and calm what is called plastic but is the original material. It will be giving its life force to that material, trying to feed it since it is so unhappy being a plastic bottle.

If tap water is all we've got, that's what we do, right?

Yes, if that's all you've got, then drink the tap water (assuming the tap water is safe), but try to drink out of glass or ceramic. Then, if you can, also try to pay attention to life-force foods.

Putting Love and Life Force into Your Pet's Food

Look at the animals around you. Look at your pets. It is clear to you that the animals, the wild animals around you, eat what is there from nature. That is obvious. But look at your pets. If you give them, say, canned dog food or canned cat food, sometimes they eat just a little bit of it. Unless they are very hungry, they eat only a little.

Suppose it is the time you normally feed your pets. They eat a little, but maybe when they smell it first, they look up at you—a "What's in that?" look. Pay attention to the expression in their eyes if you are conscious of eye expressions; you will see that it is about disappointment, not just because the food has no life force whatsoever, but also because they are disappointed that you do not know this.

The best food to give cats or dogs is something that you find out is okay for them. Check with your veterinarian, or maybe you know your cat or dog well. Obviously, do not give them candy and things like that, but maybe you can give them something like what you would give to an old dog. Make them some scrambled eggs with a little rice, if they are very old. Or for younger dogs, give them cooked meat (they'll eat it raw, but they are used to dog food, which is cooked). Then the only look they'll give you will be a look of joy, which you will be able to see clearly in their eyes.

I am saying this because a dog or cat is very often the pet you live with. There are not that many people living with other pets. Obviously, there are other animals you might live with—fish, rabbits, some of you have horses—but most of you have dogs or cats. You understand that a dog or cat is someone. You don't think of your pet as a cat or dog; you think of your pet as a friend. So that's why I speak to you like this.

In this way your animal friends tell you what is vital life force for them. It's true that maybe you buy meat at the store. You cook the meat and give it to them cooked, like that. It's not, as ranchers say, on the hoof, but it is the next best thing, because when you take the time to cook for them like that, you put a vital life force back into the food, because it is love.

You make the effort to give them that vital life force, which has to do with love. Any living being on the planet, including those who are consumed on a daily basis by animals or human beings, is filled with vital life force in the form of love. When you cook your pet's food, you are taking time. You don't curse and grumble when you're doing it—you take the time because you *want* to do this.

Maybe you are making meat for yourself. First, cook it without spice. They don't need that. If you find out they like a spice, they can have a little bit at some point, but cook a bunch of it and then leave yours to simmer on the stove while you give them theirs first. They'll never want dog food again.

Now their food has vital life force. What happens? Your beloved animals get healthier. Sometimes you see them looking kind of listless and strange. If they are not sick, they need vital life force. Cats very often (dogs sometimes, too) go out and eat a wild animal filled with vital life force. Then they come back and eat the food you give them from a can because, though it's empty food, it is filling to the belly. But it has no vital life force.

If you put that love into the food and give it to them with pleasure, saying, "Here, eat, enjoy this food. I am happy to share this food with you," then they eat and are happy, very happy. They don't leave much on the plate. Maybe a cat might leave something, because a cat is very much like a human being—if a human has almost too much food, he tends to save a little bit. But a dog will lick the plate. The plate shines when a dog gets done!

I say this to you this way because it is important for you to understand what is natural. Natural animals living out in the wild eat other natural things living out in the wild. *That* you know, but it is easy to forget this with the animals who live in your home because you have been conditioned by your culture to believe that the food you give them is good for them. Sometimes the conditioning is well-intentioned; people who have knowledge at least of the physical animal can tell you what is really good for them and what they need. I do not rule that out.

It's okay to give animals safe, healthy food with vitamins and minerals that are good for them. But food in cans for dogs or cats not only has no life force, but very often it has terrible things in it. It can actually injure a dog or a cat. And when they give you that sad look, it is not just because the food is not good for them at all and they know it by smell (they are very sensitive), but they are disappointed that you have not learned this yet.

The Natural Being and the Vital Life Force in Food

I was not simply lecturing about dogs and cats; it was intended for you to understand the natural being. It is easier for you to understand the natural being in the form of an animal than to understand the natural being in the form of yourself. But your physical body just like a dog or cat or robin or finch or snake or horse—it is just like a natural animal. Animals all know that they must have vital life force to survive. The fact that the vital life force lives in other living beings is coincidental.

I don't mean that it is an accident, but it is a fact. You must have bulk in your stomach, but you also need vital life force. So, in short, those of you who live on a farm can go out, kill a chicken, come back in and cook the chicken. This is pretty close to vital life force. Of course, a chicken raised on a farm is not free. Those of you who hunt, shoot ducks and bring them home—or better yet, camp out and prepare, cook and eat the duck—there's lots of vital life force there.

But let's say many of you, especially those who read this, are shy to eat meat. Maybe you feel it is not "evolved." Maybe you feel it is not spiritual. I honor your feelings, though I do not agree with them. So what do you do? How do you get vital life force? Some of you go to the health food market because that food was raised without chemicals. That's okay, but there is still no vital life force. The best vital life force is when you grow your own food.

Be nice to the plants when they are growing. Water them, talk to them, sing to them. I spoke to you a bit about this before. Then pick an ear of corn, for example. Go cook it and eat it as fast as possible. Generally speaking, this is how vital life force goes. If the food has been blessed and honored—you grow it yourself and it feels honored and knows that it is not just an anonymous product—it is filled with love, and lots of vital life force remains in the plant for about thirty minutes.

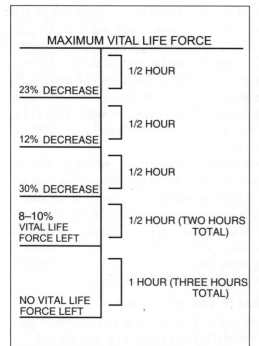

Fig. 18-1. The depiction of vital life force from the time the food is picked.

Let me draw a picture [Fig. 18-1]. This is the corn, for example, that you grow yourself. You use no chemicals, but talk to it and sing to it—not words of popular songs that have sad lyrics, but happy songs. If the lyrics are happy, it's okay to say those words. If not, then just hum the tune and be happy; don't take sadness and anger to the field. Then the plants will feel love from you, and they will take this from you. If there are three, four, five days between then and when you pick the ear of corn, then it's safe. Fine.

But if the plants take sadness from you because they love you and all natural beings around them, then if you pick an ear of corn that day, that ear of corn might have your sadness in it and it won't give you as much vital life force. Let's say this: Here is the maximum vital life force. This, of course, will have to do with many conditions in the field. Food raised in the best conditions (grown yourself or hunted in a sacred manner) in a half-hour will decrease in life force by about 23 percent. In another half-hour, the vital life force will fall another maybe 12 percent. Then after another half-hour, the vital life force will fall 30 percent—quite a bit. After two hours, the vital life force will be down to only about 8 to 10 percent. An hour after that, there is no vital life force left.

And that's in ideal conditions. So by the time we get home, what we buy in the store has no vital life force left.

The Overweight Condition

This is why so many people in wealthy countries are so fat. The physical body is not getting vital life force from food. The body is very hungry, and it feels it must eat a wide variety of different foods all the time.

You might eat a type of food that is not particularly good for you, though it's not harmful if you eat a small quantity. But you might eat a lot of chocolate, for instance. However, chocolate has other things in it that your body likes; it has a tendency to stimulate good fluids in your body. So when you eat this it feels like you are getting something from it—not vital life force, but it feels good. So chocolate is the exception.

Generally speaking, however, you might find all these different foods that you like and eat lots and lots more of them than you need because your physical body tells you that you haven't had enough. This is because most food you usually eat contains no more than 2 percent to occasionally 1 percent vital life force.

Now, not all people are overweight, but this is the general condition. Generally speaking, people who are not overweight are getting vital life force from some other thing. Maybe if they are married or in a relationship, they are getting it through love with an intimate partner. A youngster running around, playing outdoors, having fun, is getting lots of vital life force from just being in nature. And some people are slim anyway; maybe they work at staying slim. But I am trying to cover general grounds. So the vital life force in foods is very important.

Raising Food in a Sacred Manner

Now, what if you did not raise the corn (using corn as an example), but it was raised in a sacred manner? You can eat that and get vital life force at about half the rate the person or family who raised it will get, meaning that even though it was raised in a most sacred manner, *you* did not raise it. But even so, the corn is still able to impart vital life force to you in the first half-hour of picking and cooking.

In the case of an apple picked off a tree (but raised in a sacred manner), it might be able to have about 50 percent vital life force. An apple tree, for instance, has been growing in your yard for a long time. You don't do much to it, just encourage the rain to come in a sacred manner, or if no rain comes and the tree needs water, then as a last resort you give it water from a pipe. The best would be to irrigate the tree with wild water from a creek or river. Most farmers know that creek or river water is much, much better to irrigate with than something that runs through pipes.

In your day, some farmers or big business farmers don't know, think or care about this, but most farmers who work the family farm know. They irrigate with river or creek water because the plant responds better and the farmer notices this. They don't try to force it to grow with chemicals. The plant responds better because they *know*—they might not talk about it, but they know—that there is vital life force in wild water, free water.

Ways to Get the Vital Life Force You Need

It is important for you to state an objective for yourself to grow some of your own food. For some of you, it might be winter where you are or you can't really grow food where you are, but you might be able to grow a little bit indoors. You can grow sprouts or herbs in a window, where they get sun and so forth.

You surely can grow something indoors. Try lots of plants. Get literature or talk to friendly farmers or neighborhood gardeners. Ask them, "What can I grow indoors during winter?" They will tell you what to grow.

Then get used to growing these plants. Add them to your diet. In the case of your pets, you might even be able to add a little bit to their diet. Find out if your pets can or will eat such things. If the plant has enough vital life force, then your pets might eat it, even if they do not normally eat such things.

In short, you need to have in your diet every day at least something that gives you a minimum of 10 percent vital life force, or you need to be involved in a friendly or intimate relationship—friendly or intimate meaning you might hug the person. This could be a brother or sister or a husband or wife, something like that. Vital life force comes that way because you tend to give vital life force to each other.

Perhaps if you are a youngster and running around outside a lot or your job takes you outside—not just in the city with plants put in the ground by humans, but outdoors with wild plants—you can get vital life force this way. Humans plant flowers, orchards and trees to look the way they think they ought to look, but a wild plant knows where it needs to be and it grows where it is welcome in the ground. It is watered and nurtured by the Earth to grow and be strong. If it is a field where human beings have decided not to build anything for a time, where so-called weeds (otherwise known as wild plants) are growing because they have felt welcome, where they reclaim the land as much as they can for the natural expression of natural life—you can get some vital life force just by walking through that field.

Forests too, right?

Forests, of course, but many people reading this do not have a forest available, or maybe the forest is covered with a heavy blanket of snow. During a time like this, not much energy in vital life force is expressed by the trees or plants because this is a time of rest for them. Even if they are evergreen trees, they are covered with snow; they will rest quietly and tend to hold vital life force very close to themselves, not radiating much at all.

Therefore, wintertime in the forest, when there's snow, might be quiet. It might be calm. There's not much radiated vital life force then; you don't get much there.

And horticultural gardens. When people travel, there are many of those all across the United States. They are good to go to. Humans tend them, but they are still green and growing, aren't they?

Vital life is available from plants only if they have been growing naturally—not if you go to a place where humans have grown lots of beautiful exotic flowers in a glass house.

Not in a glass house.

But I speak of this: There's not much vital life force there. What do you speak of, though? Tell me.

Well, I was thinking there are great gardens like in Florida and Virginia, acres and acres.

But planted by humans, yes?

Planted by humans, yes.

That means the land did not welcome them. It will tend to sustain the plants somewhat, but if humans walk away from the garden—and sometimes you've seen gardens that people have left—immediately the wild plants take over. All of the plants that are planted by humans die off almost immediately because they don't want to be there. They might go to seed, and the seeds will blow in the wind to someplace where they are welcome, but they are not comfortable there. They die off immediately, and so-called weeds (otherwise known as natural plants with natural energies, filled with vital life force) sprout up and take over. If this happens, you know that humankind planted there.

Sacred Hunting

You were going to talk about hunting in a sacred manner.

You would first need to know what you are hunting for. Maybe you are hunting for yourself, your family, or maybe for a whole group of people (in my time, a tribe or clan). So in the case of a tribe or clan, you might know that you are hunting specifically for deer or elk.

But if you're hunting for food and you are hungry, you need to eat, then maybe you're not quite so fussy. You might be perfectly happy to get a mountain goat, for example, or another animal—maybe even a bear, though you must be cautious there, you'll need help. You're unlikely to get a bear on your own and live to tell about it. But, in short, in either case you are hunting to eat and survive.

Either way, pray in a sacred manner before you go out. Speak to the spirit of the animal. Ask the animal spirit to seek you out, because if you only seek the animal out, you might be out hunting for weeks or months. But if you ask the spirit of the animal to seek you out where you are going, an animal who is prepared to offer itself to you and your people will come forth.

Also, this will most likely result in an animal who will not be grieved for and missed by its family, one who can be spared—not a mother deer who has just had a baby. This would be an animal whom the family of that animal can live without, even though they'll be sad to see it go, just as you would be sad to see a family member go.

So this type of animal spirit comes. Bring gifts—something that is meaningful to you. In this case, maybe you have grown some food— corn, for example. Bring some of that corn. It is a personal sacrifice for you and your family to bring that corn to the forest, but bring it because it is an offering from the heart, a personal sacrifice. Bring it to the forest and leave it there for the animal.

Maybe the animal will eat it; most likely it will. In the case of food brought out that you raised or gathered in a sacred fashion, very often it is a sacrifice on your part lovingly offered and the animals know that not only are they eating the food they eat in the wild, but they are very often making it possible for that plant to grow again. When leftovers come out of their body in form of dung, the seeds in this dung live on. The animals swallow the seeds but cannot digest them, so they pass out through the body in dung and are nurtured, kept warm and survive. Then a new plant might grow out of that. Animals know this; they are not just stupidly eating seed.

In short, bring what you have. Don't bring out your last grain of rice or last ear of corn, but if you have only one ear of corn, take some ker- nels off and bring that out. It is truly a sacrifice. You must offer it to the forest with love, not with grief. Say, "This is what I have to offer." When you get out there as a hunter, as in my time, go with many people so you are safe. Follow along the line of a river or creek. Camp near water or the shore of a lake, wherever you are, because not only do you need water to survive, but you also know that animals must have water, too.

Put the food out and offer it with love. Look for tracks. Look for animals, but don't tramp all over the place. Trust that the animal spirit will come to you. Follow a traditional hunting trail or path that would be close to the natural trail or path of the animals you are looking for. But maybe don't walk right on the trail, because you do not want to put your scent on the trail of animal scent—not only because the animals are likely to avoid that, but also to honor the animals. Do not tramp on the same road they use as if to say, "This road is for everybody."

This is a path that they follow. The animal has a traditional path (you call it migration in your time), but it is not just a path that al- lows animals to have the food and water they need. Animals walk along very specific paths. They walk only where they feel welcome. Granted, an animal must look around and make sure that no preda- tors are nearby, and they might go off the path to avoid predators or to eat or drink something if the path does not have all the food they need at that moment. But they tend to stay on the same path be- cause it is exactly that ground that has welcomed their ancestors walking that path.

Therefore, as the animals walk the path, they feel welcome because the land has welcomed them. So do not put your foot on that path as a human being, because that path, that land, is for the animals. Pay attention not only to the tracks of an animal for hunting but to honor it. Equally, the animal does not walk on the traditional hunting paths of human beings. If a human being is hunting in a sacred manner, he or she will walk on land that welcomes him or her.

So animals and human beings are in a relationship, much more than they appear to be. It is not just simply that you go out and shoot animals, whoever they are, and bring them back and feed your family. Sometimes it is that way in your time, but the sacred hunter, hunting in a sacred way, does not have to go out so far. The animal will come out to you just as much as you go to it. You kill animals using the tools you have on hand in the quickest and swiftest way so the animals suffer the least.

If you do not have to touch the animal while killing it (unless you use a spear or arrow, for instance), then as the animal is dying, stand back. It is best to not look at the animal, not only because you feel bad seeing the animal suffer, but because the animal is then with its spirit. Step back if you can, at least ten paces. Look away into the forest.

You could thank the spirits, whatever you want to do, but do not talk amongst each other. Look away and let the animal commune in its own space with the spirits that will come to take its spirit on to where it will go after life. When that animal has died, stopped moving, then you can dress it and take it back to your people, or if your people came with you, you can cook and eat it right there.

But do not cook and eat it within at least a hundred and fifty, maybe two hundred paces of the animal trail, because the animals will feel grief if they go by there. It is best to walk back to camp where you live or to base camp. People might come out from the base camp, or maybe you meet halfway between and then walk back with the animal, far away from where the animal lived.

As you cook, the smell goes out. The animals can feel that, sense that. It makes those who are left feel more grief. You want to honor the family of that animal. Do not cook and eat it right there unless you are cooking and eating migratory animals who fly, as in the case of ducks. The duck probably does not live there; it just flies there, lands and goes on. In that case the hunter could cook it and eat it there. It's best to move away from water, though. There is much life force in the water.

Vital Life Force from the Sun and Stars

I speak to you about this today, even though I have mentioned it before. In your time there is so much distress, so much discomfort, so much challenge, with the experience of so many life lessons; yet there is so little vital life force available to you that all you can do is resolve one life lesson. You need all the vital life force you can get.

Of course, there are meditations you can use to connect with the Sun or whatever spirit energy you like, asking it to give you energy. You know of these things; I need not speak of that because you all know this. But to get vital life force, it's best to connect to the spirit of some plant, animal or heavenly body that you can see, such as the Sun. You probably will not get much vital life force from the Moon, but maybe you can get a little vital life force from stars. You can get some from the Sun, but the Moon only reflects the Sun. Plus, your Moon is not feeling so well, so it does not have much vital life force to give you.

I say this to you because many of you do not understand this, but you need to know it. Say these prayers and do things in this way as best you can, and recognize that I know that fully 90 percent of what you eat will not have any life force energy in it, so you will need to get some. Otherwise, you will get more and more tired as time goes on, and instead of achieving long life as you desire in your time, life will get shorter.

Why is the Moon feeling sick right now?

You have seen pictures of the Moon. It is not living. It has no soil, no trees, no plants, even in a state of natural being. Also, people have been digging things out of the Moon just as people dig things out of the Earth, lessening the vital life force. Only people have been digging things out of the Moon much longer than they have been digging things out of the Earth. So the Moon has practically no vital life force at all for itself.

As a matter of fact, the Moon has so little vital-life-force energy for itself that it tends to take vital-life-force energy from those who are digging out of it. As a result, people digging things out of the Moon very often need machines to help them. It is all they can do to operate the levers on the machines because they are so exhausted most of the time.

Life Purposes and Lessons

Can you categorize life purposes? Are there a few basic issues?

No, there are thousands of life purposes. Many times your life purpose has to do with something that you have either been unable to do or had no opportunity to do in previous lives. Perhaps it might be something that you need to understand from another point of view. If your soul has had an experience one way, it requires it to have the experience another way or many other ways—whichever other ways complement and make a whole experience out of any one circumstance. You must do that in order to fully understand the complete meaning of the circumstance or experience.

As a result, there might be many, many different life lessons. This could be in the form of an overall life lesson, if that is important to that which goes on immortally with you. We call this soul (it's a good word) or, as Zoosh likes to say, immortal personality—either one. Maybe certain lessons are more common than others, but generally lessons that are more common are not main life lessons.

A main life lesson has to do with something the soul has to do in this life, as I mentioned before, but secondary life lessons can be more common. For instance, some people might need to feel appreciated and will put themselves in circumstances so they not only feel unappreciated (so they desire and need the opposite, to be appreciated), but also so they maybe do not appreciate others, though others tell them they need to feel appreciated. These people might not always understand when others say that because sometimes they say it in anger. They might say, for instance, "You never say anything good to me, only criticism." They don't know how to say, "Appreciate me when I do something good."

Very rarely do people say "Well done" meaningfully, not just, "Well done, da, da, da." That's not meaningful. It means nothing. You must look at it, consider that it is well done and say, "Well done," meaning it. People can feel that, when it's not said meaningfully, and they say, "Oh." Maybe they don't react to you; maybe they go back and feel a little blue for a while.

I mention this because these kinds of life lessons are secondary. They are not primary life lessons. So with secondary life lessons, especially since so many people have them, you become more conscious of them. Many others are also going through them, and when you communicate with other people, it turns out that they are working on those issues, too.

But the primary life lesson is very often something singular to you as an individual. Maybe a few other people have things like that, maybe you even know someone who has something similar, but it is rarely the same exact thing. It is very specific to that individual.

So the secondary ones would possibly be self-love, appreciation, compassion, patience, things like that?

Yes. You really must put most of your energy into primary life lessons right now because you are more aware as individuals (especially people who read your magazine and books like this) of secondary life lessons since everybody around is having them. When things happen along those lines, you can pick up on them quickly and help each other: "Oh, this is about patience." You pick it up very quickly. So you do not need to focus energy on that; it will happen as a matter of course in daily life.

But energy must be focused on primary life lessons on the soul and physical levels, because secondary life lessons, as I say, might happen. They come up if you're conscious of them. Or you might not notice them if you're not conscious, but circumstances will come up. But if you are focused on your primary life lesson, which is the reason you are here in this life now, then you can urge or encourage circumstances to come up to facilitate that and you can be looking for those circumstances, which will tend to be repetitive and will not have primary experience—what you notice will not have the primary factor of that experience, will not be of the secondary life lessons.

It might have some secondary life lessons thrown into it, but the primary thing that happens and tends to repeat . . . circumstances that cause you to feel certain ways physically tend to repeat so that whatever is occurring, those feelings keep coming up for you. That will be your primary life lesson, and you can then work on those feelings and try to resolve them.

You won't be able to know (you are kept from knowing) why your soul is working on that life lesson. If you know why, you will tend to process it only mentally You can mentally process a life lesson for forty years, and even with total mental understanding of the life lesson, you might resolve the life lesson only to the tune of 1 percent, because the life lesson is intended to be resolved *physically*. That's why you have feelings; the same feelings that come up all the time are about the life lesson.

Exercise: Writing to Connect to Your Physical Feelings and Discover Your Life Lesson

This is intended to be resolved simply and easily. When those feelings come up again—"Oh no, not that"—and you have those feelings again—"Oh, I thought I was past that"—then you must work on those feelings. Try to identify what prompts those feelings. Do the actor workshop, pretend to be this and feel that, and see if those feelings come up. Then you might be able to identify some feelings. You don't have to go to an acting workshop, but you can pretend and begin to recognize those feelings.

Physically, you might feel a little nauseous or awful for a moment, but feelings can be quickly identified if you are paying attention. You might feel disappointment about something that didn't happen, for example. That is very common. Then try to write down and feel this feeling again, because this and this didn't happen. Disappointment. And then feel this feeling again, because you had only this much experience, but this and this didn't happen. In our time we could remember because we didn't have many distractions, but you have lots and lots of distractions, so write it down.

After a while, the more you write about having these physical feelings, the more they tend to resolve because you are paying attention. You might be writing down, "But I didn't get this, didn't get that." After a while, you'll begin to write other things, still focused on the feeling.

I am pointing to an area that is just left of the solar plexus. This is often a place where you get those feelings, or you might get them to the right. Generally speaking, feelings will come up somewhere around the belly. Maybe they'll be below the belly button, maybe they'll be in the solar plexus, but generally you'll get those feelings around the belly.

Then, after you write down your disappointment—what you *didn't* experience or what you *did* experience and don't like—you'll get other things. You'll write more and more, and as you are writing, you'll be focusing, paying attention to those physical feelings. After a while what occurs is that the feelings will move your hand as you write. Then you'll have a message to yourself that you can read later. You don't have to read it as you're writing it; read it later and stay focused in your feelings.

Write. Write. Write. Write. What happens in that moment is something that is intended to happen in this life for you—physical energy, material-mastery energy. It unites with mental energy to form this message. So keep writing until you either don't feel like writing anymore (meaning you're done writing), or you don't feel that physical feeling anymore. That physical feeling has communicated through your writing on the paper what it's trying to tell you. So then you'll get a message you can read, and you'll say, "Oh, this is wonderful. This is marvelous."

Now you have something you can work on. Maybe you'll still have that experience from time to time. Each time, write it down. First, make the list, and then begin writing other things. Eventually, the experience that prompts those feelings won't happen so much anymore because you are paying attention and trying to do something with the message.

In short, body consciousness speaks to mental consciousness. Because you write with words, the body and mind must work together to move the pen or pencil across the paper—in short, there's union. That is why you are all here, to experience the union of total self. So you see, this is the reason to do that. Then you begin working with feelings and discover that feelings can communicate.

Maybe for some reason you can't write—then speak. If you have a recorder, record. If not, speak; some of it you will remember. But most of you will be able to write. Writing is good because it allows you to use your mind. But even if you speak, you will use your mind. If you speak into a recorder, then write it down later exactly as you spoke it. Transcribe it exactly. That tends to support union better.

Then work on it. Think about it. What can I do differently? How can

I resolve this? Then you are consciously working on your life lesson.
So that's how people can find out what their life purpose is?

Yes.

My Life Purpose

How did you find out what your life purpose was?

A shaman person, a mystical man, took me to the top of a hill as I talked about before.

Oh, so your life lesson was your gift, then?

My life lesson was a gift, but also a challenge. The gift came in with a challenge, making the gift more appreciated.

I didn't realize that could also be the life lesson.

Yes, I was afraid, terribly afraid of heights, but once I conquered my fear, then the gift arrived. Once a life lesson is resolved, then the resolution not only comes with union, but with a gift. You get a gift and something wonderful you can do that you couldn't do before. Life opens up many, many more opportunities. Maybe life does not seem to be much different around you, but you can experience it much more. You can experience the gift of it much more, enjoy it more. You'll have many more opportunities, even if life does not seem to change, but with these opportunities, life will change. It'll get better. It did for me.

So in your time, you worked not only with apprentices, but with almost everybody in your tribe as a teacher, didn't you?

No, I would work with apprentices to pass on wisdom, but I never gave wisdom to people who did not ask for it. People needed wisdom when they needed it, but I did not go around and tell everybody in the tribe how to live. They had their own teachers. Maybe they needed to learn about plants and the medicine woman spoke to them. Maybe they were learning how to be a hunter. Certain people in the tribe were hunters. We might have all known how to hunt, but certain people in the tribe were specifically trained to be good hunters. They learned everything about hunting that our tribe knew, the sacred as well as the practical.

So, no, not everybody was meant to know these things. If a hunter came to me with something that was not given to him or her (sometimes there were hunter women) from his or her teachers and asked, "What do I do about this?" then I would offer what I have to give, but not before. *Wisdom is valued only by those who seek it.* That is known but often forgotten. If you seek it, you are going to appreciate it, value it and use it.

A Tribal Approach to Discovering Life Lessons

Was there someone in your tribe who worked with your people to help them understand what their life lesson was?

Remember, time was different then. In your time it is not easy to find your life lesson because you are all born in a big room with lots of people around; from the moment of birth, the distraction never stops. In my time there was not much distraction. When there was a birth in the tribe, everybody was interested. Maybe we had to go about our daily life, but everybody wanted to know; it was a big event in the tribe. In your time there is a birth every day—so what? But in my time it was a big event.

Very often elders or mystical people—especially mystical people—would attend births regularly. These would be women who might very easily be able to pick up the life lessons of an individual—sometimes even before he or she was born, but always right at birth—and this would be told to that person when the time was right. Not when the child was small, but as he or she was growing up, maybe when the child got to be five, six, seven years old. Then the elder or mystical person or maybe the grandmother or grandfather would begin to speak to the child about his life lesson, why he came: "You came here to be with the people again. It is wonderful to have you. We love you very much, but that part of you that lives forever came to do this, so you must be alert to it."

Now, occasionally, we would not feel (I am speaking for my people in general) a child's life lesson; we did not know it. Then we would pay attention to the experiences the child had and could usually come to a conclusion about what the life lesson was in a practical aspect. We might not have known what had driven or caused the soul to seek out this life lesson—the past experience or something the soul was interested in knowing more about. It might have been achieving balance or just curiosity. We might not have known that at all, but we could sense feelings in the child.

If feelings came up that were uncomfortable, as in the process explained before, then sometimes sensitive people, an aunt or a mystical or medicine woman or man or an elder, even the mother—most likely, though, a sister of the mother (a mother has other duties and might not always be able to easily identify the difference between her feelings and the child's feelings, but she sometimes can. It's easier to do it if you are an aunt, when the child does not live with you all the time)—could pick it up and say, "Their life lesson has to do with these feelings." And that person would talk to the child about that when the time was right.

Earth Experience Concerns the Physical

Can we then say that the way to look for the life lesson is whatever causes you discomfort?

No, that is too general. The discomfort will show up in the same part of your body all the time, every time something happens. It will be the same discomfort and will be in the same part of your body every time. Why are you here? Never forget for a moment that you can live here without a mind at all, but you cannot live here without a body. This basic Earth lesson tells you immediately that you are here because of your physical body and the physicality of the world. Everything else builds on that. If you ever forget that, you will become greatly confused, thinking you are here for some mental reason.

No one is here for a mental reason. I use the word "mental" only to explain. Say you have other things come up. Maybe you need to feel appreciated or maybe you need to appreciate others—in short, other things we talked about that are common secondary lessons. These discomforting feelings will come up in various parts of your body at different times, but your main life lesson will always be the same feeling in the same part of your body every time. It is an important landmark to know.

Remember, every single person here—you, everybody else—is here about the physical. No one born on Earth, no *human* born on Earth, is here for a mental reason. Everyone is here for the physical. This does not exclude the mental in terms of processing the physical, but you are here for the physical. Even if you have a wonderful life, then you are here to experience the joys of the physical.

And that could be a purpose.

That could. In some cases you might meet or hear about a person whose life seems to be wonderful and she is enjoying it. Maybe that's why she is here. Do not say, "Oh, lucky her. I wish I was her," or think that she is frivolous, not paying attention to the seriousness of life. Maybe she is paying attention; maybe she is living a life lesson for all you know. Saying that about others in that way gains nothing for you or them.

That's what's so hard. You can never know what someone else's purpose is.

The only way you can know is if that person has identified it and chooses to share it with you. That is the only way you can know. It is also possible to know if you are an elder, a mystical person or a shamanic person. Then you might be able to sense it, but I'm speaking in generalities. And when I say "might be able to sense," it is only *might*. Every shaman, mystical person, medicine person or elder—no one can do everything. [Laughs.] I say this in humor, but also for truth.

Gurus Must Keep a Sense of Humor

Sometimes people have a teacher or guru they are attached to, expecting or hoping that the guru or teacher will resolve all things. It is important that the guru or teacher knows he or she can never do that and maintains a sense of humor about it—can humorously impart that to the student. But sometimes a guru or teacher forgets this and gets very serious, thinking he or she must provide all things to all people. Then the teacher gets very unhappy very quickly.

Most gurus and teachers know this. That is why oftentimes they might laugh at unexpected or unusual times. Laughter might have to do with the fact that the guru or teacher understands that this is something he knows nothing about. Somebody else must be sought out. Maybe the teacher will seek that other person out, maybe the student will, but the teacher personally can be of no help; he knows nothing about that.

It is most important for a teacher to know what he knows and what he doesn't know. If the teacher feels like he must be all things to all people, the teacher will be unhappy very soon. If he stays that way, pretty soon he'll be of no help to anybody, including himself.

Resolving Life Lessons through Trauma

I don't think that everyone knows they have a life lesson.

This is true in your time; many people are not aware of this or were not brought up to be aware of this. Thus, many have to resolve their primary life lesson in an unconscious way or very often in a physical way, meaning through some drama or trauma—something happening suddenly. You might get hurt or others might get hurt, in a car crash or something like that.

I'm not saying "like that" meaning that your life lesson guarantees you'll have a car crash. But you will have some kind of drama in which, regardless of how you have been living your life, suddenly in that drama or trauma—or maybe as the drama is happening around you, like an earthquake—even if you're not hurt, you have to suddenly do things differently than you have ever done before. You must take a chance or risk to help others; then you might be working on a life lesson even though you don't know about the lesson.

For example, maybe you're desperately afraid of water, afraid of being on the water for some reason. Your life lesson might not be to resolve that fear completely but to begin. Maybe you must take a boat— you're not happy about it, but you must get from land to an island. You are with a youngster in the boat. The youngster is looking at fish, laughing at the water, and falls overboard. He cannot swim very well but can kind of stay afloat. You are desperately afraid, but you reach into the water (you do not get out of the boat, you'll just drown; it's no good to keep the child company drowning) and pull the child into the boat. Now you're very happy, shaky: "Oh, I was afraid I was going to lose you," and so on. You don't tell the child that you are desperately afraid to even stick your arm in the water, but you grab the child and pull him into the boat, saying, "Be careful in the future.

Soon you will learn how to swim, and you'll jump out of boat just fine on your own."

Then you go on with life and say, "Well, I'm still afraid of water, but I know I can stick my arm into the water if I have to. Maybe I could even wade into the water to help somebody if I had to." You have made a step, and that was what was required. You have no knowledge of a life lesson, but you have made a step, accomplished a life lesson through drama and cooperation with others. The water, boat and child cooperated, and you made a step toward accomplishing a life lesson. You can go on with your life completely, even though you do not know any of this. But if you know your life lesson, you can usually resolve it more easily without drama or trauma.

Finding an Astrologer

You said that the astrologic, or what we call astrology, is becoming more important now. That is in our horoscope. We can read our horoscope.

You don't need to read it—have an expert read it for you. Try to get an expert you feel good about as a person. You want to get someone who is really good with it, but although knowledge is important, it is equally important that you feel safe and comfortable with that person, that he or she feels like a nice person even if you are talking on the phone—that he or she does not try to say anything to scare you, only gives you advice that is useful. It is important to feel good about the astrologic person or even the astrologic company. If you don't, then even if the best advice comes from that person, you will still feel uncomfortable and maybe you won't use it.

Astrology can hand the keys to the universe to you on a plate, can unlock all the universe's secrets to the benefit of your family, your people and yourself. But if it is handed on a plate of anger, put the plate aside and never touch it. Astrology teaches each human being like everybody else, but some astrologers like some clients better than others. If you don't like a certain client too well, it is best to pass her on to another person until she eventually finds a person who likes her and whom she likes.

Sometimes a client might say to you, "I appreciate your advice very much, but I need to seek out somebody else." Don't be offended. Maybe he doesn't feel comfortable with you, even though you like him. Never be offended about this. Just say, "Okay, it was very nice to know you as long as I did. Good life or goodbye," whatever you say.

Knowledge Is What You Feel

The feelings in our body are one source that helps us come into awareness of our life lesson. Is another one astrology?

No.

We can't get our life lesson from astrology? That's what I thought we were just talking about?

No, that is not what I am talking about. I'm talking about how you relate to an astrologer and how an astrologer relates to you. You can never know a life lesson from astrology, numerology or anything like that. You know your life lesson from feelings and what those feelings communicate. You cannot know a life lesson from astrology, but you can know about circumstances and you can know about things and even places that will support you.

You can, in short, get instructions on how best to live your life, meaning what works and what doesn't work for you. What doesn't work for you, might work for somebody else. It doesn't have to work for you. Astrology is a very useful tool. Numerology and readings from various people are also very useful. But the way to find out a life lesson is the way I described, because it is the physical speaking with the mental through the physical.

In short, it is like a sandwich. You have feelings, you notice feelings. Your mind contains the words of your culture. So even though a hand—a hand or an arm and so on—is the only thing that can write, you must use the words of your culture, thus uniting the physical and mental. And as I say, it is possible that a mystical person can tell a child his or her life lesson. The mystical person might even be able to occasionally tell an adult a life lesson, so don't rule out the astrologic; it just might be able to do this. But that does not mean you know your life lesson. Knowledge is not what you *think;* it is what you *feel.*

Wisdom is what you feel and use because it works, but knowledge has nothing to do with what other people say to you, from my point of view. I recognize that this is a different description than Zoosh gives you, but it is what I believe on the basis of my experience of being a physical person. Knowledge . . . someone speaks to you about something, and you get a feeling in your body. That feeling says, "That is true," meaning it is true for you. It might not be true for everybody else, but you might even say, "Oh, that's true, and I think it is that way for everybody." Of course, you're *not* right, but you say it because it feels so true for you as well as for that other person.

In short, that is knowledge you can use. You know it is so; at least you believe it at that moment. But even with those feelings that you know might have more to say to you, even in such a condition that I just spoke of, you might put your hand down to the paper and say, "Isn't that so?" to your feelings. Stay focused just on those feelings, and write down whatever comes out. Maybe you write, "Yes, it is so, and it is so for these reasons. I'm writing down all these reasons." So your mind is speaking through feelings, but if your feelings tend to fade as you're writing it down, it means you are getting focused in your mind. Go out of your mind, and go back into your physical feelings and feel them. See if you can get another person to write down what those feelings mean to him or her. They might not always be the only truth to the other person.

It might be the physical body responding with physical feelings, saying, "Yes, I am working on this, too," meaning you have a lesson in common, similar things or truths in the body. So that truth in the physical body might get excited, and you might feel like this is true for you and everyone else, but maybe it is the physical body saying, "I want to talk to you about this." So write it down, as much you can. It is not really channeling; it is inspiration.

The physical body can inspire writing, but you have to stay focused. You have to feel your feelings as you are writing. Maybe your handwriting will not look as beautiful as normal—maybe a T doesn't get crossed, maybe an H gets crossed instead, maybe the dot on an I is in the wrong place—but you are writing or even typing as best you can. It is okay to type, but you must feel the feelings. The moment the feelings are not felt anymore, stop. Maybe you are focused in the mental in that moment—you can notice this because you will have the sensation of mental or that the feelings are done communicating. Maybe in the middle of a sentence, you'll feel that that's all for now. If the feelings come up again later, maybe you can write more.

If you have used a computer, then read it, think about it, maybe print it out. Think about it some more, but stick it into a computer file. The next time the feeling comes up, if you can, type some more. Maybe it will be the same thing; maybe it will be different. Through this process you will find out more and more about those different feelings and what they mean to you. You will find out more of how you can most easily resolve your feelings.

The more you do this kind of thing, the more you tend to resolve these lessons. Sometimes feelings are uncomfortable; other times they are very comfortable. Once you have resolved all the uncomfortable feelings, you will tend to have uncomfortable feelings come up only in life circumstances that are not safe for you in that moment, saying, "Go this way, not that way." Uncomfortable feelings simply demonstrate what is not safe.

But mostly you will tend to have only comfortable feelings come up because you have resolved not only your primary lesson, but the manner in which you live, your lifestyle, and secondary lessons as well. So feelings that come up tend to be mostly good. The only time uncomfortable ones come up is when something is *not* good for you in that moment.

Think of the uncomfortable feeling and say, "Well, I'll do something else, then." If that doesn't work, then write down more from that uncomfortable feeling. I don't want to give you too much here. I want to give you the idea that this can be an ongoing process that can help to clarify your life, help you to work on lessons and ultimately resolve them in a way that works for you.

Sometimes you will have to use a different resolution later in life, but you can have a solution that works for a time at least. Maybe it will work forever in that life. The main thing is that your physical body talks to the rest of you. Writing is very useful, even if you speak and write later. The main thing is to get this communication going with your physical body; then the physical and mental bodies will unite. Then you can embrace life, life will work for you.

The Moon and Her Cycles

Are you okay? The full moon's there. You're getting good energy, right?

Where I am, there is only a quarter moon.

Where you are?

I am in another place. I am in my own home, in my own time. In my time, we have a quarter moon. I get energy from the quarter moon.

We have a full moon here.

Good, you'll get lots of energy. It's a good time to pay attention to the details in life. The full moon is the best time to resolve the physical details of life, but it is not a very good time to resolve the mental details, mental solutions. The full moon does not support mental solutions so much, but the physical body will feel energized. If something isn't working in the physical life, you might be able to get more physical innuendo, meaning the physical body might be able to provide a method that would work better. Instinct working in the physical body is more profound during the full moon cycle (the full moon cycle meaning three days before and three days after, including the full moon).

Maybe you are doing some work: regular work or alternate work you have to do. Don't even think about it. If something comes up, just do it physically. Then think about it later and say, "I've never done it that way before, but it sure looks good." That is instinct working through the physical body because instinct and the physical body work best during the full moon cycle.

What about the Moon's other cycles? How do we best focus on them?

The new moon is a time for rest and relaxation. Not much feminine energy is coming through, so it is not a time to nurture. It's more difficult to do other things in general. With the first quarter you have a time in which good or clear mental solutions will be available (three days before, three days afterward). If there is an overlap—sometimes in cycles there might be an overlap, but not usually—that is also a good time for mental solutions. The last quarter is a good time for relaxation, fun things, family. This is not to say that it isn't good to do those things at other times, but I'm giving you a brief overview here. I'll talk more about that at some other time.

I can best speak to you about the cycle you are experiencing when I am experiencing that cycle, especially at its uppermost, or as you say, zenith. The full moon can speak to you about the full moon, but the quarter moon can speak better about the quarter moon. I can only make a casual observation when the quarter moon is not present for you.

Do you want to say something about the full moon now or at another time?

No, that is sufficient for now. I don't want to give you too much. If I tell you how to live all the time . . . some people want to follow close-order drill steps. They'll think, "We must do this, must do that." So I'll just give you a statement, a brief thing, not too much. If I give you too much, then you'll follow too closely. I speak to you about what I believe works best for me and what I believe works best for my people. But sometimes I don't tell you all those things because I know that in your time those things do not apply.

Sometimes I speak to you about things that occur in your time that do not apply in my time, which is what I spoke about initially and talked about today. And it is in varying degrees. Sometimes I say only a little bit because I do not want to interfere with your life. You are creative persons in your own right. I do not want to say, "This is how Speaks of Many Truths lives, so you live this way, too."

Right. You would be a dictator.

Not very helpful.

But what you said earlier is so important now because we're not getting enough life force at this time while our energy is being used for unity and to take responsibility for our creations. That makes the challenges even more difficult.

I bring it up because it is timely. It is good for you to know and have some solutions, things you can do.

Vital Energy and Your Food Products

Say corn is raised on a farm by a big business. They use fertilizer and spray water from pipes; they do not use wild water. In short, the corn is raised entirely the wrong way. Nobody is telling the corn how beautiful it is. No one is singing to the corn. Nothing. This is the worst possible conditioning. It is even picked by a machine, not a human hand. So the corn has maybe 1 or 2 percent of vital-life-force energy.

At the time it's picked?

Yes.

So by the time we get it . . .

Yes, it is in even worse condition. If you can eat that corn within a half-hour, you can still follow the chart by percentage, but in this case, after an hour or so there is no vital-life-force energy at all left in the corn. It might fill the belly, but it has no vital-life-force energy.

That really makes sense. I mean, obesity is becoming one of the largest problems in the United States.

This is because the physical body recognizes that there is no vital life force in food. And the physical body is doing the right thing because if the physical body feels any life-force energy at all (it might be fractional, a teeny amount of life-force energy), it will try to consume as much of that as it can.

So how do you see our future, then? Are we going to have to change the way we do everything?

It's an important thing for businesses to know. If the food you are raising has vital-life-force energy, people will naturally be drawn to it and will want to buy it over an ear of corn for sale in the supermarket, even though it all might look the same. Yours might not even look as good, but people will go right to it because their physical bodies will prompt them to do that. Only people who are really rigid or not in touch with their physical self at all (a rare situation) might go to the other ear of corn, but they will naturally be attracted to the ear of corn you grew.

An Experiment: Sacred versus Machine-Picked Corn

I grant that right now you must use chemical fertilizer, things that are practical because of dollars—as you say, the bottom line. But there is something you can do. Notice the men or women going through the field with machines. They are bored and listen to the radio. It is best to have someone go through the field singing a song—not over an amplifier, booming out, but singing a pleasant song with his or her human voice. It is hard for you to do this as a business person, but experiment.

Try to say, "Okay, here is a vast field where we are growing corn commercially, to make money." Then take one acre and tell whoever is in the business—maybe a private farmer next door or perhaps a sacred person, maybe a Native American living a sacred life or another person living a sacred lifestyle—"Raise the corn, please. I will pay you. Raise the corn in a sacred manner such as Speaks of Many Truths mentioned or in another manner, and let's see what happens at the end." Pick an acre well apart, at least three or four acres from the actual physical land where the corn is grown. Raise the corn for an experiment.

Then, in the first half-hour after the corn is picked, as an experiment, bring in people from work. These should be average people, but you don't have to bring in people off the street—use people from work. Put all the corn together in a pile. Mark the ears very carefully without making an obvious physical mark. Put an ear of corn raised in a sacred manner with three, four—not too many—other ears of corn picked by the machine.

Then ask the people to pick out some corn. Just tell them there is no right or wrong way, they aren't getting paid, this is their own time. They should just go and pick out the ear of corn that they feel most drawn to. And you'll find that at least half the time, maybe more than that, even though there's only one sacred ear to three or four ears of machine-picked corn, people pick the sacred corn over the other.

Sacred Food and the Future

So think about it. See how you can integrate this method into the food you sell to the general public. Someday corn will be raised in a sacred manner. People say, "We cannot do it; there are too many people to feed; it will cost too much money." Even so, you have to ask yourself as a businessperson, to say nothing of a population expert, "How can billions and billions of people live on the Earth. They need a place to live. How can we raise enough food to feed them?"

If corn—and I use corn only as example—is raised in a sacred manner and eaten soon after it is picked (a half-hour to an hour), it takes very little to feed people, and they will feel good. They won't need any more. The kernels of one ear of corn would probably be plenty for most people—probably not even an entire ear of corn, more like two-thirds of an ear. In the case of youngsters, one ear of corn could easily fill up and give all the vital life force needed for two children. Think how far your corn could go then. I say this to you not because I'm trying to twist your arm, but you must think about this because the time is very close now.

Even big business farmers know how much land is left. You keep building houses—all these people have to live somewhere. Where are you going to grow the food? I know you are thinking about these things. You cannot and will not be able to grow enough food for everybody when it has no vital life force, but with vital life force, you will have enough.

That's a new way to look at things. Not a new way—it's just that we've gotten so far into the unnatural way of living.

Someday you will live differently. Cities will be planned in a circle, not unlike cities in Andromeda and other places. Food, corn and other things will be grown in the city. There will be a big circle in the center. Part of this area will be buildings where people come together to do things, maybe watch moving pictures, go to church and so on, but a lot of that area will also be land where food is grown and tended. Then cities will spring up and circle around that. So there will not be one place where corn is grown and shipped to everybody; it will be decentralized.

Grown close to the people who are going to eat it . . .

Yes, so when it is picked, it will be picked shortly before the people tend to eat it. Some people, of course, like to eat at different times, but if you can get the best vital life force that will fill you up and make you feel good and strong, that will give you much energy, you will want to eat at the same time. You might eat a snack at other times that does not have much life force, simply for the pleasure of eating, but you will all eat around the same time, most likely two meals like that a day, not three.

During the waking hours, you'll wake up and get going. You'll get dressed, get prepared, then eat a vital-life-force meal. Then toward the end of the afternoon (I say afternoon, because most of you eat during the day), before you're done with work you will eat a second vital-life-force meal. Then maybe you'll have a snack a few hours before you go to bed, probably without as much vital life force in it—just a snack to fill your body, and then you'll go to bed soon after. You won't eat so much meat then for your snack; meat might keep you up.

The Sacrament of Food

Zoosh
October 6, 1998

ll right. Zoosh here.

Welcome.

The Spiritual Act of Consumption

A brief amusing comment. Oftentimes, one hears people on Earth, sometimes disgustedly and other times hopefully, say they wish that the ships would just come and take them to some beautiful other planet. Just a brief comment (it may be something worth knowing): If you were born and raised on Earth or even just born on Earth, and you went to another planet, if your body did not eat food grown on Earth at least once a week and drink water from the Earth at least once a day, in about a hundred days that would be just about it for you.

You're ruining the science fiction industry!

A person might survive but would require medical help, because the physical Earth body is so different from the cultures on other planets. When you eat and drink from Earth, you do not just consume food. It processes in your body and so on, but it is also a spiritual act, whether you are conscious of it or not. You take in the living resonance of that which you consume.

You see, when the human being comes to the end of the natural cycle, your soul departs and that's that. You do not leave a residue of your soul—or your immortal personality as I like to call it—in the physical body. But with certain animals and many plants that you consume, when their souls leave at the end of *their* cycle, whether it be natural or otherwise, they often leave some slight residue of themselves.

So involved are they in the homogeneous system on Earth, that it is an act of faith on their part. When you eat lettuce or sprouts or potatoes or carrots, there are always some vestigial remains of the soul of that being you are consuming. When you consume certain animal tissues, mostly from the ocean or from lakes or rivers, but wild, fresh fish (free fish, let's call them) or certain animals who are free (deer, as in venison, or elk)—but not generally the animals you raise for slaughter—these beings leave some residue of their soul self because of their embracing on Earth. This processes through your body and carries the wisdom of that animal or plant or fish, so even if you are living an unconscious life, you will absorb some spirituality that you might not otherwise take in.

The intent, then, is that this soul matter processes through you slowly. It does not depart from your body when you let go of waste products. The average soul residue from other creatures (and I'm including plants with this for the moment) requires a good forty days or at least one lunar month to pass through your physical body. Ofttimes it takes a few days beyond a lunar month.

While it is going through its different stages in your body, it tends to seek out like wisdom in your immortal personality or soul and attach to that, embracing it lovingly, supporting and sustaining it. If there is no knowledge that is equal to the knowledge that the vestigial soul contains, it will touch a portion of yourself (your soul, not your mind) and mark it—as you would say, put a stamp on it. That mark will tend to draw that wisdom to you in some form that you would experience in your life, if your soul deems that wisdom to be of good use to you.

In this way eating and drinking become a spiritual process designed to augment the spiritual process your soul goes through in its day-to-day life on Earth. This is why you cannot live for long periods of time in space without consuming Earth-grown food or Earth-provided water.

Now, it is possible to consume recycled Earth water, as untasty as that sounds. This has been done by the astronauts and cosmonauts, and they bring food from the Earth. It is important for you to know this so that when you do go out to explore space and other planets, you make sure you bring along what you need. Even though you may be offered perfectly wholesome foods that are safe for you to eat on other planets and they will feel good in your body, the spiritual function will not be served. The foods will be set up to serve the spiritual function of the people who grew them or who gathered them on those other planets, and it will not tie in with your overall or even your specific soul lessons, having been born on Earth.

Therefore, you will need to bring what you need with you for the sacrament of eating. I am using that term on purpose. Religion has borrowed that ceremony of the consumption of the food or wafer and the wine as a holy sacrament. I fully understand that, yet eating in general is a sacrament. Not to make any religion feel less than, because that is not my intent, but the adaptation by established religions of this level of consumption, which represents a sacred intake by the parishioners, is actually adopted from earlier philosophies that understood that the consumption of food and water was in its own right a sacrament based upon what I have explained tonight.

I'm mentioning this, not to put the kibosh on imagination strung together with good entertaining science fiction, but rather to remind you that even the seemingly most mundane and commonplace occurrences will often be totally enmeshed with the unseen spiritual world that exists between you and Mother Earth.

Sacred Farming

That's why they say you should grow your own food, because then it is suited for your own spiritual development, right?

If and only if you participate significantly in the growing of it. If you purchase a seedling, say a seedling fruit tree, you will find that the food will not be exactly attuned with you; it will be attuned with whoever sprouted it. So even though it takes longer, I encourage you to sprout your own seedlings and then plant the fruit tree, if it is something you are growing for yourself.

You want to have an understanding of sacred farming, even if you cannot do it. I recognize that if you are living a fast-paced life, there will be so much you can do and that's it. But I will at least expose you to some of these things. Rather than water the plants with the hose, try to use irrigation from a natural stream or river, because this is water that would have run free and picked up the energies of the land.

For those of you a little further down the line, as we say, I would recommend that you consider requesting it to rain (I believe exhaustive discussion of that occurred in other books in this series about encouraging the rain, so I won't go into that). The best thing for plants is natural rain—rain that comes from a cloud because it chooses to, not rain that has its departure from the clouds sped up by cloud seeding. That I would call unnatural rain.

Now, I recognize that most of you will not be able to do that shamanistic practice, so therefore, recognize that the more the water has been free and run free over the stones of a creek, the more likely it will nourish that plant. Nowadays, because you have so much pollution to deal with, you might naturally just take water out of the tap or from the garden hose (which might as well come out of the tap) and it will be treated for your consumption. This is completely understandable, yet it is not the best for plants. For them, it is like diet food. It's like unnatural rain, rain that isn't happy to be there and is grudgingly doing its job. Now, if you eat a dinner that was prepared that way, it doesn't feel quite as good. If you are around people who are grudgingly friendly rather than open and genuinely happy to see you, I don't have to tell you that the latter is better.

Ideally, you want to nurture this seed and sprout it. You want to sing to it. Singing is the natural language of the natural growing cycle, and that is why mothers and fathers naturally sing to their children. In your time you play music from a recording, but singing to your children is much better. Music (even if you can't carry a tune, by the way) encourages the natural growing cycle of all living things—including matter you don't necessarily consider to be living, but is—and to the extent that you are welcoming and happy . . . not just singing a heavy-metal song and tapping your toe, not that at all. But if you are singing a welcoming song, you can make up the words, "Thank you for coming. I hope that you will nurture me and I will nurture you as well."

Make up the words. It wouldn't be that different from what you might sing to a youngster, and this will encourage the growing being. The music sung like this from your own mouth, if you can, is the best. It is like food, because it is musical love. For those of you who can, play an instrument, but sing, too. That discordant music, like heavy-metal music, will (I'm not saying might) derange the mechanism within a physical being—a child, let's say—and make it more difficult for that child to understand true love and to respond to true love in like kind. I'm not saying that heavy-metal music is the enemy, but I am saying that it is not healthy.

How do you colonize planets? You can't take that much food to feed an entire colony?

By the time you are really colonizing planets, you will have developed a little bit more respect for your physical selves. You will bring some kind of garden with you, or at the least you will have hydroponics. This will be useful as long as the food and seed and soil come from Earth. You will probably do that, and you will have very sophisticated water-recycling systems.

You know, at some point you are going to find yourself on another planet, and for some reason you'll have to consume the food and water there when you can't get Earth food and water. What will happen after a time is that you will get more and more tired, and if you don't get Earth food and water, pffft!

Plants and the Angels

Someone said that vegetables are the most spiritual beings on the planet. That's a whole new understanding for the virtues of being a vegetarian, or at least eating a lot of vegetables.

The nature of life here is simple because all life has a great many things in common. Yet the level of complexity, as scientists have discovered and which any spiritual person knows as well, is attuned so mightily to different frequencies that one can understand the direct analogy between the different frequencies—or let's say octaves—of the different forms of life and the choir that one hears when being exposed to the angels.

The angels sing to those forms of life because many times they are not encouraged, or they are given artificial encouragement such as chemical fertilizers. Or consider plants growing by the side of the road. If someone thinks that they are messing up the road, they are arbitrarily killed, even though many of them contain chemicals that could cure diseases. I've said this before, but I'll say it again: Weeds are as persistent as they are because *they are determined to help you.* All plants that are classified as weeds are in fact loaded with curative chemicals for your diseases. You will discover this, but I need to remind you once in a while.

Think about that. The angels sing to the plants. Do the plants respond? Yes, they do. Many animals do—cats and sometimes dogs, certainly deer and birds. I'm not just talking about the interaction of the wind through the leaves; I'm talking about *sounds that actually emanate.* Track the sounds made from a plant. It might take a good ultrasonic receiver to at least see on an oscilloscope that something is happening, but I can assure you that the plant is in fact responding with sound. And this sound, if it is not communication from the plant to another plant or to another being on Earth, is always its response to the angel singing to it.

So the angels sing a specific frequency to each plant?

They usually sing a specific octave or tone to each individual plant. Think about it. Human beings might find it difficult to make more than a few tones at once—even the monks who can do two tones at once. But as an angel, you do not have to struggle with that limit, so you can make many tones at the same time—pure tones—and you can also receive many pure tones at the same time.

When Speaks of Many Truths said that the music is getting thinner, that's because so many plants have left?

Yes. After all, you all know how it feels. If you are made to feel unwelcome, after a while you just say, "Well, why bother to come back?

They don't want me." The way the feeling is in the plant is almost exactly like your feelings, except that they know who they are. Knowing who they are means that they understand that you are largely cut off from knowing who you are, which allows them to be more tolerant of your casual destruction of them and other forms of life. But it does not make it all right.

It is as if some giant came along and didn't see you, as in the case of an ant and a human being. You might understand why your best friend was stepped on and left crushed, and the intellectual understanding might make it easier to cope, but that would not cause you to grieve any less.

Good night. Thank you.

Working with the Elements

Speaks of Many Truths
November 24, 1999

This is Speaks of Many Truths. The function and purpose of the solar wind is what I'm interested in. Other people will comment on the facts and so on, and that's fine. But the function and purpose need to be explained so that people do not assume that solar wind is an anomaly or strictly something prompted by Creator in all of Its great wisdom.

The Sun and Your Physical Body

Something that is not fully understood here in your time is that the Sun has a corresponding element within the physical body of every human being. If you slide your hand down the front of your body until you get to the point where the solar plexus first starts, then if you could try with your energy (extended fingers) to curl your fingers up so that they are right behind . . . I want people to know the exact position: It is as if the fingers were curled up behind the rib cage, the fingertips pressing out on the rib cage from within the body [Fig. 20-1]. I don't recommend, of course, that you try physically try this.

Back against it from the inside?

That's right, but pulling out as it were. That is the corresponding position in everyone's physical body to the Sun. Nobody can live on any planet in any solar system without having in the physical body a corresponding position with their suns. Generally speaking, there isn't

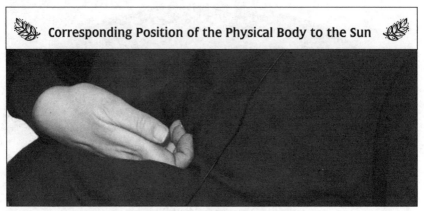

Corresponding Position of the Physical Body to the Sun

Fig. 20-1. Curl up your energy fingers behind your rib cage so that your finger-tips are pressing out on the rib cage from within the body.

a specific corresponding position per individual in each solar system with its moons. Each person might have a different position and, of course, some planets have more than one moon, so each individual might have different positions. But on Earth, this is the position for all human beings that corresponds with the Sun.

This tells you something important, that your relationship to the Sun is personal. If you know that, then the Sun becomes not only your friend, but an ally. This is important to know. Many people knew that in my time, and some people still know it in your time. People who know it tend to have a much more benevolent interaction with the Sun.

The Sun is considered a friend, and it is spoken to. Some people greet the Sun in the morning and even wish it well as the Earth goes around it each day, but I would not say that this is required. I'm simply saying that this is their way of personally interacting with and welcoming the Sun.

When the solar wind—as it is called—comes up, meaning a strong flare that emanates significant energy toward the Earth, your scientists can say, "Well, here's this solar flare coming right toward the Earth, and we can expect it." This [the solar wind] is never done because the Sun chooses it on its own, nor does Creator say, "Now do this." It is always only done because this position in your body requests that that extension of Sun energy blanket the Earth with such an impact that it can actually be measured on instruments and, more importantly, that it can be felt by your physical bodies.

You might not all be sensitive enough to actually feel it, but the feeling is significant. Different people will feel it in different ways, but very often it will tend to improve the overall physical health of all beings on the Earth. It is like an inoculation of extra energy. This also tends to improve the energy level and general health for animals and plants.

If this were to happen every day, it would have a detrimental effect. But it doesn't; it just happens once in a while. The reason I'm talking about this is because these events are relatively imminent, and it's important for you to understand their function and purpose.

Solar Winds Will Help You Process More Oxygen

I've talked about the function; now let's discuss the purpose a little bit more. As I said, the solar wind tends to augment health levels in the physical body. What does that mean? Specifically, it will have measurable effects on the hemoglobin in the blood. In some individuals it might also affect the way the blood processes oxygen in the body in ways that may or may not be measurable.

You all know that there is less and less available oxygen for your physical bodies. Something must be done; otherwise, you will gradually experience oxygen starvation. So as I see it from my time, the purpose of the radiation you are receiving in your time is to alter the efficiency of the blood system in your physical body so that more oxygen can be processed.

If more oxygen can be efficiently processed in your physical body, that will at least partially compensate for the lack of available oxygen. Now, you must understand that aside from technological supplements of oxygen (which will increasingly become commercially available for individuals as well as fed into closed air conditioning systems), generally speaking, the oxygen depletion will progress. There will be less and less oxygen available. Of course, eventually this will lead to water shortages. At some point, as a more benevolent society forms on the planet, all people of all countries and all lands will be saying, "There's only so much oxygen. We can get it from the water, but there's only so much water. We have to choose to have less people."

The people will see that it is important. It will not just involve some ruthless authoritarian government figure saying, "You will have no children," or "You and you and you will have only one child each," which is happening in some countries. If you ask those governments, they will give you a rationale, but very often most of the people just hear, "This is how it's going to be." But it won't be that way in this more benevolent society.

How does the eleven-year sunspot cycle fit in?

I am saying that it doesn't, and I'm not even considering sunspots; I'm only considering flares that radiate energy toward the Earth.

I shouldn't have used that word. The eleven-year cycle of solar energy . . . it seems to expand significantly in the eleventh year!

You will find that most likely, as you need it (your physical bodies are born to require oxygen), this cycle will gradually drop so the solar flares will be available to you perhaps on a nine-year cycle. You can't have it all the time, not even once a year. The optimum might be once every four or five years. I want to put this knowledge out now to get that going in your subconscious minds so that you can understand that this is something you can request from the Sun.

Requesting Energy from the Sun

How might individuals request this? The best time to do it would be shortly after the Sun rises in the morning. Go out onto the land—barefoot is best. If you have to have shoes on, use only those with leather on the bottom (ideally elk or deer, not cow leather, but do what you can in your time). Focus your physical consciousness on that position of the body where you connect to the Sun.

Speak to the Sun all the time, keeping your physical consciousness there. I've spoken about physical consciousness before in terms of generating or noticing the heat in your chest or solar plexus [see the love-heat exercise on pp. 7-8]. This means that if you were to put your fingertips together, your physical consciousness would suddenly become very aware of your fingertips. Then, if you were to put that same physical consciousness inside that portion of your body that connects to the Sun, you would become conscious of that physical part of your body, meaning you would feel it.

As you feel it (you have to do both at the same time), talk to the Sun and say, "Please, can we have some more benevolent energy for us now?"—us meaning you and your people, the people of Earth. If the Sun feels that it is time and not too soon—because the Sun is a consciousness as well—it will radiate energy to you.

Generally speaking, do not ask this only for yourself. Say, "Can we have this for us?" not "Can I have this for me?"—do not say that. After you ask that, maintain your focus for a few seconds (maybe ten seconds) in the physical part of your body, then relax and say a prayer of thankfulness to the Sun or whatever you would like to say, as long as it is benevolent. You might say, "Thank you," or "Good life," or something like that—just as you might say to any other life form. Whatever you say, say it and mean it. It's not just a passing thing.

Do Not Create Your Own Gestures

On the subject of body consciousness, I would like to know the dynamics of these gestures. How are the movements of the hands chosen? Is there a correspondence to suns and planets and minerals? What do these gestures mean? How can we create them ourselves?

Don't. I truly believe that I am showing gestures and not saying, "This is how you can make your own." Most people, even many spiritual people, do not understand the profound impact of their own gestures. Very often a single gesture you might make . . . for example, how often have you seen someone do this [Fig. 20-2]?

Typical Gesture That May Have an Unknown Impact

Fig. 20-2. This typical gesture often has unknown impacts, sometimes to the individual, sometimes to other people. People also might make this gesture using the flat part of the hand.

How often do you see something like that? It happens often, or people might use the whole flat part of the hand. Now, one might say, "Well, that's just a gesture . . . " Gestures like that often have other impacts, sometimes to the individual, sometimes to other people (I won't go into it all). So the hazard is that if people right now make gestures, they have no idea of the extended impact. If I said, "This is how you can make your own gestures," it could create spectacular complications and upheavals in your time.

I have not in the past been overly secretive. But in your time there is a level of—I don't like to call it *secrecy* but rather *discretion*—in communicating knowledge and wisdom to an apprentice. The communication takes place slowly. The apprentice is expected to learn, memorize and completely understand one thing before he or she goes on to the next.

On the other hand, if too much is given to the apprentice too soon because she is fascinated, excited and enthusiastic, she will very likely rush out and start doing things before she is ready. Since you and others—whom I am attempting to expose to these capabilities in these books—are not going through the apprentice process with me or any other shaman, I do not feel that it is safe to give this wisdom to you yet. That's why I'm saying, "Don't make your own gestures."

Someday, when there is more potential for working with individuals either in groups or perhaps with videos taken in groups, I will give more of this knowledge and wisdom. But to give it to you right now would be like the statement, "A little knowledge is a dangerous thing," so I will not tell you how you can do it for yourself.

But I will tell you this: The motion of the hands waiting for the physical body to respond with its heat tells me that this is the right gesture for you now, because the physical body I am speaking through right now was born and raised in and is therefore a product of your times. His physical body gives me physical signs to know that this is the exact position, whereas in my time the hand position would be different. So different times do affect the position of the hands, and many other factors weigh in as well.

Asking for Knowledge

Okay, without going into specifics then, can we get some generalities? If you move a hand and point a finger . . .

Generally speaking, the wand has been given before [see page 23]. But if you want, I'll give you a little generality. If you are using the wand, say with your right or left hand, and you want to know something about Earth, the way Earth works with the material world, then the palm faces down. If you want to know something about your immediate environment, meaning something physically here, the palm of the hand may be pointing to the side.

Vertically.

Or the hand is vertical, but the palm is pointing horizontally. Or it might be in between. More likely in your time (this is what the body is telling me), the position is going to be in between.

At a forty-five degree angle.

Yes, between the Earth position and the immediate environment position.

If you want to know something that is from the stars or from Spirit, then the palm is upward. But this may not be knowledge. As you know, very often the wand is used to feel, to sense, but sometimes the wand is used to give a blessing or to send out energy for a specific purpose.

Most of the time, most of you will not be sending out energy into space. Occasionally, some shamanic students or a shaman might do that, but most of the time this will have to do with your immediate environment or Earth, meaning a question about your immediate environment or a blessing for Earth.

The Andromedan Mind

But can't you get into the theory of it at all? The hand is obviously moving. What is it affecting?

You want a *mental* explanation for something that is entirely *physical, spiritual* and *feeling.* If I give you a mental explanation, do you know what it does? It then takes on the risk of becoming a mental science, and this is *not* a mental science. The reason your physical body is so heightened to the experience of physical evidence (such as the heat coming up for some reason) is that the mind hungers for it; this is food.

This food for the mind requires physical evidence. This is something the mind takes in. If it becomes a mental science, then the mind is no longer fed, and this becomes a precise positioning: "You hold the hands like this, *exactly* like this." The body ceases to feed the mind. Remember, the reason your mind is in your physical body is only partially (half of it, the experience) for the mind to provide to the physical body. Mostly though, 50 percent is for the mind to be fed physical proof that it can understand and appreciate. It is so the mind can expect repeated experiences and develop the capacity to move beyond knowledge to wisdom.

The mind that you have now (as Zoosh has so eloquently described)—being from Andromeda and so on—never had the capacity to develop wisdom. It could only develop wisdom in a physical body, which can give it physical evidence and proof that something works. The mind, therefore, gradually develops the capacity to learn, experience and apply wisdom.

This has been done by you on Earth, and that is why the mind is now beginning to move back to Andromeda, because it has the capability that it was sent here to get. It was unable to get that on Andromeda, because the Andromedan body does not feed back sufficient physical information and experience (feelings) to support the need for the mind to be fed in that process. It could only be done in a place like this, where the primary lesson for all beings has to do with the physical world.

That's excellent. Zoosh explained it before, but not in that way. Years ago he said the Andromedans were already harvesting the mind from those who had passed over.

Well, I wanted to communicate that to you in practical, understandable physical detail, because although we all know and love our friend Zoosh, he doesn't always provide it in the practical physical because he doesn't function in that realm.

Introducing Yourself to Water

Did you work with the elements? Can we work with the elements? With the spirit of fire?

I did not. That is not my specialty. You'd have to talk to somebody else. But I have done extensive work with water.

How did you work with water? What can we learn to do?

If you live in an area where there is any natural body of water . . . not water that has been dammed up or is part of an irrigation system, but a creek, a river, a lake or an ocean, anything natural and flowing in its own process. As soon as you can, it would be good to walk down there and introduce yourself. If there are people around, you can whisper, but try to find a place where there are not too many people. You can bring family members if you like, but everyone should know what it is that you are doing.

First, go down to the river and say, "Greetings, my friend"—I would say that. Or you might say, "Brother/sister river," however you feel. Then say, "I would like to introduce myself and my family," and say your name and maybe your spirit name if you are inclined to, if you feel like this is what to say. Then put your right hand down into the water so that the palm and the fingers touch the water [Fig. 20-3]. If the water washes up over the top of your hand, fine, but you want the palm and the fingers to touch the water because you are introducing yourself.

If you have to get your feet wet, that's fine. The main thing is, you want to touch the water. If you have brought your family, then you could

Gesture to Introduce Yourself to a Natural Body of Water

Fig. 20-3. This is the gesture to introduce yourself to water. Put your right hand down into the water so that the palm and fingers touch the water.

introduce them: "This is my wife." You could introduce her the other way, but I would say, "This is my wife." I would not say her name.

She then says, "My name is . . ." and goes and touches the water in the same way. Then the children do so, maybe the grandchildren, and so on. Everybody comes to introduce themselves. In our case, our whole people went down, and one after the other, everybody introduced themselves, just like that.

After the family introductions, ask the water to introduce itself to you. Take your other hand like this [Fig. 20-4]. Put the back of your left hand into the water, making certain the water flows over the top of your hand, but the back goes in first. Then ask, "And do you have a name you wish to be called?"

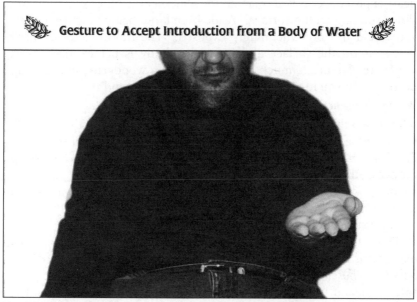

Gesture to Accept Introduction from a Body of Water

Fig. 20-4. Here is the gesture to accept introduction from a body of water. Put the back of your left hand into the water, making certain the water flows over the top of your hand. Do these introductions as soon as you can if you live near a body of water.

In your time rivers are named by other means, but we ask what its personal name is. Sometimes I will feel a sensation of a name, but other times I won't.

Like River That Runs Over Rocks or something?

Perhaps something like that. So after you introduce yourself, the river most often politely gives its name. Then that's how you and the people refer to the river from that point on.

No one ever calls it "the river," even in talks amongst ourselves. We don't say, "Oh, go down to the river." Never. We always say, "Go over to . . ." and use the personal name; in that way there is a polite introduction. This is very important. In your time this has largely become a lost art, but I have given you directions, instructions. I think it's pretty clear how to do it.

Water Is Mother Earth's Heart Exposed

This is vitally important if you live near a body of water. It is less important if you live three or four miles away, but it is good to do because bodies of water of your time are very lonely. They are completely misunderstood. People talk about droughts and floods and all of that, but it is a scientific approach only—in short, a heartless approach.

Rivers, bodies of water, are full of heart. They are Mother Earth's heart exposed. Can you imagine for a moment having your veins and fluids running on the surface? Aside from it not being practical or safe, you would feel overwhelmingly exposed. The fluid of Mother Earth that runs on the surface and inside her body is her exposed heart. Therefore, she needs much love, and this is a wonderful and easy opportunity for you to give her that love, so I recommend it.

We're polluting her heart.

But even that can be soothed quite a bit by such an introduction. Obviously, if the river is so polluted that it's not safe to touch (in some cities that might be so) or maybe if it's where the water empties into the sea or the ocean, then people might not be able to approach the water. But if you are living where the river is still clean, especially near the headwaters, then even if you are fifteen miles from the river, you will be helping those who are downstream if you perform this intimate introduction.

Don't feel shy or silly. Remember, *the world around you is sacred, and sacred does not mean that it must be feared and interacted with only by a chosen few.* In your time that has come to mean sacred, but sacred means intimate, heartfelt, necessary, beloved, appreciated. *That* is sacred. In my time, and I believe even in your time—even though that has been somewhat forgotten (perhaps unintentionally by your religions)—the world around you needs to be made more of your heart.

In your time many people's hearts, which pump the fluids of the body, are injured by the process of life. Things happen. It is grief, or this or that. A great deal of restoration and soothing is needed. This is especially true for those of you who don't have relatives nearby who would normally do this for you, people who would put an arm around your shoulder and let you cry and support you and say, "Go ahead, if it feels good"—*not*, "Don't cry." That is an unfortunate disaster in your time. Tears are important.

Receiving Solace from the Water

So if you don't have that, you can go to that body of water you have introduced yourself to. Put your right hand on your heart; then change and put your left hand over your heart while reaching out with your right hand to the body of water [Fig. 20-5]. Then touch it palm down to

🍃 Gesture to Accept Solace from a Body of Water 🍃

Fig. 20-5a. Here is the gesture to accept solace from a body of water. Go to the body of water you have introduced yourself to, and put your right hand on your heart, like this.

Fig. 20-5b. Then put your left hand over your heart while reaching out with your right hand to the body of water.

Fig. 20-5c. Touch your hand palm down on the surface of the water. If you like, say, "I am greiving, Grandmother. Can I sit with you for a time?" If you get a good feeling, then sit with the body of water. Do this when you need solace or comfort.

the water and say, if you like, "I am grieving." You could add "Mother" or "Grandmother" (people affectionately call a body of water "Grandmother"): "I am grieving, Grandmother. Can I sit with you for a time?"

If you get a good feeling, then sit with the body of water. Try to have your feet in the water, maybe touch it with your hands. If you want to, you can stand in the water, but oftentimes the water's too cold. If the water is too cold, put the bottoms of your feet in it, or touch your hand from time to time to the water. But if it happens to be a cold time of the year, if there is ice in the water, then just get close to the water and talk to Grandmother. If there is ice, then Grandmother is flowing underneath but protecting herself on top, because it is a time of restoration for her. She has the ice . . . it is not just science, where it gets cold, water freezes—that is not heart consciousness.

In our time we say ice forms over the water because Grandmother sleeps, but, in fact, I believe—even though that is the story we tell children—that this is a time when Grandmother restores herself. She needs to protect herself from the rest of the world around her.

Of course, we need water, so we have found a place where we can create an opening and draw out the water we need. Grandmother has shown us the exact place where she will allow this opening to take place, and we only go to that spot every winter to get water, if we happen to be there during the winter. Usually we will try to move south, but sometimes storms come up all of a sudden. Then it's too late. That's why you always have to have food stocked up. You never know.

So are you interacting with the water? The life force of the water is what we call a deva. Do you use those terms?

No, we think of Mother Earth and her whole body as being part of her living tissue, as in the physical body. We think of all of Mother Earth as being sacred. In your time you hear native peoples saying that this mountain is sacred or that mountain is sacred, but if you go talk to them, they will tell you that the whole Earth is sacred, sacred meaning exactly the way I described it. Sacred does not mean something distant, possibly feared. Never. It always means you are supported, that your existence is dependent upon Mother Earth. Without Mother Earth you would not be here, and that is that.

The deva idea, I believe, is something that was put forth by people in another part of the planet. It started out as a way to explain the sacredness of the land and how things worked, because children always ask why and how. They do in my time, too—no difference.

Not just children.

Yes, but if children ask these things and they are answered clearly, then they repeat those things when they are adults. So I believe that this is how the sacred process of nature was explained in this other part of the world. It has continued into your time as a benevolent way to explain to people how things work, but it is not part of my culture.

Communicating through Tears

Okay, you said it was very important: Talk about tears.

Let's consider tears. They are salty, yes? So tears tell you all you have to do. You don't necessarily taste your own tears, because if you are crying, you have to feel what you're feeling. But it's not unusual for a person to taste the tears of somebody else.

Suppose I tell you a story from my time. One day in my walks from encampment to encampment, going to work with an apprentice, I came across a young woman. This is unusual in my time. I do not usually come across people—animals, yes, but people, rarely. But I came across a young woman sitting near a river, and she was crying very hard but did not speak my language. I did not speak her language either, and she was obviously overwhelmed by something that was of great grief.

So with signlike language, I asked her if I could approach. She nodded, and then I went to help her. She could see that I was a shamanic being because I was wearing a medicine shirt. A medicine shirt in my time sometimes displayed certain things so that even if you were not of that tribe, you could understand that this was a shaman of some tribe.

She probably would have thought, "Not my people; I don't know who he is," but maybe she felt I looked safe. She nodded, which I took to mean that it was okay to approach. We could not communicate, but she had great grief. I wished to help her, but how could I?

So I touched my finger to her tear. I tasted. Then with a different finger, not the same, I touched her tear again. I smelled. Then I took my third finger and touched her tear again. I rubbed it between my thumb and finger. I never used the same finger. One finger does one thing and another does another and so on. Each finger performs an individual task.

Then—because I know my body and I know what my body feels—I knew that her grief had to do with the fact that she had miscarried a child who was very important for her people. Later on I found out from a friend, a shaman from another tribe who speaks that language, that it had to do with the fact that she was married to the son of an elder, and this child was intended to be his heir. The miscarriage was a great disaster for her. It did not happen early but well on in the pregnancy.

I was sorry she was grieving. Naturally, she was by Grandmother, grieving by the river, and I understood that she had lost a child and was grieving. So I put my left hand on my heart and my right hand toward

Gesture Meaning "Spirit Comes to Earth"

Fig. 20-6b. Another view.

Fig. 20-6a. Here is the gesture: Point to the sky, meaning Spirit.

Fig. 20-6c. And then come down with your hand, meaning Earth.

her, meaning, "I give you my heart love." The left hand receives from the heart; the right hand provides. I gave, and then she understood that I wanted to do something for her. So she composed herself a bit. She sat on the rock a little bit straighter and closed her eyes, not just lying down, weeping tears and so on.

She was still crying but was more composed, and I inquired, "Is there another spirit of a child who is going to come into her body who wishes to be born and live with her?" I heard yes. I also heard two others who wanted to.

So I pointed to the sky. She knew this meant Spirit. But just in case she didn't, I went like this and then like that [Fig. 20-6]. This, to the sky, means Spirit, and this, coming down with my hand, means Earth.

She understood. Then I held up three fingers, and she knew she was going to have at least three more children, so she brightened. She

Fig. 20-7. This is the gesture: Hold your arms up toward the sky, palms facing out.

sat up, felt better. She wiped away her tears and went like this [Fig. 20-7]. Her people do not hug. My people do not hug, either. Of course, husbands and wives are more intimate, but we don't hug everybody. So this means, "Thank you, and I give you my love."

She went like that and was so happy. She began to compose herself, started to smile a bit, and then she walked off back toward her people. I walked off toward the village or encampment where my apprentice was. I tell you this to show you that tears give not only feeling, but meaning.

Practice with Your Loved Ones

In your time if someone is crying, maybe you comfort them, but what happens if you are from Asia and you speak only the language of your region? What if you see a youngster crying and nobody is around? The youngster looks at you hopefully but does not speak any language you know. It sounds like gibberish to you.

If you have practiced with your family and with your mystical people, then maybe you can get some feeling. Don't just try to think what it is, because your mind will think up every possible thing that will ever be, that you have ever heard of. Always go with physical evidence. Use the finger method I described. Maybe it won't seem like it makes sense to you in your mind, but you will show your mind.

You might not be able to get this right away, so, as I say, practice. Your children or brothers or sisters are going to cry sometimes. Just let them know that you want to console them, you want to comfort them. If you see them crying, maybe a boyfriend or girlfriend broke up with them, then say, "Please take no offense. I console you; I love you," and taste, smell and feel their tears—just to know how tears taste, smell and feel during this kind of grief. If they know you love them, they won't mind. Just do one finger at a time as I described, and then simply pay attention.

You might have another opportunity to do that with a beloved family member who understands that you are on a spiritual path. Maybe that person will do it for you sometime when you are crying. What I am saying is, it does not have to be only a mystical thing, but at the very least, mystical people can try to practice this in your time. So should you come across an individual like this, whose language you don't understand, maybe you can help. Or at least, if you are not able to communicate with Spirit, you can find out why the person is crying.

What can you do to help? You can say a prayer to whoever or whatever you believe in, that this person be consoled for his or her terrible grief and go on. In short, it is a thing you can practice. But always go to physical evidence first.

Things are a little different in your time because some wisdom is happening now. That's not to say that there hasn't been wisdom in the past, but now the mind has the capacity to feel comfortable with wisdom and to trust wisdom over authority. Somebody else tells you or you read about how to do something, but you've always done that thing in a certain way and it works for you because that's your wisdom. Now you trust your wisdom more than an external authority.

I feel that is good. In your time this is what the mind has accomplished. What I say is this, then: If you can practice these things, go to physical evidence first. Then you'll get inspiration.

Tears Are Like the Ocean

Tears are like saltwater. I tell you that tears directly relate to the ocean, to the sea. River, creeks, sometimes even other big bodies of water, all eventually go to the ocean and come from there too at some point.

This tells you that they are bringing the feelings of the land and the people and the animals—whoever interacts with those bodies of water—to the ocean. They are bringing all these feelings, washing them off the land down to the ocean, because the ocean can restore, reenergize, soothe, calm. It can create a loving environment for excessive feelings. This is why sometimes rivers flood, especially in times of great population.

In places where there is tremendous population and the land gets saturated with the feelings of human beings, a flood comes along, but this is not intended to hurt human beings. If a flood comes with enough warning, maybe human beings can get out of the way. The flood comes along and washes the land. It takes that excess of feelings down to the sea where they can be restored, nurtured and soothed—purified.

So tears always come because human beings have feelings—they may be tears of joy, but they are feelings. Since tears have a direct connection to what you are feeling, they have a direct connection to feeling the body and heart. The ocean is also about feelings, about feeling the body and the heart of Mother Earth.

Human Emotions and the Deep Ocean Calm

How does the ocean restore water that's full of emotion?

You notice that rivers and lakes have very little, if any, wave action. The wave action, the shape of the wave, the actual curve of the wave, is churning the water at the surface and to some extent nurturing a little bit—it's bringing waters up from below. Waters from below tend to be much calmer, with soothing energy.

Nowadays people dive. They go down deeper and deeper and deeper using some kind of machine. The deeper they get, the more they might notice that the animals who exist down there are very calm, moving very slowly. Even sharks at that level move very slowly.

There's pressure.

There's pressure, yes, but many creatures who live down there are not moving slowly just because of some scientific reason. They are also moving slowly because they are calm, very relaxed. That is because what is most relaxed has already been cleansed.

Cleansing takes place at the surface. Sometimes if a great deal of human emotion or even war is going on, where humankind has ships at sea or tumultuous things going on all over the Earth, that's when you get a typhoon. It stirs up the water and tends to bring that calm water up. Deep, calm water comes up to calm the troubles of the human beings being processed on the surface. It calms at the surface, but it also must spin.

Mother Nature uses spinning to transform, to mix, to bring things together that do not normally come together, such as the cold, calm water being brought up to the surface. The surface water might be warmer, more passionate, filled with human feelings that have been washed off the land. If feeling comes to a height, then maybe a storm needs to come along and bring up that calm water to soothe the surface.

It actually evaporates up into clouds and then comes back down again?

Mother Earth does that to clean her air; the function of that rain is to clear her air, to give her a fresh feeling. You've experienced this when you come outdoors after rain. Maybe all day long it was pouring down rain, but after that nice shower, the Sun comes out and there's a tremendous sensation not only of fresh air, well-washed air, but you feel profoundly vitalized in your physical self. It is a physical thing you can feel—absolute proof. "It's true," you say.

That revitalization process brings together the water and the Sun and the water vapor—all this has to do with revitalizing Mother Earth. And Mother Earth has enough revitalization energy that she can share with a human being or a tree or an animal. All feel revitalized in that moment. Mother Earth then cleans her air and revitalizes her body in that place—her whole body, at least the surface and above the surface.

The Calming Effect of Human Crying

What about the human then, human crying? Does that help pressure or emotions? What happens inside the human as a result of crying?

In your time you have been told not to cry, especially men but sometimes women. It's terribly sad. Those of you who don't or can't cry, it's probably taking a good 10 to 15 percent off your life.

So if you feel like crying, go ahead. You will probably live longer. The body requires crying because the body is like a smaller version of Mother Earth. The tissues of a body function as a place where the calm energy is stored. At the very bottom of your lungs, there is a place where you haven't usually exhaled all the air, a layer of air or an atmosphere that is calmer. It is always calmer there.

If you've ever been around anybody crying, you've noticed that they tend to gasp when they cry. That gasping completely empties the lungs. It pulls that energy and air up out of the deepest level of the lungs, and that functions the same way that cold water functions in the sea.

In order to do that, you must actually cry. Otherwise, it will never be like that; it occurs only when you are crying. This eventually will soothe the body.

So it's that calm air rather than the tears themselves?

Tears also help, because when tears flow, some of them evaporate, and Mother Earth is familiar with saltwater from humans. When tears flow, the best place to cry is by a body of water near where you live.

Say you are near the ocean and for some reason are experiencing great grief for a moment. Even if you can't get down to the ocean, if you can smell the ocean, that vapor, it will come. It will be attracted to your face, and the ocean will actually be able to reach out. I have spoken to shamanic brothers and sisters who have told me from their personal experience that the ocean can reach inland from five to about fifteen miles. According to what they have said, it can reach that far inland to offer nurturance.

So cry, cry, cry, and notice at some point that you smell the ocean. You don't really pay attention because you are busy crying, but afterward, if you can notice, you can smell the ocean because the ocean reached out to you with its capacity to resolve and help nurture you.

This tells you something very important. You know that you can smell, but you don't often think of Mother Earth as being able to smell. She can. Mother Earth smells your tears. She comes to help.

Beautiful.

Mother Earth can smell, taste; she has all the senses you have and, in her case, more, because she is the teacher.

Sending Loving Energy with the Wind

Is there anything you want to say about the wind? I remember you said that strong wind brings you information and takes information from you for others. Is there anything else you want to say about working with air or the wind?

Let's say you hear about great grief or tragedy in some part of the world, maybe far, far away from you. Maybe there's nothing you can do about it from where you are. Or perhaps you hear about some situation that happened someplace where you have relatives living, and you can't reach them. Perhaps there is an earthquake or something like that, and you are worried.

Here is what you do. This is partly something I heard from an African brother, but I used it only once in my time. We talked to our African brothers with a long communication, and sometimes my African shamanic brother spoke to me about this circumstance I'm going to talk about.

Spit on the fingers of your left hand—not the little finger or thumb, but your middle fingers. Spit on those because they contain your body fluid. Put them down toward the palm of your right hand [Fig. 20-8]. Then turn your hands over and using the wand [again, see page 23], send a blessing, a prayer for the people. Try to aim it in the direction that has the most heat in your body. It may not actually be the physical direction, but this is the way energy wants to flow.

Energy does not always want to flow from point A to point B, in a straight line. It might want to go some other way. It might need to pick something up on the way to get to where you send it. If a relative or a loved one is there, you can picture the loved one's face and say a prayer: "My loved ones or family, may they be safe and protected, may they be nurtured and taken care of, may they be loved, and may they be able to have the capacity to do this for others as well, if needed." That's an example.

Or if there are no loved ones there, then simply say it for the people. You can also say, "May the animals . . ." If you are going to say it for the

Gesture to Send Loving Energy to a Distant Tragedy

Fig. 20-8a. Here is the gesture to send loving energy to a distant tragedy: Spit on your left middle three fingers, and put them down toward the palm of your right hand. Do this outside, if you possibly can.

Fig. 20-8b. Then turn your hands over like this.

Fig. 20-8c. Using the wand, send a blessing or prayer. Once you feel the heat begin to lessen, in ten to twenty seconds (or maybe even as long as thirty seconds), then stop. Take two to three steps back, then turn to the left. Do this when there is a tragedy that occurs far away.

animals, you must also say it for the people, because you are a physical human being. You must always include your own kind. I mention this to you because some of you really love animals, and I'm not so sure how you feel about human beings.

But since you are a human being, you must always include your own kind first. If you say it for the animals before you say it for the human beings, the animals will not trust that energy, will not take it as safe, because unless the animal has an intimate connection with you (it is a spirit animal or something like that), the physical animal will not accept that from a human being. It might be a wide open space where you know only animals are, but there could be a human being there. It's possible.

So say it for human beings first, then for animals. Then the animal can identify that this is coming from a human being who is at least comfortable with himself or herself. If you do not say this for another human being, the animal will think (or feel) that you do not trust your own kind—"How can you help me?" This is important to say because many people in your time feel good about animals, and that's good. I feel good about animals, too.

So this is something you can do with wind, even if the wind seems to be calm. There is always air around, energy flowing out. Stand on the ground outside. Do this outside if you possibly can. If you can-not—you might not be able to—then do it where you are. That's the best thing you can do. Know that energy flows right through walls—not so easily through metal, but it can. You might have to do it longer if it's going through metal, maybe two, three, four, maybe five minutes. If you're out in the open . . . ten, fifteen, twenty sec-onds—that's enough. Maybe thirty seconds if you feel it. In short, if you are feeling heat in your chest, the solar plexus area, do it as long as you are feeling that heat. But the moment the heat begins to lessen, stop, because you will need that remaining heat to recharge you a bit.

Remember, never send heat out of your physical body to others. They cannot use it. Teach others how to do the heat for the physical body. Heat in the physical body gives you physical evidence as to how long to hold the gesture. As the heat begins to diminish, then let go of the gesture and relax.

If you are outdoors, turn to the left and walk away. Not to the right. Earth moves in that energy, I believe. Turn to the left. If you wish, you can take two or three steps back and then turn to the left. Let it go; you have done what you can do. If you live in a city you can always call the Red Cross and make a donation or something like that, but do this first.

Of course, you're going to try to call your relatives first. But do this blessing and then go give money or clothes or whatever they need to the Red Cross and or a church or whatever charitable organization. So this is something the wind and atmosphere do.

Mother Earth's Difficulty Breathing and
Its Correlation to Your Health

All these centuries, except for some off-planet spacecraft coming in, the air was undisturbed. The air above us, our atmosphere, the stratosphere didn't get mixed up. Now we're blasting through. We're putting up satellites. We're coming down with shuttles. Has anything changed in this envelope around our Earth in the past couple of hundred years because of this that affects us in any way?

Mother Earth has a very hard time breathing when her atmosphere has holes in it. She breathes with her atmosphere—that makes sense, doesn't it? It is her air. She breathes. She has places in her physical body where air rushes in and out. Even some of your own scientists and explorer people have said, "I hear air rushing in and out of this place." Mother Earth is breathing. Sometimes exhaling, sometimes inhaling.

The exhale comes from within. It's easier to hear the exhalation, but sometimes you can tell she breathes in and air obviously comes from the surface. When she has holes in her atmosphere or the atmosphere is polluted, then it's hard for her to breathe. If the atmosphere ever gets terribly polluted, then it will rain, rain, rain, rain, rain. But that has not happened in your time yet.

When you say holes, do you mean what we call holes in the ozone layer?

Yes, that is part of the atmosphere. When she has holes like that, it is harder for her to breathe, and there is a corresponding situation. In the thirties and forties, there were basic rocket experiments. Nothing was too dramatic, but a few rockets were sent up in the thirties, and then in the forties a lot more, and so on. It continued to build up more and more and more.

Then, if you come forward to your time, more people per capita than a hundred years ago have difficulty breathing, have a breathing problem that directly correlates to Mother Earth having difficulty breathing. Always know this: Any time Mother Earth is sick or having difficulty, you as a human being, an extension of her, will have some difficulty in your own way. But it never works the other way, meaning that if you were having profound difficulty for some reason, that does not mean Mother Earth will have it.

If she is sick, you are sick too, in a similar fashion. Maybe it's diagnosed as this or that disease, but the symptom is noted as difficulty breathing at least some of the time, which correlates directly to Mother Earth's difficulty breathing. This tells you that pollution, mining, digging in the Earth, drilling and so on are harming Mother Earth, with a direct result on your soul.

What effect on humans does mining have, when crystal is taken out and then uranium and rare ores and all that?

Yes, and also digging holes. You dig a hole in your body—it doesn't feel too good, eh? Mother Earth has a greater survivability capacity than a human being. Human beings are meant to be fragile, because being fragile requires that you learn certain things you came here to learn as a soul being. Mother Earth is not quite as fragile. She can have holes in her body and still survive. She's not happy; she's hurting, in pain. There's discomfort, but she'll survive longer.

Is there a direct correspondence in humans, then? Are there more bullet holes? More operations?

Suppose a physician says an organ is very sick: "If you leave the organ in your body, you will die, but I can do surgery and take the organ out. Then you'll take this pill the rest of your life." The doctor does not tell you this, but you'll probably live almost as long as you would have otherwise. The doctor says you will live your normal life, but, in fact, the doctor knows it will take a little bit off your life. But this is what the doctor has to offer: take the organ out, take a pill, get along. You recover from surgery, but your body's not the same. It cannot do the same things.

Okay, but thirty, sixty years ago we didn't have these knee operations. There are operations for everything now.

Yes, but someday operations will be much more benevolent—not cutting into a body with a knife. Surgeons will change to noninvasive surgical procedures; this is coming. A step along that path is laser surgery, but that's still somewhat invasive. More will be done with light in the future.

Different types of light are very nurturing to the body, especially when done in a very specific way, meaning certain types of sounds—music, singing, tones. It's different for all kinds of people, and much of this is being experimented with now. Generally speaking, that type of healing method is different from individual to individual. In the case of a surgeon taking out an organ, that method is fixed. The organ might not always be in exactly the same place in every person, but the procedure is fixed.

And ultrasound now. They're bringing up kidney stones and all sorts of things.

These are steps along the path to other benevolent types of treatment for the physical body.

Communicating with the Earth

I think there was a teaching in the old days where you could actually go and give your pain to Mother Earth.

Don't do that anymore. She can't take it. And you cannot really process her pain by putting your left hand on the Earth and taking her pain. Don't do that either. You cannot handle that.

How would you work with earth as an element?

I'll tell you something practical you can do. As I said earlier, my people moved, came to this spot by the river and went down and introduced ourselves to Grandmother River. But before we did that, we were on the land. The land would welcome us. We knew this because we felt good in this spot, the same way an animal feels welcome on the land: "Dig a hole here, build a nest here—this is where I feel welcome. The tree welcomes me; the land welcomes me. This is where I put my nest."

For us it was no different—just like an animal. We walked around here and there. Sometimes as we walked around, the people in the group walked way up this way, way down that way. We always moved in the same direction, but people walked all over the land, because everybody was feeling, using their heat, their bodies, their feet to feel the land: "Where do we feel welcome?"

Sometimes an individual might feel welcome in a spot, and then we all went over and stood there. If no one else felt it, we might say, "Oh well, you stand up for a moment and feel that. Good. We'll wait if we can. If we can't, we'll go on and you catch up." I was just a child then.

It was just for that person, then.

Just for that person. And so we would say, "Try to remember that spot." But maybe another person or several people said, "Oh, it feels very good here." And we also noticed that we could hear the river. That was a good sign. Anytime we were close to the river, we said, "Oh, this is what we like," and we tended to walk along the river, within, say, a half mile or so—maybe on a little higher ground. When we got to a spot and we all felt good on this spot, then this was the place where the land gave us physical evidence for our physical body. The land told us, "Here you are welcome. Live here. You can build a house."

We were happy about that. Then everybody reached down to the earth and felt the dirt, scooped up a little bit of dirt where there weren't any plants but only dirt. We tried not to disturb any place where animals lived, ants and so on. I'd bring it up in my right hand; women tended to bring it up in their left hand. Either way was okay.

We would smell the dirt, pay attention to that smell, memorize it—smell the dirt for a long time, maybe five or ten minutes. We wouldn't stick our noses in it, but we tried to memorize the smell because someday maybe one of us would be separated from our people for a time. Maybe we'd have to move quickly from that spot.

Then you might not be able to walk along slowly and feel the Earth. You might only be able to run to get to a safe place. You'd run along and scoop up a piece of earth and smell it. If the smell was the same as where you were before, you could say, "Oh, I'm probably safe." You might not be able to relax and be sensitive enough to feel the sense of welcome, but you could note the smell. The smell would tell you that this was the place. If you were running from some danger, maybe you could not be so slow and sensitive, so we memorized the smell.

So here's a practical thing you can do. Memorize the smell for ten or fifteen minutes maybe. Then rub the dirt between your hands; feel it. How does it feel? Then sometimes, not always, if it feels safe—meaning you have the warmth for this—move your tongue toward the dirt. If it does not feel safe tasting the dirt, then move your tongue over to where the dirt is, as if you were licking the fumes. If it feels safe, stick the tip of your tongue on your finger where there is some dirt.

You've been rubbing the dirt around between your hands; hold your hands flat when rubbing, like this [Fig. 20-9]. If your hands are vertical, it will have to do with sky, stars, atmosphere, below Earth and so on. So have your hands flat. This has to do with the Earth below your feet.

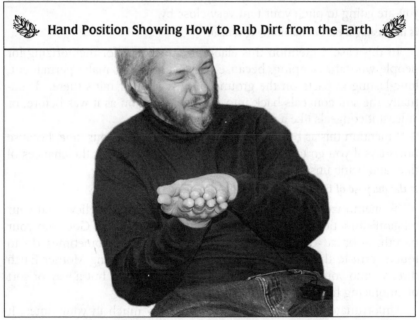

🌿 Hand Position Showing How to Rub Dirt from the Earth 🌿

Fig. 20-9. Here is the hand position. Hold your hands flat, which has to do with the Earth below your feet.

Let that dirt spread all around your hands. Then, if it feels safe, move the tip of your tongue to the tip of your hand, meaning your longest finger. Touch the tip of your tongue to the dirt. See how it tastes. Move it around in your mouth. Again, only taste the dirt if you have the heat in your body. Heat means yes—it doesn't mean safe, but you can interpret it that way. It means yes, there is love to do this. If you do not have heat when your tongue approaches the dirt, do not taste it. Only lick up the fume that you have, the smell of the dirt you have been smelling. But if you do taste it, then move the dirt around in your mouth so you'll have some idea of how the dirt tastes there. Then swallow.

I like to give you practical things because in your time you can still do this. Granted, the soil is polluted so it might not be safe to taste the dirt, but in some places it might. Maybe, for instance, you are out walking in the hills, camping somewhere. Do not go off the trail too far, but you might notice, for instance, the roots of a tree.

You might be able to taste the dirt under where the tree brings its roots up to the surface. Sometimes the soil right there is a little softer. If you want to taste the soil there, you might be able to do so safely. But only taste the soil if you have heat in your chest, and only do it by moving it around in your hand and slightly touching it to the tip of your tongue. Don't make it a habit, though. The only reason to do that is if you are going to pitch your tent very close by.

Is the tasting a part of memorizing it also?

In this case, I mention this elaborate procedure for memorizing for people who are camping, because tent pegs do not make permanent, long-lasting impacts on the ground, unless it never rains there. Eventually, the soil congeals back into a similar position as it was before, or at least it congeals like a wound healing.

I mention this as being a safe place to taste dirt in your time, because nowadays if you go to build a house, even on open land, the chances of that land being unsafe to taste dirt are very high.

Is the purpose of it to feel if it was safe or to memorize the place?

To memorize the place. But it is more than dirt. I believe that your religion's practice, where you take the symbolic taste of God into your mouth, is based on this ancient ritual that people sometimes do to touch earth to their mouth, because it is a way of taking Mother Earth directly into your body. It is not a sacred sacrament, but a way of sort of embracing her, an intimacy.

Unfortunately, I do not recommend it very much in your time. It can be done under very specific circumstances (that's why I gave the circumstance), but it has to be by a person who knows how to recognize what heat in the chest means. You say, for instance, "Is there love for me to slightly taste this dirt?" And if heat comes up in your body, then yes, there is love. Love means it's safe. So do so.

If there is no heat, then honor the dirt. Rub it around on your fingers. Smell it, if you wish. For a camping spot, smell the dirt, but don't taste it. Unfortunately in your time, you cannot do this too much. It's something you miss.

Tell me some situations in which you had to vacate your camp very quickly.

There's only one I can think of—when there was a fire. Sometimes in my time there were prairie fires caused by lightning. We saw fire coming, and in front of the fire, lots of animals were running. The animals were not running at us to do any harm. We saw clouds of dirt before we really understood that there was a fire.

The fire was moving slowly, but you never know when fire might pick up speed. We packed up everything in a hurry and ran, ran, ran to a place where there was not much grass and there were some caves. A hunter had mentioned that this was a spot where it probably was safe, where there was not much stuff to burn—maybe it had burned over sometime before. And everybody rushed and stayed in the cave near the river for a time until the fire went by.

Then, as the embers gradually went out, we returned to see if the camp was still usable.

But you were able to save your belongings. I was thinking of a wild animal or something.

Well, you try not to set up camp near any place where a bear or a dangerous animal might have to come. If you see lots of nice berry bushes, never set up camp there. You say, "Oh, a bear will come there for sure."

Or if you see bear tracks on the way to the river or something?

That's right. You avoid setting up camp there. Give sister bear plenty of room.

Communication with Fire

Do you do any ceremonies with fire? Do you bless the fire? Do you do anything at all?

Fire is not my job. Someone else does fire. The spirit in charge of fire is not always in charge of building and tending fire, but is in charge of communication with fire. She is the one to ask.

What elemental spirits were you involved with?

I have told you about water, wind and soil.

You did those for the tribe?

You want to say, "This person does this and this person does that." But I trained others how to do things because I was not always there—so I trained others. Usually, others had sufficient wisdom so they could do it when I wasn't there or if I was doing something else when I was there. Everybody did not have a specific task that only they did.

Very often women communicated with or had wisdom or interaction with and knowledge of fire. Not so often men. In your time fire is very often considered masculine, but in my time fire was considered feminine. Water was also considered feminine. Think of it for a moment. When spirit enters the body of a woman and a child comes out, that is transformation. Fire is also transformation.

Shamanic Training

As you interacted with other shamanic people, as you met them on the trail or met their tribes, did you share and learn from other shamans beyond what you learned from your teachers?

Yes, very often we talked about experience. Very often we asked each other questions. Maybe there was something I did not know how to do, but my people needed it. I asked mystical people from other places, "Has this come up for you? What have you done?" So very often we consulted with each other. Then sometimes, because I might be spending the night there, we all sat around and told stories.

So you shared. They shared. You learned.

Yes. It's not so different in your time. We told stories of what we knew.

How old was Bear Claw when you started working with him [Bear Claw is a past life of Robert Shapiro, and Speaks of Many Truths was Bear Claw's teacher while they were both in the body in the 1600s in North America]?

About three years old. Old enough to travel around and no longer drink from his mother's breast—and that's a practical necessity, because when a child drinks from his mother's breast, the mother has to be present for the teaching, which might not be appropriate for the mother. Even so, when I worked with a child, I went to him. His mother did not bring him and leave him there. I went to him because young children need to be in a very familiar area. And I did not work with him so much; it was more like play.

When children are very young, you play a game and have fun, but basic principles may be learned that way. We would go for a walk, and I would walk my way, do things my way. A little child, as anyone who is a parent knows, is very receptive to everything going on around him or her. So I would be myself and do things my way, and the child would notice. That is the beginning of teaching.

That's the whole foundation. You teach him how to walk, the look, all of it, right?

When very young, a child walks the best way that child can. He or she sort of stumbles about but notices how you walk.

The child's mother or maybe father or brother or sister would introduce me as Grandfather, even though I was not: "This is Grandfather Speaks of Many Truths." The child might not have understood that, but eventually would identify the sound. Then, as the child grew up, he tended to call me Grandfather for a long time until I said, "Call me Speaks of Many Truths, only if you wish." But most often I'd be called Grandfather from that point on.

Sometimes, though, I did not only work with people when they were little children. I might have started later because of a need in the tribe. For instance, the medicine woman in another encampment was not feeling too well. So a young man from this encampment needed to help the medicine woman—not only with gathering (she said what to gather), but to know which plants to gather. So he had to have communion with plants. I was not able to teach medicine so much. I might have been able to communicate to the spirit of the plant, but not the medicine. It's different from the mystical. So I taught him what I could.

This young man was drafted. He was hunting, but also needed to learn this. He was thirteen, fourteen years old when I started to work with him. So I did not always start with the very young.

How long did you work with Bear Claw?

Oh, I never really stopped. With my teacher, if I have something I do not understand, if my teacher's still alive, I ask him first. Bear Claw does the same thing. I stopped teaching Bear Claw physically when I died. Maybe he is still trying to communicate with me in spirit.

Yes, but is he still alive now?

Bear Claw? In my time, yes.

How old is he now?

From the moment in which I speak to you?

Yes.

About twenty-seven years. Middle-aged.

Middle-aged. And you?

I'm old now. Very old, by the time of my people. But not at this point. Sometimes I talk to you when I am younger, sometimes when I am older. It depends on what is needed.

Oh, I thought you were always fifty-four or so.

No. Sometimes I talk to you when I am in my thirties. Other times I talk about my wife, my children. Other times, I talk when I am an old man and my children have grown up or when I am very old and my wife has passed on. That's why sometimes I don't talk about my wife and children, because I speak to you from different points in my time. I can do this since I am not in linear time, no longer physical. I choose to talk to you from physical time so that I can talk to you in ways that human beings require—not just spirit talk.

I didn't know that. I've noticed that sometimes you say you had a wife and children, and I know sometimes you've said that she's passed, but I didn't realize that you were moving in time like that.

It's necessary and very useful. I say, "Good life."

Good life. Thank you.

Communication with Those Who Would Follow

Speaks of Many Truths
November 26, 1999

his is Speaks of Many Truths.

The Mandate: Messages for Those Who Would Follow

What was the invitation to your ancestors to come here? What was the stated purpose? It seems to me it was because you could teach communication. You were here to help with communication between all the beings on the planet, right?

One of the main reasons they were invited was to help to bring the different forms of life together in such a way that the human being, which would be the form they would take, would be able to see all forms of life as equal teachers. In short, what has survived, even with some tribal peoples existing in your time, is the profound impact of animals or animal figures or even diagrams having to do with animals that are so obvious in many of these tribal cultures.

With the scientific approach, some people nowadays have become overly confused, thinking this means that somehow we relate only to the animals on the basis of spirit, or that ancient man, as they like to say, related to the animals on the basis of some godlike quality. In fact, it was one of our mandates to make the importance of animals clear in the best way we could with our stories passed through time to present generations. Of course, my people do not exist in the present, but that was the plan.

So the mandate was to show Those Who Would Follow that the animals are profoundly important (that's how it was put, *Those Who Would Follow*—we did not know what that meant, but obviously, it meant your culture). Of course, this was also meant to show the importance of plants, but not many themes, especially in pictographs or petroglyphs, have been interpreted as plants. Some of them exist and have been misinterpreted as either deities or some kind of as yet unrecognized form of life. For example, here is one that has been confused. I'll show it to you [draws Fig. 21-1].

This is just a segment, but this frond has been largely interpreted as having something to do with a deity. It's about a plant. I'm going to draw another one, too [draws]. I'm not drawing it in the best way, but just giving you the idea. This was also assumed to be a deity, but, in fact, even a child would say that it's a plant. But often the childlike interpretation is discounted. So, as I say, sometimes it's understood what things are and sometimes not.

Say what plants those two drawings represent.

These weren't intended to represent specific plants, although one of them I think might represent holly. It wasn't intended to represent that so much as it was intended to suggest that plants are important, important enough to be left as a message for the future.

Generally speaking, with very few exceptions, all pictographs or petroglyphs (which are two different things) were left for future generations. An occasional mark was left for people coming through the area, meaning for the present and future present, but almost all were left for Those Who Would Follow. In that case, our people and probably others knew that this didn't have to do with our own people, since we would have stories that would carry forward. So it was understood

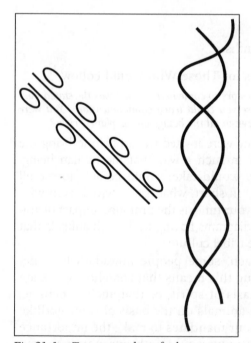

Fig. 21-1. Two examples of plant images that have been misinterpreted.

by my people that it was for others.

There are places, then, with many profound pictures left for you. I will tell you that almost all of the cave paintings as I recognize them are messages for Those Who Would Follow, regardless if they're a million or ten thousand years old—even though very often they've been interpreted as having to do with an event of the moment, meaning the hunt or something like that. Also, knowing that Those Who Would Follow could not be spoken to in any way and that language could not be left, there were attempts made by some ancients and also ancestors to show a blend between what would clearly be partially an animal and partially something intended to be godlike or spiritlike in order to show the profound importance of animals. Sometimes this would be done with plants as well.

This has also been either largely misunderstood in your time to be associated with gods of the moment, meaning that people put it down because it was some kind of spirit they thought was important, or occasionally it has been misinterpreted to mean ETs. But these paintings were always done to show that these beings all around you are vitally important. Those Who Would Follow—especially not being able to have the stories available to you that would survive through the generations and tribal situations—would need to turn to the most immediate teachers who would be available, which would be the plants and the animals wherever you lived.

We believed in the ancient spirit. I still believe in my time that wherever you are, there will either be plants or animals in some form, and that they have wisdom for you that will not only help you in your day-to-day survival, but will also help you to understand who you are as a human being (maybe not who you are in the larger sense, but who you are as a human being) and possibly even what you're doing here—meaning why you are here, why your people are here in this area and how you can live more pleasantly in terms of sources of food and water and shelter and so on. In short, every type and every clan of animal living in specific areas will have knowledge having to do with Those Who Would Follow. There might be the same type of animal distributed over wide areas just like human beings.

Speaking for my ancestors, concerning human beings of your time who do not have such wisdom readily available to you, we did not realize the full impact on your culture that would occur as a result of authority figures telling you how to live—your own kind. It's true that some of your religions are based on truly benevolent beings and wise beings who had much to offer, but those beings are no longer with you, and their words have been written down sometimes in a mistaken way and over the years misinterpreted again to reflect the culture and the deities and the political attachments of the time. In short, things have been so rewritten that the religions of your time have distanced and disenfranchised you from the animal and plant world so that you feel that it is you who is superior to the plants and animals, that it is your job to look after the plants and animals, to stay their fears, to feed the animals in a domesticated sense and to be careful of (meaning watch out for) the wild animals.

Of course, some people in your time have a fondness for wild animals and sometimes even try to support them should they be struggling in the winter or something like that. But speaking largely for your culture, with some individual exceptions, most people today are more impacted by political and religious understanding than you know. Therefore, your permission to communicate with the animals in ways that they can truly and easily communicate with you has been missing.

How to Communicate with the Animals

For example, when you come upon a wild creature (in the city, it might take the form of a small being, rarely a large being, but in the country, one might come across a large creature), stop and maintain a respectful distance, and then the animal will wait a moment for you to introduce yourself. If you do not, then the animal will give you an introduction.

The animal will probably not communicate in words, though it is possible in some places that you will hear words, meaning the communication that it offers comes through your guides or spiritual teachers, who will give you words if they believe you are unable to hear the animal's message as presented. If you are sensitive person, you might pick up the introduction as follows: The animal will present the message in pictures. Most often it will show you what it did that day. It won't give you its life story; it won't say, "I was born to this one or that one." It knows that does not mean anything to you. But it knows you can see it or you are aware of its presence, so it will present you a picture for your mind's eye. In short, it will show you something from its perspective.

It might not be from a perspective outside the animal's body. You will see life from what it does: it woke up; it moved from where it was; it went to get something to eat. The animal might show you the way it got its food and maybe a little bit about its travels to the spot where you see it, and that's it. That will happen very quickly, usually within ten to fifteen seconds, occasionally in twenty seconds.

Then the animal will stop and wait for you to do the same thing. If you do not, the animal will assume that you are not evolved enough to communicate with it in that way, in which case it will most likely become either wary of you and give you a wide berth or is more likely to wait to see what you will do next.

So should you receive that message, do the same thing. Don't show the animal what you did from the outside. Show it simple things, not complicated things. Not how you fixed or ate breakfast or that it was fixed for you by someone else, but simply that you got up. You can show it a little bit of what you ate if you want to, but you don't have to explain how it got to be in front of you. Then maybe picture a little bit of the space you were in.

You don't have to explain anything. Just picture it. Everything is pictures, just as you picture it in your own mind. Maybe show pictures along the way of how you got to where the animal sees you, and then stop. That maybe takes fifteen to twenty seconds. It might take a little longer for a human being, since you're not used to doing it. If it takes thirty or even forty seconds, the animal will wait.

When that happens, what usually follows is a period of quiet time, meaning the animal will hunker down or sit down, and you can do the same thing. Then the animal will be prepared to communicate with you in some way. Perhaps it will tell you something. You might at that point have a question. You might wonder who the animal's people are. The animal is not going to show you where it's from because it just met you, but it might show you its family or members of its family. All of this is done in pictures. The animal has stopped when the pictures stop coming. Wait for a moment to make sure that it's done, and then you can do the same.

If, on the other hand, the animal starts presenting you with knowledge that comes through in words, then most likely the animal has something to teach you and is involving your guides with that. If you can hear that, then it might be a teaching that you can use based on how the animal sees you. The teaching might also respond to something you need, because when you presented the image of yourself, you also presented your energy, and the animal might, especially if it is wise, be able to offer something to you based upon what it perceived or felt from your original introduction of yourself.

Perhaps you have an injury or a sickness. Perhaps you have a need that the animal can in some way address. If it can't respond, then it won't; it won't apologize. But if the animal does have something to offer, it will give it usually in a form associated with how the animal would relate to it. If it is something the animal has experienced, then it will show you something based upon what it feels you can understand. If it can communicate through your guides with words, then it will give you words, whatever words you understand culturally.

Then might come a period of time in which it is just quiet. It is important for you not to walk forward. Wait until the animal gets up and decides to leave. Before that, though, notice if the animal has an injury or a wound or if you get the impression that the animal might be hungry—whatever, on the basis of your impression, the animal might need. Perhaps it is thirsty. Whatever your impression is, picture what you feel would help that animal—even if it is wrong. The animal will know if it will help, just as you will know if what the animal suggests to you will help.

In short, picture things in your mind's eye, and try to show enough of the picture so that the animal can find its way. You don't have to describe every step of the way. Maybe it's something you saw, some food or water, or something that is close enough to point to. But don't talk and point; you have to be holding the picture in your mind of what would be good for the animal, and while you're holding that picture, point. So you'll probably have to point with your eyes closed—thus pointing is probably not the best way, then. The picture is the best. Then sit back down and wait for the animal to communicate more to you.

I've had these experiences myself. If you get up and the animal remains sitting—be it the smallest beetle or a bigger animal—you can then begin to move on. If the two of you are in each other's way, then begin to walk around the animal and make a gesture like this [Fig. 21-2].

🌿 Gesture to Communicate with Animals 🌿

Fig. 21-2a. Here is the gesture. First, point to yourself.

Fig. 21-2b. Then the hand comes out like this.

Fig. 21-2c. Then like this.

Indicate to the animal that it has to do with the land: "I go this way on the land."

But if the animal gets up and you can tell something by its attitude . . . maybe it's a little stiff or it's shaking its head from side to side (animals do understand yes or no in that sense, though they don't interpret it that way). Or even if it seems to block your path, meaning the direction you're pointing—it goes and sort of stands there—this doesn't mean the animal is going to walk with you. It means there is more to be said.

Fig. 21-2d. And then turn like this. Do this when you need to indicate to an animal, "I go this way on the land."

Sit back down and wait. The animal has more to say to you. At some point, it is usually best to let the animal walk off first, but I mention this because you might have somewhere you need to go in a hurry or it might be getting dark. There are reasons you might want to go. But the animal might still have wisdom for you, even if it is getting dark.

So wait until the animal speaks to you, and recognize that if it says nothing, if it appears to be blocking your path (not approaching you, just blocking your path), it probably knows that there is danger ahead for you and it blocks your path so that you will not walk into danger. Bears aren't likely to do this much because they're not as communicative as big cats. If the cat looks at you and begins walking off in a certain direction, and then looks back at you, pauses and walks off in that direction again, clearly it wants you to walk that way.

Don't walk with it unless it slows down to walk with you. This is un-likely, but it might happen if it feels very safe with you or feels a sense of connection. Don't wait for that to happen, though. A respectful dis-tance is always good. If the animal looks at you as it's walking and keeps looking at you and walking, it wants you to walk that way. The animal might walk you to a point where it stops. Then stop and just wait there. Maybe if it's getting dark, that's a good place to camp.

Perhaps the animal is trying to get you out of the way of some dan-ger. This is a danger you may or may not ever know about. Perhaps danger approaches and then veers off and never comes that way, but the animal does not know that. The animal knows only that the danger is approaching in your general direction. It might not be dangerous to the big cat, but it would be dangerous to you. The cat can run very swiftly and hide. It can do many things to survive—run up a tree or some-thing. If it is human danger, then that is something to be warned of.

So, in short, many things are possible. Don't assume that all of these things will happen; you can't necessarily expect it. I share these things with you because animals have so much to offer. I can't tell you how many times I found myself in a circumstance—maybe with an in-jury or not quite knowing where I was going in new territory, needing food or water—and an animal would tell me.

Often it was a flying or a little crawling animal, but sometimes it was a bigger one, and it would share. I would give to the animal what I had to offer; if it needed something, I would do what I could for it. Then if I needed something, the animal would do what it could for me.

The Survival of Animal Wisdom

The animals and plants have all the wisdom you need to survive here. They also know that until you understand and trust such meth-ods of communication (and there are others, but I'm giving the ones I use myself), another way for you to receive from 1 to as much as 6 or 7 percent of that wisdom and support is through your consumption of the animals. Some animals consume other animals. Plants do not con-sume that way, but animals understand this. And although they do not wish to become your dinner, they understand that if they do, this is a way for you to take in the wisdom they have to offer.

You will probably not understand this mentally as you are consum-ing them, except for the rare person who is that sensitive, but you very likely will have a dream in which the spirit of that animal or other ani-mal spirits of that type will give you wisdom. The hope is that you will retain it when you wake up. This is why some of the animals have fought so hard to survive in your time, because some of them have vast amounts of wisdom stored up, waiting for you. This is not wisdom that is left by other human beings for you. It is not wisdom that ETs or other cultures of humans have given them, saying, "Please hold this for the human being." It is wisdom that they themselves or their own cultures have, which they can clearly see applies to you in a way that you can use. It's either what they have learned on Earth or what they have brought from their culture, from where they have come from. That's why some have fought so hard to stay here, even if you are killing off all the wild animals, intentionally or otherwise.

In the case of some animals you are afraid of, such as big cats, this is perhaps intentional. In the case of some you are afraid of but who pose no serious risk to you, such as ants or beetles, this can also happen. But some of these creatures will make a tremendous effort to survive—not only for their own culture's sake, but because they are determined to pass on knowledge and wisdom to you if you are willing to take it. They know that they might be the last resort on Earth for you to receive the wisdom you need to not only survive well here, but to grow spiritually and to come to a point as a culture where you will be considered prepared in the eyes of ET visitors or wise teachers who might come to seek you out—that you will be prepared in their eyes to receive the true wisdom and assistance they have to offer you. If you are not prepared in the eyes of those teachers or visitors, they will simply not offer that wisdom because they know it will either fall on deaf ears or you might misuse it in some harmful way to yourself or to others.

So some of these beings fight to survive. One group is the ants. They have worked very hard to survive. Some beetles and many other little crawling and little flying beings have also worked hard to survive in order to pass on this wisdom to you—not all of them, but many of them. When I say "worked hard to survive," I'm talking about how you have for various reasons devised the need to kill them off or get them out of the house by poisoning them. But if a group of beings of any type can adapt to the poison and survive—they might be miserable and sick, but they survive—then you know they have wisdom for you. I say this to you very pointedly because some of you use sprays and so on to kill off or prevent the little beings from coming into your houses.

If they've adapted in some way to that, this tells you that they are not only a very important culture here on Earth and want to survive, but that they have very important knowledge and wisdom for you. They are willing to do whatever it takes to survive until you ask for that knowledge and wisdom, receive it in as many ways as possible, disseminate it to all the people in your culture and teach it to your young.

The Emissaries Speak with the Ancestors

You spoke about the mandate. Can you ask your ancestors? What was the original situation? Did an invitation go out from Earth because your ancestors' specialty was helping all beings communicate with each other? Were they invited specifically?

There was not only one reason—that's why I said *one* of the main reasons. At different times and in different books, I will speak of different reasons. The emissaries, wherever they came from, would come and talk for a long time about what was going to happen and what was needed in general terms.

Then, of course, since the emissaries would be talking to my ancestors on their planet, the ancestors would either not ask a question, they would say nothing, in which case the emissaries would say, "Well, we enjoyed our meeting with you, and we wish you good life," and go on. Or if my ancestors on the planet would say, "Tell us more about this," or "How can we help?" then the emissary would proceed to suggest that the ancestors—or people in spirit form taking the form of the people who would follow—might be very welcome to do this and this and this, or whatever they felt they might best choose to offer. They would say something like that, but this was always done very politely without any suggestion, because that's really like twisting someone's arm.

It was like an opportunity, a challenge, an adventure—all of that?

It was put to them as a story: "There's something happening that's going to have certain other effects, and we thought we'd tell you about this and then wait." It wasn't a trick. It was understood all over the universe at that time—and still is, as far as I know—that when presented like this, it is a matter of being polite.

If you wish to participate, if you or any of your people wish to involve yourselves in some way, then you will say so. You will indicate it in some way to the emissary. But if you do not, then clearly you would simply enjoy the meeting with the emissary and that would be that. You might thank them for informing you, perhaps.

Did the emissaries explain the concept of the Explorer Race? Why it was important?

They didn't even use the term. They just said in general what would happen and what the result might be. It was done very generally, and if the ancestors indicated an interest, then more would be told to those who volunteered either on the native planet or when they arrived in spirit form on the Earth. This teaching would be made available then.

The emissaries for such a project would always be very respectful and not give so much information that it might influence the culture on the planet. The planet's culture would be honored, and things would be contributed only if the culture on that planet was intended to take that in. Do you understand the difference?

The volunteers would need the specific information, but the rest of the people on the planet would need only a general overview, enough so that they could decide whether they wished to volunteer or not. And they might have volunteers who would go. Maybe the first ten or twenty might go all at once, but the rest of the individuals might volunteer over time, meaning that when they came to the end of their natural cycle on the planet, their next life would be on Earth.

When they reincarnated, they would be born on Earth and live here; that would be considered volunteering. Or perhaps it would not even be the next life in that sequence, but a life along the line of sequence. Maybe their soul hadn't intended to be born on Earth, but it decides, "Okay. How do we do that?" So the soul is matched up and at some point it is brought into a tribe of peoples to live on Earth, and then it finds out more about the Earth project.

Can you say roughly in our years how long ago your tribe came?

You can use this as a measuring stick: If you know from your best scientific estimate the age of the oldest cave pictograph or petroglyph, add about ten thousand years to that—that's when my people came.

This is not intended to be a riddle, but I cannot give you that number exactly. The oldest drawings and carvings are very old. You know just from your own knowledge roughly how old they are; some were recently found in Europe, in France, I think. You can get that figure very quickly. So we've been here for a long time.

Can I use the figures of the scientific community?

Yes, in terms of the oldest, plus ten thousand years. Excuse me, I'm not making myself clear. But say, for example (I'm not saying that this is true, but just for example), that the oldest pictograph was a hundred thousand years old.

Your ancestors would have come ninety thousand years ago.

That's right. I just wanted to be completely clear.

Messages in Cave Paintings and Carvings

As an aside, does anyone ever talk about specific paintings I could get pictures of?

Probably not, because I've given the basic overview of what the cave paintings really are. Think about it: Suppose somebody told you that it is essential for you to leave an absolutely critical piece of wisdom for people in the future whom you know nothing about, nor will you ever know anything about. The picture or diagram that you cut into the stone needs to survive into their times and cannot use words, but it must impart to the best of your ability an absolute story or artistic example of this vital piece of information.

What a challenge. Some of the drawings are so lifelike that you expect them to almost come alive.

They are sufficiently different than the way the animals actually looked. Sometimes this has been assumed to mean that the artists were not good, but very often that was not the case.

I have been able to see with my long vision two examples of people who put these cave paintings and carvings in places that have been discovered in your time, who could draw beautifully in the sand and dirt. They could draw a picture of an animal or something that would look gorgeous, even in your own time. But when they made the animal for Those Who Would Follow, they were trying to make it look larger than life. This was important so that the animal didn't exactly look like an animal—it looked like something different. The difference that would be accentuated would be that artist's culture's idea of how best to communicate the importance of this being to you.

So it was very challenging, and they did the best they could. Eventually, the meaning of these paintings and carvings will be largely understood, and I think even now there has been some suggestion and speculation that they could mean other things.

So your people came and pretty much stayed within the North American continent?

Yes, our people came to the North American continent, and that's where we were the whole time.

Was it a plan that they ceased to be at a certain time, or was there some type of catastrophe or accident?

It wasn't a plan that anybody in my culture was at all conscious of, but it occurred as a result of the western settlement of the peoples who came to establish your culture.

But because of your life, because of your abilities and Robert's, you are carrying out the dissemination of the wisdom to the people of this time in a way probably nobody there thought about.

Well, yes. I didn't think about it that way myself either, but it is . . . speaking for others, we believe it is important enough to make the effort.

Mystical Women and Men

I think your experiences with the animals are more . . . normal mystical men of the tribes did not have the clarity of communication you did. Was it because you came from a tribe who specialized in this?

No, not according to my understanding. Most of the mystical men and women I met had equal or better knowledge and capabilities in their particular areas of wisdom. This type of thing was normal. You have to remember that with very few exceptions, almost all of them were trained since they were very little children by the best teachers available to them. These teachers continued to give them wisdom until the day the teacher died or became incapacitated and unable to teach.

Also, the students would continue to acquire wisdom from the beings they interacted with when they could, if they had no particular thing that they were doing with their tribe or their family in that moment. Or if something came up that required assistance they might have to offer, they would ask other beings or creatures or spirits how to help.

So it either came up on the basis of simple communication when they had the time, or on the basis of need. Everybody I've ever spoken to (including using long vision and long hearing) had similar educations. By the time they were able to communicate at all to those around them, they had already been taught. Possibly in the case of some, I have had the impression that they might have been receiving teachings even when they were inside their mother—which would not be the case with my people, but has apparently been so with some people.

One of the reasons you had mystical men and women in the tribe was to help the tribe survive, right?

Yes, one of the reasons mystical men and women were in the tribe was to help the tribe survive and to help the people to have the best available connection to their spiritual sides as well as to the practical world. It wasn't our job to tell the people how to live spiritually, but if they had questions, we were there to give the answers we had or we were available to get answers the best way we could. Of course, the elders would also have a lot of this knowledge.

If a youngster had a question, she would likely go to her parents first, or to her uncles or aunts, and then maybe to the elders. Then as the last resort, she'd come to the mystical man or woman. That was the usual progression. This wasn't because the mystical man or woman was considered unapproachable; it was just considered a matter of politeness. It wasn't a hierarchy; it was simply that one goes to one's family first and then begins to move out further in the family. One does not go to the mystical man or woman—or in some cases, the medicine man or woman—unless one knows for a fact that nobody knows the answer to the problem.

But, for instance, maybe the child has a wound, and nobody around knows what to do. Immediately, she would go to the medicine man or woman and say, "What to do?" The medicine man or woman would know at least as much as all the others know, plus more. So in an emergency one goes straight to the being who would be the most help, just like in your time when you are in an accident and get an injury. You are taken right to the doctors who deal with that all the time; you don't ask your friends and family what to do.

So people would go to the medicine man or woman for that and come to you more for their spiritual needs, then? Or for something you could do only with long vision or something?

Yes, they would come to me or others of my tribe and other tribes if whomever they talked to advised them to. Maybe their father or mother or grandmother would say, "I know that Speaks of Many Truths could help you with this." In this case, they would come straight to me. But if their parents or grandparents simply said, "I do not have this knowledge," then they would continue along the family chain. If the elder said, "This is what I know about this, and Speaks of Many Truths might be able to give you more," then they would either come to me directly or they would try what the elder said first. Then if they needed more, they would come to me.

Every tribe has particular, unique ideas and ways of being. Can what we learn from you be considered generic to the way most of the tribes lived in your time?

No, I can only speak for my own people. Occasionally, I will say what other people do, but this is not an attempt to suggest that they do that because we all do it that way. No, I don't think that's true.

There might be some similarities, of course. We all had to survive in different and difficult conditions, and I think most of the tribes almost immediately started communicating with the plants and animals and Mother Earth to get the best advice and guidance. But other than that, you cannot assume that culturally we are the same.

But I don't mean culturally. That's what I meant by uniqueness. You were all here for the common purpose of preparing Mother Earth to receive . . .

Those Who Would Follow?

What can we call them?

Those Who Would Follow.

Those Who Would Follow. Okay, so you can say the Explorer Race.

I would call them Those Who Would Follow, because the Explorer Race was not always here. It has been a recent arrival, is that not so?

Ah well, we can never get Zoosh to tell us exactly when they came.

Considered from when we got here (that many years ago) to now, the bulk of those people were Those Who Would Follow. If you were to make a graph or a chart, only a little bit would be the Explorer Race.

Oh, I didn't know that.

The Explorer Race Focus Is Recent

Were there many humans here before the Explorer Race?

Yes, this has been discussed. Didn't Zoosh say that those souls specifically intended to be part of the Explorer Race had only been here for a few hundred years or so (occasionally earlier than that) but not for hundreds and thousands of years reincarnating over and over again on Earth?

We've never gotten specific answers to that.

Even with Atlantis, I do not think that any being who was in Atlantis was a member of the Explorer Race, with the possible exception that some of you who are members of the Explorer Race now might have had lives there. When you had lives there, however, you were not members of the Explorer Race—this was not your focus in that life.

You may have all arrived in that large experience through Creator and all that, that's true. But it's only in the past few hundred years that beings have been focused as the Explorer Race, meaning that you were here incarnated on Earth because you were working on Explorer Race problems and solutions. That has been only in the past—I can be fairly specific in your time—one hundred and seventy-five years or so.

I didn't know that.

That's why there's been confusion, because you and many of the readers as Explorer Race members might easily identify past lives you've had on Earth. It is very easy to assume that the Explorer Race was functioning in Atlantis and Lemuria and lesser-known civilizations, but from my perspective—what I've been told, what I know—the Explorer Race is not that. It's only recent. So you might have had a life five thousand years ago on Earth, but at that time you were focused on something else.

How interesting. That's totally new. I poked and prodded and never got an answer.

The Many Cultures of Those Who Would Follow

So you were preparing for Those Who Would Follow—they go back ten, twenty, thirty, forty thousand years—who had some purpose in coming here?

All of Those Who Would Follow could easily have been multiple cultures through time. In the case of ancient cave drawings and so on, just because in your time certain things have been rediscovered does not mean they weren't discovered before. So Those Who Would Follow might be a culture who lived here for a few thousand years or, even in the case of ET cultures, who camped here for some time and then went on. Those Who Would Follow would be all of those people, plus those who would even visit.

If they stayed here for more than ten years, they were no longer really visitors; they were at least encamped. We perceive ET bases as encampments, because most of the ETs who stay there, with some few exceptions, go in and out, meaning they come for a while, then others come to replace them. So it's an encampment, not quite an embracement of the planet as a home.

And since they're studying, they are going to be searching all over the planet for whatever they can find. So they might very well find as many cave paintings and so on as could be found by their methods. Sometimes they would interpret these paintings and carvings as they were intended, and other times they would interpret them in very much the same way scientists and researchers do today, depending entirely on their culture's perception.

Were there other beings such as your tribe here for this purpose: to prepare for Those Who Would Follow all over the planet? Were they in South America, Africa, everywhere?

I believe they were almost everywhere, but not where it was difficult to live, such as very volcanic areas. And there weren't so many beings in areas where there was snow and ice. There were a few, but generally speaking, only where it was possible to live and be sustained.

You're not going to like this, but I'd have to say that you need to ask them. I can ask them remotely, but my understanding is that the beings who are called the Eskimos do have some link to that continent that is near them by the chain of islands. There are some elements of shared culture and a connection to the Siberians even today, but they also have their own link. Most likely you would have to talk to one of their spirits or elders to get the best information. I can only communicate on the basis of my occasional contact with such beings.

I thought only North America needed to be prepared for these . . .

No, no, no—it is global. This is why you also have island peoples, because living on an island, especially a fairly small island, is very different than living on a massive piece of land somewhere. You have to develop a completely different kind of culture and even spiritual understanding to live on an island.

Then, of course, you become very connected to the water. You fish to survive. The water becomes profoundly important to you if you are an island dweller, especially if you go from island to island. Then you develop a huge reservoir of wisdom based upon what the water and the water creatures can teach you, which is not the same for my tribe. We knew the water, but we were land beings.

So you had that relationship with the land?

With the land and some with Grandmother River, but we would not have the vast amount of knowledge that island peoples would in relation to the waters of the ocean (or perhaps, in some cases, the waters of an inland sea that might have some islands). If the sea was big enough, you might never know as a people that there was a landmass beyond that, because your island was so far from that landmass that your people never had any reason to go there.

The sea would look infinite.

Yes.

Food That Is Wild and Free

This is maybe a silly question, but why didn't you just plant seeds and domesticate animals? They were doing this in Europe. Why did you have to walk so much and be subject to shortages and poverty?

Oh, no. We always believed that the best food and water that could support us was what grew or came up on its own, free and wild. We could identify that free spirit, that free energy, in other beings. If the food or seed or plant was planted by human beings, it would not be as welcome by the Earth—saying, "Welcome seed"—as the seed that flies through the air, rolls on the ground or comes around in the water.

The human being would put the seed someplace near where he or his people lived for the sake of convenience; he would not just let the seed go and grow where it might. The freedom of the being . . . there is nothing that can replace that. Using long vision, I and many other spiritual mystical people of other places knew about cultivating and raising food and even raising animals, but if the plant or the animal is not free and has not been able to develop its own culture and happiness or celebrate life as a free being, then the energy that it can give you as food is so greatly diminished that you have to eat maybe ten times as much and you still won't really feel energized by the food. How many people today will eat a huge meal and not only feel bogged down, but not feel energized at all?

So it was the quality of life that kept you . . . there's a word for it, not wanderers but . . .

You mean nomadic?

Nomadic.

We weren't really nomadic, because we would settle in various places and move only if the weather became extreme. Gradually, we moved farther south over time so that we weren't subject to such extremes. Sometimes there would be seasons in which we would be up higher, say in the hot season; then we would be down lower in the cold season. But that does not really qualify as nomadic. We would only move entirely if there was some reason.

So you might stay in a place a year? Five years? Ten years?

Oh, certainly in the beginning my people might be in a place for ten or fifteen thousand years, something like that. Our people were not nomadic. There are people who are truly nomadic, who go from place to place all the time. Those are true nomads. We were not that.

So your encampment was almost like a permanent . . .

It was permanent, like a village. We would gradually acquire all the things we needed, like cups and so on, but we would also learn how to survive to the best of our ability. Someone might weave a basket, or we would dry food. You had to learn how to survive or you didn't last too long.

Preparing for Those Who Would Follow

Can we say that one of your primary purposes was bringing this quality of energy and your respect to the Earth? When you say "prepare for Those Who Would Follow," what you were preparing them for was to love the Earth, wasn't it?

Well, I think maybe the emissaries must have felt that we as a people with our culture, spirit and general personalities had something to offer. It didn't only involve preparing the Earth in terms of the Earth responding to our needs. There is that for all peoples who came, but also the emissaries seem to have felt (from the best I can understand) that our culture and all of the other cultures of those who were invited had some unique characteristics that would be worth putting into the Earth in the form of human characteristics. This would ultimately lead to certain general characteristics in Those Who Would Follow.

In your time you can state that, generally speaking, all human beings do this and this and this—for instance, "All human beings are born curious." But *all* human beings—or beings who roughly take the form of human beings on all other planets—are *not* born curious.

Yes, I've talked to a lot of them.

That's right. So you perhaps are in a better position to know this. But apparently, there were cultures invited here who were born curious. Our people were not born curious on our planet, but it's safe to say that there was at least one culture, maybe more, who was invited here who was born curious, so that now in your culture you can say, "All human beings are born curious," and say that as a matter of fact. And you can prove it from culture to culture, from child to child. But it wasn't always that way.

So beings were invited to bring characteristics as well as to have the Earth respond in ways that would support and nurture the beings there, our cultures and others. This was also in preparation for Those Who Would Follow: things you would need—plants, animals, atmospheric conditions, oxygen and so on—so they would all be in place by the time you got here.

Ceremony as a Way of Life

Who of the wise men and women of the tribe—the medicine man or woman, the elder, the mystical man or woman—was responsible for ceremony? Or were all of them?

You mean the way things are done and so on?

Yes.

I would have to say that the medicine and mystical people are not responsible for ceremonies, but they suggest how to perform ceremonies that other people might wish to do from time to time. If it had to do with the plants and animals or the mystical that is all around, it would probably be the medicine woman or man or the mystical woman or man. But if it had to do with things in the culture of the tribe, my people and so on, it would probably have to do with the elders.

So what were some of the ceremonies that you did spontaneously, and what were some that were part of the way your tribe did things?

I do not think of myself and the way I function as being the way I am *plus* ceremonies. My ceremonial aspects are fully integrated into the way I am, which is what I have taught Robert. The things I do might be looked upon by someone who is not of my people as being ceremonial in day-to-day practice, such as the use of the wand as we've discussed or my stopping and communicating with any creatures should they indicate the desire to communicate by giving me a greeting message or by simply doing something physical that I notice.

The medicine people of my tribe are also like that. It's integrated. The only ceremonies that are done separate from day-to-day life are encouraged by the elders, largely having to do with the changing of seasons and births. I'm sorry, but I cannot reveal them without very easily being recognized and spotted as a specific tribe.

I see. So a lot of the ceremonies were respect for the life around you, the way you did things, right?

Yes, the way I am, the way I have been, but more specifically, the way I've been taught to interact with all life around me, including the air.

Well, we would probably call welcoming the Sun and the rain ceremonies in our time. To you this was how you lived.

Yes, somebody not from our culture might say this is some kind of ceremony, but, in fact, it is integrated into our day-to-day life. We welcome the Sun and give thanks, for we see because of the Sun. But we tend to give to the Moon; we give thanks and love to the Moon. We appreciate the Moon's love, but it is kind of like a circuit. While we give our thanks and love to the Sun, the Sun gives to us. That is clearly understood, even in your time. And we give to the Moon and the Moon gets from the Sun. So it's kind of like a connected thing.

We recognize that the Moon gives us light, but it is light from the Sun. We knew that even in our time. So we know that if the Sun is giving the Moon light, the Moon may be giving us light, but let's go back further. If the Sun is giving light to the Moon, then the Moon must need it. It may be true that the Moon gives us light, but the light is not going to the Moon to give us light; the light is going to the Moon because the Moon needs light and heat.

So then it is our tendency to give to the Moon, because the Moon is in need. We do not assume that heavenly bodies are anything other than beings like ourselves. The Sun gives us light and warmth; we need this. It also gives its heat and warmth to the Moon, so it is safe to say that the Moon must need it also.

The Gestures Are an Integrated Ceremony

The gestures didn't make sense until I realized that they were a ceremony.

But an integrated ceremony. They are done when needed.

But in a ceremonial, very respectful way

They're done in a specific way according to the way your body feeds back to you—in this case, my body and the bodies of other apprentices who have been taught the way the physical body tells one how long to hold the gesture. I have given you certain times because I do not necessarily expect you all in your time to have the capacity for your body to feed you back this heat in ways you trust.

Sometimes though, from time to time, you will wake that heat that will come up with one or more gestures because you have a specifically important role to play in that gesture, according to what it does. In the case of the first book [*Shamanic Secrets for Material Mastery*], perhaps it has excited an energy that supports a certain place on the land; in the case of this book, maybe it has excited an energy that supports a specific place in your own body. It might even have to do with a special communion that you have with that part of your body—or that part of the bodies of all beings, which is less likely—or a special communion that you have with that place on the land.

So, in short, this might be many different things. It might even be a gesture that means other things to your body. But when your body gives you feedback and you can say that this is good, hold the gesture even longer than twenty or thirty seconds; if the heat is profound in your chest or solar plexus area, then it is usually all right to hold it longer. The moment the heat starts to fade (if you're holding it past the time I recommended), gradually begin to relax the gesture. Don't immediately and abruptly stop it, but gradually relax. Have you noticed that when I stop doing the gestures, I don't immediately and abruptly stop them? I gradually dissolve them.

You can't tell from the photographs of your hands. I'd like a statement about how the gestures work without giving people information that you feel is inappropriate.

The gestures create a specific harmony in your physical body, in your immediate environment, as the gestures affect you and others in the environment of all beings.

Heightening Animal Qualities in Oneself

Did your tribe have dances where you wore masks of wolves and bears?

No, different tribes develop different manners and means to communicate with the spirits of those beings they will have wrapped around them [animal hides] or perhaps with that type of spirit within themselves, should they need it for some reason.

For instance, you might identify certain qualities of life with a wolf or a bear. Your people might say, "Well, this animal is this and this and this." Maybe for some reason you want or need to heighten those qualities in yourself—if your people did not normally have these qualities or if you as an individual did not have these qualities as much as you thought you might need them—because of something you need to do for yourself or others (most likely, it would be something you need to do for your people).

I only know this on the basis of communicating with my brothers and sisters in other tribes. You might wear the hide or part of the skin of the animal in order to heighten those qualities in yourself. This was often done that way. That might also be done to communicate with the spirit of the animal, so the person who killed it would know certain qualities the animal had and pass that on.

The qualities of a specific animal, not a generic species?

That's right, because someone, maybe you, knew that animal. You did battle with that animal. So you would know about it, or more often (if the herd survived for a while) you as a hunter would say, "This animal was this and this and this, and did all of these things. Aside from what the animal is from what our people have been able to gather over the years, the animal was this . . ."—maybe brave or strong or something.

So if you needed those qualities, then you would try to acquire them from the animal, perhaps in a dance or you might even have the animal skin there. You might sleep near it to get the capacity to dream that animal, especially if you knew that the animal was not near your people at that time of year or wherever you were. Maybe the animal migrated according to the seasons or its food or its needs or its culture. So you may or may not have been able to make a dream connection with that animal, but if you had the skin or the hide, you might sleep near it. In your time it is assumed that you sleep on the skin or you put the skin over you, but all the people I talked to in my time would never do that. It would be considered disrespectful to the animal. You would let the animal skin have its own place and sleep near it.

I grant that I did not talk to everybody; it is certainly possible that some people do things other ways, but I only really care to speak to you about what I know.

So all the tribes on the planet came from different cultures and approached survival and spirituality in different ways?

Let's extend that: In your time sometimes you use animal skins as something to walk on. Maybe it's a sheep you raised because you liked its wool, and you either walk on it or keep it someplace where it is stepped on. My people would not consider that respectful, and many of the people of my time would not either.

Natural and Unnatural Materials

Many of you have a blanket made from that animal's fur, which you call wool. Most likely you would have cotton between you and the wool, but if you sleep under the wool blanket, some of that domestic animal's experience and its tribal experience (meaning with other domestic sheep) would tend to be imparted to you—not only its culture and wisdom, but also its fear and anxiety of humans, how humans treat sheep: "They shear off our wool, either respectfully or not respectfully, and they take some of us away. We never see them again. We think they kill and eat our people." In short, the sheep would not trust the human being and would often feel uncomfortable (the only exception being perhaps the lamb, but other than that, you would have this).

Cotton is a plant. It grows. It has its own culture, its own identity, its own beliefs, its own way of being. As a result, if you put a cotton blanket or a cotton sheet over you, that cotton imparts something to you as well. If the cotton is closer to its natural state, it will impart more of its being to you; if it has been thoroughly processed through a factory, it might not impart so much of its being to you, but it will impart something, at least in the first year or two after it has been picked. So everything that touches you, especially if it comes from something natural such as a plant or an animal, will impart something to you.

It is different if the blanket or the sheet is made out of some unnatural material, meaning something from Earth made in a way that does not naturally occur. This type of thing that covers you will usually be uncomfortable, because whatever it was before it was turned into a blanket or a sheet was its own thing, and it knew and understood itself. It was happy where it was, comfortable with all those other types of beings that surrounded it, and when it was taken away from there, it was lonely, frightened and upset. I've spoken about this before in relationship to machines.

When you put that on top of yourself, you apply all of those qualities to yourself, and when you are asleep and much more open, you might unintentionally take those qualities into yourself. That is why I suggest being cautious not only about what you remove from the Earth, but very conscious about who and what you allow to touch your body during sleep time.

Exercise: Helping the Things in Your Home to Remember Who They Are

Maybe after reading this, you'll go home and look at your blankets and sheets with a newfound interest. What can you do? Take your right hand (since you are going to give) and say, "Thank you," to each blanket and each sheet, touching each one in turn, as you have the energy, with your palm down on it.

Imagine what it would have been like to be that sheep. You don't have to feel yourself as a sheep, because that might be uncomfortable, but picture it. The best way, of course, is to be the sheep, but it might be uncomfortable, and if you live with animals they might react. So picture the sheep. If you hold the picture in your mind's eye, that could help. Then hold your palm on that wool blanket for a time, as long as feels right to you or, if you use the heat method, as long as you have the heat.

When the heat begins to fade, take your palm off and rest for a while. Then do the same thing with the cotton. Picture cotton. It is probably safe to be cotton. Try to be cotton or imagine being cotton. Touch the cotton and so on.

You can do the same thing if you have a wooden frame for your bed. You can imagine being a tree or picture a tree, and while you are holding that picture, touch or even wrap your right hand around the wood. There might be metal in the bed frame. Try to touch one piece of the metal and be a mountain.

Go through and touch everything like that. If you were to do that with your whole room or the whole house, it would take a long, long time, so you can't do it all at once. But once it is done, that room will become much more relaxed. All of the beings will remember who they are. They will no longer be desperate and unhappy. You will not be putting desperate and unhappy things over your body. Anytime you touch things in the room, they will remember who they are. They will be relaxed. They will be comfortable. They will then be able to dream the dreams of their own being, connect with their own beings wherever they are on the Earth and maybe, in some cases, in the stars.

In short, they will relax, and any tension you bring into the room from work or the stress of life will dissipate much quicker. If you bring in tension from somewhere else and the room is already tense, it will just heighten the tension that is already present. But if you bring in the tension and the room is relaxed, you will relax much more quickly and the tension will quickly dissipate.

Magnificent. I think somebody said to do that with a car. But this . . .

Of course, it will take awhile if you have a big house, but if you have a small house or an apartment, it won't take as long. You can't do it all in one day, but you can do it gradually. And when you walk into that apartment, you will relax very quickly because everything in the apartment will also be relaxed and you won't take on any of its tension. So your tension will go away very quickly.

You're home. You're relaxed. You sit down on the couch. You're asleep like that [snaps his fingers]. You take a nap. You get up. You eat for a little while. Maybe you watch a little television. You laugh—whatever. You go to sleep and have a good night's sleep. Very restful. You wake up refreshed in the morning.

Good life. We'll talk tomorrow.

Elemental Connections

Speaks of Many Truths
November 27, 1999

his is Speaks of Many Truths.

Welcome.

I may have mentioned this before, but in your time you're balancing out each other's discomforts. This has been largely something you've been doing with human beings, and as the weeks or months go by, you've been gradually adjusting to it. But I must tell you about the next level.

The next experience along those lines is balancing out discomfort from things to which you have personally contributed to cause them discomfort—not other human beings, because you're working on that, but specifically I want to talk about plastic today.

Plastic is an artificial substance, as I've said before, and although it might be very convenient and helpful to you in many ways, it is not natural. The materials that make up plastic were originally natural but have come to be the ingredients that are mixed together to make this product in its many forms.

Exercise: Releasing Tension in Landfills

You will probably still use plastic for some time to come, though someday you will not. I want some of you who have time (and who can do so without feeling embarrassed, where it is not a problem with you being judged harshly in the community) to look around for places that have been filled [landfills]. Sometimes they build parks over these places and sometimes they put houses there.

First, you will have to do a little research. Find out what the natural materials originally were before they became plastic. It might have been oil in some way, it might have been other things, but even if they used chemicals to make the plastic, originally it would have been something natural. So find out what those natural things were. You can probably find out in a library or encyclopedia or something.

Now, what I'd like you to do, if you have the time, is to go out to these places where the landfill was done. (I don't suggest you go to the store or places like that where there are lots of plastic bottles and so on. It would be embarrassing for most of you.) You can go to the landfill and perhaps sit down someplace where no one will disturb you and close your eyes.

Then imagine being those natural things. Don't imagine being oil in a can, but oil underground in Mother Earth where it is very calm, very restful. If you were able to survive in such a place comfortably (which you cannot, of course), the first thing you would notice is how calm and restful it is.

Mother Earth uses what you call oil to lubricate parts of her body and to create a restful calm within her. You can do this with your lungs, with your breathing and so on. But she will do that using this fluid, less so with her breath. You have been pumping her fluid out, and that's why she is a little more agitated. She needs to have more storms and earthquakes to express that agitation, to release tension as you'd say.

So once you know what those materials are, pretend to be them as much as you can. Probably it's best if you sit somewhere by yourself, but it's unlikely that you'll make anybody sitting near you uncomfortable. If they do get uncomfortable, they can just move. Pretend to be those materials for just a few minutes with the idea, the thought in your mind (that will radiate in all directions), that while you pretend to be them—or if you are shamanic person, *be* them—that energy will radiate down to all the plastic in that landfill and might just remind it who it once was.

Do that two or three times in different places in the landfill for maybe fifteen or twenty minutes in each place. Then the landfill will become a lot calmer. With all the plastic and other things brought together that don't come together naturally, the landfill area is tense. Parks that are built over landfills are never quite as calm or fun or safe as parks that are built on natural land. Of course, some of this has to do with settling and so on, but the bulk of the tension has to do with materials brought together that don't come naturally together, that are unhappy, and this unhappiness creates tension that radiates in all directions.

Of course, some of this tension will radiate to the surface. So if you can do this, even if others have done so, it will be helpful. Just do it one time in two or three places where you can sit down comfortably. Maybe bring something to sit on, a blanket or something. And then go on about your life.

What about doing it in stores? In department stores?

I don't recommend doing this exercise in stores because it takes fifteen or twenty minutes of radiation. You are standing there next to plastic bottles for fifteen to twenty minutes with your eyes closed, and pretty soon the manager comes up and says, "Are you all right? Do you need help? Shall we call the doctor?" You do not need to draw attention to yourself like that.

You can't sit outside in your car and do it in your thoughts?

It is not a thought process, but entirely physical. See, you *become* that. You know this is physical. I'll give you an example, something your friend Zoosh said in another fashion for another example.

You go to the theater and see a play, a good play with good actors, very convincing. You sit far away perhaps, in the cheap seats, but the actors are convincing, even though you cannot see them too well without using a magnifying instrument. They are not just portraying their feelings, but they are *being* in order to convince you up there in the back row.

You feel something that's actually happening. Not only are you responding with feelings in kind, but those feelings are prompted by what these actors are radiating. That's because the actors are doing a physical thing. They might be thinking about their lines, but they know their lines well enough that they don't think about them anymore. They just become that role and say their lines in a meaningful way. This is proof that such radiation goes outward.

Dealing with Plastic in the Office

Here's what I recommend for those of you who work in an office. Maybe go to the office sometime on a day when no one else is there—work overtime or something. Take a coffee break, but instead of drinking coffee on your break, sit quietly at your seat and do the plastic exercise in your office.

There is lots and lots of plastic in offices these days. But only do this if you can sit there calmly. Go get a cup of coffee in case anybody looks at you and says, "What are you doing?" You can come out of it and say, "Oh, I'm resting, taking a coffee break," so you won't be embarrassed. Then drink the coffee later while you are working.

You don't have to do this, but that is the circumstance to do this exercise in. Otherwise, it's very distracting for you and could cause problems for you and others. But there are many places with lots and lots of plastic where nobody is around.

Metal, Leather and Plastic in the Car

I don't think cars have been discussed in this context. Can people do this to their own cars?

Yes, you can do the same thing in a car, though maybe you might park someplace where nobody is going to bother you or even out in the garage. You will need one day in your car. You could do this in the office also, but I do not want you to get paid by your boss for doing spiritual work. In short, this will take a long time.

Start with the car. The car is more than plastic. It has metal, glass, fabric, all of these things, and all of these things were originally part of other things. For instance, the leather was probably part of a cow, so you would have to be a cow.

Do this only if you feel comfortable with it. Don't have a picture of a cow in your mind's eye. That's not it. Maybe start with that, but then go into it and *be* it. Each person might feel a little different with that, but it is worth a try.

You will have to find out what the material is, but even if you do something that isn't in the car, it will not harm anything. To be any natural substance on Earth cannot harm you. It might be different for you to be a combination of metal that does not come together naturally, and it might not be right to be plastic as plastic—it could be uncomfortable. But to be the material that originally made these materials up is fine.

The metal in the car was originally rock, maybe iron ore, but you don't have to be that specific. If you want to, you can try to be a specific kind of rock or material, but to just be a rock is sufficient—a mountain, a boulder, something like that. *Be* it. Imagine it, and then try to be it for twenty minutes.

In the case of the car, you can touch the materials in the car, but you do not have to. You can, in the case of plastic, put your right hand on the steering wheel or dashboard or some place that is plastic. I recommend, however, using only your right hand. You do not want to take in the discomfort of the car. To use your left hand would take in discomfort. Once something is perfectly comfortable being who it is, then you can use your left hand, but you cannot be certain about that with the car.

The thing you call a car isn't a car; it is a mountain, oil, a cow, other things. You know that mountains and cows and oil do not necessarily come together all at the same time. So you're trying to be all those things, and you might find other materials in the car. Do this and practice someplace quiet with no distractions, if you can help it. Just practice as much as you can. This is also good practice for actors in general, but you don't have to be an actor to do this.

Using Touch to Radiate Love to Natural Materials

You don't have to touch the items in the car like metal or plastic, but it could help; it is your personal car. In the case of the landfill, you obviously cannot touch the plastic there, and in the case of the office, you can't go around and touch every bit of plastic, so you just radiate. But you can touch your personal car or your personal computer at home maybe. Touch the glass, touch the plastic, touch the metal.

Don't touch anything, even with your right hand (or fingertip in some cases), until you are totally feeling that natural material. Then touch it slowly, if it feels comfortable. When you touch, if you begin to remove your hand before the plastic or glass gets enough, you'll leave an uncomfortable feeling, so put your hand back and keep doing it.

If you get tired and you have to take your hand off and you still have that uncomfortable feeling, it's not done. You'll have to do it again. Rest up and try to do it later that day or, more likely, the next day. Do it some other time, but make sure you finish. You cannot start and not finish.

At some point, though, you'll be able to remove your hand. Probably it won't take more than fifteen, twenty minutes at the most, but most likely no more than five minutes. Then you will be able to remove your hand and feel good. You'll actually feel better than you did before, because the material radiates back some of the similar love you gave. You give love in different forms, see?

Then do that with all the different materials. Don't worry about touching metal inside the computer or inside your car. What you touch radiates to others of its own kind, and you also have feeling radiating out in all directions, past your own car or computer. So everything that is that same material gets touched, remembers who it is and then feels calm and relaxed.

That's beautiful.

Giving Love to Your House

Then if you have lots of time, you can do your whole house.

Yes, if you had a small house. You could touch the wall: Maybe the wall is made out of a wood frame, maybe it has mirrors. Maybe it's wallboard, which is made from a form of rock, gypsum or paper (which is trees). You don't have to touch every wall in the room; just touch one wall as long as the walls are connected.

In some houses the walls aren't connected, so you have to touch more than one wall. Look at your house; you can see. Maybe you have plastic in a room. If you cannot touch something—maybe it's on the ceiling—then sit down somewhere comfortably and just radiate that energy, become that natural material.

But start with something simple. I recommend a landfill, but you also can start with your car. If you have a car or a computer or maybe your own room in the house—maybe you are a young or an old person and you have your own room, but that's it— then do that. If someone comes in and asks what you are doing, you can come out of what you are doing and say, "Oh, I'm doing a relaxation exercise, removing stress." If they want to know more, you can tell them what you think they can hear. If you think they cannot hear about this, just say, "Well, I just relax as much as I can, and then I feel better." It's not really a lie, because this exercise causes you to relax in the process.

How many years before we can speak frankly about these things?

Not long. The only people who will resist it in six, seven or eight years are people who perhaps are very rigid in certain religious or political beliefs. But even such people are now beginning to look at other things because more and more of their own people are saying, "Well, I tried that and I still believe . . ." And then they talk about their religion or whatever their politics are, and say, "This is okay, too. I can see how this works in my religion or philosophy or politics. It doesn't interfere."

More and more people talk about such things and even say, "Well, this actually helps me to understand more about my politics or religion or philosophy." Then the body of people promoting that religion or politics or philosophy feels less threatened and says, "Oh well, maybe it's all right then."

Wonderful.

But it will take a little longer, though. We'll see.

Medical Uses for Natural Materials

I am not a medicine man. I cannot say, "Use this plant and so on," but I can suggest uses for plants, even drugs that might now be incompatible with a patient. For instance—this happens a lot in your time—a wonderful drug that can cure certain diseases or control symptoms so well that one can almost lead a normal life comes along, and the person cannot tolerate this drug for some reason. But he or she can perhaps take what the drug is made up of originally. Very often in your time the drug is synthesized, but it is synthesized from something that originally worked, meaning it can be traced back to its natural materials.

You can get those natural materials and perhaps put them on a palette, like an artist's palette. Or in the case of plants, you can hold them. If the material is liquid, put it on something neutral like wood. And what you do is blow on them.

For instance, in the case of a plant leaf, hold it above the person, either above the place where you would normally put in an injection, or over the place that the drug might treat, meaning a certain organ that is not working. Then blow over the plant leaf straight into the body of that person.

It's important for you to be a spiritual person, however, so that your energy is pleasant. Otherwise, you will blow your discomfort into the person. Then it is like sorcery; it harms the person. You must be in a very good spiritual state of being before you do this.

So if the doctor is a spiritual being and can do this, then it could work very well. With the doctor, if she does not feel that she can get to such a place, not knowing how or perhaps with so many distractions and stresses involved in being a doctor, then she could say, "Here is the material," and give it to a spiritual person who is in a benevolent state of being, a state of grace.

Then that person might set the material on the patient and blow gently on it, blowing energy into the person. Sometimes this can work; sometimes it can bring the organ back to health. If the person is spiritual enough, he might be able to remove discomfort from both the organs and the tubes themselves (body tubes, passageways that lead to the organ). Usually, the organ does not become that way on its own. Usually, something led to it.

Veins and arteries.

Or passageways, such as with the kidneys. The kidneys process something, and tubes lead from the kidneys to other parts of the body. Tubes run liquids and material through our body. They make a circuit. So clear that whole circuit where it runs, and then check the body to make sure it is clear. You might want to clear the body first. Make sure the patient is lying somewhere that is also clear.

A patient, if she has a disease like this, discomfort, might be a sensitive person anyway and might tend to pick things up from the environment. So the environment must be safe. It's not likely that this would be an operating room; it should be a pleasant, comfortable place, someplace where the person feels safe and calm. Maybe even do it at the patient's home, if this person is comfortable there. Have her lie on the bed and do it there.

Maybe having a dog or cat in the room—if the dog or cat is comfortable with the doctor and the shamanic person or healer—might make the patient more comfortable. It's also possible then to clear the dog or cat in the same process, but you'll have to see if the dog or cat will allow that. You can try these different things. That's what I would recommend.

Using Homeopathy

It does not always have to be with breath. For instance, you might be able to do the process like homeopathy. You might even be able to do that homeopathic treatment with the drug itself already made up, even synthesized, though I recommend always using natural materials. But say you have the drug. You can give the drug as a homeopathic treatment. The drug itself is not safe to take through the mouth . . .

With that particular patient?

With any patient. Maybe the drug is only safe to give in an injection; it's not something you would take in your mouth and swallow.

If you give it as a homeopathic treatment, you must work with a homeopathic physician. They take the drug and give it full treatment. The amount of material is so infinitesimal that taking it into your body cannot harm you. Others, say, don't want to do that with arsenic or something toxic, poison, like radiation. Most drugs when given as homeopathic treatments cannot possibly harm you. So you might be able to take them internally that way.

Many homeopathic physicians have considered doing this with modern drugs. Some are experimenting with this. It might be worth a try, but I do not recommend using synthesized drugs. Nevertheless, if that is all that is available, try it with the synthesized drug, taken homeopathically. A patient who cannot take the drug as an injection might be able to take it orally as a homeopathic. Experiment with volunteers only.

So the only reason you have to use the synthesized drug is that the plant from which the original drug came from is no longer here?

No. Some synthesized drugs have been put together by so many chemical processes that by the time you got back to the original material, it would not have the same effect as what it has become. It would do something, but it would not have the same effect at all. A pharmacologist would have this knowledge and perhaps a physician as well.

So you can try this with synthesized drugs. You can create a neutral homeopathic base. A homeopathic base is often sugar, sometimes a sugar substitute, sometimes an alcohol solution. There are many different bases for homeopathy. Look into it.

You can even do this in the case of radiation treatment. Take the normal machine that would be used for radiation treatment, and put neutral homeopathic material onto the place where it would radiate exact energy. Don't worry about depth and all that business of tissue. Just radiate it so it goes down to the homeopathic material only. You do not need to radiate for more than . . . oh, I do not know if the machine can do this for such a short time, but do it as briefly as you can make it on the machine. If you have a computer, you might be able to do a thousandth of a second or even less. Do it as briefly as possible, and then set aside the material in sterile bottles. Let it sit for at least a month, thirty days.

Some people cannot tolerate radiation, but they can try to take it internally. As a scientist, you say, "There is no radiation in there." You go to measure it, and you cannot even measure it. But try. Experiment. It might work.

Remember, homeopathic work is the opposite of allopathic. Homeopathy works by reaction, not stimulation. Reaction would be considered stimulation by some people, but reaction is different. It takes a little longer, but it works with homeopathy.

Experiments with Homeopathic Treatments

Researchers in Europe and other places have been working for years and years with homeopathy. There is lots of knowledge, and they would very much like to cooperate with a drug company in the U.S. or some other place, even in Europe. They could come out with experimental homeopathic treatments like this to try on people and see how they work. They might be able to treat more people with less side effects as well as treat those who are sensitive to medication.

That's wonderful. You say they're already doing this?

In some places researchers are doing some of these things, but very often those places do not have the equipment that large corporations would have in their laboratories. With a large and thorough laboratory, you can do interesting experiments on human volunteers.

Don't experiment on animals. That will not get you any result you can use. You must have a human being who can speak to you. It requires a human being who is able to communicate with you in some way. You need someone who can say, "Well, I feel this or I feel that."

A sensitive person?

Most people who are sick or not feeling well are pretty sensitive anyway, and they know how they feel. They know they don't feel good, and they'll be able to tell you if they feel better.

I do not recommend using too many psychologists. As any psychologist knows, if you want to have an interesting debate, fill the room with psychologists. Many of them either will be able to convince others that something is true, or will never be convinced. I do not blame psychologists. It's just that when you approach things from a mental position, it is to argue yourself either into or out of any position.

In a famous experiment done years ago and occasionally repeated in colleges and universities for term papers and so on, one individual is considered to be a patient and another individual is considered to be a doctor. The doctor is given preconditioning and is told that this patient is very schizophrenic or psychotic or something, so that whatever the patient says is a sign of his or her symptoms. The person playing doctor is predisposed to think that no matter what this person says or does, it is a symptom of that condition.

This is something that is played out for a term paper in a psychology class, or occasionally it's done in acting class. It demonstrates that if a person is predisposed to believe something, then he or she will believe it. So I do not recommend using psychologists in the homeopathic experiment unless the psychologist is also an MD or homeopathist, because if it's only a mental approach, it will not have a very good result.

You must also use a sensitive approach. Ask, "How does it feel?" not, "What do you think about it?" The volunteer has taken something orally. Ask, "Do you notice it?" "How long does it last?" "Do you feel better in five minutes? Ten minutes?" "How long does it take for you to feel better?"—questions like that. These are clinical questions, not "psychological" clinical, but "laboratory" clinical.

The Prospects for Energetic Healing

So we need to go through this stage, but eventually almost everything, if it's caught early enough, can be healed energetically, right? By what you said, clearing the discomfort?

Remember, you are a creator-in-training, yes? Many, many things on the planet now will gradually be included in your responsibilities to resolve discomfort. But I cannot say that everything can be healed simply by solving its discomfort because, of course, you have trauma and drama and things like that. Things happen. A boulder falls down the hill and rolls over your leg. You cannot blow a leaf on that and make it feel better. This is not for you right now. Maybe someday you'll have something you can do, but it's not necessary to talk about that now. You need to have first aid, then go to the doctor.

But if we are our own creator, we created that boulder going down the hill. So eventually we'll get cleared and we won't do that, right?

I cannot be so sure about that. You did not create the boulder going downhill. When you say that, you forget that the boulder is part of Mother Earth's body. Just like you, you stretch, you yawn . . . it's hard to stop yourself. There are certain things you need to do. It's part of your body motion. Your heart beats . . . boop, boop, boop, boop, boop. You cannot say, "Stop heart." You as a human are responsible only for being in the path of the boulder, but you did not create the boulder going downhill.

No, but if you were there, you created being in the wrong place at the wrong time.

You allowed that to happen, but you also have to remember that maybe you needed that to happen on some level. Perhaps you did not desire it—it's not a pleasant experience—but maybe it's part of a soul lesson, if not for you, then maybe for others. Remember, you are all connected. Maybe there is a greater reason. You cannot blame yourself and say, "Ahh, I messed up. I got hurt. It's my fault." You cannot always say that. Instead say, "Sometimes I get hurt. There's something for me to learn or something for others to learn, and I'll learn with them," and so on—not always blaming yourself. If you blame yourself because you get hurt, you tend to miss most of the big picture.

What about someone who has an attitude about the soul? I heard someone say, "If the soul thinks somebody needs a lesson, then why doesn't the soul come down here and experience it?"

That attitude would keep that person back. As long as you fight the process of life, you'll always be unhappy. Remember, you came here voluntarily. Nobody dragged you and said, "You have to come." You always have the option to step out before you are born here physically, right up to the last moment.

If you fight the process, you guarantee yourself unhappiness. But recognize that the process is this way because it is a place to learn. Maybe it's not easy, not fun. I can understand that very well, but this is a place to learn. What you are each learning is not always obvious. Sometimes you cannot learn on your own, but you must learn with those others who say something, do something.

Something happens to the process with others, even other circumstances, other places. Then, suddenly, "Ahh, I understand my part." Maybe you don't understand their part, but it's not your job to tell them their part. It's up to them to go, "Ahh, I understand."

Releasing Tension from Feeling Foolish

What about people who are afraid to look foolish and so don't try something new or different?

When a person feels foolish—people feel they might look foolish in public—the foolish feeling starts in the face. It moves down the body and gets down to here, this spot just a few inches below the belly button. That's where it stays, and then what happens is it creates a tension. It starts here and settles down into this part of your body.

It starts in the head and settles down to the . . .

Not in the head, not in the face, in front of the face. Then it goes down the front of your body, down to where I mentioned. It goes in and stays there. This is another reason many people get diseases down there. So I'll give you a series of gestures for that.

These will be gestures to release the tension of feeling the fool. This tension of feeling the fool is one of the most damaging elements of your entire society and culture in your time. Sometimes it creates wars; it always creates fights, murders, attacks, embarrassment and disease. In short, it creates misery.

Here is the first gesture to release the tension of feeling the fool

[Fig. 22-1]. Hold that position for maybe ten or thirty seconds. I am sitting here, but it can be done either standing or sitting. Most gestures can be done standing or sitting.

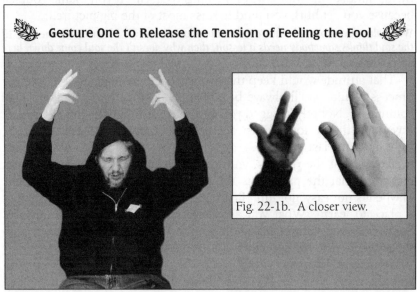

Gesture One to Release the Tension of Feeling the Fool

Fig. 22-1b. A closer view.

Fig. 22-1a. Here is the first gesture. This can be done either standing or sitting. Hold for ten to thirty seconds. Relax this gesture slowly, for ten to twenty seconds, then move on to the second gesture.

Here's the next gesture [Fig. 22-2]—do not flow to this gesture. Relax the first gesture slowly, then create the second gesture. Hold that position for about twenty or thirty seconds.

Always remember with such gestures you hold like this, if you get strong heat coming up in the chest or solar plexus area and it is very strong, then it's good for you to hold that as long as you can, as long as you have strong heat. The moment the heat begins to fade, then release the position and relax. Relax for ten, fifteen seconds, maybe twenty seconds or so between gestures.

I realize it is not easy to glance at a clock and do the gestures. Eventually, you won't have to use a clock anymore. If you do enough of these gestures, you'll know how long to hold them. Some people hold the gestures longer, others hold them shorter, and so on. The timing is a little different in different people, but the gesture eventually becomes something you make and know how to do in terms of holding it in a way that's right for you.

Perhaps even sometimes the hand position is slightly different. But

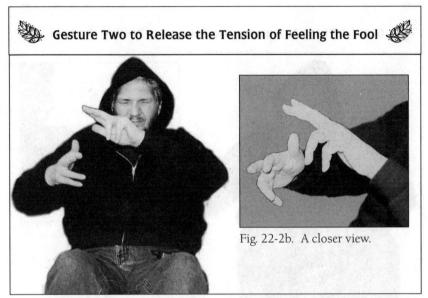

Gesture Two to Release the Tension of Feeling the Fool

Fig. 22-2b. A closer view.

Fig. 22-2a. Here's the second gesture. Hold for twenty or thirty seconds. Relax for ten to twenty seconds, then move on to gesture three.

you must be careful if you're using your physical body. If the physical body feeds back heat, then the gesture is probably just right for you. But if there isn't any heat, make sure the gesture is exact, the best you can do according to the photo.

Here is the third gesture for releasing the tension of feeling foolish [Fig. 22-3]. Hold this last position for ten seconds only.

You can do this series of gestures using the timing indicated. Do this two or three times a week until you notice a decided release of tension in that part of your physical body, meaning you feel more relaxed.

This will tend to create a feeling of general relaxation in the belly area, but first you will feel a release of tension in the specific area stated, three to three and a half inches below the belly button. Put your thumb in your belly button; then put your fingers below. Where your fingers land in that position, that is the spot. That's the way we give measurements in my time.

So you will notice that the tension is released and probably feel much better physically. If in the future you notice that the tension is up again because of feeling the fool or for other reasons, do the series again until you notice the tension release and can cease doing it. It's an ongoing process. You all feel the fool sometimes.

Sometimes others don't intend to cause you to feel that way, but because of your life, you do feel it. Other times they do intend to cause

Gesture Three to Release the Tension of Feeling the Fool

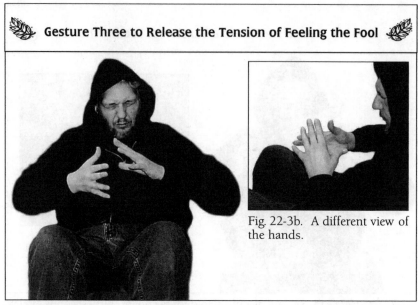

Fig. 22-3b. A different view of the hands.

Fig. 22-3a. This is the third gesture. Hold for ten seconds only. Do this series two to three times a week until you feel more relaxed in that area, three to three and a half inches below the belly button.

you to feel that way, especially if you are a young person in school or in some place where lots of people gather and are very unsure of themselves and make fun of others.

Does this include embarrassment?

It's very close. It's almost the same—when you are embarrassed or cause someone to feel embarrassed, you feel foolish. It's similar. But feeling the fool is different, because feeling the fool is not always caused by something you do. Sometimes people make fun of you, just you yourself. They try to make you look stupid in their eyes or the eyes of others around them.

Less than.

Less than. Then you feel the fool, even though you did not do anything different than you normally do. So it's not always caused by something you do or do not do.

Hundreds of Volunteers Came to Earth from Different Planets

I'd like to shift gears a little bit to what we were on yesterday. On the North American continent, how many of the tribes came from different planetary systems in response to the (I'm assuming) wide-ranging emissary travel?

I cannot be certain. Many hundreds.

Many hundreds of different groups from different planets? In just North America?

Remember, emissaries came to my planet and spoke to my people because they felt my ancestors had certain planetary qualities, certain qualities that people from this planet have. The ETs did not think, "Americans have certain qualities; Russians have other qualities." They thought that when compared by observation, all Earth people have these certain qualities.

The emissary came to our planet because people from my planet have certain qualities, and it was the same for other tribal people who have certain qualities. So the emissary perhaps felt that those qualities were right for Earth and invited volunteers.

What was the actual method of your people coming to this planet?

Remember, I said yesterday that the first ten or twenty volunteers came in their original form, but in most cases, their original form of being was not compatible with Earth.

If their original form was compatible with Earth, they finished out life there on Earth and were reborn in spirit on Earth as Earth people looking awfully like Those Who Would Follow. But sometimes the volunteers could not live on Earth, so they came in a vehicle. The vehicle had the extensive capacity to be larger inside than on the outside—special technology. And it could also go back with technology to its home planet. The first time ten, twenty volunteers came like that.

Were they supported with what was on the ship?

On the ship, yes. Brought from the planet. Maybe, in some cases, they might go to a deep cave in Earth and transform it, like an ET base. The ultimate intention was to die on Earth at the end of their natural life, so the body remained on Earth, went into the soil of Earth and was reborn there. But that was only with the first ten or twenty volunteers. Then everybody else came at the end of their natural life cycle.

And were born from some of these first ones?

Yes. That's why many volunteers had to be near the end of the life cycle. The volunteers originated the group, and some volunteers would come later. They'd have to be in different positions on the life cycle to blend different generations. Remember, they would have to die naturally and then from here go to Earth.

Some of the volunteers didn't even come to Earth . . .

. . . but died and came later. So no one's life was disrupted. They came later as later-generation volunteers. Then eventually enough people were there, and it was not necessary to do that anymore. It just kept recycling.

But the first ones, the first twenty, the ones who landed . . .

The first ten or twenty had to come physically.

And had to be childbearing.

Remember, if they came in their original bodies, then their offspring were brought about in the natural way for that culture. But when they died on Earth, the first couple or so had to be reborn by the emissary process. If the first people were volunteers . . . ten to twenty came to Earth. If the first one or two die, how are they going to be reborn on Earth? The emissary must help to create a body.

Could it be a cloned body or something?

I cannot say. The emissary used its own process to create a body that looked generally like Those Who Would Follow. This is one of the ways different races came to be on Earth. The emissary knew that later other beings would come from other planets and would want to leave some of their people here and so on. So races came perhaps, as Zoosh says, from other planets, but originally with my people, some would have to look like those races, because those races would be Those Who Would Follow. Follow far back from your time when the race first came—for example, beings from Sirius or some such thing.

In my ancestors' time, some would have to be born who looked like Those Who Would Follow. So not all people on Earth in the tribe in the old days looked alike. Some looked completely different. One looked this way, like this race; one looked another way, like that race. This was only in the beginning to prepare Earth, to introduce those races to Earth so that she could prepare to have what they might need. Those races might need something different, so the initial group might have people who looked terribly different: one light-colored, one dark-colored; one tall, one short. All were different.

But as time went on, Earth recognized—through the bottoms of the feet and the air breathed in and out and the sweat and fluids that were exchanged with the Earth—Earth knew that this was how to prepare for those beings. So succeeding generations were born in the way that the tribe's people felt most comfortable with. Eventually, tribal people all looked pretty similar, but maybe some of the original ones had light skin, some had dark skin. Then, eventually, the tribe's skin color was sort of in between. Then, of course, they lived outside, so their skin color got darker anyway.

What I was getting at was . . . if there were hundreds of tribes in North America, was this happening over a hundred thousand years or at the same time? Did they all come at different times?

They came at different times according to when the emissaries felt those qualities were needed on Earth.

Original Bloodlines

So within your tribe and within every other individual tribe, did the genetics and the bloodline stay in that tribe, or was there vast intermarriage among tribes?

There was not so much intermarriage in the beginning, or in my time for that matter. You tend always to feel comfortable with people like you, though you might have friends in other tribes, good friends even. Eventually, you have more tribal intermarriage, but this tends to happen only with another tribe you feel really good about, when elders from both tribes can see and know that the young people are truly compatible. They don't look into the future of young people so well, but they can know that the young people are truly compatible because in both tribes the young, the old and different people in the tribe are compatible with the others. Compatibility provides a pretty good chance for our youngsters. Then maybe marriage would be allowed.

But can you say that in your time your bloodline and genetics are pretty close to the original?

Pretty close, I think. I do not know for sure.

A few hundred years ago, before the Anglos went across the West, were the tribes pretty pure? Were they all pretty much representative of their home planets?

I believe so. Of course, they would not have the same blood and tissue as on the home planet. But, for example, whatever blood did when they were born as a form of Those Who Would Follow was consistent in an Earth way with the physical form of fluids (if there were fluids) on the original planet. You could say this was an Earth version of people from the home planet, yes.

The DNA would be different.

The U.S. Government's Policy of Eradicating the Tribes

How many of them became extinct like yours?

By your time?

By my time now. How many of the original tribes are extinct?

Most are no longer in existence in tribal custom fashion. Sometimes a tribe got wiped out or absorbed because of battle. When settlers came in from Europe and other places, many tribes were lost or had to go live with other tribes out of necessity. Some tribes were strong, lived longer and resisted.

Maybe, if they could, they moved to Canada or Mexico, where it was a little safer and they were not pursued quite so much. People in the United States, the original settlers, had a policy of killing, but in Canada this was not so much the policy. The government did not necessarily feel one way or the other, but the actual government policy was not to kill. So, if possible, maybe they went to Canada. This is something that is denied in history books, even today. It is denied that the U.S. government's actual policy was eradication in those times, but it was.

The government said to the soldiers, "Go out and move them from the land. If they won't move, then kill them." They made it very clear to the soldiers. The soldiers followed these orders, sometimes with disgust. Sometimes they were very, very angry at the military who said, "Do this." Some soldiers never got over it and felt guilty and miserable and maybe hateful for the rest of their lives. Some soldiers deserted. Many desertions occurred in those days because the soldier might be a moral man.

The government didn't mean to just kill warriors; they meant to kill men, women, children, babies—kill them all. Your government said to do this and is ashamed to admit it even today. I understand such shame. Your government says, "Look at Hitler. He was a monster. His soldiers were monsters." I do not say that your government was bad and monstrous, but we'll use Hitler as an example: The way he did things with his people, the basic policy was the same. It's easier for people in your time to say, "Hitler was a monster," but it's not so easy to say that early American government heroes were monsters.

Processing Discomfort from the Land

Someday, though, when you are not so involved in being an American first but an Earth citizen, you will be able to say, "Terrible things were done," because the land will have been worked on in a heartfelt way. You will have processed a lot of the discomfort of other people, and it will eventually be your responsibility to process discomfort from the land.

That's why I say that the next stage will be to process discomfort from things you make—that you as a human being make—plastic and so on. Eventually, though, it will be your job to take misery and anxiety and suffering out of the land. This is all part of creator training—not immediately, but someday.

Some people are volunteering to do that now and have been doing so for a long time. But someday it will go past the volunteer stage. You all will have it visited upon you, but not just yet. Someday someone will say, "Where are you from?" and you will say, "I'm from Earth," whether you live in Ireland or Peru or Afghanistan. You will say, "I am from Earth," and they will say, "Oh, yes." Then you will not be attached to protecting national heroes. Everybody will say, "Well, bad things were done, but we have done a lot to resolve that in the land."

Remember, the bodies of those who die go back into the land—not just the feelings incurred during death or struggle or battle, or misery or discomfort or anything you experience over a lifetime. Ultimately, the bodies of people go into the land. The land then becomes that. Someday it will be your responsibility to resolve this, but by that time you will have been working to dissolve discomforts in each other, to resolve discomforts in the materials you have made and so on.

So by the time it gets to the point where it's your responsibility to re-solve discomfort in the land, you'll be able to do it. It seems like a big task now, but always here on Earth you go one step at a time, very slowly. The slower you go, the less resistance there is. Most people do not like to be rushed. Rush, rush—resistance. Even if they do not have men-tal resistance, the physical body has resistance to being rushed. There are some exceptions, of course. If a bear is chasing you, then rush, rush. There will be no resistance at all. Run very fast. Maybe you're not as fast as the bear, so look for some way to escape.

Qualities Brought from Home Planets to Earth

Let's go back to this plan because it's fascinating. We heard a little bit about it before, but I didn't equate it wth the tribes coming like this. So all these tribes actu-ally brought qualities they had on their home planets, such as curiosity, and made them available to Those Who Would Follow on Earth? What were some other of these qualities?

Think of every nuance of feeling that human beings have all over Earth—qualities like that were brought. Sometimes certain human be-ings in certain places on Earth have feelings that human beings in other places don't necessarily have. In some countries now on Earth, when people are very rigidly controlled, certain feelings come up all the time. In other places people have vast amounts of freedom and don't have those feelings at that time in that culture. So those feelings might be needed for those experiencing rigid control.

Maybe people on certain planets are known for their endurance or for their truthful outlook (or just about anything you can think of). Earth might have the capacity to sustain such qualities in beings. Emis-saries believed that if original beings went down and prepared Earth or let Earth know that such qualities would be needed, then Earth could do what she needed to do to prepare herself to sustain such qualities in others, even if she did not have them herself.

And that's what you meant by "prepare for Those Who Would Follow."

Remember, many subtleties were involved. Think of all the diseases you have now. Sometimes a person might have a disease and have dif-ferent ways of expressing feelings. Or feelings arise for that person be-cause he or she has a disease or a wound or maybe was born in some unusual, different way. Feelings come up for that person that would not come up for others in a similar circumstance. Maybe the person is in a wheelchair. Feelings come up for that person sometimes that might come up occasionally for other people *not* in a wheelchair, but those feelings might come up all the time for a person in a wheelchair.

Therefore, people who come to Earth must also be able to help Earth prepare for such beings who will follow someday in wheelchairs. They must be able to have feelings, because even though they might be uncomfortable or painful sometimes, that is the way the body communicates with the soul and spirit and the instinct to know. If you experience feelings enough, eventually you will do something to alter those feelings—get stronger, maybe spend more time with other people in wheelchairs. In short, you will find a way to not have those feelings and qualities all the time.

So sometimes early peoples came. They did not have to be in a wheelchair, but part of their makeup would be needed much later, maybe thousands and thousands of years later, by a person in a wheelchair. Or maybe it would be needed by someone with lots of money who sometimes feels embarrassed or shy in the company of those—even good friends—who don't have much money.

Many times people who don't have much money envy others, even if they try to control themselves. A person with money also feels uncomfortable, and that's why sometimes people of a certain type, people with money, spend more time with other people with money—not because of snobbery.

Because it's easier.

They do not have to feel foolish or embarrassed or guilty because they have money. And people with less money do the same. This . . . all these qualities, I'm not saying they are good or bad, this is just a fact.

People came who could express these qualities. I believe all the original tribes came, all over the Earth, with all different qualities, some of them not needed on the Earth at that time. But they would be needed later, and Earth might need time to prepare herself to sustain those qualities as expressed by Those Who Would Follow, maybe many thousands of years later. Earth had time to prepare to sustain those qualities that would be needed by people to learn lessons, or to be able to live a physical life in a benevolent way or, in some cases, in a most dramatic way so they can learn.

In short, Earth must be able to sustain those qualities because you are born from Earth matter, which makes up your physical body. If she cannot sustain those qualities, even if the feeling came up for a brief moment (your soul might stimulate the feeling for a brief moment) . . . if the physical body cannot sustain that feeling, it will go away quickly. Then it might take a very long time to learn a lesson. This is what happens on other planets where ETs are. The physical matter of the planet does not sustain those feelings.

They have a very narrow range.

Yes, that's why a person might have to live maybe thousands of years in order to learn the lesson, because only spirit can stimulate qualities, and qualities such as feeling or emotion will not be sustained in the physical body. It will require many, many repeated experiences to learn what you came to learn, because the planet that makes up your physical body does not know and cannot support that feeling.

So when we say this is the only planet of free choice, all those choices had to have been brought here and seeded here or they wouldn't be available to us as avenues of expression?

That's right. Everything you do here, everything you can be here, was originally brought by others to make it possible. Earth reacted and so on, "This quality must be needed."

Emotional qualities, physical qualities, spiritual qualities . . .

. . . instinct qualities. And Earth says, "Okay, you are here on me, and these qualities need to be supported in you." Once a quality is supported, it is always available to be supported, no matter how far in the future you go, as long as you are on that type of Earth. I cannot say that fifth- or sixth-dimensional Earth will support those qualities, but I can say that this Earth will.

Once the Explorer Race Is Gone

Once the Explorer Race is gone, what will this Earth do with their awesome qualities? Will it become a planet of re-creation or a planet of drama?

You can say that you who are here now are also supporting those who will follow you when you go off as the Explorer Race. Perhaps those who will follow you will need some of those qualities, though maybe not all of them, just as you do not need all the qualities brought by those who came originally. But people who lived here before you needed those qualities and people who will live after you will need those qualities. Do you understand? Not all those qualities were brought just for the short time of the Explorer Race being here.

So many of them were here for all the other cultures between your time and our time?

Yes, and beyond your time.

And when the 3.0 Sirians come up . . . that's why the planet is being changed, isn't it? They don't need as much oxygen.

That's right. Beings are coming with many different qualities. Those 3.0 beings from the former negative planet of Sirius might need qualities not being used by you that have been used by cultures before the Explorer Race or even by people of your time. When they are done with those qualities on Earth and move on, other civilizations will come who might require sustenance of certain qualities available on Earth now.

It goes on and on and on. Of course, each generation might also occasionally stimulate supportive qualities not here before. Generally speaking, I believe, all qualities needed by Those Who Would Follow were brought originally because the emissaries invited people from all over to come, including my ancestors.

The Tribal Practice of Naming Children

When you were born, how much did you know? Were you just born like we are, behind the veil and forgetting, or did you have memories of who you were?

I was born like you, with no memories. We have elders, shamanic people, mystical people, medicine people, all those things. Elders are often nearby at birth, maybe grandmother elders, also grandfathers. They might be able to tell something from feeling the baby, not touching, but being aware of the baby.

They might know certain things, perhaps give a certain name to the child, a spirit name. Not all names are given immediately. Sometimes later, when the child is a few years old, other wise beings might be able to understand some things. Sometimes they might even know the child's lessons right away just by looking at the child, seeing how the child is. Sometimes it requires a few years for a child's personality to emerge. Then the lessons are obvious to many elders and sometimes to the whole tribe. It is the same in your time.

I never asked you how old you were. You were fifty-four once, but how old were you when you actually left your body?

Somewhere in my fifties, I think. Very old—considered ancient for my time.

How old were you when you got your name, which was, I assume, when they knew who you were going to be?

Speaks of Many Truths? How old? I think about two and a half.

So it was obvious very early on that you were a special being?

Well, it was obvious to elders that I had some qualities. I think maybe I was talking pretty early. The name "Speaks of Anything" would have to do with talking—so, Speaks of Many Truths. They didn't tell me too much about it. I think it might have had to do with some childlike thing I said that maybe they considered to be of value.

Using Long Smell

So you went all through your natural life as one of your tribe with mystical gifts, with the long vision. How old were you when you discovered long vision? Was it after you conquered your fear of heights?

I did not discover it. I was taught about long vision, about long hearing. I can even use long smell sometimes. I have used long smell occasionally to communicate, to understand, to speak to brothers and sisters in other places, other countries. Sometimes I try to describe an herb or a method of doing something, a method of preparation. Sometimes we have plant material and so on, but sometimes we don't. If we don't but I need to know the smell because there might be a chance for me to find that herb, then we have some brief feeling or a sensation of smell. In the case of a medicine woman, she does the long smell all the time with other medicine women in other places.

Have you ever had the experience where you remember something, some smell, and it comes back to you briefly for a moment? Maybe you remember breakfast cooking when you were a youngster. You remember a coffee smell or something, and the smell comes back to you briefly as sort of a smell memory. It's a feeling very much like that. Then you might recognize a plant if you came across it.

Letting Children Feel That Life Is Good

How old were you when you discovered there was a world beyond your tribe?

Oh, I discovered this immediately. From a very young age, I was told of ancestors on other planets and whether a nearby tribe was friendly. I had a very good friend in a tribe just down the river. Now, I speak to you in this time in my fifties, and that tribe is only about maybe a day and a half walk down the river. If I walk slowly, it's maybe a two-day walk. I have a very good friend there. We see each other two or three times a year for ceremonies, but because my friend is in a similar occupation or is in demand, we cannot always see each other. So we see each other two or three times a year when the tribes get together for ceremonies or special celebrations, and then we have lots of fun. We talk, tell each other stories, laugh and joke and so on.

As a youngster, if there was a friendly tribe nearby, we were told all about them. But if a tribe, perhaps at a distance, was not friendly, we were not told about that until later. You were not told that as a little child, since it might frighten you, make you afraid of life. It's important to let a little child feel that life is good and a celebration so he or she will want to be here.

When I was young, there was a need to want to be here. Otherwise, life was hard. If you didn't want to be here, then you might give up and say, "I don't need that. Goodbye." So little children were not told about unpleasant things too much.

But your worldview wasn't limited to the tribe. Your worldview encompassed home planets.

Our home planet, yes. And the cosmos and stars.

You were literally told as a child about the reality of life.

Yes, to some extent. As I say, I was shielded a little bit but sometimes told of things that I needed to know. For instance, "If you see a bear in the woods, don't run toward the bear"—I was told about things like that. But I think in your time your culture exposes children at an early age to things that frighten them. It's a very big mistake.

I think part of the reason many youngsters—say from teenagers down—die young in your time, is not only because of some terrible problem in your society, but also that they may have been frightened as children. Maybe they heard about something.

The Physical Impact of Shock Media

Now, natural death in the family does not have to be frightening. I'm not talking about natural death. Children do not have to be shielded when Uncle so-and-so or Aunt so-and-so dies. A curious child walks up to the coffin, looks in, sees the dead body. It's different if someone died in mortal agony—don't show children that.

But children do watch television; they go to movies. Little children get terribly frightened, even though they do not remember the movie later. When they are older, in most cases it still makes them more afraid of life, so that when a door opens—and doors open for you many times in life—they might leave sooner rather than later because of fear and anxiety about what life might bring.

Even if a movie or television show is not about Earth life—a horror show or something that would never happen—it has a physical impact. It weighs in on a feeling level. I do not understand the attraction to horror, mainly monster movies and psychotic killer movies. It's unfortunate. I consider such movies and plays to be disease-causers in your time, and many, many more murders come about as a result of such consciousness built into your society.

People who become psychotic killers, for example, do not do so because of a movie. Most often it's because of certain conditions in life—maybe not with parents, maybe something beyond family control. But a child might be born with the possibility that could be this, and something happens to trigger it. What I am saying is that in your time there is a consciousness of the psychotic killer that welcomes such an event.

Why We Sometimes Seek Out Catastrophe

From a larger understanding, why do you think we have these horrible things?

Remember, at deep levels people will respond to an emergency in ways they do not respond at other times—earthquakes, fires, floods. Almost always you forget about your differences with friends, family, strangers. Maybe you never talk to people who live on there another block. Maybe you never go there because those people don't like you there. You don't want to even be caught over there. You'll go with friends only if you have to go through there. It's like that for youngsters in a city, for instance.

But during a terrible earthquake, you forget all about that. You help each other. At a deep level, you know you are all the same, so you help one another. Usually you do so only in an extreme drama like this. So sometimes when there is much trouble between people, you feel unsettled and will sometimes seek out this circumstance.

Remember, most, if not all, psychotic-killer movies ultimately end because a group comes together, even if they do not like each other in the beginning of the drama or movie. They eventually get together to finish off the psychotic killer in some way. Then they discover that maybe they can be friends after all, even though in the beginning they didn't like each other.

Ultimately, movies portray that. So sometimes there is a desire to see this—not so much a desire for earthquakes, fires or floods, but a desire to shed differences. Everybody works together, feels good about each other, notices what is common ground. I think that because there is so much separateness in your time, people desire to come together and sometimes feel they need to create, support and sustain an artificial means to do so.

A means to an end.

Of course, there are other reasons an audience will go to a movie. The people who make movies say, "Well, it costs a lot of money to make a movie, so let's make a movie that an audience will come to for sure. Then we will make back the money we put into it, and maybe more." There is that, of course. Also, there are some people who get to the point in their lives where they like to be stimulated that way. They like the feeling in their bodies. Maybe they don't like it in the moment when it happens, but it's sort of exciting.

So there are many reasons, but I think it mostly has to do with missing and desiring the experience of being able to get along with neighbors regardless of differences. Sometimes this happens in a big battle, a war between countries. Maybe you find out that you and some other soldier you might never have been friends with outside of war come together and become friends because you're fighting for a common purpose. You might not like everybody you are fighting with, but still you have that common purpose and will often die or make great sacrifices to protect those others you may not completely like.

But along with all of the other negative things, horror movies don't have long to last, right?

They will probably go away as the global economy . . . right now some businesses are very shortsighted, but as the global economy comes more together, becomes one unit, gradually businesses will see that encouraging and supporting and sustaining such things in people is not good in the long run. So businesses will begin to discourage it and will ultimately be the leaders in this.

Many moral individuals have been decrying it for a long time, but ultimately it will be businesses saying, "Maybe we shouldn't encourage people to throw rocks through windows when we are the insurance companies." Eventually, all will homogenize: the insurance company will also process milk and might also run a private police force. Eventually, businesses will say, "This is not a good idea. We are hurting ourselves. Why do we do this?" Businesses will probably be leaders in this, even though many moral individuals and ministers will breathe a mighty sigh of relief that this phase is over. But businesses will ultimately lead.

Taking Responsibility

Speaks of Many Truths
November 29, 1999

H ere we have all these tribes from all of these other planets for thousands and thousands of years in North America. Were there wars among these tribes and bad feelings?

Early Explorers in North America and the Beginnings of Tribal War

In the beginning there was no problem among tribes. We'd see other people, sometimes nomadic people. They'd come by our camp. We were happy to see one another; it was a celebration. We'd tell stories, talk about mutual customs and so on. We would encourage them to stay for a few days on their travels, if they could, but to at least stay the day and the night—eat together and rest, and then go tomorrow.

But as time went on, explorers from other lands (Spain, France and Europe in general) began to come—not just settlers for new land, but before them, others. Remember, in those days, Mexico was much bigger. Going back five hundred years, Mexico included the western portion of your present United States.

Spain was involved for many, many years before settlers came to establish the United States. Spain, France and England—the great powers of the sea—traveled all over; some ships never made it back. They say Columbus discovered America, but of course that's not true. Aside from the fact that people were living here already—it would be like somebody coming to your home and saying they discovered your home—there were also many other European explorers, including Nordic explorers, who came many, many years before Columbus.

The Vikings came sometime before A.D. *1000, didn't they?*

I do not know the year, but many explorers came hundreds of years before Columbus. Columbus got the credit, but many others came. What happened when they came is that they not only left trauma behind them, but also their influences and ideas.

Gradually, over hundreds of years, this began to filter all over the place through nomadic tribes. Explorers landed on the west or east coast of the continent, but some came overland from Canada and Mexico, from the whole of North America and probably from South America, too. Eventually, these ideas permeated the tribes, and young people—who are always the most susceptible to new ideas, whether good or bad (sometimes they are good and of advantage; sometimes they are bad and young people don't have the discernment yet to know that)—would try things

So by the time it got to be the 1700s, there began to be more tribal wars. By then, ideas having to do with the self had spread—meaning "I" rather than "we"—and this made for jealousy, resentment, anger, self-motivated desire and so on. I'm not saying the European and Nordic explorers were bad. I'm simply saying that these explorers did not understand that the people they were interacting with were very spiritually advanced. This is because they brought their own religions, which were not always so advanced in terms of application.

From my point of view, God is about heart and love. Any God who is about anger, war or anything dangerous that could kill you or others . . . you'd have to look and say, "Maybe this is not God. Maybe this is somebody else who poses as God." But you'd say this to people as best you could without shared language, and maybe they wouldn't understand.

Some early Nordic religion was very good, I hear, but it was still very engaged in battle, because they believed early on that battle is what defines a man's courage. We believe what makes a man courageous is his ability to survive gently on the land, causing as little harm as possible to all other beings—just that man surviving in the wilderness, not against the bear, but with the bear. He gives the bear its own space, doesn't eat its food. This makes what we believe to be a benevolent citizen, a benevolent man or woman. I think many early tribes had an attitude like this, but explorers came and challenged it, saying, "We can do this better than you." At first tribes simply paid no attention, essentially thinking, "So what? We don't care. Go away." But ultimately, they interacted.

If you have something poking you in the side, eventually you have to take action. Maybe the Nordics came and tried to say, "You've got food.

We want it. Give it to us, or we'll hurt you or kill you." Maybe at first the tribes tried to be reasonable, but if reason was not listened to, then they'd have to destroy the invaders. Oftentimes, the invaders were destroyed, but then the tribes had to express qualities in themselves that would influence themselves and their people. In short, they became polluted.

So that's what happened, and then eventually the invaders and the tribes started fighting each other?

Yes.

But at the time you were alive in the 1600s, that hadn't happened yet?

It had begun a little bit. We had to be careful.

Because in the 1500s there were Spaniards wandering around.

That's right. Of course, I told Robert a story the other day about fur traders, an amusing incident in my own life. One of the fur traders was French (so France was there, too). The nice thing about the French people I myself have met (and those other tribal people have met as well), traders and so on, is that they always make an effort to learn your language. I have not noticed this so often with English-speaking traders. Yes, some individuals make this effort, but generally speaking, French traders make the effort to learn your language and respect your customs. They do not expect you to respect theirs.

So the French were more involved, I think, with diplomacy. Maybe this is why in your recent history, diplomatic services tend to focus around France. This must run deep in the French people.

Responsible Business: Facing the Consequences

Are we coming into a time now where we're going to be needing this information that you're giving us? Is there going to be a disruption in technology? Are we going back to the land or something?

Not that way. Many people in your time—some with a political point of view, some with simply a heart point of view—can see good things in technology, but they can see more things in technology that are harmful. As a result, many people are now looking for some way to do things that does not require as much technology.

It's more like that—not a movement as in a political point of view, but a desire to have another way to do things that is more gentle, more benevolent and more beneficial. So what I speak about is in response to the desire of people of your time.

In time even businesses and corporations will have to face the fact that any pollution they are responsible for will very soon come right back to the mouths of their own children. Business corporations in the United States and other places, I believe, are granted rights of citizenship, like a human being. But this is short-lived. Soon human beings in business will be granted rights of citizenship, but business in its own right will not be granted these rights, because a business is a piece of paper and cannot be responsible.

Right now, a citizen who commits a crime—maybe a crime of passion—has to pay. Perhaps you are angry at someone who sells you something, and you throw a rock through the window. You'll have to not only pay for the window, but maybe you'll have to spend time cleaning highways. You'll have to pay more than one way, plus you'll feel embarrassed and silly, and people who know you will say, "I never thought you would do that." So you'll feel embarrassed, ashamed for a time. In short, you'll pay many ways for certain actions.

But businesses pollute a river, and nobody is paying like that.

That's right. Citizens in business might pay—that happened for a time—meaning businesses get fined, but so what? You cannot take a piece of paper and send it to prison. In time that will also be tried, meaning that the corporate charter will be suspended, but that is not really a personal problem.

If someone takes you and puts you in prison, even for a week or two, when you get out, you feel awful. It might take years to get over the terrible experience, because prisons in your time, even in your country, are a terrible disgrace. They cause much more harm than good, so much more that when you finally apply the proper method to prisons and to the punishment of prisoners, you will wonder how you could have ever seen for a moment that prison in its current state of being could be in any way helpful. But that will come soon.

Now, when you have to make alterations in the way you conduct yourself as a citizen, do so. But before too long—not immediately, not soon, but before too long—the whole idea of a corporate charter will be suspended. All businesses will be private. By that time, tax systems will be much different. There will be no financial advantage to having a corporation.

So you only do business you're responsible for.

That's right. You are responsible. You do something wrong, you pollute the river, and you and everybody involved—including the man or woman who eventually opened the valve and let the stuff go, right down the line—are responsible. The person at the top, including all management, all the way down to the last person who opened the valve . . . everybody will be punished, maybe not cruelly but in a way that you feel personally ashamed.

No one will be put in stocks in the city square for people to mistreat, but they will be publicly shamed. Perhaps some individuals will do some jail time, but any jail time will always start with the person at the top and then extend to the board, then the upper manager. The person at the bottom will be the last person to go to jail.

This will come before too long, and then it will be much, much better. If you know that you are going to be shamed or seriously punished, you will not only think twice, but many times before you open the valve or order another person to order other person to open the valve and pollute. Even if you say, "It's just a little bit," just a little bit eventually comes back and goes into the mouths of your children. In short, people will embrace responsibility.

Embracing Responsibility

But that's part of what you said: We have to take responsibility for our actions. It's not just an honorable thing to do, it's an ultimatum from the Creator.

Any creator who gives you an ultimatum is not worthy as a creator. Always remember, you have been born in a time when Creator has been portrayed as wrathful. I say this: All of this "angry God" stuff . . . that is not the Creator I know. This might be some creator or god somewhere, but this is not the Creator I know, not anybody I know or recognize as the Creator of this place.

Know that Creator never gives an ultimatum; He always gives an allowance instead. Sometimes you might wish Creator would not be quite so allowing, but Creator is allowing because He trusts you to find your own way and needs you to find your own way within your own capacities. In short, a parent cannot always carry a child around. Someday the child has to walk for himself or herself.

So Creator will make it possible for you to have more of the capacity you need to be able to make free choices. This is just like in times gone by when Creator has released more heart energy for you. When you have more heart energy, you feel better, but you must change the way you live. Because you have more heart, more tenderness, more vulnerability, you have more of a need to get along with your neighbors. It's not okay to say, "Who cares about you anymore?" because your heart is more tender. So Creator gives you capacity.

But I was referring to what Zoosh said about humans now having to take responsibility for 5 percent of what we created.

Yes, but it's not an ultimatum. You have the capacity to, meaning Creator makes this available for you. But Creator doesn't put a spiritual finger in your face and say, "Do this now, or you'll be sorry." Creator never does that. Do you know what Creator does? Creator abandons that 5 percent, does not do it anymore.

You, being offspring of Creator, immediately spring into action and initially feel tense, upset, agitated. You are given something to do, but in fact, Creator does not give it to you—Creator abandons it. And you immediately pick up what Creator lets fall through spirit hands, because if you do not pick it up, your life also gets completely messed up, to say nothing of the lives of other beings. That is how Creator does it. Of course, if you as people did not pick it up, then do you think Creator might pick it up again? In the past, Creator has done that, but in your time, if you did not pick it up, then other beings on Earth would pick it up instead—then you would no longer be the Explorer Race. Other beings on Earth would become the Explorer Race instead: maybe ants, maybe deer, maybe birds.

But you pick it up. Creator knows there is a percentage of chance you won't pick it up, but you pick it up immediately. The percent is small, but Creator always saves something just in case. Maybe it would be what you would think is an animal. Then you would not be the Explorer Race anymore; you would simply finish out your lives here. So-called animals would then become the Explorer Race.

A backup plan.

Always. If there isn't one, then you cannot just abandon it and walk away. You are responsible. But you can abandon it if you have something in place to immediately pick up what you've dropped.

And so humans did that, right?

Yes, and Creator feels good about that. He knew you would do so in the beginning, that He wouldn't have to visit the responsibility of the Explorer Race on the ant world. But ants are very high on the list to have received that. Why? Because ants are durable, determined to live. They still hang around in your time, even where you make an effort to eliminate them. So a being would have to be like that, durable. Ants are very durable as a race of beings.

I didn't realize it worked like that.

It's important to know when you take on more creator duty, that someday you'll be teaching people something.

Well, we're training down here to be creators.

You have always been training to be creators, from the beginning. Us too—in my time we trained to be creators. Maybe we didn't have to, but the more the human-being body has trained to be a creator . . . by the time you come along as the Explorer Race, Creator drops the ball on purpose and you pick it up right away because the body is fully conditioned. If the body was not conditioned by those who came before (like my people and others), then when Creator dropped the ball, you would say, "What do we do?" And in two weeks, you would all be dead.

But Creator makes a plan . . .

That's very powerful, the way you explained that, the idea of conditioning the body through all these lifetimes for Those Who Would Follow. That makes a lot more sense now. You weren't just bringing the qualities and staying here to get Mother Earth used to your energy, but you were actually preparing our bodies, training the particles that would make up our bodies.

I tried to explain this in a practical way that is quickly and easily understood—heartfelt truth. We'll continue tomorrow. Good life.

Good afternoon. Thank you so much.

Creating Personal Relationships

Speaks of Many Truths
November 30, 1999

The whole point of shamanic interaction with anything is to create a personal relationship between the individual shaman and whomever he or she is touching and to pass on that knowledge of wisdom—not only to students, but to the people they live with in general, so that ultimately all people can have personal relationships with all material things around them. That is why we are doing this book.

Relating to the Natural Being in All Things

If I speak to a plant or a tree, or even if there is some reason to speak to something that has been made of a tree, maybe a box or a table—to me it is not a box or a table, it is still a tree. Even if it has metal in it, then it's a tree with pieces of stone in it. If I can relate to it like that, then there can still be some communication, but if I am stuck with the idea that it is a box or a table, then there will be no communication. None.

You must relate to whatever you are communicating with on a personal basis, how you would relate to a friend or an intimate on a personal basis. You speak to them; they speak to you. The tree is the same, and so is the mountain. They might not speak the same language, but communication is still possible.

Even if the mountain or the tree has been used in your time without its permission to form something else, it remains itself in its own heart or consciousness. If I wish to speak to its heart or consciousness, I can still do so, even if it is somewhat in the spirit form. But because it still has a physical presence there, it is sort of in between.

To Communicate with the Dead, You Must Also Relate to the Bones

When a human being dies—even though in your time you do not cherish this as we do—it is intended that the physical body be returned to Earth in the natural physical process so that after a short time, there isn't much left of the human being. There might still be something, though—bones or something. We know that the consciousness or the soul has moved on elsewhere, but there is still some physical matter left.

When people communicate—even in your time—with the spirits of those who have crossed over, they will, in fact, be communicating not only with the spirit of that person, but they must also include (if they want the best connection) a connection to the bones or what's left of that person. If they include that, then they will speak to the heart and consciousness identified with that specific human being. They do not have to be present at the gravesite, but they do have to make that connection if they wish to get the clearest possible message based upon who or what that person was when he or she was here on Earth. If, on the other hand, it is uncomfortable for them to do that, which is very possible, then they will communicate only with the spirit and get the spirit body's more expanded view, having moved through the veils.

I mention this so that you can consider the sense of personality of a human being, even deceased, as compared to a table—which is, you might say, a deceased tree—or a piece of rock used after its normal incarnation as stone (as something taken out of Mother Earth's body), processed and turned into something that holds a table together. I mention it this way so you'll understand that there is a direct connection.

Are you saying that you need to touch these bones in consciousness? You don't have to physically touch and find them, right?

I'm not saying you or anyone should. I do not do this work, but I'm talking about people who will help others speak to their dead relatives or loved ones who have passed on. There are people who do this well, but there are also many people in your time who do it not so well or try to do it as best they can. And there are some people in your time who do not do it well, but claim they do. It is actually very difficult to do this in such a way as the psychic needs in order to have a clear connection but also to feel good in his or her body, especially doing the work.

If the psychic doesn't feel good—meaning he makes the connection but it feels uncomfortable—and he continues to pursue it, it will feel worse and worse until he has to stop. Also, in this case, he will not have the best connection. When a psychic or channel makes a connection to anyone or any being to bring forth a communication from that being, if you as the channel or psychic do not feel good when you make that connection—that is, your physical body and sometimes even the spirit being are telling you that the connection is not the best one—and you go forward in the attempt to help the person anyway, it won't be the clearest message. It won't be good for that spirit, and it won't be good for you. In short, it won't be good. Most likely, your physical body will tell you, because the spirit being will not always have much experience in this.

Sometimes psychics use the same form of channeling that is going on here, where for many, many years Robert has been channeling beings such as myself and others he's connected with many, many times, so we know how to connect benevolently with each other. But in the case of a psychic trying to help an individual to communicate with a passed-over relative, most likely that connection will not have been made very many times before, if at all. So it is necessary to make sure the connection actually feels good to your physical body. Always try to make sure that your body is signaling to you that the connection is working well for you, meaning you feel good.

Relate to the Being the Way It Relates to Itself

Okay, but isn't the whole point of it to create this personal relationship between yourself, the shaman, and whatever or whomever you are dealing with?

Yes, it is intended to be personal. If I am asking a plant, which might be contributing, if it chooses to, some of its leaves or berries or roots for some purpose—to help a human being or perhaps an animal—if I'm communicating with the being and I'm asking that being to make such a sacrifice of its own personal body, how can I do so in any way other than in a personal manner?

I must relate to the being the way that being relates to itself. The plant relates to the plant as some*one*. Other plants relate to that plant as some*one*. Am I to relate to that plant as some*thing* and expect cooperation, much less assistance? Over the years perhaps you as a human being might have had someone talk to you as if you were some*thing*. You immediately felt resentment, anger, maybe disappointment or worse. The chances of your wanting to cooperate were very slight.

So even on the practical level, to say nothing of being polite, if you want cooperation, you have to be nice. And you can't just be nice on the outside; you have to feel it, you have to mean it, you have to feel good about it. It becomes your philosophy. You discover it works, so you do it.

I was originally taught this by my teacher. My teacher walked me right outside (we were in a small hutlike structure) and said, "Now I'll show you the example." And my teacher spoke to a bush in this warm-hearted way. There was no wind that day, but the bush immediately moved, physically, to let the teacher know that this was good and appreciated. The teacher then taught me how to talk to the bush.

It didn't move right away for me, because it took me awhile to understand that I had to talk in a different way. I couldn't just talk sincerely from my mind. To be clear, I had to speak sincerely from my heart. Once I realized that it was that kind of talk, that kind of personal connection, then the bush moved. So the bush worked with my teacher to teach me.

Well, the reason I'm so interested in this is that it has dawned on me that the shamanic way of life is the ideal way of being for the human. I mean, we've gotten so far away from this because of the mental and the technology and the separation, but this is our future—not just the shaman's, not just the medium's, but the future for each of us.

Interestingly enough, it is your past and also your future. You came here to Earth in your time as the Explorer Race. You arrived purposely at a time that slightly predates the age of technology as you know it now, but there still was something like technology, the wheel and other things. So there was basic technology when you began to arrive here as the Explorer Race about a hundred and seventy-five years ago from your time now.

And you progressed forward, developing technology as a society. Therefore, as you became more and more developed technologically, you no longer required in your own mind as a culture to have a personal relationship with everything because you did not need to. You could get what you wanted when you needed it without asking, almost like a spoiled child.

The Art of Finding Water

Fortunately, in the past and even today, some people in your time have made an effort to keep the art of finding water going. This goes way, way back to my time, but not to my people. My people did not believe in digging in the ground, even to find water to make a permanent well. We did not believe in that. That's why we camped near streams and rivers.

I know in my time, having talked to fur traders and trappers and people from outside our culture (including outside Native American cultures), that people still went around to find water with a stick, or even with feelings. I think in your time sometimes people use metal rods, but this can be done.

One time I was out with a group of people, and we were separated from our people for a time. We needed to find water, and we were not near any. So one of the people said he could find the water, and he did. He was one of my students.

He found the water; it was a seep, as they call it. Sometimes, even high up on the side of a hill, one finds a seep. Usually the animals know where it is, and they drink from it. So my people were sustained. There was enough of a reservoir under the seep, like a little puddle or pond, that we could get enough and still leave enough for the animals. We drank and went on.

This kind of dowsing—you call it water witching (I don't like that term, water witching, because it suggests that something not right is being done, but dowsing is an acceptable term)—is a good thing in your time and a carryover from the days when the dowser had to have a personal relationship with water in order to find it. Such talents and abilities initially allowed your people to come and populate areas far, far from any source of water. People would just look for drinkable water close to the surface, and then when they found it, they would drink by hand.

So it had to be pretty close to the surface.

Yes, but in those days the water table was higher.

Consciousness at Birth

At what point did you know you would be a mystic man?

Well, one could say that there's more than one point there. When you are born, you have consciousness from a more expanded version of yourself, and you probably know even then. For me, when I came in, I had certain knowledge that told me I would probably be a mystical or medicine man. I didn't know which.

Before birth?

When I was born.

You were conscious when you were born?

As were you. Everybody is conscious when they are born, but my people encouraged me to remember. Of course, I could not remember it all, but when I was learning words, they were asking me things. It was in my people's nature to try to communicate with the very young—not to pressure, but to try to get the child to talk or describe or even draw a picture or emote what he or she was feeling. In this way one knows the child better. Even by the time children are three or four, they remember enough about their life, their consciousness or their heart purpose (as my people say) when they came in, and by that time they speak the language pretty well, so they can communicate it very well.

In my time, by the time you were a year old (a year and a half or two years old at the most), the elders already knew why you came there.

They didn't need you to communicate to tell them; they knew. But sometimes it might still have been useful, because you might still have had some capacity to speak about the greater being that you are, even though you had to let that go in order to live a life here.

Tribal Populations

How many people were in your tribe?

During my lifetime, when I was born, there were maybe about . . . I'm not used to thinking these ways. Let me think. Let's put it like this: Given that my life span ran to my mid-fifties, the greatest number of people at any time in my tribe was about 126. During a difficult year, it dropped to about 80. This was not uncommon in those days.

We didn't have an inexhaustible supply of food. Not all the young survived as they do in your day, and not all the mothers survived the process of giving birth, even though the women who helped them were very good. They were trained by others for such duties, but still, it was different in those days, back then. And we were not looking to make a huge permanent settlement.

So that's why there weren't too many. I've talked to many people of other tribes, and the largest settlement I found—if you want to call it that (because when you're that big, you kind of have to settle)—was just a little over nine hundred. I don't think that was unusual for those times.

I have heard in your time of thousands and thousands in tribes who have managed to survive . . . and in one case, even a hundred thousand or more because the tribe managed to make a compromise it could live with: to accept modern conditions while maintaining the tribal identity to the best of its ability. I think that tribe is at least partly here in Arizona.

The Diné?

That is the proper name for what the Spanish refer to as Navajo—but that is not a Diné word.

Recognizing and Nurturing Abilities Present at Birth

Was there some kind of a commitment from the elders or the ancestors or from Spirit that there would always be a mystical man? That when one got really old, there would be the promise of someone coming in with those abilities?

You mean, did Spirit communicate to the elders and say, "You will always have a mystical man or woman"?

Was it an assumption or a promise?

One assumed nothing in those days. The more you assumed, the more trouble you would be in. One was grateful for the arrival of anyone or any type of being who would contribute to the welfare of all the people, just as one was grateful that a child would be born who would make a good midwife, who came in to do that. (Think how frightened you might become if no child was born who chose to be a midwife.) The elders would say, "Well, this is why she's here."

We always celebrated the birth of someone who was a mystical man or woman or a medicine man or woman or a midwife or any of the other necessary skills—day hunters, night hunters and so on. We would celebrate the arrival of every child simply because we were happy to see him or her. We knew that since the child was being born, if he or she survived, it meant that he or she was here to bring an ability that could be nurtured. It was vitally important when the elders or the wise ones would say, "This is what this child came here to do." That was not just to satisfy our curiosity never.

It was always done so that you would know how to nurture the child, meaning that the child came here to do something and he or she would be highly receptive to being taught anything along those lines. If you got it wrong, then the child would be resistant. Every once in a while, the elders or the wise ones would not be clear, and they'd get the feeling that the child's reason for being born would be this and then try to teach the child. The child would be resistant or wouldn't be interested, and then they'd say, "No, that's not it. That's not why this child is here."

Usually, it was pretty clear to the wise ones or the elders, but I can remember once or twice when it was not very clear. One of the times was something unexpected—someone was born who wanted to be a cook, meaning that person wanted to find new ways to cook food for our people and to instruct people on how to cook. But everybody knew how to cook.

This individual wanted to go out and find herbs and work with the medicine woman, finding new ways to cook so the food was more flavorful and maybe even good for us. This was kind of like early vitamin supplementation, but in the food, which is, I believe, better. That was the first time when anyone was born to our people who wanted to do that.

Passing on Mystical Knowledge

Were there times when there wasn't an appropriate candidate for mystical or medicine person, and then they would just sort of have to make do?

No.

There was always someone?

No, but I have heard that sometimes a mystical man or woman—mystical women were just as common as mystical men—would be born when the present mystical woman or man was very old.

With nobody to train him or her?

No, not that. You would train. You would pray and communicate to everyone to try to get that mystical man or woman to live as long as possible. Usually, then, with such encouragement and support from other members of the tribe (meaning that the mystical man or woman might be excused from doing certain duties so that he or she could preserve as much energy and strength as possible), the mystical man or woman might live as long as possible to pass on as much knowledge as possible to that youngster before he or she died.

But, generally speaking, the mystical woman or man did not give knowledge to somebody else to pass on to the tribe because . . . see, in your time people do that because they don't remember that knowledge is felt as well as spoken. So if I give all my knowledge in some way to somebody and then he tries to teach it to somebody else, if he does not practice it in a way that works for him, then when he teaches it, it is words, but the student gets no feeling from it. The feeling is vitally important.

Otherwise, it is just like somebody telling you how to cook deer meat so that it is tender. It is interesting, but as the student you don't feel it on the heart level and, at the same time, you don't fully feel how important it is to you personally. In short, there is no personal connection. So we come back to the original exploration.

In most tribes, then, it somehow worked out in the process of reincarnation that they had a mystical man and a medicine person and . . .

I cannot say that. You must remember that I only spoke to certain people in a small area. What I believe is, because the mystical man or woman would have frequent communication with the medicine man or woman . . . if a child was not born to receive such wisdom, then that wisdom might come to an end for that tribe with the mystical man or woman. But if the whole line died out because a child was not born in time, and then a child was born later, ready to be a mystical man or woman but the teacher was gone . . . in some cases, some of the knowledge could be preserved because of communications with the medicine man or woman. It wouldn't be the same. The instruction wouldn't be the same, but the medicine man or woman would teach the child born to be a mystical person only what was communicated to him or her on the basis of the mystical. The medicine man or woman would not teach medicine unless the child was born for that.

So some knowledge might be preserved, but it wouldn't be taught to the child with the same feeling. The medicine man or woman would try to make it the best they could, but that's all. So that's how some tribes died out. It wasn't all wars and battles. Tribes would sometimes die out if they didn't have the right people to sustain the tribe.

Day-to-day sustenance is possible very often except in a crisis, say a drought. For example, sometimes another crisis comes up where you need a mystical man or woman or a medicine man or woman to survive. If you don't have him or her, then that's it. Think how it would be for us if we didn't have any hunters. If we had day hunters or night hunters, that was good. Then we always had a hunting party out if needed. If we didn't have any night hunters, we would not have night-hunter food but would get by on day-hunter food.

Childhood Knowledge of the Abilities You Are Born To

So many challenges! So you have a lineage of mystical people that goes back to the beginning?

Yes, I must, or I would not be a mystical man in my time. If my lineage were broken, I would not be here, or if I were here, I would be trained for or doing something else, maybe not what I came to do. If nobody is there to teach you everything about what you came to do, you might feel kind of unsettled, your whole life spent doing something else. But that happens. I have known that to happen.

When you were standing on a peak, when you were a hawk, working on your fear of heights, did you know then?

You mean when I was a youngster, a child?

Did you know then that you were going to be a mystical man?

I knew before then.

So what was the first mystical thing you did?

It is hard to say, because I was born with the knowledge that I would be that and it was sustained in me by others—elders and wise ones. If you could not communicate the language, then they would sing to you or they would dance. They would do things, and it was sustained. So for me, I always knew.

So how did it feel the first time you did long vision as a result of looking through the eyes of the hawk?

It was wonderful, exciting. It was not the usual way long vision was taught, but it was the way that was right for me. It was kind of like a reward, and I thought it was fantastic. Of course, as is typical for children everywhere, I assumed everyone could do this. I was very surprised when my teacher told me that only mystical men and women and sometimes medicine men and women could do this.

In the time of visioning, maybe some elders could do it, but I was really surprised that other people in my tribe in general could not do this. I was told that it wasn't so much a matter of "couldn't do it"; it was just that they were born to do other things. When I got older, I would have the duties of a mystical man, but I might not have other duties that other people have. So that is how the teacher explained this to the child I was, and it made sense to a child. It was very simple, straightforward—"Oh, I get it," and you go on.

The Student Becomes the Teacher

How old were you when your teacher died?

My teacher died when I was about nineteen years old. I was fortunate to have my teacher for so many years. Then I had another teacher, so I was fortunate to have more than one. I worked with one teacher mainly, but then I worked with the other sometimes, too—and that person was alive a long time.

So there were two mystical men or women when you were born?

There was a mystical man and a mystical woman. The mystical woman was also very unusual and worked so closely with the medicine woman that both individuals acquired many of the skills and abilities of the other. This is how I had a teacher who lived on into my middle age. I was very lucky.

How old were you when you started teaching students?

Well, you'd be surprised. Even as a child—say seven or eight years old, certainly nine years old—I had some knowledge, and one of the teachers might say, "Okay, you work with this other youngster," because sometimes youngsters learn better from a young man. They called you a young man when you were nine years old because things were different then, and they also wanted to compliment you. That's considered a compliment with my people.

Teaching the Touch Walk

Then they gave you a simple assignment: to teach a child how to walk, for instance. They'd say, "Take the child out." The child might be two or three years old, a toddler, and you would walk this kind of walk so the child would see it and then would be encouraged to walk that way. You would recognize that the child was just learning how to walk like you did once. So you were not teaching the child exactly, but were supporting this type of walk—meaning, for instance, the touch walk, where you put your toes down first.

Of course, most of my people put their toes down first, but a child has to learn how to do this. If a child is not taught the touch walk where toes go down first, then the child might learn to walk by putting the heel down first. So he or she must see people putting their toes down first.

If you and the child were to go out for a walk—in the little one's eyes, even though you are big, you're still a child, not an adult—then the child would identify this as something he or she wanted to do. This is not just something adults do—you don't always relate to that the same if you are a child. But if another child is doing it, you want to do it.

And then sometime, maybe, if other boys or girls had the time, you would all go for a little walk near the village with the young child—take turns. Everybody would walk the touch walk and maybe the child would want to do it. You all would also look around—not just walk the touch walk. But you would all get your feet walking that way. In this way the child would look down at his or her feet and notice them, and then walk that way.

At that age children don't really understand what it's for or how it helps, but they just want to do what others are doing. So even if they can't do it because their muscles and bones aren't developed so well, they try to do it, and then it gives them motivation. As children are growing up, they keep trying to do it until their bodies grow into the task and they are happy they can do it. Of course, with that, they want to do it. That's how a child learns, of course. You teach a child to do something not by discipline, but by encouraging him or her to want to do it. Then the child does it his or her whole life to that child's benefit.

Family Life in the Tribe

How old were you when you got married?

When my wife and I came together and started our own family? I think it happened for me a little later than others, at about seventeen and a half or eighteen years old.

But some of them started younger?

That was normal. I'd say when you are about fourteen, fifteen years old, you're ready to take on the responsibility of marriage, but the physical body is usually ready in girls a little sooner. The female physical body is ready to have a child maybe around twelve or thirteen, but a girl is probably ready before a boy. My people usually encouraged youngsters to not take a wife or husband before fourteen or fifteen. But if the boy and girl have a profound connection that is very obvious to everyone, then thirteen is okay.

So then they go to their own tent or something?

They might create their own living space. They have to do it themselves. If you don't do it yourself, you'll never feel comfortable in it.

There is a division of labor. Everyone has a purpose. The hunters provide food, and the medicine woman provides for the whole group with plants. Each is on his or her own. When we had a chef, the chef would make something. Hunters would provide meat and so on, and people would prepare it. But the chef person (I say instead of cook, because she was creating all styles) would be experimenting with little bits of meat in different ways and eventually would find something that made the body feel better. She would prepare the whole thing for everybody and patiently explain how to make it. Then everybody would make it in their own family grouping—except for ceremonies, of course, or special celebrations when everybody made food for everybody else.

Inviting the Rain

We don't have that many examples of your work. Tell us of different times when the tribe would turn to you when it was life or death, or really serious.

Once we had a drought situation. The drought came from a particular direction. For us, the rain would usually come from the west, sometimes from the north. But we stopped getting rain from the west, and for a while we were only getting rain from the north.

When we used to send out hunting parties, we generally sent them out to the west and to the north because you're not going to find too many animals where there's no water. Our hunting parties reported that it was getting drier and drier there and there weren't very many animals. Hunting parties then just went out to the north, and the elders talked to me and said, "What do you think here?"

Since the elders had knowledge and wisdom passed on to them from previous generations, they said, "We have heard of this before. As long as we continue to get rain from the north, we can respect these conditions," meaning that the drought was considered part of the natural cycle. "But if the rain slows down from the north, then we have to move north obviously, since the rain stopped coming from the west first."

We believed that if we needed to move, we would move north. If it was the other way, rain coming from the west and not from the north anymore, then we would move west. So the elders said, "Do you think it is time to move? We felt we wanted to honor this drought, but we're concerned."

And I said, "Well, I will go north for a while. You can spare me?"

They said yes, so I said "I will go north for a few days"—meaning just north of the tribe—"and see if it is much wetter."

I walked maybe three or four days—walked a little bit at night—to see if it was a lot wetter in comparison. I did that and came back and said, "It was not much wetter when I walked three and a half days north than it is here."

So the elders said, "It might be time to ask when you need to invite the rain."

I did not invite the rain very often. Usually we would welcome the rain and the Sun and all of this, but we'd only invite the rain in conditions of drought. We'd have to be very respectful of Mother Earth's cycles. But after walking north and discovering that the ground was not much more saturated up there than near us, I felt I had sufficient permission to go invite the rain.

You cannot just look at the blue sky and invite the rain. We believe you have to talk to the clouds—in this case, not the clouds too obviously near where we were, but on the mesa. So I took a few days of food and water—rations—climbed up to the top of the mesa and waited for a cloud. I always looked and talked to cloud beings at a distance and could feel (using the wand) where the cloud beings were.

Up on top of the mesa, I could see farther than I could from the ground, of course. So one night the clouds were off in the north. I saw lightning flashing, but from the top of the mesa I could see clouds. I talked to the clouds and invited the rain to come. Because I was talking to the clouds that are in the north, I was also talking to the north.

Then I smelled the rain and the lightning, and this told me that the north wind blew down to me from the rain to feel me. (Otherwise, this storm was off far enough where I would not smell the rain or lightning very well—maybe just a hint of it—but I smelled it very strongly, as if the rain and lightning were right there.) This told me that the rain was bringing a storm of rain to me to smell me, to see what I was about and by so doing to see what my people were about.

I asked the clouds and wind to give me a sign whether my people needed to move farther north for a time, or whether the rain just needed to be welcomed more and feel strong feelings. The wind came up strong from the north, and I felt that the rain and storm were trying to embrace me using the wind. This told me that I needed to invite the rain.

So I worked on inviting and welcoming the rain. I stayed up on top of the mesa for about three days. Once the contact was made, then I could communicate for a while. All the time the smell was present, I could communicate—meaning that even though the storm had moved off, the wind was still bringing me the storm, hugging me, embracing me. So the rain still wanted to be encouraged, touching me.

I stayed up all night as long as I could strongly smell the rain and invited the rain, felt the rain, did certain things to call the rain. In short, I interacted with the rain. When the next storm came, in about another day and a half, I saw it coming very big from the north.

I did not see lightning, but I saw big clouds, cloud tops, before I saw the storm coming from the north. It was moving very slowly down with no embracing. I did all that I could to invite the rain, to welcome the rain, and the rain knew this. It did not need any further invitation. It came down from the north and stayed with us awhile.

People could not really go out and hunt, but we had things stored up. That's why we dried meat. I stayed up on the mesa and had to ration my food a bit, but I had plenty of water. I stayed up on the mesa another two days while the storm stuck around and gave us full rain. The streams that had not been running for a while were now running again, and everything was all right then.

So that would be an example of how to know when and how to invite rain so it feels welcome, instead of having everybody pack up, leave certain things and go north. And what I know is that the wind cooperated, brought me the rain's love. I smelled the rain and lightning that time and felt it blowing all around me. It was like the rain hugging me from a distance, and that's how I knew.

Wise Ones, Young and Old

How old were you then?

I do not think in terms of age, so it's difficult for me, but . . . maybe thirty-two, something like that. Already getting old.

Compared to your people, right?

My people would have an average life span (not a mathematical average)—taking out things like children dying at birth—a general lifetime of maybe mid-thirties, late thirties, something like that. Elders sometimes got to their early forties, but when you think about my age, I'm not exactly clear on that.

Mid-fifties, you said.

Yes. Fifty-four, fifty-five—I'm not clear on which year. That is very old. That's why I say ancient.

The elders and the wise men . . . did you know what they knew, or did they know things other than what you knew?

Wise men meaning elders, wise people? Sometimes we'd have elders with wisdom, but sometimes young people would be born with natural capacities for wisdom. They might bring wisdom into the tribe, but also they might be able to just have wisdom from inspiration, or maybe plants or stones gave or communicated wisdom to them—not unlike the process here [the channeling process], inspired wisdom from other beings, other times, something like that. So sometimes the elders and wise ones were not always the same beings. The elders were generally wise ones, but wise ones were sometimes younger.

Ocean Dreams and Bear Claw's Quest

Tell me of another time when who you are and what you can do made a difference because people learned from what you said. These are teaching stories.

Well, once I had a dream about a place that was not typical for my people: the ocean. I saw the waves coming in—peaceful, though. In my ocean dream it was just as if I was standing on the beach. I was curious about this dream. I asked several of my teachers, "What is this dream about?" They did not know.

I did not know what this dream was about for several years. Normally, I knew what dreams were about. I did not have the dream again, but remembered it. Many years later, working with Bear Claw, my student, he told me that he had been having a dream since he was a child. He had it about once a week, in terms of your calendar (we did not use a calender).

And I said, "What is this dream?"

He said, "It's like I'm standing on a beach looking at the ocean."

He described the exact same dream I had had, and I realized that the dream I had had was not my dream; I just shared his dream. This was a message for him.

So I said, "You are having this dream how many times?"

"Many, many times."

"You must go to this place. It will probably take you a year or two to get there. Stay there as long as you need to, to do whatever you're supposed to. Then come back."

He said, "When should I go?"

And I said, "Probably pretty soon. If you start at all having dreams, say, every other night, let me know. Then it will be time to go. If we do not see each other for some reason for a while, just go. When I come to your place and you are not there, your people will tell me you left. I will know."

So that's what happened. I didn't see him for a while, so I walked over to his place, but he was not there. People said, "Oh, he told us that he was supposed to go to this place. He's gone." Someone told me, "He will be gone for several years."

And I said, "Yes, most likely, but when he comes back, he will have vast amounts of knowledge and wisdom he'll be able to use."

I stayed there that night, and we exchanged some stories. They insisted I stay for dinner and tell stories, and I stayed. Then I walked to the next place.

The Story of Bear Claw and His Journey to the Ocean

About four or five years later, I saw Bear Claw again. He told me that he went to this place, had to walk. First he started to walk north and then realized he needed to walk south once he got to the ocean. He walked south for many, many days until he found the exact spot where the dream took place. He went down to the beach and stood in the exact spot where the dream took place.

He stood there with a feeling like he was expecting something. Nothing happened, so he found a place where he could sleep and stayed there for many weeks. Finally, he thought, "What a beautiful place. I have wonderful dreams here." He had learned a few things, but he was thinking about leaving, going back. By this time he had a family, a wife, children. He missed them very much, and he knew they missed him.

So he was thinking about going back. He said, "If nothing unusual happens, I'll go back in a day or two." Right then, an interesting thing happened. He heard sounds, woke up and saw whales. This was the first time ever any person I knew saw whales.

He saw something like light from behind one of the whales. Bear

Claw thought, "Is the Moon rising? Is that its glow behind the whale?" That would be the natural assumption, but this whale was moving very slowly.

As he glanced around the sky—kind of sleepy, as when you wake up and see that—then, of course, the Moon was over there. He thought, "It's not the Moon!" So he looked. When the whale came to the surface the way whales do, every time it hit the surface, there would be light behind the whale, but it was not the Moon. Bear Claw stayed up and watched this. Some whales went by, then other whales. Many whales went by.

Every time a whale broke the surface, there was light behind that whale. "What does this mean?" he thought to himself. He told me later, "I wish you were there to tell me what this meant."

When he told me this later, I said, "Probably I would have had no knowledge any better than you." Then we laughed about that.

Finally, just a little while before the Sun came up, he saw no more whales, but he did see the light. The light started coming closer, but it felt good, so he was not frightened or anything. The light got very close. It came up on the beach and stopped at just about the point where the water comes up to the beach and recedes. It did not come up on the dry part of the sand, but only so far out of the water, headed straight for Bear Claw.

Bear Claw got the feeling to walk toward the light. He walked toward it, and the light sort of leaned toward him, meaning welcome. So he walked toward the light, and it got brighter. As he got up to it, kind of shielding his eyes, he heard a gentle feminine voice say, "Step forward." So he kept stepping forward until the light was practically all over him, and still he heard the voice saying, "Step forward."

He stepped forward, and suddenly he was not on the beach anymore. He was somewhere else. He felt like he was asleep for a while —you could say like he "lost consciousness," but it didn't feel like blacking out; it felt like he went to sleep. He woke up and was somewhere else: not, I think, on the planet, very unusual. People there talked to him in a language he could not understand, and he wondered why not.

He walked around there for what felt like about a day. He did not get sleepy there, nor hungry or thirsty. There was no need for any of that. He walked around there all the time, and people talked to him in this unusual language. He did not know what it was about, but they gave him the freedom to walk all over. He said it was big, like a city. I know it was a city, though he did not describe it in that language. The buildings were clear; he could see through all the walls.

Sometimes people took him by the hand and led him all over the place, but he never understood what they were saying. He was kind of sad about that, because in my time we often ran across people we could not communicate with at all, but usually we would do some sign language or something. But to do sign language, you have to have a common culture at least—you have to come from the same planet.

On Earth, you can use sign language. You know you all have to eat and drink and so on, so basic sign language is readily available. But on that planet, the culture was different. People were short, shorter than Bear Claw. Bear Claw, by your standards, was not a tall man, but these people were much shorter, maybe two and a half feet tall. They were very cheerful, laughing all the time, with twinkling eyes. Bear Claw said he liked them very much, but he wished he knew what they were saying.

So at some point, he was outside the city, and then the light came. The next thing he knew, after a little sleep, he woke up on the beach. The water was close by but not washing up over him, and he said, "I do not know what that was about."

When he got back to the ocean, it was coming up on night again, so he said, "I will stay one more night, and then go back." That night he had an extraordinary dream and remembered every word. When he woke up in the morning, he still remembered most of the words—like a very intense dream, but pleasant. He woke up in the morning still a young man but with completely white hair. Unusual. It did not turn white from fear, just from some reason he never knew.

Bear Claw's Voice of Wisdom

His hair was all white, including his body hair. (And when it grew out, it was still white.) He did not know what this meant, but he discovered something interesting. When he noticed his long, white hair, he did the thing that people would naturally do. He immediately reached up to touch his hair—not that this would make it change back to its original black color, but it's natural to touch your hair.

The moment he touched his hair, a voice talked to him, saying things about the universe. And the minute he took his hands off his hair, the voice stopped. From then on he would grab his hair, hold it and hear a voice talking about the universe, the people in the universe. It was like thinking out loud. He said, "I wonder if this voice can tell me about the people I visited."

Immediately, the voice told him all about the people he visited and said that these people have the capacity to give to others this characteristic. The way the characteristic affects Earth people is that they always turn their heads away. The voice said that the people who gave him this ability do not know why, so they cannot prevent this, but they did not believe it would be a problem between Bear Claw and his family.

Bearclaw

Sakina
8 - 91

When Bear Claw realized he could communicate with the voice, back and forth, he asked the voice, "Can you tell me anything about life here on Earth?"

And the voice said, "I can tell you anything."

And so from that point on, Bear Claw used tales of cultures on other planets to tell stories to people only when they wanted to hear them. The voice talked to him, and he repeated what the voice said later on when he got home. Other than that, any time Bear Claw saw some plant being or animal being, he already knew how to talk to that being. After communicating with an animal or plant, he then asked the voice (holding his hair every time), "Is there anything about this communication that I can do better?" Or would say things like, "Is there anything you recommend I say to this being?" Or, "Can you help me to know when the plants or animals need help that I can give?"

In short, Bear Claw had a teacher, even though he was far from that teacher. He was unable to pass the skill on; he could not pass it on himself. But for the rest of his life, aside from doing mystical-man work, he was also available not only for his own people, but to spread the word around a little bit to any other tribal people who had questions. That voice seemed to be able to answer many questions. To no question did the voice say, "I don't know," none of that.

So Bear Claw passed this wisdom on whenever it was needed. Sometimes at a celebration or gathering, after everybody told their stories, if the gathering lasted long enough, people might ask Bear Claw to ask the voice to talk about other places where "people like us" live, meaning tribal peoples—"Tell us about other places where people like us live. Where are they and all of that?"

No one ever asked, "Tell us about home," because tribal people always knew about home. This was passed on from your ancestors, so you always knew who you were—that you were living on Earth, that you love her nurturing you, but home was elsewhere.

That's wonderful. Did you ever find out who . . . do you know who the voice was?

Never knew.

Can you ask from your expanded state now?

I do not need to know. It's like questioning a gift. If someone brings you a gift, you don't say, "Where did you get this?" You say, "Thank you."

I just wondered if it was Zoosh or something.

I do not think so. I know Zoosh well enough to say that I do not think this was Zoosh.

So how did you feel when he told this story? That was incredible!

Oh, it was wonderful. We were both very excited, and I said, "Can you show me?" He said, "Oh, yes," and grabbed his hair and started telling me what the voice said. The voice was describing whatever it was talking about then. Then he asked the voice to tell me something about mountains. He said this and that—nothing worth repeating now, but interesting things for us—and I said, "This is wonderful."

Did you ever go to get information on something that . . . ?

No, I have things in place. Spirit. Animal. Plant. Stone. Mother Earth's body. I never have to do that. Most mystical men and women do not do that. Bear Claw also trained with me in a traditional way. He does not really have to ask that being about things, but it is like a link. After a while, we all thought of it as a link through this being between us and other places. Anyway, I found out why I had a dream about the ocean.

Oh, that's a wonderful story. How old did Bear Claw live to be? How many years did he have this gift until he died? Five? Ten?

I could tell you about how many years Bear Claw was when he died. Bear Claw was maybe forty-nine when he passed away.

Oh, so he was a young man in his twenties when he went to the ocean?

Yes, a young man.

More about Bear Claw's Journey

Do you realize what an awesome, incredible thing this is . . . one person crosses half the United States by himself?

It was a long way. It took him a little over a year to get there—a long walk. Of course, he could not just walk, but had to stop to hunt, eat and do the other things of life. Sleep. Survive. And if he came across other people . . . since Bear Claw was already trained, at least partially, to be a mystical man, he might come across people he could help. He'd have to be cautious sometimes. He didn't know these people, if they were friendly. But he could usually tell from a distance whether people would be friendly or not.

He would also come across different animals sometimes. He didn't know who the animals were, but if he needed to know, he could walk over to the tracks after the animal was long gone. He would try to make sure that he was not in the animal's scent, that he was downwind, and then he'd walk over to the track, feel the track, get a feeling whether the animal was safe or dangerous and so on—like that—and then go on.

What about the people? How did he know from a distance? Long touch?

No, that would not be right. But he was trained to look for certain qualities, like kindness, and also to look for the people's communication with others—with animals or plants or their spirits, at least some kind of communication. When communication was going on, he could tell at a distance, without invading their energy, whether the people talking were speaking from the heart or speaking from the head. When they were speaking from the heart, he could feel at a distance very gently without taking energy, because the body responds with warmth in the chest.

If they were speaking from the heart, probably they were good people. But if they were speaking from the head, he'd keep his distance. I do not recommend that everybody do this, because it has to be done very carefully so as to not invade the energy of other people. You use the long touch but do not touch the person. Rather, you touch the energy body way out at the outer boundary so it is not invasive.

But that would be a survival tactic.

Yes, it is a survival tactic, but also, if you feel these people have heart, then maybe you come out and wave or something, and they wave and go on. Maybe you feel they have something else to do or they wave and come over and ask who you are, and you try to communicate. "I am a mystical man on a quest," you say, but in your own way of communicating. Maybe you go like this: You point your hand up to the sky, then down toward your heart, then forward in the direction you are going. They understand you are on a quest.

Where was this beach Bear Claw journeyed to?

It was mid to northern California.

So he needed to cross the Rocky Mountains.

Yes, but he was guided. He took the easiest possible route, mountain passes, you understand—what would now be considered to be natural routes where they would put highways. Then it just took awhile. He walked, he hiked, he tried to do it in the warmth of day. He also went in the time of year when it's fairly warm, and he didn't go up to the peaks, if he could avoid it.

Of course, he brought along a few things. Not too much stuff, because he would have to carry everything, but he brought along a blanket, something to cover himself with. It was not exactly a blanket, but something he covered himself with. When it got cold, he had his garment set up in such a way that he could wear it.

What about the whales? Were they spirit whales or were they real whales?

Bear Claw said they were real beings.

Black and white or big sperm whales? Can you describe them?

Looked like a gray color.

Real whales?

Whales. Whales must have something to do with the beings. I do not know what.

That's a wonderful story. These stories are just beautiful. Thank you very much.

Speaks of Many Truths
December 1, 1999

For you readers, especially those who have read *Shamanic Secrets for Material Mastery*, you can see that my intention in creating this book for you is to help you to move forward on the path of physical things that you can do in your day-to-day life to create greater harmony—not only for you as an individual, but as with the *Material Mastery* book, what you can do for the Earth.

In the next book we will be talking about spiritual mastery. These are things that can help to unify you even more with the world of spirit around you, which might even take form from time to time. I will also give you things that you can do to connect better to spiritual beings from other places and even from other times who might be able to help you here.

The books in this series are all designed to actually simplify your life, to give you physical things that you can do that have physical effects on you and sometimes on others, as in the case of the *Material Mastery* book. That is the intention so that you can improve your day-to-day life in ways that can move you through the blocks and barriers that seem to be present all the time, that you can never get past. When you cannot get past blocks and barriers, it is because you need to do something physical and spiritual.

It's not just something mental. When you do mental things, it is very useful. It can help you to think in a new way, which is very often helpful. But if you focus only on the mental, it may *not* be able to help you very well with changing your physical and felt and day-to-day experiential life into something more benevolent.

Thank you for your interest in these books. I can promise you that the next book, which will be called *Shamanic Secrets for Spiritual Mastery*, will be as detailed as this and the previous one, *Material Mastery*. We will make some effort to give you more visual things to use and understand, and to apply, perhaps, to your own part of the world, so that you can feel an increasing and greater intimate connection with the physical, spiritual and material worlds all around you.

Appendix A

Living Prayer

Speaks of Many Truths

Living prayer allows you as an individual to give to the Earth. So many of you ask, "What can I do for the Earth? What can I do for the animals? What can I do for people suffering in other parts of the world or in my own town or family? What can I do?"

If people are suffering on the other side of the Earth, you can say, "May the people be nurtured and know they are loved. May their hearts be healed and may they find what they need, or may it be brought to them in a benevolent, beneficial way for all beings."

Say this key phrase—"I will ask," or "I am asking"—out loud, though perhaps softly. This way it is understood that what you are asking is about physical things. In the case of a war on the other side of the world, you might say, "I ask that everyone's heart be healed and that they find peace together in the most benevolent and beneficial way for them."

Let's say you are driving through the forest and there is no one else around. Suddenly your heart hurts. It is a dull ache. When you get used to this living prayer, you will look around and say, "I will ask." The moment you say that key phrase, Creator knows that you are saying a living prayer. "May the heart of the forest be healed. May the hearts of all the trees, plants, rocks, animals and spirits who like to be here be healed. May they enjoy their time in the forest and feel welcome."

Then go on. Your heart will probably feel better. If you get the feeling again farther up the road, say it again without looking at them, "May their hearts be healed. May they feel welcome wherever they go or where they are."

Remember, you have to say these blessings only once for each place, person or group of people. You are more sensitive now, and the plants and the animals and the stone and maybe even other people are more sensitive, too. You all need each other more now than ever, and here is something you can do to help others and feel better yourself.

Try not to look directly at people who cause your heart to hurt. Some other part of your body may hurt sometimes when you are near people who are suffering in some way. First ask that their hearts be healed, then add other parts of them according to what hurts on you. You don't have to name the organ unless you feel sure; just say the place on the body.

It is intended now that many people begin giving and asking for such prayers. As Mother Earth and her rocks, trees, plants and animals come under more strain in your time due to so many people and their needs, these natural forms of life may no longer be able to give you the healings and blessings they have been doing simply by being and radiating their good health. So you can now give to them in return for all their generations of benevolence. These prayers are all they ask.

Appendix B

Mantras of Feeling and Optimistic Vision

Zoosh

A few years ago it was popular in New Age circles to speak as if something had already taken place that you desired to take place—"speaking as if," they called it. It wasn't really about whether it would work or not; it was to prepare you.

Many have had dreams and nightmares of [catastrophes, but now that] you are Creator juniors (not quite on Creator level—a little ways to go yet), it is time for you to say, "Well, these concerns might be legitimate. However, I feel that it could be better. Better things could happen. More benevolent things could happen—unification, comforts, loves, insights and so on," whatever words you wish to say. Keep it simple.

While others around you are saying, "Woe is me," say, "Well, it could get better." Say it with feeling, not just words. Say that, and you will fulfill the function and the purpose of such visions, which is to trigger your Creator-junior status to change it.

That is what these things are about. If enough of you do that, it [a catastrophe] not only will not happen, it *cannot* happen.

Appendix C

Claiming the Good Life

Zoosh

Accept on a personal level that you deserve to have a good life and that you can most easily attain it if everyone in the world has that same opportunity and feels and knows that it is possible.

Say, "I claim the good life for me."

Build a time-line toward the future: "I deserve the good life."

When you feel good as you say it, that means you don't have any blocks to it in the way at that moment.

If you are uncomfortable saying it, do the love-heat/heart-warmth/physical-warmth exercise [pp. 7–8]. Then say, "I deserve the good life. I am safe; it is safe for me to have the good life."

Appendix D

A Lesson in Benevolent Magic

Zoosh
January 23, 1999

Let's start off with benevolent magic. It is time to take a conscious, aware step toward changing your reality. It has been useful in the past to experience what exists, then unconsciously change it or work with it. Now one cannot wait any longer for changes to occur.

I'm going to suggest what to do about changing your reality. If you are around children, this will be easier. If you are not around children, then you will have to wait for your opportunities. Your opportunities are as follows:

When people around you are laughing, cheerful, happy or joyful, simply take note of it and observe from a distance. If you are involved, note your cheerfulness, your laughter, and be that quite sincerely. If you are observing, however, look at the happy people, especially if they are laughing just for fun, or because they heard an amusing story, or because, being children, they are having a good time. Focus on it, then turn away and look at something else. Try to look at a neutral scene such as trees, the sidewalk, cars—whatever is available—and stay in that feeling of joy.

What is going on in your society all the time are moments of joy and happiness, but these moments of joy and happiness are bursts of happiness, yes? They are not sufficient to sustain benevolence for you all anymore, so I'd like you to begin to spread it around. After you have glanced quickly at it, notice that it cheers you up. It is especially important to smile at it if it cheers you up. Then look at something neutral, and if you can, glance back to the cheerful scene and again look at something neutral. Hopefully, it will be something in your environment that you see every day. Now, this will not work if you are looking at a movie or a television program. The emotion has to be demonstrated by *living people*.

If you can, then look at something that is either unpleasant or that usually annoys you, and you will notice that it doesn't annoy you as much. This is not a profound revelation. You all know that if you look at something that annoys you while you are laughing, it usually doesn't annoy you as much. This is a way of becoming consciously involved in that process so that you are like a farmer—you are reaping the excess happiness. You are not draining it from people; you are just an observer. It's just like picking an apple off a tree that has many apples; one will not be missed.

Look at something that might be annoying or is usually annoying for a moment; don't dwell on it. Notice that it doesn't annoy you as much. When you can do this around your home, ultimately things that annoy you—even if people aren't around laughing—will not annoy you so much.

This is really a way of seeing your world and making it different. It is simple. You will not remember to do it all the time, but when you do, it might be something to experiment with. Consider it an experiment, because we will build on this later. It is interesting to note that the electronic media (such as television) are not things you can draw energy from. It has to be people. It can be people laughing at the television, but it must be people. It can be people laughing at something on the radio, but it cannot be pulled *from* the TV or the radio. If you do that, you will simply pull the electromagnetic radiation and will not feel very good.

It is not that there is an immediate crisis, but there is a tendency now to become overinvolved in the dramatic. The dramatic is there to catch your attention, to relieve you of the need to create dramas of your own. But it is necessary to begin making an effort to change your reality, not through your will, but through a conscious effort to utilize the excess joy. There is not a crisis. I just want you to begin to do this.

Appendix E

Disentangle from Your Discomforts and Pains
Become Your True Self

Ssjoooo
July 12, 2000

---

the
DISENTANGLEMENT
Basic Process

Lie on a flat surface on your back, hands by your side, palms down and slightly away from your body—preferably three hours after eating and before you go to sleep, but it works anywhere, anytime. Do not cross your legs or feet. This position allows you to get used to being vulnerable in your most receptive area.

Say out loud (if possible), "I ask golden lightbeings to disentangle me from my pains and discomforts. If other teachers or guides or lightbeings of other colors want to help, I ask them to assist the golden lightbeings."

Squeeze your eyelids shut and then focus on the light patterns—don't think. If you catch yourself thinking, gently bring your attention back to the light patterns and continue. Do this for an hour or as long as you feel to do it or until you fall asleep. This can be done twice a day.

After a few weeks, make a list of every person and event in your life that makes you feel uncomfortable. Say the above statement and add, "I am asking to be disentangled from the discomfort and pain of _____," reading one or two names or events from the list. Do each name for two or three days or until you feel clear with the person/event.

Speaks of Many Truths Adds:

"You may notice that if you say those specific words or names during the course of your day, after you've done disentanglement on them three or five times, you no longer feel as physically uncomfortable about them as you once did.

"This means the disentanglement is working. The objective is to feel physically calm. Keep saying those specific words or names in your disentanglement process until you feel physically calm. When you do, move on to other words or names, never more than one or two at a time."

I will speak of postcreation now. You understand, postcreation . . . a leaf lives its life, seasons change, it falls from the tree, say, where people don't rake it up [chuckles], and then gradually it disintegrates into the ground. As it's disintegrating and becoming soil, we can say that that's postcreation. You can think of a number of other examples, of course. For the human being, however, this form of postcreation does not mean that your body is returning to Earth.

There is a point where a creation of the moment starts to uncreate itself; though things may or may not actually dissolve, creation starts to move on. Creation can be something as simple as seeing your friend on the street unexpectedly and saying, "Oh, it's so good to see you!" You give your friend a hug or shake hands or give a pat on the shoulder, and go on. That moment is a creation, and when you go on, it dissipates—it goes away. So let's use that as an example of the form of disentanglement we're going to do. You can understand that more easily because it is clearly a moment.

Now, you all have moments throughout your life where you connect with things, with people. Let's say you have a friend you have known for years, but you had a misunderstanding. You see him on the street and you are happy to see him. You give him a pat on the back and shake hands and so on, yet you are uncomfortable and so is he. You're both rushing somewhere and you say, "I'll call you!" And off you go. But you have an uncomfortable feeling. This tells you, aside from having to talk things over with your friend, that it would be of value to disentangle from that past situation.

The Disentanglement Exercise

So postcreation, disentanglement—I'm not going to give all the instructions, but I want to give people homework. For those who meditate, simply do your basic relaxation/meditation. Try not to think of too many words. After you're relaxed, request that gold lightbeings come and remove the discomforting cords that connect you to all your past discomforts in this life, period. Say no more than that—it's a good beginning. If you've had an upsetting incident—some person, a circumstance, a problem at work—you can be specific. But you need to be *generally* specific: You'll ask that the gold lightbeings come; you'll say that opening statement, but instead of saying, "Disentangle me from all discomforts of the past," you will say, "Please disentangle me from that argument I had at work today." You don't say, ". . . that I feel so bad about." You're very specific, but at the same time you don't give a lot of details. They'll know, but you need to say it when you're beginning to do this work.

You don't write it; you say it.

Don't write it; say it out loud. You can take notes before and after about your impressions if you want to, but during it, you just lie there. And you need to make an effort to not think. For those of you who can already do that, just go ahead. For others, I'm going to give you a trick you can use: Squeeze your eyes really tight (it would be best for this to be in a darkened room, even if it's daylight), but not so tight that it's uncomfortable. Then release them, and you will be able to see light patterns if you stare at your eyelids. Keep your eyes closed, though, during the process, and look at those light patterns. Or if you can imagine standing in front of a white wall, look at that. In short, do things that are inclined to cause you to think less. If you catch yourself thinking, don't worry about it; go back to looking at your eyelids [chuckles]—closed, of course—or the white wall as best you can. That's the beginning of disentanglement. It is going to evolve, but that's how you begin.

A Second Stage of Homework

For those who want a second stage of homework, I'll give you that now as well. After you've done this for a few weeks—and when you're not doing the disentanglement exercise—write down a list of all the people you're in any way uncomfortable with. You don't have to write it down in any order, but write it down—everything you can think of, including all the incidents or circumstances you can remember that make you feel uncomfortable when you think about them. When I say "uncomfortable," I don't mean sick to your stomach; I mean even annoyed. Something happened and there was a misunderstanding, or there were times when you felt someone might have judged you—anything, all right? [Chuckles.] And you don't have to write it down in detail; write down just enough that you know what it's about. It will take a few weeks, because you'll add things off and on.

Then you can do the second stage of the homework. It would be best to say this before you lie down to do your relaxation. Say, "I request that gold lightbeings disentangle me from . . ." You can either say, ". . . all these things I've written down," but you have to glance at the pages (don't read it; just glance at it), or you can pick out two or three—no more than that—and say, ". . . disentangle me from," for instance, "that event," and use a key word: "that happened in 1987." Something like that. Be to the point so that you know what it's about, but don't dwell on it. Lie down and relax, and it will take as long as it takes. You cannot time it and say, "Well, it'll take a half-hour."

The best time to do this is before you go to sleep at night, but you need to lie on your back with your arms at your sides and your palms touching the mattress or the couch or the ground. That's what I recommend.

Some of you will fall asleep during this, so it will be accomplished to some degree, or not. I really feel that the first stage is the most important, because the gold lightbeings will find what you need to be disentangled from. They will also tend to take things out of your body that are discomforts. So you could say it's a healing practice. But the reason I want you to consider using it for specific things is that there's a follow-up observation you could make. It's not something you need to keep notes on, but you can if you like. At some point you're going to work all the way through your list. Saying two or three things a night, naming names or events, "Disentangle me from . . ."—at some point you'll work through your whole list. Then you can say, "Disentangle me from all my discomforts," going back to the first original statement.

Attitudinal Changes after Disentanglement

You will notice either that you feel different physically or attitudinally; you're not thinking about things the same way you did. It can change your whole life. Because Earth is a school, most people here are affected by everything they have created or have participated in with somebody else, which then becomes somewhat your creation as well, at least your part of it. Because of that school effect, your personality is driven by the events that have happened to you in your life—including the good things, of course. You're not going to ask to be disentangled from benevolent things or good memories; you don't do that.

So most likely you will notice attitudinal changes. You will also notice that many things might change. I don't want to say too much. You can keep notes on that if you like. Now, how long might you expect it to take and what might you expect to feel? Some of you might feel a sense of electricity in your body; it might be difficult to remain perfectly still, which is helpful for the beings who are working on you. (This is at all stages, not just the second stage we're talking about here.) If you feel that electricity or if your body suddenly . . . I'm doing this as an example.

It looks like an electrical tremor.

Yes, if your body suddenly jerks like that, do not worry about it. Since some of the beings will be working in the electrical realm, those who are working in the magnetic realm will have a different effect on you, but you might feel as if you have to move. Don't be afraid; it's just that your muscles are being stimulated with electricity, and basic science tells you that if you do that to a muscle, it contracts. So you might feel tense; don't worry about that. It will go away.

Ask to be given a sign that you're done for that session. You can do it any time of the day, but the best time to do it is before you go to sleep at night. That may not be best for everybody because of other things you might be doing. You might be exhausted and fall asleep, or turn over on your side or your stomach. They can do a little bit when you're asleep, but they can't really do a lot. So you can lie down in the afternoon or the early evening, before you would go to sleep (most people sleep at night, but not everybody), or if you sleep during the day, then try to darken the room and proceed. Try to make sure that phones are not going to disturb you because that will break the flow. I'm not going to go over everything like this because most of you are doing some of these things as it is. If there are questions later, I will respond to them.

When you ask for a sign, ask for something benevolent; don't ask for the phone to ring [chuckles] because it might happen. It's better to say, "I would like to have a feeling when it's over." It is most likely going to take anywhere from twenty minutes to an hour and a half. If you've managed to stay conscious for the first half-hour to forty-five minutes or so and then you fall asleep, that's all right.

Now, there is another matter. Some of you are more electrical than others in your basic makeup. There are many gold lightbeings who are magnetic in nature as well. You will feel something that is your opposite. You will start to feel more relaxed; that is all right as well. I'm mentioning this because some of you, by your nature, are more electrical. Any questions about the process so far?

You answered one of my questions—"If you fall asleep, do you lose some of the value?" You said yes. What are you saying that we can clear? You use the word "discomforts."

Everything. I am saying you can clear almost everything. Obviously, if you've been in an accident and you're missing a finger or something, you're not going to grow a new one. Or if a loved one was killed in an accident, he or she is not going to reappear in your life. The whole point is to disentangle you from the pain in your past that is driving you to display certain personality traits that are not your actual personality. When your personality is not being driven by past pains and miseries, most of you become much different. You'll tend to be very calm and your sense of humor will be up. You might even notice that you're more polite [chuckles]. It is not a politeness driven by conditioning or culture, but a greater consciousness of the needs of human beings in general. You simply become more gentle with people.

More respectful, more aware, more . . .

Yes, but it is not your job to know what everyone is feeling. Rather, it is your job to allow others to feel that way and to offer help if asked, if you choose to and if you have something that will benefit them.

The Long-Term Process of Disentanglement

When the disentanglement process has gone a long way, after you've gone through your list, you will think of other things over the weeks and months, and you'll write those down. Many times they will disentangle you from things you can't remember, things that happened when you were a baby, things that were so traumatic. Everybody has those. They will do that, but of course they would like to disentangle you first from things you perceive as priorities. You don't have to keep a book about how much better you feel after the first night or the first session of doing this. This is a long process.

Even though you might go through your whole list, the disentanglement process has to continue because there are often things that you haven't noticed happening in your life, things that you need to disentangle yourself from. Maybe you hurt somebody's feelings without knowing it; maybe somebody hurt *your* feelings but you didn't notice it. This happens profoundly often in your society, because people (I'm speaking to people in the United States at the moment) are used to a certain level of pain. Adults and even young children get used to a level of pain, and it tends to make you somewhat cynical, to say nothing of wearing you out and making you sick. Very often your body will get sick to tell you, "Hey, something's wrong. Let's remove this pain; let's do some disentanglement." Your body knows how to do disentanglement; you don't have to instruct it on how to do it. But you need the help of beings who can do the disentangling who will not be affected by it. That's why we request gold lightbeings; they function very well on Earth, and the gold light contains the other colors of the spectrum.

During the first few weeks, just do stage one of the homework. Then after you go through your list, start keeping notes if you want, if you see that there's a difference in you. Notice that this might make you more sensitive, but that is a good thing. I want to give you something you can do so that other people's discomforts or the discomforts in general around you—animals' discomforts or Mother Earth's discomforts and so on—do not always affect you. You can radiate, do the heat-in-the-chest exercise [see pp. 7-8]. You can also picture gold light inside you, make a tone, any tone, and let that gold light radiate outward. Always try to start it inside you and let it radiate. That way it will tend to push out the discomforts that are in there.

If you create a shell around you, it will simply trap the discomforts within you [chuckles] inside that shell, sustaining that level of pain. The whole point is, we want to let go of pain. We want to let go of the things that prompt and drive people to be the way they are—submissive, bossy, angry (fill in whatever adjective you want to), fearful, aggressive, violent, enraged and in pain. It's profoundly true that without disentanglement, in most of your societies on Earth, adults are not really adults. They're living out the pain of their childhood. They might learn to do things as big children [chuckles], but they are still living out the unresolved pain. That's why I do not expect you to remember to list everything. But once you do the first stage and then make the list and do the second stage and go through that, the gold lightbeings will then understand what you are trying to do. And they will continue to do things.

When you get to the second stage, don't eliminate the first stage's statement; you'll say you want to be disentangled from all your discomforts. We're using "discomforts," but you can say, "from all my pain," or other things, but be careful not to say, "from all my anger." Anger, actually, is useful sometimes. I'm not saying that self-destructive anger is useful, but sometimes it is the energy—on a low-key level of anger—that causes you to be more assertive at a time when you need to be and so on.

It is better to say, "Disentangle me from all my discomforts." When you say "discomforts," that is something you know will pass. You have something uncomfortable, but you've had uncomfortable things before and they passed and you went on. Understand? So "discomforts" is an accessible word to people, a free word. It means that there's motion in and out, whereas if you say, "Disentangle me from my pain," you can say it only if you have something specific going on. Your mind might say, "Gee, I've had that pain for years and years." In short, it may not seem like something you can go in and out from. We want to use a word that describes it sufficiently to the gold lightbeings, but doesn't sound crushing to you. So the choice of words is sometimes useful.

Now, at some point you're going to feel that you've gone through your list and you can't think of anything else to say. By that time you will have come up with other words that work for you, or you will have been inspired to come up with other words. Always ask for what you want; don't ask for what you *don't* want. At some point, then, you will simply be saying these words that work for you, to preset what you want the gold lightbeings to do for you. You don't have to be exclusive; if you sense that there are white or pink lightbeings or something like that around, you can welcome them. But you'll need to say something like, "I will welcome gold lightbeings and other lightbeings" or "white lightbeings"—whatever—"who can work through the gold light or through gold lightbeings." Say it just like that.

Some of you will know white lightbeings whom you'll want to participate. Don't use names if you can help it, because they will come with lots of other connotations. That's what I'd recommend. Not only are there lots and lots of gold lightbeings you've never heard of or will probably never hear of here (and white lightbeings, for that matter), but if you say a name you might normally feel good about, at deeper levels you might not feel that way. You can say what you want and see how it works, but it is my job to teach the way I feel is best. People might want to say "Jesus" or someone who is a deity to them. But when you say that, you will think of that being the way you know that being to be *at that time* of your life, whereas by simply saying "gold lightbeings" or "white lightbeings," that being, if it can help you, will be there. That's sufficient. Words that *describe* the being will be limiting. Otherwise, it will be able to come in its entirety, or in its pure state, without being limited by your preconception of what that being is.

The process of having yourself disentangled can easily take months. It is an ongoing process that is something you do on a daily basis. It's very helpful once it gets going for you, and you can feel it. Your personality will change, but you will not become something you don't know. You will, in that sense, have demonstrated various characteristics in your personality that you're conscious of (or not) that either you or other people perceive. In short, you will be happy to notice that you are acting and being and feeling so much more like yourself.

Some people will react well to this. Some might be people you don't really know, and they might become new friends. Other people may not react so well, and you will have to decide whether you want to keep them as friends. As more of your pure personality comes forth (by "pure," I do not mean something that is more spiritual than other people; I simply mean your actual personality, not restricted by the pain of the past), you'll have to decide whether you want to continue to see people who might criticize you for not being this painful personality they used to know. You can tell them as much or as little as you think they can hear about your process, tell them why it's working for you and what you're getting out of it. It's up to you. I'm not trying to drag you away from people or break up relationships or friendships; it's just something you need to know could happen. People who are with you might perceive you in ways that draw relationships more closely together. This is much more likely. But the unexpected is also possible, and you need to know about that.

Connection Homework

After several months of doing this, you will most likely notice changes. I'm not telling you everything about it, but I will perhaps say more about it at some point in the future, or Speaks of Many Truths or Zoosh or Isis will. Someone else might comment on it, and that's fine, too. I want to say a bit about the other aspect. It's a little too soon to talk about connection, and I don't want you to work on connection first. But I want to give you an outline of how connection works.

After several months of doing disentanglement, after you work through your whole list . . . your list will probably be pages and pages and pages long, but don't let that alarm you. It takes awhile, but it's worth taking the time. Sometimes you might say two or three names, and the next night you may say the same two or three names because you don't feel finished. This could go on for a week. That's all right, and it's not unusual, especially with people in the past or even in the present (don't eliminate the present) with whom you have a great deal of enmeshment (I think that's the popular word of today)—that is, it's uncomfortable. It could take a long time, but that's all right, because it's intended to be homework that you do for the rest of your life. [Chuckles.] It's not temporary. It's homework that you were intended to be able to do when you were born here. In ancient days, societies knew about this. They called it something else, but they knew about it. And some societies still know about it.

The basic connection homework, though, is this: You've gone through all of that [your list] and are now just using the basic words to disentangle things that you don't know about, but the gold lightbeings are working on it. You will already have asked for gold lightbeings and said your disentanglement words. Then you will say, "I will also request that connections be made for me with beings or other energy sources that will improve the quality of my life." These connections will be made and the energies will connect to you. It won't be for specific incidents, but it will be an ongoing thing. You don't say it just once; every night (or whenever you do your disentanglement work), you say your disentanglement words first, then you say your connection phrase, and then you lie down and the work is done. That's as much as I want to say now, because I've really given you about six months' worth of homework.

The reason we don't do the connections work first or with the disentanglement right away is that it's too complicated for the gold lightbeings. Picture yourself inside a ball of yarn or something like that—a massive amount of cords are going every which way. They want to clear you off first as much as they can. Then doing the connections is easier for them and better for you. That's why I've given it in that order. I gave you a little more than I intended to right now, but it's the basic work and I feel that it will be very helpful to a great many of you. With the disentanglement, you let go of all that stuff, but with the connections, we are helping to improve your life. You first become yourself, then we improve your life with what you want. You don't say, "I want connections to get a new car"—not any of that stuff. The connections will be the energy that will support whatever you want in your life. And later on, maybe other beings, or even myself, will give other things you can say for connections. But this is sufficient for now.

Connections Knowledge in Ancient Tribes

This is absolutely awesome! You say that some ancient tribes knew this, but when was it decided to give this to everyone?

When human beings as you know them today started running around on the surface of planet Earth, they were much more open to spirit. They didn't know that they had to be certain ways [chuckles]. In short, they were people living more by the sacred. The sacred, in the early days, had to do with paying attention to how things are here and trying to get along with all life—in short, harmony. This is often identified in your time by shamans or mystical people who will almost always have a relationship with what is called here the natural world—meaning the Earth, plants, animals, elements, rain, lightning.

Now, these people were given this homework, and you can relate to some of them. I can't say that all Native American tribes still have this wisdom, but some do. Some have been given the wisdom more than once, when the tribes were decimated. The same goes for native peoples who can trace their roots back in Australia, New Zealand, Canada, Africa and all these places, even peoples in Scotland in the early days, going way back.

You see, in the early days people didn't really populate cold areas very much because they couldn't live there. Granted, the climate was different and the planet was more temperate. Ice ages, as you know them scientifically, came later. You could live in northern Canada and it would be balmy year round. There is scientific evidence for this; it's been thoroughly researched and discussed in other books. I mention this to suggest that the native peoples were born in those lands not only because their souls chose to be, but because in the early days they were setting the pattern on Earth so that Earth would know how to respond to their needs. They were also setting their internal patterns for their cultures so that those born to those cultures all over the Earth would be inclined to be cooperative with those cultures and want to embrace their interaction with Earth and all beings upon it.

So that disentanglement and connections work was given to them, but in those early days when harmony was much more of a factor, disentanglement and connections did not seem any more important than anything else. As a matter of fact, it seemed in some ways less important because of the harmonious condition of life.

Well, they didn't have all the strings in the yarn like we have now.

That's right. It seemed to them like something that might be useful in certain situations. It would be something they'd be more inclined to not pass on. It would be something they didn't remember. Thus it was something that sort of fell away after a while. Some peoples managed to maintain it for longer, or it was given again in inspirations.

The early peoples had it, and some have managed to maintain it over the years or else had it renewed if they've maintained the contact on a spiritual/inspirational level with the ancients who preceded them. That's how some peoples who still exist here have managed to maintain this wisdom. But a great many people in this modern society—especially those involved in the pursuit of the intellect for its own sake—don't know about it. In your time and in these conditions, it is vital and really can change your life. It requires a great deal of patience. Because of your societies, you are culturally conditioned to rush, rush, hurry, hurry—"What can I do fast? How long will it take?" But if you know that it's intended to take the rest of your life and if it works for you, you will pass it on to your children or to those who ask as you become more familiar with how it works. Then it doesn't become rush, rush, hurry, hurry. It just becomes something you do on a daily basis because it improves the quality of your life.

Disentangling from Soul Lessons and Cellular Memory

This is absolutely astounding. One of the beings said through Robert that a soul comes into this life and wants to do certain things, but it sets up certain lessons first. But what happens is, those lessons create such trauma in the cellular memory of the physical body that the soul can't really do what it wants to do.

But you remember, some time ago your friend Zoosh told you that karma was over. What he didn't say is that you do not have to come in with lessons anymore. Think about what that means. When Zoosh said, "Karma is over," it was a while back. That meant that the children being born then were without lessons. This does not mean that they do not experience things in their lives, that they didn't come in to learn new things, but that they didn't come in with soul lessons in the same sense. That's why people have noticed, "The new children—oh, look how they are!" and so on. What I will say is that yes, you need to disentangle from that stuff.

The result of the lessons we took on.

That's right. But if lessons are no longer so vitally important, then it is possible to change your life. If you could let go of your karma . . . the whole point of the disentanglement is to disentangle you from your pain, but it also disentangles you (those of you who were born before recent times) from those lessons you came in with. That's why it takes time. If you were born with those lessons, you continue to do your disentanglement until you die. But if you were born without those lessons (you can track when Zoosh said that—it was pretty close to the precise moment), the disentanglement will be easier for you. So this is a process that youngsters can do, those youngsters people like to call the "new children." The disentanglement process will go at different paces for different people. Youngsters may not even feel the need for it, but if you're a youngster experiencing some pain, you can do it, you can try it. It can't hurt you; it's very benevolent. You don't have to give up your religion to do this [chuckles]. I can assure you, one of the first things all religious deities do when they start communicating to those who make notes or try to leave messages or pass on the wisdom these beings have to offer, is tell you how to live on Earth in a better way. [Chuckles.] Therefore, this is one of the first things they talk about.

This will clear what we have called cellular memory, where trauma is in our cells? We aren't aware of them, but they still run our attitudes, our emotions, our feelings, our choices . . .

It will clear it if you maintain it. If you do it a couple or three times and stop, it won't. If you do it for six months and stop, it won't.

It's the continuous application.

It's continuous, that's right. It will clear the drive to resolve things, but that doesn't mean things won't happen in your life. It does mean that you will react in ways that are more clearly your own personality rather than in ways other people told you how to be. This will allow you to give the gift of your personality to many more people than have seen it. Sometimes people will say, "Oh, that guy, he's such a jerk." But then you talk to people who know him better, and they'll say, "Well, he can be annoying sometimes, but if you know him, you'll see at times he does these wonderful things." You'll often find in relationships that someone will say, "Well, he can be annoying, but I've seen him when he's really on, and he does these great things." When he's doing those things, he might be exhibiting his true personality. That's the sort of thing that's going to come to be more common.

Understand that because you are in Creation School here, I cannot simply wave a wand and say, "Okay, everything's all better now."
We have to do it.

You have to do it because it's school. But in order to do it, you need to be instructed in *how* to do it. The first hows always have to do with your own body, because your first responsibility is your body and what you do in it. Obviously, you are immortal—your personality goes on— but your body is the vehicle made up of Earth and what she has to offer. This allows you to learn these most profound lessons that cannot be learned anywhere else, because just exactly the right balance of challenge and discomfort exists here that will allow you to quickly learn lessons. You can learn lessons other places, but not quickly. And of course, as more people do disentanglement and are less driven by pain, over the years the percentage of discomfort will begin to drop and your relationship with animals and Mother Nature and plants and so on will gradually begin to improve. Many of the things that animals and plants and Mother Nature—rain and lightning and so on—have been trying to show to *all* of you (not just to mystical and shamanic and sensitive people), you'll be able to understand even without instructions. In short, you will not only become clearer mentally, you will become clearer in your feeling self, clearer in your physical self and clearer even in your spiritual self, because your spiritual self will not have to keep trying to balance you on that one leg of the chair, to do a little of this and a little of that so you don't fall over. In short, it purifies the process over time so that life is simpler and better.

You don't have to give up comforts, to give things up. You might in time do things differently. As time goes on and people begin doing this more, you might notice that some things are less necessary. Obviously, you can't keep building cars and using oil indefinitely—in time people will choose to do other things. But that doesn't happen immediately, because you need to do your homework and it's one . . . step . . . at a time.

Disentanglement and Earth's Negativity
What is the percentage of the negativity on the planet at this time?

Understanding that it's in constant fluctuation, taken as a gross potential on the planet, it does not exceed 47 percent. This, you understand, means that some places might have a huge amount and other places wouldn't have as much. The huge amount might be in a war zone, for instance, and in a war zone, death is not uncommon. If you get negativity up around 62 or 68 percent, that creates conditions where death is sometimes welcomed. You don't think of it consciously, but if you're suffering from a terrible wound, death may not look so bad.

Disentanglement could also be called discreation, couldn't it? It's one of the techniques to get down to the 2 percent negativity that we will carry in the future?

I'd rather call it postcreation than discreation, because discreation can happen before the fact.

Ah, and disentanglement only after.

Yes.

This is one of the gifts, then, that will bring this negativity down to something tolerable before we go out to the stars, right?

That's right. It will bring it down in time, and it gives you something practical and not very complicated that you can do no matter where you are. As Zoosh gives in his favorite example, you can be in prison and do this, and it can change things for you. It might not get you out of prison, but it's not impossible.

It could change you.

It could change circumstances in your life. And if it works for you, if others want to know about it, you can tell them. Don't tell them unless they want to know. It's not a new religion; it's a way to live.

Benevolent Magic and the Disentanglement Process

Can we call it benevolent magic?

You know, I don't think we want to call it benevolent magic, because magic has connotations to people. I'd rather talk about it as such a foundational element of life that it can't be something you *add* to life to improve it; it has to be something *upon which you build life*. This capacity to disentangle and to create connections has to be in place before anybody [extraterrestrial] ever comes here to these kind of societies. So no, we can't really call it benevolent magic. Benevolent magic is used to improve specific conditions or specific circumstances.

Can we say that once we disentangle to at least a good degree, we will be more able to use benevolent magic?

Yes, and it may not even be as necessary, because the more disentangled and clearer you get, the less likely that certain things will continue to happen in your life, especially those that prompt, "Oh no, not this again." That is a pattern that you reproduce in your life (granted, often unconsciously) because of some old pain in this life.

By the way, you can do this more than once a day if you want to, but no more than twice a day. If something major but temporary is going on for you, you can do it three times a day. But I would prefer that you do it no more than twice a day, then after a while, once a day. I don't want it to take over your life. If you've got nothing else to do, all right, but most of you have other things to do.

And don't feel that just because you're eighty-five years old and your life is, as you might see it, coming down the home stretch, it won't benefit you. It can benefit you at any age. I might add that it's a process that naturally goes on for babies, at least until they're six months old—basically before they start to speak or have any real understanding of what verbal language means. They will have understanding of what being held and loved means, of course; they'll have the basics. But usually it is naturally in place for the first five to six months. That is also how you can learn to do it. It's not complicated, because you were born doing it.

Disentanglement and Dying

If you disentangle and then come to the end of your natural cycle, will this eliminate some of the pain of the life review?

It may, although it won't eliminate things you have done in life that need to be felt and understood. Because your personality will change as a result of the disentanglement, it's less likely that you'll eventually be causing pain to others. It raises your consciousness and your sensitivity, of course. And it is also less likely that your feelings will be hurt by others, because you'll be much clearer when others are still causing pain. You will be clearer that something they're saying or doing is not actually directed toward you—it might be a self-destructive impulse on their part. It does not create enlightenment in its own right, but it gives you many more of the natural tools you were born with, without the encumbrances of all the complications of your past pains and multiple pains. In short, it's a clarifying activity. It probably won't directly change your life review, but it can indirectly change it.

You don't have to change your religion at all; it's up to you. But it can improve the dying process. It doesn't necessarily mean that you'll have a lot less pain; there might be *some* less pain. But in the dying process, you can still do disentanglement and your connections. You'll want to be connected to the most benevolent energies, and in that case, the connections will be to energies that will support you through the death process, perhaps in a slightly more benevolent way. So don't assume that if you're toward the end of your life, this can't help you.

Can we add here that because humans are becoming more filled with light, when beings die . . . Zoosh wanted us to say that you ask to go to your own guide and not into the white light.

Oh, yes; we can add that here as an aside, if you like. If you're sitting with or near someone who is dying, that person doesn't normally have to be instructed, but if you want something to say to him or her, say,

"Look for your guide; he or she will take you on your journey." That's all; something simple. Or you can say, "Look for the loving light from your guide," because that person will actually see someone radiating gold and white light. It's especially useful posttrauma—meaning a car crash or war or something sudden—when you know the person is dying. If you're an emergency worker, you're probably busy trying to save that person or help him or her feel better. In that process, you might not be able to say that, but you might. If the person is frightened, you can say, "Look for your guide" or "Look for your angel," if you like. These beings come. Of course, they don't really have wings. That was an artistic interpretation that has become popular. But you can say either "guide" or "angel," that they'll "take you on your journey." Just say, ". . . on your journey." That person will get it.

Appendix F

Disentangling Cords of Discomfort

The Spirit of Transformation

I am the Spirit of Transformation. It is my intention to help you understand the meaning of disentanglement as compared to its impact on you. It is not my job to analyze it, but rather to help you appreciate how it works.

Disentanglement is intended to extricate you from the uncomfortable ties that bind you to portions of your demonstrated personality, which for the most part have very little to do with who you actually are and who you will show yourself to be once disentanglement is well under way. You might say that it performs a clarifying function, but clarity in your time is often associated with the mind. Disentanglement, however, is more associated with the physical body, the feeling self, the spirit self, the inspirational self and the instinctual self.

You haven't heard about the inspirational self before because this has largely been referred to as the soul self or the spiritual self. But the inspirational self is that which can act quickly on the best feelings and instincts passed to you from all sources who respect and appreciate you as you are without having to be something to please others. In short, it is what is focused to you as a unique personality, as an individual designed to reflect that portion of Creator.

The inspirational self works like this [holds index and middle finger together straight up] with the soul self or the spirit body. But it also works just as compatibly with the feeling body and the physical body. It tends to think of the mental body as a child and does not indulge it, but rather will simply ignore it if the mind wishes to exert its will. The inspirational self will disregard that will, which it can do, and provide the pathways for inspiration. I am talking about the mechanism by which your instinctual self can pass wisdom or awareness to you that you might need to apply in your physical life. Equally, it functions to create a welcoming atmosphere for benevolent beings, guides, angels and others who might wish to pass on a message, either felt or heard as a word or two into the mental process. This is to inspire the best quality of life for you and perhaps even for others around you. That is how it functions. The circuit from the spirit self comes from one direction and the instinctual self from another.

The Value of Disentanglement

I am coming through to speak tonight in order to provide the necessary understanding of the *value* of disentanglement, because the value allows you to gently, without trauma, release the portions of yourself that are the masks you have taken on to survive in your culture, family or society. Disentanglement allows you to gradually, gently remove these masks while gradually, gently counterbalancing that removal as the weights and measures tilt toward balance. You understand that disentanglement allows this process to take place slowly, so that as the mask is gradually removed, the feeling that is generated is one of the emerging natural personality you were born with.

This is directly connected to the essence of your true self, meaning that which bears the marks of your immortal personality. These are the marks by which you might be recognized by someone you never met in a given life because there is a familiarity, a sense of feeling exchanged between you and someone else. You come up to someone in a crowd, you begin to chat, and pretty soon you're like old friends. Without doubt, that kind of connection allows you to disentangle from the old timeline of the third dimension and directly connect to the new timeline in the most easy, gentle and accessible way. The attempt to grab on to the new timeline does not become a hit-or-miss thing, something there is no apparent way to accomplish other than what may sound insufficiently substantial. When you do that, it then becomes easy to make the shift, even though your body might still be in that old timeline with others in that society.

Here is the old timeline [draws line on the left] and here is the new [draws line on the right]; you have these dotted lines here. The disentanglement essentially allows you to do this [draws an X with broken lines].

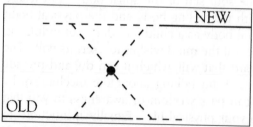

Fig. F-1. Disentanglement allows flexibility between the old and new timelines.

It does not disenfranchise you from your world, but it allows you to move flexibly between the old and the new, similar to the way alternating current pulses. Alternating current is essentially like a switch: it's on, it's off; it's on, it's off. The process of disentanglement is not a matter of being on or off, but the switch can happen so quickly that those in the old time with whom you may very well be interacting on a daily basis are not aware that you are, in some senses, between worlds. And those in the new timeline with whom you interact in your day-to-day life are not aware that you are also available to access the old world (using "old world" interchangeably with "old timeline").

So it allows you a greater degree of flexibility and, perhaps most importantly, safety—that is a key factor. When one feels safe, one is much more inclined to reveal the personality qualities that one treasures or feels shy about in a group of unknown individuals. Therefore, the safer you feel, the more likely you are to demonstrate that "new" disentangled personality, which is your actual personality. ("New" is in quotes here because it's not really new. It's the personality you came in with when you were born out of your mother.) Disentanglement essentially sheds that which does not serve you. But—and this is important—it does *not* shed the valuable experience that provides for you the necessary discernment to live your life. In short, it does not shed your wisdom.

Wisdom is the key here. You are here as the Explorer Race largely to assimilate wisdom that can be applied on many different levels, and that works in concert with responsibility for consequences. You have, then, an ideal situation in which something you would do to improve the quality of your life anyway is actually easing your way to a newer, better world, a world in which complications, discomforts and other things that seem random (but really are not) are much less a portion of your day-to-day life.

Disentanglement does another important thing: It helps you to feel less attached to the behavior of others as a reflection of your own. So many people feel the need to apologize for the acts of family members or of someone else, even if that person is not even related to you in given circumstances. I grant that there are times when such apologies are appropriate, but when this is done all the time, it simply allows that rebellious family member to be constantly offensive, because he or she has an explainer, a person saying, "Oh, please forgive him," or "Don't pay any attention to him."

This disentanglement allows you to feel more complete as an individual and gives you much greater flexibility and motion. Perhaps it also allows you to feel what is an opportunity and what will simply lead you down a path to unhappiness. In short, it clarifies your body's physical messages to you through feelings you can understand, not something vague. A warmth is love or good for you in that moment, whereas a tightness or discomfort might mean it's not good for you in that moment.

Such clear and simple *feeling* messages take the place of an analytical process, which can always and only be based on the manners, mores and values of the culture you are in—not just the ideal manners, mores and values, but the actual ones you live in. That's the key. Even though a given society might say wonderful things, might have ideals that are definitely worth looking up to and striving for, what occurs on the day-to-day level are the real values.

One can always be clear about what those values are when one observes twelve- to thirteen-year-olds, because it is at this age that they are moving away from their parents as their models for behavior, albeit temporarily. They are adapting not only to their peers, but also to the values presented to them en masse—not just religious, spiritual or personal values from parents and other concerned family members. When you observe the behavior of the average twelve- to thirteen-year-old in your society, whatever that society is, you will be able to quickly understand that the actual values of your society may not directly connect to the ideals you were raised with. Of course, when these youngsters get older and begin consciously or unconsciously emulating their parents or the adults who raised them, they may shed some of this apparent rebelliousness. But I call it "apparent" because rebelliousness is usually a direct reflection of actual values, not promoted ones.

I am telling you this to help you appreciate and apply the means of disentanglement, and to allow you to rationalize these means so that your mind can feel it is being given an understanding of either the value of disentanglement, which your mind is not clear about, or its purpose and function, which the mind will accept over value anytime. This is why the physical body and the feeling body provide a much better way of knowing heat, warmth and other good feelings within you. This is a much better way of knowing whether something serves you—and hence others—than what your mind tells you, which is always based on something abstract, based on words or motivations compelled by having to adapt to a given society's rules or, more often the case, behaviors and reactions to what you've been exposed to as a youngster. What we have here, then, is a mental explanation of disentanglement, which is my intention to give you tonight.

Exercise to Connect to Your Personal and
Professional Goals

Say, "I am asking . . ." ("I am asking" is in the present) " . . . that cords of support, nurturance, love and strength be brought to me and connected to me in the most loving and gentle way to bring energy from resources who have a great abundance themselves, who wish to lovingly support me and provide strength and insight, and who support my wisdom process in the most gentle way for me, in order that I may achieve my personal and professional goals."

Now, here's a little homework to do before this request. Briefly write down your personal and professional goals. Make sure they are practical and things you can live with. Your goals can't be pie in the sky. They have to be something down-to-Earth that you would like to experience on a regular basis, not something you think you *should* experience.

Say more about "pie in the sky." Do you mean unrealistic?

Yes, not grounded, as people sometimes say. Make sure that your goals are grounded in reality. Say what you want, but make sure that it is a real thing, not something that is associated with . . . for example, "I want to fly around in spaceships with all my space friends."

The gold lightbeings can do a great deal. They do their best work if you are lying on your back, with no folded arms or legs. If you fall asleep, you might tend to roll over on your side, in which case they can do some things, but every time you fall asleep during the process, you might have to add a few more nights.

Trusting the Process

Are they basically untangling the solar plexus? Is that where most of the stored trauma is?

Oh, no. It's all over your body and your auric field, everywhere. It is a worthy process and it's not difficult. One gives oneself permission, then basically other beings do it for you, but you must be receptive. Not everyone can be receptive right away, so it takes time. Over time, one develops a degree of trust and faith in the process. It is not something you do for a year and then go on to do something else. It is essentially a lifetime thing, because it performs its initial task and then functions as maintenance for you—the gold lightbeings can remove discomforts that have become attached to you during the day on a daily basis, not just cords and connections rooted in the past.

Let me go back to the drawing [Fig. F-1]. Now, the bottom triangle extends up and the upper one connects to the new timeline.

Not a solid triangle, you understand; it's a broken line.

But are we at any moment physically, mentally or in any way conscious of being on that other timeline, or does the movement happen so fast that it doesn't have a chance to filter down to the mental body?

It's not intended that it feel like anything other than a benevolent change in your personality that you feel better with and that very often others react to in a better way. The world around you does not apparently change, though your attitude about the world around you will. So it is a subtle difference, but also profound in that it greatly improves the quality of your life and often the lives of those immediately around you—family, friends and so on.

I'm hoping facilitators will pick it up, use it, teach it, share it.

That process has already begun. I do not intend to speak only to the mind, but since the mind is that portion of the total being that can withhold permission because of the way you've been conditioned, it is my intention to soothe its fears. In this way, the mind can potentially, at least, offer permission without feeling it is being coerced. The mind often feels coerced and then becomes truculent in terms of allowing benevolent change for any individual who might desire that change.

When you are going through this process, sometimes you will feel angry and resentful because those feelings were happening when you were donning a mask and suppressing your actual personality. So as you disentangle, some of those feelings are released. It will, for the most part, have nothing to do with what is going on in your life, though it might seem like that sometimes, and this might be a minor influence. But largely it has to do with the release of those feelings you are actually feeling. Because you are actually feeling them, they can be processed. But when you suppress them and stubbornly wear the mask, the feelings cannot be processed, resolved, nurtured or healed, and they build up into a coagulated and often destructive mask.

Is it okay for the reader to ask the Spirit of Transformation to help with this? Or is that not something you want to get involved with?

No. It is my job to inform, to educate and to enumerate, but it is not my job to activate.

Some Effects of Disentanglement

You've given some side effects, but are there other results of disentanglement that people should be aware of so they don't think something strange is happening to them as they go deeper into this process?

It is possible to experience a change in attitude toward those around you. For instance, in a relationship, perhaps your loved one does something maddening, something that might have driven you to the edge many times. It is very possible that this maddening thing will either no longer bother you or will trigger a decision that prompts you to seek other companions or, more likely, friendships, so that you no longer require your companion to fulfill all things for you.

Very often in relationships in your time, there is the mistaken impression that the husband or the wife must also be the best friend. I do not feel that this is required. It is required that he or she be a friend, and a good friend, but not the best friend. The best friend is usually someone a bit more objective in terms of the relationship, someone you can speak things to that you would never say to your companion because it might hurt his or her feelings. Therefore, know that such things might come up.

It is equally possible that the behavior, whatever it is, however small or great it might be, will simply become something you have less of a feeling about. You don't really take it as seriously anymore. It doesn't bother you. Furthermore, you have no desire to change it, so you will stop trying over and over again in direct and indirect ways to change this behavior. You might even come to find it amusing, which is a very good way to break the tension, as you know.

It is also possible that you will change your attitude toward animals and plants—in short, toward nature all around you. You will probably begin to feel better about it even if you are living in the middle of a city that is all concrete and steel. You might, when you see the weed growing up through the sidewalk, find beauty in it instead of seeing it as something that needs to be removed. You may have a different attitude about your lawn. In short, you will stop seeking artificial perfection in what you are creating—in your lawn, in your children, your companion, your students. Instead, you will begin to allow and encourage the nature of the true personality of those beings to emerge.

You might also find that your wardrobe can change. Certain colors once favored by you might go out of favor for a time. Sometimes you wear certain colors as a way to support or nurture some condition that is beyond your means to take action on, or this becomes a compensating factor. As you begin to experience this disentanglement process over a period of months, you might notice that although you were once attracted to wearing, for example, purple or red or black, you suddenly are enchanted with orange, yellow or pink. And you begin to integrate them into your daily wardrobe regardless of whether they are in fashion or not. It doesn't necessarily sharpen your fashion sense, but it will very likely affect the colors and possibly even the fabrics you choose to wear.

How do the colors you wear reflect your level of development or your feelings?

Let's not call it your level of development. Rather, let's say that the colors you wear might support what you are feeling in a given moment. For instance, if you are feeling stressed or put upon to do much more than you want to do or are even capable of doing, you might be attracted to a given color. It is not the same for everyone. The assumption is, "This means this and that means that," but this is not so, just as a dream symbol for one person might be different for another. Granted, many dream symbols are similar for all people, but all dream symbols are not the same for all people. Therefore, it is not good to say that this color means this and that color means that.

So just enjoy it; don't analyze it.

It's important not to analyze, because in analyzing you support the mind's desire to be approved of at all costs. You are not born with that desire, but it is conditioned into you by your physical environment, not only in the formative years, but as you come into your teenage years and so on. You want to please and be approved of by those peers you admire or at least want to be liked by. So I would say that the demonstration of personality is a fragile issue and must be treated gently.

Disentangling from Authoritarianism

You must understand that personality requires nurturance in order to feel confident about demonstrating itself, especially in a world of polarity. One cannot stand in front of the mirror and demand, "Be yourself." You can say other things, but the mind, remember, has been conditioned to make demands. Those in authority when you were a youngster—your parents or grandparents, your teachers at school, those you had to look up to or whom you did look up to—often made demands that might have seemed completely reasonable to those adults. The adult does not always know how to explain the reason to the child or does not feel the child can understand it, so the adult will simply make a demand. Thus the child learns, in a very powerful way, that making demands is appropriate behavior and ought to be emulated for the sake of approval and love. That is why little children will often sound authoritarian to their younger siblings or to dogs and cats around them, and it is cute up to a point. But as they get older, that authoritarianism can constrict the demonstration of their true personalities, to say nothing of how it might constrict those around them.

Can you give us words to use for disentangling from the authority issue?

Why don't you say, "I am asking that unnatural-for-me authorities who make demands on me that are not natural and not in my best interest, that these easily fall away from me by a mechanism supported within me by loving, generous and nurturing gold lightbeings and lightbeings." Understand that I am stating this in a clear way because I am speaking to your mental bodies. This might not be the most heart-centered thing to say, but the whole point at this time is to get the mental body or the mind to release restrictive control and to allow the process to go forward in the most nurturing and gentle way, rather than demanding that the process, even the disentanglement process, be done in the fastest, strongest and most authoritarian way.

It will be fun for people to see who's under their masks.

Most of you are much more gentle, spontaneous, artistic and affectionate than you now know. Many of the qualities that you and others like about you will remain in some form, but many of the qualities that make you feel guilty will fall away. That is because those qualities are conditioned into you but are not part of you. That is how the gold lightbeings can remove, in that sense, a cord you have sent out to something because you are trying to understand your world.

Cords can be with you for a lifetime. A child sends out cords all the time to parents and peers that are intended to help that child to understand, because very rarely can parents communicate in the way the child needs to hear and understand. A child does not learn only from pronunciation of words; a child learns from feeling and touch. These cords provide a more profound connection to the child's learning mechanism. This is understood nowadays in special education classes where children who have been unable to learn in conventional ways are nurtured and perhaps touched by those who are attempting to teach them life skills. This nurturing helps them survive easier, get along on their own or perhaps learn things not unlike what other children are learning, but in such a way that the child feels safe to learn and does not feel a demand to perform like a trained being.

Cording at Birth

Say more about these cords.

You completely understand the function and value of cords when you are born, even while inside your mother, because there is the tube from your mother's body to your body. As an infant within your mother's body, you understand that cords are good, that your life depends on cords, that you are corded to something greater, some spiritual thing beyond you. Often you understand it much better in your early years, as well as in utero, than you might as an adult. The infant inside the mother is presented with obvious physical lessons. And at that stage, one is not interested in complexities and complications; one is interested only in what is pure, clear and true. Therefore, since there is a cord that you can clearly understand is supporting your life, you will immediately assume that life is supported by cords.

The child growing in the mother is not only receiving from the mother but also giving back, so the cord is going both ways. The child, the boy or the girl, reaches out along the cord for what it needs, but also tends to give back a sense of personal enjoyment about life. The mother is much more aware of this when the child is kicking inside, flexing its muscles, but sometimes she is simply happily aware of the happy being inside her. Sometimes the glow (as it's called) of a pregnant woman is equally prompted not only by the mother's feelings about being pregnant, but also by the child within. So the glow is real.

Once the baby is born, does the child put cords out?

Think about it. The child is raised in a water environment, inside the mother in a saline environment, so it is essentially at that stage of its life a water being, not an air breather. Picture an extraterrestrial who normally lives under the water coming to Earth. It's as if you are demanding, in the baby's physical process, that the extraterrestrial suddenly become a terrestrial—with very little warning. The child goes from a water being to suddenly being something else, an air breather. This is startling and often done in ways that are not so nurturing, though it can be done in more nurturing ways, such as water birth. When it is done in this nurturing way, the quality of life greatly improves because the child learns as he or she emerges from the mother that life on Earth is an extension of the mother, not something other than the mother.

When the child believes that life on Earth is something other than it's mother, the first thing it does is send out cords to understand what it is. The infant will plant those cords in whatever adults are around it in those first few hours of life as you understand it. Therefore, it might quickly cord the doctor, the nurse and the midwife—and the child may not ever pull those cords out. So whatever the doctor, the nurse or the midwife go through, the child might be feeling that on a stimulating level.

To the same degree, the child might cord the parents. This is why some children demonstrate qualities beyond their years, whereas others seem to have great difficulty in learning simple things about acceptable and unacceptable behaviors from parents and siblings. What often happens here is that the child gets mixed messages along the lines of the cords. Remember, if you are suddenly thrust into the unknown world of Earth, you don't go, as in water birth, from being a water being inside your mother to being a water being on the Earth who can choose to be an air breather as well. Water birth is best done in a large tank so the child can swim out of its mother. It will swim naturally; it doesn't have to be taught. If you are presented with a loving water birth, then you are much more likely to send cords out to beings who demonstrate an ongoing love for you. For instance, you will send a cord out to your mother and perhaps your father or brother or sister, but you will tend to send it out that way to beings who have an immediate sense of connection to you.

But if you don't know where you are and you are thrown into a world that is completely unfamiliar, you will do what people do (whether they are adults or children) when they are thrown into an unknown situation: You will either withdraw or you will seek anywhere and everywhere for stimulation to understand what it is and where it is you exist in that moment. In short, you will use no discrimination whatsoever. But if the child, for instance, swims out of the mother or is gently welcomed by loving family members and sung to and cooed to and so on—it doesn't always have to be a water birth, though that's the easiest way. It can be a nurturing birth in other ways, too. If that happens, then the child is more likely to feel that this air world may be safe, compared to the water world.

How We Cord in Childhood

Okay, but let's consider the typical case in the hospital. The infant cords to people in the hospital. It goes home and cords to people at home. Then it goes to school and it cords—it just keeps going through life cording, then?

Yes. Just think about it. In your modern culture, in a society where a child's education is often more academic than based on values and principles, the child becomes confused. The child thinks that learning about the life of Abraham Lincoln or George Washington may be exactly the same value, no greater or less, as learning how to be a good citizen—meaning how to share your toys with your brothers and sisters. At that level, citizenship training immediately takes place. So in terms of cording, when understood in a spiritual, mystical or medicine society, it is understood that one is asking to have these things gently resolved in some way. A disentanglement is more direct in the mental society of your time. You are, in that sense, demanding that children be mental and insisting that they be mental above all else. It is small wonder that so few relationships are lasting, in terms of husbands and wives, girl-friends and boyfriends, and even among friends. Because if you approach a relationship on an intellectual level, aside from a sexual one in the case of an intimate relationship, you are missing the vast reservoir that can be given and shared and appreciated. In short, what do people want in intimate relationships? They want to be loved for who they are. But by the time most people come to the age where intimate relationships are acceptable, they are already confused about who they are. However, they do know when someone is being kind and loving to them as compared to when that person is being cruel.

I'm bringing water birth up because it will become increasingly common in the future. One of the reasons for this is so people can begin to regard water as something that not only keeps them alive, that entertains and amuses them and fosters growth in the plants and animals they need, but is also a sacred fluid that welcomes them into the world and therefore must be allowed to be itself. In short, the whole water-birth impact is going to encourage people to allow water to be safe and to find technological means to transform pollution. And this, of course, will be very good for economies. Those technological means all exist right now; people just need to want to do them. These technologies will certainly give many people a lot of work and create good businesses for many, and of course over time they will improve the water and the Earth and human relationships with both. Now, in order to embrace physical life on Earth, one needs to feel safe and nurtured by life around you. Water birth will provide that means to allow the connection between the academic, the technological and the heart-centered worlds. I realize this is not a new thing; people have been giving birth in the water for hundreds of years, which has been documented in your time. But only recently has it come into greater popularity once again. So it is not something unnatural; it is just something that requires a different shift, an allowance.

I want to understand these cords. So as the child, the adolescent and the young adult, we send these cords out all during life to things or to people or what?

You might even think of your childhood, how sometimes you had a favorite chair or a bicycle. You may have very well sent a cord to that object because it is something you drew a string from or felt nurtured in. In short, you have no limit to the amount of cords you can send out.

So someone might have cords to his motorcycle, automobile and all the houses the person's lived in?

That's right.

Cording in Adulthood

So here's the adult now, and there are cords to everything the person ever contacted?

Possibly. Only possibly.

How do those cords affect the person now? Are they pulling on her energy? Are they confusing her? How does it work?

It tends to keep people in the past, and if your past is loving and nurturing and supporting, then that is fine. But this is not the case for most people in your society in your time.

So everything traumatic that's ever happened, you have a cord to that trauma?

Not necessarily a cord to an event, no.

To the person who caused the trauma?

Or even to someone who witnessed the trauma. Maybe you were spanked for something as a child, and you did not understand, as children often don't, the mental concept of what you did and why you were being punished. You might not, in that circumstance, send a cord to your father or mother who's spanking you, but you might very well send one out to your brother or sister or your dog or cat because they are there and you're hurting, you're fighting tears and trying to understand. Perhaps later the parent found a way to explain it to you that you could understand, but the cord is still there.

Are there many cords to the same person—for instance, to parents or siblings, or if you are married a long time, to people in relationships?

Let me just give you an idea. Let's take an average forty-five-year-old adult in the United States in the average social and workplace conditions. In your time, this average person could have several thousand cords.

The purpose of disentanglement is to disentangle you from the pain, discomfort and restrictiveness—in short, from the discomforting aspect of whatever that cord was connected to. Therefore, you might easily be able to change attitudes without someone saying, "You should forgive your brother or your sister or your uncle or your aunt. That happened thirty years ago. Why are you still angry at him or her?" You will try to mentally rationalize why you are still angry because you feel the anger and it's real, but you may not be able to say it in a rational way to another person. Maybe you can, but most often you cannot. Therefore, regardless of the best intentions of those who are trying to convince you to let go of this old grudge, you don't know how because you are corded to the pain and the anger of the time—you are not corded to the pain and the anger per se, but you are corded to something physical of the time. *Cords go to physical things,* whether they are physical in this dimension or other dimensions. They are, in fact, things of substance. That's why I say, one does not cord an idea.

Disentangling Your Cords

Since cords represent your vast means of understanding the world around you, then what happens during disentanglement when these cords are removed? Not all cords are removed, you understand. Obviously, the connection cord between you and Creator is never removed; it might be clarified or purified so that discomforting things attached to it are removed. But *all* cords are not removed. Some cords are simply clarified and nurtured, meaning that some cords might be going to things that are nurturing you right now. In that sense, one never says to gold lightbeings, "Please remove all cords." One does not do that because some cords are feeding you in the moment, especially if you have asked for something to be fed to you, to support and nurture you in some specific way or for some specific circumstance. If you ask for all cords to be removed, you might unintentionally have those removed as well, because the beings will tend to follow what you say—not because they are stupid, but because it is their job, just like all other beings in your society, to serve your learning process as well as your needs.

So they don't just remove the discomfort, they actually remove the cord?

If a cord was sent out prompted by discomfort, then the cord itself will be removed, purified and allowed to come back to your body in a purified state. It is not cut off and discarded. They never do that.

So you get the energy back that you used to send out the cord?

That's right, and that's why often over time with disentanglement, one begins to feel physically stronger or more mentally clear, or finds it easier to adapt and accomplish spiritual goals. In short, you have more energy to do more things.

So at this moment the cords are physical, but we can't see them or feel them?

Sometimes you can. Occasionally you will get a stinging vibrational feeling, and unless it is associated with a disease, it might be associated with your bellybutton. Sometimes in your bellybutton—being the initial physical cord through which you understood the cording process inside your mother (aside from your spiritual connection to Creator)—you might get a resonating pang, as it were, like an echo, when you are being corded by someone else. You will sometimes get a discomforting feeling.

It works both ways.

That's right. So if this resonant feeling suddenly occurs and you get this discomforting feeling at the root of your bellybutton, which goes inside your body, it is your physical body's way of telling you that something has just entered your body that needs to be released.

The gold lightbeings remove the discomforting cords you send out, but what about all the ones that are sent to you?

There are just as many. When I said that the average forty-five-year-old might have thousands of cords, I was including cords from others. Now, animals do not cord, so you're not going to be corded by your dog or cat. You might cord them, but they won't cord you. They don't do that, because they aren't here to learn anything. Human beings are the ones who are here to learn.

If you're asking to remove the discomfort from a cord from someone else, will the gold lightbeings remove that from you and send it back to that person? Is that how it works?

That's right. They will extract it from you and resolve the physical discomfort around it to the best of their ability, unless it has festered into something over the years, in which case a trip to the physician might be necessary before or after, but you will usually know that. You may have a discomfort that is ongoing, but I won't go into that; you can resolve that on your own. In short, the cord will be removed, purified and clarified, and sent back to that other person.

Even though they didn't ask for it to be sent back?

They might not want it and they might very well try to cord you again, which is why disentanglement needs to be an ongoing thing indefinitely. In some societies, when children are nurtured and welcomed as one often hears about with extraterrestrials and so on, the cording process does not take place, because one is nurtured and loved and raised that way. And nothing ever happens to the child, even as he or she grows up, becomes a young person and then an adult . . . nothing ever happens to him or her that is not easily and nurturingly and lovingly felt as well as mentally understood, if there is a mental body. Therefore, the cording process is not only unnecessary, but does not take place, even if the physical birthing mechanism is similar—meaning that in utero, one has a cord in the mother. But that cord is understood. It is often suggested in the religions and philosophies of those cultures that that cord is the connection to your mother in that stage and that your mother's cord is connected to the Creator. It is thought that your mother splits her cord, and that when you come out of your mother she essentially shares or gives life to your cord to the Creator.* Now, I'm not saying that this is necessarily always and only true. But I'm saying that in cultures not associated with Earth at this time, if birth takes place in a similar fashion, it is usually considered to be that way. This allows the child to feel that his or her mother is not only a wonderful being that the child loves, but that she is also a sacred instrument.

Cord Removal after Physical Death

Okay, but let's get back to Earth. What happens when someone dies and all these cords are running back and forth?

Often what happens is a long period of resolution after death. That means the soul, the essence of one's personality, leaves the body, but the

---

*You need to understand the sacredness of the mother herself. The mother becomes part of Creator during conception and the entire birth cycle. This allows Creator to come as close as a creator would like to come to joining the human race through the mother as a representative. Of course, during this time the mother must be herself, so this is why she often has mood swings, sometimes even major ones. It is also why on occasion mothers take a long time recovering their own personality, even well after the birth.

All souls who become women on this planet are instructed by their teachers before life that they will have a special obligation to Creator to carry a portion of Creator's consciousness during conception and birth. Of course, before life this sounds and feels wonderful to the souls. However, during their lives, it does not always feel so good. If the mother were treated and honored as bearing a portion of Creator as well as the soul of the child, most women would have a better pregnancy experience. It is unfortunate that during your time and in your culture, a mother does not receive this respect and, perhaps even more importantly, does not receive the guidance she needs to comfortably accommodate Creator's personality within her own.

soul still has somewhat of a responsibility. Remember, these cords are physical; you don't see them, but some sensitive people might sometimes see them. I really do not recommend preserving the body—let it return to Earth without boxes and concrete bunkers around it. As the body returns to Earth, it gradually dissolves all those cords, not only the ones it sent out when the personality was in it, when the soul was in the body, but the connections that others sent. In other words, it dissolves cords coming in from the outside, but only if the body is allowed to decompose in a natural way.

If the body is preserved, then those cords you may have sent to that person can create a problem. The soul will tend to stick close to Earth if that problem exists, if the body is unnaturally preserved. It might hang around, maybe thirty days in Earth time, hoping to resolve it, working with teachers, guides, angels and so on to continue removing those cords, which can be done very quickly since the personality is no longer in the body. But it requires that the soul hang around to do that, whereas if the body naturally dissolves on its own, then the soul can leave. It might hang around for a short time, but not very often. If you, for instance, sent out a cord, you did not necessarily send out that cord hatefully. The vast majority of cords are sent out simply because you need or want something. If you've sent out a cord to this person when he was alive, and he dies and his body is preserved, it then becomes harder for you, the individual who consciously or unconsciously sent the cord, to let go of that person. In short, grief might take longer, and the natural process of transformation is greatly slowed down because of the desire to unnaturally preserve the apparent innocence of life.

Aside from commercial and industrial motives, the whole idea and appeal of preserving the physical body—so one can gaze on it not only at a funeral, which is understandable, but when the body is in the Earth and no one's ever going to see it again—is that the body is formed by after-death artists at the mortician's, and they are artists. The face especially is formed into something that looks idealistic, not unlike the way one considers babies to be. The babies are idealistic, they are pure, and likewise, this is an attempt to re-create that pure innocence of childhood so that the friends and relatives can have the memory, the last memory (if one goes to the funeral and looks in the coffin) of seeing the pure innocence of this person. This is the appeal on the deepest level. I am not saying that this is a bad desire, but I feel that you are greatly complicating your lives by it, from my perspective. It is the unnatural desire to preserve the quality of life for the passed-over loved one rather than putting enough attention toward the quality of life for the living. That is why one often overdoes a funeral. But you know, it is not my job to criticize your society; it is my job to help you to understand it better.

What about cremation?

Cremation is acceptable, but only marginally so, because it is not natural. The natural way is for the body to decompose on or under the surface of the Earth. Under is acceptable, but the purely natural way is for the body to be *on* the surface of the Earth and decompose. Now I realize that in your time this is not acceptable; too many people are on the surface of the Earth, and thus you would be tripping over bodies. The smell, in short, would not be pleasant. But think about the societies you have read about where a bier of some form is built and the body is laid upon it and allowed to gradually decompose in nature. Even though the animals might come and do things, this is allowed because it is considered a returning to the Earth. I am not, in this sense, trying to tell you how to live your lives. That is entirely up to you. But in time, I feel that death will be celebrated in a different way, that the recollection of the loved one and all these things going on in the funeral ceremony—be they religious, philosophical or heart-centered—will evolve on their own. But it would be best if the physical body was placed in such a way, perhaps wrapped in a sheet or something, on or within the Earth so that it can simply dissolve on its own.

You said cremation was barely acceptable. How does that affect the cording process?

In the sense of the soul hanging around Earth, with cremation it might hang around for twenty-eight instead of thirty days. So it is better than preservative and wooden boxes and concrete bunkers and all that, but only marginally. Now, I will give you another choice—burial at sea is considered completely natural, but only if the body is wrapped and dropped into the ocean as one often finds in seagoing societies or navies. This is also considered natural and completely acceptable.

Cord Connections and Disentanglement

Let's say a man or woman has many sexual relationships over the course of his or her life. Is he or she corded to every one of those?

Oh, certainly.

What effect does that have on his or her life, then?

Well, of course, every succeeding relationship is still tied to the one in the past, to say nothing of being tied to your parents and so on. This tends to color the ongoing relationship cycle, which is why people often have similar experiences from one relationship to the next. It's the cording, not the karma. Karma, to my understanding, is a philosophical way of explaining the circumstances of your life, but it is not intended, nor was it ever intended, to become an iron rule.

What about those we read about who are contactees, or as they're now called, abductees? Are they corded to the ETs on ships?

If they are little children, it is less likely they will cord unless they are in that moment missing mom or dad or dog or cat or something. It is less likely that they will cord, because if they are, say, three, four, five, six, seven years old, and especially if they've been nurtured by their parents to accept and appreciate different appearances of other human beings, they will simply accept the appearance of the extraterrestrial at face value. But if they are older and have to deal with the complexities of society, or if they were raised to feel afraid of other people in general, they will always and immediately not only cord all the extraterrestrials they see, but will run cords around the vehicle and cord beings they don't see as well as attempt to cord the ship itself. But in most cases, if the extraterrestrial society is advanced enough, the ship will have a living element to it and will reject the cord. The extraterrestrials will probably have the cord in them and accept it during the time the individual is actually on the ship, or they will integrate it into their society in some way—sometimes contactees are taken to the place of culture of these beings—so the cord will be allowed. But once the person is returned to Earth, the extraterrestrials will release that cord so they can go on with their lives, with a process not unlike the one you are being taught now.

How do people ask for disentanglement when they don't know the names or descriptions of the beings who corded them?

Just let the gold lightbeings do their work. If the cord is not supporting you, if it is associated with discomfort in any way, it will be removed and resolved. You do not have to specify ETs unless you want to, but sometimes cords connected to ETs might be nurturing. Still, ETs do not cord you. Nevertheless, if you are asking for certain energies and supports, one might liberally interpret that to mean energy coming from ETs. Therefore, if you ask for all cords connected to all ETs to be removed . . .

. . . you are shooting yourself in the foot.

So it might be good to be specific, asking for only the discomforting cords—either from you to extraterrestrials or from them to you—to be disentangled from you (which is unlikely, but you can say it like that). Adapt it—it doesn't have to be what I said per se.

This will also help the person who may have an attitude, such as an individual who believes ETs are dangerous. Granted, this might be fostered by fictionalisms in your society, but if you have that attitude, you need to honor it within you. If the gold lightbeings do not see any ET cords running to you, they will simply ignore it.

If you go into a public place and see thousands of people who each have thousands of cords per person and they are walking down halls and in and out of rooms, or they go to the opera or to the baseball stadium . . . how does all this work as far as keeping cords straight?

You understand that the cords, while they are physical, are not of the same kind of physicality you experience as a solid substance. If they were, you obviously wouldn't be able to move. But they are physical in the sense that they prompt physical experience and, of course, they are associated with feeling.

So they're very flexible? You can travel around the world and cords still connect you with others?

That's right. Of course, once you begin disentanglement, that number reduces quite a bit. Eventually, if you do disentanglement long enough, cords will essentially be down to a single digit on any given day. But you must remember, it's not that you are exclusively cording others or that others are exclusively cording you. It happens all over. You do them; they do you. It might be unconscious because you've been trained in your society to do it and you weren't sufficiently nurtured to *not* do it. Don't feel bad; just allow the gold lightbeings to resolve it for you as you ask them to do it in the way you prefer. That's why it needs to be an ongoing process. Initially, of course, for the first year, year and a half or so, a lot is going on. But after a while, when there are very few cords connected to you, less goes on and the disentanglement becomes a maintenance procedure.

And at that point then, when the cords are down to very few, is that when you can start asking to be corded to abundance and energy connections? You don't say how to do it yet, but what are the possibilities ahead relating to connections?

I think it's best for the first six months to not become overly involved in asking for connections. But if you feel tired and feel the need for connections, you can ask for them within three months. Now, some people will ask for connections immediately, but what will happen is that they won't be made.

So there's discernment on the part of the gold lightbeings as to which of our requests to honor?

That's right, the gold lightbeings know how to do their work. They are not subservient to your requests.

When people try to use this for some purpose that is not benevolent to themselves and others, will the gold lightbeings ignore that?

They will ignore it.

So there's a fail-safe?

Yes, there is. And if one even asked lightbeings to do the work without the use of gold lightbeings—lightbeings might be benevolent, wonderful beings, but given the specific light they are, they may not be able to protect you during the process. That's why you can ask for gold lightbeings or for lightbeings who can work through gold lightbeings or radiate or emanate toward them for your greater good. You can use your name. But gold lightbeings *need* to be present. Simply by their presence and by working on you, gold light tends to protect you like a shield during the procedure. When cords are being removed or brought back to you, this creates a vulnerability. If it is only, say, white lightbeings, they can give you all the love that exists, but they cannot protect you. They may very well have the wisdom or the experience, but the mechanism of protection is not a portion of white light. White light loves everything all the time, no matter what. So you can ask lightbeings to support the process, but gold lightbeings must do the process so that you are safe.

I think we have contributed vastly to the understanding of this process. You are wonderful.

We may talk again about the process as time goes on and you develop other curiosities, but for now I will say good night.

Good night. Thank you.

Appendix G

Creating Safety in Your Life

Speaks of Many Truths

A letter was sent to Robert from a reader in Texas who wanted to know more about something I had mentioned in one of our columns about being safe and creating safety around oneself, about creating an avenue of safety to arrive at whatever place one needed to go, and then creating that same avenue back. So I'm going to talk a little bit about this for that fellow.

In your time people are constantly exposed to people they don't know and have never met, whereas in my time that was almost unknown. Oh, there was the occasional person you didn't know and had never met, but after you talked for a moment or two, you discovered that you had friends and family alike or in common. Or you discovered that his father or your father or someone like that was somebody your relatives had met, because there were not that many people around in my time where I lived.

In short, common ground was easy to find, but I understand in your time that it can be a bit more challenging, and sometimes you feel like you're really out of place in a community and you're worried about what people might be thinking about you.

First, you need to be familiar with the *love-heat/heart-warmth/ physical-warmth exercise* [see pp. 7-8]. I want to talk about other things, but I'm going to build on that for those of you who have done the love-heat.

The First Method: Using the Love-Heat Exercise
to Prepare the Way

I'll give it in two different ways, and this is the first. For those of you who can do the love-heat exercise, if you know that you're going to have to go somewhere you're not sure about—and I'm not just talking about going down to the grocery store or supermarket; it might be a trip halfway around the world or to some other spot where you don't know anybody—this is for you.

What I'd like you to do is to get that heat going real good inside your body, and just stay in that heat. You don't have to say any words, but while you are in that heat, just blow out of your mouth anytime you're ready to exhale. (But don't blow that heat out of your body, because that's not what it's about.) Just exhale sharply, blowing out, then get a quick picture of your drive to the airport and see that heat blowing down there ahead of you before you get to the airport, then as you walk into the airport, and finally as you travel to where you're going to go.

Every once in a while when you exhale—all the while focusing on the heat—just blow in the direction of your trip. This plants seeds, plants some of your love there for you so that when you do get to those places, there will be love of your own there for you. But don't do this for the way back until you're ready to return. Do it one way at a time.

Maybe someone's driving you to the airport, or you're in a bus or in one of the little shuttle planes or a van. At some point, you might even focus into that heat in your chest or solar plexus and just blow forward, looking out through the windshield or toward the windshield.

Blow forward to just blow some of that love in front of you, and picture that love going to the airport. From time to time, go into the love-heat and just blow in the direction in which you're going. It can't possibly harm anybody else because it's love. Now, don't blow unless you've got that heat, with one exception, which I'll tell you about later.

And so having done this, you arrive safely at your destination. It's planting safety and love for you, but it's all right to be courteous to others and as nice as you can be. Don't try and take advantage of it, though I'm not too worried that you will.

Do this every leg of the way until you get to your hotel or destination. If you have a presentation to make or people to visit, continue to do it every once in a while, just blow when you're in that love-heat.

That heat in your chest or solar plexus will help you to be safe and have a good experience—or as good as you can have, meaning that there might be some challenges that come up. But the challenges won't be as extreme as they might have been otherwise, because you would have already seeded some love there. If the experiences are challenging, there will be something good about them, because you've already seeded love there for yourself and it ought to make a significant improvement. That's really all you can ask for.

Then when you're on your way home, follow the same procedure. Now, if you had decided to do this love-heat exercise all the way back before you'd even gotten there, before you'd even left, you would have unintentionally erased what you already did. So do it one way first and that will be good; then you're there. When you're done at your destination and ready to come back to the hotel, to the airport and all that business, then just repeat that cycle going all the way back to your home. That will work for you.

The Second Method: Picture a Gold Light inside Your Body

I want to give you the second way to do this because for some of you, you've had trouble getting focused in that love-heat. You'll get there eventually, but it might take you awhile. So I'd like you to do something else. Picture gold light inside your body. Picture it like a light bulb or as a glowing spot of gold light, and let it radiate around you.

Imagine the gold light, and if you know about the wand position, which has been shown before [see p. 23], then take that position with your right hand. You can aim your left hand down toward the ground if you want to, whatever feels good to you. Imagine the path you were doing that love-heat on. Just imagine the drive to the airport and the flight as you did earlier, and using your right index and third fingers as a wand, send a ribbon of gold light all along your route.

Again, do this one way at a time. When you get done at your destination and you're ready to come back, do the same thing with your wand and the ribbon of gold light for the return trip. Now, it's not quite as good as the love-heat, but it's pretty good. If you make a good connection, ask your angels and guides to help you out. You can also ask the planets to help you out and the Sun and the Moon, if you like. You can ask Creator. Ask anybody you want, but do it yourself as well.

Make the physical gesture. Aim your right hand out there. Move your hand around if you want. If you can picture the way the road curves, move your hand in sync with the curving and the road. You can do this if it happens to be the part of the trip you see, but you don't have to. Just imagine that gold ribbon all the way there. And when you're done there, repeat this for the way back. This will help make it safer for you and give you a little more confidence. There are other ways to do this, but these two ways are the ways for you to start.

The Safety Exercise

What about the long safety exercise for those who are seriously unable to go out of their homes? Is that something you can give?

That's very elaborate. Generally, Zoosh and I will give that exercise in some form to individuals in private sessions because it takes anywhere from twenty to forty minutes to explain. But I will give it here because it's important.

This is for people who feel not only unsafe or nervous or worried, but really frightened. Sometimes it will be a fear that's justifiable, someone you have reason to be fearful of. Other times, you won't be able to put your finger on it, but it's really complicating your life. Maybe it makes you shy to go out and about and do things, to meet people and go places. I realize this is particularly challenging in your time because your technology enables more people to stay home and have everything they need for work, entertainment, shopping and communication available in their homes.

Most of you who are alive today, with the possible exception of a few oldsters, will be alive for an electrical instrument that will be able to check your body at home and make recommendations for prescription medications and even some herbal medications in time (when the established medical profession broadens its point of view). It will be necessary for you to go see a doctor only if the instrument does not understand what is bothering you.

In short, many of you will be encouraged to *not* go many places. It's not because anybody is trying to control you, but the technology exists to provide for almost all your needs without you really having to go anywhere. In more technological cities, this is now becoming increasingly available. That's why even simple things, such as an actual awareness of the true population of a given state or country, are really often unknown, because many people are just not available. They don't answer the door for one reason or another—sometimes for good reasons, sometimes just because they don't want to. And sometimes you don't even know who's living in your own building. You might not see those people very often, or even people in your own neighborhood or town.

This is why from time to time there is the creation of power blackouts. Sometimes you can say, "It's this or it's that," but in the larger sense, it's just a creation that you're all involved in, or something you allow for one reason or another. But a future reason will be that it's important for you to understand just how many people are out there, that you've got neighbors in the general area where you live that you've never even met. Blackouts will become more common in the future, but for right now this is just something to mention as a coming event. And I'm not predicting catastrophes or anything like that; it's just that you have more reasons to stay home if you want to.

But I'm now talking to people who stay home because they're afraid to go out. There is an exercise that Zoosh and others and myself refer to as the safety exercise, which involves many stages. Other people have given bits and pieces of it over the years, but this is a long, elaborate exercise that will help some of you, especially those of you who have trouble getting to that love-heat thing. The love-heat exercise is the quick way to get to feeling safe and more comfortable. But if you can't do it the quick way, then here's another way.

Step One: Create the Physical Feeling of Safety

Imagine you're in your apartment or your home, and let's say that you're either alone or you've managed to create some alone time during the week. I'd like you to lie down in your bed if you can or sit in a chair, whichever is most comfortable for you. If you can do the love-heat exercise, that's the best, but if you can't, I'd like you to just imagine yourself feeling loved or appreciated. If that's awkward or difficult or it's not something in your life that you experience much, then I want you to remember a time or imagine yourself being loved or appreciated or protected so that you're imagining an experience of being *safe*.

Once upon a time when you were babies, there was always, for all of you (even if it was a short time for some of you who had a harder life), at least one adult who would pick you up, and you felt completely safe with that person. Maybe that person wasn't even an adult—he or she might have been an older brother or sister—but when he or she held you, you knew you were safe. So try and remember that time. If you can't remember it, then imagine it so that you can have that feeling in your body, the physical feeling of feeling safe. That's what I want you to do for the first seven times of this exercise.

If you can do it one day after another for seven days, that's fine, but if you can't, just count up the times you're doing it so you have that physical feeling inside your body that you can recognize as feeling safe. Or you might feel loved or comforted or nurtured or appreciated, but these all have to do with the feeling of safety.

After doing it seven times, you'll be able to recognize how it feels to feel safe in your physical body. Of course, it will also remind you how rarely you do feel safe as you go about the rest of your life, but this exercise is designed to give you the opportunity to generate your own safety rather than relying on external circumstances to create it for you.

So after doing this seven times and accomplishing the feeling—not just trying it seven times, but accomplishing it—then you can go on to the next level of the exercise. I want you to take as much time as you need with all these things. The full completion of this exercise might easily take a year or longer. For others of you who have more time to devote to it, you might be able to accomplish it in a couple of months, but it does take awhile.

Step Two: Stay in Your Safety Zone

The next level is this: Sit in a chair or lie down on a bed, and while you're sitting or lying there, simply go into that feeling of safety. Then move your arms and legs around. If you're sitting in a chair, that will be easy to do; if you're lying on a bed, it will also be easy.

Stay in that feeling of safety all the while. If the feeling goes away, stop moving and go back into that feeling of safety and into the exercise on that feeling. Now, perhaps not immediately, because it might take five or six tries or more, but you'll be able to maintain that feeling of safety and move your arms and legs around. You can have your eyes closed if you want to; that's perfectly fine for the beginning stages of the exercises. It might make it easier for some of you.

If you're taking this time in the middle of the day, you might want to put your phone machine on or unplug your phone for a little while so you can minimize any concern you might have about being distracted. Do the best you can. At some point you'll be able to go into that feeling of safety at this level of the exercise, and you'll be able to move your arms and legs around while still maintaining that level of safety. But just remain lying on the bed or sitting in the chair—that's fine.

Step Three: Stand Up and Feel Safe

Once you've done this three or four times and you accomplish it every time, then you are ready for the next level of the exercise, which involves the following: You are on the bed or in the chair. Go into that feeling of safety. Then swing your legs over the edge of the bed (if you're on the bed) and stand up. Now, if you don't have your eyes open, open them. You don't have to open your eyes though, because probably you can stand up without opening them. But you don't have to do that just yet if you don't want to.

If you're sitting in the chair, just stand up, all the while maintaining that feeling of safety. That's the groundwork for this. Practice this seven or eight times so that you can go into that feeling of safety. Stand up (don't walk around); just stand up and stay close to the bed or the chair. Maintain that feeling of safety, and then sit or lie back down. Do this seven or eight times.

Step Four: Open Your Eyes

Here's the next level of the exercise: Go into that feeling of safety and get ready to stand up, but open your eyes, all the while maintaining that feeling of safety. If that feeling ever goes away, lie or sit back down, close your eyes and get that feeling of safety back, and that's the end of the exercise for that day. Don't feel bad about it; it takes time for you to build up experience and learn how to do it well. And when you don't rush yourself this way, you know you're making progress. Remember, no one's taking notes or putting a red check mark by your name.

At some point you'll be able to stand up with your eyes open. Don't look around the room too much, but if there are things in the room that sometimes upset you to look at, if you'd like to for the exercise, you can put a towel over those things so you don't have to see them. Obviously, if it's a human being, there's nothing you can do about that, but if it is some object or picture that just has to be in the room but you don't really like it, cover it up with something.

Step Five: Take a Few Steps

Now you're ready for the next level of the exercise, and you're making progress. Go into that feeling of safety and open your eyes—all the while maintaining that physical feeling of safety in your body—and I'd like you to take a few steps. Just walk over to the nearest wall and touch it. You don't have to touch any objects on the wall. You can touch it with your fingertips or the back of your hand; it doesn't make any difference.

Just walk over and touch the wall and turn around and walk back. If it's a closet door, that's fine. Turn around and walk back, sit or lie back down and stay with that feeling of safety. Then the exercise is over. I'd like you to accomplish this about ten times.

Never do the exercise more than once a day. You can do it for up to twenty or thirty minutes if you want to, but no more than once a day. You want your body to be able to adjust to this slowly and not feel rushed; that's really important.

Step Six: Walk Around the Room

After you've done this ten times, you'll be ready to do more. Each time we build on what we've done before. So go into that feeling of safety, open your eyes and get up. This time walk around the room; don't examine things but simply touch them casually. Just touch them with the back of your hand or your fingertips. You can pick something up if you want to, but if you pick it up, it has to be something that doesn't mean much to you, such as a stone or a blank piece of paper or something like that.

All the while you are maintaining the feeling of safety. If at any time the feeling of safety goes away, go back to the chair or the bed and go back into that feeling of safety that you've learned how to do well, then end the exercise. You can hold the feeling of safety as long as you want, but just end the exercise with that. So that's that level of the exercise. I'd like you to do this at least five times, all right?

Now, as I say, it won't be easy to accomplish these things, because you're educating your body. This isn't about creating safe conditions that you can be in; it's about creating safety within your body and learning how your body works so that you are essentially projecting a field of safety around yourself, even though it won't feel at all like you're doing that. It will feel as if you're going inside your body to feel safety and that it's all you can do to walk around the room and open your eyes and touch a few things casually while you're so focused in your body. But it's a way of relearning how the physical world can work. That's why you need to take your time and go slow.

Step Seven: Interact with a Friend

After you've accomplished that level, you're ready for the next big stage. This will involve leaving the area you've been using to do this exercise—your bedroom or den or whatever place you could get away from it all. The next stage will also involve someone you care about, someone you know who cares about you enough to help you.

It might be better if the person is not a family member, just so there is little effect of the outside, but you need a person you are able to trust. If a family member is the only one who's available, ask him if he'll help you.

Explain that you're doing an exercise to learn how to feel safer and you'd like some cooperation. If the person asks you how it's done, tell him as much as you know so far, but don't discuss it—no pros and cons, and no arguments. A good friend won't need an explanation. Just say it's something you're working on, and when you feel that you've really got it down, you'll not only be happy to explain it, but you'll be happy to show how it works. Because once you've got this down, you can show it or teach it to anybody.

If you've been doing the exercise in your bedroom, ask your friend to come over at a certain time and sit in the living room, maybe on the couch. Serve tea, put out magazines and books for him, and then say you're going to do the exercise pretty soon. Don't turn on the television for him though; it's always best not to have the TV on during these things.

Then go into the bedroom and do the exercise all the way up to that point. You've accomplished this before, and that's why the person needs to be a friend, because if you can't get past any one of those stages, you have to lie back down and go back into safety, and then do the exercise again. That's why I had you practice these things so much. Your friend might still have to make several trips back and forth before you're ready.

At some point, you're going to be able to walk around the room and touch those things, all right? And that was where we left off. Now, all the while maintaining that feeling of safety so that you're really focused into your body, feeling that safety, I'd like you to open the door. Maybe you've had the bedroom door shut, maybe not, but open the door and go out and sit on the couch with your friend, still maintaining that level of safety.

If at any time the feeling goes away, just go back and lie down, go back into safety and it's over. But remember, this is a big stage. So at some point you're going to be able to sit down and look at your friend. You can close your eyes to begin to do this with the person. Just keep your eyes closed and talk about simple things that have practically no meaning, such as, "It's a nice day outside today," or "That was a lot of rain we had today." You've all had these conversations that don't really mean anything; just keep it simple like that. Nothing complicated, you understand: "Nice weather we're having lately." "It sure is." No more than that, something simple. And then if you can, open your eyes, all the while maintaining the safety and talking of simple, innocuous things that have no meaning to you.

When that's done, say, "Thank you." Then, maintaining the feeling of safety, walk back to the chair or the bed (wherever you started the exercise). Lie down, go into the feeling of safety and thank your friend. It's going to take a good friend to do this; that's why I recommend a friend, not a family member, because it takes someone who really cares about you and is not attached to anything that goes on in family relations. It can be a family member, but it's often easier if it's a friend, maybe a next-door neighbor.

I'd like you to accomplish this at least ten times with the friend, all the while maintaining the safety. Now, we're getting near the end of the exercise, arriving at kind of a graduation day. We're not quite there yet, but we're getting there. That's why this part is so important.

Step Eight: Leave Your House in Safety

If you can accomplish that level ten times, you'll be ready to go on to the next level and the next level after that. We're going to keep it simple, but we're going to involve your friend again if that's possible or someone you know who doesn't need to talk because I'd like you to have a quiet ride. The next level of the exercise has to do with leaving your house, and this might require a lot of back and forth and going back into that feeling of safety, perhaps even ending the exercise.

Talk to your friend and ask if he will drive to the department store or the supermarket or a mall or someplace where a lot of people go to shop for different objects. Now, this is not to be a trip that you *need* to take, all right? I want you to go to the store at a time when you *don't* need anything, because I don't want it running around in your head, "Oh, I need some aspirin," or "I need to pick up some tissue," or "I need to pick up some apples."

I want you to have all that done before you go there. It would actually be best to go to a store where you never go because you never buy or need any of their stuff. That would be the best way, but if that's not available, go to what is available.

Have your friend pick you up at your door and drive you to the store. All the while you're going to maintain that feeling of safety. You're going to go through all the steps you normally go through. You're going to walk out to the car. Have your friend open the car door for you and close it after you—you're maintaining that feeling of safety, so you don't want to have to think about those things.

Fasten your seat belt, but stay focused in the safety. Once you're in the vehicle, if at any time that feeling of safety goes away (this is the exception), just relax, go back into the feeling of safety, then end the exercise, and you and your friend can go get a bite to eat or something. We're going to make the exception here because it's just so elaborate and it involves your being considerate of another person.

But let's say, after so many tries—no one can say how many for each of you—you manage to get to the store, all the while maintaining the feeling of safety (so you're not talking with your friend other than to say hello). You get to the store, and your friend might say to you, "Okay, we're there now," or "Okay, this is as close as I can get." Maybe you are driven up to the door of the store or perhaps the car is parked right near the door.

Graduation Day

This is graduation day. It will be complicated because you have to open your eyes and step out of the door on your own. This time your friend doesn't open the door for you. All the while you are maintaining your feeling of safety, and you know what to do if at any time that feeling goes away. You will walk back out to the car, get in and go back into that safety and hold it for as long as it's comfortable to you. Then you can relax, and that's it for the day.

But this is what is intended for the graduation exercise. You go into the store. If it's a supermarket, you can pick up a little basket—you don't have to get the kind you wheel around. You don't even have to get a basket at all, but if you want to, you can get the kind you wheel around. I want you to simply walk up one aisle and down the other. You don't have to walk around the whole store. You can stop sometimes and touch some of the objects, but you don't have to buy anything; in fact, I'd rather you didn't.

If people say hello, you can nod to them and smile, and you can say hello, but don't pay too much attention to them because they might want to engage you in conversation as is normal in such places. But all the while I want you to be focused on maintaining that feeling of safety. Now granted, this is complicated compared to what you've been doing, so it might take you many tries to do it.

But if you can do that, walk slowly up one aisle and down the other; don't rush yourself. You might make it part of the time and it might take you awhile to accomplish the whole thing, but walk up one aisle and down the other, still maintaining that feeling of safety. You haven't bought anything, so just walk. Park your empty basket and walk back out the door, get back into the car, still maintaining the feeling of safety. Then relax and sit back. Go into the feeling of safety and come out of it, smile at your friend, and go out and have a nice lunch or dinner or do whatever you want.

You've graduated. Now it's true that the feelings of being nervous or upset might come up again, but once you've accomplished this safety exercise for yourself, you'll be able to use it a lot. You'll find that you'll be able to quickly focus on being safe, whether it's at work or perhaps at the airport or some other place. When you suddenly feel those old feelings of nervousness and stress, you'll be able to focus in on feeling safe and continue what you are doing.

Practice It

Practice this, and if any of you need any other, more elaborate instructions, please write a letter to the publisher addressed to me, and I will elaborate on it if you feel it's necessary. I know this doesn't cover all situations, but I'm giving you this because this young fellow from Texas wrote and asked about safety in a world that can sometimes be complex and a little upsetting. And I know you've all had this experience, so that's the safety exercise.

Appendix H

Asking for Energy

Isis
September 21, 1999

Ask that the energy of all creation be fed to you in the most benevolent way for you. Do this, either as people have done in the past [see Fig. H-1], or if you prefer, this [see Fig. H-2]. Good night.

Fig. H-1. Here's the gesture to ask for energy.

Fig. H-2a. This is an alternate gesture to ask for energy.

Fig. H-2b. Here you can see the position of the fingers.

Appendix 1

Theoretical Consequences

Robert's Vertical Wisdom

Robert Shapiro: Is gravity becoming greater?

Yes, gravity is relative to the conscious mind's capacity to solve its limitations! As we work through our limitations from the starkly physical to the application of theoretical consequences (which allows a vehicle to travel beyond the speed of light and remain intact), we release gravity's effect. In short, we transform the limiting constriction of gravity and are pulled forward by our own natural capacities, without limits, to remerge with our true spirit selves or that which is of our true essence.

Conversely, when we allow ourselves to be constrained by the limits of others, the effect of gravity becomes greater and our mass requires greater quantities of energy to propel us. In short, we become "heavier" and have to use greater energy to move.

So we now have a choice. Will we choose the "heavy" path burdened by the limiting beliefs found all around us, or will we choose the "lighter" path, which removes our limits and allows us to be our true selves with all of our true capacities and unlimited applications? The application of theoretical consequences defines the capacity of one body to exceed the limits of another body when that body is moving in the opposite direction, as long as both bodies are exceeding their own capacity of forward thrust.

This can happen only in an environment of electromagnetics. In short, picture an armature spinning in one direction, surrounded by its opposite field member spinning in the other direction. Add an environment free of friction, as might exist in space, and the two bound together by the magnetic field, and nothing else can exceed their own capacities.

Appendix J

Humanity Chooses Species Consciousness

Zoosh
September 22, 1999

Alll right, Zoosh speaking.
What is the process of gravity becoming greater? How does our conscious mind create this heavier gravity?

Your timeline is based, or let's say rooted, in the idea that the wider the experience an individual has, the more likely he or she is to be able to solve some problem, whatever line that problem occurs in. If you have your full capacity (if you remember your past lives and experience), the more experience you have, the more likely you are to be able to resolve anything that comes your way. But in your situation, where you do not have access to your past-life wisdom along the horizontal plane or time experience, you are simply laden with an accumulation of experience that has to do with what I call *species experience*, meaning the human race in your time.

Species Knowledge

Right now you all have the capacity to have *species knowledge*, which is the accumulation of knowledge of all human beings alive on the Earth right now (not in the past, not in the future, just in the Now). What Speaks of Many Truths was talking about was that in order to have that gift, you also have to have the responsibility—the other side of the situation, in which all parts of the mechanism (if we can call it that) of humanity must be in equal share of all other parts. You cannot have some people who are suffering while other people are, not happy, but oblivious to the suffering. That's the key. That is why your current-events programs are so important, because they get a lot of information out to a lot of people about what's going on in other places—through TV, radio, newspapers, magazines, conversations between people, the Internet and telephone calls.

All this is important because it is vital that in order to achieve species consciousness of the moment, which is a step toward having species consciousness of the past, present and future, you must make an effort to provide physically for the needs of all people. That's why people like President Clinton and others in the United Nations who are making some effort to provide for the well-being of all human beings on Earth are to be saluted and congratulated. Even though the methods, manners and means may not always be the most benevolent, it is a step, an intention, that is necessary for all human beings to pay attention to.

That's why the Internet is so important. People talking to each other around the world are finding out what's really going on for individuals elsewhere, not just countries and political systems.

Science Will Find Its God in the Heart

Information that has been talked about [see Appendix I] purports to give to physicists the potential for physics to become what physics students have known for many years—that physics and spirituality must join in order to achieve the promise of physics. This promise is not just the explanation of what is; it must also, in order to be the true promise, contain the instructions for how to re-create what is in order to make what is more benevolent and benign for all beings. Therefore, spirituality must join physics. This document points the way for physicists and spiritualists, if I might call them that, to join together to deliver the promise of physics.

There is no reason science cannot find its god in the heart rather than in the mind, which allows for painful mistakes. Needless to say, if at the end of WWII it would have been possible for the U.S. or the Allies to drop a bomb on Japan that would have simply radiated energy that created peaceful sensibilities in all beings, they would have done so. But they didn't have that available to their minds. That loving energy that binds all beings together who wish to be joined together, not abstractly or against their will, is the means by which you will solve the impossible physics problems of today. And that is required, because it is these people who have the desire to solve the unsolvable problems.

Yes, to a degree, benevolent magic will help. But it will be necessary for people who want to solve the problems to be able to instruct others in the means to solve them; to have the tools, technology and heart sense to give to others; and to easily be able to instruct others to, for instance, transform toxic waste to something benign.

How does this relate to what was given to us earlier [see Chapter 8], this sudden happening where everyone's energy is being used to bridge to those who are suffering or connect all of us to a unity of consciousness?

To have *active species consciousness*, you must not only access all the knowledge that all human beings alive on the Earth have ever known or will ever know, in addition to what all human beings on the Earth now know in this moment, which continues moment to moment, but also you must have the other side of it—responsibility.

This evidently just happened, and no one knew that it would deplete human energy so drastically?

I wouldn't say that no one knew. Some beings did not know, and it was alarming to Speaks of Many Truths, heart-centered being that he is, loving being that he is. It was alarming to him. Understand that. But from my point of view, it is strictly a challenge that you can rise to. Each individual right now must negotiate with your future-anchored existence. It is not actually your future self. If you try to negotiate with your future self, it will be unnecessary.

Two Easy Remedies

What you need to do is this: For those who have the spiritual ability to extend beyond their physical body, this will be easy. For those people, the quick instructions, which you probably already know, are to not exit the body entirely, but to send out your physical energy to its future, to a point in that future where you feel comfortable. Then bring that comfort back into the physical body you occupy now and notice how it feels. Keep doing that until you can memorize the way your physical body feels under those circumstances, and work toward achieving that feeling all the time. Then you'll have more energy than you'll know what to do with, and you may actually have to moderate that a bit so you can sleep at night. Those are the instructions for those who are able along those lines.

Now, for those of you who do not know how to do that, write yourself a letter and say, "Dear Future, I need to feel physically my benevolent future being in my Now body. Please allow me to feel it often. The best time for me would be (then you write down the time) between this and this time." For some people it will be just before sleep. For others it will be when you wake up. For others it will be during the time of the day when it is most convenient for you to relax. You could ask for a specific time. Then just relax during that time and try not to think. Try to keep your mind as free of thought as possible and see how you feel. Also, during the time preceding that relaxation time, you can read the letter you wrote.

Creator School Challenges

I told you a long time ago that the challenges and lessons in Creator School will get greater and greater because Creator believes you have the capacity to achieve positive results. A fairy godmother will not come along with her magic wand and wave it over your heads to make everything hunky-dory. It's not going to be like that, and you know that

darn well. It has to be placed upon you in such a way that you will notice. It can't just be a mental conundrum—"How should we do this?
Let's discuss it philosophically."

No, it has to hit you in the home spot, and the home spot is your
physical body, which is where you reside. You will find that almost all
your challenges that come up in the next few years will strike you right
smack in the physical body, because that's what you cannot avoid and
what you are most likely to take immediate umbrage to—in short, ask
about. So don't be surprised. You might also pat yourselves on the
backs, saying, "Well, we must be doing something right, or Creator
wouldn't be dropping such a problem on us."

*Speaks of Many Truths said that all humans decided this, but was it decided on a
higher or broader level than that?*

From Speaks of Many Truths' point of view, he saw it that way, but
from my point of view, I do not see anything happening for humans
without the Creator's allowance. It may very well be true that at one
point all human beings decided that "this is the moment when we are
going to make this happen." But Creator always has the capacity to say,
"No, wait." But Creator did not. I am not saying that what Speaks of
Many Truths said is false. I am just expanding on it a bit more. If the
Creator does not interfere, that is by way of Creator saying, "Yes, you are
ready for this now."

Creator would have checked with His friends and advisers for their approval also?

Theoretically, but Creator did not do that.

In this instance?

Correct.

*This was a further result of the astronomical lineup of planets in August [1999],
right?*

The astronomical lineup is not separate from this. Everything is
planned. Such astronomical lineups like this occur more than once, so
you might say that in the larger sense, Creator brings this about from
time to time.

The opportunity . . .

. . . the opportunity with such astronomical lineups. The Creator
brought it up again, and this time you said, "Okay, let's do it." If you accomplish the challenge, it is likely to shorten the time for the availabil-
ity of species consciousness, at least in the Now, by sixteen to eighteen
months.

*It would've taken X years; now it's going to take eighteen months less. What's the
time period had we not done this?*

Maybe seven years.

So it's from seven years to five and a half now?

Yes, but think about it: How many people would suffer needlessly during that time? It gives you a chance to improve the lot of all beings and to eliminate that much suffering.

How does this decision by humanity and the Creator speed up the process by achieving unity earlier?

It will allow you to make the preparatory steps to get to 3.50 dimension. You see, the challenges are not complicated. The formula is stated in a wordy and complicated way, but it's stated that way to be very specific, precise. It's not stated that way to confuse anybody. The words need to be kept absolute—no changes at all. But the challenge in its own right is not complex.

It just means that the golden rule needs to be applied across the board to everyone, even if they say something offensive to you. It does not mean that you have to be beaten up or killed and still apply great love. You can defend yourself to some degree. What I'm saying, though, is that it is not all right to remain ignorant of the suffering of other people.

Now, think about what I'm saying. You can be aware of the suffering of other people, and you may or may not do something physical about it. Maybe you'll contribute to the Red Cross, maybe you'll organize something on your own or maybe you'll simply say a prayer associated either with your religion or a living prayer:

> **"MAY ALL BEINGS BE AT PEACE, LOVE AND HARMONY WITH ALL OTHER BEINGS NOW."**

Say a living prayer such as that or add other things that suit the situation. That is what is required: *do what you can.*

It is essential, then, that you know about it. In short, it is no longer acceptable to be ignorant of the suffering of others. You must know about it. You see, if you know about it, in most beings it will automatically create a desire to make it better. So even if you did nothing, but you heard about it and then went to sleep at night, your spirit selves would be instructing your physical selves what to do, whether you did it or not. And at the least, you would talk it up to people and you would likely do something.

The Redistribution of Human Energy Will
Force Your Attention to It

Precisely how is this energy being used or redistributed? What does that mean when 20 or 30 or 5 percent of our energy is being used to bridge to this unity consciousness?

If you had three generators—one operating at 20 percent, one operating at 30 percent and one operating at 50 percent—that would give you perhaps the 100 percent energy you need in order for your business to function. But suppose the 50-percent-operating generator dropped to 40 percent. Then what needs to happen doesn't happen as well as before, or maybe it gets completely messed up. You need to have that 100 percent of energy. This means that someone somewhere has to bring in a 10 percent generator or else some other means must be found to provide the energy needed.

You all know that the brain and nervous system can be measured for its electrical capacity. The energy that evacuates your body to go to the bodies of others comes directly from the electricity in your nervous system. This usually happens in the most benign way, which is when you are asleep. Think what would happen if energy were being tapped from your mental and neural systems when you were awake. You could have accidents, you could make mistakes— you could, in short, hurt yourself or others. So it has to happen when you are at the deepest levels of sleep, when you can afford to let it go because you are less likely to be injured.

A percentage of our energy is being sent in sleep to other humans on the planet who need it, and we need to learn how to replenish that by calling for energy from the future timeline.

Yes, that's the temporary solution—and/or you need to resolve the sufferings of people on the Earth. Even saying a simple living prayer will help. You need to *do* something about it.

This is an attempt to force us to do something about it—not force, but . . .

No, it's all right. Let's say it: It's an attempt to force your attention on this point. Disease is also an attempt to force your attention onto your physical body.

How do we focus on this future energy?

You pull it from . . . what is the present? The present is energy, mass, love, motion, all these things. It is something tangible, something that you can't quite grasp, like the air, but you can feel its effect on you if you move your hand around quickly. In short, it has tangibility. It is easier for you to understand what is the past, having lived it. But it is no easier for you to understand the past in physical terms because you can't go back and grasp the past any easier than you can go forward and grasp the future—unless you know how to do that, as I gave instructions to those who do.

Isis said to ask for energy from all creation in a way that's benevolent.

Yes, that's fine. Understand that it is my tendency to speak about things in mental terms. It is Speaks of Many Truths' tendency to speak of things in physical and feeling terms. And it is Isis' tendency to speak in terms of loving spirit.

I'm concerned about the people who don't know what to do, people whose energy is being used but who don't understand what is happening to them. They're going to feel depleted, but it's not going to cause depression or breakdowns?

It might.

What about all the people on the planet who don't understand that there are ways to increase their energy? I'm concerned about them.

I appreciate your concern, but as it is with all discomforts, the discomfort is not intended to be a punishment; it's intended to be a message, and the response to the message is ASK FOR HELP! If something is giving you difficulty, ask. Eventually, someone will tell you. Try many different things. Some will work for a while, others won't.

At the end of five years instead of seven, we should approach 3.50?

No, I didn't say that. I said that it's a preparatory step to allow you to approach 3.50. I didn't say it would be the result. You always want the solution, but the solution is not in the answer; the solution is in the process. The answer is obvious once the process has been started or is in the middle or sometimes when the process is completed. But the answer is almost useless in a physical world.

Apply the Process and Juggle Your Challenges

The process is essential. Thinking about it doesn't accomplish it. So I am less interested in your knowing the answer than in your *applying the process*. You are here in this profoundly physical world—you and everybody else—in order to understand how physicality can make a profound difference in the expansion of all beings. Yes, there are great risks involved, because if one goes the wrong way, it's very easy to create contraction out of necessity. Contraction is essentially going back to the starting point, because the process is going in the wrong direction. If you *don't* go back to the starting point, everything will contract [to understand this remark, see the loop of time illustration on page 168 of *The Explorer Race*]. That's why Creator took such risks. [See *Explorer Race: Origins and the Next 50 Years* and *Explorer Race: Creator and Friends*.] That process is the key to it all.

Of constantly taking risks?

Of doing things, of attempting the process, of accomplishing it or at least trying and saying, "Well, that's not for me, but at least I tried. I did what I could do. I couldn't climb to the top of the mountain, but I got partway up. I feel pretty good about that. I know now that I might not be a mountain climber in this life, but I can climb partway up if I ever have to." You, the reader, cannot know that by thinking about it; you can only know that by *doing* it.

We can look forward to being motivated and responding to this challenge, and at the end of five years, we will create another interesting challenge?

There is no reason to assume it will take that long. What makes you think it is one at a time? Certainly there are other challenges going on while this one came up. There are always many hats in the air to juggle. To be a creator even on a small scale, such as having children, what is it like having four or five children running around? You have to pay attention and take responsibility. You have to do many things at once. What is it like having uncountable numbers of beings running around, and you have to pay attention to all of them? You are a creator now, but you are taking necessarily slow steps. Why do you think life is the way it is here? Why do you think you perpetuate this species by birth rather than by cloning, as happens in many cultures on other worlds? It is so that *you will experience in every moment the responsibility of creation on a detailed scale.*

The process of creation.

That's right, a process.

THE EXPLORER RACE SERIES

ZOOSH AND OTHERS THROUGH ROBERT SHAPIRO

Superchannel Robert Shapiro can communicate with any personality anywhere and anywhen. He has been a professional channel for over twenty-five years and channels with an exceptionally clear and profound connection.

The Origin . . .
The Purpose . . . The Future . . . of Humanity

If you have ever wondered about who you really are, why you are here as part of humanity on this miraculous planet and what it all means, these books in the *Explorer Race* series can begin to supply the answers—the answers to these and other questions about the mystery and enigma of physical life on Earth.

These answers come from beings who speak through superchannel Robert Shapiro, beings who range from particle personalities to the Mother of all Beings and the thirteen Ssjoooo, from advisers to the Creator of our universe to the generators of pre-creation energies. The scope, the immensity, the mind-boggling infinitude of these chronicles by beings who live in realms beyond our imagination, will hold you enthralled. Nothing even close to the magnitude of the depth and power of this all-encompassing, expanded picture of reality has ever been published.

This amazing story of the greatest adventure of all time and creation is the story of the Explorer Race, of which humans are a small but important percentage. The Explorer Race is a group of souls whose journeys resulted in incarnations in this loop of time on planet Earth—where, bereft of any memory of our immortal selves and most of our heart energy, we came to learn compassion, to learn to take responsibility for the consequences of our actions and to solve creation's previously unsolvable dilemma of negativity. We humans have found a use for negativity—we use it for lust for life and adventure, curiosity and creativity, for doing the undoable. And in a few years, we will go out to the stars with our insatiable drive and ability to respond to change and begin to inspire the benign but stagnant civilizations out there to expand and change and grow, which will eventually result in the change and expansion of all creation.

Once you understand the saga of the Explorer Race and what the success of the Explorer Race experiment means to the totality of creation, you will be proud to be human and to know that you are a vital component of the greatest story ever told—a continuing drama whose adventure continues far into the future.

the EXPLORER RACE

Zoosh, End-Time Historian
through Robert Shapiro

Book 1...
the EXPLORER RACE

You individuals reading this are truly a result of the genetic experiment on Earth. You are beings who uphold the principles of the Explorer Race. The information in this book is designed to show you who you are and give you an evolutionary understanding of your past that will help you now. The key to empowerment in these days is not to know everything about your past, but to know that which will help you now.

Your souls have been here on Earth for a while and have been trained in Earthlike conditions. This education has been designed so that you would have the ability to explore all levels of responsibility—results, effects and consequences—and take on more responsibilities.

Your number one function right now is your status of Creator apprentice, which you have achieved through years and lifetimes of sweat. You are constantly being given responsibilities by the Creator that would normally be things that Creator would do. The responsibility and the destiny of the Explorer Race is not only to explore, but to create.

$25⁰⁰ SOFTCOVER 574 P.
ISBN 0-929385-38-1

Chapter Titles:

Book 2...
ETs and the EXPLORER RACE

In this book, Robert channels Joopah, a Zeta Reticulan now in the ninth dimension, who continues the story of the great experiment—the Explorer Race—from the perspective of his civilization. The Zetas would have been humanity's future selves had not humanity re-created the past and changed the future.

14^{95} SOFTCOVER 237 P.
ISBN 0-929385-79-9

Joopah, Zoosh and others through Robert Shapiro

Chapter Titles:

- The Great Experiment: Earth Humanity
- ETs Talk to Contactees
- Becoming One with Your Future Self
- ET Interaction with Humanity
- UFOs and Abductions
- The True Nature of the Grays
- Answering Questions in Las Vegas
- UFO Encounters in Sedona

- Joopah, in Transit, Gives an Overview and Helpful Tools
- We Must Embrace the Zetas
- Roswell, ETs and the Shadow Government
- ETs: Friend or Foe?
- ET Presence within Earth and Human Genetics
- Creating a Benevolent Future
- Bringing the Babies Home

Book 3...ORIGINS and the NEXT 50 YEARS

This volume has so much information about who we are and where we came from—the source of male and female beings, the war of the sexes, the beginning of the linear mind, feelings, the origin of souls—it is a treasure trove. In addition, there is a section that relates to our near future—how the rise of global corporations and politics affects our future, how to use benevolent magic as a force of creation and then how we will go out to the stars and affect other civilizations. Astounding information.

14^{95} SOFTCOVER 339 P.
ISBN 0-929385-95-0

ORIGINS and the NEXT 50 YEARS

Zoosh, End-Time Historian through Robert Shapiro

Chapter Titles:

THE ORIGINS OF EARTH RACES
- Our Creator and Its Creation
- The White Race and the Andromedan Linear Mind
- The Asian Race, the Keepers of Zeta Vertical Thought
- The African Race and Its Sirius/Orion Heritage
- The Fairy Race and the Native Peoples of the North
- The Australian Aborigines, Advisors of the Sirius System
- The Return of the Lost Tribe of Israel
- The Body of the Child, a Pleiadian Heritage
- Creating Sexual Balance for Growth
- The Origin of Souls

THE NEXT 50 YEARS
- The New Corporate Model
- The Practice of Feeling
- Benevolent Magic

- Future Politics
- A Visit to the Creator of All Creators
- Approaching the One

APPENDIX
- The Body of Man/The Body of Woman

ORIGINS OF THE CREATOR
- Beginning This Creation
- Creating with Core Resonances
- Jesus, the Master Teacher
- Recent Events in Explorer Race History
- The Origin of Creator
- On Zoosh, Creator and the Explorer Race
- Fundamentals of Applied 3D Creationism

Book 4...
CREATORS and FRIENDS
The Mechanics of Creation

Now that you have a greater understanding of who you are in the larger sense, it is necessary to have some of your true peers talk to you, to remind you of where you came from, the true magnificence of your being. You must understand that you are creators in training, and yet you were once a portion of Creator. One could certainly say, without being magnanimous, that you are still a portion of Creator, yet you are training for the individual responsibility of being a creator, to give your Creator a coffee break.

This book will give you peer consultation. It will allow you to understand the vaster qualities and help you remember the nature of the desires that drive any creator, the responsibilities to which that creator must answer, the reaction any creator must have to consequences and the ultimate reward of any creator. This book will help you appreciate all of the above and more. I hope you will enjoy it and understand that maybe more will follow.

19^{95} SOFTCOVER 435 P.
ISBN 1-891824-01-5

Chapter Titles:

Book 5...
PARTICLE PERSONALITIES

All around you are the most magical and mystical beings. They are too small for you to see as single individuals, but in groups you know them as the physical matter of your daily life. These particles remember where they have been and what they have done in their long lives. We hear from some of them in this extraordinary book.

14^{95} SOFTCOVER 237 P.
ISBN 0-929385-97-7

Particle Personalities and Zoosh through Robert Shapiro

Chapter Titles:

- A Particle of Gold
- The Model Maker: The Clerk
- The Clerk, a Mountain Lion Particle, a Particle of Liquid Light and an Ice Particle
- A Particle of Rose Quartz from a Floating Crystal City
- A Particle of Uranium, Earth's Mind
- A Particle of the Great Pyramid's Capstone
- A Particle of the Dimensional Boundary between Orbs
- A Particle of Healing Energy

- A Particle of Courage Circulating through Earth
- A Particle of the Sun
- A Particle of Ninth-Dimensional Fire
- A Particle of Union
- A Particle of the Gold Lightbeing beyond the Orbs
- A Particle of the Tenfold Wizard
- A Particle of This Creator

Book 6...
EXPLORER RACE and BEYOND

With a better idea of how creation works, we go back to the Creator's advisors and receive deeper and more profound explanations of the roots of the Explorer Race. The liquid domain and the Double Diamond portal share lessons given to the roots on their way to meet the Creator of this universe and finally the roots speak of their origins and their incomprehensibly long journey here.

14^{95} SOFTCOVER 360 P.
ISBN 1-891824-06-6

Explorer Race Roots, Friends and All That Is with Zoosh through Robert Shapiro

Chapter Titles:

- Creator of Pure Feelings and Thoughts, One Circle of Creation
- The Liquid Domain
- The Double-Diamond Portal
- About the Other 93% of the Explorer Race
- Synchronizer of Physical Reality and Dimensions
- The Master of Maybe
- Master of Frequencies and Octaves
- Spirit of Youthful Enthusiasm (Junior) and Master of Imagination
- Zoosh

- The Master of Feeling
- The Master of Plasmic Energy
- The Master of Discomfort
- The Story-Gathering Root Being from the Library of Light/Knowledge
- The Root Who Fragmented from a Living Temple
- The First Root Returns
- Root Three, Companion of the Second Root
- The Temple of Knowledge & the Giver of Inspiration
- The Voice Historian, Who Provided the First Root
- Creator of All That Is

THE EXPLORER RACE SERIES

Book 7...
COUNCIL OF CREATORS
ROBERT SHAPIRO

The thirteen core members of the Council of Creators discuss their adventures in coming to awareness of themselves and their journeys on the way to the Council on this level. They discuss the advice and oversight they offer to all creators, including the Creator of this local universe. These beings are wise, witty and joyous, and their stories of Love's creation create an expansion of our concepts as we realize that we live in an expanded, multiple-level reality.

SOFTCOVER 237 P. $14.95 ISBN 1-891824-13-9

Highlights Include:

- Specialist in Colors, Sounds and Consequences of Actions
- Specialist in Membranes that Separate and Auditory Mechanics
- Specialist in Sound Duration
- Explanation from Unknown Member of Council
- Specialist in Spatial Reference
- Specialist in Gaps and Spaces
- Specialist in Divine Intervention

- Specialist in Synchronicity and Timing
- Specialist in Hope
- Specialist in Honor
- Specialist in Variety
- Specialist in Mystical Connection between Animals and Humans
- Specialist in Change
- Specialist in the Present Moment
- Council Spokesperson and Specialist in Auxiliary Life Forms

Book 8...
THE EXPLORER RACE AND ISIS
ROBERT SHAPIRO

This is an amazing book. It has priestess training, Shamanic training, Isis' adventures with Explorer Race beings—before Earth and on Earth—and an incredibly expanded explanation of the dynamics of the Explorer Race. Isis is the prototypical loving, nurturing, guiding feminine being, the focus of feminine energy. She has the ability to expand limited thinking without making people with limited beliefs feel uncomfortable. She is a fantastic storyteller, and all of her stories are teaching stories. If you care about who you are, why you are here, where you are going and what life is all about—pick up this book. You won't lay it down until you are through, and then you will want more.

SOFTCOVER 317 P. $14.95 ISBN 1-891824-11-2

Highlights Include:

- The Biography of Isis
- The Adventurer
- Soul Colors and Shapes
- Creation Mechanics
- Creation Mechanics and Personal Anecdotes

- The Insects' Form and Fairies
- Orion and Application to Earth
- Goddess Section
- Who Is Isis?
- Priestess/Feminine Mysteries

ROBERT SHAPIRO

SUPERCHANNEL ROBERT SHAPIRO can communicate with any personality anywhere and anywhen. He has been a professional channel for over twenty-five years and channels with an exceptionally clear and profound connection. Robert's great contribution to an understanding of the history, purpose and future of humanity is his epochal work, the Explorer Race series, of which this book is number nine. The series includes Robert's channeling of beings from particles to creators to generators of pre-creation energy. He is also the channel of the six books in the Shining the Light series.

through ROBERT SHAPIRO

Book 9 of the EXPLORER RACE
THE EXPLORER RACE AND JESUS

The core personality of that being known on the Earth as Jesus, along with his students and friends, describes with clarity and love his life and teachings 2000 years ago. He states that his teaching is for all people of all races in all countries. Jesus announces here for the first time that he and two others, Buddha and Mohammed, will return to Earth from their place of being in the near future. And a fourth being, a child already born now on Earth, will become a teacher and prepare humanity for their return. So heartwarming and interesting, you won't want to put it down.

16^{95} SOFTCOVER 354 P.
ISBN 1-891824-14-7

*Each book weighs 1.07 lbs.
28 books per carton
30 lbs. per box*

Chapter Titles:

- Jesus's Core Being, His People and the Interest in Earth of Four of Them
- Jesus's Life on Earth
- Jesus's Home World, Their Love Creations and the Four Who Visited Earth
- The "Facts" of Jesus's Life Here, His Future Return
- The Teachings and Travels
- A Student's Time with Jesus and His Tales of Jesus's Time Travels
- The Child Student Who Became a Traveling Singer-Healer

- The Shamanic Use of the Senses
- Other Journeys and the Many Disguises
- Jesus's Autonomous Parts, His Bloodline and His Plans
- Learning to Invite Matter to Transform Itself
- Inviting Water, Singing Colors
- Learning to Teach Usable Skills
- Learning about Different Cultures and People
- The Role of Mary Magdalene, a Romany
- Traveling and Teaching People How to Find Things

Light Technology Publishing • PO Box 3540 • Flagstaff, AZ 86003
Phone: 928-526-1345 • Fax: 928-714-1132

Visit our online bookstore: www.lighttechnology.com

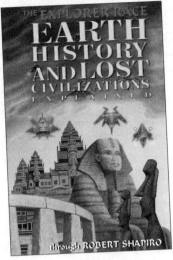

THE EXPLORER RACE SERIES

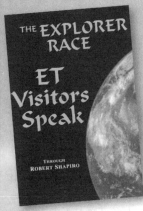

Book 11...
ET VISITORS SPEAK
ROBERT SHAPIRO

"There is one channel who's writing for [Sedona Journal of Emergence] who shouldn't be missed. His name is Robert Shapiro and he channels the spirits who inhabit dogs and rocks and penguins. Shapiro talks to Bth-ah-ga-la, who came from the planet Teth-Thia to oversee Earth's cats in their secret mission, which is to initiate humans into the realm of mystery. He talks to Cha-Cha, a sixth-dimensional being from a planet that is 'like an expressive dance school' who came to Earth to study our dancing.

Shapiro is Amazing. Either he has cracked the mysteries of the universe or he's a genius of science fiction."

—Peter Carlson
Washington Post

Even as you are searching the sky for extraterrestrials and their spaceships, ETs are here on planet Earth—they are stranded, visiting, exploring, studying the culture, healing the Earth of trauma brought on by irresponsible mining or researching the history of Christianity over the last 2000 years. Some are in human guise, some are in spirit form, some look like what we call animals as they come from the species' home planet and interact with those of their fellow beings whom we have labeled cats or cows or elephants. Some are brilliant cosmic mathematicians with a sense of humor presently living here as penguins; some are fledgling diplomats training for future postings on Earth when we have ET embassies here. In this book, these fascinating beings share their thoughts, origins and purposes for being here.

SOFTCOVER 350 P. 14^{95} ISBN 1-891824-28-7

Highlights Include

- Stranded Sirian Lightbeing Observes Earth for 800 Years
- An Orion Being Talks about Life on Earth as a Human
- Sentient Redwood
- Qua: Earth Religion Researcher
- Visitor to Earth Talks about Pope Pius XII
- Observer Helps Cats Accomplish Their Purpose: Initiating Humans
- A Warrior of Light, the Ultimate Ally
- Penguins: Humorous Mathematicians
- Xri from the Ninth Dimension
- Sixth-Dimensional Cha-Cha Dances with Humans
- Starlight for Regeneration of Earth's Crystal Veins

- Nurturing the Birth Cord
- ET Resource Specialists Map and Heal Planetary Bodies
- The Creation and Preparation of the Resource Specialists' Ships, Part 3
- Future Zeta Diplomat Learns to Communicate with Humans
- Sirius Water-Being—A Bridge between ETs and Humans
- The Rock-Being Here to Experience Movement
- We Need Benevolent Alien Implants to Go to the Stars
- Ketchin-sa—ET in Dog Form
- Balanced Beings Attempt to Remove Earth Beings' Discomfort

ROBERT SHAPIRO
ZOOSH AND OTHERS THROUGH ROBERT SHAPIRO

Superchannel Robert Shapiro can communicate with any personality anywhere and anywhen. He has been a professional channel for over twenty-five years and channels with an exceptionally clear and profound connection.

LIGHT TECHNOLOGY
PUBLISHING

To order from our Book Market, call us at 1-800-450-0985 or log on at:
www.lighttechnology.com

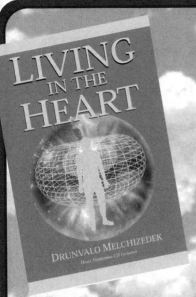

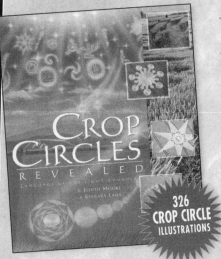

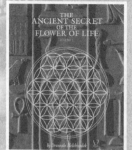

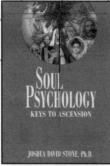

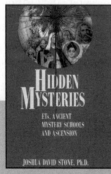
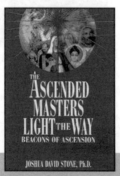
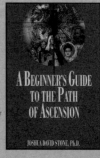

GOLDEN KEYS TO ASCENSION AND HEALING—REVELATIONS OF SAI BABA AND THE ASCENDED MASTERS

This book represents the wisdom of the ascended masters condensed into concise keys that serve as a spiritual guide. These 420 golden keys present the multitude of insights Dr. Stone has gleaned from his own background and his path to God realization.
ISBN 1-891824-03-1

MANUAL FOR PLANETARY LEADERSHIP

Here at last is an indispensible book that has been urgently needed in these uncertain times. It lays out the guidelines for leadership in the world and in one's life. It serves as a reference manual for moral and spiritual living.
ISBN 1-891824-05-8

YOUR ASCENSION MISSION —EMBRACING YOUR PUZZLE PIECE

This book shows how each person's puzzle piece is just as vital and necessary as any other. All aspects of living the fullest expression of your individuality.
ISBN 1-891824-09-0

REVELATIONS OF A MELCHIZEDEK INITIATE

Dr. Stone's spiritual autobiography, beginning with his ascension initiation and progression into the 12th initiation. Filled with insight, tools and information.
ISBN 1-891824-10-4

HOW TO TEACH ASCENSION CLASSES

This book serves as an ideal foundation for teaching ascension classes and presenting workshops. It covers an entire one- to two-year program of classes.
ISBN 1-891824-15-5

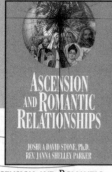

ASCENSION AND ROMANTIC RELATIONSHIPS

Inspired by Djwhal Khul, Dr. Stone has written a unique book about relationships from the perspective of the soul and monad rather than just the personality. This presents a broader picture of the problems and common traps of romantic relationships and offers much deeper advice.
ISBN 1-891824-16-3

ASCENSION INDEX AND GLOSSARY

Ascension names and ascended master terms glossary plus a complete index of all thirteen books.
ISBN 0-891824-18-X

Coming Soon! BOOK 15

How To Be Financially Successful: A Spiritual Perspective

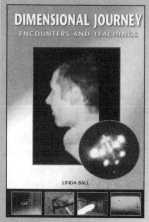

The Amethyst Light

Perhaps you are standing in a bookstore thumbing through the pages of this little book, wondering if this book contains the insights you are looking for. Perhaps you are wondering who the Ascended Master Djwhal Khul is and whether he really exists or ever did. Ultimately, it does not matter who the source is, but whether the contents are enlightening and useful to you and whether, after reading this book, you can understand more metaphysics and the significance of the present time in Earth history.

My perspective is that of one who has been a Tibetan Buddhist monk who eventually presided over a monastery. In that life I focused on meditation, contemplation, study, simple chores and training and teaching younger monks. This life culminated many others spent in the monasteries of the Orient and in more mundane activities. The contemplative life makes it possible to raise consciousness to higher levels, and it is a testing ground to see how well one has learned the principles one has studied.

The goals of my Tibetan incarnation were to attain my true Buddha nature, demonstrate my compassion for all sentient beings, break free of the bonds of reincarnation and join the Noble Ones. Thus I am writing this book as one who has attained these goals and who now dwells in what might be considered a different dimension. Or I might be referred to as a mind without a body! At the time when I transcended to a higher level, I gained insights into a greater realm of knowledge and wisdom than had been available to me as a man incarnated on Earth. So I am not writing from the perspective of a Buddhist, but from that of one of the spiritual hierarchy who guides the life on this planet.

ISBN 1-891824-41-4   **$14.95**

Topics Include:

- The Seven Rays as Fields of Endeavor
- The Evolution of a World Forum
- The Planetary Chakras and the Angelic Beings
- The World Economy as a Reflection of Human Values and Creativity

- Replacing the Word "Love" with "Kindness"
- You Came to Earth on a Mission
- Meditations
- Giving Personal Channeled or Psychic Readings
- Astrology Works through the Collective Unconscious Mind
- Reflections on the Immediate Future
- A Word on the Great Invocation
- Links to the Stars

LIGHT TECHNOLOGY PUBLISHING

Call us at
1-800-450-0985
or log on to
www.lighttechnology.com

The Diamond Light

The purpose of this book is to present esoteric teachings similar to those given to Alice A. Bailey during the period between the two great world wars and offer them to the public in an updated form that is short, concise and simple. The original teachings from the Master Djwhal Khul were presented in lengthy volumes that were somewhat difficult to understand without a thorough background in the religion known as Theosophy, founded by Madame Blavatsky in the late 19th century. It is the Master's current wish that he contribute a short book to the world that is simple and clear to the general New Age reader.

The Master is one member of a planetary council of spiritual beings who exist within another dimension and who guide the spiritual destiny of this planet and the life forms on it. Although a spiritual government exists, it does not interfere with the free will of humanity but occasionally sends teachers to guide us.

The Master would like to convey the concept that he is accessible to average mortals and does not reserve his communication only for the most well-read and well-known advanced souls. Rather, he is available for those who most desperately need him, who feel as if they are struggling to survive in the modern world without a message of hope.

ISBN 1-891824-25-2 $14.95

Topics Include:
- Toward a Cosmic Psychology of Being
- The Seven Rays
- Time and Probability
- Atlantis
- Dealing with Daily Life
- Thoughts on Love, Sex and Relationships
- Shaping your Future
- The Language of Mythology
- The Ascension Process
- Into the Millennium and Beyond
- Inhabitants of the Fourth Dimension
- The Etheric Levels
- Creating Prosperity
- The Arthurian Legend
- Karma, Reincarnation and Morality
- The Christ

LIGHT TECHNOLOGY PUBLISHING

Call us at
1-800-450-0985
or log on to
www.lighttechnology.com

WES BATEMAN, FEDERATION TELEPATH

Wes Bateman is a telepath with direct, open contact to ETs from the open state, who are not subject to Earth humankind's Frequency Barrier-caused closed brain and limited consciousness. Bateman has 30 years of ongoing information on the open state; the Federation; the Frequency Barrier and how it affects humanity; ETs and evolution; a wide spectrum of technical and scientific information, including mathematics and the universal symbolic language; and the three trading houses of this system—all part of the Federation's history of this part of the galaxy and beyond.

THROUGH ALIEN EYES

The accounts given by extraterrestrials in this volume are about events that occurred in our solar system many millions of years ago. In that ancient time the solar system consisted of four planets and four "radiar systems" that orbited the central sun. The four planets of the solar system are known today as Venus, Earth, Mars and a now-totally shattered world that was called Maldec.

The term "radiar" applies to the astronomical bodies we presently call Jupiter, Saturn, Uranus and Neptune. The original satellites of these radiars are generally called moons by Earth astronomers, but the extraterrestrials prefer to call them planetoids.

This book reflects the personal views of a number of different types of extraterrestrials regarding the state of the local solar system and the state of the Earth.

19^{95} **SOFTCOVER 507 P.**
ISBN 1-891824-27-9